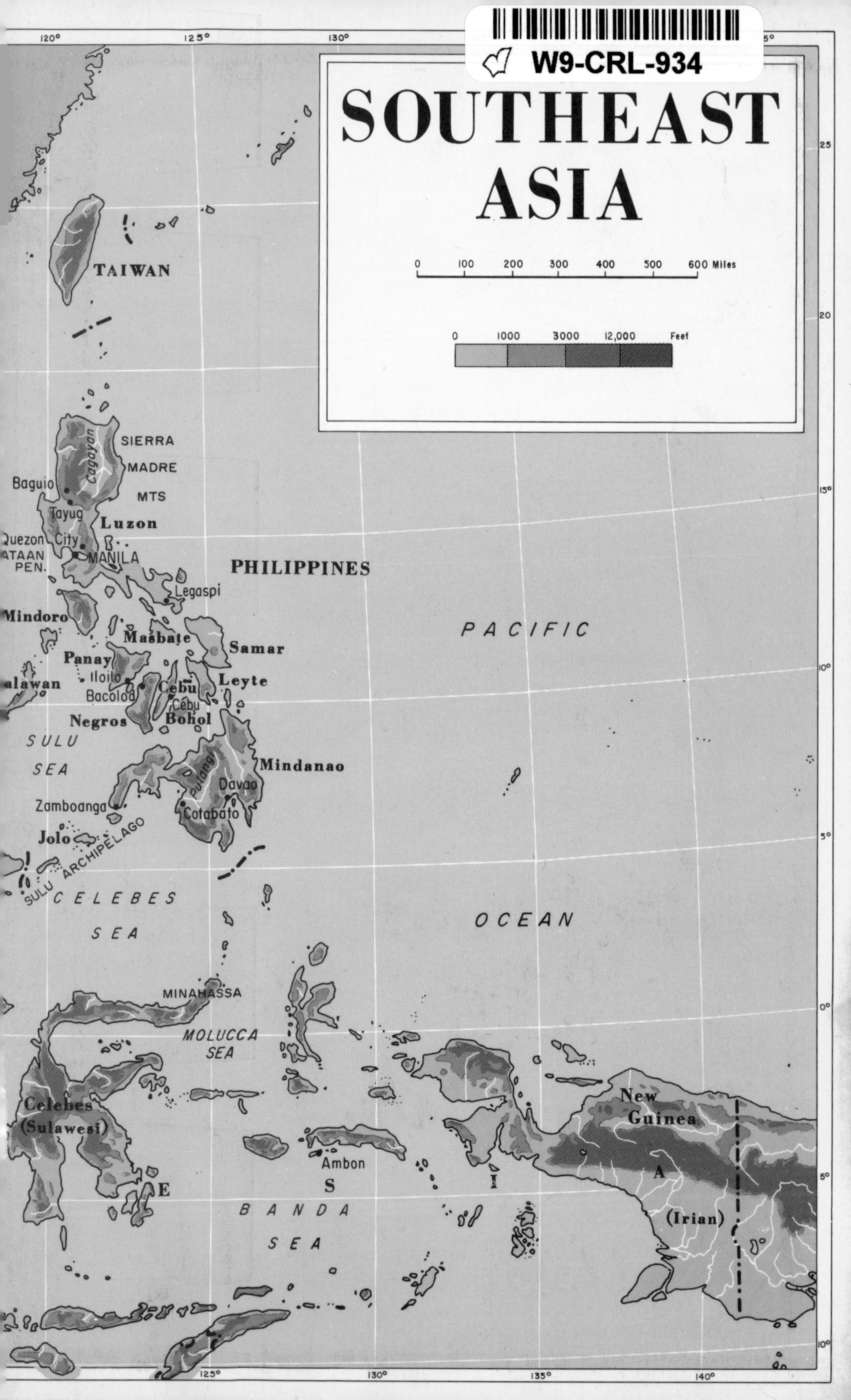
SOUTHEAST ASIA
0 100 200 300 400 500 600 Miles
0 1000 3000 12,000 Feet
TAIWAN
SIERRA MADRE MTS
Cagayan
Baguio
Tayug
Luzon
Quezon City
MANILA
PHILIPPINES
Legaspi
Mindoro
Masbate
Samar
Panay
Iloilo
Bacolod
Cebu
Cebu
Leyte
Negros
Bohol
SULU SEA
Mindanao
Pulangi
Davao
Zamboanga
Cotabato
Jolo
SULU ARCHIPELAGO
CELEBES SEA
PACIFIC
OCEAN
MINAHASSA
MOLUCCA SEA
Celebes (Sulawesi)
Ambon
BANDA SEA
New Guinea
(Irian)
120° 125° 130° 135° 140°
25 20 15° 10° 5° 0° 5° 10°

STEINBERG

WOODSIDE

CHANDLER

WYATT ROFF SMAIL

DAVID JOEL STEINBERG, Associate Professor of History, University of Michigan, and Secretary-Treasurer, Association for Asian Studies, earned his doctorate at Harvard University in 1964. His book *Philippine Collaboration in World War II* won the 1969 University of Michigan Press Award.

DAVID K. WYATT earned his Ph.D. in 1966 from Cornell University, where he is Associate Professor of History. He is the author of *The Politics of Reform in Thailand,* a co-author of *Hikayat Patani: The Story of Patani,* and editor of *The Nan Chronicle.*

JOHN R. W. SMAIL, who was born in Egypt, received his doctorate from Cornell University in 1964. Now Associate Professor of History at the University of Wisconsin, he is the author of *Bandung in the Early Revolution, 1945–46.*

ALEXANDER WOODSIDE earned his doctorate in history and Far Eastern languages from Harvard University in 1968, where he is Assistant Professor of History and a member of the East Asian Research Center. He is the author of *Vietnam and the Chinese Model.*

WILLIAM R. ROFF got his Ph.D. in 1965 from Australian National University. Now Associate Professor of History at Columbia University and a member of its Southern Asian Institute, he is the author of *The Origins of Malay Nationalism* and other books on Malay society.

DAVID P. CHANDLER, after years in the U.S. Foreign Service in Cambodia and in Washington, returned to Southeast Asia in 1970 to write his dissertation for the University of Michigan on Thai-Cambodian relations in the nineteenth century.

In Search of Southeast Asia

STEINBERG, David Joel and others. In search of Southeast Asia; a modern history. Praeger, 1971. 522p map bibl 70-121850. 12.95, 5,95 pa.

The collaboration of six skilled and well qualified historians has resulted in a most insightful volume on the history of Southeast Asia during the past two centuries. While obviously closely integrated, the chapters are clearly individual essays which describe and synthesize with judiciousness and skill the complex developments in each area. Especially useful for introductory history courses of Southeast Asia, this volume should come to supplant most of the standard works such as D.G.E. Hall, *History of South-east Asia* (3rd ed., 1968), J. F. Cady, *Southeast Asia; its historical development* (CHOICE, Sept. 1964) and J. Bastin and H. J. Benda, *History of modern Southeast Asia* (CHOICE, Sept. 1969) for the coverage of the modern period. A splendid bibliographical essay of some 60 pages, a map, and a time chart in the endpapers enhance the value of this book. Generalist and specialist both will find much of interest and value in this book.

CHOICE *MAY '71*
History, Geography & Travel
Asia & Oceania

In Search of Southeast Asia

A MODERN HISTORY

David Joel Steinberg
Alexander Woodside
David K. Wyatt
William R. Roff
John R. W. Smail
David P. Chandler

Edited by David Joel Steinberg

PRAEGER PUBLISHERS
New York • Washington • London

PRAEGER PUBLISHERS
111 Fourth Avenue, New York, N.Y. 10003, U.S.A.
5, Cromwell Place, London S.W.7, England

Published in the United States of America in 1971
by Praeger Publishers, Inc.

Library of Congress Catalog Card Number: 70–121850

Printed in the United States of America

CONTENTS

Part Three: *Frameworks for Nations*

Part Four: *Social Change and the Emergence of Nationalism*

Part Five: *The Preoccupations of Independence*

MAPS

Note: In the paperback edition, maps listed here as endpapers appear at the back of the book.

NOTES ON THE AUTHORS

David Joel Steinberg was born in New York and educated at Phillips Academy in Andover, Malvern College in England, and Harvard College, where he graduated *magna cum laude* and Phi Beta Kappa. In the process of gaining an M.A. and a Ph.D. from Harvard University, he held Fulbright, Woodrow Wilson, and National Defense Education Act fellowships. At present, he is Associate Professor of Southeast Asian History at the University of Michigan and Secretary/Treasurer of the Association for Asian Studies. He has received awards from the American Council of Learned Societies/Social Science Research Council, the National Endowment for the Humanities, and the Office of Education, among others, and has served as a consultant on the Philippines to the Ford Foundation. His book *Philippine Collaboration in World War II* (Ann Arbor, Mich., 1967) won the University of Michigan Book Award in 1969.

David K. Wyatt, Associate Professor of History at Cornell University, was born in Massachusetts in 1937. He studied philosophy at Harvard University, where he graduated in 1959, and received an M.A. degree in history from Boston University in 1960. After research in Thailand in 1962–63 on a Ford Foundation Foreign Area Training Fellowship, he completed work for his Ph.D. degree at Cornell University in 1966. He was Lecturer in the History of Southeast Asia at the School of Oriental and African Studies in the University of London from 1964 to 1968 and spent five months as a Visiting Fulbright Lecturer at the University of Malaya in 1966–67. In 1968–69, he taught at The University of Michigan. He is the author of *The Politics of Reform in Thailand* (New Haven, Conn., 1969), co-author with A. Teeuw of *Hikayat Patani: The Story of Patani* (Leiden, 1970), and editor of *The Nan Chronicle* (Cornell University Southeast Asia Program, 1966), and has published more than twenty scholarly articles.

Born into a different colonial world in Cairo in 1930, and coming to Southeast Asian history by way of studies in English history and literature at Harvard (B.A., M.A.) and two years of military service in Japan, John R. W. Smail did his doctoral work at Cornell University, specializing in Indonesia. His published works include the monograph

Bandung in the Early Revolution, 1945–1946 (Ithaca, N.Y., 1964) and the influential essay, "On the Possibility of an Autonomous History of Modern Southeast Asia," which was published in the *Journal of Southeast Asian History*. He is Associate Professor of History at the University of Wisconsin, Madison.

ALEXANDER WOODSIDE was born in Toronto, Canada, in 1938. He received a B.A. with honors in modern history from the University of Toronto in 1960 and went to graduate school at Harvard University on a Woodrow Wilson Fellowship the same year. He received a Ph.D. in history and Far Eastern languages from Harvard in 1968. He studied both the Chinese and Japanese languages at Harvard and began his study of modern Vietnamese while he was attached to the Southeast Asia program at Cornell University in 1964–65, during a year's leave from Harvard. In 1965–67, supported by a Foreign Area Fellowship Program grant, he continued his language work and did research in Saigon, Hong Kong (where he studied with Ch'en Ching-ho), Tokyo, and Paris. He is currently an Assistant Professor of History at Harvard University and a member of the staff of the Harvard East Asian Research Center. His book *Vietnam and the Chinese Model* (Cambridge, Mass., 1970) deals with one of his research interests, traditional Vietnamese government and society. He is also interested in Sino-Vietnamese relations, past and present, and has so far published three papers on the subject: "Early Ming Expansionism, 1406–1427: China's Abortive Conquest of Vietnam," in *Harvard Papers on China*, 17, 1963; "Vietnamese Buddhism, the Vietnamese Court, and China in the 1800's," in Edgar Wickberg, ed., *Historical Interaction of China and Vietnam: Institutional and Cultural Themes* (Center for East Asian Studies, University of Kansas, 1969); and "Peking and Hanoi: Anatomy of a Revolutionary Partnership," in *International Journal* 24, No. 1, 1968–69.

A native of Glasgow, Scotland, WILLIAM R. ROFF first became acquainted with Southeast Asia during six years in the British Merchant Navy. After settling in New Zealand in 1953, he worked as an editor and feature writer for the Broadcasting Commission and attended Victoria University of Wellington part-time. Graduating with a B.A. in 1957, and an M.A. (First Class Honours in History) in 1959, he held a research scholarship from the Institute of Advanced Studies, Australian National University, in 1959–62, and spent two years doing research in Malaya. He received his Ph.D. in 1965. He was a Lecturer in Southeast Asian History at Monash University, Melbourne, in 1963–65, and Senior Lecturer, University of Malaya, Kuala Lumpur, in 1966–69. He is now Associate Professor of History and a member of the Southern Asian Institute at Columbia University. His publications include *The Origins of Malay Nationalism* (New Haven, Conn., 1967), recently translated into Malay; two collections of writings by nineteenth-century Malayan administrators, published by Oxford University Press in 1967 and 1968; a short history of Malay newspapers, *Sejarah Surat2 Khabar* (Penang, 1967), and a bibliographical *Guide to Malay Periodicals* (Singapore, 1961); and numerous articles on Malaysian and Indonesian history, including the chapter "Southeast Asia in the Nineteenth Century" in the *Cambridge History of Islam* (London, 1970). He is now interested mainly in the sociological history of Islam in the Malay world.

David P. Chandler was born in New York City, and graduated from Harvard in 1954 *magna cum laude*, Phi Beta Kappa. After a year at Oxford and two in the U.S. Army, he joined the Foreign Service, where his posts included Phnom Penh, the Cambodian Service of the Voice of America, and the chairmanship of Southeast Asian area studies at the Foreign Service Institute. He resigned in 1966 and earned an M.A. at Yale in Southeast Asia Studies in 1968. He is now a doctoral candidate at the University of Michigan. His dissertation will focus on Thai-Cambodian tributary relationships in the early nineteenth century. He received a Foreign Area fellowship for research in Thailand, Cambodia, and France in 1970–71.

PREFACE

On the small island of Mactan in the Philippines there is a monument erected by the Spanish in the nineteenth century to glorify God, Spain, and Ferdinand Magellan. In 1941, during the American era, a historical marker inscribed "Ferdinand Magellan's Death" was erected nearby. It stated: "On this spot Ferdinand Magellan died on April 27, 1521, wounded in an encounter with the soldiers of Lapulapu, chief of Mactan Island. One of Magellan's ships, the *Victoria*, under the command of Juan Sebastian Elcano, sailed from Cebu on May 1, 1521 and anchored at San Lucar de Barrameda on September 6, 1522, thus completing the first circumnavigation of the earth." Exactly a decade later, the by then independent Republic of the Philippines erected a second marker, entitled "Lapulapu." It read: "Here, on 27 April 1521, Lapulapu and his men repulsed the Spanish invaders, killing their leader, Ferdinand Magellan. Thus, Lapulapu became the first Filipino to have repelled European aggression."

This example illustrates vividly the historian's predicament. In the wake of such wide variation of interpretation of what at first appears as fact, the attempt of the historian to impose order on the past may seem a dubious undertaking. This book rests upon the assumption that in the interaction and expertise of collective authorship greater coherence can be found in the welter of human events. Starting in the fall of 1966, we began exchanging outlines and debating assumptions; in the summer of 1969, we gathered in Ann Arbor for a working seminar on modern Southeast Asian history. Together we rewrote the outline, divided our responsibilities and criticized each other's work in the constant hope that we might produce a history that would examine the totality of modern Southeast Asia as well as its elements. There were handicaps, of course, including, for some of us, the inaccessibility of source material and, for all of us, limitations of time. None of us is an expert in Burmese history, and we probably have not been able to give that country the kind of treatment it deserves. We have come away from our joint effort convinced, however, that there is wisdom in studying Southeast Asia as a whole, not only because of the insights it offers for the comparative historian but also because, in the words of the motto of the Republic of Indonesia, there is unity in its diversity.

The depth and perspective we have gained by viewing the region as a whole has enhanced our understanding of its parts. This said, it has to be conceded that there were of course some occasions on which, even after debate and recrimination, we had to agree to bicker.

The list of people we wish to thank is at least six times longer than would have been the case if only one of us had been involved. Our debts range across the world. We want to acknowledge our particular gratitude to Professors Gayl Ness and John Broomfield, of the Center for South and Southeast Asian Studies at the University of Michigan, for their support and enthusiasm at every stage of this project. Without Dr. David Pfanner, of the Ford Foundation, and Dr. William Bradley, of the Rockefeller Foundation, the book would not exist; we are deeply indebted to them personally and to the foundations they serve so ably. We also acknowledge with appreciation the financial support given to us by the National Endowment for the Humanities and by the Horace Rackham School at The University of Michigan. The maps have been prepared by Ronald Edgerton and the cartography was done by Karen Ewing. We all owe a debt to our students and would like especially to thank Stewart Gordon, Patricia Herbert, Theodore Grossman, and Norman Owen of the University of Michigan. Our sense of gratitude to Ronald Edgerton for his assistance, his accuracy, and his good cheer at every stage of this project is profound. Finally, we apologize to our five wives and eight children, who somehow endured while the summer, the autumn, and then the winter wore on.

Ann Arbor, Michigan
July, 1970

In Search of Southeast Asia

INTRODUCTION

Over the past two centuries, as a result of the human energy unleashed by the scientific, industrial, and nationalist revolutions, Southeast Asian societies have changed profoundly. This change, which continues unabated, can be dated from approximately the middle of the eighteenth century, when Europeans in the region first had the power and the inclination to impose on others their technical skills and new world view. The nature of Southeast Asian history has been partially obscured, however, because many historians have interested themselves primarily in external stimuli, to the detriment of the study of indigenous institutions, thereby elevating foreigners beyond their position as actors on a common stage. From this perspective Southeast Asians have been reduced to passive receptors, too weak to do more than reflect the brilliance of other civilizations. Southeast Asia faced similar challenges in earlier eras; indeed, it has perhaps interacted with a greater variety of external cultures for a longer period of time than has any other area of the world. From the Southeast Asian vantage point, therefore, what is important is the process of acculturation through which Southeast Asian societies adjusted to their changing environment.

Social change does not take place in the abstract. The evolution of values and the concomitant development of social institutions in a society are a complicated aggregate of individual human reactions. Change takes place in a community because people interact—sometimes consciously, sometimes not—with those around them. Occasionally, new ways are adopted because they seem attractive or promise some reward; at other times, people are forced to accept change as a result of coercion or more subtle forms of compulsion. The dissemination of ideas and the development of institutions are gradual processes, involving a few key people at first and then gradually spreading to the larger population. Since there is always a wide variety of attitudes, and since most social organisms are constantly evolving, any attribution of consensus is arbitrary. The designations "new" and "old," "traditional" and "modern," "alien" and "indigenous" can be no more than relative.

In the daily reality of living, people naturally adjust to their environment by making the best use they can of the ideas and institutions that surround them. They rarely notice the inconsistencies that seem so obvious to outsiders. To the devout Muslim of Arabia, who defined Islamic orthodoxy by his own practice, the Malay Muslim may have seemed heretical. The Malay, however, commonly saw no problem in the way he expressed his faith or reconciled it with pre-Islamic custom. Perspective, therefore, shapes perception. To the Indian, Arab, or Chinese, who saw the culture of Southeast Asia as an extension of his own civilization, indigenous modifications were interpreted as perversions of his own value system. Similarly, observers from the West, looking for what was familiar to them, have for many years seen Southeast Asia in ethnocentric terms. The task of the historian is made the more difficult by deeply ingrained value judgments and subconscious biases of this sort. This book strives to treat each society in Southeast Asia as a separate species and the region as a distinct genus.

There is natural and spontaneous change in all culture contact. In the process of transmission and translation, terms, values, and institutions are altered. Local context shapes the contours of abstract concepts and specific structures. Whatever the meaning of a word or institution in its original environment, it changes as it takes its place with other forces in the new setting. The term "guided democracy," for example, can be understood only after one appreciates Sukarno and the Indonesian social matrix as well as the development of the concept of democracy in the West. "Buddhist socialism," a term in use in Burma and Cambodia, is a similar example. From the Southeast Asian point of view, the origin of the concept is far less important than its meaning within the local environment. Similarly, it is often only marginally relevant whether a man's place of origin is Hong Kong, Calcutta, or Amsterdam, if he is acting in a Southeast Asian milieu. This does not deny his distinct identity or alien ways; it simply fits him properly into the indigenous scene. While a Singapore Chinese merchant had ties to a Canton business firm, and a French naval administrator in Vietnam was part of an imperial enterprise with headquarters in Paris, they must first be seen as participants in the history of Southeast Asia.

Acculturation is not a simple linear development; interaction generates too many variables. The displacement of established tradition by new patterns of behavior is rarely easy. Accepted values are finely interwoven into the social fabric and usually have stanch defenders. The rate and character of change are determined by such things as the strength of existing institutions; the receptivity of the society to new ideas; the physical, intellectual and moral power of the new concepts and of the men who transmit them; and the compatibility of the new values with the old. Some institutions seem to develop along a single line and then suddenly fragment; others appear to retrogress or to remain motionless. Some established values crumble upon the first encounter with competition; others continue to develop as if no challenge existed. Very often the institutions and values that seem strongest prove to be the most vulnerable.

These observations concerning society and change supply one dimension to the Southeast Asian history. A second dimension stems from the physical and climatic environment. The relationship of land to people, the general ecological balance, and the margin of surplus have ordained many of the priorities by which Southeast Asians live their lives. Unlike China and India, most Southeast Asian societies have not been troubled by overpopulation in the past. The history of China and India has been, in part, the struggle of man to establish social organisms that can maximize yields to minimize starvation. Except, perhaps, on the island of Java and in northern Vietnam, Southeast Asia has been spared this awesome constriction, at least until very recent times.

Southeast Asia may be defined as the area south of China and east of India. Known to the Chinese and Japanese as the South Seas (*Nanyang* or *Nampō*), the region has only recently been called Southeast Asia by most people. During World War II, the term gained wide currency to designate the theater of war commanded by Lord Louis Mountbatten. It includes the present political units of the Union of Burma; the Kingdoms of Thailand, Laos, and Cambodia; the Democratic Republic of Vietnam; the Republic of Vietnam; the Federation of Malaysia; the Sultanate of Brunei; the Republics of Indonesia, Singapore, and the Philippines; and Portuguese Timor. While there are arguments for expanding the definition to include certain other territories for religious, ethnographic, linguistic, or topographical reasons—Taiwan, Hainan, or Ceylon, for example—or contracting it for similar reasons, the general consensus accepts current usage. As defined, Southeast Asia has a population of approximately one quarter of a billion people living in a total land area of just over one and one-half million square miles (a little smaller than the Indian subcontinent). Slightly more than half of the territory is on the Asian mainland, and the rest is unevenly fragmented into the ten thousand islands that make up the archipelagos of Indonesia and the Philippines. More than half the population, however, lives on the islands.

A pilgrim who journeyed from one end of Southeast Asia to the other would note a similarity of flora and fauna, of climate, and of human cultivation. While the languages and architecture would change, he would be struck by the repeating patterns of wet-rice and slash-and-burn agriculture, found from Burma to Bali. Traveling on the mainland, east or west, he would move from delta to coastal mountain ridge to river valley, and then across a series of river valleys and mountain ridges, until he finally reached the next delta on the other side. He would note that the mountain ridges frequently determined political boundaries and that the river valleys were fertile zones of civilization. Where water was plentiful he would find wet-rice farming; where it was scarce he would find fewer established communities and less plentiful cultivation. Similar patterns would be evident through the island world. Moreover, wherever he went he would observe the close relationship between rainfall and fertility and the importance of the monsoon in the seasonal lives of the people.

Southeast Asia lies within the tropical belt on either side of the equator. The tropics are all too often conceived of as exotic and endlessly fertile by those who live elsewhere. Visually they display a deceptive richness of vegetation. While there are areas of great soil fertility created by volcanic action, as in Java, and by alluvial deposits, as in the Mekong delta, the apparent fecundity of much of the area is caused by rapid photosynthesis rather than soil chemistry. A precarious ecological balance exists within the region, especially in the tropical rain forests, where the forest cover derives its nourishment from the rapid decay of plant life and humus at its roots. The forest is, in effect, a hothouse where the cycle of nature accelerates sharply. The topsoil may be only a few inches deep, and yet the growing cycle can support itself with seeming ease, provided that equilibrium is maintained. If the virgin growth is cut or otherwise destroyed (as with defoliants in Vietnam), the rainfall is too much for the soil to absorb; the earth is quickly leached of its nutrients, becoming a useless savanna.

This ecological fragility has made much of Southeast Asia unfit for large concentrations of people. Only in the so-called ecological niches of alluvial riverbank and volcanic loam have dense population centers formed. Heavy rainfall and resultant erosion have carried massive silt deposits down from the mountains and made fertile the banks of such rivers as the Mekong, Čhaophraya, Irrawaddy, and Red. A rather similar process has taken place along the shorter but steeper rivers on the islands. Where there was sufficient human need or incentive, generated by population pressure or profit motive, painstaking labor was employed to build extensive irrigation systems, but for most of the area the prospect this opened up of a double rice crop was not worth the effort. Many of the delta regions remained nonproductive until the nineteenth century, since the potential wealth of the soil was difficult to utilize without drainage and other technological skills. The Mekong delta, for example, was sparsely inhabited until the late eighteenth century, and the "rice bowls" of the Burmese and Thai deltas were barely cleared until the late nineteenth century, when a worldwide demand for rice produced boom conditions.

The ecology of Southeast Asia has played an important part in the area's history, especially by influencing the relationship between the concentrations of people who live in the fertile niches and those who dwell on the much less fertile periphery.[1] Since the flood plains were ideal for wet-rice, and since the hinterland was generally better suited for migrant slash-and-burn cultivation, very different cultural and social institutions emerged. Wet-rice permits a density of population and a social wealth far greater than is possible in the less-favored regions. The major agrarian kingdoms in Burma, Thailand, Vietnam, Cambodia, and Java had authority that radiated outward from their capitals.

The farther from the center one traveled, the less influence the center wielded. Prior to the nineteenth century, the wet-rice societies rarely established total control over the outlying areas. Whenever one state did attempt to impose dominance over an adjacent buffer zone, geopolitical tensions increased, because the balance of power was endangered. The upland people who were threatened were likely to appeal for support to one of the lowland societies, because highland groups often maintained ties with all their powerful neighbors. Mutual defense agreements were part of traditional tribute relationships. Only Cambodia among the major wet-rice societies lacked the luxury of buffer zones; its exposed position between Thailand and Vietnam eventually led to its destruction as a major power.

The concept of national boundaries, as defined by the West, did not exist in Southeast Asia until the nineteenth century. One must not imagine the map of traditional Southeast Asian states as if it were a map of Europe in 1764, with Burma one pastel shade, Thailand another, and Vietnam a third. Southeast Asians were not much concerned with the demarcation of frontiers. The inconclusive Vietnamese-Lao wars of the seventeenth century, for example, were resolved when the Lê emperor in Vietnam and the Lao king agreed that every inhabitant in the upper Mekong valley who lived in a house built on stilts owed allegiance to Laos, while those whose homes had earth floors owed allegiance to Vietnam. It is only quite recently that the rulers of the traditionally dominant societies have sought to establish a modern sense of allegiance to the notion of a nation-state identity, with its concomitant demand of loyalty from all citizens living within sharply defined national boundaries.

The technological power developed in the West was used to rework the ecological balance in Southeast Asia. Unhappy at the discomforts and dangers of tropical existence and unwilling to leave, Westerners used their power to sanitize and soften nature. Conceptualizing this power as the white man's burden, they recognized an obligation, in Kipling's words, to "fill full the mouth of Famine and bid the sickness cease." Personal and humanitarian concerns fused with economic ambition. Drainage projects in the deltas of Burma, Thailand, and Vietnam made humanitarians millionaires. In the Klang area of Selangor, the British first succeeded in eradicating the malarial anopheles mosquito in an effort to reduce the mortality of rubber estate workers. Whatever the motivation, such manipulation of the environment produced radical change not only in the life cycle of the flora and fauna but also in human demography. The doctor or sanitary engineer was an important force for change within the human environment; modern transportation, new crops, and instant communications altered the world in which traditional Southeast Asia had existed.

The last two centuries have created a community of experience for the societies of Southeast Asia. Linguistic, religious, ethnic, and social isolation within each of the countries, if not always between them, has been lessened. As a result, each society has undertaken a search for a new and broader consensus—one that would harmonize established social institutions with changing conditions. Increasingly, as people participated in a range of new organizations and activities, they broadened their frame of reference from the village or the province to the nation. This new congruence of values has restructured allegiances, challenging primordial loyalties. Earlier distinctions of culture, society, and state have become blurred as nationalism has developed; the importance of genealogical and geographical origins has lessened, for some if not for all. Whereas the term "Burman," for example, is limited to a single ethnic community, the national term "Burmese" embraces all ethnic groups within the Union of Burma. The process of national development throughout Southeast Asia has involved both a reassertion and a reformulation of authority.

Like Manila rope, which is the strongest cordage in the world because of the intricate and specific way thousands of abaca fibers are entwined, history is difficult to unravel. For the sake of clarity, historians sometimes halt history, like a strip of movie film, in order to examine it frame by frame; this can be no more than convenient artifice, however. The story must be run through the projector carefully at the right speed. If the pace is too fast, the viewer sees only a blur; if it moves too slowly, the illusion of the recaptured past flickers in parody. Although the historian cannot fully portray the dimension and drama of a past reality, he can at least strive to illuminate some of its richness and color.

PART ONE

The Eighteenth-Century World

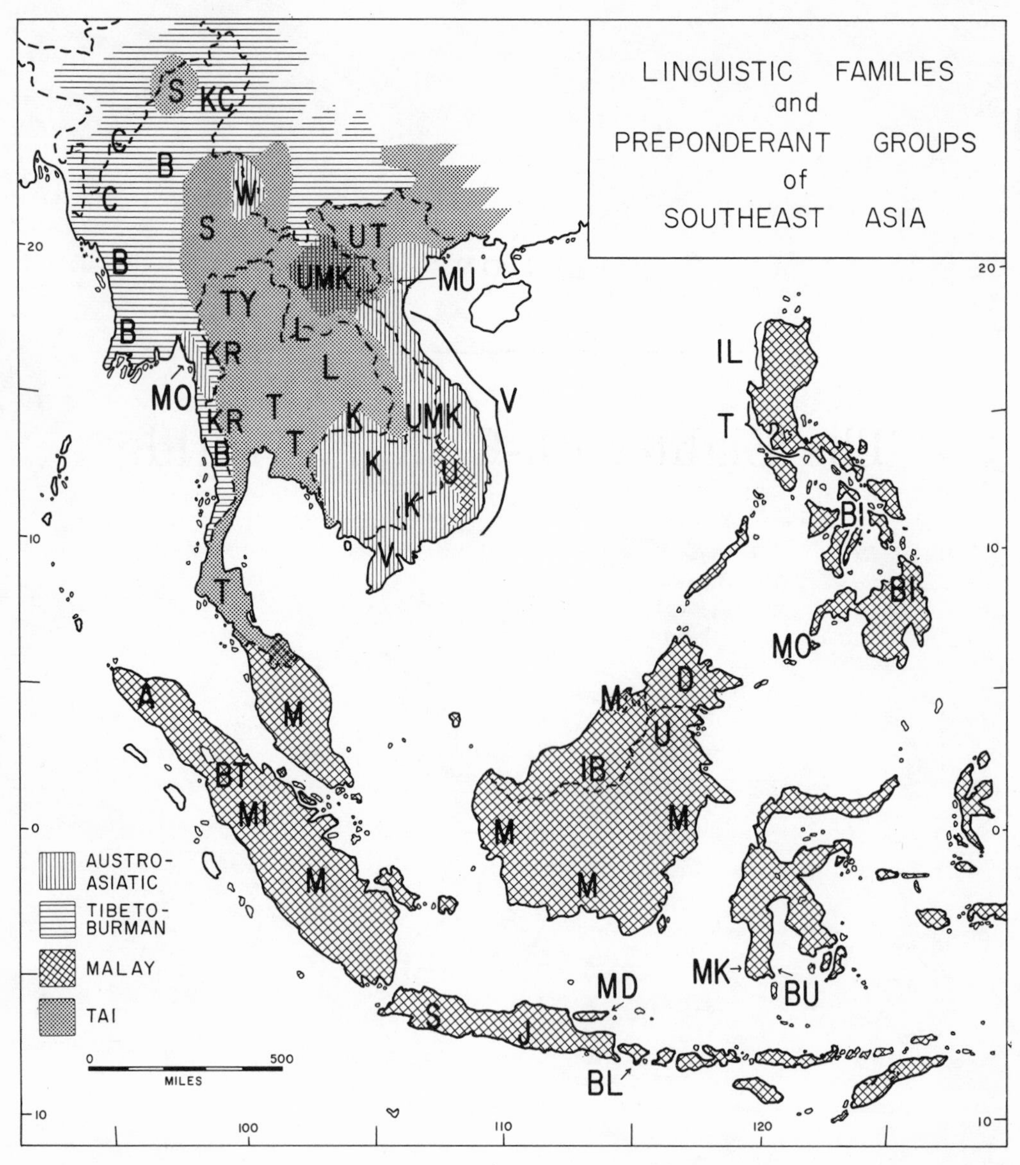

KEY

Austro-Asiatic

K	Khmer
MO	Mon
MU	Muong
UMK	Upland Mon-Khmer (Sedang, Bahnar, Pear, Hre)
V	Vietnamese
W	Wa

Tibeto-Burman

B	Burman
C	Chin
KC	Kachin
KR	Karen (Red Karen, White Karen)

Malay

A	Acehnese
BI	Bisayan
BL	Balinese
BT	Batak
BU	Bugi
D	Dayak
IB	Iban
IL	Ilocano
J	Javanese
M	Malay
MD	Madurese
MK	Makassarese
MI	Minangkabau
MO	Moro
S	Sundanese
T	Tagalog
U	Upland Malay

Tai

L	Lao
S	Shan
TY	Tai Yuan
T	Thai
UT	Upland Tai (White Tai, Red Tai, Black Tai, Striped Tai)

1

THE PEASANT WORLD

If, as certain sorts of science fiction suggest, modern man had the power to retreat to eighteenth-century Southeast Asia, it is unlikely that he would find himself in the palaces tourists visit today. More probably, he would happen instead upon a dusty road (a muddy one in the rainy season) and head toward a patch of green and gray on the close horizon—the nearest village. With emerald green ricefields on either side, he would pass occasional ox- or buffalo-drawn carts piled high with rice; old women taking fruit to market; or young men carrying a caged cock for fighting. A rise in the road would bring him into the shade of heavy trees arching over a huddle of bamboo and thatch houses. There he might stop at the communal well to quench his thirst and to wash off the dust and sun-glazed perspiration around his eyes. At various times of year, he would see whole families engaged in the never-ending pursuits of farmers everywhere—harvesting, or milling grain, or fishing; weaving, sewing, gossiping, courting, and cooking; fashioning implements of wood and bits of metal; celebrating birth or mourning death; tending the ill and educating the young.

The modern reader, like the traveler, might wish to hasten on to the city, where "real" history occurred. Although rural life in eighteenth-century Southeast Asia—or in the twentieth century, for that matter—has lacked its chroniclers, the activities of peasants then and now are no less important for their obscurity. Neither visiting Europeans nor keepers of court records described the lives of peasants, as both took for granted their importance in the daily life and functioning of the state. Present sources provide meager information to fill the resultant vacuum; however, the combination of scattered historical references and a retrospective application of the insights of modern social science make it possible to sketch the broad outlines of Southeast Asian life two centuries ago.

WET-RICE FARMERS

Such concentrations of population as there were depended upon complex agricultural techniques for the irrigated cultivation of rice. The peasant farmer placed less importance upon land than upon the muddy water of streams and rivers, which everywhere crossed the landscape, bringing with the floods of each rainy season rich nutrients washed down from the hills upstream. His rice paddies or *sawah* were basins to hold the seed and the water required for its growth. The prosperity of village and state thus required a sufficient supply of water for the irrigation of thousands of ricefields spread across the plains and valleys. Fields and their accompanying dikes were a capital investment for the peasant. In these fields, generations of peasants harnessed nature by setting their roots perhaps as much in water as in soil.

The varieties of rice, differing from place to place, were bred over centuries to survive and yield grain under particular climatic and soil conditions. In the Red River delta lands of northern Vietnam alone, there were at least 300 types of rice, each with its own properties, from which the peasant chose to suit his fields and local climate.[1] Even under considerable variation in growing conditions, peasants throughout the region could expect to harvest 20 to 25 bushels of grain per acre, so that even on very small holdings a family could sustain itself and meet its obligations. Where land holdings or yields were smaller, peasants grew two crops of rice a year, if weather or irrigation facilities permitted, as in northern Vietnam. Generally, however, peasants grew only a single crop of rice each year, and thus provided the basis for their prosperity and health.

The agricultural cycle of wet-rice growing was consistent from place to place, although the schedule could vary according to the length or timing of the monsoon rains. Where a single crop was grown, it was begun in small seedbeds sown densely at the approach of the rainy season. While the seedlings took root and grew, the farmer and his family prepared the nearby fields, weeding them and breaking up the soil with hoes until, with the soakings of heavy rain, the seedlings were transplanted by hand with enough space between them for each plant to grow. While the crop matured, the peasant worked at repairing his dikes and regulating the flow of water as the rains reached their peak and the floods descended across the plains to the sea. As the water receded, the fields drained, and then the sun did its work to ripen the grain. The harvest was a time of festivity, with whole families in the fields working side-by-side amid songs and jokes, which spilled with the rice across the threshing floor. During the dry months that followed, as the fields baked hard and dry, they were cleared of stubble. Then the farm tools were sharpened or repaired, in preparation for the cycle ahead, while religious feasts and festivals, marriages and merrymaking filled the dusty, rainless days.

To grow and harvest his crop, the peasant employed a few simple implements. Agricultural technology was least elaborate in regions where only one crop of rice was grown each year and where landholdings were comparatively large, and most elaborate where the opposite conditions prevailed. Plows generally were of wood, sometimes tipped with an iron point, and wagons or sledges were often used to cart produce. Harvesting was much too important—economically, ritually, and supernaturally—to be undertaken with more than a single, hand-held blade. Throughout the region, draft animals were employed, especially in plowing and milling; the water buffalo was found everywhere, and oxen or bullocks were also used. Rudimentary wooden or stone threshing and milling implements existed in every village, worked by human and by animal power. Wooden treadmill or waterwheel pumps raised muddy water to the fields from streams and ditches. In northern Vietnam, where the Red River had to be kept within its banks and double-cropping of rice was the rule, the dike system had attained a total length of some 1,000 miles by the nineteenth century. Most northern villages used canals and ditches to conduct water to their fields, and many dug ponds to hold water for use in the dry season.

To supplement his rice diet, the peasant grew vegetables and fruit; raised chickens, ducks, and pigs; and joined his sons to fish not only the nearby streams but also his own fields when the floods came. Poultry and fish were crucial to the health of his family, for they provided protein, which had either to be found or bought throughout the year. Normally, through most of Southeast Asia, the peasant village was economically almost self-sufficient. Only items such as salt and cloth had to be purchased. The greater the need for such items, the more numerous were the outside trading contacts of the village and the more important the production of a marketable surplus either of rice or of secondary crops. Only in a few areas, however, such as the south central provinces of Vietnam, the cotton areas of Upper Burma, and the coastal regions of the Indonesian archipelago, was a predominantly market economy a significant part of village life before the nineteenth century.

Through most of Southeast Asia, the lands the peasant worked were not fully his own. Although kings claimed sovereign rights to the soil, communities joint proprietary rights, and villagers the right of actually using land, these claims did not approximate Western property ownership. For the most part, villagers themselves worked out how the resources available to them might best be distributed in order to serve the interests of individuals, families, and state. The patterns of rights to the use of land, strongly defended against external challenges, were well-established in customary law and practice. In the Philippines, the Spaniards had transformed a pattern of land utilization rights into one of private ownership; they pre-empted for the Crown all lands not specifically identified as belonging to an individual or village, thereby restricting the expansion of village lands to accommodate the needs of expanding populations. In Vietnam, strong pressures encouraged the accumulation of lands by officials and landlords, which by the eighteenth century had the effect of rendering many peasants landless. These developments, the harbingers of increasingly difficult economic circumstances, were deviations from an earlier general pattern in which peasants passed land on to their children—sons and daughters alike.

The traditional mode of easing population pressure on agricultural land had been through the constant clearing and opening up of new areas, where these existed, by ambitious farmers or by deliberate government effort.

Southeast Asian rice-growing villages took a variety of physical forms. In some areas, like present-day Northeast Thailand, where settlement was dispersed, villages might be composed of a single, family-related group connected loosely to a larger political unit some miles away. Older villages on a densely settled plain might have larger populations of between sixty and one hundred families, either grouped in a single cluster or strung out on both banks of a canal. Around a central core, the groups within these villages were clearly and elaborately organized in terms of carefully differentiated social and functional roles. Still other villages were composed of a number of smaller units, the whole village being an aggregate—natural or artificial—of units that might have separate familial, economic, religious, or administrative identities. The basic unit of peasant life in the Philippines, for example, was the *pueblo,* which was composed of a number of *barrios,* while the Vietnamese village (*xa*) was made up of a number of hamlets. Between the Burman household and the provincial capital there could be a wide range of potential social and administrative units. Southeast Asian villages varied considerably in size, organization, and appearance.

The variation in housing was similarly wide. Almost everywhere in Southeast Asia (except in eastern Java, Bali, Lombok, and where Vietnamese or Chinese lived), houses were built on piles or "stilts," raised some six feet or more off the ground. There was a considerable difference, however, between the communal dwellings of the Minangkabau of Sumatra, built to accommodate an extended matrilineal family, and the thatched bamboo hut of the Malay peasant. Fashioned of local materials, such as teak or bamboo, sometimes with stone pillar-bases, houses could be simple or elaborate. The chief architectural elements were a front porch, one or more interior rooms almost bare of furniture, enough windows for ventilation, and a steeply pitched roof to ward off the torrential downpour of the monsoons.

The few public buildings in villages might be the result either of common labor over a period of years or of the benefaction of a local notable or prosperous peasant. Only the larger village units would support major religious edifices—the parish churches of the Philippine *pueblos,* or the village mosques of the Malay states or north-coast Java (which could not be established unless there were at least forty adult males in the community). The Vietnamese village often constructed its own bamboo palisade, and the Thai, Cambodian, or Burman village its monastery. The talents of local craftsmen and of itinerant artisans were lavished on these structures; those that survive are a vivid reminder that by no means all the important art of Southeast Asia was concentrated in capitals.

PEASANT FISHERMEN

Throughout Southeast Asia, river, lake, and sea together provided a welcome and necessary addition to man's food. Fish, sometimes fresh but more often dried or otherwise cured, was the most frequent accompaniment to rice in the peasant meal. The seas of Southeast Asia are particularly rich in fish, and, though riverine communities often devoted a major portion of their energies to fishing, it was on the endless coastlines of the Malay peninsula and the Indonesian archipelago that the fishing village most clearly represented a distinct form of social and economic organization.

Fishing villages, seldom prosperous even by peasant standards, tended to be small and scattered. Set on white sands beneath waving palms and casuarina trees, and situated near the outflow of a river or creek for fresh water, the typical fishing village was the home of a dozen or so families housed in rough bamboo dwellings along the beach. The methods of fishing varied with locality, seas, and kind of fish, but line-hooks, fish-stake traps, casting nets, shellfish pots, and boats and nets of many sorts were used. Although most of the equipment was simply constructed from materials available within the village, it represented considerable capital outlay for the fisherman, more than could be raised by single individuals or families. In addition, many fishing methods were facilitated by cooperative labor—running the larger boats, for example, or hauling dragnets. These two facts taken together—the need to mobilize resources and to share work—led to patterns of cooperation of a kind peculiar to the fishing village economy. One might find in a village several "rings" of fishermen working independently, each headed by an individual directing operations. Sometimes the leader was chosen for his larger share in equipping the venture, but more often, perhaps, he earned his position by experience and technical skills thought to be above the ordinary, by his presumed knowledge of the movements of fish, and by his ability to propitiate spirits, thus ensuring a good catch. Marketing also, in which shares taken out reflected a complex assessment of shares of time, capital outlay, and skill put in, was often a complicated joint enterprise.

VILLAGE ARTISANS AND CRAFTSMEN

Larger peasant communities usually included among their members artisans and craftsmen as well as religious practitioners, the devotees and specialists required to deal with the uncertainties of the world. These professionals were peasants who, having acquired special skills by study or practice, often pursued the traditional sideline of their family. There were experts in villages who were able to tell the farmer when to sow or the young man whether he had chosen the right bride, or who, like the Javanese or Malay *dalang*, could perform the shadow-play, a mixture of magic, ritual, and entertainment. There were mediums, sorcerers, astrologers, and medical practitioners. Other villages had skilled artisans, village metalworkers, and carpenters, or perhaps women especially noted for their weaving or plaiting, working usually in the dry season, when their fields did not require labor.

There existed villages specializing in a single craft or trade to the exclusion of agriculture. Some produced salt by evaporation from shallow ponds of sea water, for example. Other villages concerned themselves with potting, papermaking, brick-making, hat- or umbrella-making, weaving, and jewelry-making. In a few places, such crafts were the private property of hereditary caste groupings, as on Bali, though family and village groupings, as in Vietnam and Thailand, were more common. Generally, because of the restricted availability of materials, one craft per village was the rule. In Vietnam, villages attempted to keep special industrial traditions and expertise to themselves by forbidding their women to marry outside the village or by refusing to teach skills to outsiders. Artisans, more susceptible than others to official exactions, were more heavily dependent upon marketing than were their neighbors. Their specialized functions were recognized by the government, hence they often were exempt from the seasonal labor and taxation required of other peasants. Nevertheless, they had to pay heavy taxes and to supply their products to the court at fixed prices—or none at all. Labor slavery of this kind probably inhibited the growth of industry by market restriction and price manipulation. Village handicrafts survived more because of the necessity of producing basic commodities than because of their inherent desirability or profitability as an economic enterprise.

SLAVES AND BONDSMEN

In the eighteenth century, slavery was practiced through most of Southeast Asia. There were hereditary, nonhereditary, temporary, and permanent slaves. Hereditary, nonredeemable slaves were usually descended from war captives, criminals, or traitors or were the result of slave raids into the highlands. In the archipelago, both Christian and Muslim law forbade the enslavement of believers. Since, however, it allowed that of infidels, there were some Muslim and pagan slaves in the Philippines, and pagan slaves in some of the Malay sultanates. In Burma, Cambodia, and peninsular Thailand, there were monastery slaves, the descendants of persons condemned for various crimes who remained exempt from normal labor service and state taxation. They lived in villages as ordinary peasants and devoted the produce of their assigned lands to the upkeep of Buddhist monastic establishments. In Vietnam, those who entered slavery as punishment for crimes were often sent to military camps in frontier areas to open up new lands for cultivation. They could become peasant farmers on the land they worked when their sentences as labor slaves expired. Apart from ordinary slaves in Java, there were a number of special slave outcaste communities serving the state in special functions like rope-twisting and maintaining harbor fire beacons. Usually they were outsiders by origin or had fallen by their actions from positions of respect. These people, few in number, were never extensively employed outside personal household service for the elite.

Debt bondage was undoubtedly more common than outright slavery in the late eighteenth century, especially in Thailand and perhaps Malaya, where the rural economy had become increasingly monetized. A peasant in economic difficulty, needing cash for a wedding or to settle a gambling debt, might seek or have thrust upon him assistance from his neighbor or local chief, receiving either money or goods with a time limit for repayment. If he had not paid up at the end of this period, he and his immediate dependents became debt-bondsmen until the debt was cleared. During this period, he might remain in his village rendering services or goods to his creditor by way of interest, or he might be taken into the creditor's household and provided with food, clothing, and protection in return for labor. He was paid nothing, hence repayment of his debt was hard. Many debt-bondsmen became obligated for life. The institution of debt-bondage was particularly well developed where manpower was in short supply. It offered obvious advantages to creditors, who were assured of cheap labor and of a force of men for use in war or in their bids for political power. The bondsman, however, might benefit as well. He remained in theory a free man, not a slave, and his social position was sometimes improved by his link with a member of the ruling class. Through the institution, in return for his surrender of freedom, he might gain protection, reasonably good living conditions close to a source of power, and exemption from the harsh labor and taxation imposed on his fellows. Although in some cases bondsmen and their families were ill-treated, escape to the hills was possible for those willing to give up the settled village life of the plain. Customary law generally provided detailed rules for the conduct of masters toward their slaves.

PEASANTS OUTSIDE THE VILLAGE

For the most part, the peasantry stayed at home. All the major countries of Southeast Asia, however, had established outlets for the young, adventurous, and unconventional of the village community. In many cases, these outlets were thoroughly respectable. The young Minangkabau who went roaming as a peddler for a few years on the trade routes of Sumatra and the Straits came home with riches and experience. Admired by the village, he could then claim a bride and settle down. Similar customs existed among most of the peoples of Sumatra, among the Lao of what is now Northeast Thailand, and elsewhere. Pious Muslims sought renowned Islamic scholars in their wanderings, and Buddhists took long pilgrimages. All these societies embraced less respectable wandering troupes of actors and musicians. In addition, banditry was a frequent outlet throughout Southeast Asia for those displaced by warfare, in trouble, or unwilling to endure the restrictions of village life. Bandits—*djago* in Java, *tulisanes* in the Philippines, to mention only two of the best-known types—were organized in regular groups, with their own established customs and group culture, headed by leaders renowned for their magical powers and bravado. Their depredations were sometimes later celebrated in folklore.

Many other villagers regularly went away from home to perform compulsory labor service for the government—the *corvée* of the mainland states and Java, called *kerah* in the Malay states and *polo* in the Philippines. Generally speaking, it took two different forms: services rendered personally to local lords, and services owed impersonally to "the government." The latter form was probably best developed in the mainland states, where the *ahmudan* classes of Burma and the *phrai luang* classes of Thailand were required to give three or four months each year to the service of the king. They might be gathered and sent off to dig canals or accompany a military expedition, leaving their families behind. They might be supervised for extended periods of time by men whom they had never seen. If health conditions were good, and often they were not, their annual labors might provide an opportunity for adventure, financial gain, and amorous exploits. The dangers, unpredictability, and possibilities of harsh treatment or living conditions, however, rendered this type of labor service, in Thailand at least, something men usually tried to escape, preferring personal service in the establishments of officials. The personal service rendered by the *athi* classes of Burma and the *phrai som* of Thailand, which was often spread more evenly throughout the year, was usually closer to home. It was frequently carried out under a local personage, who was given control over men as part of his remuneration of office. Performing their labor service in the households of local officials and rulers, and maintaining a relationship with a single master or family over several generations, these peasants had close personal ties to their patrons. The peasant could count on the support of his master or supervisor if he became involved in litigation, for example, and his master in return could expect the backing of his men in political moves. If this latter form of labor service was more heavily dependent on individual than on institutional arrangements and, thus, less secure over time than the formalized government labor service, it was more personalized and predictable for the people involved. It helped to integrate the village into larger political units.

In time of war, the role and importance of the peasant's labor changed radically. Few Southeast Asian states, dependent upon conscription to raise the troops they needed, had large professional armies. Vietnam maintained a particularly well-developed system of military conscription, which operated even in peacetime, with peasant conscripts serving four months each year and longer if campaigns demanded. While in Vietnam the service came under the impersonal supervision of a professional officer corps, elsewhere in Southeast Asia forces were usually raised through the normal channels of forced labor, going to battle as local or provincial units under their own chiefs and leaders; transporting their own food, equipment, and weapons; and sometimes, as in Burma, buying their own ammunition. Philippine mercenary forces, by garrisoning Pampangan troops in the Bisayas, for example, were organized to play upon the animosity between linguistic groups. As elsewhere in the eighteenth century, wars could bring large casualty lists and great hardship to many people, although often campaigns or desultory warfare could take on the aspect of organized, large-scale brigandage, offering the young man opportunity for prizes and adventure, as well as for a rapid rise in social status after demonstrated skill on the battlefield.

SOCIAL STRUCTURE

The immediate world of the Southeast Asian peasant was peopled by his close relatives—his nuclear family and his kin. Through most of the region, maternal relationships were as important as paternal ones. Though subject to stress from the patrilineal biases of Islam, Spanish Christianity, and the Confucian ethic, inheritance patterns indicate that bilaterality and the high position of women generally were cultural factors of enduring strength. As villages often contained only a small number of families, they were interlocked or joined to other villages primarily by marriage. Kinship ties provided the individual with a set of primary loyalties and defined his place in village society.

There were various forms of social interaction beyond the family. The patron-client relationship allowed for mutual understanding between superior and inferior in the social hierarchy. The client received protection and assistance in return for his support, service, and respect. In Thailand, where the system was elaborately developed, these interactions occurred both within the formal structures of the bureaucracy, from the village upward, and outside formal administrative hierarchies through private relationships.[2] By becoming a client of an official, a peasant could make more personal an often distant system of law and administration, perhaps obtaining the preferment that could secure his social advancement. Similar ends were served in a very different framework in the Philippines through a system of ritual kinship associated with Christian baptism; there, the ties of godparenthood linked individuals and families within and outside the village, both laterally and vertically in the social hierarchy.

VALUES

Some of the strongest values of Southeast Asian societies are immediately apparent in their languages, which contained elaborate sets of pronouns used to express social distance and relationships among superiors and inferiors, intimates and strangers. The Javanese language had almost distinct dialects for use in speaking to superiors, equals, and inferiors on the social scale. The same is true of Cambodian and Thai, where, in addressing officials, peasants referred to themselves with a self-abasing set of pronouns which emphasized their own low status. The maintenance of these hierarchical relationships was very important to Southeast Asian societies. The ultimate in social disapproval was reserved for those thought guilty of shamelessness, presumption, ingratitude, or disrespect.

The life of the peasant was filled with risks. Infant mortality was high and life expectancy low. To meet and explain the threat of the incalculable or unexpected, throughout Southeast Asia an ancient animism supported peasants in their daily lives. It was characterized by a belief in myriad universal, local, and sometimes personalized spirits, which could interfere in human lives for good or ill and which controlled the unusual events in human life. Called *phi* in Thailand and *nat* in Burma, they were believed to be everywhere present and everywhere in need of propitiation. They might, like witches, be exorcised; their intentions might somehow be accessible by divination; and measures might be taken to ward off their evil effects or encourage their assistance.

The complex rituals associated with rice cultivation at every stage of the agricultural cycle were based on a recognition that the seed, the crop, and the land that bore it were inhabited by spirits or soul-substances that had to be exorcised, assuaged, or nurtured in order to secure the success of the harvest upon which life itself depended. In Malaya, the community, led by the village magician, celebrated the clearing of the ground before planting with rituals designed to insure the casting out of malign influences. Later, the tools used to break the ground and plant the seed were ceremonially prepared and cleansed to facilitate their work. The act of planting itself was a carefully prescribed enactment of conception, accompanied in its initiation by charms and prayer. After ripening, the crop was harvested with the tiny knife that, concealed in the hand, would not frighten to flight the beneficent soul of the rice now grown to maturity.

Tutelary and ancestral spirits abounded, often as village guardians. In Vietnam, the village tutelary deity actually received a seal of investiture from the imperial court. Representing the founder of a village or, for example, a general who had defeated Chinese invaders, the deity's tablet in the village communal house evoked village solidarity and participation in the community's past. Ancestor worship and hero veneration were highly developed only in Vietnam, where they constituted a regular part of everyday life. There, news of all important events was communicated to the souls of ancestors. The primary function of tutelary, ancestor, and associated observances was to emphasize, by the regular performance of rites, the stability and identity of place and the immutability of family and hierarchical connections.

Though they overlapped with the more universalistic beliefs of the world religions—Buddhism, Christianity, and Islam—the animistic traditions were by no means superseded by them. The many elaborate ceremonies, rites, and festivals of the year were major events in the lives of rural communities.

LAWS

The religious life of the community enhanced as well as symbolized its solidarity. Consent of all village members to the rule of local tradition, particularly as expressed in customary law, was necessary for the successful functioning of communal life and for the ability of the village to live in peace. Throughout the region, there were developed legal codes. Some were the product of secular and ecclesiastical bureaucracies, administered through courts of law or through the acts and decisions of district chiefs and magistrates. For the peasant, formal litigation of this sort, often carried out in inaccessible places, could involve high costs, "presents," and written documents which the litigants could not easily read. In addition to these difficulties, the outcome could not be assured. As most litigation was local and treated as if civil in character, it was in the interests of peasant society to solve disputes within the village community rather than invoke outside authority.

Living in villages more stable than most courts or bureaucracies, men already had well-tested rules for living together and reliable means for resolving their differences. In the Malay and Indonesian world, this system of customary law was known as *adat*. In its original sense, *adat* simply means "custom," the right and proper conduct for all the incidents of life from birth to inheritance. It was often local in character, and minor individual variations were a matter of pride and distinction to the communities concerned. Although codifications of *adat* were sometimes recorded, one of the principal characteristics of the system was that, generally, it was not written down and consulted. Rather, it resided in the memories of the older and more knowledgeable members of the community. Even though elaborate written codes were more prominent in the mainland monarchies, there, too, law was primarily a matter of local custom, a standard of equity and justice and a body of local precedents against which most local disputes could be assessed and settled within the community.

Village life was an insular life, a life directed against impingement from without. Close proximity for generations bred strong attachments among its dwellers—for the locale where they mourned life's passing, for the field where they drew sustenance, for the ground where they buried loved ones. Rarely did the lure of town or city pull the villager away from his roots. The gulf between peasant and distant ruler was to the peasant perhaps greater than that between himself and the spirits around him.

2

THE UPLAND PEOPLES

The uplands of Southeast Asia presented a very different world from that of the plains below. The hills and mountains of the mainland, and the hinterland of the islands of the archipelago, were and are peopled by a wide variety of ethnic groups speaking a multitude of languages. These groups had much in common with each other, from their agricultural techniques to similar experiences with the people of the valleys and plains. Seldom, however, were they given their due in the written records of the more developed states downstream.

While small numbers, notably the negritos of the Malay peninsula and the Philippines, led a primitive nomadic existence as hunters and gatherers of food, most lived by slash-and-burn agriculture, known widely as swidden. Usually living in houses raised on piles, and occasionally in communal dwellings ("longhouses"), they practiced a complicated cultivation that provided them with dry rice, grown without irrigation, as well as millet, sugar, bananas, and root crops, frequently all grown together in a single plot. They had much land in the sparsely inhabited uplands and on the fringes of the jungle, but it was generally poor and seldom level. The agricultural cycle for swidden peoples began with the clearing of brush from new land. The cuttings were allowed to dry out and then burned, their ash contributing to the fertilization of the soil, and then the small fields were sown, often broadcast, in time to take advantage of the rains. Weeding was carried out through the long growing season, followed by harvest, sometimes spread over months. The cycle might be repeated for one or two more years, but the soils were rapidly depleted, and soon the hill farmers would begin the clearing of new fields, allowing old ones to lie fallow for as many years as possible. Crops grown under such circumstances were varied widely to take advantage of different growing and market conditions. Dry rice (nonirrigated) was the essential staple attempted by all groups, while other crops could include millet, corn, taro, yams, chili peppers, cotton, ginger, and the opium poppy. It was a life of often backbreaking labor, lived in relative isolation.

The ethnographic map of Southeast Asia in the eighteenth century was as complex, as fragmented, and as particularized as the topography itself. In the upland mountains and plateaus of the mainland, most of the groups were related linguistically and ethnically to some of the peoples down below. Speaking languages akin to Burmese were such groups as the Karen and Kachin. There were numerous Tai peoples, related to the Siamese, Shan, and Lao, spreading from northeastern India to northern Vietnam. Along the length of the mountains dividing Vietnam from Laos and Cambodia were many groups, some speaking Vietnamese and Tai languages and other languages related to Khmer (the language of Cambodia) or to Malayo-Polynesian languages. Almost without exception, the upland peoples of the archipelago, from Malaya to Luzon, spoke languages of this family, but in very few cases were these intelligible to speakers of Malay, Javanese, or Tagalog. Although only five major language families were to be found in the region, even such a limited area as the Philippines counted more than eighty recognized dialects in six principal language groups.

The peoples of the hills shared many characteristics of social organization with the lowland peoples. Their villages were woven out of kinship and personal relationships into a strong and resilient fabric, which kept them cohesive in their relative isolation and facilitated their styles of agriculture and trade. Each group had its chief, and most had specialists for the propitiation of the spirits, which were a profound part of everyday life. The complexities of upland social organization tended to be a product of internal elaboration rather than external extension, as the dispersion of people over rough terrain made supra-village organization difficult. Although little is known about relationships among the upland groups themselves, evidence would suggest that, despite the small size and scattered nature of the separate communities, there was a good deal of contact between them. Migration, intermarriage, barter trade relations, intergroup political structures, shared value and belief systems, and warfare all paint a picture of interacting social systems. Though they cannot be delineated clearly and should not be overstressed, the indications that exist about the relationships among and within at least the major groups should serve as a corrective to any general propensity to characterize individual groups as discrete, homogeneous, and isolated. Their isolation and political fragmentation were relative. Different Karen and Tai groups, for example, were sufficiently aware both of their own distinctiveness and of the general identity of their larger ethnic group to call themselves "White Tai" and "Striped Tai" or "Red Karen" and "White Karen," sharing as they did a common culture while remaining fiercely independent in their own mountain valleys. But the ecological structure of swidden agriculture limited the density of settlement and organization.

The highlanders were also differentiated from lowland Southeast Asians by their greater isolation from cultural and commercial influences. Their societies had not been stimulated or fertilized in any direct and major way by Buddhism or any other of the world religions. Situated outside the ambits of Sanskrit, Pali, classical Chinese, or Arabic, most upland societies were preliterate, with rich but local oral traditions. Differences in agricultural techniques were indeed an important historical force shaping the highlander-lowlander dichotomy. They must not, however, be exaggerated, since some highland peoples, like the Tai and Muong in northern Vietnam, practiced wet-rice agriculture rather than the slash-and-burn variety. What really explained the dichotomy was the fact that selective cultural borrowing was far more an essential art of the civilizations of the lowlands than it had been of highland societies.

The upland peoples inhabited the fringes of states throughout Southeast Asia and came into frequent contact with them. Living where they did, in the mountainous regions separating the major states, the hill peoples affected the security of their neighbors. The Karen, tribal Tai, Meo, and Muong, for example, scattered from west to east across the highlands of Burma, Thailand, Laos, and Vietnam, played pivotal roles in the military expeditions mounted by the lowland states, both as objects of attack and as participants. They could provide troops, rice, supplies in and guidance through difficult terrain, and intelligence. In some places, the tribal peoples provided the lowland monarchies with products important in foreign trade, goods often termed "jungle produce." In Cambodia, for example, the Pear in the southwest were exempted from taxation and labor service in exchange for an annual quota of cardamom, a seed much in demand for Chinese medicine. Likewise, other tribes provided such exotic products as rhinoceros horns and deer nerves, for which Chinese traders would pay large sums. In many areas throughout the region, the hill peoples were the frequent objects of slave-raiding expeditions, carried out either by the lowland peoples or by their own neighbors and enemies; in this way, many men and women brought down from the hills were incorporated into lowland societies. In the Philippines, many hill groups remained for centuries the object of missionary endeavors. Generally they were regarded as uncivilized and as heathens or infidels by the lowland groups.

Throughout mainland Southeast Asia, from Burma to Vietnam, courts sought to relate themselves to the minorities of the fringe by demanding that they accept tributary status. These arrangements were entered into for a variety of reasons, on both sides, and created a complex matrix of economic and political relationships. For the hill peoples, tributary status offered a truce in their battles with lowlanders, as well as an outlet for some of their produce, in return for goods, especially salt, that they lacked. The power of the suzerain might be invoked to maintain peace among warring groups or to recognize one leader at the expense of another. The lowland kings and emperors could hope for stability on their frontiers, assistance in warfare, and sources of goods important in the export trade. Some felt their own prestige as rulers strengthened by maintaining lengthy lists of tributaries padded with numerous hill tribes, as the Vietnamese emperor did in recognizing the two sorcerers of the Malayo-Polynesian Jarai as the "kings" of "Water

Haven" and "Fire Haven"—while the two were also tributaries of the King of Cambodia.[3] The continued legitimacy of the kings of Luang Prabang commonly was held to rest in part on a tributary and ritual relationship to the Kha, the Mon-Khmer hill peoples of Laos.[4] Similar relationships were less well developed in maritime Southeast Asia, though the matrilineal ruling house of Negri Sembilan in Malaya, for example, claimed a right to the soil based on real or supposed marriage alliances with tribal women of the interior. There were widespread trading relations between the coastal peoples and the upland groups, the latter collecting jungle produce, such as rattan and bamboo, in return for salt, cloth, and iron. Everywhere, however, they remained unincorporated into the Buddhist, Muslim, Confucian, and Christian societies of the lowlands.

3

AUTHORITY AND VILLAGE SOCIETY

Considered individually, peasant villages and upland kin-groups were similar in many ways. Lowland villages, however, were integral parts of larger frameworks, linked to a supra-village world through local leadership, in which the key, though not the only, figure was a village headman.

The manner in which village headmen were chosen tended to reflect the power structure and values of the village as well as governmental concerns; when these were seriously opposed, the relationship between central authority and village was strained. The basic variables in the status and function of such headmen were the relative degree of social or economic division within the village, the degree to which external control was regarded as alien by the peasants, government attitudes toward villages and peasants, the administrative hierarchy through which control was exercised, and the demands that central authority placed on village society. A limited set of examples drawn from different parts of the region should suggest some of the different relationships in which the headman functioned.

In the customary Malay village, consisting of one or more groups of kinfolk linked by intermarriage, the position of primary authority fell to the headman (*penghulu*), who was usually a member of the principal or founding family and often had assumed the office by direct inheritance. Though from time to time a *penghulu* might have connections with the district chief or other members of the aristocracy, he was more frequently from the peasant community to which he ministered and a farmer like his fellows. Though his appointment might in effect be hereditary, it was commonly vested in him by the explicit gift of the ruler of the state, whose sealed document of authority he might well bear. This imprimatur, and the suggestion (perhaps more often than the reality) of external sanction it carried, gave to the headman what little coercive authority he had. Apart from this, he relied for the most part on respect and on the mobilization of social disapproval. For this reason, it was usual to find that the *penghulu*, besides belonging to the traditionally most important family in the village, had somewhat more material wealth than his fellows and was perhaps acknowledged to have unusual force of personality, piety, or particular success in the techniques of agriculture and husbandry, in which all were in common engaged.

The Malay *penghulu* was responsible, along with other village notables—for it would be a mistake to see the office as a solitary autocracy—for keeping the peace in the village and surrendering serious malefactors to the district chief, for exercising a judicial function, for providing *kerah* labor and sometimes produce from the village, for the allocation of surplus land, and for functioning as the eyes, ears, and sometimes the right arm of his chief and overlord.

In sum, as the sixteenth-century Malacca Code provided, *penghulu* had to

> make themselves well acquainted with the following subjects, otherwise their functions are thrown away upon them: first the *Hukum Shera* [religious law]; second, the *Hukum Akl* [principles of natural justice]; third, the *Hukum Faal* [principles of right conduct]; and fourth, the *Hukum Adat* [custom, and customary law]. This done, they may be termed men.[5]

In the Philippines, an essentially Malay system of village organization was the basis upon which Spanish rule built its administration. The pre-Spanish chief, known as a *datu*, was retained in office and renamed *cabeza de barangay* (village headman). His allegiance to the colonial regime was co-opted by increasing his privileges and guaranteeing his status. Since each village had a number of key families, the elders (*principalía*) reshaped the Spanish system to accord with the high value placed on consensus. Although the headmanship was initially a hereditary position, it came in time to be rotated among the *principalía* who formed the village elite, from which the petty governor (*gobernadorcillo*) was selected. With the priest, the *gobernadorcillo* was of critical importance, since he was the fulcrum between the foreigners above him and the peasants below. He was usually the highest *indio*[6] official in the Spanish bureaucracy, governing a *pueblo* composed of several *barrios* and at least 500 adult tribute-tax–payers. Always deeply involved in the infighting among the *principalía*, this man also had clear administrative obligations to his superiors. He was expected to deliver tax revenues, goods, and labor for the *polo* tax and to serve the myriad other functions of government, and he was expected to remunerate himself for his efforts. As his ties were basically downward to the peasantry, his need to extract the required exactions, plus his own maintenance, put a constant strain on his relationship with the community.

By the middle of the eighteenth century, there was developing in Philippine rural society an economic elite increasingly interlocked with the *principalía*. This group, the *caciques*, derived wealth and power from landholding. Some inherited title to land, while others gained wealth through money-lending and foreclosure. Many of the latter emerged from the *mestizo* (mixed-blood) class. The impact of the *caciques* on the structure of the village was immense, as they came to play an increasingly important role in every aspect of village life.

Village headmen in northern Burma, the *ywa thu-gyi* or *myei-taing,* generally came to office by hereditary succession through the male or sometimes the female line, or through marriage. Their succession appears to have reflected a social hierarchy in the village based on wealth and "right to rule," reinforced by continued possession of the office over generations. Their appointments were confirmed by the court only after their rights to succeed had been checked against written records and testimonials from their immediate superiors in the area in which they lived. Their responsibilities were heavy, for Burma's rural tax system was extremely complex and the administration of justice often tortuous. Although they lived in the village, they had a regular working relationship with the township headmen nearby. As these latter, too, received their positions by hereditary succession, patterns of personal and familial relations must have developed elaborately in the course of time; and indeed, the effectiveness of the village headman in representing the interests of his neighbors to higher authority must have depended on his ability to utilize these relations.[7]

Most of the same considerations applied to the role and functions of headmen throughout the rest of the Buddhist world of mainland Southeast Asia. Through Lower Burma, Thailand, Laos, and Cambodia, however, headmen generally were informally elected from among the elder men in the village. Their age gave them an automatic high status, and their experience gave their judgments weight. Being the wise old men they were, however, they employed consultation and persuasion to perform the acts required of them by central authority and to settle disputes by conciliation and compromise. These were part of a style of leadership inculcated by folk tradition and encouraged by the values of village society, which put a high premium on avoiding conflict. The popular literature is full of tales about heroic provincial governors who in battle saved their towns and about brash country lads who by wit and winning ways won power and the governor's daughter, if not his wife. Village headmen were not such heroic characters; both government and village respected their critical mediating role, but this left them, as often as not, the bearers of ill tidings to both parties.

Village leadership in Vietnam shared some of the characteristics of the above systems. Vietnamese villages were governed by chiefs (*xa truong*), who were chosen by their fellows. But although the village notables may have chosen the village chiefs, the court had to approve them. They had to carry out the orders of the court and, of course, collect its taxes. They were also the servants, rather than the masters, of the village council of notables (*hoi dong hao muc*), which exercised the real leadership in the village. As a Vietnamese proverb put it, "The village association is a small court"—as opposed to the large court at the imperial capital. An elderly retired village chief who had become a notable after retiring from office enjoyed more prestige as a notable than he had enjoyed when village chief.

A basic reason why the notables were the true village ruling elite in Vietnam was that they did not perform specific tasks for the court in the way the village chief did. Their status was informal. While an active village chief served a specific three- or five-year unpaid term, the notables constituted a permanent body of members for life. The notables were a heterogeneous group, the composition of which varied from village to village. Wealth, old age, and academic attainment by themselves were not enough to legitimize authority, although they were cardinal qualifications. Illiterate landlords, for example, found it difficult to become notables. Among the notables, the man with the highest status who presided over their meetings might be the villager who had achieved in his lifetime the highest scholarly or bureaucratic grade or might simply be the oldest retired village chief.

Unlike their opposite numbers in Thailand and Burma, the village notables in Vietnam were not the clients of town-based officials. If they served the ends of the court, as they usually did, it was not because of patronage extended down to them, but rather because they were part of a theoretically open class system that encouraged their orientation toward the societywide bureaucracy. Many of them were the heads of literate families who dreamed of having their sons and grandsons pass the civil service examinations. In their eyes, the good reputation of the village depended upon its interaction with the court, at least to the extent that its communal self-esteem was directly related to the number of successful examination candidates it had produced over the centuries. The importance of this is that, while no traditional Southeast Asian court commanded mass communications media or mobilization systems or desired socio-economic identity with the rural masses, the variety of styles of integration prevailing in societies as geographically close as Thailand and Vietnam was as crucial to the premodern history of the region as the uniform reliance upon rigid stratification and control over social mobility.

The Vietnamese case exemplifies the critical importance of consensus as both the source and the nature of village authority. The vital issues in village life were social and economic; they affected the relative status of each member of the community by easing and resolving conflict, by assigning labor and tax obligations, and by distributing the use of land. Customary law ultimately depended on village consensus and consent for its successful operation. In strongly hierarchical societies, the interests of individuals were given weight according to their social and economic status. The greater the variation in status, the more important it was for the village power structure to be representative.

4

PROVINCIAL POWERS

Ascending the social and administrative scale from the village toward the court or capital, it was in the provincial towns or district centers that one first encountered individuals acting in their everyday lives according to more broadly based loyalties. The Thai word for politics, *kanmüang,* means literally "the business of the province." Villages had to deal with the *müang* of the governor and his officials, rather than directly with the king. The provincial capital had direct connections with both ends of the administrative hierarchy. These strands met in the country towns where national and regional identities were shaped and made alive. Provincial and district towns, however, differed greatly from one part of Southeast Asia to another. Some were but larger villages, while others took on much of the appearance of a royal court.

There were at least three basic systems of bureaucratic administration. The first type was represented by the provincial administrations found in Burma, Thailand, Cambodia, and Java, which were essentially based upon the control of manpower rather than the control of land. As far as the court was concerned, the primary function of the provincial administration in these places was to collect the taxes levied on the activities of the peasants and to mobilize the peasantry for labor service and warfare. Governors in the mainland states commonly were said to "eat" their provinces, and much of the time their rule may indeed have been as extractive as is suggested in popular literary tradition. Often, however, provincial administrators had to reciprocate with protection and services for what they obtained.

In such systems, provincial governors and district chiefs usually had two essential qualifications for office. First, because their fathers or other relatives had held the same posts before them, and because their uncles and cousins filled minor posts in the province, they had a network of family connections and a set of dependents or clients that, as patrons, they normally inherited. Their position within the local social hierarchy could not be ignored by the central government. Second, they had, by virtue of their social status, training for the tasks they came to assume. The sons of provincial and local officials were brought into public life at an early age, involved even as boys in the work of ruling. In Thailand and Cambodia, they frequently served a period as pages at court and then returned home to begin climbing an administrative ladder that eventually would bring them to succeed their fathers. In Java, they went to the distant court less often, but they usually served in the households and retinues of their fathers and uncles, where they learned the family traditions and gained a knowledge of the working assumptions of political life. In all these societies, unlike Vietnam, academic training beyond a basic literacy was a minor qualification for office in comparison with practical experience, social grace, and the patterns of speech, dress, and manners that marked them as men of the ruling class. Even among such gentlemen, there was considerable scope for conflict, for primogeniture was not well-established and polygamy was widespread among officials. Fraternal jealousies ran rampant, and competition for public office and inheritance was intense.

Thus, provincial government in Burma, Thailand, Cambodia, and Java was for the most part hereditary government by a provincial elite that had firm roots in the provinces. The nature of their rule stemmed principally from the manner in which they were integrated into the society of the province by kinship connections and informal patron-client relationships. Because of their connections upward, they must also be considered part of the state's bureaucracy. In most cases, there were regular contacts between, say, Burman or Javanese provincial towns and the capital. Governors paid annual visits to the court to pledge their loyalty, deliver taxes, or attend state functions. A great many orders and reports flowed back and forth, and officials from the capital frequently were sent out to check tax or labor rolls or to invest new governors. The governor and his men were involved in transmitting the demands of the capital upon the villages, and they used its methods in doing so. By the eighteenth century, Thailand had reached the point in administrative development where some provincial ruling families had won by marriage relations and political alliance a role in the politics of the capital, but, on the whole, such developments were exceptional. The provincial administrations in most of these countries remained rural; their importance came from their ability to control and mobilize the manpower of villages.

The provincial elite in Vietnam, in contrast to its Buddhist and Javanese counterparts, was characterized by the possession of land, leisure, and classical learning. A Vietnamese landlord who had not used his leisure to acquire scholarship could not normally be considered a member of the elite, since he had no hope of an official career and could not serve as an intermediary or "broker" between the court and the local community. The provincial bureaucracy itself, that is, the group of commissioned officials actively on duty in the provinces, was merely a specialized division of the more general provincial elite. It included provincial governors-general, governors, financial and judicial commissioners, prefects, and district magistrates who served in the provinces, prefectures, and districts of the country. Sub-bureaucratic clerks and underlings linked the district magistrate to the 30,000 or so villagers whom he governed. Poorly paid and poorly educated, their misdeeds could subvert the entire system unless they were strictly controlled. As Emperor Gia-long put it in 1811, "He who loves his ox first drives away its flies; he who loves his people first punishes the sub-bureaucrats. This is a well-established theory of government."[8]

While the provincial elite in Vietnam, in and out of bureaucratic office, enjoyed a security of economic position most of the time, the fortunes of its members could improve in times of dynastic weakness. Like their counterparts elsewhere in Southeast Asia, once they discerned through their bureaucratic connections that a dynasty was declining, they transferred the focus of their ambitions from the context of the court to their own families and native villages, determining to build up their position locally so as to survive the dynastic tempests they saw ahead. They attempted to accumulate more land and enjoyed a greater opportunity to do so, once the court's controls began to weaken. Trends at the end of a dynasty actually improved the opportunities of elite provincial families to check the downward social mobility of their sons. The dynastic cycle was a strange mixture of the increasing isolation and incompetence of hereditary emperors, who had not fought for their throne, and the conditional allegiance of provincial bureaucratic families to the throne, an allegiance dependent upon the capacity of the court to guarantee stability and to satisfy family ambitions for bureaucratic success. In the provinces, the downswing of the dynastic cycle meant the economic polarization of social classes. Independent producers, the middle level of the society, almost disappeared, while there was both a small movement toward the upper level of the society (landowners) and a very large movement of people toward the bottom level, that of the landless who sold their labor to others. This landed character of provincial power contrasts sharply with the labor-oriented provincial elite of the countries to the west and south of Vietnam, though the rhythm of dynastic decline was essentially similar for both.

The third bureaucratic model of provincial administration was that of the Spanish in the Philippines. There, the top positions in the social and political order were filled by foreigners. Born either in the Iberian Peninsula (*peninsulares*) or in the Empire (*creoles*), they rarely lived their whole lives in the Philippines. They came as bureaucrats, soldiers of fortune, and political appointees, and most considered the islands a hardship post. They clustered in the administration in Manila or served as the provincial governors (*alcaldes-mayores*). This latter office offered great power and opportunity for the individual, especially because of the geographic fragmentation of the archipelago. Despite extensive legislation designed to keep the provincial governor from abusing his authority, he was rarely sympathetic to the native population. Moreover, the high turnover rate and specific prohibitions against marriage or other long-range ties in the region kept the institution an alien one. The usual provincial governor was far more involved with events in Manila,

Mexico City, or Madrid than he was with those in his province. As a result, he tended to be insensitive to local interests.

On the whole, and especially in Java and Vietnam, provincial authorities were securely integrated into the social and administrative hierarchy of the capital. By way of contrast, the nonbureaucratic systems in the Malay states of the peninsula, in western Indonesia, and in the Shan and Lao principalities tended rather to be localized systems of hierarchical order held together by tributary relations. In the Malay system, the key to political organization above the village was the district chief. Indeed, the ruler of a state was, in effect, a chief within his own royal district, his exercise of authority within the state as a whole deriving from his control over territorial chiefs scattered throughout his domains. These offices were essentially hereditary, though appointment and continued tenure depended at least theoretically on the pleasure of the ruler. Chiefs commonly held, under commission from the ruler, rights of control over a specified area of the state usually based on a stretch of the main river or one of its tributaries. These rights included the collection of taxation and tolls on riverine trade, the granting of concessions and monopolies, and the right to demand produce and labor from the inhabitants of the district. Because rivers were the principal means of transport and communication, district chiefs usually placed themselves advantageously at some strategic point on the main waterway of their territory, facilitating both tax collection and defense. Although the ruler's situation at the mouth of the principal river frequently gave him an economic advantage over the chiefs, they were virtually autonomous in their territories and jealous of their powers. The resultant tendencies toward strife and fission were counterbalanced only by a common recognition of the values and virtues of the institution of the sultanate as a validating mechanism for the whole system. It was to the advantage of the chiefs to maintain the sultanate, the symbol of state and source of legitimacy, as a basis for their position vis-à-vis each other, as a source of reward in dynastic maneuvering, and as the embodiment of the larger political entity, with its advantages for trade and defense. Thus, although the real power of a ruler might be little greater in political and economic terms than that of some of the senior chiefs, there was a general acceptance of his office, if not necessarily of his person, as formal head of state.

The chiefs in most of the Malay states, stretching from Acheh and Kedah to Sulu, were members of a hereditary ruling class and were ranked in complex orders of seniority, which served to define and determine relative position and influence. All rank and dignity was held to be served by unseen forces that punished insults to lawfully constituted authority. The concept of differential status and concern for its expression were of abiding interest to the traditional elite, with a correspondingly exclusive attitude toward those not privileged to belong to it. It was rare for a man to cross the barrier from the subject class, particularly in his own state, where his origins and background were known. Marriage outside one's own class also was exceptional, though marrying children into advantageously positioned families was a well-established means within the class of chiefs itself for indulging in the constant preoccupation with rank and influence. The main advantage of the rank of chief, apart from the values inherent in the prestige it bestowed, lay in the right it gave the holder and his kin to a share in the economic resources of the state. The basis and emblem of authority was manpower, so that much depended upon the ability of a chief to gather and retain a following, both from among his own kinsmen and from the peasantry. A typical chief's household consisted of dependent kin performing the necessary tasks of administering his lands and acting as secretaries or accountants and tax-gatherers, or mercenaries and free volunteers who provided a permanent, if often idle, armed force—the feared *budak-budak raja*, or raja's bully boys—and of debt-bondsmen and slaves.

In the Lao and Shan principalities of Burma, northern and northeastern Thailand, and Laos, a similar system prevailed in which, more often than not, the "king" was a first among equals rather than a monarch set above his officials. The key political units, *müang*, were semi-autonomous, ruled by hereditary princely families. Their relations with their neighbors and distant suzerains generally consisted of sending annual gifts as symbols of submission, made substantial only in time of warfare, when the interests of all were served by joining together to repel invasion.

Through most of Southeast Asia in the eighteenth century, political and economic power were synonymous. Because property was usually subject to arbitrary confiscation by the ruler or his officials, and because manpower generally was more important than land, real wealth in most of the states lay in the right to the service and produce of others. Major exceptions were the landlords of Vietnam and the Philippines.

In Vietnam, landlordism was most extensive in the southern and south-central provinces, even though the population pressure was significantly lighter there than in the north. A consistent feature of rural Vietnam was the struggle between private landlordism and the ancient Vietnamese ideal of communal, village-owned property. Villages as communities owned public or communal lands that amounted generally to less than 20 per cent of the land of the state and were meant to ensure that no peasant remained landless. Plots were assigned and reassigned regularly to members of the village by the notables, who usually kept the best ones for themselves. An undeniable trend was the growth of private estates carved out of these public lands, which in theory could be leased to private individuals only for publicly documented three-year terms.

Similar developments in the Philippines stemmed from different conditions and causes. There, the Catholic Church emerged as the greatest landlord, its holdings geographically concentrated and unevenly shared by the various religious orders. The Church, which had become an important source of credit to the colony through its charitable agencies lent money with land as collateral, much as patrons elsewhere lent money on the collateral of labor. The problems of a landless peasantry were, unlike the case in Vietnam, new to the country. In the late eighteenth century, the orders began to give concessions to individuals to clear and improve its land. These men, called *inquilinos*, were allowed a certain number of years of tenure without rent and were thereafter charged rent-in-kind by the order. They, in turn, sublet their concessions to sharecroppers for about 50 per cent of the yield. The peasant perennially went into debt, and the system was abused, as the sharecropper was forced to pay out more and more of his crop. The friars, who increasingly needed the rents from the estates to maintain their mission work, often failed to see the repressive quality of this institution, and how their economic dealings compromised their authority.

Provincial and port towns, the headquarters of district chiefs, and upriver trading posts were modeled on the court or capital they served. A few carried forward the dignity and traditions of earlier days of independence, like Nakhọn Si Thammarat in southern Thailand, which had its own court and bureaucracy on the model of Ayudhya. Many more, however, had as great a need for specialists and professionals as the capital, in order both to represent higher authority and to service its administrative functions.

A provincial government, such as that of Nakhọn Si Thammarat, could be extremely complex. The titled officials there numbered 424, while the districts under its control contained 322 more, each man with specified rank, title, and responsibilities. For the most part, their functions were narrowly restricted to the administrative sphere, involving such duties as the control and supervision of conscripted labor; the collection of taxes, tolls, and duties; and the administration of courts of law. There were clerks, foremen of slaves, judges, policemen, customs and toll collectors, elephant trainers and keepers, translators for the port, accountants, and a host of others. There were Brahmans to consult with judges on points of law, and physicians and astrologers to minister to the governor and his city.[9] Some governors of that town had been noted in the past for their patronage of the arts, especially poetry and the dance-drama. With his officers, and surrounded by an elite of technical and professional expertise, artistic talent, and religious devotion, the governor was more than an individual administering an area: He was the center around which the cultural life of a wide territory revolved.

In Java and Madura, the major provincial officials and local hereditary lords presided at courts (*dalem*) that were smaller replicas of the royal court in Central Java. The *dalem* was a large complex of buildings, often walled, containing the residence of the lord himself and his principal wife, separate apartments for his other wives, children and relatives, halls for official meetings and for *wayang kulit* (shadow drama) and dance performances, kitchens, stables, and numerous outbuildings for servants and grooms. The *dalem* was also, like the royal palace-city, the center of a universe, in this case, the region ruled by the provincial lord. Before it, to the north, stood the *alun-alun*, a grassy square with one or more great banyan trees at its center; on one side of the *alun-alun* stood the mosque; and around this complex spread the town, not usually very populous in this period, but the place where virtually all nonpeasants in the region (apart from the rural ulama) were concentrated. The *dalem* was the political, in a sense magical, and cultural focus of the whole region; in the Sundanese areas of West Java and on Madura, moreover, it was the major institution through which Javanese culture spread out to the common folk in the outlying areas.

The actions of individual governors and chiefs did as much to determine the character of provincial rule as did any strength or weakness of administrative institutions. One could argue that inactive or inert or self-concerned administrations predominated in Southeast Asia in the eighteenth century. Certainly, a considerable insensitivity to the problems of the peasantry existed where, as in Vietnam and the Philippines, problems of landlessness were building up; where labor was being abused, as in Burma and Thailand; or where political strife dragged whole states into warfare, as in Cambodia and Java. A nineteenth-century Cambodian treatise on the interpretation of dreams stated that if one dreamed of a person without arms or legs, one was destined to become a governor.[10] Such limbless creatures could do nothing else but eat, and in the eighteenth century there was no shortage of appetite or food.

5

RELIGIOUS LIFE AND LEADERSHIP

In the course of its long history, Southeast Asia has known all the world religions, and since the seventeenth century three—Buddhism, Islam, and Christianity—have commanded the adherence of most of the region's population. All but Mahayana Buddhism are relative late-comers to the region. They share similar concerns for personal salvation and the religious life of individual communities, which distinguish them from the Brahmanical religion, distant and esoteric, so typical of the earliest kingdoms of Southeast Asia. The most important effect of the great religious changes of the thirteenth through the seventeenth centuries was the creation of religious systems and hierarchies that bridged the distance between the village and the court and encouraged the growth and dissemination of a culture that became vernacular and popular.

MAHAYANA BUDDHISM

Mahayana Buddhism is the "northern school" of Buddhism, which spread historically from India to Nepal, Tibet, Mongolia, China, Korea, Japan, and northern Vietnam. Theravada Buddhism (sometimes called Hinayana) is the "southern school" or "southern family," which spread from India to Ceylon, Burma, Thailand, Cambodia, and Laos. To cite some of the differences between the two schools, Theravada Buddhism strictly follows the words of Gautama Buddha, whereas the Mahayana insists upon broader interpretations and is more eclectic. Theravada venerates only the Buddha himself as the founder of the religion and considers Mahayana, with its worship of bodhisattva (men, lay or ecclesiastical, who had become Buddhas-to-be but who compassionately helped others to reach *Nirvana* before entering it themselves) to be idolatrous. Theravadins practice religious devotion to save themselves, Mahayanists to save themselves and others. Mahayana tends to allow laymen and women a greater role in its religious community than does Theravada, which strictly separates monks from lay people. Theravada monks in such countries as Thailand and Burma wear saffron robes and beg for their food, while Mahayana monks in Vietnam wear brown robes and do not beg.

On the whole, Vietnamese patterns of cultural borrowing from

China dominated the evolution of Vietnamese Mahayana Buddhism. Because the Vietnamese were generally under the Chinese cultural sway, they were more likely to read Buddhist scriptures and religious tracts written in classical Chinese than those written in Indian languages. Buddhism in Vietnam, moreover, intermingled with Taoism and with popular refractions of Confucianism and existed as one element in a religious compound the Vietnamese themselves called "the three religions" (*tam giao*). The Chinese and Vietnamese religious worlds overlapped so much in the eighteenth and nineteenth centuries that many southern Chinese priests could emigrate to Vietnam from Kwangtung and Fukien and develop large religious followings there. But Vietnamese Buddhism also had its "Southeast Asian" side.

Vietnamese Buddhists themselves like to stress that, in Chinese Buddhism, the two possible courses of action—"participation" in worldly affairs (*nhap the*) and hermitlike "abstention" from them (*xuat the*) —were usually kept rigorously separate from each other, as two mutually exclusive categories, rather than being dynamically combined. Vietnamese Buddhism, on the other hand, attempted "to reconcile the two aspects of participation in the world of men and abstention from the world of men, in order to create a special way of life for Buddhists: an emperor could be a monk and a monk could be the secular leader of his country."[11] Far more than his Chinese counterpart, the Vietnamese Buddhist believed that he possessed the theoretical license to engage in a life of both private "spiritual experimentation" and practical politics, basing the latter upon the former.

This synthesis of "participation" and "abstention," although an integral part of Vietnamese Buddhist political thought, remained an unattainable ideal in the eighteenth century, when institutional Buddhism was at an unprecedentedly low ebb. At that time, the Confucian court feared Buddhism not as a highly organized political rival but as an indirect ideological influence that could undermine the court's intricate bureaucratic order. The greatest writer of the period, Nguyen Du (1765–1820), under Buddhist influence, quite explicitly declared, in his poem "Chieu hon ca" ("Song Summoning Back the Souls of the Dead"), that in paradise "the superior and the lowly of this world are reseated in rank." In his poem, he also reminded the wandering souls of former court officials that "the more prosperous you were, the more hatred you accumulated. . . . Carrying such a weight of hatred, do you really think you should seek a way to reincarnate yourselves?"[12]

The court embarked upon a policy of religious control, manipulating the recruitment of Buddhist monks and priests. To become a Buddhist ecclesiastic in Vietnam in the early nineteenth century, a peasant or scholar required an "ordination certificate" (*do diep*) from the court. Applicants for these ordination certificates had to travel to Hue itself, where they were given religious examinations. Furthermore, no Buddhist temple could be built in Vietnam at that time without the permission of the Nguyen court. The numbers of monks and acolytes at the larger temples were fixed by law, and village chiefs who did not report surplus monks at local temples were punished. The court itself paid the salaries of the head monks at the major temples. It endowed important temples with their land and even gave them their names. It bestowed upon them teas, paper, incense, candles, and drugs, which it imported from China. At its command, Buddhist temples would celebrate a "land and water high mass" (in origin, a Chinese Buddhist ritual) for the souls of dead soldiers who had served the dynastic house. In addition to controlling the temples, the court sponsored and financed the construction of new ones, usually in the vicinity of Hue, where they were easier to supervise. Hue's emergence as a center of Vietnamese Buddhism dates from this period of court patronage and control.

Considered purely as an organized institution, Mahayana Buddhism occupied a much more modest place in Vietnamese society than Theravada Buddhism occupied in the Burman, Thai, or Cambodian societies. Needless to say, the heavily patronized Vietnamese Sangha became little more than a political instrument of the Nguyen emperors. By itself, it was poorly organized. There was no hierarchy of temples controlled by a central monkhood as well as by the court. There were no societywide Buddhist religious organizations to compete with the Confucian bureaucracy. The Vietnamese Sangha of the early 1800's was small compared to the Sangha of the Theravada states. The values of Confucian familism and filial piety (which required the procreation of sons to continue the family and its ancestor worship) made monasticism less popular in Vietnam than in neighboring societies. Widows and elderly women, on the other hand, commonly joined the important associations of temple nuns (*hoi chu ba*) in every village that possessed a temple. These women did good works, participated in temple worship at least on the first and fifteenth days of every lunar month, and paid rice dues to the temple in the same way that village men contributed dues to village communal feasts. Village religious life tended to be more stable—and more parochial—in the north than in the south. Pilgrimages to religious shrines in the agricultural off-season were a feature of Vietnamese rural society. But such pilgrimages were especially popular in the south, in regions like Ca Mau and Rach Gia, where there were few long-established temples to cater to worshippers or where the monks did not yet have sufficient prestige.[13]

THERAVADA BUDDHISM

Theravada Buddhism from Ceylon spread rapidly between the eleventh and the fifteenth centuries through the countries of mainland Southeast Asia from Burma to Cambodia and Laos. Every village had a monastery for its monks. A village was considered incomplete without one, though it might consist only of a small preaching hall (*vihara*), an *uposatha* building for ordinations and rites, and a dormitory for the monks. Around these, other buildings and tower-like monuments (*cetiya*) containing relics of ancestors or exceptional men might in time be built, and a sacred tree, reminiscent of that under which the Buddha preached his first sermon, planted. The monastery was inhabited by a small group of celibate monks clad in saffron-orange or yellow robes who had taken vows of poverty, chastity, and devotion to a life of religious study and meditation. Their activities were governed by 227 specific disciplinary rules. Forbidden to touch money and bound to beg for their food, they began each day with a walk through the village accepting the food offerings of willing householders. The monks returned to eat at their monastery, where food was prepared for them by students and pious hangers-on. Food obtained from the faithful was supplemented by garden produce and delicacies, never including meat, offered to the monastery by people eager to gain merit.

The Buddhist monkhood in village society provided all males time and opportunity to perfect their moral being, seek enlightenment, and to preach the *Dhamma,* the teachings of Buddhism, to the community. In a subsidiary fashion, the Sangha served as an outlet for the community's desire to perform meritorious deeds, particularly for women, who could best improve their moral state and hope for rebirth as men in their next incarnation by regularly offering food to the monks, attending preaching services, and offering a son to the monkhood for ordination. In day-to-day terms, the monkhood's most important function was to offer boys and young men a rudimentary education in reading and writing and the principles of their faith; for this reason, probably more than half the men of Thailand, Burma, and Cambodia in the eighteenth century were functionally literate, at least able to read a simple piece of vernacular prose. To those who had the time or were unusually talented, monks offered advanced instruction not only in religious subjects but also in the arts and sciences of Indian civilization, from mathematics and astronomy to poetics and medicine. Such advanced instruction, however, was not often available. It was generally concentrated in the monasteries under royal or noble patronage in the towns, which could encompass large monastic populations, support paid government teachers, and provide incentives for the best trained, offering them official position or ecclesiastical advancement. At every level of society, however, the monastery was the repository of whatever the population (which, after all, provided the monks) admired and needed in the way of sciences and arts. In out-of-the-way monasteries, some of this learning was uncanonically connected with manipulating events, interpreting dreams, and setting astrological rules for conduct.

In village society, the institutions of monastery and monkhood provided a coherent model of religious action and belief, which transcended village concerns and tended to draw villages together by ties that were wider and deeper than those provided by language and agricultural custom. The abbot and monks of the village monastery belonged to a hierarchical ecclesiastical organization that extended, parallel with the civil hierarchy, all the way to the king. The organization was a channel for the transmission of information in both directions, up and down, and a vehicle of social advancement for those inside it. Monks frequently carried the complaints of their villages to higher authority, bypassing secular intermediaries, and the village abbot often was the most respected leader in the village, sometimes more effective in his leadership than the village headman, who deferred to him. Ambitious young men, who found the secular social avenues to their advancement tightly closed by law and custom, could, through ecclesiastical education and promotion, circumvent the restraints against social mobility and advance to positions of ecclesiastical authority. Moreover, if they found the monastic life too encumbering, they could leave it and be "reborn" into the secular world at a point higher than the one at which they had left it.

The Buddhist ecclesiastical hierarchy was for the most part organized territorially in each of the Buddhist countries, save that the forest-dwelling Ārañnika monks were organized separately. Each district and province had its own chief abbot, who was subject to the authority and discipline of his patriarch and the supreme patriarch (Sangharaja) in the capital, whose decisions and injunctions were given force by civil authority. The Burman Sangha had a long history of sectarian divisions, which weakened its cohesion and authority. The Thai monkhood, by contrast, was carefully supervised by the crown, and, during some periods, prince-monks held high ecclesiastical offices. Royal patronage, steadily strengthened, had reached the point in Thailand by the seventeenth century where the monarchy was fully supporting religious education through the sponsorship of royal monasteries, which became virtual universities for religious and secular studies. The teachers of noble and royal sons and preceptors of monarchs found it difficult to remain free of political entanglements, in spite of their discipline. Popular literature and chronicle accounts suggest that, on the whole, theirs was ultimately a strong moral influence. Monks could, and probably did, mobilize public opinion for or against kings and officials. They had so established their moral influence by the last half of the eighteenth century in Thailand that no king could rule long without their approval.

Between the fourteenth century and the eighteenth, there were major intellectual and institutional developments in the Buddhist life of mainland Southeast Asia. On its arrival in the region, Buddhism had to contend not only with well-established animism in both village and court (the royal oaths of allegiance in all the courts included the threat of being punished by spirits if one broke the oath) but also with both court and folk Brahmanism in Cambodia and central Thailand. The Brahmanical tradition, unlike Buddhism, offered absolute and "scientific" certainty in its explanations and predictions of natural and human events. As long as Buddhism was incapable of giving people certain answers when asked whether a military campaign should be undertaken or a marriage entered into, Brahmanism remained of primary importance in everyday life. With the gradual secularization of Indian science, the strengthening of Buddhist scholarship and popularization of sophisticated cosmological ideas, and eventually official and popular disapproval of Brahmanical rites and practices, the Brahmanical element in the religious life of much of the mainland weakened. The same developments worked more widely to reduce animism to an essentially residual category for the explanation of phenomena beyond moral and scientific reason. Hindu religious sites, such as the temple of Angkor Wat in Cambodia, and Brahmanical institutions, such as the concept of the *devaraja*, or god-king, fitted easily into Buddhist terminology and practice, producing no pangs of conscience or sense of contradiction. As if to mark the success of Buddhism's domestication in Southeast Asia, monks from Ceylon were visiting Thailand and Burma in the eighteenth century to obtain valid ordinations and copies of religious texts then lacking in Ceylon, the original source of Southeast Asian Theravada Buddhism.

ISLAM

The Muslim world of Southeast Asia stretched in a 3,000-mile crescent from the northern tip of Sumatra (where perhaps Islam had first arrived) to the islands of the southern Philippines. Whether or not it had come as an adjunct to trade (and the point continues to be disputed), Islam, in contradistinction to the landward Buddhism of the region, retained a close association with the coast, with the maritime pathways that threaded the archipelago, and with the port towns and riverine states—in short, with that complex of geographical and cultural factors known in Indonesian as the *pasisir*. Islam was organized in no church—despite the persistence of European observers in finding "popes and priests"—but nonetheless possessed institutions, structures, and patterns of communication that knitted its adherents together and joined them to the heartland of Islam in the Middle East. Chief among these, perhaps, was simply the movement of people. Itinerant Arabs, mainly traders but including teachers, had been a feature of the port societies of the archipelago for centuries. Some had formed settled communities, and individuals were often found in religious advisory capacities at the courts of local rulers or moving among the villages as teachers or simply "holy men." Youths traveled regularly to preachers of this sort, whether Arab or indigenous, forming around them communities of scholars known variously as *pondok* in peninsular Malaya, *langgar* in Sumatra, or *pesantren* in Java. Parts of the area—Kelantan and Patani, for example, or Demak in north coastal Java—were particularly well known for these institutions, which attracted students from far and wide and acted as dissemination points for a zealous form of the faith. The *pondok*, too, were often centers for another of the institutions that linked Islam within and without, the Sufi *tarekat*, or orders of mysticism, which, sometimes to the disapproval of the rigorous, afforded a more emotional approach to God than other more restrained forms of worship. Ubiquitous in the region, the *tarekat* brotherhoods (of which the Shattariyah was in the eighteenth century perhaps the most prominent) were not highly organized and consisted mainly of individual *shaykhs* who claimed common teachers, along with groups of village or *pondok* followers. Knowledge of belonging to the *tarekat* added to the sense of commonality given by Islam. Yet another form of movement within Southeast Asia was the pilgrimage to Mecca, the *haj*, which afforded both ideological renewal to the body of Islam and considerable status and prestige to returning practitioners.

Within Southeast Asian Islam, it is common to make a broad distinction between two basic patterns, one might almost say intensities, of the faith—that related most specifically to the *pasisir* areas already described, which included the Malay world and the eastern islands, and that found in Central Java. Doctrinally, the Javanese form of Islam was characterized by an idiosyncratic blend of indigenous, Hindu-Buddhist, and rather florid Sufi mysticism. In its more nativistic forms, it has been described by the term *abangan*—a term distinguished from the *santri* form held to characterize the *pasisir* regions. The *abangan* had absorbed Islam, along with elements of Hinduism, Buddhism, and animism, into a larger, Javanese, complex of belief, whereas the *santri*, taking their self-identification as Muslims more seriously, were more exacting in their observances of Islam. Organizationally, the ruling class in bureaucratic central Java relied for the administration of Islam upon what came to be an appointed hierarchy of officials, who functioned more or less as adjuncts of secular rule, staffing mosques, prayer houses, and religious courts—the "priesthood" of contemporary Dutch observers. Within central Java, the *santri* element was represented by the independent *ulama*, teachers and propagators of the faith at the village level, who based their knowledge of Islam on their esotericism as initiates in the *tarekat* and their espousal of an outwardly as well as inwardly Islamic mode of life. Standing aloof from, and at times fiercely critical of, Islamically imperfect secular governments, they formed a powerful focus for peasant discontents in times of trouble.

Pasisir Islam, exemplified particularly in the Malay states of the peninsula and Sumatra, possessed little or nothing in the way of structured Islamic authority. It is true that the sacral powers of the rulers of these states included responsibility for the defense and good governance of the faith, but in the realm of religion, as of political organization, these sparsely settled riverine states lacked either the resources or the stimulus for centralization of control. Though the theoretical responsibility of the traditional secular ruling class for the religious life of the people was never seriously questioned, it was seldom seriously tested either. From time to time, individual rulers and chiefs did, for pious or other motives, appoint religious officials of various sorts beyond those attached to their own mosques, but there was a marked absence of anything approaching hierarchical organization or systematic control. In these circumstances, religious authority tended to dwell in those members of village society who, by their piety and some pretense to learning and, perhaps, through having made the pilgrimage to Mecca, were accepted as fit to exercise it—as *imam* of mosques and religious teachers, or as *guru tarekat*. The rural *ulama* thus described did not constitute a separate social class. In the absence of anything more than an attenuated religious officialdom, the Malay states were without the tradition of institutionalized opposition between independent *ulama* and religious bureaucracy that marked central Java.

The focus of village religious life was the mosque of general assembly, or the smaller *surau*, where the men congregated for prayers, met nightly during the fasting month (and at certain other times) to recite the Kuran, and held the religious exercises associated with the Sufi orders. For Malay youths, it was frequently also the sole place of education, where young boys learned by rote to recite the Kuran and were taught the basic tenets of their faith. If the intensity of religious life varied from place to place, it did so chiefly in response to particular individuals from within the village itself, who, through force of piety or esoteric knowledge, communicated their enthusiasm or ardor to others; there was neither hierarchy nor system to impose it from without.

Village mosques of assembly, as a rule, had only a small number of officers, chosen from among the villagers themselves. The principal functionary was the *imam*, who led public prayers, was responsible for running the mosque, celebrated marriages and recorded divorces, arbitrated (assisted by other elders) in disputes concerning religious law or practice, and was probably also the village teacher. Other officers were the *khatib*, who gave the prepared admonitory address (in Arabic) at the Friday prayer, and the *bilal*, who made the daily calls to prayer. Some of them may have been to Mecca, but most had derived what learning they had from attendance at a *pondok* for some years, or simply within the village. This, and a small knowledge of the Arabic language, sufficed to ensure them recognition as *ulama*, a standing shared with those itinerant Malay, Indonesian, and Arab divines who, throughout the area, found respect and sometimes veneration for their saintly qualities (allied sometimes, it must be said, with commercial acumen) and necromantic skills. The authority wielded by traditional religious leadership of this kind, though persuasive within its terms of competence, was essentially derived from the peasant community itself, of which the *ulama* were a part, and was devoid of external sanction, except where the ruling class found an interest in enforcing it.

Nevertheless, there did exist a clear, if frequently inactive, association between the secular power and the religious life of the people. Indeed, to speak of the "secular" power in this context is inapt, for the relationship between ruler and ruled defied simple classification and certainly embraced the spiritual as well as the material well-being of the state as an entity. In many of the Malay states of the peninsula and East Sumatra, there were, from time to time, state *kathi* (magistrates), responsible to the ruler, who, at least in theory, had a general oversight of all mosques in the state. In Perak, and possibly elsewhere, there was an office corresponding to that of state *mufti*, or legal adviser, exercised in this instance by one of the eight major hereditary chiefs of the state, who, it was said, together with the heir presumptive to the throne, held religious jurisdiction over the subject class. Jurisdiction over the aristocracy was held by the heir apparent. The assimilation of religious authority to customary political authority suggested here was a common feature of the region, potential or realized, and was later to be of political importance.

What has been said so far tends to suggest that eighteenth-century Islam in Southeast Asia was a stable system at rest. It is important to emphasize, therefore, that quite apart from the inbuilt tensions to which attention has been drawn—between Javanist and Islamic elements in central Java, between religious bureaucracies and independent *ulama*, and between traditional secular leadership and the expression of religious authority—Islam was still at that time an expanding religion. In Borneo and Sumatra, for example, and even in Java, *pasisir* Islamic society formed a kind of fringe, within which were populations with indigenous religious systems that knew nothing of Islam or were resisting incorporation. The expansion of Islam was a process that was to accelerate and become far more complex in the years following.

CHRISTIANITY

Spain colonized the Philippines as an act of devotion. The proselytizing zeal to make the archipelago a "showcase of the faith" colored Spanish institutions with ecclesiastical concerns. To the Spanish monarchs, glory in this life and the next was to be found through mission work, and there could be theoretically no divergence of goals between the religious and temporal spheres. Priests and bureaucrats were dedicated to the service of crown and cross; the resultant congruence established an interpenetration of functions. The colony would not and could not have survived without the priests, and by the end of the Spanish era the country was described as a "friarocracy." The friars, who came originally to spread the faith, were the only Spaniards willing to live in the rural communities for their whole lives. They enforced Spanish law and molded peasant (*indio*) values. As the result of the early decision of the Synod of Manila in the 1580's, priests learned and then taught in the vernacular languages rather than in Spanish, so that, except for the urban centers, where a patois called *chabacano* was spoken, most Spaniards could not communicate with the *indios* except through the priests.

The actual relationship between Church and crown was very complex. By a series of papal bulls, the Spanish monarchs were given the right of exclusive patronage over the Spanish missionary effort. In return, the crown provided transportation, paid each priest's annual salary, and guaranteed support of the Church. The priest became a salaried government official, and the crown, through another concession, the *recurso de fuerza*, was able to intervene in ecclesiastical jurisdiction if its interests were jeopardized.[14] These concessions, which were enlarged through legal interpretation by Spanish jurists, gave the crown two bureaucracies, one ecclesiastical and the other temporal. While this system remained effective during the first era of Spanish control, it became awkward as the interests of Rome and Madrid grew apart. By the mid-eighteenth century, there was no longer the congruence of interest that had once existed.

The tension between the crown and the Church was exacerbated by the struggle between the diocesan hierarchy and the religious orders. The Philippines had been converted initially by the friars (also known as regulars, from the Latin word for vows), who received from Pope Adrian VI the right to administer the sacraments and hold parishes free from supervision by the local bishops. Diocesan (often called secular) priests, in contradistinction to people in orders, were only to be given parishes that had not been assigned already, and, because the whole of the Philippines had been divided into spheres, there were few parishes left for diocesan priests. In theory, the friars were supposed to be shock troops, converting the heathen, transferring authority to the diocese, and then moving on to new areas. Moreover, the Council of Trent had attempted to curb the worldwide independence of the friars by ruling that a bishop had the right to episcopal visitation in any parish in his diocese. The bishops maintained that they must have the right to inspect and control all parish work and priests, whether regular or diocesan; the friars, in turn, argued that they had their own hierarchy, reaching up to the Pope.

What complicated the issue was the crown's dependence on the friars in running the colony. Since the friar was usually the only Spaniard in the hinterland, and since the crown discovered that only friars were willing to live and die in the *bundok*, the crown was unwilling to alienate the various religious orders. Each time the diocesan authorities in Manila attempted to impose the right of visitation, the friars would threaten to resign en masse. In 1750, after almost two centuries of trying, the diocesan authorities had only 142 parishes out of 569. More significantly, they were poor and small compared with those of the orders.

Indio priests were an obvious solution for diocesan officials unable to persuade Spanish diocesan clergy to endure the hardship of migration. Some Spanish temporal officials saw ecclesiastical advantages in using *indios* as a means of reducing the power of the orders. The friars savagely opposed such a move. For example, Fray Gaspar de San Agustín felt that the *indio* who went into the priesthood would do so "not because he has a call to a more perfect state in life, but because of the great and almost infinite advantages which accrue to him. . . . If the [*indio*] is insolent and insufferable with little or no excuse, what will he be when elevated to so high a station?"[15] Friar resistance effectively limited the number of *indio* priests to those trained by the orders to serve as assistants. Thus, they had only a smattering of education, enough to perform their subordinate jobs but not enough to make them learned in the faith.

The secular-religious controversy began as an administrative struggle within the Church. In time, however, it evolved into a racial tension between the friars, who remained almost exclusively Spanish, and the diocesan priests, who increasingly were non-Caucasian. The issue was to spark nineteenth-century Philippine nationalism. Since the clergy was an essential arm of the government, the struggle for *indio* parity transcended its ecclesiastical confines. While the Spanish crown and the Roman Catholic Church fell out of perfect union, they were so intertwined that they could not easily be separated.

The presence of four distinct religious traditions in the region, with the boundaries between them frequently political as well as cultural, may give a false impression of cultural compartmentalization in Southeast Asia. What worked to soften the impact of religious division was the mutual and creative accommodation that each religion and each society continued to make in the process of conversion and domestication. The ideas, institutions, and practices of society and religion were to some extent transmuted in their interaction with each other. Earlier animistic and Indianized traditions were not wiped away, nor did imported religious traditions survive their transportation without modification. The earlier Hindu-Buddhist mystical ideas and practices of the archipelago, for example, made the adoption of an Islamic mystical tradition easier than the adoption of sterner forms of that religion.[16] In the Philippines, Roman Catholicism was adopted passionately but selectively, and the grafting of this Western faith on indigenous beliefs changed both scion and stock. The relatively homogeneous Chinese-style Mahayana Buddhism of northern Vietnam, when it migrated south to the Mekong delta, suddenly encountered, and became sensitive to, the Theravada Buddhism of the Cambodian population there. The craftsmen of the mainland Buddhist states worked from Indian and Ceylonese treatises, which specified the physical characteristics of the Buddha, to produce bronze and wood images that satisfied their own aesthetic standards. As long as Brahmanical and animistic ideas remained pleasing and useful to their subjects, Buddhist kings were enmeshed in ceremonies primarily expressive of those traditions. The spread and intensification of Islam among peoples who had not so far adopted it or been greatly affected by it was similarly accommodated to regional ways. The interaction of Southeast Asian and imported religious traditions was a continuing process that gave dynamism to the cultural and religious life of the region.

6

TRADERS AND MARKETS

In the eighteenth century the village was, as it is today, the primary unit in the life of the people of Southeast Asia. Its links to larger units were administrative and cultural, through its own headmen and provincial governors or chiefs, and monks or friars. In addition to these connections, however, and sometimes transcending them, were economic relationships that might extend a short distance to local markets, beyond them to a riverine or coastal port, to the capital, or even overseas. It is common to consider these economic relationships as flows of commodities, or networks of trading connections; and on both these subjects recent research provides useful information. However, they also may be seen as the relationships of groups and individuals, given substance by the exchange of goods and services and providing grounds for actions of a political nature.

As an economic unit, the first concern of a village was for self-sufficiency through production of the grain on which its life depended. The minimum economic requirement was that it should produce sufficient rice to sustain itself. No village, however, lived on rice alone, and all required animal protein, vegetables, fruit, condiments, and salt to balance the daily diet. Most of these could be produced as secondary products but were not always available when needed, or efficiently produced, or—like salt—locally obtainable. Moreover, manufactured products, like iron and cloth, had to be found elsewhere. Thus, out of both convenience and necessity, peasants looked to local marketing and informal exchange to obtain the staple foodstuffs and other commodities they required for life.

In addition, by definition both fishing and craft villages were deficient in rice, as were many upland farming villages, while they all produced commodities the rice-farming villages desired. Fishing villages usually would work out informal exchanges of fish for rice with the rice-growing villages in their hinterland, carrying their fresh or dried fish and fish-paste upstream or along the coast to other villages or to regular or intermittent markets. Craft villages might market their basketry or pottery or cloth across the countryside in bullock-drawn carts or on long boats piled high on seasonal trading expeditions in the months following the rice harvest, when roads and tracks were passable and rice stocks high. In the market places of towns, at a periodic village market or annual fair, or informally along their route, a peasant might barter a chicken for good basketry, pottery, salt, or chili peppers. The meat of an old bullock or water buffalo might go toward the purchase of gold for a maiden's dowry or matron's vanity. Especially on the mainland, this was often a trade among women, who enjoyed the opportunity to gossip and arrange the marriages of their children. It was a vital and simple trade, little affected by government and international prices or wars and insecurity. No village could survive without it.

Tangential to this widespread trading was the commerce between the lowlands and highlands of the interior. It may have been best developed along the length of Vietnam, where highland woods, bamboo, and lacquer were traded for lowland fish sauce, dried fish, salt, and lime. Often the highlanders came for this trade to lowland rural markets, which were periodic, every three or five or fifteen days. The trade could become more complex when, for example, in central Vietnam the Hre people assumed the role of serving as commercial intermediaries between the Vietnamese and the more isolated Sedang and Bahnar peoples, though Vietnamese might still serve as peddlers—especially of salt—to the highland peoples.

Salt was the most important of the imports of inland villages, a commodity beyond the scope of purely local barter trade. With few exceptions, it was a coastal commodity, produced, as on the island of Madura off the east coast of Java, by evaporation from great salt pans constructed along the shore. It and other imported goods were distributed by traders of the coastal towns to the villages of the interior. On Java, the Javanese and Chinese merchants of the coast traded up the Solo and Brantas and other rivers, carrying salt, Chinese earthenware, textiles, and opium. There and elsewhere, peddlers and small traders set out from coastal ports with such goods for extended tours of inland towns and villages, bartering coastal products and imported goods for foodstuffs for the towns and goods suitable for export. On the whole, theirs was a difficult and often hazardous enterprise. They had to run a gamut of market and shop taxes; ferry, bridge, and road tolls; and, in the riverine states, the exactions of district chiefs or petty bureaucratic officers. Martaban in Lower Burma and Nakhọn Si Thammarat in southern Thailand, for example, were ringed with stations for the collection of transit dues on every road and waterway. Similarly, along the Solo River in Java, where such stations are recorded as early as the fourteenth century, tolls were heavy, increasing in the late eighteenth century to the point of constricting trade.

One important category of goods entered trade from producers with little or no compensation whatever. These were the goods accepted or required by some governments in lieu of, or as part of, taxes. Although a substantial proportion of this probably was rice, a large number of other products were involved. In Thailand, they were collected on a number of different bases. Some were given over as a substitute for labor service, particularly when the crown desired the product and the producer lived in a remote area—for example guano (for the manufacture of gunpowder), ivory, sappan and other exotic woods, and swallows' nests (for Chinese soup). Others reached the royal warehouses as a proportion of a peasant's produce taken in tax, as on ricefields, orchards, or market gardens. In some areas, rice or other goods could be demanded of peasants at a fixed price set by government; this was the case in the Philippines, Dutch Java, and portions of Thailand, although in such cases cash payment was involved. Elsewhere, goods were demanded as a substitute for taxes. The kings of Mataram in Java, for example, distributed their household requisitions among villages, one supplying the king's coconut oil, another his fish, others his rice, and still others the fodder for his horses. These were highly particularistic, personal, and direct economic relationships. All along their course upward through the administrative and social hierarchy, the commodities were subject to the exactions of intermediary officials, so that many groups and individuals were linked by their passage, each in some way dependent on the other.

Some of the above goods were deliberately produced for export and were usually collected through the same administrative and revenue devices, but also—and, in the eighteenth century, increasingly—commercially, in a much less particularistic and personal fashion. By that date, commercial agriculture had begun in two locales. In West Java, commercial sugar production began in the seventeenth century when Chinese entrepreneurs "leased" the labor of villages from local authorities and made the peasants grow sugar cane. They built small processing mills to extract the sugar and exported most of the product through the Dutch East India Company (VOC). In Vietnam, sugar was produced for export in provinces like Quang Nam, where the Internal Affairs Office or imperial household treasury purchased it by an exploitative operation, euphemistically known as "harmonious buying," in order to control its export.

Just as specifically, commodities for export were the products of mining operations in the region, especially the tin of the Malay Peninsula and the gold of western Borneo. The most valuable article of trade in the peninsular Malay states was alluvial tin. Dutch records for the seventeenth century describe the large trading expeditions of the Sultan of Kedah, carrying tin across the Bay of Bengal to the Coromandel coast; in the course of that and the following century, the Dutch made a determined effort to monopolize, by means of treaties with local rulers, the export of tin from Kedah, Phuket, Perak, Selangor, and Sungei Ujong. This monopoly was extended in 1755 to the island of Bangka, off the southern coast of Sumatra, after tin had been discovered there early in the century. The peninsular ore was worked for the most part by Malays, though communities of Chinese miners were known before 1800. The industry was controlled by members of the ruling families of the Malay states, either by direct ownership of the mines or by levying tribute on production and export. Encouragement was given to the tin trade in the 1780's by a shortage of tin in China, and prices remained inflated until beyond the end of the century.[17] The Chinese gold-mining in western Borneo began around the middle of the century. On a large scale—tens of thousands of Chinese miners are alleged, even for the eighteenth century—this was commercial production by independent frontier groups organized into their own *kongsi*, or working communities, which paid some of their yield in tax to the coastal sultans. Similarly, Spanish attempts at mid-century to develop iron-mining in the Philippines were contracted to an entrepreneur who imported Chinese labor for the task. Such developments cut two ways—toward an economic division of labor between indigenous peoples and the Chinese, and toward monopolistic policies aimed at keeping mining activity under strict control, particularly where (as in Burma) precious metals and gems were involved.

Generally, then, agricultural and imported commodities and the products of local mines entered the market and trading systems of Southeast Asia either laterally through direct barter trade between producer and consumer or vertically through administrative institutions, and only rarely through monetized commercial transactions. Though the quantities of goods traded within the region must have been considerable, a large proportion of them was traded in the village or market town by peddlers and merchants traveling inland individually and by Malay and Bugis traders along the coasts, rivers, and streams. In the absence of written records, such trade, by nature small-scale and local, is virtually inaccessible to the economic historian. It is only where international trade tied into the local economy that more distinct patterns come into view; in this situation, state trading monopolies (like that of Ayudhya, based on the export marketing of commodities obtained through tribute and taxes), and large-scale Chinese and European seaborne commerce developed. These may be conveniently viewed in terms of geographically defined trading networks, which everywhere touched, but rarely overshadowed, local commerce.

There were, first of all, systems of local and long-distance highland and hinterland caravan and peddling trade. Well-established caravan routes crisscrossed the interior of the mainland, stretching from northern Burma and Thailand into Vietnam and South China and carrying hill cotton, tobacco, silver, and forest produce by pack horse, oxen, mule, and elephant to periodic markets in return for horses, salt, and silk. Among those engaged in this trade were Chinese, Shans, and other Tai peoples. In Burma, the main center of such trade was Bhamo, where Chinese caravans brought warm clothing, silks, and copperware in return for cotton. To the east, there was a substantial overland trade between Vietnam and China, directed mainly by China's need to obtain the silver of Vietnamese mines in order to offset the bullion drain caused by the import of opium. These well-organized trading systems made a considerable profit for the Burman and Vietnamese courts.

Southeast Asia's seaborne trade with China took place within an ancient framework of international relations usually referred to as the Chinese tributary system. China in theory regarded itself as the suzerain of all the states of Southeast Asia, receiving homage from each at specified intervals, at which time the "vassal" states presented their tribute of local products and in return received from the emperor Chinese goods of equal or greater value. The tributary system in practice was a regular system of legitimizing official trade and, at an early date, accommodated private trade on the side, first by Southeast Asian traders and later by Chinese merchants. By the time of the Ming Dynasty (1368–1644), the private trade was predominantly Chinese and far outweighed in volume and value the official exchange of goods in tribute and gift.

On the Southeast Asian side, a large proportion of the goods involved in trade was both bought and sold by royal trading monopolies. The Thai and Cambodian kings, for example, who collected in their royal warehouses large amounts of goods in lieu of taxes or by monopolies of production and marketing, depended on external trade with China for much of their revenues. Roughly one-fourth of the revenues of the court at Ayudhya came from the profits of the royal monopolies. Malay sultans marketed some pepper and tin in this fashion, and, where the system was best developed, as in Thailand, an elaborate bureaucracy was created to run this trade, collecting in the provinces goods most salable on the Chinese market, processing and storing them, and arranging for the wholesaling of goods imported through the same channels. In time, the system was extended to include the building and staffing of ships, often by Chinese immigrants who had settled down in the country to engage in the trade. The existence of such organizations was a source of some strength to the Thai government, though it did create a vested interest in the China trade as such, as well as monopolistic practices not readily tolerated by European trading interests.

The South China Sea network was the most extensive and elaborate in the region. Strung from the major ports of the China coast, it extended in two directions: the "western" route to Vietnam, Thailand, and Malaysia, and the "eastern" route to the Philippine and Indonesian islands. The Chinese court was hostile to the growth of this trade, since Chinese shipbuilders and shipowners were the potential creators and owners of independent and politically uncontrollable navies. Although the Chinese court frequently attempted to ban such trade, Chinese ports continued to develop. In 1741, for example, it was pointed out that the ban, then under reconsideration by the court, would result in unemployment for more than 500,000 people in South China alone.

The word "junk," an English derivation from the Malay approximation of the Amoy pronunciation of the Chinese word *ch'uan*, "ship," itself aptly symbolizes the multicultural nature of the South China Sea trade. In 1821, the overseas Chinese in Thailand operated a fleet of some 136 junks, of which 82 operated in the trade with China and 34 sailed to Vietnam, Malaya, and Java. The ports of Vietnam traded primarily with the South China ports, sending about 100 ships north each year. A great many junks traded to Manila with merchandise for two annual galleons sent from the Philippines to Mexico. These junks were manned by Chinese crews, often resident in the foreign countries to which they regularly sailed, and generally remunerated by permission to load the junks with small cargoes of their own for trading at their destination. They became thereby modest shareholders in the venture.[18]

Extending the length and breadth of the South China Sea, this essentially Chinese trade was quite comprehensive. The major Chinese exports carried south were such luxury goods as silk and porcelain. Southeast Asian ports depended on such imports and on an export market for a wide range of local commodities, ranging from foodstuffs, such as rice, to luxury articles, Chinese-desired medicinals and aphrodisiacs, jungle produce, and such exotic products as birds' nests. The southern end of the route, including the Straits of Malacca, Borneo, and the southern Philippines in particular, was a difficult region for trade because of the multiplicity of petty ports and small cargoes, which were often carried by single traders on small ships, resulting in small-scale, complex trading systems. But by the eighteenth century the Chinese, through diversification and even third-party trade, had built up an extremely important trade in the region of the South China Sea, upon which the Thai court and the Manila government, as well as many smaller ports (Sulu's exportation of pearls, and Timor's trade in sandalwood, for example), depended for a high proportion of their revenues.

Within the South China Sea trading network, traders other than Chinese were widely active. Malay, Sulu, and Bugis traders in their small *perahu* handled much local trade among the islands in the south; Vietnamese and Thai junks occasionally extended existing Chinese trading patterns. Both the local and long-distance traders worked to integrate and expand this trading network. At three points on the fringes of the South China Sea—Manila, Batavia, and the Straits of Malacca—it was tied into other trading systems.

One of the reasons for the Spanish conquest of the Philippines was that Manila was a natural entrepôt for the China trade. The lure of the China market and the ease with which Chinese junks could bring goods to Manila made it a way station between China and the New World. Indeed, so much silver and Chinese silk were transshipped that the merchants in Spain soon forced the Madrid government to impose strict limits on the value and volume of the annual Manila galleon. The galleon trade, which lasted about 250 years, was carefully controlled so that it yielded enough to keep Manila financially afloat but not so much that it crippled Spanish home industries. Space in the galleon was divided into shares, or *piezas*, of a fixed size, and the Spanish community of Manila lived on the income from the sale of space to shippers. The Church supplied most of the capital to buy the Chinese goods, outfit the galleon, and tide the community over, and it received

30 to 50 per cent in interest when the galleon returned. When a galleon was lost or captured, the colony was virtually bankrupt. In 1743, for example, when the British admiral, Anson, captured the *Nuestra Señora de Covadonga,* he seized about 1.5 million pesos in silver.

The impact of the galleon trade on the Philippines was stultifying. Since the colony was heavily dependent, and since the galleon siphoned off most available capital, there was little interest in developing the country internally. By the mid-eighteenth century, the rigid mercantilist restrictions of this quasi-monopoly inhibited the development of trade patterns with other Southeast Asian states. The ease with which the colony could survive encouraged torpor and, for better or worse, kept the Spanish, except for the priests, isolated and uninvolved. The various restrictions also created endemic corruption, since the myriad restrictions were more honored in the breach than in the observance. The frequency of proscriptions against violating the rules indicates the universality of the abuse.

Most of the coastal and interisland trade in the Philippines—including that between Manila and the Muslim sultanates to the south—was handled by the Chinese or Chinese *mestizos*. The Chinese resident in the Philippines also had close ties with firms in China. These traders imported, through the South China Sea trading system, Chinese, Indian, and Southeast Asian goods destined for transshipment on the galleon and required in the colony itself. In turn, they exported the silver bullion through the same channels. Although the Spanish community was heavily dependent on the profits of the galleon, relatively few Spanish merchants and traders lived in Manila. Political connections with the Distribution Board—controlling available galleon space—proved a more effective way to make money than trading on an open market. Widows and Church charities had automatic rights to shares, which they sold annually to the few merchants. The number of traders participating in the galleon steadily contracted as the advantages of money and connection drove the small trader out of business. In the middle of the eighteenth century, there was neither a free enterprise system of entrepreneurs nor a great trading company; the Chinese did the work and shared the profits with the Spanish.

A second trading network centered on Batavia (Jakarta), the Asian headquarters of the Dutch East India Company (Vereenigte Oost-Indische Compagnie, VOC). The VOC (1602–1799) was a many-sided, far-flung enterprise—a trading company that was also a state. It was an ancestor of modern Indonesia as well as a pillar of the Dutch state in the seventeenth and eighteenth centuries; it was also the founder of modern South Africa, a major actor in the history of Ceylon, and the agent of an important movement in early modern Japanese intellectual history. Its home office was in Amsterdam, where its directors, the so-called *Heeren Seventien,* the Gentlemen Seventeen, exercised a general supervision over its trade and political policy, ordered goods for the home market, sent off consignments of goods and reinforcements of officials and troops in the outgoing fleets, received and sold the cargoes of the returning fleets, and paid the stockholders' dividends. In time, however, its activities in the East, centered on the governor-general's castle in Batavia, came increasingly to have a life of its own. The governors-general were appointed by the Gentlemen Seventeen, a circumstance that gave the VOC a bureaucratic stability not shared by the kingdoms and powers it dealt with. But once in Batavia, half a year's sail from Amsterdam, and with full autocratic powers over all company servants east of the Cape of Good Hope, they had virtual autonomy. Inevitably they and their subordinates—like the officials and private traders of the English East India Company and like the captain-general and priests of the Spanish Philippines—accommodated themselves to the real world in which they operated, with its own opportunities, dangers, and historical patterns.

In the first century of its existence, up to about 1700, the VOC grew into the classic trading-post empire, carrying on a busy trade along all the coasts of the Indian Ocean and China Sea from a network of bases at Capetown, in Arabia and Persia, along the Indian coasts, in Burma, Siam, and Vietnam, on Formosa, and at Nagasaki in Japan. From the beginning, however, its interest was focused, and its successes greatest, in the seas of the Indonesian archipelago. Obsessed, like all European merchants of the time, with the cloves and nutmeg that grew only in the Moluccan Islands at the eastern end of the archipelago, the Dutch concentrated their naval power on these small places. By the middle of the century, they had subjected their sultans, destroyed or enslaved their peasants, and secured a virtually complete monopoly of production and trade of the precious spices. This, in turn, unhinged what had been a historical axis of trade running along the Java Sea from the Moluccas to the north-coast port-states of Java, from there to the entrepôt of Malacca, and onward to India—a trade that had brought Indian textiles to Java, Javanese rice to the Spice Islands and Malacca, and the spices to the outside world in general. The north-coast states of Java were conquered in the 1620's by the inland state of Mataram. The Javanese traders, who had dominated the trade over the whole route, were driven out of business by the VOC, which also captured Malacca in 1641. The company extended its naval dominance in the 1660's and 1670's, reducing the major Islamic trading powers, such as Makassar, Bantam, and Acheh, to vassalage and imposing a great variety of restrictive commercial treaties on them and on lesser trading states along the whole Java Sea route. It could not monopolize the major products of the rest of the area—pepper from Sumatra and Borneo, tin from the Malay peninsula—for they were too widely distributed and their producers too numerous, strong, or agile, and so other traders, such as the Chinese and English, continued to do a large business. Nor was the company either inclined or able to monopolize the trade in the great variety of forest and sea products coming out of the islands along the Java Sea. Archipelago peoples, such as the Bugis and Malays, continued a lively trade in these departments. By the late seventeenth century, however, the VOC was the paramount naval power from Acheh to the Moluccas, dominating trade in these waters, carrying all the lucrative cloves and nutmeg, half or more of the tin and pepper, and much else besides.

From its height in the late seventeenth century, the VOC's naval and trading power along the Java Sea and Straits of Malacca declined steadily in the course of the eighteenth century. Two factors stand out among the causes of this long decline at sea. One is that, from the 1670's on, the company was increasingly drawn into the affairs of Java, so that by 1757, if not earlier, it was lord of the whole island with its several million inhabitants. This development was in the long run fatal for the VOC as constituted and for the interests of the Gentlemen Seventeen at home, but the governors-general and their subordinates found it both easier and more profitable for themselves than the wearisome business of naval patrol and trade through the archipelago. This tendency was reinforced by the continuing vigor of the maritime peoples and Chinese traders of the area and by the steady rise of English naval power and commercial activity throughout the century. By the mid-eighteenth century, this process was already far advanced. The VOC was well on the way to transforming itself into a territorial rather than a naval power, and the trading world of the Java Sea routes was reverting to the more open and pluralistic pattern it had had in the early seventeenth century and before.

Finally, there extended into Southeast Asia from the west a trading network linking the ports of the Indian subcontinent with others on the eastern shore of the Bay of Bengal, notably the Burman ports of the Irrawaddy delta, Thai ports on the isthmus of the Malay peninsula, and Malay ports dotted along the western coast of the peninsula and the opposite shore of Sumatra. In an exchange well established many centuries earlier, when the Malay port of Malacca was considered richer than London, the chief commodities were Indian cloth; rice and teak ships from Burma; the local products of western Indonesia and Malaysia, especially pepper and tin; and products, like spices, gathered in the region of the Straits of Malacca from farther afield. In this trade, a wide variety of peoples and states were involved in competition, including European traders and trading companies; Gujeratis, Muslims, and Chulias from India; occasional Persians and Arabs; and a few Armenians and Syrians in Burma.

Probably the most important single element in the Bay of Bengal trade was the English East India Company (EIC). Like the Dutch Company, the EIC was a semigovernmental trading corporation directed from Europe. Unlike the Dutch, however, the EIC had virtually no territorial possessions in Southeast Asia in the mid-eighteenth century—the single exception being the out-of-the-way trading post at Benkulen on Sumatra's west coast. The company's major trading ports in India, however, and its slow-developing trade with China stimulated the Bay of Bengal trade generally. And, although the EIC itself conducted little trade with Southeast Asian ports, English private merchants—"country traders"—were particularly active in the Bay of Bengal. As their activities grew in importance and as the Company's trade with China increased, the EIC was slowly drawn into a more active role in Southeast Asia.

Of the trading groups that conducted this international trade throughout Southeast Asia, the most widespread and important was the overseas Chinese. A common explanation for their commercial ascendancy argues that their extended family organizations and kinship networks provided them with greater capital resources than any that Southeast Asian traders could muster; yet among Southeast Asians the Vietnamese had a similar kinship system without being able to withstand the competition of overseas Chinese merchants any more successfully than their neighbors. The commercial supremacy of the Chinese was really based upon a variety of other factors.

History itself favored the overseas Chinese merchants, since the vast commercial world of the mainland Chinese Empire from which they came antedated the economies of Southeast Asia in development and transcended them in size and sophistication. The fact that overseas Chinese merchants still maintained relationships, familial and cultural, with the South China trading communities of their ancestors gave them an unchallengeable position as middlemen between the markets of their homeland and those of Southeast Asia. Southeast Asian political elites found it convenient to permit outsiders to manage international trade. Chinese merchants were mobile, freed of compulsory labor, and located by government policy and their own preference in port areas. Southeast Asian governments found it desirable to restrict the contacts of their people with foreigners and strange ideas, thereby insulating them from a commercial frame of reference as well.

In general, then, outsiders, whether Chinese, Arabs, Indians, or Europeans, were most active and widespread as traders in Southeast Asia in the eighteenth century. This is not, however, to argue that they remained an indigestible lump in the stomachs of Southeast Asian societies. The contrary is true; the Chinese, for example, seem to have assimilated to Thai, Cambodian, and Javanese society more completely in the eighteenth century than they were to do in the twentieth. The skills of the Chinese community were important in economic life and soon came increasingly to be appropriated or exploited by courts and governments that lacked them. In the Philippines, where Chinese *mestizos* retained a separate identity more than their counterparts in Thailand, they slipped into entrepreneurial and commercial roles when economic opportunities presented themselves.

Many of the same considerations apply to the Arabs living throughout most of the archipelago. Whether or not—as traders—they were responsible for the spread of Islam, they certainly served to perpetuate contacts between Islamic Southeast Asia and the heartland of the faith, and they had a religious and economic status that enabled them to enter society at a higher level than that of indigenous traders. This was true of many outsiders in Southeast Asia, who thereby were often much more socially and geographically mobile than most of the populations in which they worked. The effect of such developments was that economic, commercial, and professional organizations and accomplishments created parallel to Southeast Asian societies could, through the integration or assimilation of individuals or institutions connected with them, be appropriated to the use of the indigenous society.

Even on an economic level, the West was by no means the dominant actor on the Southeast Asian stage in the eighteenth century, except in the Philippines and small Dutch-ruled portions of the East Indies. The trade it conducted and generated had wide ramifications, but it was not exclusively a European trade. Indeed, it depended upon Asian traders, as did the galleon trade in the Philippines. If peasants in interior villages bought or bartered for Indian cloth brought to the region by Dutch or English traders, the trader operated in the same fashion as his Indian or Arab predecessor. Outside the Philippines and western Java, Asian traders were much more active than Europeans, and Arab or Malay or Vietnamese cultural and political influence was immeasurably more significant than Western influence. There was apparent by the mid-century, however, a thrust to European commercial and political expansion that was beginning to draw more European attention to the region and to create conditions more favorable to the introduction of European political power. As European ambitions extended to the world and as European industrial development created capital and demanded Southeast Asian raw materials, the earlier commercial pattern in Southeast Asia was challenged by new political complications. Not all the eighteenth-century states of Southeast Asia were equally prepared to meet this new phenomenon, a challenge as much cultural and technological as political and economic, which strained Buddhist monarchies and Muslim sultanates no less than the colonial outposts of Spain and the Netherlands.

7

THE BUDDHIST KINGS

The Theravada Buddhist monarchies of mainland Southeast Asia were products of a period of political upheaval and cultural change, which followed the collapse of earlier Indianized empires, as Theravada Buddhism spread through the area between the eleventh and the fifteenth centuries. The most prominent of these, extending from the border regions of Southwest China to the neck of the Malay peninsula, were the monarchies in Ava in Upper Burma, in Phnom Penh in Cambodia, and in Ayudhya, north of present-day Bangkok.

From these states emanated magical authority and physical power, which diminished as distance from the capital increased, until their hold was too weak to secure the allegiance of remote principalities, or until they encountered the power of a neighboring kingdom. In the less populated areas on their fringes were lesser Buddhist states, the Shan and Lao states of northeastern Burma, northern and northeastern Thailand, and Laos. The power and independence of this second group of states over time rose and fell in inverse relation to the strength of the monarchies in Ava and Ayudhya.

The institution of the monarchy played an important role in Theravada Southeast Asia by providing a system of social and political authority, which overlapped and transcended the values of Buddhism. Indian and Buddhist theories of kingship blended with indigenous political patterns and with such techniques as tributary diplomacy, which may have been derived from China, to produce an institution unique to Southeast Asia. Although the monarchies of Laos, to be sure, would be recognizable to a Burman, there were sharp differences from country to country that reflected the historical experience of each.

Hindu-Buddhist traditions of kingship, introduced into Southeast Asia by the seventh century A.D., saw the monarch as a repository of *karma,* or merit, linking the kingdom to the cosmos, and as possessing, both in his person and in his office, a relationship to the invisible world by which his body and his actions were made sacred. The king's advisers fixed the dates of the calendar that regulated the agricultural year. The monarch was also the patron of Buddhism and the arts. Indian and Buddhist literature offered to rulers and subjects models for kingly behavior like the hero of the *Ramayana,* an Indian epic, whose graceful and ordained victory over evil symbolized the ideal behavior of the monarch.

By portraying his subjects as "dust under the royal feet" or "slaves of the lord," court language and its accompanying etiquette kept the ruler at a distance from others. Physically concealed behind the walls of his palace, the Buddhist monarch often found his capacity to influence events outside his entourage limited; in many cases, the historical records, composed at court, exaggerate the king's effectiveness and importance. Inside the palace, his actions were regulated by Brahman advisers, and his opinions were formed from conversations with favorites. Constricted by a costume that, in Burma, weighed more than 50 pounds, acting on information that was always secondhand and frequently false, and stifled by protocol, astrology, and precedent, the Buddhist monarch of eighteenth-century Southeast Asia was frequently a prisoner of his situation. Since the population often viewed the monarch as godlike, an imminent Buddha, Buddhist monarchs occasionally proclaimed themselves gods. Twice in eighteenth-century Thailand and Burma monarchs were deposed for proclaiming this delusion.

The palace crowned the kingdom; its construction repeated the symbolic design of the Hindu cosmos. The monarchy provided the ultimate coherence for societies organized socially, politically, and linguistically on hierarchic lines, justifying by its existence the wisdom and permanence of that kind of organization.

AVA

The Burman monarchy in Ava was heir to the empire of Pagān. Between the tenth and thirteenth centuries, this empire had united the Burmans of Upper Burma and the Mon people of Lower Burma in a single Buddhist state organized on a common cultural base and administered through a loosely structured bureaucratic system. The strength of the capital was based on the ruler's personal control of the Kyaukse valley, the rice bowl of Upper Burma, while the critical administrative and political links on which the unity and security of Ava depended were personal (as opposed to institutional) relationships between the governors of individual provinces (*myo*) and the king. Ava's armies were drawn heavily from Upper Burma, and its economic and political strength attracted the willing and unwilling allegiance of local ruling families to the monarchy, to which they pledged a share of their revenues and manpower. At the capital, these resources were apportioned to various princes, officials, and members of the royal family, who were said to "eat" the provinces (*myo-za*). In 1783, for example, the *myo* of Sagaing was given to the newborn son of the crown prince "to eat as a snack."[19] The "town-eaters" in the capital, in turn, delegated their powers to local governors in return for fixed sums.

The chief function of the government in Ava was to coordinate labor and collect taxes. The bureaucracy was concentrated in the capital, where a ministerial council, the *hlutdaw,* held executive and judicial authority from the king. No act of state was valid unless sanctioned by and registered with the *hlutdaw*. Of its four members, *wun-gyi* or chief ministers, each had his own sphere of operations, but these were not functionally defined, and the work of each depended largely on the vigor and skills of the minister. To assist them, the *wun-gyi* had a large staff of officers, including messengers, clerks, heralds, marshals, surveyors, and registrars of oaths, in addition to men responsible for public works. They lacked, however, financial independence. Control over the finances of the state was reserved to the king, who exercised it through his privy council, the *byè-daik,* which was composed of four "inside ministers," *atwin-wun.* Revenue matters, as well as the affairs of the palace, were in their hands, and they often enjoyed status and power equal to that of the members of the *hlutdaw*. Numerous other officers, however, operated more or less independently of both *hlutdaw* and *byè-daik* and had their major contacts directly with the king in audience. This seems particularly true of the regiments of the regular army and the royal bodyguard, which provided crucial military support for the regime.

In Burma, as elsewhere in Buddhist Southeast Asia, the rules governing royal succession usually qualified whole sets of men, rather than individuals, because of royal polygamy and the lack of any traditional rule of primogeniture. Within the *myo-za* system, which attached individual royal princes to different elements of the capital bureaucracy and provincial towns, the administrative system positively encouraged the fragmentation of power upon the death of any king and during the reigns of weak ones. A king usually nominated his successor, although he frequently succeeded only in setting up a target for the enemies of the prince he enthroned in the Eastern Palace. With competing sets of ministers in the *hlutdaw* and *byè-daik,* military officers only loosely controlled by them, and a multitude of princes entering into direct relations with nobles and officers, the stage was always set for the cyclical drama of court politics, which played regularly to a climactic crisis at each change of reign.

From a collapse of the empire of Pagān in 1289 to the middle of the eighteenth century, the region now called Burma was stretched between two poles by cultural and economic differences. In the south were the Mon people (related by language to the Cambodians, or Khmer) centered in Pegu, whose Buddhist state resisted incorporation into any larger entity until the middle of the sixteenth century. Upper Burma, the heartland of the Burmans, was dominated by the neighboring Shans and pulled apart by localism until Tabinshwehti, ruler of the Burman state of Toungoo, conquered and absorbed both regions between 1539 and 1555. The nature of the resultant empire, however, was always in question; the Mon tradition of independence did not die easily. Tabinshwehti's successors eventually found it necessary to keep the capital in the north, at Ava, near the rice supplies and Burman military levies of the Kyaukse region. This location, however, encouraged a relative cultural and economic isolation, although Ava was never shut off from the world. Ava managed to conduct a considerable overseas and overland trade across the Bay of Bengal and northward into China. It would be more fruitful to see Ava's problems of political, administrative, economic, and cultural integration as stemming from the fact that, unlike any of its neighbors, the kingdom had two distinct foci, each of which had clear cultural and economic interests to be defended. Strong personal leadership on the part of the Burman kings and flexible social and cultural institutions were required to maintain the unity of the state.

AYUDHYA

The kingdom of Ayudhya was founded in 1350 as a petty Tai principality on the edge of the Cambodian Empire centered at Angkor. Within a century, it had reduced its eastern rival to a shadow of its former self, while extending outward in all directions. The Ayudhyan monarchy borrowed heavily from Cambodian models in order to enhance the magical dignity and authority of the crown, to make of it a symbol capable of commanding at least the fear, if not the respect, of the culturally and racially mixed populations that fell under its control. Its administrative and political institutions resembled those of Burma in many respects, though they were considerably more capable of withstanding internal and external pressures.

Ayudhya was only fifty-five miles from the sea, connected to it by a stretch of the Čhaophraya River. It was a cosmopolitan city of many peoples and a wide variety of ideas. From its foundation, it was visited by merchants from China and the Middle East, and its distant contacts were maintained throughout its 400-year existence. The kings of Ayudhya thought of themselves partly in international terms. For example, King Naresuan in 1593 offered to assist the Chinese empire by attacking Japan, and King Narai in the 1680's was sufficiently attracted to European ideas and techniques to appoint a Greek adventurer, Constantine Phaulkon, as his prime minister (replacing the grandson of a Persian immigrant). The Thai sent tribute to the Chinese emperor, yet they never were so constrained by that relationship that they failed to see the opportunities of alternative arrangements.

As at Ava, the court of Ayudhya was the center of the cultural life of the kingdom. In addition to its specialized bureaucracy, the Thai court maintained a full complement of artists, performers, and craftsmen, who filled the city with carvings, statues, monuments, and a succession of dramatic and musical performances. Talented poets and dancers, wherever found, were brought into the court or the households of high officials, who took pride in their writers-in-residence and dramatic troupes. Buddhism flourished under the patronage of the court; the hundreds of monasteries in and near the capital were major centers of secular as well as religious learning. The diffusion of the literary and scholastic writings of the capital into the provincial towns and even villages suggests that, at least by the eighteenth century, the culture and language of the kingdom were becoming increasingly uniform.[20]

The Thai Kingdom was run by a quasi-hereditary class of nobles dominated increasingly by a small group of families. The functions of government were concentrated in a single body of high officials, the six *senabodi*, who were ministers of state. Although the administrative system laid down in the fifteenth century envisaged ministers each carrying out specialized tasks throughout the kingdom, four of the six ministers of the eighteenth century in effect ran omnibus ministries, carrying out a full range of governmental functions in particular geographical areas—the *kalahom* in the south and west, the *mahatthai* in the north and east, the *phrakhlang* in the provinces at the head of the Gulf of Siam and the *krom müang* in the districts immediately surrounding the capital. Each ministry collected taxes, administered law courts, constructed public works, and attempted to maintain order, yet each retained some vestige of its original functions—the professional army and mercenaries remained under the *kalahom*, the *mahatthai* kept the elephant corps and various specialized civil departments, the *phrakhlang* was still the treasurer of the court and conducted its foreign trade and foreign relations, and the *krom müang* policed the capital. The ministries of lands (*krọm na*) and the palace (*wang*) were less favored ministries performing specialized functions.

To a much greater extent than in eighteenth-century Burma, centralized administration was an accomplished fact in the kingdom of Ayudhya. This was undertaken among the provinces of the Čhaophraya River valley in order to ensure the military security of the kingdom. To withstand Burman and Cambodian invasions, successive kings had found it necessary to strengthen their control over nearby provinces and to gain their resources of manpower. Farther afield, primarily in peninsular Thailand but also in the southeastern provinces bordering Cambodia, the extension of central control over provincial administration responded to the increasing importance of those areas in international trade. For example, local ruling dynasties and families in the provinces of the south—Nakhọn Si Thammarat, Phattalung, and Songkhla—were replaced by governors sent from Ayudhya during the seventeenth century, as the economic importance of that region increased with a rise in international trade.

The court of Ayudhya was relatively stable in the seventeenth and eighteenth centuries, primarily because of the relationship between the king and his nobles. The Thai practice of minimizing direct relations between the princes and the nobles undoubtedly reduced political temperatures considerably. Succession contests usually concerned only a small number of candidates and rarely resulted in the slaughter of the losers, which at times was an element of Burman succession. Political conflicts in Thailand tended to reflect the competition of major noble families for power more than royal preoccupations and infighting. The nobles were the real element of continuity in the system, single families continuing for as many as seven generations with a member in a ministerial position. The nobles put and kept kings on the throne, and kings maintained the substance of royal power only by carefully manipulating public appointments so as to balance the noble families against each other or by bringing in others to compete with them. Royal rule was a delicate business for high stakes, not to be indulged in lightly by ambitious amateurs, and for the loser there was only the velvet sack into which he was put to be ceremonially beaten to death with sandalwood clubs.

From the sixteenth century on, the Thai and Burman courts were preoccupied with each other's affairs. They were bitter competitors and mortal enemies in a war that, with some silences, lasted over three centuries. Each king was jealous of his own prestige and mindful of the importance of repute in holding together an extensive empire. An event, act, or gesture at court that could be interpreted as a sign of weakness might lead to the defection of enough provinces and tributary vassals to bring about the downfall of the empire. The kings solicited vassals, promising them protection from other powers. In return, they demanded loyalty and assistance, as well as regular and substantial tokens of submission, such as the gold and silver ornamental trees regularly received in Ayudhya from the Malay sultanates of the peninsula and the northern and eastern Lao states. To the rulers of such second-level states, it was a complex world indeed. They had to measure carefully the strength of all their neighbors, taking the greatest care to avoid offending dangerous enemies and useful friends. It was not unusual to find in the Lao and Shan world of the north, on the Malay peninsula, or in Cambodia what the Thai called a "two-headed bird" looking in two directions at once, paying tribute to both its neighbors.

PHNOM PENH

In the seventeenth and eighteenth centuries, Thai and Vietnamese territorial expansion, to the east and south respectively, had the effect of drastically reducing the area under Cambodian control. The pressure of its neighbors, principally by reducing sources of revenue, loosened the power of the Cambodian court. By the middle of the eighteenth century, the court was small, fractured, and institutionally brittle; its members and their clients were engrossed in the politics of personal and dynastic survival. In order to survive or to overthrow one another, royal or bureaucratic factions sought support wherever they could find it, especially from Ayudhya and Hue but also from regional leaders and minority groups. The prices paid to the neighboring states were large, in terms of territory, tribute, and the loss of freedom, and the size of the political debts incurred by each new monarch on his way to the throne frequently crippled his capacity to rule. As Cambodia's territory shrank along with the availability of manpower for warfare and production, so too did the range of options available to the court and to factions seeking to overthrow it. A "Vietnamese" or a "Thai" monarch would assume the throne in Cambodia, surrounded by advisers helpfully provided by his patron state. Perhaps motivated by patriotism, and in any case without an alternative, the king's rivals would then seek help from the power not responsible for his accession.

The Cambodian court in the eighteenth century must be studied with this background firmly in mind. The court had little leisure in which to act out its traditional role. Cut off from access to the sea by Sino-Vietnamese adventurers who controlled the coast and by the Vietnamese who were migrating into the formerly Cambodian Mekong delta, the court was also isolated both from outside observers and from the benefits and hazards of extensive foreign trade.

The king's revenue, such as it was, came from a 10 per cent tax levied on all rice production, as well as from a monopoly of both export and import trade and supervision of the production of (and internal trade in) products within the kingdom like lumber, dried fish, and hides. The king also received one-third of all legal fines (one-third went to the judge, and the rest to the party winning the case). Royal expenditures were light, since goods and services commandeered by the palace were seldom paid for.

In the late seventeenth century, a Cambodian king married a Malay, took the name of Ibrahim, and embraced Islam. Assassinated by his nephew, he reappears in later Cambodian literature as the "king who left religion." In a less publicized case, a prince in the 1740's was secretly converted to Catholicism by a Bavarian missionary he had befriended. Either event would have been unthinkable at a more stable Buddhist court, and both indicate the kinds of looseness, or perhaps the tensions, that characterized the Cambodian court throughout this period.

Eighteenth-century Cambodian legal documents stress that deference was due to the monarch, but they indicate by many of the cases they recount that hierarchic restraints maintaining distance between the people and members of the royal family frequently broke down. One case relates that a monarch, out hunting in this period, strayed into a field and jostled a buffalo tender. Not recognizing the king, the tender addressed him angrily as "you." Relating the story later to his ministers, who accompanied the king on expeditions of this sort astride saddled oxen, the monarch boasted that it was proof of his great *karma,* or merit, that he had not killed the buffalo tender for his breach of courtesy. His ministers disagreed. What the story meant, they told him, was that the king had little business outside his palace, where etiquette was properly observed.

It should be stressed, however, that from the peasant's point of view the primary function of the Cambodian king was to enact, as in a dance, the moral victories appropriate to a monarch as reflected in classic and popular stories. Secondarily, the king was patron of the agricultural year. Each spring, as in Ayudhya and Ava, he plowed a ceremonial furrow on the palace grounds, initiating the agricultural cycle throughout the kingdom. In November, he held ceremonies to mark the end of the rainy season. His patronage of Buddhism and his enormous fund of *karma* were other aspects of the monarch's "image" for his people. In times of crisis, such as famine or invasion, villagers built models of his palace out of sand, attempting to gain for themselves the harmony with sky, earth, and under-earth that the king commanded.

THE LAO AND SHAN WORLD

Compared to their neighbors, the mountain-valley states of the Buddhist Lao and Shan areas across the northern edge of mainland Southeast Asia were indeed petty principalities with small populations and limited wealth and power. They had personal links between one valley and the next and were much less affected by the state symbolism common to the more heavily Indianized world to the south. The Shans and Chiangmai took pride in their more rigorous Buddhism and expressed disdain for the court Brahmanism of Ayudhya; however, their own symbolic "magic" was localized and politically less efficient.

The most common form of political and administrative organization in the northern states was based on a hierarchy of five princes or chiefs, the topmost being the ruler of the principality—its *čhaomüang* or *sawbwa* or "Lord of Life." Each of the five had his own separate domain of districts or households providing him with taxes, products, and labor services, and each had his own separate administration to deal with them. This highly personal system worked well in small mountain valleys with limited populations, developing personal relationships into a framework that was as much a social as an administrative hierarchy.

Ava and Ayudhya followed different policies in dealing with the Shan and Lao states nearest them. Ava encouraged conflict among the Shan states so as to minimize the threat they might pose to Burman control and, in addition, to provide opportunities for the court to step in to assist candidates in any succession disputes that might develop in the future. Particularly in what is now North Thailand, Ava posted military governors and garrisons to exert a direct control for more than 150 years. Ayudhya, on the other hand, because it rightly feared Burman ambitions in the area, was more defensive in its dealings with its northern neighbors. It encouraged the consolidation of the Lao states under their own leaders and for the most part confined its dealings with those states to diplomatic missions.

In the first half of the eighteenth century, both Ava and Ayudhya were too preoccupied with court politics and internal affairs to pay much attention to their vassal fringes. Ava faced serious raids from Manipur, on its northwest frontier, and then a Mon rebellion in the south. Confident that the Burmans were no longer a threat to their security, the kings of Ayudhya could afford to relax efforts to maintain good relations with the Shan and Lao. The effects of the withdrawal of both these powers were readily apparent. Chiangmai rebelled against its Burman governor in 1728 and soon entered into friendly relations with rebellious Pegu. The ancient kingdom of Lan Xang in Laos disintegrated on the death of King Suliyavongsa without heir in 1698 and split into three small kingdoms, each ruled by distant claimants to the throne, in Luang Prabang, Vientiane, and Čhampassak. Furthermore, even within the orbits of these principalities, district and provincial towns resisted the authority of their overlord, as the constant warfare of Lamphun, Lampang, and Chiangmai shows. Legitimacy was lacking, as was authority that could transcend an individual claimant to a throne or one of a group of towns. In a situation of great complexity, when the future and intentions of Ava and Ayudhya were in doubt, no new order was possible until the great monarchies again could define and order the tributary systems that made sense of and to the Lao and Shan principalities.

8

THE VIETNAMESE EMPERORS

If one dominant feature of the premodern political history of mainland Southeast Asia was the cultural variety of its royal despotisms, the Vietnamese monarchy stood at the opposite end of the cultural spectrum from the Ava and Ayudhya monarchs. The imported political theories that it attempted to incarnate in Southeast Asia were Chinese rather than Indian. In Vietnam, as elsewhere, a fundamental parallelism was believed to exist between the world of nature and the world of men, and human institutions were intended to harmonize with and reflect the natural order.

The Vietnamese emperor was called the "Son of Heaven," the deputy on earth of the natural forces of the universe. The test of whether or not an individual Vietnamese ruler was a successful "Son of Heaven" was his practical capacity to ensure a minimum standard of living for his people. Sudden floods or droughts that damaged the livelihood of the Vietnamese peasantry were interpreted as cosmic expressions of disapproval with the emperor himself. The association between agricultural productivity and the moral credibility of the monarchy was so strong, for example, that Minh-mang (r. 1820–41) would penitently cancel court banquets if he received news that the dikes had burst in a northern Vietnamese province. As the vassal of Heaven, the Vietnamese emperor prostrated himself, prayed, and sacrificed a buffalo to Heaven at the end of every winter at the "southern altar" (*nam giao*) outside his capital. But as a patron of agriculture, the emperor also performed a plowing ritual with a gilded plow every spring, while his court astronomers were charged with the task of producing yearly agricultural calendars.

Mediating between nature and man, the Vietnamese monarch unified politics and ideology. The emperor was required to be a scholar, a Confucian teacher, a man who could set a moral example, and a sage. Traditional Vietnamese political theory did not concern itself with externally imposed limits upon power—i.e., the rule of law—since a sage could be expected to wield power wisely. At the same time, that theory favored a largely passive style of authoritarianism, which stressed moral example rather than more dynamic goals. "Prestige" (*uy tin*), the indispensable quality of all leaders in Vietnam from the emperor to the village chief, combined the concept of fearsomeness (*uy*) with the capacity to induce trust and even affection (*tin*). One without the other was, in the long run, useless. The ideal ruler was not a "direct action" despot so much as a man who could attract scholars to him and make them his officials.

The key to the Vietnamese sociopolitical structure was familism rather than monarchism. Loyalty to the family hierarchy was the single most important virtue, since it was believed that a man of great filial piety could never commit an improper political act. Society revolved around the hierarchical relationships of the famous "three principles" (*tam cuong*) that were the operative ideal of Vietnamese life: namely, a subject's loyalty to his ruler, a son's obedience to his father, and a wife's submission to her husband. This meant that the emperor was only one of three ideal authority figures. And, although he was supposedly the senior one, filial piety yielded to loyalty to the throne in theory more often than in fact. Indeed, as in China, the emperor was even required to excuse from active service under him bureaucrats whose parents had just died, since the morality of familism demanded that they return to their villages to observe an extended period of mourning. In sum, the one unlimited and apotheosized loyalty that existed in Vietnamese politics was loyalty to the family. There was never a clear point where loyalty to the family ended and loyalty to the ruler began.

Furthermore, the bureaucracy, not the monarchy, effectively controlled Vietnamese state ideology, exercising the kind of leverage over the emperor that the Christian Church exercised over medieval European kings. In the eyes of his officials, trained in the Chinese Confucian classics, he had to exemplify right conduct or "cultivate himself," before he could rule his country. Besides these two constraints of familism and lack of control of state ideology, every Vietnamese dynasty was also circumscribed by its need to prove its own legitimacy. The Nguyen Dynasty (1802–1945) collected materials for the preparation of a history of the Lê Dynasty (1427–1788) and spent large sums restoring Lê Dynasty temples in order to prove that it was the dutiful heir of a previous ruling house. It also recruited former Lê officials and recreated many Lê institutions and laws. More important, such forces of convention affected individual emperors as well as whole dynasties. No new Vietnamese emperor could openly reject or even drastically modify the institutions his father had devised and bequeathed him without violating filial piety and thus losing his moral ascendency. In the beautiful Buddhist-flavored poem, "Cung Oan Ngam Khuc ("Song of the Disenchantments of the Palace"), written by Nguyen Gia Thieu (1741–98), the view of the abandoned imperial concubine that a nunnery would be preferable to the court expressed a common Vietnamese belief that court life could easily pass from glory to a form of predestined servitude.

From the early eleventh century until 1802 the Vietnamese monarchy ruled from the environs of modern Hanoi, a city known as Thang-long before 1802 and as the "northern citadel" (*bac thanh*) in early nineteenth-century documents. In 1802, the first Nguyen Emperor, Gia-long, moved the capital to Hue in central Vietnam. Here the monarchy was domiciled at the heart of three concentric walled cities: the outer "capital city," the inner "imperial city," and the "forbidden city" within the "imperial city." Although the arrangement of Hue gates, throne halls, and palaces was meant to approximate that of similarly named gates and buildings in Peking, the capital's monthly parade of elephants suggested Southeast Asia. If the Vietnamese capital was not quite a magic center of empire in the way that neighboring Southeast Asian capitals were, it did possess tutelary spirits, which watched over its walls and gates, and it was considered to be a repository of benevolent supernatural influences, thanks to its favorable geomantic position.

The two centers of power in the Vietnamese central government were the emperor and his inner court, on the one hand, and the regular outer bureaucracy, on the other. An Internal Affairs Office (*noi vu phu*) served as the private treasury of the imperial household. Its nine subtreasuries stored the tribute goods received by the emperors from foreign countries, as well as imported luxury goods (brocade, drugs, porcelain), which the emperors dispensed to their officials as rewards. Only a shadowy distinction might exist between public tax revenues and the private income of the emperor. Yet, in fact, the fiscal foundations of the Vietnamese monarchy were weak and vulnerable. The capital received only a small share of the annual tax collections throughout the country, since large sums were first deducted from these collections for provincial and district administrative needs before the balances were remitted to the capital. The emperor ruled more through personal control of his bureaucrats than through direct economic control of the government's purse strings. Revenues from the taxation of foreign trade, however, were considered almost an imperial monopoly.

The administrative structure of Vietnamese central government was crowned, as it had been since the fifteenth century, by the Six Boards (*luc bo*). These were, in order, the Boards of Appointments (the commissions of civil bureaucrats), Finance (taxation and other fiscal matters), Rites (education, the civil service examination system, foreign relations, court rituals), War, Justice, and Public Works. Coordination among them was weak, and it was not until 1829–30 that Minh-mang created his Grand Secretariat (*noi cac*) to control the flow of state papers in Hue, preserve state seals, and draft edicts and decrees in the emperor's name, subject to his approval. Only in 1834–35 did the emperor create an even more important executive organ, the Privy Council (*co mat vien*), a small body of the highest civil and military officials in Hue, to plot military strategy (for example, in Cambodia in the 1830's) and attempt to resolve domestic and international crises.

Ever since 1075 A.D., the Vietnamese court had recruited its civil officials through a Chinese-style examination system. The system possessed two main levels: the lower regional examinations, which took place at a number of provincial sites, and the higher metropolitan and palace examinations, which occurred at the capital. At both levels, examinations were commonly but not always held in three-year cycles. Only unqualified success in the regional examinations permitted a student to take what the poet Cao Ba Quat called "the unfathomably long road" to the capital in quest of a higher degree. Theoretically, the poorest peasant could compete in the examinations and in local eligibility tests that preceded them, although village chiefs were required to notify provincial officials of the names of "unfilial" or seditious villagers who should not be allowed to participate. Soothsayers might issue cryptic predictions about individual candidates before the examinations. They could develop large local followings if they predicted successes in the examinations accurately. The vocational ideal in Vietnam was the career of a government official.

The passport to becoming a mandarin through the civil service examinations was an academic knowledge of the centuries-old Chinese Confucian Four Books (the Analects, Mencius, the Doctrine of the Mean, and the Great Learning) and the Five Classics (the Classic of Songs, the Classic of Documents, the Classic of Changes, the Record of Rituals, and the Spring and Autumn Annals). This meant that the traditional Vietnamese scholar-bureaucrat was a generalist well versed in Chinese classical philosophy rather than in specialized administrative knowledge. In his society, he was the local scholar who was also a court official or an aspiring one, a "broker" who owed allegiance both to his native village and to the societywide bureaucracy. He did not occupy a number of different roles at the same time, nor did he normally serve as a patron to a host of clients, like the Thai official. The court lacked enough revenue to pay its officials adequately, but official status did confer other privileges, above all exemption from *corvée* and taxes, and entry for bureaucrats' sons into the National College (*quoc tu giam*) at the capital, where students received stipends, special training for the examinations, and, sometimes, lowly clerical official posts.

The existence of the examination system raises questions in comparative history. Upward social mobility was relatively high by the standards of a premodern agrarian society but very low by the standards of the industrializing West. In the latter, the number of elite positions—that is, the number of teachers, doctors, engineers, and so on required by society—typically increases faster than the population does, so that upward mobility for the non-elite improves steadily. In traditional Vietnam, the population increased more rapidly than the number of bureaucratic posts. And, although there was a shortage of eligible scholars, schools of the kind needed to give village children enough knowledge of Confucian scholarship to pass examinations were far from widespread. Also, the cost of such education, in time and money, was extremely high for most Vietnamese peasant families.

To control his mandarins, the Vietnamese emperor resorted to a number of devices. An institution known as the Censorate (*do sat vien*) supplied him with officials who resided at the capital and traveled in the provinces, scrutinizing the conduct of regularly commissioned officials and sometimes impeaching them in memorandums to the throne for misbehavior. The emperor tried to keep his bureaucracy small in numbers so that he could manage it. The partial truth embodied in the Vietnamese proverb, "The laws of the emperor are less than the customs of the village," was a cogent reminder not merely of village parochialism and poor communications but also of the premodern monarchy's unwillingness to create an officialdom vast enough to govern some 17,000 villages directly. The court also attempted to circulate its bureaucrats, moving them from one post to another every three or six years. This was intended to prevent them from developing local power bases. As another form of surveillance, it received triennial "rating" (*khao tich*) reports on its officials, usually written by their superiors in the eighteen-grade civil service hierarchy.

In foreign relations, the chief efforts of the monarchy were directed toward the maintenance of the myth that the Vietnamese emperor, as Confucian "Son of Heaven," was the cultural beacon of the lands about Vietnam. In communicating with Lao rulers, the Vietnamese court habitually styled itself "the central country" (*trung quoc*), or "middle kingdom," borrowing and Vietnamizing the Chinese term for China. Neighboring societies like Cambodia, which had not espoused Sino-Vietnamese culture, were denigrated as "barbarian." Although the Vietnamese ruler himself was a tribute-sending vassal of the Chinese court at Peking, and each new Vietnamese emperor received a seal of investiture from Chinese officials in formal ceremonies at Hanoi, the Vietnamese court also strove to create its own tributary system of vassals who would pay it political homage and economic tribute. Because its monarchical institutions were modeled upon those of China, its interstate diplomacy had to be a reasonably plausible copy of that of China. Tributary envoys from Luang Prabang, Vientiane, and Phnom Penh were expected to bring tribute to Hue every few years, as well as on special anniversaries.

All this meant that the Vietnamese court faced the problem, never publicly acknowledged, of balancing the shibboleths of its borrowed political ideology against the exigencies of its Southeast Asian environment. *Realpolitik* in mainland Southeast Asia was more than the intersocietal tournament of cultures that Vietnamese diplomatic archives sometimes pretended it was. When the Thai monarchy, operating under its own ideological assumptions, challenged Vietnamese ambitions stemming from such cultural evangelism to convert Cambodia into an exclusive tributary (and protectorate) of Vietnam, wars with Thailand resulted.

9

THE MALAY SULTANS

While the eighteenth-century states of mainland Southeast Asia are recognizable today, those of island Southeast Asia (including the Malay peninsula, which, brute geography aside, belongs for most historical purposes among the "islands") are not. The eighteenth century Spanish colony of the Philippines, somewhat expanded, is the ancestor of the present Philippine Republic, but 200 years ago there was no such thing as Malaysia or Indonesia. Instead, across this great arc of islands, there was a bewildering variety of societies and political structures. To begin with, there were the innumerable small stateless societies of hunters and swidden cultivators found mostly in the interiors of the islands throughout the archipelago. Then, in the string of islands east of Java were two lively survivors from earlier historical eras: Bali, the last heir of the age of Hindu-Buddhist states in Southeast Asia, and Portuguese Timor, with its small Catholic *mestizo* community, as fiercely independent of Lisbon as it was exceptional among its Muslim and pagan neighbors. In addition, there were those rather anomalous powers, the Dutch and English East India Companies, states of a sort but in any case armed merchants that exerted political influence along the seaways and in the ports of most of the archipelago. There were also two large and comparatively homogeneous societies, containing the only sizable concentrations of population in the islands: the Catholic Philippines, under Spanish rule, and Java, which in the mid-eighteenth century was largely controlled by the Dutch company.

Finally, and most characteristic of island Southeast Asia as a whole, were the Malayo-Muslim sultanates and chiefdoms of the coasts and rivers. The Muslim societies and states of the archipelago differed considerably among themselves. Java was a case apart, for its coastal sultanates had been overwhelmed in the seventeenth century. The relatively large wet-rice–cultivating populations of the Bugis and Makassarese in southwestern Celebes and of the Minangkabau heartlands in west-central Sumatra were also distinct in some respects. But even these two societies shared much of the common pattern of the Malayo-Muslim polities spread widely throughout the eastern archipelago—in Mindanao, the Sulu islands, the Moluccas, and some of the islands east of Bali—and concentrated more densely in the western archipelago along the coasts of the Malay peninsula, Sumatra, Borneo, and on the small islands in the vicinity. The western archipelago, which for convenience may be called the Malay world, was the historical home of the Malayo-Muslim pattern, and in the mid-eighteenth century its numerous states still best exemplified that tradition.

Much of the Malay world was inhospitable to human settlement. Tropical, covered in dense rain forest, often mountainous, fringed by mangrove swamp, its soils leached by heat and torrential rain, the area offered little encouragement to extensive habitation. Only the rivers, with which the coastlines were deeply and frequently incised, made it possible, given available technology, to develop complex polities. Movement across the grain of the country was virtually impossible, and communications were therefore nonexistent except up into the headwaters of usually independent river systems or along the seaways of the coast.

These circumstances shaped the social, political, and economic structures that developed in the Malay world. They were rivermouth societies, for the most part, centered on port towns lying where the river debouched into the sea, placed so as to control what came down and to participate in what passed by. The political power, the "state" or *negeri*, at the mouth of the river, sought to establish sufficient authority over the peoples up-river and, in the interior, to ensure a flow of produce that could be taxed or sold. At the same time, it engaged in a complex power game with other rivermouth *negeri* in the area to take advantage of international trade and thus to increase or maintain its wealth. State boundaries tended to be vague and relatively unimportant, for what mattered was control of waterborne traffic, not land. The scale of political organization these activities either permitted or required was small in comparison to that of the great deltaic and agrarian states of the mainland and Central Java. Although from time to time concentrations of power were built up—systems of suzerainty, dependence, hegemony, alliance, and even commercial empire—they were vulnerable and impermanent. For the counters that bought them, made of political intrigue, dynastic maneuver, promise of immediate trading gain, periods of more efficient leadership, or military prowess, were available to all.

At the apex of the political structure of the *negeri* was the sultan, though this personal honorific from Islamic Turkey was less used in the eighteenth century than the ceremonial Malay *Yang di-Pertuan* (he who is made lord), often abbreviated to *Yam Tuan*, or the Indian-derived generic title for ruler, raja. The role of the *Yam Tuan* was first and foremost to express the symbolic unity of the state and to protect its order and integrity. In his person were embodied both *daulat*, the mystical reinforcement of personality conferred by kingship, and *kuasa*, supreme temporal authority. The aura of sanctity with which he was invested found outward expression in an elaborate apparatus of ceremonial practice and belief, which was of real importance, although sometimes it represented no corresponding concentration of administrative strength or power.

Surviving accounts of the installation of rulers make clear the sacral and magical importance of the office. Succession was confined to members of a single royal lineage, usually male, with final confirmation by the principal chiefs. A ruler's ascent to the throne was marked first by ritual lustration, signifying exaltation from the ranks of his kinsmen and the creation of a new and larger personality. He was then equipped with the royal regalia, the emblems of office, ranging from symbolic weapons, drums, and special dress to the state seal and ritual ornaments, all held to share in the supernatural qualities of kingship. A senior official of the court mosque uttered the Kuranic text, "Lo! We have set thee as a Viceroy upon the earth," to mark the ruler's position as defender and arbiter of the Islamic faith. And finally, the assembled chiefs performed before their raja a symbolic act of homage, repeated at intervals throughout his reign at gatherings specially convened for the purpose. The accepted norm of conduct toward the ruler was characterized by careful respect for proper forms of address and approach and by the ideal of strict formal obedience to his commands.

In the Malay world of the eighteenth century, the life-style of a raja in his riverine principality, though doubtless splendid in comparison with that of his subjects, was modest when contrasted with that of his fellow rulers in the great agrarian states of Southeast Asia. Though occasionally built of stone, his *istana*, or palace, was more probably a piled wooden structure thatched with nipa palm (*attap*) and set in a bamboo-fenced compound otherwise occupied by a motley collection of huts and outbuildings for the members and servants of the royal household. The compound, usually not more than two acres in extent, was, as a rule, set near the river bank commanding all movement on the principal artery of communication; it was a scene of busy activity at the cooler hours of morning and evening. The center of public life in the *istana* was the *balai*, or audience hall (which might, on occasion, be a separate building), in which the business of the state was daily or at intervals conducted. Within stood the royal throne, draped in yellow hangings for royalty. Before it was a shallow-stepped platform on which, at either side, squatted the principal attendants of the ruler or, on occasion, the carefully ranked chiefs.

Malay society was clearly graded. Its topmost rank, among whom the ruler was naturally paramount, was the royal family itself—a numerous group, especially by virtue of the practice of polygyny, which tended to provide candidates for disputed succession and idle pretendership. Below this came the nonroyal nobility or aristocracy, whose claim to privilege lay in belonging to families with traditional rights to office or position and to a share in the economic wealth of the state. It was from this group, for the most part, that the "pillars of the state" were drawn, though, as with the royal family, functioning positions were seldom as numerous as candidates. Few of the Malay sultanates were equipped with (or indeed required) anything resembling an elaborate bureaucracy, though titular offices based on the system in force in fifteenth-century Malacca often remained. One result was that the ranking of social class depended more frequently on noble descent or connection than on actual administrative office. During periods of social conflict, traditional but functionless nobles, away from the fountains of power, might well, like dissident members of the royal family, afford source or support for disaffection.

Nevertheless, there were ministers and administrators. One common pattern had at the top level three or four principal officers of state (the number often followed what had been Hindu cosmological theory): a *temenggong* or *mentri* (first minister, as it were), *bendahara* (treasurer), *laksamana* (commander-in-chief; literally, "admiral"), and a *hakim*, or judge, who was probably also the chief religious dignitary. Below these, though relative positions sometimes differed, might be a number of officers of trade, including a customs or port-dues official and a *shahbandar*, whose task it was to act as liaison officer between the sultan and, in particular, foreign traders.

The above officials served in the *istana*, or at least in the port town itself. In addition, there were usually district or territorial chiefs who held, under commission from the ruler, rights of control over a specified area of the *negeri*: a tributary or upper stretch of the main river, or another river farther down the coast. District chiefs were entitled to draw revenue from the area they commanded and were often largely independent of the capital. They may be said, however, to have shared in a general way in the management of the state, and their position often entitled them to consultation and participation when important matters of foreign or trade relations were being discussed.

Though a certain amount of the business taking place in the sultan's *balai* might concern outlying parts of the *negeri*, interstate matters, trading policy, or other great affairs, much of it from day to day was certainly local or domestic in character, for the *Yam Tuan*, though first among equals, was in an important sense merely a district chief. Much of his time was devoted to administering his own parish, settling appeals and petitions, arranging for renewal of licenses for monopolies or concessions concerning fishing or mining rights or the performance of shadow plays and similar entertainments, receiving intelligence of crop production, surrender of produce, taxation on river trade, or incipient disaffection, and making a host of minor decisions in connection with all of these. His revenues were commonly sufficient only to pay for the administrative apparatus here described, to maintain an armed force of some description, and to support the royal household and its customary array of dependents.

The elements of weakness in this political system—vulnerable to sudden changes in prosperity or trading conditions or to attack—are fairly clear. There was a permanent residue in the *negeri* of well-born persons who considered themselves, for one reason or another, deprived of their due or at least of that which, with some effort, they and their following might obtain. Intriguing with people of this sort was a standard means, within interstate relations, of subverting one's neighbor. It was resorted to particularly, perhaps, by the European powers, which were by definition disqualified from the traditional dynastic power games. In addition, central financing (if indeed one can use this term), devoted largely to maintaining the royal household and some form of armed force, was seldom sufficiently secure to permit the accumulation of reserves adequate to withstand prolonged periods of stress. And the relative independence of districts led to inherent instability in the polity as a whole.

The European powers—the Portuguese in the sixteenth century, most strikingly the Dutch in the seventeenth century, and the English after the mid-eighteenth century—were able to exploit the vulnerabilities of the individual Malay polities and to disturb the system of which they formed a part. Recent historians have argued, plausibly, that European powers in the early centuries of their participation in the maritime trading networks of Southeast Asia, operating by means and on a scale no different from those of their Asian counterparts, did little either to alter the system radically or to affect the lives of the other participants. By the eighteenth century, as the effects of these intrusions accumulated, however, it becomes difficult to press this view with the same confidence, and the point has stimulated much discussion. The debate essentially has concerned whether the context—the actual structure and dynamics—was changed, or just the participants. As to the latter there is no doubt, as the Dutch East India Company, for example, substituted itself for Makassar in the eastern seas and replaced Acheh in relation to the pepper ports of Sumatra. Is it really the same play with a new actor taking some of the parts, just as the Indonesian *wayang kulit*, after the advent of Islam, acquired one or two new characters and a few alterations in emphasis? Or did the whole plot change, throwing the other actors into confusion, while everyone tried simultaneously to write his own script? A good case can be made for the second interpretation.

In particular, it can be argued that the European presence, increasingly superior in arms and relying especially on the exaction of commercial treaties from weaker powers, the compulsory stapling of trade in its own entrepôts, and the detachment of vassals and dependencies, contributed to the decay of the larger political units in the Malay world and to their fragmentation either into weaker states or into squabbling bands of marauders. The loss of commerce and revenue to the ruler and chiefs of a riverine Malay state produced a corresponding diminution or loss of political control—either inside the *negeri* or between it and its dependencies. In effect, in the eighteenth century the forces of instability represented by pretenders, rivals, opportunists, and knaves gained a freer rein for longer periods than had traditionally been the case. One result was the success of interlopers, adventurers, or usurpers, like Raja Kechil in Siak, the Bugis in Selangor, or Sayyid Abdurrahman in Pontianak, who set themselves up inside the boundaries of previously established Malay realms of commercial empire. Another response was a great increase in what is often described as "piracy," which, like Clausewitz's definition of war as an extension of diplomacy, can be described as the continuation of trade by other means. It was the heyday of tough, lawless marauding communities, such as the Balanguingui and Ilanun of Mindanao and Sulu. Occasional marauding also became the recourse of many Malay chiefs, no longer fully able to sustain themselves and their followers in more settled ways.

How, then, did the Malay map of the western archipelago look toward the end of the eighteenth century? Acheh, at the northern tip of Sumatra, having reached the peak of its greatness in the early seventeenth century under Sultan Iskandar Muda, had since been on the decline. This appears to have been due in part to a succession of female sovereigns (a circumstance that gave free play to the energies of fissiparous territorial chiefs), but Dutch pressures exerted from their newly acquired base in Malacca (taken from the Portuguese in 1641) greatly assisted the process. The principal Dutch concern in the Straits of Malacca at the time was to control the trade of the peninsular Malay tin *negeri,* of which the most important, Perak, was a dependency of Acheh. The resulting decline of Acheh in this trade was accompanied by a loss of its control over the Minangkabau pepper ports of west-coast Sumatra, which found themselves forced to accept Dutch in exchange for Achehnese suzerainty. By the mid-eighteenth century, Achehnese power was largely confined to the northern half of Sumatra, and even there English private traders were evading Achehnese dues by dealing directly with its dependencies.

To the south, the Johore Empire, which had fluctuated in fortune since inheriting the mantle and royal lineage of Malacca after the fall of that emporium to the Portuguese in 1511, was able to take advantage of the conflict between the Dutch and Acheh to strengthen its own position both in the peninsula and in east-coast Sumatra, where the *negeri* of Siak and Indragiri came under Johore authority in the mid-seventeenth century. Its situation, however, remained highly unstable. The next seventy years saw a series of complicated maneuvers for power and advantage, involving constantly changing alliances and feuds with the *negeri* of Jambi in South Sumatra, Bugis adventurers from the Celebes, the Dutch at Malacca, and the Minangkabau ruler, who had usurped the throne of Siak, and attended also by dynastic changes and power struggles around the throne of Johore itself. Together these events, which centered on the contest for control of the trade in Siak pepper and South Sumatran tin, brought the Johore Sultanate to its knees. The principal advantage in the situation, however, was taken not by the Dutch but by bands of Bugis adventurers who were engaged in fashioning a new commercial empire based on a dual policy that combined indirect but effective control of some areas, as in Johore-Riau, and direct assumption of power in others, as in Selangor, on the west coast of the peninsula.

The Bugis, who had emerged from the Celebes in the late seventeenth century after the destruction of their Moluccan spice trade by Dutch monopolization, were an energetic maritime people known throughout the Malay world for their fierceness and courage. With some already established, first as marauders and then in more settled communities, in parts of Borneo, others were able, by intervention in Johore politics, to become in 1722 the virtual rulers at Riau, the Johore capital. From there, they proceeded to assert effective control over the tin states of Kedah and Perak and to create their own *negeri* in Selangor. These activities necessarily brought them into direct conflict with the Dutch in the peninsula and South Sumatra, in which the possessions of both contestants changed hands several times before the eventual Dutch occupation of Riau. This occurred not many years before the onset of the Napoleonic wars in Europe ended, for the time being, Dutch ascendancy in Southeast Asia.

Meanwhile, effective British interest in the area, born as much of strategic considerations related to the East India Company's China trade as of any desire to intervene largely in local trade or politics, increased first in Sulu and northern Borneo with the attempted establishment (1773) of a new entrepôt at Balambangan. When this venture failed, others were considered, culminating in the acquisition in 1786 of the island of Penang, ceded by the Sultan of Kedah in the hope (scarcely fulfilled) of gaining assistance against renewed Thai interest in controlling his own *negeri*. British participation at this point resulted in a further economic imbalance in the area, as both Kedah and Achehnese trade became diverted in part to the new settlement, with a consequent loss of revenue to their respective rulers. Dutch power collapsed in the wars of the French Revolution, but the British took over, at various times, all Dutch possessions in Southeast Asia. Though these were for the most part ultimately returned, it was clear that maritime Southeast Asian politics and trade had to accommodate yet another powerful European power in residence, for all the foreseeable future.

10

THE JAVANESE KINGS

The Javanese political tradition, like those of the Burmans, Thai, and Khmer, goes back to the Hindu-Buddhist era in the first millennium A.D., when the introduction of Indian political-religious ideas provided a new and more capacious framework in which Southeast Asian political life could develop. From the eighth to the fourteenth centuries, a series of kingdoms in Central and East Java expressed themselves in terms very similar to those used by their contemporaries on the mainland. The kingdom was conceived as a representation on earth of the cosmos, and the king therefore as an incarnation of Shiva, Vishnu, or the Buddha, served by a priestly caste of literati and by ministers who crouched reverently before him.

The political histories of Java and its mainland counterparts, however, took very different turns in the "religious revolutions" of the thirteenth century and after. The mainland monarchies adjusted easily to Theravada Buddhism, which came out of an already familiar Indian tradition, and the patterns of political life continued much as they had before. On Java, by contrast, the last great Hindu-Buddhist state, Majapahit, sagged abruptly around 1400, and for the next two centuries the political affairs of the island were dominated by a string of small Islamic trading states stretched out along its north coast from Surabaya to Bantam. In economic terms, this development reflected the new importance of trade along the Java Sea between Malacca and the Spice Islands, a trade dominated by Javanese merchants. In religion, the north-coast Javanese—prince, merchant, and peasant—went over to Islam along with the other trading peoples along the trade route. Politically, too, the Javanese of the north coast—the *pasisir*—turned to face outward, and their string of sultanates joined the community of small Islamic trading states spreading through the archipelago.

But whereas trade and Islam served to unite the scattered peoples of the archipelago, they were divisive forces on Java, with its large agrarian base and its own strong cultural tradition. In this period, the outward-looking *pasisir* drew apart from the agrarian interior, where claimants to the grandeur of Majapahit lingered on into the early sixteenth century and the Hindu-Buddhist tradition was as yet hardly challenged. In the *pasisir* itself, the introduction of Islam inaugurated what was to be an abiding tension in Javanese culture. The ambivalence fostered in this way is best illustrated by the myths that grew up around the careers of the half-historical Nine Wali, the reputed bringers of Islam to Java and founders of the *pasisir* states. Reduced to their fundamentals, the tales reveal one central preoccupation, an effort to reconcile Islam and Javanism. Thus, characteristically, the Nine Wali are credited with introducing not only Islam but also the *wayang kulit,* the shadow drama that is the epitome of pre-Islamic Javanese culture.

The balance of power between coast and interior shifted abruptly in the early seventeenth century, when a new dynasty, Mataram, with its center near present-day Jogjakarta, conquered all Java. But Mataram did not thereby simply obliterate the *pasisir* pattern. In a devastating series of campaigns, Sultan Agung (r. 1613–45) restored the political unity of Java, destroyed forever the independent existence of the north-coast sultanates, and, with the help of the Dutch, condemned the once-flourishing Javanese merchant class to centuries of obscurity in the backwaters of Javanese life. But it was also in Agung's time that *pasisir* Islam rooted itself permanently in the Javanese interior. Agung himself was a pious Muslim who sought confirmation of his Islamic title of "sultan" in Mecca,[20] consorted regularly with *ulama,* and established new courts using Islamic law.

Agung thus confirmed the cultural tension inherent in the *pasisir* pattern and presided over its extension to most of the Javanese population. His son, Amangkurat I (r. 1645–77), moved back toward the Javanese pole of the synthesis, remaining Susuhunan but dropping the title of sultan, abolishing his father's Islamic courts, and, on one occasion, slaughtering several thousand *ulama* whom he had collected at his court for the purpose. But the fine ambivalence of religious syncretism was now permanently entrenched, most strikingly symbolized, perhaps, in the Javanese calendar that Agung introduced in 1633, numbering its years according to the Hindu Shaka era (1 Shaka = 78 A.D.) established from early times on Java, but nevertheless using the shorter Islamic lunar year in place of the Hindu solar one.

Leaving aside for a moment the role of the Dutch East India Company, the political structure of Java in Mataram times began—and, theoretically speaking, also ended—with the king. Since Mataram was an Islamic state, the king was no longer explicitly a god-king, as he had been earlier; he was, nonetheless, a sacral figure. One recognized a king by the *wahyu,* the divine light that descended upon him or shone from his eyes, and when the *wahyu* left him, one knew that his time as king was up. He was, to take the names of some of the Javanese kings, "He who holds the World on his Lap" (Hamengku Buwono) and the "Axis of the World" (Paku Buwono). As such, the king's function was to maintain the natural order in the kingdom, encompassing and reconciling perturbations if they occurred, so that the microcosmos would mirror the harmony of the cosmos. Thus, Sultan Agung's calendar of 1633 characteristically resolved the tension between the two different calendrical traditions, Hindu-Javanese and Islamic, by incorporating them in a new and harmonious unity. It goes without saying that there could, in theory at least, be no limits to the powers and rights of such a king.

The kingdom over which the Mataram king ruled had no boundaries. It was conceived of as a series of four concentric circles going outward from the capital into the indefinite distance. At the center was the *negara*, a Sanskrit word that, significantly, meant both "kingdom" and "capital," the palace-city from which the king sent forth the rays of his influence. The *kraton*, to give it its other, more familiar name, was moved three times before the division of the realm in 1755, being located in the area of modern Jogjakarta until the 1670's and after that near modern Surakarta (Solo). Wherever it was, the *kraton*—like its counterparts in the Theravada countries—was a vast complex of buildings and squares enclosed by walls and moats, its essentially sacral character shown by the fact that it was oriented to the points of the compass. Inside were the king, his queens and concubines, officials, royal dancers, the corps of female guards, and multitudes of servants.

Outside the *negara* walls was the rest of the kingdom, the *negara* in the other sense of the word. The next circle was the *negara agung*, the core area, which in the seventeenth century consisted of the immediate Jogjakarta-Surakarta area and which grew considerably in the eighteenth century. Next came the *mantja negara*, the outer provinces, which, at its greatest extent in the seventeenth century, occupied all the rest of Java but the western and eastern tips. Finally there was the *tanah sabrang*, the lands overseas, consisting of distant states, such as Palembang and Banjarmasin, which acknowledged Mataram suzerainty and sent tribute.

In this respect, at least, Mataram's political theory and practice fitted very closely. The king's power, radiating outward from the *kraton*, was felt less and less strongly the farther it reached, until it faded out somewhere among the islands of the archipelago. The different concentric circles, too, were ruled on different principles.

In governing this kingdom, the Mataram kings generally did not use members of the royal family; their policy was to keep them at the court, as far as possible politically neutralized and content. In part of the *mantja negara*, notably in some of the former distant states and in the Sundanese highlands of West Java, they incorporated hereditary local lords into the administration of the state. Otherwise they ruled through officials, men who, however independent they might be in practice, were, formally speaking, servants of the king. The operation, and even the formal structure, of this administration is not yet fully understood, but its general principles can be sketched. For practical purposes, it consisted of two main parts: officials who resided at court and constituted the central administration and officials who resided outside, particularly in the *mantja negara*.

The structure of the central administration was particularly elaborate. It was encrusted with special offices and titles, many of them—such as the office of *patih*, the chief minister—going back to Majapahit times or earlier. It also had a pronounced sacral or magical character. There were, for example, four chief *wedana* under the *patih* (two of the left side, two of the right) and exactly twice as many lesser *wedana;* and the four plus the *patih* made a group of five found in state structures all over Indianized Southeast Asia, representing the center and the four compass points. The functions of these officials, in contrast to the structure, were imprecise; individuals' areas of responsibility and relative importance seem to have depended more on their personal relations with the king or their strength in court circles than on the particular offices they occupied. In Mataram, formal structure was as much political aesthetics as table of organization; a proper pattern was, after all, essential for the proper functioning of a microcosmos. Meanwhile, practical political business was conducted primarily in terms of personal relations.

The officials of the central administration did the king's own business in the populous *kraton* itself and the *negara agung* and acted on his behalf in his dealings with the more distant *mantja negara.* The outside officials, on the other hand, were primarily concerned with the local worlds they governed. Even under strong kings like Sultan Agung and Amangkurat I, when the *kraton* watched them jealously and discipline was swift and harsh, they had a good deal of autonomy. Many ruled in what were natural geographical regions with an old history, and all had their own courts (*dalem*), sometimes very substantial, amounting to smaller *negara* within the larger one. Their territories varied widely in size, importance, and history, and the men therefore held different titles in the Mataram hierarchy of official ranks, but it is convenient to call them all *bupati* (regents), which was the general title later under the Dutch. In all these respects, they closely resembled the hereditary local lords alongside them in the *mantja negara;* in time, too, their posts tended to become hereditary.

The tax system that supported this administration is better understood. "Tax system" may be misleading, because it suggests money taxes. Some taxes, notably port, river, and road tolls and a head tax on peasants, were normally levied in cash, but Mataram Java had very little cash in circulation and no currency system of its own (it used Spanish silver dollars and Chinese copper cash, among others). Most of the taxes, therefore, were taxes in kind (consumer products, such as food for the nonagricultural elite, and commercial products, such as pepper and rice), and taxes in labor (*corvée* duty for building roads or a new *kraton* or *dalem,* personal service to king and officials, military duty).

The tax system reflected the concentric pattern of the realm very clearly. First, at the center, the king drew food and labor for himself and dependent members of his large court partly from royal lands sending their taxes directly to him and partly indirectly, as described below. Second, the rest of the royal family and the officials of the central administration were granted appanages by the king—that is, the right to collect for themselves a certain amount of produce or labor owed to the king as tax. Most appanages, other than tolls, were calculated in *tjatjah* (peasant family heads), and many lists have survived showing how many *tjatjah* in what region were assigned to various officials or princes. Most appanages were in the *negara agung*. Appanage-holders acquired what was due them by appointing a Javanese or sometimes Chinese *bekel* (bailiff, tax farmer), who did the actual collecting and sent them the proceeds after subtracting a share for himself. Third, officials or local lords in the *mantja negara* collected their own taxes and brought a specified proportion of them to the *kraton* once a year when they came to attend the *Garebeg Maulud* (the celebration of the Prophet Muhammad's birthday) and pay homage. Inside their territories they granted appanages for the support of their own relatives and subordinate officials. Fourth and last, the vassals overseas had complete autonomy in taxation and simply sent tribute at longer and more irregular intervals.

The king and the local lords of the *mantja negara* were hereditary, while officials were commoners and their sons were in theory no more likely to be appointed by the king than peasants' sons. In fact, however, there was a tendency for particular official posts, especially in the *mantja negara,* to become hereditary in the family of the holder. In any case, even if they did not succeed their fathers in particular offices, the sons of officials almost invariably remained in the official class, the *priyayi*. Javanese society had a marked hierarchical character and pronounced class differences, most basically between the peasant (*wong tjilik,* the little man) and the elite (*priyayi,* plus the few hereditary families above them).

The *priyayi* had a strong Java-wide cultural pattern, which they shared with the royal family and the hereditary local lords. *Priyayi* culture was very sensitive to status differences and expressed itself in an elaborate code of etiquette. Proper behavior, however, was more than a mere mark of social standing; it was an outward sign of inward refinement and spiritual accomplishment. A *priyayi* was *halus* (refined, able to control his emotions, attuned to God's will), and *wong tjilik* were *kasar* (coarse, excitable, little more aware than the animals). Alongside this in *priyayi* culture was a strong knightly ethic: devotion to one's lord, a strong sense of honor, readiness to die in battle. In Mataram times, *priyayi* rode horses to battle, and there were weekly tournaments at the *kraton* and the various *dalem*. *Priyayi* culture found its fullest expression in the shadow drama, the *wayang kulit,* a vast storehouse of religious learning and moral teachings as well as high art and simple entertainment. Its stories, developed out of the Indian classics, the *Mahabharata* and the *Ramayana,* inculcated the knightly ethic and *halus* behavior and offered to the young *priyayi* an ample choice of character types on which to model himself.

Two features stand out in a general view of Mataram Java. One is that the Javanese economy was simple, laborious and stiff. It rested almost exclusively on the most elementary of bases, raw peasant labor. It had very little currency for lubrication. Transport was rudimentary, a few roads hardly better than paths, short rivers going every which way and linked only by the Java Sea. In fact, only in a very limited sense was there a Javanese economy at all. There were local economies, in the thousands of villages and to some extent in the natural regions. Individual *priyayi* had what might be called private economies of their own, each one taking care of his economic needs himself through his own channels—his appanage, his *bekel,* his toll on the Solo River. All these local and private economies were only very loosely and precariously associated in a kingdom-wide economy.

Laid over this congeries of local economies and societies was a political and cultural pattern wonderfully suited to the severe requirements of making a Java-wide system. The king had very few economic means of control; he could not stop *mantja negara* officials' salaries, for example, because there were none. He could use military force only when his officials came to the *kraton* bringing their peasant levies, for he had only a few companies of his own. Java as a political entity rested on three things: a common language and culture, a political myth that was universally accepted because it rested on and expressed common religious beliefs, and the shared values of a Java-wide *priyayi* class. As the Mataram dynasty rose under Sultan Agung in the early seventeenth century and consolidated its power under Amangkurat I in the middle of the century, these three factors overrode the patchwork of the island. Mataram in that time was the strongest dynasty in Javanese history, and Java was effectively a political whole.

The other side of dynastic glory is dynastic decline. What Sultan Agung's armies and his *wahyu,* reverberating through the *priyayi* and folk of Java, could build up could also be torn down by other armies and other men's *wahyu* and by the intractibility of the Javanese economic landscape. In 1672, the volcano Merapi erupted, followed soon by a comet and a great drought—signs that Amangkurat's *wahyu* was departing. Rebellion seethed and then burst out, driving him from the *kraton* to death in exile. The legitimate heir soon was installed as Amangkurat II, and the pieces on the political map were properly reassembled —one pretender killed, another brought to homage at the court, Madurese and Makassarese intruders sent home, and the Dutch rewarded for their help with economic concessions and small pieces of the *mantja negara.* But it could not hold. Even the transfer of the *kraton* to a new and auspicious site did not help. Mataram was falling apart, and Java had entered on a time of troubles, which lasted three-quarters of a century and ended with the realm dismembered and Batavia suzerain of the whole island.

The Dutch East India Company had established its overseas headquarters in Batavia in 1619, but for a long time Batavia remained on, but not really of, Java—a fort, a lively port town, and a few miles of lowlands on which Chinese grew vegetables and some sugar for export. The company's interests were in the spices of the Moluccas and the trade of all the archipelago. Batavia barely escaped obliteration at the hands of Sultan Agung in 1628 and 1629—from his point of view it was simply another *pasisir* state to be conquered in its turn. For half a century it worried about Mataram's might, sent missions bearing tribute, and bought its rice there.

In the early 1670's, when the rebellion against Amangkurat I inaugurated the dynastic decline of Mataram, the VOC was at the very peak of its success as a naval and trading power in the archipelago. It was not really interested in Java but was drawn into the developing vacuum of power by the need to protect its flank and by the possibility of certain economic advantages. The Dutch were not the only ones to be drawn into the affairs of Java in this way; during the next three-quarters of a century, not only Madurese and Makassarese but also Java Chinese and Balinese played major roles of their own in the wars that accompanied the disintegration of Mataram. All were participants in a Javanese historical process.

By 1757, a new political Java had emerged, one that remained undisturbed for half a century and, in its formal structure at least, largely unchanged until 1945. The kingdom of Mataram was divided among three houses, two senior ones (the Paku Buwono's of Surakarta and the Hamengku Buwono's of Jogjakarta) and a junior one (the Mangku Negara's of Surakarta). They ruled, with their territories and appanages all tangled up together, over the old *negara agung* and the inland parts of the *mantja negara*, a long rectangle on the south central coast of Java. Along with the sultans of Bantam, these three houses were vassals of the VOC, still largely autonomous in their internal affairs but tied to Batavia through treaties, Dutch-appointed *patih*, and a certain habit of subordination. The rest of Java—a great bracket of lands enclosing the Mataram principalities—was VOC territory, ruled through *bupati*, bureaucratic nobles in their own lands, like their forebears, the *bupati* of Mataram's *mantja negara*. Alien though it was, the VOC was now enacting a role in Javanese history. Its earlier naval dominion in the archipelago was decaying; it had gone ashore on Java and was now the successor to Mataram. The circles of the realm were reversed—coastal Batavia was now the center, the *bupati* now faced west and north, and Mataram princes were now outer vassals. But politically the underlying structure of Java had hardly changed. Socially, below a small conquering elite of Dutchmen, *priyayi* still lorded it over *wong tjilik;* a multitude of local economies still sent tribute through political channels to a greedy but distant center. A Javanese writing of the eighteenth century, indifferent to the company's outside connections but sensitive to the imperatives of Javanese history, could explain this. "Jang Kung" (Jan Coen, the governor-general who founded Batavia), it said, was the son of a wandering foreigner and a princess of West Java who was destined to bear kings. Through her, therefore, descended a legitimate dynasty of Java.

11

THE SPANISH GOVERNORS

The governor and captain-general of the Philippines appeared to be one of the most powerful rulers in Southeast Asia. From his position in the massive walled city of Manila, he was commander-in-chief, the king's own representative, and vice-patron of the Roman Catholic Church. As virtually all connection between the Philippines and Spain was via Mexico, the governor was insulated by time and space. Because all instructions and replacements had to await the galleon's arrival from Mexico, it could take close to a year before an order from the court reached Manila. If the governor chose to request clarification, he could avoid carrying out instructions he did not like. However, despite the pomp and his position at the head of the civil, military, and ecclesiastic bureaucracies, the governor's powers were but a fraction of what they seemed.

First, the governor's tenure was insecure and dependent entirely on the whim of the monarch. Since it was a patronage position for the king, he appointed his friends and supporters rather than men dedicated to the job. It was clearly understood, if rarely articulated, that the governor was to profit personally, provided he did not plunder too grossly. The whole system was predicated on presumed malfeasance; before an outgoing governor could depart for home, he had to undergo an official investigation, or *residencia*. Bribery was endemic to the system, and each outgoing official knew that he would have to use a certain percentage of his profit to buy his way out. Second, the administrative structure of the colony was such that the governor usually had to compete with his principal assistants in the Royal Council (*Audiencia*). The bureaucracy was generally unresponsive and often openly hostile to the governor. Because petty officials also came to the Philippines to make their petty fortunes, few devoted much attention to the directives from Manila. The provincial governors, usually called *alcaldes-mayores*, established nearly autonomous fiefdoms, which were frequently on different islands or in remote areas. Third, the major Spanish concern in the colony was the galleon trade. Manila, the entrepôt, was a parasite, drawing what it needed from the interior but fundamentally uninterested in indigenous developments. The only viable link between the small urban community in Manila and the mass of peasants was the

Church. The governor, therefore, was dependent upon the friars. Although he was the vice-patron of the Church, he could not command their allegiance automatically. He was in the anomalous position of requiring support from the clerics to rule the archipelago. The scope of his power seemed far more impressive in Madrid than in Manila; however, because he usually viewed his tenure as brief, his goal as staying alive in the tropics and returning home rich, and his legacy as perpetuating the system, he was rarely concerned over these restraints.

Most of these men were not ogres, however. They did not see any contradiction between personal ambition and official function. They were loyal to their monarch and devoted to propagating the faith. What is significant is that the office defined their actions and that even the so-called enlightened governors accepted the system without any hesitation. However, their strategy of perpetuating the system did not preclude change. One of the clichés of Philippine historiography is that the colony was inert from the early seventeenth century until the accession of the Bourbon king, Carlos III, in 1759 and the conquest of Manila by the British three years later. In reality, there was constant ferment below the seemingly placid surface. Indeed, many of the Philippine governors who seemed most interested in maintaining the *status quo* actually proved to be catalysts for change. The pressure of events forced them to make decisions with unforeseen ramifications. If we examine, for example, the problems of Governor Don Pedro Manuel de Arandía (1754–59), we can see the process clearly.

At the minimum, military weakness could not be tolerated, since it jeopardized the colony. Consequently, Arandía, like many of his predecessors, attempted to reorganize the militia. He augmented the salaries of the troops to curtail venality, established the King's Regiment, and created four brigades of artillery and an artillery school. He reorganized the operations of the Cavite Arsenal. Arandía also attempted to reform the galleon trade, since this trade operation, which was the lifeline of the Spanish community, was riddled with corruption. He appointed a committee of distinguished citizens from Manila to oversee the apportioning and appraising of goods. When the committee itself was caught using its position for personal gain, he censured it sharply and began the process again. His efforts, conservative in conception, proved ineffective in application.

His equally conservative effort to break Chinese economic influence by expelling non-Christian Chinese, however, had radical consequences. Arandía did not foresee that his expulsion of the Chinese would have lasting impact on the development of the next two centuries of Philippine history; inadvertently, he opened the opportunity for the growth of the Chinese *mestizo* community, which up to then had been overshadowed by the Chinese themselves. Arandía specifically ordered the unconverted Chinese of Manila reconcentrated into a new ghetto (*parián*) and then repatriated. In his effort to lessen Chinese dominance of trade and commerce, he also ordered that the Christian Chinese who remained behind till the land rather than trade. He hoped to fill the domestic economic vacuum with a joint stock company of Spaniards. The company went out of business within a year and, through Chinese bribery and Spanish need, the Chinese slowly regained a part of their prior position. Arandía was not the first or the last governor to expel the Chinese; however, by making conversion the determinant in expulsion he reinforced the established Spanish policy of defining the alien on religious grounds and thereby stimulated the development of the Chinese *mestizo* community.

While marriages between Spaniards, usually creoles from the New World, and native women (*indias*) formed a small Spanish *mestizo* community, the great majority of the *mestizos* were children of these Chinese-*india* marriages. The Chinese *mestizos* had distinct legal and political rights and an increasingly desirable social status. Their existence permitted the Spanish to harmonize economic interest, religious conviction, and political stability.[21] The Spanish needed these people to keep Manila functioning; the Church welcomed them, since they were eligible for salvation and the sacraments. The Chinese, in turn, had an incentive to convert, in order to remain in the colony. Even if an individual had a wife in China, eventually returned there to die, and once home apostatized, he left behind *mestizo* children who were brought up entirely within the faith by their devout *india* mother. These children, integrated culturally into the community, moved freely, traded easily, and created their own subculture, which was not quite *indio* and not quite Chinese. The Chinese *mestizos* had their own section of Manila, Binondo, and became the most dynamic element in the society. In Arandía's time, they probably represented 5 per cent of the total population, though they were a much larger proportion in the Manila area.

Arandía's efforts to reform the galleon trade and to break the power of the Chinese in Manila were prompted by his need to increase government revenue. The growing poverty of the colony not only inhibited the functioning of government but also severely restricted personal opportunities for Arandía himself and the whole Spanish community. The colony was dependent on the annual subsidy (*situado*) sent from Mexico, since it had no major revenue sources other than the galleon and taxes on the *indio*. Lacking the efficient bureaucracy needed to collect such taxes and unable to tax properly its one major revenue source, the galleon trade, it had to operate on a hand-to-mouth basis. This chronic poverty in the public sector would continue as long as the colony limped along on the restrictive practices of the mercantilist galleon. It was clear to Arandía, as it had been to his immediate predecessors, that either new trade routes had to be developed or some sort of internal development had to be effected. The efforts at developing iron-mining were matched by increasing interest in agricultural products, especially pepper, cinnamon, indigo, and tobacco, in an effort to emulate VOC successes in the islands to the south. A whole series of schemes advocated reforms designed to turn the colony into a profitable operation.

The endemic warfare with the Muslim (Moro) sultanates in Mindanao and Sulu placed intolerable military expenses on the government, inhibiting the development of the economy, since the Bisayan islands and Mindanao were the regions in which the proposed developmental schemes would take place. The Muslim raids of 1754, for example, killed thousands, ravaged the coasts of Luzon and the Bisayas, subjected thousands more to slavery, and forced Arandía to devote prime attention to this security menace. He did so by reorganizing the military, strengthening Spanish garrisons in Zamboanga and elsewhere, shuffling his command, and, most importantly, attempting to establish peace through diplomacy.

At the core of his Moro problem was the Sultan of Sulu, Muhammad Alimuddin I (r. 1735–73). Shortly after his accession, he had entered into a peace treaty with the Spanish, which, among other things, offered aid to either party if the other was attacked. This commitment by the Spanish to Alimuddin achieved temporary peace, but it sucked the Spanish into the internal affairs of the sultanate. Almost immediately, Alimuddin called on Spanish forces to overcome an incipient rebellion. Alimuddin, a remarkable man, interested in Christianity or in what he could get from Christians, invited Jesuits to his capital city, Jolo. This generated such opposition within the Islamic community that Alimuddin had to house the Jesuit priests within his palace. Before long, Alimuddin was forced out of power by his brother, Bantilan, who nominally ruled as regent but soon proclaimed himself Sultan Muhammad Mu'izzudin. Alimuddin, now deposed, fled to Manila, where he again asked the Spanish to restore him. In 1749, whether out of conviction or for expediency, he was baptized over the skeptical opposition of the Archbishop as Don Fernando I, Rey Christiano de Jolo. While the Spanish in Manila celebrated with four days of holiday, the response in Sulu was all-out war. In 1750, the Spanish took Alimuddin to Zamboanga, where they prepared to force Bantilan to accept his brother back. The Spanish discovered, however, that Alimuddin had been corresponding with various Moro chiefs and, claiming betrayal, brought Alimuddin back to Manila as a prisoner and declared unceasing war.

When Arandía arrived, he attempted to negotiate an end to the bloodshed. The Spanish lacked the power to defeat Bantilan, so Arandía agreed to a peace conference in Jolo. It collapsed over the issue of the release of Christians seized in Moro raids, since Bantilan claimed that he no longer possessed the prisoners, who had been sold as slaves throughout the Malay world. Arandía also attempted to operate through Alimuddin, whom he paid a monthly stipend and treated royally. When, in 1755, Alimuddin asked to marry as a second wife a former concubine who had become a Christian, Arandía overruled the Archbishop's objections and had Alimuddin married in the governor's palace. Arandía's efforts were cut short by his own death and by further complications caused by British and Dutch interest in Sulu and northern Borneo. What is significant is not Arandía's failure, since Spain never fully succeeded in "pacifying" the Moros or establishing suzerainty, but rather his efforts to grapple with a massive and rapidly changing situation whose ramifications influenced every aspect of Philippine life.

Arandía's efforts to solve the Moro problem put him in conflict with the Church. The political expediency of diplomacy prompted him to make decisions that seemed to violate Church concerns. By the time of his death, perhaps by poisoning, his relationship with the clerical hierarchy was antagonistic; there was no longer the automatic congruence of interest implicit in the established phrase, "in the service of both Majesties," cross and crown. The interpenetration of functions tied the temporal and ecclesiastical worlds into an alliance that neither side found satisfying. For example, as a result of Jesuit insensitivity to *indio* sensibilities on the island of Bohol in the Bisayas, the governors from 1744 to 1829 found themselves involved in trying to suppress the Dagohoy Rebellion. The ebb and flow of this war forced twenty governors to divert meager resources to support the Church in its demand to be restored on the island. Arandía's preoccupation with more pressing issues forced him to assign a low priority to the Dagohoy Rebellion; however, the friars on whom he relied saw his priorities as distorted. The governor and the friars needed each other, but the growing divergence of interest strained the structure.

While the governor's weakness was due in part to a general decline in Spanish power throughout the world, it was due even more to the constrictions under which he operated in the archipelago, for his theoretical power far exceeded his actual ability to govern. Isolation—geographic, linguistic, and racial—circumscribed his power to a limited community and a limited area. The unresponsiveness of his bureaucracy and the subtle strength of other forces in the society combined to modify his decisions.

The Spanish governor-general of the Philippines was not alone in finding the full exercise of his powers checked by other forces in the society. Like him, the rulers of Thailand and Cambodia, for example, found the strength of provincial authorities sufficient to resist the full imposition of central control. Religious authorities throughout the region wielded a moral force that few rulers could ignore, and none could do wholly without the merchants, who rendered viable the taxation systems, in which commodities frequently were as important as currency. The traditional autonomy of the village community everywhere was a counterbalance to the sometimes overambitious designs of the capitals. As long as social and economic change proceeded at a slow rate, the often delicate political systems that were a feature of the first half of the eighteenth century could survive without upheaval.

PART TWO

New Challenges to Old Authority

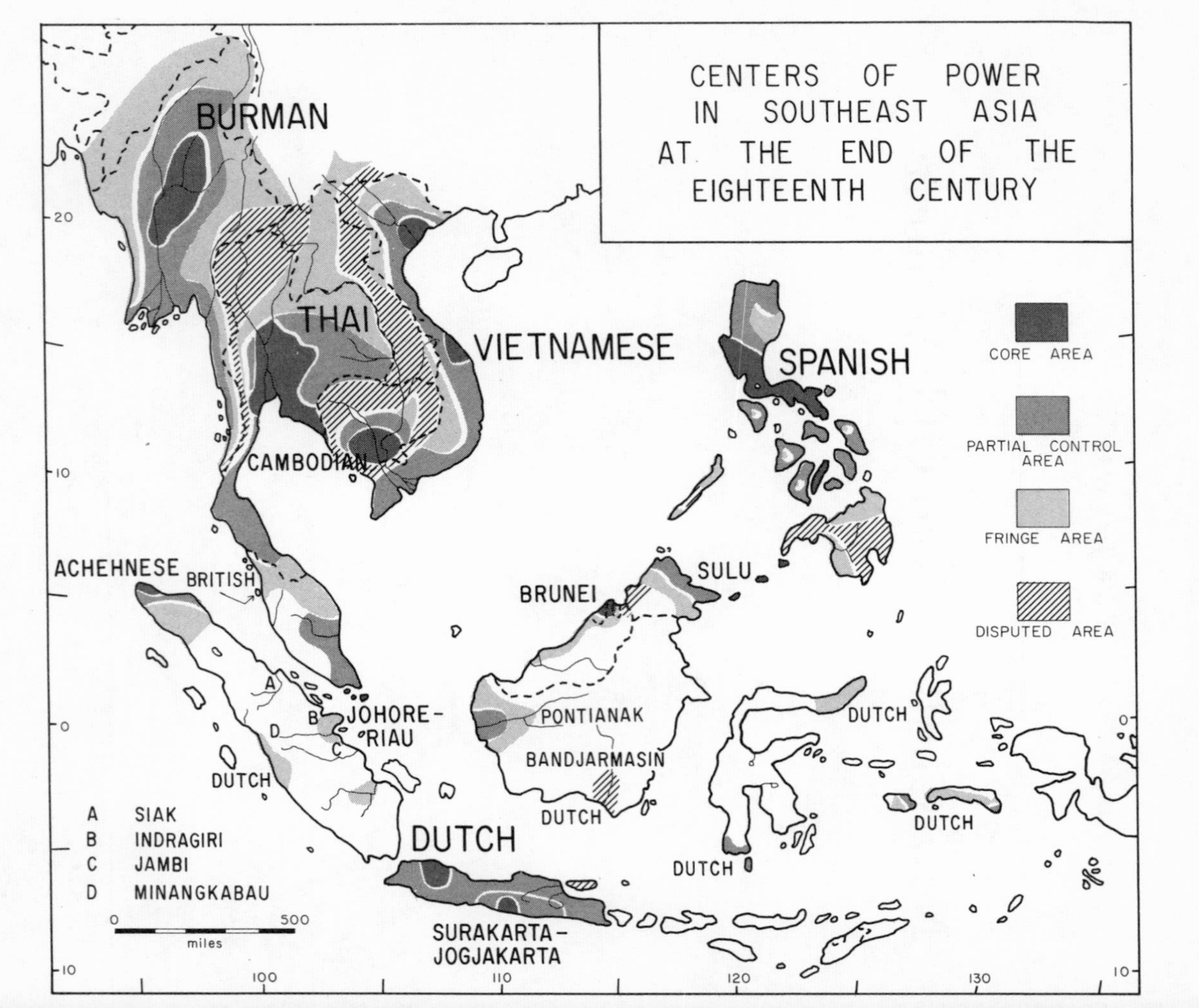
CENTERS OF POWER IN SOUTHEAST ASIA AT THE END OF THE EIGHTEENTH CENTURY
CORE AREA
PARTIAL CONTROL AREA
FRINGE AREA
DISPUTED AREA
BURMAN
THAI
VIETNAMESE
CAMBODIAN
SPANISH
SULU
BRUNEI
ACHEHNESE
BRITISH
JOHORE-RIAU
PONTIANAK
BANDJARMASIN
DUTCH
SURAKARTA-JOGJAKARTA
A SIAK
B INDRAGIRI
C JAMBI
D MINANGKABAU
0
500
miles
20
10
0
10
100
110
120
130

For purposes of analysis, the history of Southeast Asia for the century preceding 1870 can be broken into two periods. The first, extending to the early 1820's, was dominated by indigenous issues and themes. In those years, the role of the West was limited primarily to trade, which in most of the region was only a small percentage of the whole volume. Even in the Philippines, and in the other enclaves where the Europeans already governed directly, the West lacked the power it was to acquire subsequently. During that period, new groups of Southeast Asian leaders emerged to alter the power structure in virtually every society of the area. It was also an era of warfare, dynastic upheavals, population displacements, and intensifying struggles for both power and wealth among bureaucrats, merchants, landowners, and nobility. New states rose and others, like the Mon kingdom centered on Pegu and the principalities of Vientiane and Čhampassak in Laos, disappeared. Peasants were summoned to do the fighting, feed the winners, and finance the social changes from which they derived few benefits.

During the last half of the eighteenth century, three new dynasties came to power in the major mainland states. The first was the Konbaung Dynasty in Burma (1752–1885). The wars the first kings of this dynasty fought against Thailand broke the power of the Thai court at Ayudhya and set the stage for the appearance in 1782 of the Chakri Dynasty, with its capital in Bangkok. Twenty years later, the Nguyen Dynasty assumed power over Vietnam, placing its new capital at Hue. At first, the new dynasties were primarily concerned with legitimizing themselves, consolidating their administrative grip, and imposing their presence upon neighboring states. In Thailand and Vietnam, and to a lesser extent in Burma, the first years were also marked by a far-reaching cultural and political renaissance caused partly by the energies released as newcomers gained power. Those events greatly influenced Southeast Asian history for this period and beyond; the last Nguyen emperor abdicated (to Ho Chi Minh) in 1945, and the Chakri Dynasty, albeit limited by the constitutional reforms that followed the Revolution of 1932, still reigns today.

Unconcerned about events in Europe, Southeast Asian leaders were unprepared for the kind of commercial and political offensive the Europeans began to launch against the region after the Napoleonic wars. British intrusion in Southeast Asia, partly at Dutch expense, reflected new commercial and maritime ambitions brought on by the industrial revolution. Southeast Asia's position on the sea routes between India and China, which had always been a feature of its economic and political history, resumed importance now. By a series of moves in the first quarter of the century, Britain sought to secure the eastern flank of its empire in India and to protect its routes to China. These included the establishment in 1819 of the city of Singapore, a war with Burma, and a commercial treaty with Thailand. As the century wore on, Britain moved deeper into Burma and the Malay peninsula. Industrialization in Europe also contributed to the development of export agriculture in the Philippines and in the Indonesian islands and to a new market for such export crops as sugar, coffee, and rice. As a result, new economic and social structures, as well as new landowning elites, appeared in Southeast Asia.

As the years shaded into those dominated by the West, many Southeast Asians sensed the rapidity of the process of change. At several points, leaders or their advisers sought either to deflect or to accommodate the West. Most notably in Thailand, but also in Vietnam and Burma, internal reforms were enacted in an effort to stave off European control. Agricultural production, increasingly monetized, was shaped by world market conditions. However, as European influence began to spread after 1825, Southeast Asia became increasingly compartmentalized. By 1870, much of Southeast Asia's territory had passed formally into European hands, with the result that imperial interests began to inhibit interregional contact. Each colony became linked closely to the mother country. The area as a whole did not share, as it had previously and would in the future, a true community of experience. The middle fifty years of the nineteenth century saw a wide diversity in Southeast Asia's response to the West. Indeed, the themes of that period vary more sharply from country to country than they do in the high colonial era that followed; each must be traced carefully for an understanding of the tangled interaction of Western and Southeast Asian interests that developed in the period.

12

BURMA, 1752–1878

The Burman capital was moved six times in the rule of the Konbaung Dynasty (1752–1885). Capitals were located on sites deemed auspicious by court astrologers, and when the kingdom suffered grievous defeats or blows to its prestige, the state, as represented by the capital, was out of harmony with the cosmos and had to be moved. Similarly, kings took seriously their personal identification with the fortunes of their kingdom, and several rulers, sorely taxed by their responsibility, had to be "moved" from the throne. Although the records of the Konbaung period are considerable, they have hardly begun to be studied. The dynastic decline of the period is discernible in outline in a series of events at court and in external conflicts, which left Burma by 1878, at the accession of the last Konbaung king, Thibaw, a fading image of its former self.

By 1750, the Toungoo Dynasty had ruled Burma for three centuries, considerably longer than any of its predecessors. The troubles it faced were not much different from those that had brought on the collapse of the kingdom of Pagān in the thirteenth century. With a succession of figurehead kings on the throne in the first half of the eighteenth century, the dynasty fell prey to divisive forces within and opportunistic enemies abroad. Plundering parties of Manipuris raiding from northeastern India in the 1720's and 1730's undermined the credibility of Ava's military power. Burman rebels in the Mon lands of Lower Burma in turn made a bid for power, only to be defeated themselves by a Mon counterrebellion. Internal dissension, faltering royal leadership, and administrative weakness in the provinces around the capital further crippled the dynasty. Ava, the capital city, fell to the Mon rebels in April, 1752.

Alaungp'aya, deputy to the lord of Shwebo, a town a few days' march north of Ava, was a Burman fiercely proud of his home. Three times he repulsed progressively stronger Mon forces sent north to exact his allegiance, and his patriotism soon became an example to which other Burmans could respond. The magic of the news from Shwebo swept across the north, and Alaungp'aya's troops and reputation grew as he moved to the offensive. By the end of 1753, he camped under the walls of Ava; within a month, the former capital had been liberated and all of Upper Burma had been cleared of Mon troops. Alaungp'aya shifted the capital from Shwebo, established a royal genealogy for himself, and became the first king of the Konbaung Dynasty.

Alaungp'aya led a Burman people conscious of its identity and purpose when he carried to the south the battle against ethnic separatism and for the reconstitution of a Burman monarchy. His power was his army, a force unparalleled in recent times. The momentum of his victories and the legends that swept around the new king surrounded him with an aura of supernatural power. By chain letters and sponsored ballads, he sowed fear among the populations ahead of his armies, thereby weakening the will of his opponents and creating massive defections. In promising release from slavery, he won over additional groups of men.[1] During 1755, his armies moved as far south as Rangoon, and Pegu fell to his forces in May, 1757.

Compelling local and political considerations moved the king and his officers to warfare with Thailand in 1760. That war grew out of a local rebellion in Tavoy, in which the Thai in neighboring Mergui and Tenasserim—at that time Thai provinces—were thought to be involved. When local Thai authorities failed to provide satisfaction, the Burman king felt that a display of his force was necessary to maintain Burman authority in Lower Burma. He wanted to make it clear to potential dissidents that they could not hope for Thai assistance in any challenge to his authority. Once begun, the war could not easily be abandoned by the Burmans, especially after Alaungp'aya's fatal wounding before the walls of Ayudhya, in May, 1760. In eight years, the king had created a state as extensive and powerful as any in Burman history, and his successors and generals were fully conscious of the extent to which its survival depended upon the respect they commanded, both within and outside the kingdom.

In the next twenty years, Burma was constantly at war. The failure of the 1760 campaign against Thailand was not soon repeated; subsequent campaigns were better planned and provisioned. The Burman armies gained a commanding strategic and political advantage by moving through the Shan and Lao states and the isthmus of the Malay peninsula before launching their final assault; they took and sacked Ayudhya in April, 1767. Alaungp'aya's second son, King Hsinbyushin (r. 1763–76), soon found himself threatened from the northeast, where Burman activities in the Shan states provoked a reaction from the Chinese governor of Yunnan, who launched four invasions of Burma between 1766 and 1769. The Burman defenses held, and the Chinese were forced to conclude a treaty at Kaungton late in 1769. Hsinbyushin, however, was displeased. He felt that the war had not been carried through to a victory, that his generals had negotiated without authority to do so, and that the king's prestige had been damaged. Fearful of facing Hsinbyushin's wrath, his generals marched on Manipur to place a Burman nominee on the throne. Even with this additional victory, the venerable Thihathura, one of Burma's finest generals, was made to dress as a woman when he finally returned to Ava. With his colleagues he was sent into temporary exile in the Shan states.

Over the two decades following the death of Alaungp'aya, there was increasing political instability at court. Relations remained strained between the crown and its highest officers. Naungdawgyi had executed two generals on his accession to the throne in 1760, provoking an army rebellion. Neither he nor his succesor, Hsinbyushin, ever felt completely secure. Hsinbyushin's treatment of the generals following the conclusion of the China wars was perhaps symptomatic of a certain rigidity in the life of the court. Any challenge or slight to the king provoked ruthless and sometimes indiscriminate retaliation, intensifying the atmosphere of fear and suspicion that permeated the court. The armies clearly suffered from the irrational climate and, by the 1770's, their performance in the field declined as commanders quarreled and morale sagged. As Thailand recovered under Taksin and the Burman foothold in the Lao states was lost, Burma was forced onto the defensive on its eastern frontier, retaining of Alaungp'aya's conquests only the Tenasserim littoral.

It was Bodawp'aya (r. 1782–1819), the fifth and last of Alaungp'aya's sons to reign, who managed to restore a measure of equilibrium. The early years of his reign were marked by the same kinds of warfare his father and brothers had conducted. He conquered Arakan in 1784 and resumed warfare with Thailand. Conquest soon abated, however, and Bodawp'aya turned instead to the administrative work neglected by his predecessors. His general revenue inquests of 1784 and 1803, for example, were of critical importance. The country was canvassed, lands and rights assessed, tax and labor service obligations and exemptions scrutinized, and the population enumerated—at a figure of barely 2 million in a country capable at the time of supporting many times that figure. At the very least, these inquests reminded the king of the limits to his country's resources, which warfare had so severely strained. They may have prompted him to husband those resources more carefully, and they certainly revealed inconsistencies and injustices, which he endeavored to correct, most notably by revoking many of the tax exemptions for religious communities.

Bodawp'aya's attack on the economic foundations of the monkhood, as well as his intervention in clerical disputes to favor one sect at the expense of another,[2] reflected one dimension of political conflict during his reign. Elements of the monkhood were hostile not only because of Bodawp'aya's economic reassessment and his favoritism but also because they rejected what they considered to be the king's religious excesses, such as his claim to the status of a bodhisattva. There were other divisions and conflicts. The *hlutdaw* (supreme council of state), for the most part composed of elderly descendants of entrenched official families, got on poorly with the *atwin-wun,* the ministers of the royal household and privy councillors of the king. The king rewarded loyal soldiers and civil servants with land grants often made at the expense of others.

Advancement was frequently tied to kinship or geographic origin. The usual jealousies within the royal family and the jockeying for position and preferment among members of the official class increased the number of potential combinations that might challenge the throne. While Bodawp'aya sought to regulate by law the conduct of public business, private morality, and the administration of justice and revenues, his personal force, his strong political sense, and his ruthlessness in balancing the forces at court and in silencing his opposition were much more effective. The climate of fear and suspicion, however, severely restricted the flow of information to the king, who came to be told only what he wanted to hear.

Although he was seventy-five at his death in 1819, Bodawp'aya retained a strong grip on public affairs to the end. His military campaigns continued, but never in so ambitious a fashion as in 1785, when he had dreamed of conquering Thailand, China, and India in succession. Apart from occasional forays into Thailand and the quelling of rebellions, as in Arakan in 1797 and 1811, the king's attention focused mainly on the small states of India's northeast frontier, chief among them being Manipur and Assam. These states reflected the confusion that had encouraged British intervention among the states of India. Through them, Burma encountered the economic and political reality of the British presence to the west. From 1804 onward, Burman troops regularly campaigned in the region, often at the behest of ambitious local figures. The success of Burman armies in establishing hegemony over these states led Burma to an exaggerated sense of its own power and to take seriously the idea of challenging the British in India itself.

Many irritants in Anglo-Burman relations developed during Bodawp'aya's reign, and little was done by either Britain or Burma to salve the potential for conflict. Though diplomatic contacts at the end of the eighteenth century were motivated on the British side primarily by Anglo-French rivalry, the principal issues after 1800 were local. The frontier between Arakan and British Bengal was particularly sensitive. The British saw a demarcated frontier there, but the Burmans and Arakanese saw only a zone of overlapping influences. Both sides felt their sovereignty violated by what each perceived as the intransigence and irresponsibility of the other. The English East India Company (through its governor-general in Calcutta), convinced of its moral superiority, wanted to encourage local trade to provide capital for its operations in China. It was incensed at the poor treatment meted out to merchants in Rangoon. Furthermore, the British were disturbed by Burman activity in Manipur and Assam, since it threatened to collide with the defensive commitments of the company. For its part, the Burman Government could not understand British ideas of frontiers, extradition, and trade, which it viewed as eccentric deviations from a system of interstate relations in which it had long worked comfortably. Most serious were the misjudgments of each side as to the strength and intentions of the other. The Burmans were insulted by the governor-general's insistence on carrying on relations with the Burman court as though he himself were a royal equal of the king. Although the Burmans regularly sent missions to India, ostensibly for religious purposes (but actually in order to seek allies and assess British strength), and although some at court saw the real dangers inherent in the situation, most such information never reached the king, or reached him in mutilated form. The British were aware of the difficulties of reminding the Burmans of British interests and strength, yet, mainly because they were busy elsewhere in India, they never made the effort required to do so. Diplomatic contact ceased in 1811, and conditions along the Arakan frontier deteriorated without any serious effort on the company's part to indicate the limits of its patience.

King Bagyidaw, who succeeded his grandfather, Bodawp'aya, in 1819, saw no reason to change the old man's policies. Faced with revolts against Burman intervention in Manipur and Assam and with the beginnings of British efforts to assist those threatened, he appointed the ambitious and brilliant General Bandula to be Governor first of Assam and then of Arakan. In 1823, he confidently sanctioned a major campaign against Bengal. When Burman troops crossed the frontier, the English, this time free of military commitments elsewhere, responded in force. A large seaborne expedition took Rangoon without a fight in May, 1824. The hope of making the Burmans submit by holding the delta region and merely threatening the capital failed as Burman resistance stiffened. In 1825, the company's Indian troops began a slow advance north toward Ava. When they reached a point only one day's march from the capital, the Burmans were forced to accede to terms that they found humiliating and incomprehensible within the customary framework of Southeast Asian interstate relations. The Treaty of Yandabo, concluded in February, 1826, required them to cede Arakan and the Tenasserim provinces to the East India Company, yield their position in Assam and Manipur, pay an indemnity equal to $5 million, and agree to the exchange of diplomatic representatives and the conclusion of a commercial treaty. What had begun as a minor irritant to the Burmans on their western frontiers had been exacerbated by deep misunderstandings and misinformation until it became a catastrophe of the first order.

To the Burman court, the British victory was more a triumph of wealth than a vindication of human qualities or a just cause. "The English are rich," an official boasted, "but they are not so brave as we are."[3] For the time being, with the army beaten and scattered, the court impoverished, and the British in possession of large tracts of the kingdom, Bagyidaw had no alternative but to play a waiting game. John Crawfurd, who came to Ava at the end of 1826 to negotiate the promised commercial treaty, found the court determined to yield no further concessions without compensatory gestures on the British side. When Crawfurd refused to discuss political questions, the Burmans conceded to him a vague and meaningless commercial treaty, and did so only after he had agreed to give them more time to raise money for the third and fourth installments of the indemnity required of them by the Yandabo Treaty.[4] Bagyidaw felt he had a good case at least for the rectification of the borders between Burman and British territory. He was encouraged by accurate reports that the Tenasserim provinces were proving too expensive for the company to administer and that it was considering their retrocession. The king therefore sent a mission to Calcutta.

The mission, however, was unproductive, and it was not until the appointment of Major Henry Burney as British Resident in Ava in 1830 that meaningful negotiations between the two states were undertaken. Bagyidaw liked Burney, who learned Burmese and made a sincere effort to understand the king's concerns. On examining Burman records, Burney became convinced that their case for possession of the Kabaw Valley east of Manipur was justified and persuaded his government to yield it, while he persuaded the Burmans to pay over the last sums due on the indemnity in February, 1833. This was one of the few high points in nineteenth-century Anglo-Burman relations. In the following month, the British Government decided to retain possession of the Tenasserim provinces. When this decision became known in Ava, the prospects for conciliation dimmed. The territorial cessions not only had weakened Burma physically and strategically vis-à-vis Thailand but also were a blow to the prestige of the monarchy and a counterattraction to the population of Lower Burma. Over considerable opposition, Bagyidaw had committed himself to a conciliatory policy of attempting by diplomacy and reluctant performance of his treaty obligations to regain the lost provinces. As the hopes for this policy's success evaporated, Bagyidaw came to fear for his continued security on the throne.

From 1831 onward, Bagyidaw's uneasiness verged on paranoia, and by 1834 he was a recluse, while power devolved on his low-born queen and her brother. In 1837, Bagyidaw's own brother, the Tharrawaddy prince, seized the throne and had the queen, her brother, and Bagyidaw's only son assassinated. Bagyidaw himself, perhaps in deference to his great popularity, or in recognition of the fact that he had become indifferent to power, was allowed to live in seclusion near the palace.

In its origins, Tharrawaddy's rebellion had little or nothing to do with foreign affairs, being a reaction against the self-seeking rule of the queen and her brother in the absence of Bagyidaw, but it came to have a decisive effect upon Anglo-Burman relations and the politics of the court. Though Tharrawaddy did denounce the Treaty of Yandabo, he refused to go further, either openly to espouse the cause of the war party, which retained considerable strength in the capital, or to attempt to improve relations with the British, which had continued to deteriorate. Burney, who had tried to restrain the new king from massacring his opponents and had offered Bagyidaw asylum in British territory, soon was forced to retire from the capital. His successors found the atmosphere of Amarapura, Tharrawaddy's capital, and Rangoon so inhospitable that attempts to continue the residency were abandoned in January, 1840, and Anglo-Burman diplomatic contacts lapsed.

In terms of court politics, the rebellion of Tharrawaddy and his accession to the throne in 1837 was a critical turning point. Tharrawaddy's advisers were new men who had joined him in rebellion.[5] When Tharrawaddy took the throne, he had a number of Bagyidaw's family and ministers killed, replacing the latter with his upcountry friends and supporters. These men survived two subsequent palace revolutions—the accession of Pagan Min in 1846 and that of Mindon Min in 1852—and they provided a strong element of continuity through the next decades. Although Tharrawaddy's reign began with an overt gesture to revanchist sentiment, he and Pagan Min after him seemingly tolerated the *status quo* with England. The loss of territory was certainly unpleasant to Burma, but the king and his ministers were much too realistic to attempt to reconquer it.

In Rangoon, meanwhile, Maha Minhla Mingaung Kyawhtin, also known as Maung Ok, was appointed *myo-wun* in 1850. He followed his predecessor in practicing extortion on the trading community in Rangoon and in bringing indiscriminate criminal charges in order to bolster his income with bribes and fees. This time, however, the customary complaints to the British Indian Government did not go unanswered. In November, 1851, the Indian Government sent a naval officer, Commodore Lambert, to Rangoon with three ships to investigate the cases of two British shipmasters, who complained of having been imprisoned for murder by Maung Ok and of having been forced to pay nearly $5,000 for their release. Lambert ignored his instructions from India and single-handedly brought about war between the two states—seizing a ship that belonged to the Burman king and taking it out of Rangoon. The British Government in India had no real desire to avoid war, partly, perhaps, because it saw advantages to be gained in Burma, but primarily because it was afraid of losing face. As Lord Dalhousie, Governor-General of India at the time, expressed it, "We can't afford to be shown to the door anywhere in the East; there are too many doors to our residence there to admit of our submitting to that movement safely at any one of them."[6] By July, 1852, a well-organized British expedition had captured the ports of Lower Burma and begun a march on the Burman capital.

Pagan Min, who lost control of affairs, was trapped as the course of the war worsened. Parts of his army and many of his ministers deserted him and threw their support to his younger brother Mindon Min, who had opposed the war from the beginning and had withdrawn from the capital in December after a plot against him was uncovered. Mindon went to Shwebo to gather his forces and associate himself with the legend of Alaungp'aya, then returned to take the capital and be crowned king in February, 1853. Meanwhile, the British armies had taken Prome and advanced fifty miles beyond, so as to include a rich belt of teak forest within Lower Burma—a designation they invented after announcing its annexation. Mindon sent two Italian priests to meet with the British commanders in January, asking them to advance no further and await his envoys. When the king's envoys reached the British camp in March, they attempted to persuade the British to give up their conquests in Lower Burma. The British, flushed with victory, refused. And so, as in 1826, the two sides were at an impasse—though now on a line much farther to the north. The British wished to have a treaty confirming their possession of Lower Burma and defining the conditions under which future relations would be conducted. Mindon refused to sign any such treaty, despite the almost unanimous urgings of his ministers. He is said to have reasoned that "it behooves me to be more cautious than anyone in an affair of this importance. I am responsible for the honor of the kingdom. If I were a Minister, or a Prince, perhaps I should give the same advice that they do."[7] And he steadfastly refused to sign.

Early in 1853, hostilities simply ceased. Commercial and political relations remained as before or as worked out informally between Rangoon and Mandalay, where Mindon moved his capital in 1857. The untidiness of an artificial frontier drawn by British military commanders (which was neither recognized nor openly challenged by Mindon), the British-dominated riverine commerce between Upper and Lower Burma, and the relations of the two governments with the Shan and Karen states to the east all constituted potent issues for continued conflict. There were those on both sides—Englishmen increasingly attracted by the idea of trade northward into China and impatient with half-conquest, and Burmans who had expected that compliance with British demands would bring a British evacuation such as that which had followed the Treaty of Yandabo—who thought that the second war had ended prematurely.

Mindon saw himself as a virtuous man, sincerely religious and peace-loving. He had come to the throne hoping that his goodness and his eagerness to set right that which had led to the war would persuade the British to relent. He long persisted in such hopes, with little encouragement. He was greatly helped by his ministers. Three of his four chief ministers of the *hlutdaw* had been *atwin-wun* under Tharrawaddy and Pagan. They brought him skills that were to serve him well, restraining him on several occasions when his patience wore thin. Their tasks were difficult. Burma in 1853 was cut off from the rice-producing areas in the south on which it had come to depend, and many members of the royal family and nobility had lost the appanage districts there that had supported them. Mindon realized the need for new ways of ruling Burma, and the reforms he undertook were significant departures. He seems to have made them not simply to please the British; rather, he seems to have believed that the era of misunderstandings was really past, that he could look forward to coexistence with British Burma, and that a revitalized Burma could live on.

The war in some ways made reform easier; it had underlined the gravity of the kingdom's situation, and the territorial losses had undermined the old revenue and administrative systems until they had become unworkable. Fundamental reforms, therefore, had to be implemented in Burma two decades before they were executed, for example, in Thailand. In 1861, Mindon moved to abolish the old *myo-za* system by paying princes and officials regular salaries and stipends, thereby increasing their dependence on the capital and his control over them, which he further strengthened by instituting an inspectorial system for provincial administration. To pay for this, he introduced a new income tax assessed on a household basis according to the relative prosperity of each, and he abolished the *ahmudan* service class, requiring its members to pay taxes where they lived instead of to their personal masters. By the 1870's, the new tax was providing some two-thirds of the royal revenues, while the remainder came from traditional sources, like the royal monopolies on teak, petroleum, and gems. To strengthen his revenues further without increasing the household tax, Mindon sought money from royal sponsorship of trade and commerce, through both the old monopolies and new state enterprises. He purchased and ran several river steamers. He constructed factories containing European machinery—manned sometimes by European technicians and managers—to process such agricultural products as lac, cutch, sugar, cotton, and silk. Mindon also went to some lengths to stimulate rice production. Although his measures had some success, the kingdom was by no means changed overnight; it was not as easy to restructure a political system, after all, as it was to purchase steamships or to build factories.

In a number of ways, Mindon tried to bring his kingdom into greater contact with the rest of the world. He sent some of his sons to study with an Anglican missionary, and he encouraged modern studies at his court. Short of compromising his principles, he did all he could to establish good relations with the British. He sent a mission to Calcutta in 1854, and he openly welcomed Arthur Phayre, who came to the capital in 1855 seeking a treaty to end the war. In 1862, Britain and Burma concluded a commercial agreement that eased the path of Upper Burma's exports into the newly created province of British Burma (combining Arakan, Pegu, and Tenasserim) and raised British hopes of trading overland with China. The treaty was further expanded in 1867. The agreements served the immediate interests of both parties: Burman desires to import arms and to establish a relationship with Britain in which some retrocession might be possible, and British hopes of entering China through its "back door." The primary issues in Anglo-Burman relations, however, were ignored. The gradual improvement was illusory. It disappeared late in the 1860's, when the British failed to keep their promise to allow the Burmans to import arms and when they fully integrated the province of British Burma into the Indian Empire. The British then adopted a position of such arrogance that they were willing to forego diplomatic relations with the Burman king rather than to allow their envoy to remove his shoes for royal audience, as court etiquette demanded.

Internal changes at the court at about the same time also worked to hinder Anglo-Burman relations. Most of the ministers who had been prominent in the life of the court since the days of Tharrawaddy passed from the scene in the 1860's. The men who replaced them were not of equal caliber. A palace coup attempt in 1866, during which two of Mindon's sons shot up a meeting of the *hlutdaw*, killing the crown prince and several ministers, left the king unwilling to name another crown prince, a decision that opened up court politics into a free-for-all from which only the most unscrupulous emerged on Mindon's death in 1878. In the 1870's, Mindon was rather more adventurous in foreign policy than he had been earlier. His flirtations with France and Italy during this period, however, seriously compromised his kingdom's position vis-à-vis the Indian Government, which disliked the prospect of third-power interference on the frontiers of India. It has been suggested that the fate of Burma was sealed by the first Anglo-Burman war, which gave the British two of Burma's major areas and involved Burma in conflicts that would not be settled until the complete annexation of the kingdom.[8]

13

THAILAND, 1767–1868

In the century following the sack of Ayudhya by Burman armies in 1767, the Thai state, now centered on Bangkok, gained a coherence it had never known. While the old kingdom of Ayudhya had been a political center of gravity, the strength of its pull lay in its armies, kings, and prestige. When these failed, its dominions fell apart. The re-established kingdom, founded in 1782, was enabled to extend its power from the borders of China and Tonkin through to the Malay sultanates by its acquisition of a new strength in techniques, resources, and leadership, which it had previously lacked. After 1824, the Western threat and example played an important role in the development of the techniques, although Siam's ability to respond positively to the challenges was as much a product of internal development before that date as it was of the events that followed.

A new dynasty had established itself upon the throne of Ayudhya in 1688, in the aftermath of a court revolution provoked by French interference in Thai affairs. Its early reigns were filled with strong personalities and almost constant court intrigues. Political conflict centered on the succession to the throne, and the absorption of the major noble families in court politics left provincial administration neglected. No king or noble felt sufficiently secure in his position to devote to non-dynastic matters the attention they required. Consequently, the invasions by Alaungp'aya and his successors from 1759 onward caught the Kingdom of Ayudhya in a weak position internally and in regard to its vassals and client states.

The capture of Chiangmai in 1762 gave the Burman kings access to additional troops and supplies. It put the invading armies in a strategic position from which they could squeeze Ayudhya from the north. After a bitter siege of fourteen months, the ancient capital fell on April 7, 1767. Thousands were captured and led away to captivity in Burma, while many more died in battle or of sickness and starvation. The royal family and nobility were decimated, families were broken by death or captivity, and conventional morality could not easily withstand the pressures of hunger or the breakdown of social and administrative controls. The kingdom, so heavily dependent upon personal relationships and upon an ordered patron-client structure, came apart.

The Burman armies, having plundered and destroyed the Thai capital and kingdom and having been forced to fight the Chinese on their own northern borders, rapidly withdrew, leaving small garrisons behind. At least five Thai immediately moved to contest for the succession: the governors of Phitsanulok in the north and Nakhǫn Si Thammarat in the south; a survivor of the royal family in the northeast; a group of Buddhist monks near Uttaradit in the north; and the half-Chinese former governor of Tak, named Sin, who had fled from Ayudhya and had begun his campaign at Čhanthaburi in the southeast. This last-named official—generally called Taksin—had the initial strategic advantages of easy water communications, a position nearer the center of the old kingdom, and a personal following. Within months, his shrewd generalship and force of personality won him a commanding position in the area around the old capital. He defeated the remaining Burman forces on the western edge of the central plain and was crowned king in December, 1767. He constructed a new capital at Thonburi, across the Čhaophraya River from present-day Bangkok. In the next two years, while the Burmans were distracted by wars with China, he defeated his rivals and built up his own administration.

As king, Taksin's lasting achievements were military. In subduing his rivals and in pressing renewed campaigns against the Burmans, he restored the configuration and influence of the Ayudhya kingdom in the 1770's. Campaigns in Cambodia had restored Thai influence there by 1779. In the north, Chiangmai was captured in 1773, and a Thai-backed ruler, Čhao Kavila, was successfully established a few years later. Major expeditions further east enforced Thai hegemony over the separate states of Laos in 1777–79.

The king of Thonburi, however, was not successful as a politician. He retired from the personal command of his armies in 1775 and stayed in his palace, where he was increasingly attracted by the notion of his own divinity. Like Alaungp'aya, he attempted to force the Buddhist monkhood to accept him as a bodhisattva, thereby alienating them profoundly. His arbitrary and highhanded rule, undiminished in severity after the Burman threat receded, increased the opposition of the surviving nobility. Traders and those economically involved with them found their former privileges revoked. Taksin gave his country firm leadership and martial skills when it needed them most, but he spread the white umbrella of kingship too narrowly to shade under it all the interests of his court and kingdom. A revolt against the excesses of some of his officers broke out in Ayudhya in March, 1782, quickly rallying all the opposition to the king until Thonburi was taken and the king surrendered.[9] Čhaophraya Mahakasatsük, the chief of Taksin's generals, who had been campaigning in Cambodia at the time of the revolt, was named king by the rebels and began his reign as King Rama I in April, 1782.

This reign, which lasted until 1809, was critically important. Taksin had re-established the Thai state, now centered at Thonburi/Bangkok, but he had failed to nourish the political institutions that could help it prosper. In his policies and actions, Rama I set a new tone, establishing patterns of rule that went beyond a simple restoration of the *ancien régime* of Ayudhya. Most important, the relationship between the king and the elite was qualitatively changed. Rama I came to the throne without the rivals or opposition that had forced his predecessor to adopt a hard line, even though, like Taksin, he was himself in some sense a usurper. He was able to gain and to hold the confidence of the nobility by granting them representation in high office and by carefully consulting his officers in his decisions. He made clear his expectations for the performance of his officers, using his powers of appointment and dismissal early and well. He attempted to conciliate the royal survivors of his predecessors. He restored the orthodoxy and ecclesiastical hierarchy of the Buddhist monkhood and regularly asked its advice on moral issues. The reign of Buddhist morality gained substantially at the expense of older, non-Buddhist traditions. In general, his leadership was marked by open consultation and discussion, while the rule of principle reduced arbitrary authority and factionalism.

Something of the style of Rama I's reign is evident in his religious, legal, and literary work. Each new king was expected to extend his patronage to the Buddhist monkhood and to commission the copying of a new set of the scriptures, known as the *Tipitaka*. A new king was also expected to confirm or deny the laws of his predecessor and to demonstrate his cultural legitimacy by poetic composition. Rama I went far beyond what was conventionally expected of a king. He called a council of the Buddhist monkhood in 1788 to undertake a thorough revision of the *Tipitaka* to restore accurate Pali texts. In 1805, he convened a legal commission to reorganize and edit the whole corpus of Thai law and to bring it into conformity with contemporary standards of justice and equity. The king composed in flowing Thai poetry perhaps the most monumental work in Thai literature, the *Ramakian*, a version of the Indian *Ramayana* which runs to more than 3,000 pages of modern print. In proclamations and decrees reviving the ceremonial and official life of the court, the king took pains to explain himself and to justify his actions. Though all these works were, in a sense, traditional and orthodox in their orientation, the spirit and energy that moved them was new. They were suffused with self-consciousness, objectivity, and selectivity, and they took place within a more open framework of a new relationship between the king and his nobles.

Rama I's reign was marked by the extension of Bangkok's influence in the central portion of the Indochinese peninsula and by the reduction of Burman military and political power. After a series of Burman invasions in the south, west, and north between 1785 and 1797, the last major battles were fought in the extreme north in 1802–5. At the conclusion of these, the Burmans were expelled from Chiangsaen, and Thai contacts were established with the Lao and Shan states as far north as the Chinese frontier. In this warfare, the Thai troops were joined on various occasions by levies from Chiangmai, Nan, Luang Prabang, Vientiane, and Čhampassak, all of the Lao states in the north. In the south, particularly after the Burmans invaded the Malay peninsula in 1785, the Thai encountered considerable disaffection among the nearer Malay states. Strengthening their control over Nakhọn Si Thammarat and Songkhla, the Thai then moved to bring Patani, Kedah, Kelantan, and Trengganu under closer supervision and surveillance. Generally, instability or divided loyalties anywhere on the periphery of the kingdom were viewed as a threat to Bangkok's security. The combination of forceful leadership, increasing domestic strength, and the distractions to which Burma and Vietnam were subject in the last two decades of the eighteenth century made possible a major revival and extension of Thai power and influence.

Rama I's success culminated in the uncontested succession of his son to the throne as Rama II in 1809. The following years were sufficiently peaceful to permit the court to build upon the foundations laid down by Rama I. Rama II was even more a poet than his father had been, and though he withstood easily the small military challenges presented on his eastern and western frontiers, he was sometimes thought to be too lenient with his dependencies and client states. The major developments of his reign were political. Uncertain, perhaps, of his ministers and officials, he encouraged his brothers and other senior princes to take an active role in the administration, appointing some to act as superintendents over the affairs of various ministries. An important working relationship developed out of this policy between his eldest son, Prince Čhetsadabodin, who was given superintendency over the ministry of foreign affairs and trade (*phrakhlang*), and a high official of that ministry, Dit Bunnag, who was from a prominent noble family of the Ayudhya period and was closely related to the king's own mother. These two worked together to develop trade with China, to the profit of both official and personal accounts; both gained politically valuable new wealth as well as access to profitable foreign contacts. Through Dit, who later became minister—Čhaophraya Phrakhlang—in 1822, Chinese planters introduced commercial sugar production around 1816. The crop soon became an important item of a new export trade with Western merchants, concentrated after 1819 in Singapore; in exchange, the Thai were able to import, among other things, arms from American traders.

The British hoped to secure recognition of their possession of Penang; to restore the sultan of Kedah, who had been expelled from his state by Thai troops in 1819, after surreptitious dealings with the Burmans; and to increase Thai trade with Penang and Singapore. These hopes led the governor-general of India in 1822 to dispatch John Crawfurd as an envoy to the Thai court. His mission was almost totally unsuccessful, as he could offer the Thai no more than rational arguments for free trade in return for the substantial concessions he demanded. By the time a second mission, headed by Captain Henry Burney, reached Bangkok late in 1825, however, conditions there had changed.

Prince Čhetsadabodin, though the son of Rama II by a concubine, had succeeded to the throne as Rama III in 1824, primarily because of his maturity, his administrative experience, and his political backing. His younger half-brother, Prince Mongkut, born of a queen and barely twenty years of age, had recently entered the monkhood. Burney came seeking Thai participation in the Anglo-Burman war on the side of the East India Company, but he failed to obtain it. As soon as the news of the Treaty of Yandabo reached Bangkok, the Thai reacted quickly to the presence and threat of a new neighbor on their western frontier by opening discussions with Burney. After protracted negotiations and maneuverings, the two sides reached agreement. In return for British recognition of the Thai position in the Malay states, the Thai conceded to British merchants changes in trading and duty procedures in Bangkok. The court agreed to take an immediate cut in its revenues in the long-run hope that it would make up in volume what it lost thereby. Čhaophraya Phrakhlang (Dit Bunnag) played a critical role in gaining acceptance of this arrangement, even though he personally and officially stood to lose most if the arrangement did not work out as planned. However, it succeeded. Thai foreign trade increased dramatically, a new system of tax farming designed to circumvent the treaty was instituted, and the political threat of Britain abated for some decades. This success was the result of the strengths of the Bangkok monarchy—an open working relationship between the sovereign and his officials, a high institutional capacity for assessment of situations and solutions, and a quality of genuine receptiveness to the outside world through involvement in overseas trade.

For most of the reign of Rama III (1824–51), the West only indirectly affected the economic and political life of the kingdom. This is not to say that the West was unimportant to the Thai in that period, but only to emphasize the fact that Thailand's rulers, and probably the British as well, interpreted the 1826 treaty as an accommodation with which both sides could live and still be free to attend to more immediate matters. The seaborne trade through Bangkok increased, especially the export of sugar to Singapore, while the Phrakhlang and his supporters continued to strengthen their economic and political position. The new system of tax farming, under which the rights to collect internal taxes, transit dues, and commodity levies were awarded to private individuals (frequently Chinese immigrants), worked well. The combination of a new government determination to maintain its own labor supply by tattooing those considered liable for labor service and new economic developments, such as the rapid increase of bulk commodity exports, elicited quite different responses from some of the old nobility, whose wealth traditionally had stemmed from personal control of manpower and official position.[10] Those who continued to think in terms of the old system effectively subverted the intent of the labor regulations by amassing large forces of debt-slaves for their personal service. By the 1850's, foreign observers estimated that half the population of the kingdom lived in a state of voluntary servitude, easygoing though it may have been. In contrast, the Bunnag family, some other elements of the nobility and royal family, and the Chinese immigrants based their wealth on new economic patterns of foreign and domestic trade, tax-farming, and commercial agriculture. External developments like the world sugar markets and the heavy influx of Chinese immigrants newly available for wage labor, entrepreneurial services, and retail commerce made this latter response both easy and natural. It is not surprising that the *phrakhlang* refused to leave his posts as minister of treasury, trade, and foreign affairs when he assumed concurrently the post of *kalahom* (minister of war and the southern provinces) in 1830; in his old ministry, he maintained a position from which he could keep up his trade and his contacts with the Chinese.

The British annexation of the Tenasserim provinces blocked the main route by which Burman armies formerly had attacked the Thai capital and reduced Thailand's security risk on its western flank, at least so long as Anglo-Thai relations were friendly. On the other hand, the conclusion of the Burney Treaty in 1826 encouraged the Lao ruler of Vientiane, Čhao Anu, to believe that his suzerain in Bangkok was weak and seriously threatened by the British. At the end of 1826, he launched a major attack on Thailand across the Khorat Plateau and was within three days' march of Bangkok before the Thai could respond. Their counterattack, initially a small-scale punitive expedition, escalated for two years until it spread over most of the area of present-day Laos, from Čhampassak in the south to Xiang Khouang in the northeast, and it included troops from the northwestern Lao principalities of Nan and Chiangmai. Faced with the difficulty of administering and defending the Lao areas east of the Mekong River against civil strife, dynastic quarrels, and Vietnamese ambitions, the Thai decided to move tens of thousands of Lao from mountain valleys in eastern and southern Laos and to regroup them across the Mekong in the northeastern half of the Khorat Plateau. The small kingdom of Luang Prabang, isolated in the north and long friendly to Bangkok, was left alone, although Thai interest and contacts there increased. These were the years when the Thai first actively intervened in Laos on a permanent basis by encouraging and forcing the establishment of Lao provinces on the Khorat Plateau and by initiating their integration into the Thai political order.

The Thai armies, busy in the south and northeast in the 1830's, gained considerable field experience. Their officer corps, under the leadership of Čhaophraya Bodindecha (Sing Singhaseni), became more professional. They began to experiment with tactics and imported American weaponry. In the Cambodian crisis of the 1840's, the Thai were in a much better position than they had been in earlier decades to compete against Vietnamese forces, which had benefited from French training and arms. The agreement with Vietnam of 1846 allowed the Thai to maintain a resident at the Cambodian court. This capped the efforts of nearly two decades to adjust to the changes in the local balance of power in mainland Southeast Asia occasioned by Vietnamese expansionism and by the Treaty of Yandabo. The Thai had dealt successfully with regional challenges to their authority in the Lao states, in Cambodia, and in the Malay states. Their military efforts had been followed by greatly increased use of royal commissioners, who frequently visited the tributary states, and by tightened administrative control over provinces where populations had been regrouped and defenses strengthened.

The influence of the West was quietly and selectively felt in Bangkok in this period. As late as 1850, there was seldom more than a handful of merchants and only a few missionaries present in the capital. However, a small group of important Thai sought them out and learned from them. Prince Mongkut, passed over for the succession to the throne in 1824, began a personal quest for sustaining religious commitment and a satisfying intellectual system within the Buddhist monkhood. He rejected a life of meditation as well as what he felt was the laxity of traditional Buddhism, and, after an encounter with Mon monks, whose discipline was especially strict, he sought a return to what he felt was the rigor and universalism of canonical Buddhism. In 1828, he informally established a new Buddhist sect, the Dhammayut. With time to study and travel through the countryside, and later with ecclesiastical authority as the abbot of an important monastery, Mongkut soon began to extend his understanding of the world through the study of languages, science, and foreign ideas. He was not alone in these endeavors. Similarly engaged in such studies were Mongkut's full brother, Prince Čhuthamani, several other important princes, and the eldest sons of the Phrakhlang (Dit Bunnag), among others. Some gained immediate practical advantages thereby: Prince Wongsathiratsanit studied medicine as the head of the royal physicians, Chuang Bunnag learned navigation and shipbuilding, to the profit of his father's trading efforts, and Prince Čhuthamani studied military affairs by training and equipping a company of troops. Whatever the practical advantages or concrete knowledge gained, the significant legacy of these studies was simply the fact of close contact with the West and with each other on a regular basis over an extended period of time. These men, who closely followed the course of the "Opium War" in China and the activities of the Western powers in the region, were less likely to underestimate the West than their fathers or neighbors had been.

Envoys of the American and British governments came to Bangkok within a few months of each other in 1850–51, demanding free trade and extraterritoriality. Neither was able to conclude a treaty with the Thai. They found the court divided and the progressives fearful of making concessions that might compromise their chances of manipulating the succession to the throne. Prince Mongkut and Chuang

Bunnag appear to have been convinced that their country's future depended on a policy of generous accommodation with the West, which only those members of their generation who understood the West could accomplish successfully. They temporized, however, privately assuring the envoys that their demands would be met once Rama III and the older men around him had passed from the scene.

Quietly gathering support, partly through the use of their economic power and official position and partly through the manipulation of family relationships, the party of accommodation prepared for the end of the reign as Rama III fell ill in January, 1851. The political climate became charged as Rama III attempted to elevate one of his own sons, whose supporters subtly attacked Prince Mongkut, the other most logical candidate for the throne. To prevent civil war, an extraordinary meeting of the highest dignitaries of the realm was held on March 15, when Čhaophraya Phrakhlang (Dit) made an impassioned plea on behalf of Mongkut—the "rightful heir," as he termed him—and declared that any who would challenge Mongkut's right would have to fight the Phrakhlang first. He carried the day; he had too much power for others to cross him, and the case he was pleading was clear. Accordingly, on March 25, Mongkut was approached by the Phrakhlang's officers and invited to ascend the throne. He agreed to do so.[11] A guard was posted around Mongkut's monastery residence and remained there until early on April 3, when Rama III died, and Mongkut was escorted to the Royal Palace to be crowned. Mongkut insisted that his full brother, Prince Čhuthamani, be elevated to rule jointly with him as his coequal and "second king," an arrangement that at least temporarily succeeded in neutralizing any potential rivalry from within the progressive party. Chuang Bunnag was appointed Čhaophraya Si Suriyawong, minister of war and the southern provinces (*kalahom*), and chief among the king's ministers, while his younger brother, Kham Bunnag, became minister of treasury and foreign affairs. Their father and uncle, who together had run both those ministries for more than twenty years, were given honorific royal titles and, having reached old age, began to retire from public life.

Western demands soon were revived by Sir John Bowring, the British governor of Hong Kong and minister to China. By the time he arrived in Bangkok in March, 1855, the second Anglo-Burman war had taken place. Mongkut's reading of the Singapore newspapers and his prior correspondence with Bowring had made clear what was expected of him. Mongkut and Suriyawong handled themselves skillfully with the British envoy. While Mongkut sat chatting with Bowring, offering him cigars and pouring wine, Suriyawong casually revealed his detailed acquaintance with European economic theory and the principles of good government. Bowring was thoroughly impressed. Though they exuded self-confidence and conviction, however, Mongkut and Suriyawong had political battles to fight at court and a thirty-day deadline, set by Bowring, against which to work. Extraterritoriality, the legal jurisdiction of consular officials over their own nationals, could be easily conceded, but Bowring's insistence on free trade at nominal duties and on the abolition of all Thai Government trading and commodity monopolies threatened the economic interests of many at court and elsewhere. From Bowring's journal, it appears that Suriyawong's belief in the benefits of free trade—his conviction that the country could make up in trading volume what it lost on the duties paid by each ship and on each commodity—and his faith that alternative sources of income could be found to replace those lost by conforming to the treaty, won the day against considerable opposition. The Bowring Treaty, signed in April, 1855, served as the model for more than twenty such agreements signed between the Thai Government and foreign nations in subsequent years. Under its terms, the Thai accepted extraterritoriality, the abolition of both royal and farmed-out commodity or trading monopolies and transit dues, and the establishment of *ad valorem* rates of 3 per cent on imports and 5 per cent on exports. Taxes on land held by British subjects were fixed at low rates, hindering the Thai Government from increasing the land taxes charged to its own citizens; earlier prohibitions on the export of rice were removed. The only concession to the Thai was the stipulation that the import and sale of opium was to be a government monopoly. The Thai gave away a great deal for the sake of security, without any way of knowing that they could withstand the sacrifices. They did so because they believed that they had to, because the threat of foreign intervention or war was real. They recognized this fact, because they had followed so closely what had been happening in Burma and China.

To make the treaty work, Mongkut and his ministers had to undertake what Bowring recognized to be "a total revolution in all the financial machinery of the Government."[12] The old monopolies and tax farms were replaced with new excise monopolies farmed to Chinese—the opium, gambling, lottery, and alcohol monopolies—which provided the major share of government revenues well into the twentieth century. In addition, the economic possibilities of foreign trade were developed as rapidly as possible. The number of foreign ships visiting Bangkok soon increased more than tenfold, and Thailand became one of the world's largest exporters of rice and teak. Government revenues recovered within one year and soon began a steady rise; the possible domestic political dangers to which Mongkut and Suriyawong had exposed themselves declined.

With greatly expanded foreign trade and contact, the tone of life in Bangkok rapidly changed. Harbor facilities, warehouses, and shops were constructed, and the king himself invested funds in new streets of shops. Following the traders came more missionaries, artisans, and professionals, and soon a few Westerners were formally employed by the Thai as tutors, translators, police officers, labor officials and shipmasters. These numbered fourteen during Mongkut's reign.[13] Their impact was echoed by the larger community of diplomats and missionaries, whose contacts with important Thai officials were both regular and intense. Men like Mongkut and Suriyawong were aware that their country's fate in large measure depended on how much they learned from the West. They took pains to borrow and adapt Western ideas and techniques where their security was at stake, in the conduct of foreign relations, and in the organization and equipping of military forces. Foreigners were employed to represent the Thai Government abroad, later to be replaced by well-trained Thai. Europeans were engaged to advise the foreign ministry, Suriyawong, and the king in Bangkok. The Thai Government hired drillmasters to train troops, and it imported new arms. A start was made in providing new government services required for the conduct of international trade or for the convenience of foreigners, for example telegraphic and mail service and paved streets.

Although he had made these accommodations with the West—a supremely important commitment for his nation—Mongkut did not attempt to promulgate any fundamental reforms. The bureaucratic nobility remained essentially semi-hereditary and unsalaried, and its educational preparation and recruitment were virtually unchanged. No substantial revisions were made in Thai law or in the system of slavery. Most of the military forces were untouched by reform, and the provincial administration remained both inefficient and resistant to central control. It is likely that Mongkut and Suriyawong felt that they had done enough and that the worst was over. They may have thought it foolish to proceed too rapidly with change, particularly since the pressure to reform, as voiced by the foreign consuls, was still not strong as late as 1870. As with most governments everywhere, reform for its own sake, or for practical purposes, was less a political issue at court in the 1860's than was political power, pure and simple. The nobility and royal family were divided on the issue of reform, its pace and extent, and on the issue of the relative balance between royal and bureaucratic noble power. These issues at times conflicted, pulling individuals in opposite directions. The climate of the political environment suggested caution; changes could not easily be introduced without upsetting the balance of power at court. However sincere Mongkut or Suriyawong were about reform, they believed that changes had to be introduced gradually and great care taken not to disturb established interests.

Two incidents occurred in the 1860's that might have caused the Thai to reconsider both the nature of their relationship with the West and the relative urgency of domestic reform. First, the shelling of Trengganu by a British warship in 1862, after Suriyawong had been intriguing to extend Thai control there and in Pahang, reminded the Thai of the fragility of their relationship with Britain and of their own weakness in countering Western attacks upon the sovereignty of the kingdom. In 1863 came the first stage in the elimination of Thai power and influence in Cambodia to the benefit of the French. King Mongkut was deeply distressed at the severance of a long-standing paternal relationship with the king of Cambodia, and he was frightened by the undisciplined behavior of the French naval authorities in Saigon. Mongkut's response to these events was idiosyncratic. Essentially optimistic and frequently naive in his dealings with Western nations, he seems to have hoped that his own charm, rationality and good intentions would convince the West of Thailand's right to survive as an independent nation. Neither incident was serious enough to force Mongkut to alter his basic policy, but both were harbingers of more difficult times ahead. The era of high imperialism had not yet reached Southeast Asia, and Mongkut was able to deal successfully with the West. One of these diplomatic efforts was to invite foreign consuls and the governor of the Straits Settlements to accompany him on a visit to the peninsular village of Wa Ko to witness a total eclipse of the sun in September, 1868. There, he contracted the illness that caused his death five weeks later, at the age of sixty-five.

The ability of the kingdom to deal with the challenges thrust against it stemmed from a century of domestic developments. After the sacking of Ayudhya by the Burmans, the first kings of the Bangkok dynasty had reconstructed a kingdom that was alive to the dangers and opportunities around it. The smooth relationship between Rama I and his ministers led to the formation of durable interest groups at court, which lent flexibility to the workings of government and broadened the range of alternatives in the consideration of national economic and foreign policy. Economic innovation diversified the bases of wealth that could be brought to bear on the political process. The growing resident Chinese community rapidly proved a source of great strength, first in operating the tax-farming system of the third reign and then providing a rapidly expanding tax base, which kept the national treasury solvent at a critical period. Perhaps most important, though least tangible, was the self-confidence of a few Thai leaders—their conviction that they could concede to the West without losing much—and their faith that they could persuade their countrymen to accept the sacrifices required of them. They felt strong enough to take economic and political risks for the sake of security. Each risk successfully accepted, from the treaty of 1826 to the treaty of 1855, strengthened the party of accommodation.

As a result of the long period of political and economic changes in Thailand up to 1868, the political spectrum was expanded. New interests, ideas, associations, and commitments multiplied the alternatives in policies and political positions open to the court. The royal autocracy of the past became more difficult to sustain in the face of noble challenges to royal authority in defense of both established interests and radical change. The role of the monarchy, in the face of external demands, was to lead the nation to the acceptance of what was minimally necessary for its survival and to balance the personal and institutional interests at court in order to prevent conflict and paralysis. Mongkut trained his son Chulalongkorn to assume this delicate role, but his training was far from complete when the prince ascended the throne at the age of fifteen. The tests he would face were certainly no less severe than those his forebears, who provided him with a demanding example, had mastered.

14

CAMBODIA, 1779–1863

Cambodian history for the years preceding the establishment of the French protectorate in 1863 has often been inaccurately portrayed merely as a struggle for survival on the part of its governing class or as a footnote to the histories of Thailand and Vietnam. Those years were marked by territorial losses, political disorder, and wars. They damaged Cambodia's stability, strained its institutions, and humiliated its people.

Dislocations and violence, moreover, had far-reaching economic effects. As the size of the kingdom diminished, so did its population and the revenues available to the court. As revenues fell, the court's eagerness to collect them increased. Pressure from the court for taxes and manpower alienated regional leaders, who frequently led their followers, or were pulled by them, into rebellion. Rebellious factions, in turn, were both a cause and a result of instability at the center. Disorder in Cambodia attracted the notice of the newly consolidated regimes in Bangkok and Hue, which offered assistance to one Cambodian faction or another for a price either disregarded or underestimated by the Cambodians at the time. The price was generally high, ranging from outright grants of territory or workers to the requirement that royal succession be determined by the protecting power. As the court slipped further into dependent status, the cycle continued. From Cambodia's point of view, the pattern of history in this period was a descending, narrowing spiral.

In the course of the eighteenth century, the Cambodian court lost control successively over the southwestern portion of the Mekong delta, a strip of coastline between Ha Tien and Kompong Som, and the northwestern provinces of Battambang and Angkor. In 1814, Thailand annexed two small provinces on Cambodia's northern frontier and, at the time the French intervened, was preparing to administer two more, northwest of the Cambodian capital. Although each of the losses occurred for different reasons, all four had the common effect of cutting Cambodia off from outsiders and from the benefits of trading directly with powers other than Vietnam and Thailand. Significantly, when the court resumed the administration of the coastal strip in 1847, the Cambodian king, Ang Duong, quickly had a road built there and a port constructed from which Cambodian ships sailed to Singapore.

Dynastic turmoil was a constant feature of the Cambodian court. During the first three-quarters of the eighteenth century, nine kings, five of whom reigned more than once, occupied the throne, often for only a few months. Disaffected members of the court fled into the no man's land of the Mekong delta or to the more formal protection offered them by the Thai. In both places, these princes gathered troops, usually an ethnic hodge-podge under a mixed command, with which to regain power in Cambodia. In the late eighteenth century, Thai ascendancy over the Cambodian court, backed by frequent Thai invasions, reduced the turnover in the Cambodian royal house. Vietnam, racked at the time by civil war, was forced to accede temporarily. In 1779, a six-year-old prince, Ang Eng, was selected as king, while power remained in the hands of his pro-Thai advisers. For the next eighty years, only three other monarchs, all direct descendants of Ang Eng, occupied the throne. Dynastic stability, however, was not accompanied until the 1840's by any real power on the part of the monarch.

In 1794, Ang Eng traveled to Bangkok to be crowned by Thai officials, an unprecedented event in Cambodia's history. Shortly afterward, the Thai court placed a pro-Thai Cambodian official, Ben, in charge of a large tract of land in northwestern Cambodia containing the provinces of Battambang and Angkor. Those provinces soon severed their administrative connections with the Cambodian court and remained under loose Thai administration, governed by Ben and his descendants, until they were restored to the French protectorate of Cambodia in 1907.

When Ang Eng died in 1796, the Thai named no successor but continued to rule Cambodia through approved Cambodian officials. In 1805, Ang Eng's fifteen-year-old son, Ang Chan, was crowned in Bangkok. Upon returning to his capital, he quickly sought recognition from the recently constituted Nguyen Dynasty in Vietnam. Emperor Gia-long, following Sino-Vietnamese diplomatic practice, replied by sending Ang Chan a Vietnamese seal of office and court costume for his entourage. Cambodia's quadrennial tribute to the Nguyen court was also set at this time. It consisted of the same kinds of forest products that Hue demanded in tribute of the intervening upland peoples. That the Vietnamese court saw as its duty the "civilizing" of Cambodia must have galled Ang Chan and his ministers, but, in the face of Vietnam's growing power and of the need to balance it against Thai hegemony, they had no visible alternative.

Three of Ang Chan's brothers had remained at Bangkok in the custody of the Thai court, and they accompanied a Thai invasion of Cambodia in 1811, which cast Ang Chan aside for several months. In 1812, Ang Chan resumed the throne, aided by troops provided him by the eunuch overlord of southern Vietnam, Le Van Duyet. By 1816, his court had become a "two-headed bird," paying tribute to Bangkok as well as to Hue. The next fifteen years pass almost unnoticed in Cambodian sources. Their silence suggests the possibility that Thailand and

Vietnam, preoccupied elsewhere in any case, reached some sort of *modus vivendi* regarding Cambodia, perhaps legitimizing their separate spheres of influence.[14] A British traveler, passing offshore in 1823, reported that the kingdom was divided into three parts—Thailand and Vietnam each administered one, and the third, containing the court, remained independent.[15]

Between 1829 and 1832, disorders in the provinces bordering Thailand, in which the Cambodian court accused officials of being sympathetic to the Thai, dismantled whatever diplomatic arrangements Vietnam and Thailand may have made. In 1833, a Thai army, accompanied again by Ang Chan's disaffected brothers, swept through the kingdom and into Vietnamese portions of the Mekong delta. The Vietnamese responded by invading Cambodia themselves, expelling the Thai and reinstating Ang Chan, who died shortly afterward, in 1834. After his death, the Nguyen court renamed Cambodia Tran Tay, or "western commandery," and proceeded with plans to administer the kingdom directly, using Vietnamese officials.

Although Vietnamese motives for that decision remain obscure, they were probably related in some way to the recent death of Le Van Duyet. Perhaps no longer afraid that a Vietnamese advance into Cambodia would enlarge that overlord's extensive power vis-à-vis the court, the Vietnamese court felt the time ripe—and more convenient because of Ang Chan's death—to realize a long-standing ambition.

In Phnom Penh, in a move perhaps calculated to insult Cambodian institutions, the Vietnamese installed Ang Chan's teenage daughter as queen. The bewildered girl named her two sisters as vice-reine and heir presumptive, respectively, but real power fell to a group of Vietnamese bureaucrats who began to arrive in 1834 to remodel Cambodian society and administration. In contrast to the Thai, who had been content in periods of overlordship to work through Cambodian institutions, which in any case resembled their own, Vietnamese concepts of government were too different and their contempt for Cambodia's administrative style too great for them to temper or delay what they viewed as an urgent civilizing mission. Vietnamese pressure against nearly every point of Cambodia's institutional structure soon produced revolts, at least one of which was ignited by Buddhist monks. The Cambodians particularly objected to the related imposition of cadastral records, census, and land taxes, although other features of Vietnamese administration, such as the recostuming of Cambodian officials and the renaming of the kingdom's provinces, must also have been offensive to the bureaucratic elite.

In 1841, after the Vietnamese had exiled the Cambodian queen to Hue and imprisoned one of Ang Chan's brothers there through a complicated ruse, revolts broke out among the Cambodians who were living in southern Vietnam. As a result, when the Vietnamese troops temporarily had to withdraw from Cambodia, the Thai moved in, hoping to install Ang Chan's other brother, Ang Duong, on the throne. For the next three years, the chronicles state that no rice was planted and that the people lived on roots, while the Thai and Vietnamese, aided by rival Cambodian factions, fought each other and devastated the landscape. Peace negotiations calculated to save face for the exhausted armies lasted until 1846, when both sides agreed to withdraw from Cambodian territory and to accept Ang Duong as king. The treaty marked the resumption of Thai influence at the Cambodian court. To seal the treaty, Ang Duong was crowned in his capital in 1848 by representatives sent there from both Thailand and Vietnam.

Ironically, Ang Duong's divided fealty to both Thailand and Vietnam had the effect of liberating him to some extent from both. The chronicles and other reports give the impression that Ang Duong, who had remarkable administrative gifts, was unwilling to be anybody's puppet. Although he had spent most of his life in Thailand, for example, one of his first actions on reaching the Cambodian throne was to forbid the use of Thai administrative terminology, which had long been widespread. In 1853, moreover, he secretly communicated with the French court, transmitting a letter to Napoleon III in which he offered homage in exchange for friendship. The presents accompanying the letter were lost en route, and with them the French opportunity for intervention, since Ang Duong interpreted Napoleon's silence about the presents as indifference. In 1856, a French official named Montigny came to Cambodia to negotiate a full-scale commercial treaty, but Ang Duong backed away, partly because Montigny had discussed his plan already with the Thai court, which had disapproved of it. Urged to accept France as an ally, Ang Duong said, "What do you want me to do? I have two masters already, who always have an eye fixed on what I am doing. They are my neighbors, and France is far away."[16] The monarch would have welcomed informal French guarantees with which to strengthen his hand in relation to Thailand and Vietnam, but the French in the late 1850's already had larger ideas in mind.

When Ang Duong died in 1860, he was succeeded by his eldest son, Norodom, then in his twenties. During the next five years, Norodom rode out a series of dynastic and religious rebellions, which broke out in northern Cambodia and on both sides of the Vietnamese frontier. Two rebel leaders claimed to be heirs to the throne; a third was Norodom's younger brother. Meanwhile, as the French consolidated their hold on the Mekong delta, where they had intervened in the late 1850's, they began to be interested in Cambodia, whose economic potential they considered enormous. Norodom, friendless and uneasy, welcomed the presents and attention given him by French naval officers, who traveled upriver to his court from their headquarters in Saigon. In 1863, he signed an agreement with the French whereby he accepted their protection as heirs to the suzerainty held by the Vietnamese, which the French asserted had lapsed with their intervention in Vietnam. Norodom neutralized this action by negotiating a secret protocol with Thailand, pledging loyalty in order, perhaps, to be crowned king of

Cambodia, for the Thai retained his coronation regalia at Bangkok. Invited by his monastic sponsor, King Mongkut, to be crowned in the Thai capital, Norodom set off in 1864, only to hear that the French flag had been hoisted above his capital while he was traveling to the coast. Hurrying back to his palace, Norodom apologized to the French, who hauled down their flag. It was the last time the French would do so for nearly 100 years, for French control was less than a year away.

15

VIETNAM, 1802–67

In 1802, the Vietnamese state stood on the brink of a golden age unparalleled since that of the Hong Duc period of the late fifteenth century. From 1771 until 1802, the country had experienced a socially explosive peasant rebellion, led by the three Tay-son brothers of Binh Dinh in south central Vietnam, which had destroyed the already moldering Lê Dynasty (1427–1788) and then placed two Tay-son emperors upon the Vietnamese throne. The first of these emperors, Quang-trung (r. 1788–92), defeated a massive Chinese invasion of Vietnam aimed at restoring the Lê Dynasty and bequeathed to his successors memories of his epic victories over Chinese armies, like the famous battle of Dong-da, near Hanoi, in 1789. By 1802, Tay-son power had collapsed in turn, vanquished and superseded by the new Nguyen Dynasty (1802–1945), which now ruled Vietnam from Hue. For the first time in history, a single Vietnamese court governed a united polity that stretched from the Kwangsi-Yunnan border all the way south to the Gulf of Siam. The predecessors of the Nguyen Dynasty had never truly controlled both the Red River delta and the Mekong delta simultaneously.

The creation of the Nguyen Dynasty in 1802 meant the dissolution of the bureaucracy that had supported the Tay-sons. Families that had been privileged under the Tay-sons now became outcasts under Gia-long (1802–20), and families that had been outcasts under the Tay-sons became the newly privileged after 1802. One senior Tay-son official was even publicly beaten to death before the Temple of Literature in Hanoi in 1803. Yet, although the scars of the eighteenth-century civil wars were slow to disappear, Gia-long's revival of the civil service examination system in 1807 permitted many families to ride above the political storms of the period and to maintain a continuity of influence and power. For example, Phan Huy Ich (1750–1822) served the Tay-sons, his son Phan Huy Chu (1782–1840) served the Nguyens, and their descendants are active in Vietnamese politics today. Vietnamese officials of the early 1800's came on the whole either from long-established scholar families, mostly in the north, that had survived the Tay-son interregnum by such pursuits as teaching school, or from loyal officers in Gia-long's army and navy who had come mostly from the center and from the south. At first, the court rewarded them by giving them "allotment lands" (*khau phan dien*) on a hierarchical basis, the largest estates going to the highest officials. Since bureaucrats lacked private administrative power over their lands and could not subdivide them and give them to clients, and since any sufficiently talented scholar could enter the official class, this arrangement was not "feudal" in the medieval European sense. It soon gave way to a more centralized system of remuneration, which replaced the distribution of "allotment lands" with that of cash salaries. The Nguyen bureaucracy depended upon a communications system that was probably superior to any found in neighboring societies, thanks to the famous Mandarin Road (*quan lo*) with its regular relay stations, which ran from the north to the Mekong delta. Even in 1804, when the road was still being built, the officially specified rates of travel were thirteen days between Saigon and Hue and five days between Hanoi and Hue. Couriers were flogged if they were more than two days late.

In 1821–22, a European visitor who had also lived in India, Java, and Thailand wrote of Hue that its "style of neatness, magnitude, and perfection" made the achievements of other Asiatics look "like the works of children."[17] Yet the Nguyen golden age never really materialized. Two Vietnamese Marxist historians have counted 105 large and small peasant uprisings against the court in the period 1802–20 alone, impressive evidence that the Hue bureaucracy, for all its relative efficiency compared to other Southeast Asian governments, had failed to create an adequate standard of living or security for its villagers.[18] Compulsory labor service weighed heavily upon the peasants, who were conscripted to construct irrigation canals, city walls, roads, bridges, and above all the walls and new palaces at Hue. At higher levels of society, a minority of the intelligentsia indulged in satirical skepticism about the entire Vietnamese imperial system, which, from its court ceremonial to its Chinese-style Gia-long law code, was a calculated imitation of the more useful institutional features of the Ch'ing empire. A subversive woman writer like Ho Xuan Huong, for example, might employ such techniques as rhetorically transferring general discontents to the more visibly grotesque incarnations of Hue dynastic politics like the court eunuchs. The eunuchs were lowly inner officials whom Vietnamese emperors trusted because they lacked family connections to divert their loyalties, in much the same way that medieval European kings had confided in celibate clergymen. Delivering what amounted to a covert attack on the court itself, in one poem Ho Xuan Huong mockingly asked its eunuchs,

> Why do the twelve midwives who cared for you hate each other? Where have they thrown away your youthful sexual passions? Damned be you if you should care about the twitterings of mice-like lovers, or about a bee-like male gallant caressing his adored one. . . . At least, a thousand years from now you will be more able to avoid the posthumous slander that you indulged in mulberry-grove intrigues.[19]

To be fair, this view—that the practical advantages of the imperial system were, like those inherent in the plight of its eunuchs, purely of a negative kind—was not a typical one in the early nineteenth century. Bureaucratic centralization in the Chinese manner was the weapon with which Emperor Minh-mang fought centrifugal trends, military and political, in the provinces. Vietnamese regionalism is sometimes overemphasized by foreigners: The society's possession of a common family system, its common memory of folk tales and folk heroes, and its lack of any unconditional symbols of regional solidarity, like entirely separate languages, should be borne in mind. Yet under the first four Nguyen emperors southern Vietnam remained a frontier land, which participated only very poorly in the affairs of the empire. Of the 1,024,338 officially recorded male taxpayers in all of Vietnam in 1847, only 165,598 of them lived in the six southern provinces. The Hue court did not survey southern land-holding patterns until 1836. Then it discovered the existence of landlords, of poor people who lacked even enough land "in which to stick an awl," of squatters from one village who illegally occupied the lands of another, and of village chiefs unacquainted with methods of calculating acreages and marking land boundaries.[20] Southerners found it easier to win positions of power in the government by remaining outside the civil service examination system, for example, by working through the army. Of the fifty-six doctoral degree-holders who won degrees at six Hue metropolitan and palace examinations in the period 1822–40, only one was a southerner. "The people of the Gia Dinh area are very refined, but recently laziness and negligence have become the customs there," Minh-mang complained in 1832.[21] Poorer educational facilities and fewer resident families with long civil service traditions really accounted for much of the south's problem.

But it is an error to assume that, within the Confucian elitist context of "traditional" Vietnamese society, no technically advanced, culturally unifying forces were at work. A dynamic process like that of the vernacularization of the symbols and styles of politics—a process sometimes mistakenly considered to have occurred in Southeast Asian societies only after their collision with the "modern" West—manifested itself in Vietnam during the Tay-son Rebellion and continued into the next century. The Tay-son Quang-trung Emperor attempted, with limited success, to restrict the use of Chinese characters at his court in favor of the indigenous Vietnamese writing script, *nom*, which was employed to transcribe more effectively the language ordinarily spoken by the peasants. A special literary genre, which emerged during the 1771–1802 civil wars, the funeral oration (*van te*), which often began with the stock phrase "Alas!" (*than oi*) and was written in *nom*, was composed to praise illustrious soldiers who had died in battle. But although the funeral orations originated as relatively private literature, they soon metamorphosed into propaganda read before the public. In this way, the political controversies of the civil war were dramatically purveyed to wider audiences. A slight broadening of popular participation in elite culture was also heralded in the nineteenth century by the appearance of a court-sponsored work like the *Dai Nam Quoc Su Dien Ca* (*The National History of Imperial Vietnam in Explanatory Songs*) about 1865. The work popularized "great-tradition" history by converting it into colorful poetry, making it more real to Vietnamese outside the upper mandarin class.

For the intelligentsia, moreover, the definition of the moral universe in which they lived and the ways in which hardship had to be suffered in order to accumulate secret merit in this universe were expanded in a semi-revolutionary way by the literary masterpiece of the early 1800's, Nguyen Du's 3,254-line poem, "Doan truong tan thanh" (roughly, "A New Song about Great Heartbreak"), better known by the names of its three leading personages as the *Kim Van Kieu*. Although Du borrowed the story of this poem from a seventeenth-century Chinese novel dealing with the fortunes of a sixteenth-century Peking family (just as Shakespeare wrote about Romans and Italians), his poem's subject was actually the decadence of Vietnamese society as he personally had known it. The heroine of the poem, Kieu, displayed her filial piety by ignoring her own future happiness with her betrothed lover and selling herself into a life of prostitution in order to redeem her arrested father. At the end, however, her virtue triumphs over a maleficent destiny and earns her happiness. Vastly superior to its Chinese model, and indeed one of the great literary landmarks of Southeast Asia, the poem caused a stir because it depicted the weaknesses as well as the strengths of its admired characters, described decadence more realistically than symbolically, and unflinchingly gave its upper-class heroine a culturally and morally disapproved lower-class life as a bordello slave before returning her, at its conclusion, to the pinnacle of society by reunion with her mandarin lover. In a sense, it represented a vernacularization, or at least a permissive reorientation, of court conceptions of social mobility that hardly harmonized perfectly with conservative views of official morality. In Vietnam today, students write essays on the poem, newspapers use its characters as editorial paradigms, merchants sell wares like the "Kieu numbers game" (*lo to Kieu*), and soothsayers draw prophecies from it.[22]

The world of the *Kim Van Kieu* was one in which predestination and the omnipresent evils of society were prominent causal factors but in which supernatural elements rarely received much emphasis. Proud of their rationality, the Vietnamese Confucian elite reacted with hostility to what they regarded as the irrational superstitions of the French Roman Catholic missionaries who were arriving increasingly in Vietnam around that time. Jesuit missionaries had been active in Vietnam as early as the seventeenth century. Some of them, like Alexandre de Rhodes (1591–1660), had attempted to convert the Vietnamese writing system from Chinese characters to European letters, a proposition that many mandarins considered subversive, since the wholesale adoption of romanized Vietnamese by the Vietnamese population would have temporarily severed Vietnamese society's connections with its Confucian texts and Buddhist sutras, both of which were written in classical Chinese and Chinese characters. During the civil wars of the late 1700's, the future Gia-long Emperor had been aided in his successful campaign against the Tay-sons by a French bishop, Pigneau de Behaine (1741–99). On the future emperor's behalf, Pigneau had journeyed to Paris in 1787 to negotiate a treaty with the court of Louis XVI—known as the Treaty of Versailles—in which France promised to commit frigates and soldiers to the anti–Tay-son cause in return for commercial privileges in Vietnam and territorial concessions at Da Nang (Tourane) and Poulo Condore. The French Revolution made the treaty obsolete, but Pigneau appears to have converted to Christianity Gia-long's eldest son, Prince Canh, who had visited Paris with him. The prince's refusal to prostrate himself before the altar of his ancestors in 1792 provoked the future Gia-long into warning Pigneau that the conversion of too many of his officials to Christianity without some compensatory indulgence of Confucian forms would weaken the Vietnamese monarchy, since it would force the emperor to perform state ceremonies almost alone.

By the time the Nguyen Dynasty was founded in 1802, both Pigneau and Prince Canh had died. But the sociopolitical repercussions of Vietnam's version of the Christian-Confucian "rites controversy" did not die with them. Independently of any arrangement with Paris, nearly 400 French sailors and soldiers of fortune served Gia-long until 1820. Many of the citadel walls around Hue and assorted provincial towns in Vietnam were devised and constructed by French engineers at that time. Yet Gia-long's evanescent corps of French advisers failed to serve as a modernizing leaven in the Vietnamese body politic. From the beginning, they made themselves the spokesmen for French Catholic Christianity. Foreign ambitions of religious proselytization became fatally entangled in Vietnamese politics both at court and in the provinces. The most extreme example was the intimate association French missionaries achieved with Le Van Duyet, the semi-independent regional overlord of southern Vietnam, who hoped the missionaries could obtain Western guns for him. Since Duyet had also unsuccessfully attempted to block the accession to the Vietnamese throne of Minh-mang, Gia-long's fourth son by a concubine, who became emperor in 1820, Minh-mang not surprisingly considered the Catholic priests whom Duyet befriended at Saigon to be both the auxiliaries of his major political enemy in Vietnam and the fifth column of an aggressive foreign power. He issued his first decree outlawing the dissemination of Christianity as a heterodox creed in 1825, after a French warship had called at Da Nang and had landed a priest who soon began to preach the Gospel. Real persecution, with the execution of missionaries, began in the 1830's.

Despite the Nguyen court's ban upon proselytization and its execution of missionaries, Christianity continued to spread. Societywide inflation (*bach lang*, "blank coins," as the Vietnamese peasant called it), natural disasters, a long coastline that the court could not efficiently patrol, the temporary decline of Vietnamese Buddhism, and the absence of a resisting "gentry" class in the provinces numerically and qualitatively as strong as the one in China—all were possible explanations. In 1847, one year after the diocese of Vinh was founded, it claimed 68,000 Vietnamese Christians, more than half the 118,000 it was to claim, after a quarter-century of colonialism, in 1909.[23] Believing that Christianity was a "trick" by which Western nations planned to conquer Vietnam, Minh-mang created "canton teachers" among local scholars in Christianity-affected areas to lecture on Confucianism and circulated an imperial edict in 1839, about a year before his death, declaring that "those priests come from distant lands and are not members of our race. . . . Their followers' need of crosses greatly stems from what is not classical and is completely unadoptable." [24] He also sent an embassy to France to negotiate acceptable methods of controlling the religion with the French Government (1840), but his envoys were not received.

On matters other than the religious question, ironically enough, the posture of the Vietnamese court toward Western civilization was hardly, as French missionary literature tried to pretend, one of static fanaticism. Minh-mang himself, more innovative and more technologically minded than any other Southeast Asian ruler of his era, was a scientific amateur who dabbled in experiments: For example, he personally manufactured a water wheel that would pump water through a conduit into his palace so that coolies would not have to carry it.[25] He was an explicit admirer and user of Western products, like glass, cotton textiles, English gunpowder, and French brandy. By 1840, he had read the Old Testament in Chinese translation, informing his officials that he found it "absurd." In the late 1830's, like Mindon of Burma some twenty years later, he not only purchased several Western steamships but also built a factory at Hue in 1839 to construct steamships independently. That enterprise was a failure, however, essentially because the Vietnamese court attempted to copy the extrinsic features of the steamship without mastering the internal principles of the steam engine. As of 1839, the Vietnamese elite, led by Minh-mang, exhibited a naive optimism that Western technology could be privately appropriated by Vietnamese artisans without their having to cross any cultural barriers. The existence of Western machines was recognized empirically before the existence of a Western scientific culture was acknowledged philosophically.

During the Thieu-tri reign (1841–47), French gunboats visited Vietnam on behalf of imprisoned Catholic missionaries, a move inspired by the success of British imperialism in South China. This was only a prelude to more systematic violence on both sides. Between 1848 and 1860, it has been estimated, some twenty-five European priests, 300 Vietnamese priests, and as many as 30,000 Vietnamese Catholics were killed in Vietnam.[26] The response of the French Navy was to attack and seize Saigon and the three southeastern provinces around it (Gia

Dinh, Dinh Tuong, and Bien Hoa) in 1859–62. The Treaty of Saigon of 1862 between France and the Vietnamese court, which ratified this conquest, in effect created the French colony known as "Cochinchina." The French military occupation in 1867 of three more southern provinces—Vinh Long, An Giang, and Ha Tien—completed the territory of colonial Cochinchina. It was accompanied by the dramatic suicide of Phan Thanh Gian (1796–1867), the southern bureaucrat who had been leader of the "peace party" favoring negotiations with the French rather than military resistance at the now faction-torn Vietnamese court. In addition to their conquest of southern Vietnam, which had been fought more effectively by local leaders than by the Nguyen emperor, the French forced the court to concede them freedom to disseminate Christianity in Vietnam and to promise them that it would no longer obstruct the conversion of Vietnamese.

The territorial diminution of the Vietnamese state in the 1860's may well have been less significant than the schisms in Vietnamese society that preceded it and developed along with it. Quite unprecedented was the specter of religious conflict, which was induced in part from the outside and which changed the nature of traditional intervillage disputes in Vietnam so drastically that they were no longer resolvable in terms of the existing values of the society. Christian villages like Duong Son in Thua Thien Province in central Vietnam were constantly at war with their non-Christian neighbors. New religious differences coincided with old patterns of neighborhood separateness. The wide-range sociocultural system of Western Christianity, which was global in scale, impinged upon the unaltered narrow-range sociocultural system of Vietnamese villagers. Furthermore, the increase in scale of the system of cultural relationships of the Christian Vietnamese peasant was not balanced by a corresponding increase in the scale of his social relationships outside his village in Vietnamese society. For example, not only did the Christian peasant cut his hair, but his conceptions of time and of history became partly Westernized. He counted the years from the birthday of Christ, rather than clinging to the less ambitious, cyclical Vietnamese method of counting time by the reigns of individual emperors. His sense of historical time thus became related to Western history rather than to traditional Vietnamese political ideology. Yet his social parochialism as a Vietnamese villager remained undiminished. What had emerged was the formidable problem of the interaction of competing large-scale cultural systems with small-scale village politics, which lacked traditions of physical and social mobility and of "shared respect" in relations with strangers.

French intervention in Vietnam amounted, at least at first, to the opportunistic military exploitation of Vietnamese resistance to Catholic religious evangelism. The Vietnamese traditional order could not tolerate such evangelism, because Vietnamese institutions were based not upon the modern Western concept of the separation of church and state but upon the concept of the state as the political expression of the elite Confucian ideology. Catholicism, if it made inroads among the elite, would obviously qualify the nature of elite ideology. As Gia-long had implied to Pigneau in 1792, the nature of the state, which expressed elite ideology, would then have to change as well.

The traditional Vietnamese political system was not well organized to allow the indefinite peaceful competition and expression of many different and antithetical points of view, especially when such points of view were suggested by an aggressive alien culture. Conflict was regulated less by specific institutions than by the reflex of personal deference to superiors like one's father, one's emperor, or one's senior in the bureaucracy. The method, which was merely a political abstraction of the familial ethic, was simply not strong enough to withstand the merciless, unprecedented pressures of the 1860's.

The long reign of the Tu-duc Emperor, from 1847 to 1883, has been neglected by scholars. One conventional picture of Tu-duc himself is that he was a reformer at heart, a prisoner of his Confucian bureaucracy. Whether or not this picture is correct, the internal history of his reign was stormy. Because there were few legitimate channels of fundamental dissent at Hue, apart from obliquely worded memorials to the throne, an emergency that threatened the system could generate extraordinarily explosive conflicts and opposing interests within the Vietnamese elite—conflicts that were all the more explosive because they were normally repressed by the mechanisms of filial piety, loyalty to the throne, and ritualistic self-deprecation. Typically, the position of Tu-duc himself was threatened during those years both by pro-Catholic and anti-Catholic rebellions against his authority.

As the Vietnamese imperial family had grown larger in the nineteenth century, it had begun to lose cohesion and to develop factions. The process accelerated under Tu-duc. While his predecessors had confronted insurrections only in the provinces, Tu-duc had also constantly to guard against a *coup d'état* within his own court and household, a new feature in the history of the dynasty. The first attempt to overthrow him was made in 1851–53 by his half-brother, Prince Hong Bao, who had hoped to succeed Thieu-tri in 1847. Scheming to take the throne by force, Hong Bao formed a party of supporters at Hue, linked together by a blood oath, which attracted the allegiance and help of virtually every Vietnamese Christian in the area. Hong Bao apparently promised Vietnamese Catholics freedom and even privileges if he succeeded in displacing Tu-duc. He was arrested and imprisoned for life in 1853.

In 1864–65 the throne was shaken by another attempted coup, this time with anti-Catholic overtones. After the signing of the 1862 treaty, which ceded the three southern provinces to France, the Confucian elite turned its wrath against all Vietnamese Christians and Tu-duc himself. Scholars at the regional examination sites of Thua Thien, Nghe An, Hanoi, and Nam Dinh demonstrated against the treaty and had to be suppressed by soldiers. The Vietnamese elite feared "traitors" within its own ranks; an edict of the early 1850's had significantly given court officials who were secret Christians one month to recant, provincial officials three months, and ordinary people six months. Because the 1862 treaty gave Frenchmen the right to spread Christianity in Vietnam, it precipitated a religious war between Vietnamese Christians and non-Christians. And in 1864, an imperial prince named Hong Tap formed a party at the court whose purpose was to recruit an irregular army to kill Christians and assassinate certain bureaucrats. Members of the party included a prince consort, a grandson of Minh-mang, a district magistrate, and some twenty others, some of whom were the sons of high provincial officials. But this party's plot to gain control of the Hue citadel fizzled.

There was a more positive side to the spread of Catholicism among a stubborn small minority of Tu-duc's officials. While some crypto-Catholic officials in Hue, alienated from the emperor and unable to express dissent legitimately in Vietnam's traditional monistic political culture, were willing to participate in plots like the Hong Bao conspiracy, some Vietnamese Catholic scholars did blend their Catholicism with loyalty to Tu-duc. Beginning to function as constructive middlemen between Western civilization and the Vietnamese court, such Catholic loyalists favored far more changes in the *status quo* than the usual bureaucrat. For one thing, they knew more about the West. Furthermore, being Catholic, they could not increase their own power in the bureaucracy, at the expense of Confucian conservatives, without some changes in the system. But they were not pro-French, and they sought to preserve the monarchy. This small group of loyal Catholic middlemen within the elite could not have existed under Minh-mang. The disorder of the 1860's gave them their opportunity.

Their most famous member, and perhaps the most unusual official in nineteenth-century Vietnam, was Nguyen Truong To (1827–71). To had received a traditional education and wrote superb classical Chinese. On the other hand, he had become acquainted at an early age with a French missionary priest, Gauthier, who taught him French and took him back to Italy and France in the 1850's. In Europe, To visited factories and was received in audience with Pope Pius IX, who made him a present of 100 Western books. Back in Vietnam, as a provincial official, between 1863 and 1871, To sent a stream of memorandums to Tu-duc in which he proposed, in effect, that the emperor lead an institutional revolution in Vietnam. The revolution To proposed might have strengthened the monarchy but would have transformed the bureaucracy.

Among other things, To suggested that the court reduce the numbers of provinces, prefectures, and districts in Vietnam in order to reduce the numbers of officials who were performing useless tasks. The stipends of the officials who remained could then be increased as a measure against bribery and graft. Furthermore, To believed that the administrative and judicial powers within the bureaucracy should be explicitly separated, in conformity with the "separation of powers" doctrine of

Western democratic theory. (To's endeavor to create a more specialized judicial administration was an attack on the Confucian ideal of the "generalist" bureaucrat, whose omnicompetence was a function of his supposedly superior morality.) To wanted to create military schools, directed by foreign specialists, which would train officers and produce a modern Vietnamese army. As a means of supporting his program of internal reorganization, To demanded a more equitable taxation system, based upon a new population census and land survey, which would increase the taxation of landlords, tax luxury goods, and increase the taxation of imported merchandise, so that the prices of imports would rise and the consumption of indigenous goods would be encouraged. He also hoped that cooperatives could be organized to expand Vietnamese commerce.

In addition to wishing to dismantle Vietnam's unspecialized Confucian bureaucracy, To attempted to revolutionize the social stratification that had produced it, ending the traditional dichotomy between the literate rulers and the illiterate ruled. He wanted the use of Chinese characters in Vietnam abolished and replaced by romanized Vietnamese that every peasant could quickly be taught to read. He hoped that romanized Vietnamese newspapers could be founded and distributed among the masses. (This proposal—the creation of newspapers to educate the masses—was also made to Tu-duc by another Catholic spokesman, Huynh Tinh Cua (1834–1907), a southerner who served as an interpreter to the French and eventually became Vietnam's pioneer journalist.) If the civil service examinations survived, To maintained, their survival should be conditional upon their testing knowledge of specialized subjects, such as law, science, and agriculture. In foreign affairs, the Hue court should emulate the example of Thailand, not China, and send ambassadors abroad in order to understand international relations better.

This visionary blueprint of institutional revolution, created by a Catholic who believed passionately in the survival of his society but not of its traditional elite ideology, transcended the Tu-duc court's capacities for carrying it out. Its assault upon vested interests was total. Confucian scholars and bureaucrats, landlords, and the foreign merchants who would have been more heavily taxed would all have been its victims. Vietnamese legend has it that when To died in 1871, it was of acute melancholia at seeing his country drifting toward disaster and being unable to prevent it. What is significant, however, is that, as early as the 1860's, the outer fringes of the Vietnamese elite had produced a reformer many of whose recommendations were already more ambitious than any of the feeble modernizing policies the French colonialists would pursue in Vietnam between the 1880's and 1954. The French colonial regime, in a sense, was out of date before it was created.

A number of minor reforms were carried out at the Tu-duc court in the 1860's. In 1864, for example, the court launched a program of French-language training, inviting a Vietnamese Catholic priest, Nguyen

Hoang, to come to Hue to teach students and to translate Western books. But French pressure was most insistent in Vietnam at the one point the Confucian bureaucracy could not concede without agreeing to its own extinction: the French right to transform Vietnam into an ideologically differentiated society, in which Catholicism could compete ideologically and institutionally with the bureaucracy. Since the Vietnamese tradition had not produced a political framework that could accept and accommodate the conflict that would have resulted—the very syncretism of the traditional "three religions," Buddhism, Taoism, and Confucianism, had minimized the need to devise European-style means of regulating the coexistence of different religions—many Vietnamese construed what the French called "religious freedom" as the beginning of political, ethical, and social paralysis.

16

THE MALAY PENINSULA TO 1874

For the maritime Malay *negeri* of the peninsula, the last quarter of the eighteenth century was a tumultuous and confused period of changing alliances and fortunes. The century as a whole is sometimes called the Bugis century because of the political ascendancy achieved by those fierce and warlike traders from Makassar, who had established themselves as the paramount power in Malay waters as far back as 1722, when Daing Parani secured effective control over the Malaccan successor state, Johore. From the Johore capital on the island of Pulau Penyengat in the Riau Archipelago, where Parani's brother became "underking" to a puppet Malay sultan, the Bugis extended their control over the tin *negeri* of Kedah and Perak, against the rival ambitions of the Minangkabau ruler of Siak in eastern Sumatra, and, in 1742, a Bugis was installed as first sultan of the new *negeri* of Selangor, carved out of the western coast of the peninsula.

Malays and Dutch alike were disconcerted at the rise of Bugis power, which undermined established political relationships and threatened the tin trade, and a number of alliances were made at mid-century in an attempt to control a common foe. The Bugis responded by attacking Dutch Malacca in 1756, an enterprise in which they suffered defeat mainly as a result of Malay aid to their enemy. Bugis fortunes were at a low ebb for a time, but by the 1760's they had recovered, owing to the military prowess of the great warrior of the time, Raja Haji, under whose influence Johore-Bugis authority was reimposed on the principal Malay *negeri* flanking the Straits of Malacca, including Jambi and Indragiri on Sumatra and Kedah and Perak on the peninsula. Riau, the Johore capital, with a population allegedly of more than 90,000 (50,000 Malays, 40,000 Bugis, and a mixture of others), prospered, and, by the late 1770's, with Raja Haji as underking, its harbor was regularly frequented by hundreds of Bugis, Javanese, Thai, and Chinese vessels, trading in fine goods and staples ranging from European chintz, Siantan silk-weave, and Javanese batik to the best shellac and top quality Thai rice. The best and most vivid Malay-language history of the time (the *Tuhfat al-Nafis*, written by a grandson of Raja Haji) adds that Riau was also a great religious and cultural center and a stopping place for itinerant Arabs from the Hejaz.[27]

Riau's greatness did not last for long undisturbed, for in 1782 the Dutch and the Bugis again fell out, and after an unsuccessful siege of Malacca (during which Raja Haji lost his life), the Dutch in 1784 expelled the Bugis from both Selangor and Riau. At Riau, they extracted from the Malay Sultan Mahmud a treaty permitting the establishment of a Dutch garrison and resident on Pulau Penyengat, but this arrangement had scarcely become effective when Ilanun sea raiders from Borneo, summoned by Sultan Mahmud, expelled the Dutch in turn—though Mahmud and the Malays also left, fearing Dutch revenge. The Bugis remained for the moment in Selangor (which they had regained) and in their possessions in Borneo.

In the meantime, in 1786, the British had established themselves at Penang by means of an agreement with the Sultan of Kedah; the agreement rapidly proved unsatisfactory to the latter, who was under strong pressure from an aggressive Thailand. The two rival European powers—the Dutch to the south of the Straits, the English to the north—now became the target of an unstable Malay coalition, led by the homeless Sultan Mahmud of Johore-Riau, which set out to drive the aliens from the Malay world. The coalition was ineffectual, and the hope vain, though the Dutch were to be effectively removed from the scene for a time as a result of war in Europe. Ironically, however, the attack by revolutionary and expansionist France on the Netherlands in 1794 led to a temporary cessation of the rivalry between Britain and monarchist (though not revolutionary) Holland. William of Orange, having fled to London, instructed all Dutch governors and commanders overseas not to oppose the entry of British troops into Dutch possessions, to forestall the French. In return, the British undertook to make restitution of all colonies placed under their protection when peace in Europe was restored and the Dutch state reconstituted. So began the uneasy alliance between the two great European maritime powers with interests in Southeast Asia, which was to result, before the next century was out, in the extinction or subjugation of virtually all indigenous political authority throughout the Malay world.

Already the empire of Johore had all but disappeared as a political force, for, even after the restoration of Sultan Mahmud to Riau-Lingga by the English in 1795, persistent argument and feuding between Malays and Bugis concerning the succession to Riau itself and to the mainland dependencies of Johore proper and Pahang was tearing it apart. Sultan Mahmud's death in 1812 merely intensified the conflict, and a new era of British and Dutch cooperation commenced, with the Malay powers in disarray in the south and under attack from Thailand in the north. The outcome could scarcely be in doubt.

Not all the Dutch possessions in Southeast Asia had obeyed Prince William's injunction, but in the course of the fifteen years following 1795, most fell to the British by one means or another, though some for only brief periods of time. From being an Indian power interested primarily, where Southeast Asia was concerned, in the free passage of trade through the Malacca Straits and beyond to China, the East India Company suddenly found itself the possessor not merely of a proposed naval station on Penang island but of numerous other territorial dominions and responsibilities. Nor were some of the company's servants at all reluctant to assume these responsibilities and, indeed, to extend them. Chief among the visionaries and expansionists, perhaps, was Stamford Raffles. When Java, which he coveted for England, was being given back to the Dutch in 1816 by a company anxious to return to a situation in which it was concerned not with territorial governance but with the through trade to the Far East, he urged upon his superiors the acquisition of the small fishermen's island of Singapore at the foot of the Malay peninsula. What Raffles sought, aside from his desire to continue to thwart the Dutch, was a base from which to carry on "communication with the native princes; for a general knowledge of what is going on at sea, and on the shore, throughout the archipelago; for the resort of the independent trade, and the trade with our allies; for the protection of our commerce and all our interests; and more especially for an entrepôt for our merchandise." [28] The above arguments were of much the same force and nature as had characterized maneuvers for commercial power in the archipelago throughout the eighteenth century; indeed, one can as easily imagine their use by "native prince" as by English trader or company servant. When Singapore was acquired by Raffles for the East India Company in 1819, the tactics employed were based on a time-honored means of subverting one's neighbor—the exploitation of disputed succession and the playing off of one claimant to territory against another. In this case, the Dutch, who had returned to Riau and were in effective control of the claimant to Singapore island, and who in addition feared the establishment of a rival entrepôt in the area, were annoyed. A long diplomatic wrangle followed. But Singapore survived as a British base, establishing one particularly important departure from the patterns of the past—it was set up as a "free port," living not by taxation upon trade but on trading activity itself. Its free status was to turn the island within a few decades into the most flourishing exchange port Southeast Asia had ever seen, the center of a vigorous and politically demanding mercantile community.

During the first few years of Singapore's existence, the British sought to reduce systematically the potentialities for disturbance, and hence for expensive political or military involvement, in the area in which they were then interested. They wanted both to reach an understanding with the Netherlands in the archipelago consonant with a foreign policy of supporting the Dutch in Europe as part of the balance of power against France and, in the interests of untroubled continuance of the trade between India and China, to secure peace in the environs of Singapore and, more especially, Penang, where Thai-Kedah tensions were proving disruptive. Underlying all this was a firm determination not to become involved in any major way in the internal affairs of the Malay *negeri* of the peninsula or to engage in any form of territorial aggrandizement.

The attempts to reach understandings with the Dutch and the Thai were, on the whole, successful, though less so for a time in the latter case. By the Anglo-Dutch Treaty of 1824, a final settlement of the confused position following the Napoleonic wars was reached, and guidelines were laid down for the future. Under the treaty, Singapore was retained and Malacca turned over to the British in exchange for the surrender of their settlement at Benkulen in western Sumatra and for a recognition that Dutch interests were paramount in Sumatra and in the islands south of Singapore. In return for British willingness to abstain from all political interference in Sumatra, the Dutch gave a similar promise to stay out of the Malay peninsula, a division of interests that, in the changed conditions of fifty years later, was to lead to the final separation of the political destinies of those two parts of the Malay world, breaking centuries-old patterns of interdependence as well as conflict.

Two years after the conclusion of the Anglo-Dutch Treaty, Henry Burney, a British envoy to the Thai court, was successful in 1826 in concluding another treaty, which, while limited, did offer some real satisfaction to British interests in the Malay area. Under it, the Thai agreed to accept the southern boundary of Kedah (whose sultan, in exile in Penang, the British undertook to restrain) as the farthest extent of direct Thai control on the west coast and to recognize effective Perak and Selangor independence, putting an end to the harassments that had marked the preceding decade. Despite some years of uncertainty concerning the implementation and effectiveness of the 1824 and 1826 treaties, the result by mid-century was to establish the East India Company as the paramount power in the Malay peninsula. The interests of the company, and relative peace in the neighborhood of its settlements, had been secured, though they were based on new notions of international law deriving from Western practice that were not fully accepted by all the participants and on political considerations that did not take sufficient account of the changing nature of trade or of the interests of traders.

In the years following its establishment, Singapore rapidly achieved paramountcy in the maritime commerce of Southeast Asia, a position earned partly by its strategic location but most importantly, perhaps, by its jealously protected free-port status. Before long it overhauled Penang in importance (also a free port, but less well situated for trade), and in 1826 it became the governmental center for what were known henceforth as the Straits Settlements of Singapore, Penang, and Malacca. Demographically, Singapore grew from a fishing village to a flourishing port town, which, by the time of the census taken in 1840, had a total population of more than 35,000. Variegated though this population was —and mid-nineteenth-century accounts of Singapore seldom fail to describe the concourse of Tamils, Arabs, Javanese, Bugis, Minangkabau, Trengganu and Kelantan Malays, Bengalis, and countless others who thronged the streets and markets—by far the largest part, at least 50 per cent, was Chinese.

Though the first Chinese immigrants to Singapore were from the neighboring settlement of Malacca, they came increasingly from South China itself after the arrival of the first junk from Amoy in February, 1821. One observer listed the Chinese as engaged in 110 separate occupations.[29] They were concentrated primarily in trade and merchandising of all kinds, in agriculture (from vegetable gardening for Singapore's growing population to pepper and gambier cultivation on the north side of the island), and in laboring of every description. The Chinese brought with them distinctive forms of social organization, which continued to characterize their life in Nanyang, the southern seas. None has occasioned more comment (and often misunderstanding) than the *hui*, or "secret society," which, in its various manifestations, formed the principal means of social solidarity among the Chinese and the means whereby recruitment to the community, absorption of newcomers, maintenance of discipline, and the organization of new economic enterprise could be undertaken.

With the access of settled trading conditions on the periphery of the Malay peninsula, sheltered under British power and free trade practice, and with the expansion of population and trade that resulted, Straits Settlements merchants and financiers grew increasingly interested in the Malay *negeri* of the interior as a field of investment, while the rulers and chiefs of the *negeri* began in turn to look to the Settlements as a source of both money and manpower. Already in the 1830's, the ruler of Johore, long independent of the old polity at Riau, had encouraged Chinese agriculturalists to plant pepper and gambier in the interior of the state, and there were few major rivers on which Chinese shopkeepers and peddlers were not to be found in increasing numbers.

The real economic prize, however, was tin, or the opportunity to mine it in the tin-rich west coast *negeri*. European and Chinese merchants in Malacca, the natural outlet for Negri Sembilan (and later Selangor) tin, appear to have been the first to engage in large-scale investment in the mines, followed before long by Penang interests operating in Perak. Though loans were sometimes made to Malay chiefs, who used the money to make speculative advances to Chinese miners, the more usual pattern in the long run was for Chinese traders in the Settlements to make advances direct to Chinese miners and mine managers in the fields, while the Malay chiefs tapped the resulting production by drawing tribute and certain taxes. As a result of this process of expansion, which was accompanied by Chinese innovation in the actual techniques of mining, production greatly increased, and in the 1850's and 1860's there was a "tin rush" marked by large-scale Chinese immigration into the west coast states. As one example, Larut, in northwestern Perak, which had few Chinese residents in 1848, when tin was first found there, had an estimated population in 1872 of between 20,000 and 25,000.[30]

Changes of this magnitude placed severe stress on the Malay political system. The traditional balance of power within the *negeri*—both between ruler and chiefs and among the territorial chiefs themselves—was based on relatively small differences in wealth. Access to greatly increased revenues, such as were open to those chiefs fortunate enough to be in control of the richer tin-bearing areas, introduced into the system radical elements of imbalance and desperate rivalries over the possession of the important fields. Rivalries among Malay chiefs were paralleled by those among different groups of Chinese miners, the latter usually organized by competing secret societies, which in turn were backed with men, money, and arms by wealthy Chinese merchants in the Straits Settlements. The interaction of these factors, complicated by Malay succession disputes and by piracy bred of the breakdown of traditional patterns of trade and of the increasing climate of lawlessness, led to a situation on the west coast of the peninsula that, by the late 1860's, seemed to many observers in the Straits (most of whom, it must be said, had never set foot on the peninsula) to be degenerating into anarchy.

Already hard hit by a general trade recession east of Singapore, the Straits merchants, unable to pursue sustained economic exploitation of the western states (or to develop markets there for the increasing flow of cheap industrial goods from Europe), and irritated by what they felt to be the unduly restrictive operation by the Dutch of the tariff provisions of the 1824 treaty, began to press the Straits Settlements Government to intervene. They were encouraged to do this by two independent developments: the gradual extension of Dutch authority up the east coast of Sumatra after 1850, and the transfer of authority over the Settlements from the English East India Company to the India Office and then, as a Crown Colony (after the Indian Mutiny), to the more amenable—or so the merchants hoped—Colonial Office in 1867.

Following upon the 1824 treaty with Britain, the Dutch, weakened economically in Europe by the Napoleonic wars and by continued disturbance on its borders, were largely preoccupied in Asia with the development of Java. By the 1840's, however, with the success of the system of forced cultivation known as the Culture System there, energies were released for further insinuation into what were Javacentrically known as the Outer Islands, in order to bring those areas within the scope and control of the Dutch tariff system. By 1865, the Dutch had extended their presence in Sumatra to the southern boundaries of Acheh and were beginning to threaten the independence of that state as well, using the suppression-of-piracy provisions of the 1824 treaty as a pretext.

Throughout the period, the English East India Company, and then the Indian Government, had remained adamantly opposed to involvement in the internal affairs of the Malay *negeri* of the peninsula. Despite official policies, however, actual commitments in the area had tended to grow, though certainly not fast enough to satisfy the Straits merchants. Governors on the spot were prone to take action first and to explain it later. In this way, for example, Malacca found itself embarked on a "war" in 1831 with the tiny neighboring state of Naning over disputed tax collection. And in the early 1860's, in the course of the

Pahang civil war, Governor Cavenagh took decisive action in Pahang and Trengganu to forestall Thai intervention. At all times, the officials in Singapore and Penang found themselves under pressure from commercial interests to safeguard British subjects, British trade, or British protected persons in the peninsular states. Partly to relieve pressures of that sort and assuage mercantile anxieties over the downturn in trade and partly from motives that had nothing to do with Southeast Asia, the British Government in 1871 concluded another treaty, by which, in return for a promise of equal treatment for British traders in Sumatra, the Dutch were given freedom to extend their sovereignty over the whole of that island. The treaty was Acheh's death warrant as an independent polity, although execution had to await the conclusion of a thirty-year war of resistance. Though these imperial maneuvers may have improved, for the moment, the position of British commerce, they did little to lessen the demands for similar aggressive action in the Malay states. Three years later, in 1874, in an about-face of policy that has been discussed by historians ever since, the Colonial Office gave approval to limited intervention in the confused affairs of Perak. The British forward movement had begun, and as an appropriately realistic Malay proverb acknowledged, "Once the needle is in, the thread is sure to follow."

17

THE ARCHIPELAGO, 1750–1870

For the fifteenth through the seventeenth century, the great formative age in the history of island Southeast Asia, it is possible to deal with the history of the area as a whole—from Acheh and Kedah to Luzon and the Moluccas—in terms of certain great common themes. In that age, trade, stimulated by intense demand for cloves, nutmeg, and pepper, flourished and widened; along the trade routes, Islam spread throughout the islands, and Catholicism came to the northern Philippines; everywhere new port states arose and the Europeans made their entrance in force. These broad movements introduced or deepened certain commonalities of experience through much of island Southeast Asia—the Malay language as a lingua franca, the widespread fraternity of Islam, the general importance of trade as the economic base of politics, and European naval paramountcy.

By the mid-eighteenth century, if not earlier, these general movements had spent their force. The spread of Malay had halted, not to resume until the twentieth century. Islam was no longer a revolutionary force, and Catholicism too, in its area in the northern Philippines, was then simply the established religion. Cloves, nutmeg, and pepper were no longer the prizes of world commerce; the economically important products—coffee, sugar, tobacco, and tin—were, or came to be, concentrated in the three centers of Java, the northern Philippines, and the Straits. The rest of island Southeast Asia was economically marginal.

It was also politically marginal. The Spanish had settled down in the northern Philippines, playing no part, aside from perennial disputes with their immediate Muslim neighbors, in the broader politics of the archipelago. The Islamic port states of north-coast Java had been reabsorbed into the agrarian life of Java, and so, in their own way, had the Dutch. Between the mid-eighteenth and late nineteenth century, the Dutch were mainly occupied with exploiting the economic possibilities that political control of Java's large population offered, having neither the capacity nor the inclination for the far-flung naval and commercial dominion they had exercised in the seventeenth century. A third major center was beginning to take shape in just this period, as the English East India Company moved in to establish bases in the Straits Settlements and to exert its influence over the affairs of the Malay Peninsula. But, though the British Navy dominated the seas, and Singapore the commerce, of the archipelago, the British had no desire for territorial rule in those years.

Economically and politically peripheral, the peoples of the rest of the archipelago felt the commercial pull of Singapore. They were harried by British antipiracy raids in the 1840's and after and by a series of Dutch military expeditions to Sumatra, Borneo, Celebes, and Bali between the 1820's and the 1860's. But it was not until after 1870 that they were caught up again in historical movements as broad and powerful as those before 1700: the advance of imperial rule, of Christian missionaries and Reform Islam, and of new export industries. During those 100 years or more, there was still room for the many societies spread out across the wide island world to pursue their own many histories and for a crowd of different actors and movements to flourish and collide. The novels and short stories of Joseph Conrad give an appealing picture of the vigorous and still autonomous life of the coastal Malayo-Muslim peoples of the western archipelago as late as the 1880's, when he served there as a seaman.[31] Elsewhere in the archipelago during those years, still other varied local histories were being enacted.

Among those unrecorded by Conrad were various new communities of Chinese miners like those moving into the gold fields of western Borneo near the modern Indonesian city of Pontianak. There, the Sultan of Sambas, the leading local *negeri* of the time, brought in Chinese miners in the middle of the eighteenth century. They soon organized themselves into the typical Chinese frontier institution of the *kongsi*—at once secret society, mine management, and government—and negotiated new terms with the sultan, allowing him some share of the gold and assuring themselves complete self-government in their mining districts. The mines prospered, more kinsmen arrived, new and rival *kongsi* were founded. By the early nineteenth century, there were some 20,000 or 30,000 Chinese flourishing in an area where previously there had been only forest, some coastal Malays, and a few Dayak swidden cultivators. The affairs of their society took a drastic turn at mid-century, when a series of Dutch expeditions overwhelmed its resistance, while at the same time the gold began to run out. But Dutch rule was for a long time merely nominal, and the miners turned readily to subsistence farming, continuing into modern times as the largest element in the population of western Borneo.[32]

While the Chinese mining community was taking shape in the lower basin of the Kapuas River, another development was taking place far upstream. There, small numbers of Iban Dayaks began to cross the watershed into the headwaters of the Lupar River in present-day Sarawak in search of new swidden areas. By the early nineteenth century, they had come into contact with Malay and Arab coastal chiefs subordinate to the Sultanate of Brunei. The warlike Iban soon joined the coastal chiefs and, under their leadership, took up the profitable and exciting business of local short-range marauding—hence the later name for the

Iban, Sea Dayak. In 1839, an English adventurer named James Brooke arrived on the coast and, finding it to his liking, entered vigorously into its politics. It was typical of the situation in the archipelago at the time that the domain he set about building was from the beginning a purely personal and dynastic one, like that of many a Bugis or Arab wanderer in the period. Recognized in 1842 by the Sultan of Brunei as chief of the small Sarawak River district, he took his place in the Malay political system of the coast, styling himself raja—the most successful, it turned out, of the many white rajas in the archipelago in the nineteenth century.[33] In his early years he obtained help from the British Navy in fighting Iban marauders, but thereafter he and his successors were largely on their own. His nephew and successor, Charles Brooke, who had served his apprenticeship among the Iban on the Lupar River, found the crucial formula. He managed to detach the Iban from their association with coastal Malay chiefs and to attach them to his own person instead. Thereafter, the Iban went to war on land under Raja Charles, helping him to extend his rule, while at the same time they continued the dynamic of Iban expansion begun a century earlier and spread over most of what was becoming the Brooke *negeri* of Sarawak.[34]

It would be too simple to call the Iban pirates, though that is what contemporary Europeans called them, and they certainly seized innocent *perahu* on the high seas. Marauding was a recognized means of political advancement as well as a form of economic activity throughout the archipelago. It played an important role in the affairs of the Sultanate of Sulu, which Europeans considered the most notorious pirate and slave-raiding state of the time, and is therefore worth examining carefully in that context, as a number of recent studies have done.[35] Sulu, founded in the fifteenth century, reached the peak of its importance and prosperity in the eighteenth and early nineteenth centuries. As much as anything, its rise then was due to strong demand in China for luxury goods, such as birds' nests for soup, obtainable in the Sulu Sea area. Merchant shipping of the South China coast thronged the harbor of Jolo, the Sulu capital, and from there a net of trade routes reached out all over the northeast part of the archipelago.

Unlike the situation that developed in nineteenth century Malay tin states, the Chinese came only as merchants; it was Sulus and their allies who procured the luxuries and sold them to the Chinese. Sulu society was like that of other Malayo-Muslim *negeri:* a pyramid of personal relations in which, at each level, a man's status and wealth depended on the number of followers he could successfully control and support. Below the Sultan was a class of *datu*, corresponding to Malay chiefs—independent-minded aristocrats who heeded the sultan only when he was a strong leader and who were constantly competing among themselves for greater prestige. Their followings consisted of freemen—who could themselves hope to become *datu* if they were successful in trade and raid—and of slaves. It is important to note that "slavery" in Sulu, as generally in the archipelago, was primarily a method for incorporating more people into the organized community. Slaves were sometimes sold as chattels, but they were usually enrolled in a *datu*'s following, alongside freemen. Their children could expect to become free.

It was ambitious Sulu *datu*, then, who acquired the birds' nests, pearls, and other specialties sold to the Chinese merchants in Jolo. As river chiefs on the north Borneo coast, they mobilized their followers to dive for pearls or to exact tribute in birds' nests from non-Muslim peoples in the interior. In exactly the same spirit, other Sulu *datu* (or leaders of the related groups called Ilanun, Balanguingui, or Bajau) went out marauding. They sought tribute, slaves to sell or add to their followings, and even ordinary trade. It was a harsh system—perhaps especially for the *indios* of the Bisayan Islands to the north—but not unusually so by the standards of the time. One should not be too hasty in accusing its contemporary European critics of hypocrisy, for they knew little about the workings of Sulu society, and they mistook the Malayo-Muslim version of slavery for their own older and far more brutal one. Still, it is evident that the British and Spanish gunboats that ravaged Sulu villages in the antipiracy campaigns of the mid-nineteenth century practiced the same merciless aggression as the Sulus in their raids on the Bisayas or Borneo.

Although the general religious pattern of the archipelago remained stable until the latter part of the nineteenth century, there were important exceptions in particular areas. During the expansion by the Balinese in the first half of the eighteenth century, at which time they played an important role in the East Hook of Java, they also took control of the western half of the neighboring island of Lombok, and Balinese Hindu-Buddhism came to root itself permanently there. In the early nineteenth century, the Minahassans of the northern arm of the Celebes, loosely associated politically with the Dutch Company since the seventeenth century, converted to Protestantism, laying the foundations for a long-standing special relation with the Dutch in the colonial army and civil service. The most intense and complicated religious movement of the period, however, was that of the Padri among the Minangkabau of West Sumatra. The Minangkabau, mainly wet-rice farmers, constituted one of the larger ethnic groups in the archipelago. They had accepted Islam in the seventeenth century on their own cultural terms. Around 1800, however, a number of *haji*, returning from Mecca under the influence of Wahhabite fundamentalism, called for a return to Islamic purity and for abandonment of such forbidden practices as gambling at cockfights, drinking, and smoking. This Padri Movement, growing steadily in the first two decades of the nineteenth century, stimulated a reaction by the established leaders of Minangkabau society, the *adat* chiefs. There had already been fighting when the Dutch returned to the coast at the end of the Napoleonic wars determined to re-establish their suzerain powers of the seventeenth century. They soon made common cause with the *adat* chiefs—not only those in the coastal lowlands, to which Dutch claims had hitherto been confined, but also those in the interior highlands—who were seeking allies against the Padri and were willing to accept Dutch suzerainty in exchange. The ensuing skirmishes in the early 1820's had two aspects. From the Minangkabau point of view, they were a continuation of the internal struggle, with the Dutch now helping the *adat* party, while, to the Dutch, they represented an effort to enforce newly acquired claims to authority in the interior against the resistance of the Padris. In the 1830's, however, when a series of large Dutch expeditions and heavily fought campaigns made clear to all that the Dutch were aiming at full control of Minangkabau, the colonial issue increasingly overshadowed the original religious one. Some *adat* chiefs ceased to support the Dutch, and others turned against them, though it helped little; the rule throughout the nineteenth century was that, whenever the paramount powers were willing to pay the price, they could have their way. By 1840, the Dutch had added Minangkabau to the still small list of areas outside Java that they directly and closely administered. In the 1840's, they were able to inaugurate a compulsory coffee cultivation system there modeled on their practice in Java. The religious tension within Minangkabau society died down, to revive again at the turn of the century with the rise of Reform Islam.[36]

18

JAVA, 1757–1875

In the 1670's, the Mataram Dynasty had begun to fall apart, and, in the course of the civil wars of the next three quarters of a century, its place in the political life of Java was gradually taken over by the Dutch East India Company (VOC). The process reached a more or less stable conclusion with the partition of Mataram under VOC auspices in 1755–57. Between that time, when the Dutch may be said to have attained full political control of the island, and the late nineteenth century, when the history of Java merged into that of the new Netherlands Indies, falls the last era in which Javan history is intelligible by itself and must be treated separately.[37] It was a period in which Dutch and Javans came to terms and created a common society. Dutch-Javan institutions, born in the confusion of the civil wars, became entrenched during the last years of the VOC. Although challenged from the outside in the decades of disturbance between 1808 and 1830, they resumed their development until increasing pressures brought many, but not all, of the old formulas to bankruptcy by the end of the century.

Though the VOC gained an increasing say in the political affairs of Java from the late seventeenth century, its military control was always precarious and its purposes unclear. In the seventeenth century, the Dutch on Java had been diligent servants of a great merchant company, and in the nineteenth century they gradually became civil servants of a colonial state. In the eighteenth century, however, they were essentially an alien war band, extracting what they could from conquered territories by the most expedient means. Culturally remote in their polyglot enclaves on the coast, seldom venturing into the interior except on military expeditions, generally uninterested in governance, and no longer even very dutiful servants of the company, they were nevertheless masters of Java. In this situation, the Dutch and local elites in different parts of Java found it necessary to come to terms with each other. Company rule, therefore, even where it brought changes, expressed itself in essentially Javan terms.

Dutch rule on Java was not imposed all at once but grew historically and hence was full of oddments and local variations. Everywhere but in Batavia itself, however, it rested on a variety of special arrangements with local elites. Batavia and its surrounding area of a few hundred square miles, with its polyglot population of Chinese, Chinese *mestizos*, Eurasians, Dutch from Holland, Bugis and German soldiers, Balinese, Makassarese, and Indians, was ruled directly by Dutch officials. Here, too, in the eighteenth century were an increasing number of permanent appanages ("Private Lands," the Dutch called them, describing a modified Javan institution in their own terms) whose Dutch, Chinese *mestizo*, and Eurasian owners in effect ruled their own peasant subjects. Beyond Batavia, the Dutch ruled the areas ceded to them by Mataram—most of West Java, the north coast of Central and East Java, and the whole of the East Hook—through "regents," local lords whose credentials usually dated from Mataram times. Relations between the VOC and its lesser vassals, Bantam, Cheribon, and Madura, were marked by special features. Cheribon was an old ally; Bantam, formerly a trading rival, delivered large quantities of pepper at low, fixed prices; the Madurese were military allies. Finally, the VOC treated its still very large and dangerous vassals, the principalities of Surakarta and Jogjakarta, very cautiously, maintaining the forms of independence, exercising control discreetly through Dutch-appointed *patih*, and demanding less tribute than from their other vassals.

Certain effects of Dutch rule were felt everywhere in Java. The company recognized and supported the local authority of regents and vassals because it was both unwilling and unable to govern millions of Javans without their aid, because it hoped thereby to gain their political support or appease their hostility in an always dangerous military situation, and because it wanted their help in exploiting the island. By recognizing the authority of these *priyayi* rulers, the VOC necessarily accepted the Javan system—charismatic rule, patron-client relations, appanage, and the rest—within which they continued to operate. In this way, Dutch power maintained Javan institutions. Dutch rule, however, also changed the practice of Javan government in various ways. When Dutch officials on the north coast, for example, took bribes on a large scale from *priyayi* wanting appointments, new forces entered the political system. The VOC, too, was a politically stable and militarily powerful overlord, and its support greatly strengthened the position of *priyayi* in their dealings with the peasants beneath them, a change with important long-term consequences.

Other effects of company rule were more typical of the areas on which it made the heaviest economic demands, notably the interior of West Java and the north coast, areas ceded to it by Mataram and over which it had greater control. The company's economic arrangements, like its political ones, were extempore and varied widely: It levied tribute in rice in one regency, in teak or indigo in the next, and only in coffee in another. There was a clear contrast, however, in the systems of exploitation in the two main areas of West Java and the north coast.

In Priangan, the hilly interior of West Java inhabited by Sundanese, the Dutch concentrated their efforts on coffee to the exclusion of all else. They introduced the coffee bush from Arabia around 1700, found that it flourished there, and experimented for a time with cash payments and more or less free peasant cultivation before settling down to a more profitable system in the 1720's. The company required its subordinates, the Priangan regents, to deliver specified annual quotas of coffee, which the regents in turn levied from their subjects as a tax in kind. In return (as well as paying the regents a small price for the coffee), the VOC levied no other taxes in Priangan, which left the regents free to continue their own traditional taxes in labor and rice. Under this "Priangan system," coffee became by far the most valuable export from Java and remained so until the 1860's. The Sundanese regents, rescued from insignificance in what had been a poor hinterland, became great lords. The Dutch commissioners for native affairs, occupants of an obscure old Batavian post who gradually took charge of all Priangan coffee, made fortunes lending money to the regents. The peasants, put to harsh work, built a new economy for Priangan and—in times of complete peace and increasing wet-rice production—had more children.

The economic arrangements arising in the older regencies of the northern coast, most of them under the governor of the north coast, were very different. The area produced little in the way of export products—mainly sugar and indigo—but it was more accessible to Dutch and Chinese, more heavily populated, and relatively advanced economically. A great variety of devices were developed to extract produce and cash from the peasants for the benefit of the company's overseas trade and its establishment on Java, and for the profit of Chinese merchants, of regents, and of the company's servants—especially the governors, who made even larger fortunes than the commissioners in Priangan. The Dutch coastal towns built houses and ships from the wood of the area and ate its tribute rice. The company farmed road and river tolls and market taxes to Chinese and also "leased" many villages to Chinese, who used the labor rights thus acquired to grow sugar and other crops.[38] *Priyayi* normally paid bribes to Dutch officials to gain office, gave them "presents" on various occasions, and began themselves to lease out villages. All profited except the peasants and the company as an institution. But the long-term effect of such apparently sweeping changes was obscured or negated by the characteristic inclination of all concerned to operate in terms of traditional Javanese institutions. The Dutch ruled, but daily government remained in the hands of *priyayi;* production was increasingly commercial, but it continued to be organized in the feudal forms of tribute or appanage.

Politically and economically, the Javan and Dutch elites were closely entwined, but culturally they were estranged. The Dutch themselves were hardly touched by Javanese culture in this period—less so, indeed, than their more consciously superior successors in the nineteenth century. In the eighteenth century, they had not yet penetrated deeply into the interior of the island, and only a handful were stationed there. Living in towns on the north coast, they accommodated (when they did) to the cosmopolitan life long established in the ports of the archipelago, took Balinese or Makassarese slaves as concubines, and fathered Eurasians who spoke Portuguese or Malay, rarely Dutch or Javanese.

The same was true on the other side. Dutch culture in this period and through most of the nineteenth century held no interest for the peoples of Java. Javanese *priyayi* and Dutch captains communicated in Malay, nourished suspicions about each other's religions, and misunderstood each other's political beliefs. The cultural gulf mattered little to the conquering Dutch, and perhaps it mattered little to the Javanese *priyayi*, too—we know too little of Javanese cultural history to be certain. It seems likely, however, that they were sorely disturbed about the alien ways of their new lords, for the ideal of harmony so basic to Javanese culture was thereby threatened. The earlier intrusion of Islam had posed a similar threat, eliciting an intense effort at reconciliation and synthesis. But the new disharmony was more intractable. Hence the poignance in a passage like the following from an eighteenth-century chronicle describing the decision of Paku Buwono II in 1743 to move the *kraton* of Mataram from Kartasura:

> The appearance of the Honored Lord did not differ from that which was usual when the times were still prosperous, but in his heart were darkening clouds as he continuously brooded over the destruction of the capital. . . . If one thought about it the pain grew greater, as one felt it the sadder one became that Kartasura was destroyed. The Patih was addressed, 'Listen, Adipati, it is my heart's desire which cannot be resisted to move the capital. . . .'[39]

The feeling that the times were out of joint was one of the factors that influenced the remarkable flowering of *priyayi* culture in the eighteenth and early nineteenth centuries. A large new court literature grew up in this period, the art of *batik* achieved its classical form and colors (indigo blue and rust brown), the repertoire of the *wayang kulit* was enlarged and its music refined and developed, and a new dance drama, *wayang orang*, grew out of the *wayang kulit* tradition. Most characteristically, perhaps, the Javanese language was polished into an instrument of superb social precision, so that Javanese came to speak what were almost different dialects, according to whether they were addressing social superiors, equals, or inferiors.[40] Through all the branches in which the cultural movement expressed itself ran a dominant tendency toward refinement and stylization. One effect, therefore, was to define ever more sensitively and completely the gulf between *priyayi* and peasant. A second was to make available an ever more capacious and perfect cultural world as a refuge from the disharmony in the political world of the time.

A very different kind of cultural change was going on in Priangan in the same period. Priangan had been a sparsely populated, swidden-cultivating region when it first received Islam from the Javanese port states in the sixteenth century and then came under Mataram rule in the early seventeenth century. In Mataram times, the *dalem* (courts) of the Sundanese regents were centers from which Javanese culture began to spread, and around which Sundanese swidden cultivators began to settle and to grow wet rice like the Javanese. Dutch rule and the Dutch-run coffee system brought no corresponding influence of Dutch culture. Instead the "Priangan System," by elevating the prestige of the Javanized regents and by stimulating economic activity and population growth, promoted the older trend. Javanese cultural influences, in increasingly well-rooted Sundanese variants, spread steadily through Priangan. The Sundanese did not become Javanese—they continued to speak their own language, for example—but, by 1900, the process was complete; they belonged in all that was important to the general Javanese tradition.

The VOC, in whose name Dutch activity on Java was carried forward, was of course a much wider enterprise. The complex relationship between the hybrid Dutch-Javan society and the parent Dutch company is demonstrated by the growth and consolidation of the former in the second half of the eighteenth century, while the VOC as a worldwide trading company was falling apart. The causes and symptoms of the decline were a matter of Dutch, not Javan, history. It is enough to say that stiffening joints of oligarchic rule in Holland, the rising naval and industrial strength of England, rapidly mounting deficits, and universal corruption brought about the abolition of the VOC and the assumption of its debts, assets, and possessions by the Dutch state on the last day of the eighteenth century.

That event had no immediate effect on Java; the VOC system continued unchanged for almost a decade more. But new forces had risen in Europe, their roots in the Enlightenment, in the wars of the French Revolution, and in the industrial revolution in England. After 1808, those forces were brought to bear in a rapid succession of assaults on what was by now the *ancien régime* of VOC Java. First, in 1808, came the new Governor-General, Herman Daendels, Dutch by birth, a Napoleonic marshal by career and inclination; then, between 1811 and 1816, English conquest and rule under Lieutenant Governor-General Stamford Raffles, an Adam Smith liberal of great charm and energy; then, after 1816, restored Dutch rule for a decade and a half under a commissioner-general and two governors-general of varying but still non-"Javan" persuasions. Thrusting noisily through the revolving door, these successive regimes rewrote the rules of government every five years and created a tangle of conflicting legislation—much of it merely on paper—as testimony to their reforming zeal.

Daendels and his successors came out from Europe determined to govern rather than simply to control Java; they challenged the whole system of arrangements by which company servants and Javans had accommodated to each other for more than a century. Between 1808 and 1830, the company's great vassals, the principalities of Central Java, lost most of their territory to direct Dutch rule, while the Sultanate of Bantam was abolished and its whole territory annexed.[41] In exactly the same spirit, the great Dutch satrapies of the governors of the north coast and the commissioners for native affairs were broken up. In their place a uniform administrative hierarchy of residencies (headed by European residents), regencies, and districts (with Javan regents and district heads) was applied to most of the island.[42] As the logic of the bureaucratic system required, the successive regimes strove to transform the regents from what amounted to petty vassals, ruling their own territories in essentially traditional ways, into ordinary civil servants. At various times, they were denied hereditary succession, were paid salaries instead of permitted customary land and tax rights, and were largely removed from the judicial system. Finally, Raffles introduced, and his immediate successors continued, a general cash land tax intended to shift the government's basic economic role from "a system of tribute" (with the government itself collecting and selling agricultural products) to a more modern "system of taxation" (in which it would collect taxes and provide general services, leaving production and commerce to private citizens).

Coming after the simpler greeds and comfortable collaborations of late VOC times, all this purpose and policy was impressive. The new regimes did in fact inaugurate important changes; Java, by 1830, had in some respects a more modern administration than most of Europe. But the process was slower than optimists like Daendels and Raffles wished. In part, this was due to difficulties peculiar to the period: short-lived regimes, chronic war conditions, and constant pressure from home governments to make Java pay. For example, Daendels, who wanted to abolish *corvée*, levied an unprecedented quantity of *corvée* labor to build a great post road for the defense of the island. In a period when more and more of the island was coming under direct rule and Batavia was developing a more uniform administrative control, financial difficulties obliged Daendels and Raffles, in particular, to sell off great stretches of coastal West and East Java as "Private Lands," which was a step in just the opposite direction. During the whole period, for the same financial reasons, the new policies were simply not applied to Priangan; the urgently wanted coffee flowed out and the Priangan System, an archetypal arrangement of the *ancien régime*, continued undisturbed.

There were more fundamental obstacles, however. The institutions of Dutch-Javan society, developed over a century or more, were deeply rooted. A handful of Europeans, ahead of contemporary thinking in Europe itself, were attempting a social and economic revolution against great odds in a peasant population of some 10 million. Javan peasants, on the basis of past experience and current conditions, saw little advantage in growing export crops themselves, as Raffles had expected and as his system required. The majesty of a regent and the high status of *priyayi* in general, enlarged by the experience of VOC times, could not be abolished by administrative fiat. Most Europeans on Java were equally at home in the old institutions. Thus, when they took to producing commercial crops in the Central Java principalities in this period, they found it natural to buy rights to peasant labor from appanage-holders at the courts, as Chinese had leased villages previously.

The Java War, a great rebellion that ravaged the Javanese lands between 1825 and 1830, was the final crisis, which brought the confusion and experiments of the transitional years to an end.[43] Out of it emerged the Culture System, introduced by a new Governor-General, Johannes Van den Bosch, in 1830. Like his predecessors since 1808, Van den Bosch set out to govern, not simply to control, Java. He kept the land tax (though in an ancillary role), and he continued the development of a regular bureaucratic administration centering in a corps of European officials. Unlike his predecessors, however, Van den Bosch determined to govern with the grain of local custom, and the key provisions of his Culture System harked back to VOC practice. Under the Culture System, Javan peasants were required to deliver specified quantities of export produce—or the land and labor necessary to produce them, which amounted to the same thing—as their principal obligation to the government. The government no longer exported the products itself, as under the VOC; that was done by the semiofficial NHM (Nederlandsche Handelsmaatschappij, Netherlands Trading Company). But dividing the VOC's old functions between the government and the NHM did not alter the essential fact that Van den Bosch had returned to the "system of tribute." The government of Java was once again to be a machine for collecting export goods to ship home. In the same spirit, he formally recognized the traditional patterns of hereditary succession and rights over land and labor for the regents and, by thus restoring their prestige, aimed at the old practice of ruling in the Javan manner, through the personal authority of the *priyayi*.

The Culture System lasted for three or four decades as the basic regime of Java and during that period achieved just what Van den Bosch had hoped for. It produced an enormous surplus in goods, which revived Dutch shipping, made Amsterdam again a great entrepôt for tropical products, and paid off Holland's public debt. Absolute peace returned to Java, the *priyayi* were content, and the people acquired a new reputation as "the most docile folk on earth." In 1861, an admiring Englishman, called (unbelievably) J. B. Money, summed it up in a book entitled *Java, or How to Manage a Colony*.

That is how the period looks from the point of view of a purely colonial history. The importance of the Culture System from the point of view of Javan history, however, was that it entrenched a peculiarly intimate association between the modern and the traditional, between metropolitan Dutch and Javan elements, which persisted long after the system as such was given up. A typical example of the symbiosis, and one with profound implications, was the way the sugar industry developed. Though there had been substantial sugar exports from the seventeenth century, the industry in its modern form was very much a child of the Culture System. Sugar cane has the same major requirements—a great deal of water and labor—as wet rice. Under the Culture System, the government required peasant villages in many wet-rice areas to devote sections of their land on a rotating basis to cane cultivation. At the same time, it gave out contracts to private individuals to process the cane, lending them funds for the expensive milling machinery and requiring them to deliver the sugar to the NHM for shipment on government account. As this pattern spread and took root, the various parties involved became more and more deeply enmeshed in each other's affairs. The Dutch mill owner *cum* sugar contractor owned no sugar land and had virtually no full-time labor; he borrowed them temporarily, and very cheaply, from surrounding villages by orders from Dutch residents and Javanese regents. They in their turn were paid "cultivation percentages" based on production in their areas. Peasants continued to grow rice (more intensively, since part of their land was under cane) but they also cultivated the cane and, in the harvest season, worked in the mills for small wages. Their *corvée* obligations continued. They still served in the retinues and kitchens of *priyayi* officials, and they also built, by mid-century, the best road system in Asia to meet the needs of the sugar mills and other export industries.

At mid-century, Dutch liberals began a long and bitter campaign against the Culture System, and in the years around 1870 they succeeded in eliminating some of the most characteristic features of the system—culture percentages, compulsory use of land and labor for export crops, and sugar contracts. It is customary to speak of the fall of the Culture System in 1870 and to label the last thirty years of the century the Liberal Period. The distinction, however, is much sharper within the internal affairs of the small Dutch minority than it is for the general social history of Java. In sugar areas, for example, villages became in theory free to withhold land and labor from the mills. In practice, however, they were subject to informal pressure by Dutch and Javanese officials working through headmen, who were enrolled as agents of the system. In any case, the peasants were by then habituated to the sugar system, and they appear to have welcomed the higher cash income accompanying the new land leases and cultivation wages. With such adjustments, the basic symbiosis of village and mill continued, while government irrigation projects opened new land to the sugar-rice combination, and the system spread rapidly in boom conditions.

In this way, more and more Javanese peasants were absorbed in a system that allowed (or required) them to carry on inside the shell of a familiar cultural and psychological universe, while they participated in what was emerging as one of the world's largest and most modern agricultural industries. Similarly, although Liberal policies reduced the prerogatives of the *priyayi*—their claims to *corvée* services for example—and Dutch officials steadily took over more of the actual work of government, peasants still abased themselves before *priyayi*, and the Dutch honored the feudal compact in its essentials. The *priyayi* ideal carried on in an increasingly modern bureaucratic Java. There is the same quality of paradox about all the social life of Java in the later nineteenth century—the Javans embedded, by Dutch design and by their own preference, in familiar but eroding institutions, while at the same time carried swiftly on the currents of change.

The same interlocking of what was Javan and what was Dutch—and in this case Chinese, too—can be seen in the cultural life of Java in the nineteenth century. As the Dutch moved inward from their eighteenth-century coastal enclaves, they came to terms in many ways with Javan, especially Javanese, culture. Dutch officials and planters, isolated amid a large and culturally vigorous population, kept Javan mistresses and adopted a mixed *Indisch* (Indies) culture. Officials kept retinues and used the *payung* (the sunshade of high rank, carried by an attendant); all took to the *rijsttafel* (the Dutch term for the Javan meal of rice with many side dishes) and to Javan clothing when off duty; the more important or richer of them maintained large open establishments much like regents' *dalem*. Eurasians were even more thoroughly immersed in *Indisch* culture, and substantial numbers merged into the Javan community in the course of the nineteenth century.

The economic expansion of the nineteenth century drew increasing numbers of Chinese, mostly Hokkiens, to Java. In that period they became middlemen for the whole island, farming various taxes for the Dutch and trading in all sorts of imports and exports. The government treated them in the same spirit as it did Javans, recognizing them as a separate community with their own customs and leaders (*kapitans*), but it interfered less in their internal affairs, while at the same time requiring them to live in Chinese quarters in the towns and restricting their movement with a system of travel passes. This did not prevent the Chinese from responding strongly to Javan cultural influence, if only because most of them before 1900 came as single men and therefore married Javans. Some became fully Javan—some regent families in East Java in particular were largely Chinese in origin. But the great majority adopted a mixed Javan-Hokkien cultural pattern called *peranakan*, which had its roots in the eighteenth century and earlier but was consolidated and stabilized in the nineteenth.

Priyayi, for their part, adopted some items of Dutch material culture, such as chairs, and in some respects took up the *Indisch* style, but mainly they nurtured their own great tradition, watching Dutch, Eurasians, and Chinese shifting culturally in their direction. In part this was due to Dutch policy, which aimed at keeping Javans as they were, culturally and otherwise. Until late in the nineteenth century, the government discouraged its officials from using Dutch in dealing with *priyayi*, preferring Malay, and made little or no provision for Dutch-language or any Western-type education for them, or for anyone else. But their own high culture had a deeper significance for the *priyayi* in the nineteenth century; it was a cloak they wrapped tighter about themselves as the winds of modernity blew more harshly. Not until early in the twentieth century did more than a handful have the courage or the desperation to cast it off.

19

THE PHILIPPINES, 1762–1872

The most important phenomenon in Philippine history from 1762 to 1872 was the emergence of an elite whose membership transcended earlier social groupings and whose prime identification was with the archipelago itself. This elite, composed primarily of Chinese *mestizos* but also including Spaniards born in the islands, Spanish *mestizos* and *indios*, shaped Philippine nationalism. Known as the *ilustrados*, or enlightened ones, these men gained education and self-awareness because of the radical economic, social, and political changes in the life of the colony. During the period, the Philippines was integrated into the world community to a greater extent than in previous centuries, partly because Spain was helpless to control developments and partly because the shifting focus of economic power transformed the archipelago into a major producer of certain export crops.

Philippine isolation was shattered by the British occupation of Manila in 1762. The attack, which came because Spain had allied itself with France against England, found the colony unprepared and ignorant of the alliance. Although Manila quickly fell, a member of the *Audiencia*, Don Simón de Anda, escaped to the interior, repudiated the surrender, and organized an effective resistance which limited British power in the Manila Bay area. Although the British restored the whole archipelago to Spanish control two years later, powerful social forces had been unleashed in the islands. The Chinese, misjudging English intentions and still smarting under the expulsion order of Governor Arandía, openly supported England, thus incurring increased Spanish hostility. The collapse of central Spanish authority also prompted a spate of *indio* uprisings of varying intensity in Pangasinan, Laguna, Cavite, Tondo, Iloilo, Zamboanga, Samar, Cebu, Panay, and Ilocos. Of these, the Ilocano revolt led by Diego Silang was the most serious. The uprising, which grew out of local grievances, prompted Diego Silang to ally himself with the English, since he felt that the English would not molest or disturb the *indios* but would instead treat them with regard and consideration.

When the Spanish Government regained control of Manila, the colony was bankrupt. The British had captured the outbound galleon, *Santísima Trinidad*, in 1762 and seized about 3 million pesos. The inbound galleon, *Filipino*, did finance Anda's war resistance, but thereafter this vital lifeline stopped. The British had sacked Manila, seized the ships in the harbor, and departed with whatever bullion they could find. Moreover, by 1764 the seemingly limitless wealth of the Spanish empire had been spent, and rehabilitation could not be financed by the mother country. Entry into the China market by other European traders forced the Spanish to pay much more for Chinese goods than they had in the past. Bringing back the galleon was not enough; to restore authority, the Spanish needed a means of making the archipelago self-supporting.

The postwar governors, most importantly José de Basco y Vargas (1778–87), attempted to apply new ideas to reform the system. The most famous of a whole series of reform plans was written by Francisco Leandro de Viana in 1765. Among its recommendations were direct communications with Spain via the Cape of Good Hope, the establishment of a trading company with permission to develop trade between Cadiz, Manila, and Canton, the encouragement of Spanish immigration, the creation of plantations, and the reform of the army, bureaucracy, and tax structure. Such ideas were profoundly disturbing to the conservative elements in the colony. As Governor Basco noted in 1780, "the first task must be to level the massive mountain of prejudice that stands in the way of the enlightened purposes of the central government."[44]

In 1781, Basco established an agricultural society to promote production by granting prizes, printing texts on techniques of cultivation, and publicizing the study of agronomy. He imported mulberry trees, for example, to grow silk in Bicol. In the private sector, a remarkably atypical entrepreneur named Francisco Salgado started to develop copper at Masbate, iron at Santa Inés, cacao, indigo, canvas weaving, and, most persistently, cinnamon. Among the many efforts, the only "success" was the establishment of a tobacco monopoly in 1781. The monopoly freed the Manila government from dependence on the galleon trade and the Mexican subsidy. In a pattern new to the Philippines, the government rigidly controlled crop volume, price, and market sale. By establishing forced delivery in the tobacco areas of northern Luzon, it created many of the hardships already familiar in the Moluccas. While the imposition of this system led to revolts in the tobacco region, it proved to be immediately profitable, and within a few years the insular treasury was able to remit money back to Spain.

The effort to develop export crops required a restructuring of the patterns of trade. It was here that the Bourbon reformers encountered the most intense opposition, since the galleon merchants clearly perceived the threat to their way of life. A Spanish man-of-war, the first ship to sail directly from Spain to Manila in 1765 in order to trade, was ignored by the galleon merchants, even though it was trading for the king's own account. The galleon merchants were a small and powerful group. Organized as a guild (*consulado*), they tried to use their collective power to stifle change. However, the need for revenue and the new opportunities for profit were too great. Private traders, including some non-Spaniards, entered the trade with California, for example, bringing back sea-otter pelts for sale in China. Although this trade violated the monopolistic regulations governing all Spanish trade with the Americas, the galleon merchants could not stop it. They were also unable, in 1785, to block the establishment of the Royal Philippine Company. Designed to promote a worldwide Spanish trading network, the company was granted broad powers by the Spanish monarchy. It was permitted to sail around the world in either direction and was enjoined to stimulate Philippine economic development by investing 4 per cent of its profits in economic development schemes in the archipelago. By 1790, more than forty voyages had been made; the company was investing in Philippine indigo, pepper, sugar, and cotton crops; and Manila had been opened legally to foreign ships if they carried Asian rather than European goods. But, despite its name, the company derived most of its profits from inherited Latin American routes. As a result, even before the chaos caused by the French Revolution, the company directors wanted to drop Manila as an enforced port of call, preferring instead direct access to China.

A campaign by the successive Bourbon governments against the friars paralleled their efforts in the economic sphere. As men of the Enlightenment, the Bourbon rulers were anticlerical; as social reformers, they wanted to challenge friar dominance in the archipelago. Governor Simón de Anda, for example, in a memorandum to the king, maintained that the friars should not meddle in worldly affairs and that they should sell their estates, even though they were just owners, since such business was inconsistent with their ministry. Anda argued that many of the estates, if not all of them, had been usurped from the *indios.* Indicting the friars on numerous counts, he urged the king to limit their power by episcopal visitation, to establish native seminaries for diocesan clergy to replace them, and to expel them from the colony if they failed to heed the king's command. In 1767, the Spanish king expelled the Jesuits from the entire Spanish empire. Under threat of the same treatment, the Dominicans in Manila reluctantly agreed to accept visitation by the king's confidant, Archbishop Basilio Sancho de Santa Justa.

The specific technique used in the antifriar campaign was the appointment of diocesan priests to parishes formerly held by friars. Centuries before, the Pope had granted the Spanish kings extraordinary powers as Royal Patrons of the Church in the Spanish empire. The governor, as Vice-Patron and representative of the king, had the right to appoint. Working in close harmony with the archbishop, who was seeking to strengthen diocesan authority at the expense of the friars, the governor selected diocesan priests for those parishes formerly held by the Jesuits and others that had been left vacant by death. Since there were fewer than ten Caucasian diocesan priests in the whole archipelago, *indio* and *mestizo* clerics had to be promoted. Their educational level was low, since the friars had never made any effort to train a native clergy. The conservative community in Manila, already deeply resentful of the movement, was delighted when some diocesan priests proved unable to bear their new burdens. The issue became a racial one, with the native priest held up to derision by the Spanish community. A joke of the time was that there were no longer any men to row the ferry boats in Manila because the archbishop had ordained them all. Although the Bourbon governors optimistically predicted that friar influence would yield gradually to the spread of enlightened ideas, the effect was to polarize the society and to force the friars into an even more reactionary position.

The friars started to regain their position as early as 1776, when they obtained from Madrid a temporary suspension of the replacement procedure. Under the wartime conditions of 1803, they successfully won the governor's support in their fight to retain three parishes, including an important one near Manila.[45] In 1826, Ferdinand VII returned most Philippine parishes to friar control. The *indio* priests, now fully aware of Spanish clerical attitudes, were demoted to curates. Pro-friar advocates argued that the moral fiber of the colony had deteriorated primarily because of the *indio* and *mestizo* priests. They maintained that it was the friars who gave the Spanish their moral ascendancy.

The restoration of the clerical *status quo ante* was not matched in the economic sphere. The Royal Philippine Company, although maintaining the fiction of its interest in the islands, had more or less abandoned its effort by 1789. Only sixteen direct voyages were made to Manila between 1785 and 1820; the company was caught up in the worldwide disruption of trade caused by war. Although its charter was reissued in 1803, by 1819 the company showed a heavy loss. The hopes of its planners were never achieved. Moreover, the collapse of Spanish rule in Latin America ended the galleon age. In 1820, the Mexican revolutionary Agustín Iturbide seized the 2 million pesos realized that year from the sale of Manila goods. That *coup de grace* bankrupted the Manila *consulado;* by 1825, the total trade with the new world was less than 2 per cent of the 1810 level. The demise of the galleon also ended the *situado*. Perhaps some 400 million pesos had flowed from the silver mines at Potosí to Manila during the galleon's long life. The termination of the flow caused not only economic dislocation but also Philippine dependency on Spain. The galleon had been a constant channel of communication and personnel and had kept the Spanish empire racially catholic as well as Catholic religiously.

The period from 1820 to 1825 was a watershed in Philippine history. The key issue, creole equality, was related to the existent economic dislocation, political uncertainty, and social change. During those years, many *peninsulares* arrived in Manila. These Iberian Spanish, recently expelled from Latin America, looked down on creoles. The *peninsulares*, including the friars, distrusted not only the creoles and *mestizos* born in

Latin America but also those native to the islands. As empire loyalists, they saw as their duty the protection of the Philippines for Spain. However, since the Philippine bureaucracy was traditionally staffed by creoles and *mestizos*, the tension rapidly polarized the upper echelons of society. Pushed from power, the locally born creoles (*Filipinos*) saw the region as rightfully theirs and viewed the *peninsulares* as alien rulers. The frictions exploded in a revolt within the King's Own Regiment. Led by a Mexican *mestizo* captain named Andrés Novales, the revolt involved 800 troops. Although it was quickly suppressed, it seemed to confirm the worst fears of the *peninsulares*, who failed to realize that they themselves were the cause of the rebellion. Twenty-three of the ringleaders were executed, and many liberals were exiled, even though they were not implicated directly. The tightening of caste within the Spanish empire stratified Philippine society, forcing the creoles to identify themselves with their place of birth rather than with ancestry. Philippine nationalism emerged eventually from the process.

Restoration of the economic system, however, was the most immediate need, but the Spanish lacked the capital, the entrepreneurial skill, and the inclination to take charge of development. Mercantilist exclusion gave way to free trade and foreign commercial domination. By 1879, the Philippines had become "an Anglo-Chinese colony flying the Spanish flag." It developed an agricultural export economy, its cultivation occurring on small holdings. The only large estates were those owned by the friars, and they were rarely run as plantations. The key to development came with the arrival of the non-Spanish merchants who hooked the Philippines into the world community. These entrepreneurs, often tied to the great banking and trading companies of America, Europe, and China, did business in dollars or pounds rather than in pesos. Functioning initially as commission merchants who would advance the money for a future crop of sugar, copra, coffee, or hemp, they evolved into sophisticated merchant banking and insurance concerns with agents throughout the archipelago.

The Philippine sugar industry is a good example. Although sugar had been exported in the eighteenth century, old-fashioned processing curtailed production. In 1856, the island of Negros produced 280 tons of sugar. In 1857, Nicholas Loney, an Englishman working for Ker and Company, moved from Manila to Iloilo and opened the island of Negros to industry by offering Western machinery for which the planters could pay out of profits. Within a few years, there were thirteen modern mills on the island; by 1864, they produced 7,000 tons of sugar. Loney, noting that "most extensive tracts of fertile soil easily cleared, and well situated for shipments of produce, [were] to be had at Negros," observed that the *mestizos* were drawn to Negros by "the promising future of sugar planting interest."[46]

The development of an export economy is clearly reflected in the trade statistics. In 1825, the volume of trade was nearly 3 million pesos; fifty years later, it was fifteen times as large. Moreover, since Spain bought its sugar and tobacco more cheaply from Puerto Rico and Cuba, Philippine goods moved directly onto the world market. The Philippines was not integrated into the Spanish economy. The key exports of sugar, abaca, tobacco, and coffee, representing more than 90 per cent of the total volume, had to find outlets throughout the world. The Spanish were forced, therefore, to open Manila and other cities as ports, if the colony was to survive. Moreover, to maintain a balance of trade, foreign goods had to be allowed into the islands. Except for wine, olive oil, and a few Spanish luxury items, the English dominated the import market with textiles, machinery, and other finished goods. These economic developments had lasting consequences for rice production. Prior to 1850, the islands had consistently exported rice, primarily to China; however, as the distance traveled by exports and imports increased, rice land was shifted to sugar or other crops, and after 1870 the islands began to import rice. Since the Philippines, unlike Java, had a relatively sparse population and little irrigation development, the process of "agricultural involution" (as Geertz has termed it) rarely took place. The worldwide conditions, however, were important in explaining why the population increased greatly and the economy drifted away from self-sufficiency.

The economic changes had a profound effect on Philippine society. Within the Spanish community, the impact was divisive. The loss of economic control created a sense of malaise and frustration. Political tensions between liberal and conservative in peninsular Spain, which were evident from the 1812 constitution through the Carlist wars to the end of the century, broke the Philippine Spanish into two camps. The problem was exacerbated by the Spanish policy of deporting political prisoners of all persuasions to the islands. Moreover, since the liberals in Spain retained their strong opposition to the Church throughout the century, the friars in the Philippines became the rallying force for all conservatives in the archipelago. After they had been banned from Spain itself, many friars moved to Manila, where the atmosphere was more congenial. Technological improvements, which made it easier to reach Manila and to live comfortably there, also increased the willingness of lay Spaniards to emigrate with their wives. Madrid governments, which came and went with dazzling speed, bestowed patronage so lavishly that the Spanish bureaucracy in Manila, decreasing in effectiveness, doubled or tripled in size.[47] Very few Spaniards ever left the comforts of Manila for agriculture. Thus, government service was the chief means of employment, corruption the fastest road to wealth. The weight and avarice of the bureaucracy, characterized by the institutionalized disregard for the commonweal that plagues the country even now, paralyzed governmental function.

The loss of the empire in Latin America was a trauma from which the Spanish never fully recovered. Since they also were helpless to control the economic changes of the nineteenth century, they grew increasingly defensive. The specter of rebellion and bureaucratic inertia prevented them from undertaking the reforms the colony needed. Suspicious of everything, they alienated even the creoles, who were, of course, also Caucasian. The hostility from the Novales rebellion simmered during the entire century. In 1837, the Philippines was permanently banned from representation in the Spanish Parliament (Cortes) in Madrid. In the islands, legislation was passed to mark by dress and privilege the different classes within society. Thus, for example, only Spaniards were permitted to wear ties; *indios* and *mestizos* were forced to wear their shirts loose, without any neck ornaments. The current national dress, the *barong tagalog*, evolved from the proscription. Stratification was the device the Spanish used with the hope of keeping people in their place. Since economic developments unleashed new social pressures, their hope turned out to be naive.

If the Spanish retreated from change, the Chinese advanced toward it. The eighteenth-century Spanish desire to prohibit Chinese immigration eroded under nineteenth-century economic exigencies. In 1839, the Chinese were given "complete liberty to choose the occupation that best suits them." Subsequently, they were permitted to live anywhere in the archipelago,[48] developing a symbiotic relationship with the foreign traders wherein they supplied raw materials and distributed imported goods. Operating through the *cabecilla* system of a central manager and rural agents—many of whom were related to each other—the Chinese created the bridge between the *indio* producer and the foreign export community. The Chinese population, which had been stable at 4,000 to 5,000 from the 1750's to the 1840's, reached about 18,000 in 1864; by 1876, it was about 30,000, mostly males. The opening of Hong Kong in 1842 and the unrest caused by the Taiping rebellion of 1850–64 were powerful inducements for immigration, but the opportunities in the Philippines itself provided the prime force.

The Chinese migrated partly in order to enter local trade. From 1754 to 1844, the Spanish had permitted the Spanish governors to dominate local trade, even though technically the Law of the Indies prohibited this. The provincial governor was allowed to pay a fine in advance, *indulto de comercio*, in order to make his fortune. This privilege, badly abused, so greatly restricted the flow of export goods that the central government felt compelled to abolish it in 1844. Although the Spanish officials had hoped that Spaniards would move into business, it was the Chinese who soon controlled retail trade by combining low overhead, hard work, and patronage with a developed credit network. Intense competition among the Chinese led to trading efficiency, permitting the colony to prosper. After 1857, when some economic restrictions were removed, the Chinese bid successfully for the right to collect taxes.

The repercussions of the Chinese penetration affected the Chinese *mestizo* community, which had profited from the anti-Chinese legislation of the earlier period and was threatened by the changing situation. Without access to credit and unable to operate on tight profit margins, the *mestizo* community shrewdly shifted its economic base into land

and export crops, migrating to the Negros sugar lands, for example. *Mestizos* also played a major role in developing indigo for export. Most importantly, Chinese *mestizos* moved increasingly into rice production. The development of export crops, the conversion of land from rice to sugar, and the increasing shortage of the grain staple drove the price of rice upward and made rice production a profitable business. *Mestizos* acquired land in two ways. Some became lessees (*inquilinos*) on friar estates; they would open new land and would develop and sublet it to *indio* farmers for a percentage, usually high, of the crop yield. This system, in which the *mestizo* became the intermediary between the peasant and the friar landlord, was known as *kasamahan*. It became widespread in those areas around Manila where the Church had holdings and where the demand for new land was high. The second method was money-lending. Spanish law limited the *indio*'s debt to twenty-five pesos. To circumvent that statute, the *mestizo* would buy the land, granting the *indio* an option to repurchase later. Known as the *pactos de retro*, this system usually meant that the money-lender gained ownership. The farmers thus became tenants of the *mestizo* money-lenders, and the process became so prevalent that Father Zúñiga warned, "If no remedy is found, within a short time the lords of the entire Archipelago will be the Chinese mestizos."[49]

Despite the *mestizos*' successful economic response, the upsurge of Chinese immigrants posed a direct challenge to them. The new Chinese carried with them a sense of cultural superiority; they saw the Filipinized *mestizos* as cultural apostates. This attitude hurt the *mestizos*, who, despite their distinct legal status, lacked secure cultural roots. Adrift, although powerful, they tried to fuse with the creoles and Spanish *mestizos*, who were themselves, as we have seen, in the process of losing their Iberian identity. Thus, both groups searched for an identity together, and together the *mestizos* changed the term *Filipino* from its previously narrow meaning of a Spaniard born in the Philippines into a more national concept. The Chinese *mestizos* developed a set of values that was their own blend of *indio*, Spanish, and Chinese ideas. Most *mestizos* responded to the challenge of Chinese immigration by practicing Catholicism more devoutly, by adopting Spanish mores and style, and by becoming anti-Chinese. Moreover, lacking the standards of ethnic origin or family ancestry, the *mestizo* community stressed wealth as the arbiter of social status. Wealth was judged by land ownership; it became an empirical standard against which individuals could define social standing. Thus, Chinese immigration forced economic accommodation, setting in motion a process of "social Filipinization" with profound consequences for the future.

The impact of the above changes on the *indio* community was also profound. Since the Chinese *mestizo*, through his wealth and power, was close to the *indio* community, he transmitted to it values like the concern for wealth as a social arbiter, the appeal of ostentation as proof of status, and the new meaning of the term *Filipino*. By the mid-nineteenth century, the term *indio* was becoming a pejorative. Some of the *caciques* and *principalía,* especially those near Manila, had participated in the era of rapid economic development, interacting with both creoles and *mestizos.* The increasingly interdependent character of society opened new networks of communication. There were dislocations inherent in the process, but a growing congruence of loyalty was developing among sectors of society that had previously been legally distinct and socially distant.

The emergence of a sense of identity can be observed in the changing character of institutional life, especially in education. One Spaniard, noting that the "work-hand . . . [and] the goatherd do not read social contracts," warned in 1843 that the colleges in Manila should be closed, "because in a colony, *liberal* and *rebellious* are synonymous terms"; however, the number of people eligible for advanced education constantly grew.[50] Whereas previously the educational system had been limited to creoles, Spanish *mestizos,* and a few children of *indio principalía,* it was now broadened to include all groups. The process was greatly hastened when the Jesuits, readmitted into the archipelago in 1859, established Ateneo de Manila, a school that accepted *indios, mestizos,* and creoles without distinction. Enrollment at the University of Santo Tomas increased dramatically, and some of its "Royal and Pontifical" character was localized. A new and critically important elite social group emerged from these schools, an *ilustrado* class, which stood at the apex of the new Filipino community, cutting across all prior social and economic boundaries. Because it could speak articulately for the emerging Filipino community, it gained high prestige as an indigenous intelligentsia.

Many of the new *ilustrados* hoped to become priests but found that the hostility of the Spanish friars barred their advance. Clerical equality was the earliest major issue of Philippine nationalism. Conservative Spaniards were convinced that nothing would promote Philippine emancipation faster than the ordination of native priests. At the end of the century, a Spanish critic would note that the native priest was "a caricature of the priest, a caricature of the *indio,* a caricature of the Spaniard, a caricature of the *mestizo,* a caricature of everybody. He is a patchwork of many things and is nothing. I put it badly; he is something, after all; more than something . . . he is an enemy of Spain."[51]

The combination of racism and fear eventually contributed to the realization of the Spanish anxiety. The uprising of Apolinario de la Cruz in 1841 began because Cruz, a devout provincial Catholic, discovered that he could not enter a monastic order. Cruz then established a native religious brotherhood, the *Cofradía de San José,* which spread rapidly in the area near his home. His efforts to gain recognition for this order were rejected by the Spanish, and eventually Cruz and his followers found themselves under attack. When the government attempted to suppress the movement, Cruz was able initially to defeat Spanish troops, killing the governor of Tayabas. The Spanish subsequently defeated the *Cofradía,* killed Cruz, and hung bits of his body throughout the *Cofradía* region. Thereafter, the Spanish responded by increased repression and hostility to Filipino clerical nationalism. They rounded up ranking Manila *mestizos* on suspicion of secretly assisting de la Cruz.[52] In 1849, seven key parishes in Cavite were transferred back from diocesan to friar control. In 1859, with the return of the Jesuits to their eighteenth-century mission stations in Mindanao, the displaced Recollect friars were given all the remaining diocesan parishes in Cavite. By 1871, Filipinos staffed only 181 out of 792 parishes.

The decline of diocesan parishes coincided with the growing self-awareness of the intelligentsia. As a result of the Jesuit restoration, Father Pedro Pelaez, a Spanish creole who had risen within the diocesan ranks, led the fight against friar dominance. After he was killed in an earthquake in 1863, his place was taken by a *mestizo* named José Burgos, who wrote a manifesto in 1864 calling for clerical equity. Burgos, as synodal examiner of the Archdiocese, wanted newly arrived Spanish priests to learn the local language before receiving parish assignments. The arguments of clerical *ilustrados* like Burgos received unexpected support when, in 1868, Spain swung back into the liberal camp. In 1870, the new archbishop of Manila petitioned the king that "propriety and equity" required support of the Filipino priests. When, as a result of an earthquake, the remains of Simón de Anda had to be moved, a massive crowd turned out to laud this friend of the native clergy. The benign reforms of Governor de la Torre encouraged a growing confidence that was shattered with the conservative restoration in Madrid—and with the appointment of a new governor, whose policy was to govern "with a cross in one hand and a sword in the other," to repeal de la Torre's liberalizing reforms, and to restore the friars to preeminence. In 1872, a mutiny against local grievances by the garrison at the Cavite Arsenal afforded the new governor, Rafael Izquierdo, an opportunity to arrest, try, and execute the leading advocates of Filipino religious nationalism, including Father José Burgos, Father Jacinto Zamora, and Father Mariano Gómez.

The archbishop refused to excommunicate the three priests, despite the pressure of the governor, because he believed they were being executed for their liberal views. His view is corroborated by the numerous arrests and deportations of many lay *ilustrados*. The repression led many others to flee to Europe or Hong Kong. It made martyrs of the three priests. Forty thousand came to witness the execution. Crowds heard Burgos cry out, "But what crime have I committed? Is it possible that I am to die in this way? My God, is there no longer justice in the land?"[53] Izquierdo, by his ruthless and heavy-handed action, had created a symbol for the evolving Filipino intelligentsia. The greatest of the *ilustrados*, José Rizal, a fifth-generation Chinese *mestizo*, dedicated his novel, *El Filibusterismo*, to the memory of the three executed priests. The Philippine nationalist movement, the first in Southeast Asia, can be dated from their martyrdom in 1872.

PART THREE

Frameworks for Nations

The most obvious feature of Southeast Asian history in the period between 1870 and 1940 was conquest, and subsequent political dominance, by the West. During the three or four decades after 1870 the Western powers rapidly completed their seizure of the area, subjugating the remaining kingdoms and peoples and leaving only Thailand independent, though within the British sphere of influence. From conquest emerged strong colonial states which remained in full power—yielding only where they chose to, as in the Philippines—through the early decades of the twentieth century and up to 1940. It is not without reason that this three quarters of a century is often called the high colonial age.

But if colonial rule spread swiftly and planted itself solidly, it departed even more swiftly in the 1940's and 1950's. It went through these remarkable ups and downs because it was part of a much larger historical process, the scientific and industrial revolution, which has transformed the whole world, including the West itself, in modern times. In the light of that revolution, direct Western rule in Southeast Asia may be seen as a short-lived frontier institution in a worldwide process of political change.

The colonial powers did not simply seize control of pre-existing states. Cutting across established lines of political association or amalgamating previously separate societies, they created new political frameworks. On these they imposed modern bureaucratic systems and, over the decades, enlarged and perfected the apparatus necessary for such systems: government departments of all sorts, railroads, modern fiscal and tax systems. In this they acted as agents of a universal process, laying the foundations for modern nations just as others were doing in Europe, Japan, and elsewhere. The same process occurred in independent Thailand under the management of a domestic elite.

While the grids were being extended over the Southeast Asian landscape, imposing on it a new kind of order, economic change was altering the substance of Southeast Asian life. Export industries, involving millions of people, rose rapidly after 1870; by 1940, most parts of the area had export-dominated economies. Population, hitherto stable or rising slowly, almost tripled between 1870 and 1940. The rise was accompanied by large migrations into and within the area. The money economy, centering on modern institutions in the burgeoning cities, spread widely through the countryside. These changes, too, were consequences of the scientific and industrial revolution, as Southeast Asia was caught up in the world economic revolution and took its place in the emerging world economy.

20

THE MAKING OF NEW STATES

The twentieth-century historian, who lives in a political world made up of "nations" neatly interlocking in a global jigsaw, must carefully wipe the windows of his mind if he is to see the political map of Southeast Asia in 1870 as it was for contemporaries. That map was made up on different principles; it comprised an indefinite number of political centers, imposing or petty, whose influence receded through circles of more or less autonomous provinces and vassals until it reached and overlapped with other circles of influence. Six such centers were large old states rooted in the political traditions of fairly sizable and homogeneous populations: the Theravada kingdoms of Mandalay and Bangkok, the Confucian and Catholic states at Hue and Manila, and the grafted Franco-Cambodian and Dutch-Javan polities centering on Phnom Penh and Batavia. Three were novel colonial creations: the Commissionership of British Burma, the Colony of Cochinchina, and the Straits Settlements Colony. Beyond were two broad zones of petty centers: the belt of Shan-Lao principalities of the interior mainland and the predominantly Malayo-Muslim world stretching from Sumatra to Mindanao and from the Malay peninsula to the Moluccas. Scattered around and among all these, finally, were innumerable small stateless societies.

The political map of Southeast Asia had always been organized on the above principles, but it was not to remain so much longer. The rather abrupt appearance of the newly fashioned colonies centered at Rangoon, Saigon, and Singapore foreshadowed the coming change throughout the area. In the next four decades, the map of Southeast Asia was redrawn to conform with the emerging world political order, a reorganization that had two closely related aspects.

One was a process of conquest and incorporation, as the numerous political centers of the old order were marshaled into six new units. Three of the larger old centers were conquered—Mandalay by the British, Hue by the French, and Manila by the Americans—and the peoples involved (Burmans, Vietnamese, and Filipinos) then became the cores of the modern colonies of British Burma, French Indochina, and the Philippines. The Shan-Lao and Malayo-Muslim zones were divided up among the powers, usually under forms of indirect rule. The mainland zone was partitioned among the British, Thai, and French, becoming what are today the Burmese Shan States, North and Northeast Thailand, and Laos; the greater part of the island zone was incorporated into the Netherlands Indies, while the Malay peninsula and Northwest Borneo came into British hands, and the easternmost islands became what is now the southern Philippines. Cambodia was joined to Vietnam and Laos in French Indochina, and the multitude of small stateless societies fell into one or another of the larger units, often by a combination of political and missionary activity. By about 1910, the process was complete. Essentially all of Southeast Asia was incorporated into the six new states, defined now not by the power of centers radiating outward through successive circles of receding influence, but by demarcated boundaries around their outer edges.

Implicit in this change in the scope of political power was a restructuring of the basis of political legitimacy. Most of the authority of the traditional centers, both small and large, was derived from religion and was based on the sacral qualities of the rulers' persons, regalia, and palaces. On the other hand, the rulers' power to govern, in the practical sense, rested more on the control of military force than on routine administrative machinery. Even Hue, Manila, and Batavia, the least "traditional" centers in this respect, had their Son of Heaven and the overseas deputy of His Most Christian Majesty; Philippine villages were governed by friars, and Dutch officials went about under the *payung* (ceremonial sunshades) of erstwhile Javanese god-kings. The basis of rule changed rapidly between 1870 and 1910. The prestige of the colonial governors of Burma, Indochina, and Malaya came from their efficient military establishments and civil service, not from a sacred majesty; the Americans did away with friar rule; the Dutch gave up their *payung* and invented new secular ceremonies. One of the earliest acts of Chulalongkorn as King of Thailand was to order his officials not to prostrate themselves before his godly person. He was not thereby abdicating power; like the colonial rulers in neighboring lands, which he visited in his youth, he was setting forth toward a much more comprehensive kind of authority.

Everywhere, especially among the folk, the sacral royal traditions lived on, for, deeply embedded in the traditional arts and languages, they described the nature and meaning of political power as men knew it to be. But everywhere, too, actual political authority came to be exercised on secular bureaucratic principles. Modern administrative networks spread out over the new political units; alongside them arose a great variety of specialist services to serve new functions. The nature, as well as the geography, of government had entered on a profound transformation.

THE SHAN AND LAO PRINCIPALITIES

In 1870, the whole mountainous zone of Shan and Lao principalities stretching from the upper Irrawaddy to the Black River in northern

Vietnam and from Yunnan to the foothills north of the Čhaophraya River plain remained much as it had been for a long time, a sparsely populated and independent world of its own in the interior behind the larger monarchies and peoples of mainland Southeast Asia. It played an oddly important role, however, in the European imperialism of the mid-nineteenth century. While the main European challenge was to the major monarchies near or on the coast—as events at Rangoon, Bangkok, Tourane, and Saigon in the 1850's demonstrated—European interest at the time focused (in large measure ignorantly) beyond the coastal areas and upon the Shan and Lao regions in the interior. The granting of trading rights to Western powers in the treaty ports of China following the Opium War (1842) failed to generate the volume of trade that Europe and America had expected, and so the myth of a rich and populous inner China, inaccessible from the China coast, captured the imaginations of French and British commercial interests. Their immediate target was the province of Yunnan, which they hoped to reach by water or rail from Upper Burma, or up the Salween River, up the Mekong from Cambodia, or up the Red River from Hanoi. The traditional suzerainty of the Burman, Thai, and Vietnamese monarchies over the principalities along those routes was misunderstood and denied. Particularly where such principalities were the tributaries of two or more larger states, there existed openings for conflict.

To the west, the non-Buddhist Karen states on the southern fringe of the Shan Plateau became one scene of strife following the Second Anglo-Burman War. Situated in the undefined border region between British Lower Burma and Mindon's kingdom, the two chief states were Eastern and Western Karen-ni, which by 1868 were divided between British and Burman influence. In 1875, the British declared a protectorate over Western Karen-ni, while Eastern Karen-ni remained in closer relations with Mandalay. Mindon's diplomatic defeat by the British over the creation of the protectorate was the immediate cause of the unwillingness of either side to give way in the famous "footwear" controversy.

The more than two dozen Buddhist Shan states were, with a few exceptions, tributaries of the Burman kings. However, they became the objects of numerous expeditions sent from Lower Burma from the 1820's onward as they came to be of economic and strategic importance to the British. The Burman court responded with renewed efforts to recover their allegiance. British, Burman, and sometimes Chinese and Thai interference tended to encourage local autonomy and civil strife. From mid-century onward, many states like Hsenwi in the extreme north were embroiled in political troubles as they resisted Burman efforts to restore pro-Burman rulers. With independent revenues from the increasing hill trade and with access to modern weapons, such states lay beyond the effective power of the Burman court of the time. The principality of Kengtung, farther east, was the object of pressure from many directions. It suffered three Thai invasions between 1849 and 1854, repulsing them with Burman and Shan aid, though at the cost of increased Burman influence. King Thibaw, in particular, attempted to tighten Burman control over Kengtung but succeeded only in provoking a rebellion in 1881–82. It soon spread to neighboring principalities, and it ultimately developed into the "Limbin Confederacy" of 1885, an alliance of Shan rulers under the Burman Limbin Prince, who came up from British Burma shortly before the outbreak of the Third Anglo-Burman War. Its purpose was to end the warfare between the Shan states in order to enable them to withstand Burman pressure and, perhaps, British designs.

The Kingdom of Lanna at Chiangmai, in what is now North Thailand, had been brought under the loose suzerainty of Bangkok in 1774, after forty years of almost constant warfare. Once the Burmans had been expelled from the area in 1804, the state was left more or less alone while it regrouped its depleted population in defensible towns and mounted occasional raids into the Shan states to capture slaves. After mid-century, as a result of new European interest in Chiangmai's teak forests, of disputed forest leases, and of what British Burma viewed as unacceptable restraints on its trade in the region, the Bangkok monarchy became alarmed at the possibility that the rulers in Chiangmai might bring on a collision between themselves and the British. Bangkok therefore put its own candidate on the throne of Chiangmai in 1870 and, five years later, appointed the first Thai resident commissioner there to guard its interests and to prevent further conflict with the British.[1]

Similar unrest occurred in the Lao states to the east. Bangkok's suppression of the Anu Rebellion of 1826 and the massive resettlement of the population of the middle Mekong valley on the Khorat Plateau had left as independent Lao powers only the kingdom of Luang Prabang and a few minor principalities to the east and north that were tributary to it. From 1872 onward, the whole northern region was threatened by bands of Chinese (known as Hǫ) from Yunnan who roamed the whole region, burning and plundering every settlement in their path, and reaching even to Vientiane in that year. Unable to cope with the intrusions himself, the king of Luang Prabang appealed to his suzerain in Bangkok. Through the 1870's and 1880's, the Thai Government sent repeated military expeditions northward. Coming only for short campaigns and moving too slowly to keep up with the Hǫ, they achieved little. In 1887, indeed, the Hǫ sacked Luang Prabang itself. The king managed to escape, with the aid of the French Vice-Consul, Auguste Pavie, but his faith in his Thai suzerain was severely shaken, and French hopes for an easy annexation were encouraged.

On the whole, the influence and control of the Burman and Thai monarchies in the Shan and Lao region were no stronger in 1885 than they had been a century earlier. Although they attempted to strengthen their position, essentially they did so within a traditional framework of suzerainty and vassalage. Among the Shans, Burman attempts to increase control by greater use of the suzerain's powers only provoked rebellion, which encouraged or facilitated the later extension of British power. Though similar Thai efforts were more subtle (as in Chiangmai) or forceful (as in Luang Prabang), the Thai monarchy could achieve no lasting change with the old methods. The outcome here, as elsewhere, was a new map of mainland Southeast Asia, drawn between 1885 and 1909 by French and British fiat and new Thai initiative.

THE PROVINCE OF BURMA

British Burma grew step by step. It began with the Tenasserim provinces and Arakan, acquired in 1826 after the First Anglo-Burman War, and was enlarged by the acquisition of the provinces of Lower Burma during the second war (1852–53). Each initially was only a "division" of the Government of India, headed by a commissioner, but in 1862 the three were amalgamated under a chief commissioner in Rangoon. The Indian Government, in its effort to unify and centralize India, was never very sympathetic regarding the special character of Burma. After 1871, because the chief commissioners in Rangoon were men with Indian experience who looked to promotion in the Indian Civil Service, they remained insensitive to the differences between India and Burma. British colonial administration in Burma, for example, was founded upon Indian patterns of village leadership and land rights. The traditional relationships among village, township, and circle headmen in Burma were largely ignored, and an Indian system of direct administration was imposed. Efficiency and economic development, involving especially the export of rice and teak, were the watchwords of the government, as it steadily extended its new, uniform, and alien administrative system over the countryside.

British economic interests, coming to center in Rangoon after its capture in 1852, contributed to the shaping of administrative policy and, ultimately, to the extension of British rule over the kingdom of Mandalay in Upper Burma. Shipping and financial firms involved in foreign trade, along with such extractive industries as teak, had an interest in extending their area of operations along the Irrawaddy River into Upper Burma, as well as farther afield into China. Through the Rangoon Chamber of Commerce and similar organizations in Britain, they exerted constant pressure on the Rangoon, Calcutta, and London governments for more commercial concessions from Mindon, and (when Mindon and his successor failed to abolish all their own royal trading monopolies) for the annexation of Upper Burma.

Anglo-Burman relations deteriorated rapidly in the 1870's, as Mindon lost faith in the goodwill of the British and as they in turn increasingly lost patience with him. In 1872, desperate for recognition of the independent status of his kingdom, Mindon sent envoys to Europe. They were allowed an audience with Queen Victoria only when accompanied by the Secretary of State for India (and not the Foreign Secretary). They then tentatively sought recognition from the French and Italian governments but gained only commercial treaties. Mindon was boxed in by increasing British hostility and suspicion of his dealings with other European powers and by the reluctance or inability of France and Italy to assist his landlocked kingdom, which was accessible only through British Rangoon.

The accession of King Thibaw in 1878 was a power play gone wrong. After the abortive palace coup of 1866, in which the previous heir to the throne had been killed, Mindon feared to name his successor. In an atmosphere of uncertainty, foreign danger, and intrigue, court politics intensified as factions prepared for the struggle over succession. The situation was used by a faction led by a discarded queen of Mindon, Hsinpyumashin (distantly related to a ministerial family of Thailand through a woman taken captive in Ayudhya in 1767), and a minister of the *hlutdaw*, the Taingda Mingyi.[2] They persuaded the ministers to choose a minor prince, Thibaw, by encouraging them to think they could control him. Once he was crowned, all other rivals for the throne were killed, and then the old dowager and her daughter Supayalat, Thibaw's queen, took effective control of public affairs.

The British Government in Rangoon shared the righteous indignation of the British community there at these untidy affairs and saw in them an opportunity to increase pressure on the Burman kingdom. It dispatched troops to Mandalay forthwith, on the pretext that the British representative there needed protection; the following year, it reversed itself and withdrew the representative as a sign of its moral disapproval. When Thibaw sent an envoy to Calcutta to appeal for the resumption of friendly relations and to discuss a new treaty, his mission was completely ignored. But war in Afghanistan temporarily reduced British willingness to go any further in Burma. Thibaw tried, amid a difficult political situation and perhaps at the instigation of the most able of his ministers, the Kinwun Mingyi, to conciliate British opinion and to seek an accommodation through negotiations in 1882. Thibaw's envoys first claimed for Burma the right as a sovereign state to send ambassadors to the Queen in London and then, when their claim was denied, asked for at least a treaty drawn up in the names of the two sovereigns. In return, Thibaw offered to receive British representatives at his court with their shoes on. The British would not yield, offering only a royal treaty of friendship and a separate commercial treaty with the Indian Government. Thibaw felt he had no choice but to withdraw his envoys. He then embarked upon a more forceful and dangerous policy in 1883 with the dispatch of envoys to Europe to seek full recognition and aid from the French Government.

The heightened Anglo-French tension that ensued was the result not so much of French designs (as the British thought) as of a logical Burman initiative, given France's newly acquired position in Vietnam. Indeed, the official French role in what followed was passive. The Burman mission to Paris succeeded in gaining no more than a revival of the dead-letter commercial treaty of 1873; in particular, the French refused in 1884 to sign a declaration that they would come to Burma's assistance if it were threatened by a third power. Early in 1885, when the Kinwun Mingyi earnestly sought some assurance of French support, all that Premier Jules Ferry would concede was a letter promising arms shipments overland from Tonkin—*if* "this is judged compatible with our interests." Individual Frenchmen went somewhat further, agitating for railroad and banking concessions, and almost gained the ruby monopoly from Thibaw. In particular, the French consul in Mandalay, M. Haas, took part, with approval from Paris, in Burman litigation concerning the British Bombay-Burma Trading Corporation, in the hopes that the French might succeed to its teak interests in Burma.[3]

In August, 1885, just as the Ferry letter of January became known to the British, the Bombay-Burma Trading Corporation was assessed a fine of £73,333 by the *hlutdaw,* which found it guilty of under-reporting its extraction of teak logs from forests in Mandalay's territory north of Toungoo. The events that followed sprang from the issues raised by these coinciding developments, from the treatment Mandalay was according British commercial interests, and from the heightened Anglo-French rivalry following the conquest of Tonkin. Successive Liberal governments in London had been unmoved by the economic arguments for annexation put forward by British commercial interests in Rangoon, especially when British Indian armies were occupied elsewhere. But in late 1885 the armies were idle, a Conservative government, more open than the Liberals to expansion, was in power, and both economic and political fears of France urged them on. Thibaw was presented with a bully's ultimatum—that the teak case be put to the arbitration of the chief commissioner in Rangoon, that a British resident be installed in Mandalay with a guard and direct, shod access to the king, and that all Burma's foreign relations be put under the control of the Indian Government.

The French tried to ease the crisis by offering a demarcation of British and French spheres of influence, but the British would have none of it. The Kinwun Mingyi urged a conciliatory reply to the ultimatum but was overruled by the Taingda Wungyi and Queen Supayalat, who did not take it seriously. Instead, an unyielding reply was returned. When the twenty-day ultimatum expired in mid-November, British forces promptly headed north, occupying Mandalay in a fortnight. The annexation of Upper Burma was announced on January 1, 1886, bringing to an end the Konbaung Dynasty and Burman independence.

The Third Anglo-Burman War really began only after it had "ended." Although the Burman Army disappeared from the field, resistance broke out all over Upper Burma and quickly swept over British Lower Burma as well. With the deportation of the king and the dissolution of the *hlutdaw,* royal government collapsed, but authority was not automatically transferred to the British. Disbanded Burman troops, bandit groups, and peasant patriots were joined by Shans in opposing the imposition of British control. Their lack of coordination made their suppression easier, but it still remained a formidable task. More than 40,000 troops and Indian police were in the field by February, 1887, while a Christian Karen militia was raised to help quell the rising in the south. The "Pacification of Burma," to use the title of the most complete contemporary account of the subject, was a good deal bloodier than the murder of Thibaw's relatives, as British troops burned down villages and carried out mass executions of people they termed rebels. Resistance gradually subsided in Upper and Lower Burma, while columns of troops sent into the Shan states brought about the collapse of the "Limbin Confederacy" in 1887. Finally, by about 1890, British military power succeeded in establishing full control over the whole of Burma, which was defined by new frontiers, bringing to an end a conflict of more than sixty years.

THE KINGDOM OF THAILAND

The strongest pressures of Western imperialism reached Thailand a decade or two later than Burma and Vietnam, giving the Thai extra time. The kingdom needed the extra time, most immediately to resolve critical problems of domestic politics. King Chulalongkorn (r. 1868–1910) was fifteen when he succeeded to the throne, and for five years he was powerless in the hands of his regent, Čhaophraya Si Suriyawong (Chuang Bunnag). The young man traveled abroad—to the Netherlands Indies, Singapore, Burma, and India—and he gathered about him a large group of young men, many of whom had received a Western education. When he became king in his own right in 1873, he embarked with their support on a series of fundamental reforms, announcing the abolition of slavery, changing the judicial and financial systems, and establishing a council of state and privy council to advise him. The changes provoked a strong reaction. The "second king," Wichaichan, who had been nominated in 1868 by Suriyawong in the expectation that Chulalongkorn would soon die of illness, was alarmed at the forceful moves by the king and his supporters.[4] Fearful of his own fate, he fled to the British consulate early in 1875. The British and French consuls, each moving beyond his government's instructions, attempted to make the incident an occasion for strengthening their influence in the kingdom, and for a time its survival seemed threatened. But they were thwarted by their home governments, who refused to act, while the king rallied his support. Chulalongkorn, it would appear, survived the crisis only by making promises; in the next ten years, many of the earlier reforms were rescinded, and no new ones were launched.[5]

Only in the mid-1880's, as the ministers of his father's generation began to pass from public life, could King Chulalongkorn resume his reform program. Because most families of the old nobility were slow to send their children to modern schools, the king's own brothers (he had 27) were easily the best-educated men of their generation. One by one, they were put in charge first of departments and then of ministries.

In 1885, following the urgings of some of the more impatient of his brothers and supporters, the king began the reorganization of the government into ministries structured on functional lines. The new system was inaugurated in March, 1888, with the young ministers-designate, all brothers of the king, attending cabinet meetings before their ministries were formally proclaimed. Over the next four years, departments were rearranged, new ones were created, and men were prepared and trained for the new cabinet government, which finally went into operation in April, 1892.[6]

Among the most important of the changes accompanying the reorganization was an expansion and extension of the capital's controls over the provinces and distant dependencies. Patterning their system somewhat on the model of the British in India and Burma, the Thai grouped their provinces into *monthon* (circles), controlled by commissioners who in many cases were also brothers of the king. Commissionerships were established at Luang Prabang, Chiangmai, Phuket, and Battambang in the 1870's, and then at Nongkhai, Čhampassak, Nakhọn Ratchasima (Khorat), and Ubon in the 1880's. The commissioners' powers and activities, however, became substantial only around 1890, when they began forcing the pace of reform, building local military units, and regularizing financial and judicial administration.

In most of the areas concerned, the new system marked the beginning of an important development, as the authority of Bangkok, like that of the colonial powers in the same period, spread outward, absorbing former vassals and consolidating its administrative control. But in Luang Prabang and Čhampassak it was too late, as the thrust of French imperial ambitions against Thailand increased rapidly through the 1880's. The French chose to regard Thai efforts at improving their control over outlying dependencies and at quelling the disturbances caused by the Họ in Laos as a new imperialism, which challenged the suzerain rights of Vietnam over the Lao principalities east of the Mekong.[7] They manufactured claims to territory and posted agents there, provoking incidents that were blown up into a *casus belli.* They sent columns of troops into the regions of the lower and middle Mekong, where they met stiff Thai resistance. In the tense days that followed in July, 1893, the Thai shore batteries at Paknam fired on two French gunboats forcing their way up the Čhaophraya River to Bangkok. The Thai, lacking sufficient force to roll back the French naval blockade then imposed, or to resist the military forces then in preparation on the Lao frontier, had no choice but to accept a French ultimatum demanding the surrender of all Lao territories east of the Mekong and the payment of a large indemnity.

Thai survival through the period was to a considerable degree a product of Anglo-French rivalry. Each was anxious not to border the other or to allow the other a disproportionate advantage. Bangkok played upon the rivalry and made Thailand a fulcrum for balancing the powers. The most that the French and English could agree on was to guarantee the independence of the Čhaophraya River valley in 1896. This left in doubt the fate of Thai rule on the Malay Peninsula, in the southeastern provinces bordering Cambodia, and in the whole of what is now Northeast Thailand. Bangkok was able to retain most of the above territory only through a combination of good luck, timely modernization, and diplomatic skill.

Through the king's personal diplomacy with the monarchs and governments of Europe, and through the workaday consular and embassy contacts that were Prince Devawongse's responsibility as foreign minister for forty years, Thailand cultivated a reputation abroad for responsibility and for willingness to accommodate Western demands and to reform along Western lines. The image was in part sustained by the prominence of foreign advisers in the Thai Government, with Englishmen in the Ministry of Finance, Frenchmen in the Ministry of Justice, Danes in the provincial police, and Germans in the Railways Department. They made an impressive display and contributed much useful technological advice, but it was the basic policies of the ministries for which they worked that were decisive for the future of the country. This was particularly true in the case of the Ministry of Interior under Prince Damrong Rajanubhab, which extended an increasingly modern administration over the provinces remaining in the kingdom. Prince Damrong enlarged the system of "circles" and high commissioners after all the provinces were handed over to his ministry in 1894, creating a system of provincial administration that made good use of limited numbers of modern-trained officials to administer vast areas through only eighteen *monthon* capitals. The powers and prerogatives of the princely and governors' families in the provinces rapidly eroded as they were displaced by men from the capital, or as their forest leases were bought out by the central government. This was not accomplished without resistance. In 1902, three separate rebellions broke out—in the north, in the northeast, and in Patani in the south; suppressing them with its modernized army, the central government clearly demonstrated the new techniques and strength at its disposal.[8]

Thailand survived the crisis of 1893, but the Western powers still threatened its territorial integrity from without while encroaching on its sovereignty inside. Unresolved claims and undrawn boundaries preserved the possibility of further inroads on its territory. The treaties of the 1850's restricted many of its basic taxing powers, and an oppressive system of extraterritoriality placed not only Europeans but thousands of Chinese, Lao, Cambodians, Shans, and Burmans with French and British registration certificates outside Thai legal jurisdiction. The difficulties with France were resolved in a series of treaties, which, by 1907, gave Thailand its current eastern border at the expense of territorial cessions in Laos and Cambodia, in return for an end to further claims and to French abuses of extraterritoriality in the kingdom. The British price for similar concessions was equally high; it was finally paid in 1909, when the Thai ceded four of their Malay dependencies in the south—Kedah, Perlis, Kelantan, and Trengganu—to the British.[9] The basic principle of extraterritoriality and the treaty restrictions on taxation remained in effect for some time. But the agreements after 1900 eased the pressure on Thailand's sovereignty and, above all, secured the territorial boundaries of an internationally recognized state. When the *Entente Cordiale* brought Anglo-French rivalry to an end in 1904, and when World War I broke out, Thai fears of Western imperialism rapidly diminished.

It was in the same quarter-century after 1885 that the real transformation of the internal structure of the kingdom began, with the creation of a nation knit together by administrative control and countrywide institutions within defined boundaries. A system of modern government schools spread throughout the country between 1898 and 1910, as enrollments jumped from 5,000 to 84,000 pupils. The drafting of modern legal codes, the creation of modern military services and financial and tax administration, and the ending of compulsory labor service were all accomplished within a limited space of time. Ultimately, the chief obstacle in the way of reform and modernization was not conservative opposition, which died out in the decade after 1885 as the necessity of change became clear, but rather the extremely limited educated leadership available to carry it out. When this leadership, composed for the most part of young men trained abroad, came to prominence at the very end of Chulalongkorn's reign, the success of the reform program was assured, though it was far from completed.

FRENCH INDOCHINA

Of all the political creations that the age of imperialism brought to Southeast Asia, none was more artificial than French Indochina. Loyalty to the concept of a greater Indochina never germinated among the inhabitants of that multisocietal colony, although the concept clearly had its uses for Vietnamese nationalists with traditionalist designs upon Cambodia and Laos. French rule meant different things to and evoked different responses from the Vietnamese, Cambodian, and Lao peoples, whom its ambitious framework briefly covered.

The structure of French Indochina was complex. Of its five separate administrative regions, southern Vietnam (Cochinchina), under the ultimate authority of the colonial and naval ministries in Paris, was the only colony in the narrow constitutional sense. Central Vietnam (Annam), northern Vietnam (Tonkin), Cambodia, and Laos were technically protectorates under the ultimate authority of the French Foreign Ministry. After 1887, however, all five regions were brought under the sway of a single governor-general, with headquarters in Hanoi. Five regional heads served under the governor-general: the governor of Cochinchina and the *résidents supérieurs* of Annam, Tonkin, Cambodia, and Laos. There was a general budget for the whole of Indochina and also local budgets for the five regions. By a decree of 1899, the proceeds of indirect taxes (customs, taxes on opium, alcohol, salt, etc.) were reserved for the general Indochinese government, while the revenues from direct taxes (land and poll taxes) were assigned to the regional and local administrations.

Paul Doumer, Governor-General from 1897 to 1902, was the outstanding architect of colonial institutions for Indochina. He centralized and presided over the specialized services of the colony—customs, the postal and telegraph service, forestry, and commerce—and also introduced the common general budget. During the Doumer regime, the Indochina Geographical Service was created, as well as the famous French School of the Far East (*École Française d'Extrême-Orient*) at Hanoi, a combination of language school, scientific establishment, and administrative service dedicated to the preservation of historical monuments. The governor-general was advised but not controlled by a Government Council (known as the *Conseil Supérieur de l'Indochine* from 1887 to 1911, and as the *Conseil de Gouvernement* after 1911), which considered in secret the general budget and tax assessments. It consisted of about twenty high French officials and five "indigenous high functionaries," Vietnamese, Cambodian, and Lao members chosen each year by the governor-general himself. Like the immense Doumer Bridge at Hanoi, such centralization improved communications, administrative and otherwise. But it could not impose anything more than a make-believe unity upon three quite different societies, one of which, Vietnam, was soon in revolutionary ferment.

Vietnam. The first stage of Vietnam's loss of sovereignty to the French had come in 1858–67, when the French had absorbed southern Vietnam and converted it into the Cochinchina colony. The second stage was the period 1873–85, when the French established a preponderant military presence in the north, blundered into war with China, and successfully made protectorates of northern and central Vietnam. In 1873, Admiral Dupré, the Governor of Cochinchina, sent a military expedition to the north under Francis Garnier—both to bring the north within the sphere of French colonial commerce in Saigon and to acquire such a well-defined hegemony over the Vietnamese court itself that no British or German counterinfluences could ever be established there. Styling himself "the grand mandarin Garnier," he seized the Hanoi citadel briefly but was killed by a counterattack of Vietnamese soldiers and Chinese "Black Flags" (Chinese veterans of the Taiping Rebellion who, like the Họ in Laos, had streamed across the Vietnamese frontier as organized brigands). Nine years later, another French expedition, led by Henri Rivière, arrived in the north. The Hue court, exploiting its status as a vassal, requested Chinese intervention to save northern Vietnam from French occupation. Rivière was killed, the French rejected Peking's demand that they evacuate the north, and the Sino-French war over Vietnam that ensued (June, 1884–April, 1885) resulted in the defeat of China and the loss of all independence for Vietnam. That humiliating chapter in the age of imperialism is not forgotten today in either Peking or Hanoi.

One judgment that can be made about the French colonial administration of Vietnam is that Vietnamese society was much more fragmented and the differences in customs, thought, and ways of life among its three regions more acute in 1954 than they had been in 1885. The unprecedented division of Vietnam into three formally separate administrative areas—"Cochinchina," "Tonkin," and "Annam," (the last meaning "pacified south," a T'ang Chinese colonialist term for Vietnam which the French revived)—has been noted. In the long run, the cultural impact of the French was to be strongest in the south, where they ruled directly. It was to be weakest in the center, owing both to the survival of the traditional court at Hue and to the relative absence of French entrepreneurs and capital investment in central Vietnam. But administrative fragmentation was also the practice at the subregional level. Precolonial Vietnam was divided into thirty-one provinces. Under the French, the number of provinces virtually doubled to sixty: twenty-one in the south, sixteen in the center, and twenty-three in the north. This was precisely the opposite of what Vietnamese reformers like Nguyen Truong To had proposed in the 1860's—the reduction of provincial government in the interests of efficiency and better salaries. The creation in 1888 of special French extraterritorial sectors within the three cities of Hanoi, Haiphong, and Da Nang, which the French chose to govern directly, was another example of the multiplication of local administrative barriers.

French colonial policy in Vietnam moved between the two extremes of "assimilation," which meant the cultural and institutional Gallicization of Vietnam, and "association," which implied the maintenance of traditional Vietnamese institutions as legitimizing props for French rule. The history of the colonial government at Saigon in the early 1860's demonstrated the difficulties of either course of action. At first, all higher Vietnamese mandarins were removed from power and replaced by French officers. No Vietnamese was to occupy an administrative position higher than that of canton chief. Since the French did not have enough personnel of their own to make the scheme work, it lasted only until the end of 1862, when the mandarins were returned to their posts. But because many of the Vietnamese provincial officials were anti-French, this policy also had to be jettisoned. In the third, and compromise, formula, the most important agents of the new Saigon colonial regime were the officials known as inspectors of indigenous affairs. The inspectors (of whom there were about thirty in 1868, one to every 70,000 southern Vietnamese) were officers, surgeons, or engineers of the French Navy. But in order to win promotion they had to pass tests in which they demonstrated a rudimentary knowledge of Vietnamese, of the Vietnamese law code, of Chinese characters, and even of Cambodian and Thai.

In central and northern Vietnam, the colonial government expanded its authority after 1885, not so much by installing a new administrative system of its own as by the piecemeal confiscation of traditional Vietnamese authority. The legal bases of French rule, treaties concluded between France and the Vietnamese court in 1874, 1883, and 1884, had left the Vietnamese emperor at Hue a small but unmistakable residue of power. In 1897–98 Doumer, the Governor-General, appropriated that power. In 1897, he forced the Emperor Thanh-tai to issue an edict transferring all the powers of the court's highest representative in the north (the *kinh luoc*) to a French official. To tighten French control in central Vietnam, Doumer forced Thanh-tai to permit the French *résident supérieur* at Hue to preside over meetings of the Vietnamese court's Privy Council. This meant that the ministers of the court now became the ministers of the *résident supérieur*, not of the emperor. In addition, the *résident supérieur* for central Vietnam was given the right to approve the drafts of all imperial edicts before the Vietnamese emperor could sign them with his vermilion brush. Although the Six Boards of the traditional bureaucracy continued to exist in Hue, a French official was installed at each one. He had to agree to every decision of his respective Board before the decision could be sent to the *résident supérieur* for final approval. Finally, the French appropriated the power to administer the finances of central Vietnam, denying the Vietnamese court the independent revenues the 1884 treaty had allowed it.

The form that the French consolidation of power took in the late 1890's potently influenced the course of modern Vietnamese political development. By quietly confiscating the political power of the Vietnamese court, the French destroyed the prestige of the one remaining symbol of Vietnamese unity, the monarchy, without creating any significant non-Confucian institutions to replace it. It could be said that they ruled central and northern Vietnam more through the exploitation of traditional institutions, which thus became useless to later Vietnamese patriots, than through the creation of exemplary new institutions.

Local government in central and northern Vietnam under the French was a diarchy. Day-to-day government in the thirty-nine provinces of Annam and Tonkin was handled by two parallel but separate administrations, one French, one Vietnamese. Each province had a French province chief who governed Europeans, foreign Asians, and those few Vietnamese in his province who had become French citizens. Each province also had a Vietnamese hierarchy—governor-general, governors, financial and judicial commissioners, prefects, and district magistrates—responsible for the governing of the Vietnamese. The Confucian examination system was not abolished in the center and the north until 1919, so that down to the 1930's most Vietnamese provincial officials in these two regions possessed anachronistic examination-system backgrounds. Perceptive anti-French scholars like Tran Te Xuong (1870–

1907), a degree winner of 1894, could observe that "out of ten students, nine have stopped going to school. The girls who sell books by profession close their eyes in slumber."[10] But to all appearances, the classic provincial mandarinate continued long after 1885.

In the full-fledged colony of Cochinchina, such an indigenous administration by Vietnamese officials according to Vietnamese rules did not exist. All Vietnamese were ruled by French officials according to French laws. In the south, for example, it was the French province chief who was responsible for ensuring that the land registers of each village were kept up to date, whereas in the center and north it was the Vietnamese district magistrate. But colonial rule was more uniform over all three regions than appearances might suggest. In the north, the French *résident supérieur* headed both the French and Vietnamese provincial administrations. In the center, the French *résident supérieur*, through his control of the imperial Privy Council and Six Boards, was able to control all appointments in the mandarinate down to district magistrate. Thus, even where Vietnamese continued to play a role on the political stage, they were mimes acting out a French scenario.

Cambodia. In June, 1864, following ancient custom, Norodom crowned himself King of Cambodia. He received his crown from a French naval officer sent up from Saigon and his regalia from a Thai official, for Cambodia was still a "two-headed bird." Thai influence at court, however, ceased after the treaty of 1867, by which France recognized the Thai claim to the ex-Cambodian provinces of Battambang and Siem Reap, while Thailand accepted the French protectorate over Cambodia.

Over the next twenty years, French efforts there consisted largely of ineffectual attempts to curb Norodom's powers and to tidy his fiscal procedures, with a view to siphoning off some of his revenue to pay French administrative costs. Norodom balked at the reforms, and in 1884, when he refused to allow the French to administer Cambodian customs fees, France presented him with an eleven-point ultimatum, disguised as a convention, which permanently limited his powers. The document abolished slavery, permitted the alienation of land, extended the French resident's powers, and stated that Norodom was to agree to "such administrative, judicial, financial, and commercial reforms as the French Republic might, in the future, consider useful."[11]

While Norodom objected most to the reduction of his fiscal independence, the provisions relating to land and slavery cut across the interests of the provincial elite, heretofore unaffected by the French presence. In early 1885, the provincial elite precipitated a rebellion against the French. Hostilities lasted until the end of 1886, when the French agreed to postpone application of the controversial portions of the convention.[12]

Norodom's role in the rebellion is obscure, but the part played by his younger brother, Sisowath, in helping the French to put it down was well known. Before and after the events of 1884–86, the French made no secret of the fact that they preferred Sisowath to Norodom, and a French *résident* in the 1890's tried unsuccessfully to have Norodom declared insane with the aim of accelerating Sisowath's accession. After Norodom died in 1904, Sisowath was placed on the throne. He was too frightened of his brother, even in death, to officiate at his cremation. Shortly after his own coronation, in 1906, Sisowath left on a state visit to France, where the Parisians were "delighted with his blandness and courtesy."[13]

During their first forty years in Cambodia, which coincided with Norodom's reign, the French destroyed a few Cambodian institutions, renovated some, and froze others into place. The traditions of provincial autonomy, debt bondage and dynastic warfare, for example, were slowly eroded, while the machinery of tax collection, royal monopolies, and palace administration was rebuilt to meet French needs. On the other hand, the Buddhist Sangha, the local judicial system, village education, and the nonadministrative aspects of kingship, to name only four, were allowed to function undisturbed. Paradoxically, as the French reduced the powers of the king, the stability their presence brought to his realm had the effect of gradually increasing his prestige. The annual allowance granted Norodom by the French from local taxes, for example, probably exceeded the revenues of any other nineteenth-century Cambodian king. Although Norodom was, in effect, a hostage of the French, they made no effort to diminish the ceremonial and religious aspects of the monarchy, which were the ones that linked Norodom directly with his people. By reducing the king's freedom of action, the French increased the effectiveness of the Cambodian monarchy as an ongoing institution.

In 1907, when Thailand returned the provinces of Battambang and Siem Reap to the French protectorate of Cambodia, the kingdom had filled out to its present size. Minor frontier adjustments were made until the 1930's, always by the French without consulting the wishes of the Cambodian monarch or his government, whose functions had shrunk to those connected with ceremonies and provincial administration.

Laos. The political entity called Laos, confined for the first time in its history almost entirely to the eastern bank of the Mekong River, united for the first time since 1693, and with three of its four principalities ruled (without princes) by the French, formed a new state in Southeast Asia, largely by virtue of the lines the French had arbitrarily drawn around it.

Until the end of World War II, Laos was governed under rather casual *ad hoc* arrangements. In the north, the protected principality of Luang Prabang, where a single monarch, Sisavangvong, reigned from 1905 until his death in 1959, was under indirect French rule. The three other Lao principalities—Xieng Khouang, Vientiane, and Čhampassak

—were administered more directly. Both forms of governance were in the hands of a French *résident* in Vientiane.

French rule in Laos, such as it was, was lightened by the cooperation of traditional leaders, the mildness of French economic involvement, the country's isolation, and the compliance of the Lao population. French novels about Laos alternate between rapture and glassiness, without suggesting that administrative matters occupied much of a typical Frenchman's day.[14] Financially, the administration ran at a deficit, balanced by profits from operations in Cambodia and the components of Vietnam. By 1943, less than 30,000 of its population—estimated very roughly at a million—inhabited provincial towns, including the capital, and two-thirds of those were immigrants from Vietnam. As in Cambodia, the French arrived just in time to remove the Lao from Thai protection. By drawing lines on the map, freezing the Luang Prabang dynasty in place, and securing the fondness of key figures in the Lao regional elite, the French bought time, for the Lao and for themselves, in which to proceed slowly on what they viewed as their civilizing mission there and elsewhere in Indochina.

ISLAND SOUTHEAST ASIA

Between 1870 and 1910, the dominant political processes of incorporation and internal reorganization were much the same in the islands as on the mainland of Southeast Asia. But the results showed up more strikingly on the map, for in 1870 much of the geographical expanse of the archipelago had not yet been painted in any imperial color. It consisted of a whole world of small societies and *negeri*, predominantly Malayo-Muslim, still intact, and carrying on their own separate histories. The zone resembled that of the Shan and Lao principalities of the interior mainland in its political fragmentation and autonomy, but it stretched over a far wider area, its population was substantially larger, and, as events showed, it had greater economic potential. Perched around the rim of this vast no man's, or many men's, land were the stronger states of the archipelago: Dutch Java, with the largest population in Southeast Asia, the Catholic Philippines, and the naval and commercial power represented by the British Straits Settlements.

Just as the larger mainland states had always possessed spheres of political influence in the Shan and Lao world, so the British and Dutch had long been paramount naval powers among the islands, and they, together with the Spanish, maintained their spheres of influence there. These spheres had been growing more distant in the half-century before 1870. The small societies and *negeri* within each sphere—vassals, allies, and victims—were often rather severely cramped by the attentions of the paramount powers. Nevertheless, as on the mainland, these were still spheres of influence—an influence only as strong as the most recent punitive expedition or the latest grateful pretender helped to a throne.

Around 1870—somewhat earlier in the case of the Spanish—the imperial powers began to press more heavily on the lesser *negeri* and peoples around them. Within a few decades they had divided up the whole island world and imposed effective administrative control on all but a few areas inside the new boundaries. It is a measure of the political creativity of those accomplishments that all three major nations of island Southeast Asia today have names of European rather than local origin.[15] The changes after 1870 were least significant for the Philippines; it had acquired its Spanish name and its Catholic core in Luzon and the Bisayas in the sixteenth century, adding only a modest-sized Muslim region in the south in the late nineteenth century. The British-controlled area, finally sewn together formally as Malaysia in 1963, was a new creation of the high colonial period, a sector carved more or less arbitrarily out of the Malayo-Muslim world itself. Around the massive old core of Java, finally, the Dutch built up a 3,000-mile arc of island possessions into a new Netherlands Indies, which became Indonesia—much the largest, most heavily populated, and culturally diverse of the new states of twentieth-century Southeast Asia.

The Netherlands East Indies. The political system centering on Dutch Batavia in 1870 may be viewed, in a thoroughly Southeast Asian way, as a series of circles of influence. At the center was Batavia itself, where the governor-general controlled a small but relatively efficient bureaucratic apparatus, a small but relatively well-trained and effectively led Royal Netherlands Indies Army of about 35,000, and an even smaller naval force. The core of Batavia's domain comprised Java (with Madura), whose population of more than 17 million people was governed in the first instance by an elite administrative corps of not much more than 100 Dutch officials. Alongside and below them was a somewhat larger class of *priyayi* officials headed by some 80 quasi-hereditary regents. The next circle, outside Java, embraced a number of areas under direct Dutch administration, notably Ambon and several other islands in the Moluccas acquired in the great age of the spice trade in the seventeenth century, the tin-rich island of Bangka off South Sumatra, and the Minangkabau heartlands in West Sumatra, conquered in the 1830's and yielding a modest profit from forced coffee cultivation. Finally, Batavia exercised a general suzerainty over most of the small *negeri* and societies on the broad sweep of islands from Sumatra to New Guinea, a suzerainty that required frequent and costly raids to maintain and that went little deeper than acceptance of Dutch overlordship by still-sovereign local polities.

As its familiar local name—*Kumpeni,* from the old Dutch East India Company—suggests, this wide and loose political system was as much a Southeast Asian state as a Netherlands domain overseas. The *Kumpeni* was founded on Dutch power, but Dutch power working mainly through the institutions of those subject to its influence, and thus through Javan *priyayi* and archipelago sultans and chiefs. Its internal organization reflected two and a half centuries of association between the Dutch and the peoples of Java and the archipelago under conditions in which the Dutch enjoyed few real advantages, apart from superior discipline and organization, over the overwhelmingly larger local populations.

After about 1870, however, the cumulative effects of the scientific and industrial revolution began to overturn the ancient parity between Dutch organization and Malaysian numbers. The *Kumpeni* began to change internally and at the same time to extend its area of direct rule, much as Bangkok was doing in the same years under Chulalongkorn. The new forces at work in the areas outside Java during the last decades of the nineteenth century are well illustrated by events in three adjacent areas of North Sumatra that around 1870 were in or just beyond the outermost circle of *Kumpeni* influence. Among the Toba Bataks, a sizeable wet-rice–growing people in the interior not far north of Minangkabau, the decisive development was the arrival of German missionaries of the Rhenish Mission in the 1860's. The Tobas, still pagans on a largely Muslim Sumatra, responded promptly to the prospects opened by this encounter. By 1900, a large proportion had adopted Christianity, channeling through it a new dynamism that was to give them a disproportionately important role in twentieth-century Indonesia. Drawn along in the wake of this folk movement, Batavia found it fairly easy to extend systematic administration over the whole Toba area by the 1890's.

In the coastal area centering on modern Medan, to the north of the Tobas, the prime agent of change was the development, after 1863, of Dutch tobacco plantations. The petty sultanates of the area owed a shadowy allegiance to the sultan of Siak, farther down the coast, and he in turn had nominally ceded all his domains to Batavia in 1858—political formulas quite typical of the *Kumpeni* period. But the success and rapid expansion of the plantations brought in immigrant Chinese, Javanese, and Dutch to overwhelm the original inhabitants, and by 1900 their sultans were stuffed (with emoluments) and mounted on display in what was now a thoroughly Dutch-administered East Coast Residency of Sumatra.

Batavia's most important late-nineteenth-century attempt at direct military expansion outside Java, in the large independent Sultanate of Acheh on the northern end of Sumatra, was for a long time spectacularly unsuccessful. The effort began in 1873 as little more than a conventional *Kumpeni* raid, stimulated by fear of imperial competition and intended simply to enforce subservience on an unruly "native state." It proved tolerably easy to occupy the capital and for a time to envassal the sultan, but, as in Upper Burma and northern Vietnam after 1885, the move only opened the way for lesser chiefs and the folk to begin a widespread guerrilla resistance. Indeed, for the next quarter of a century, it was often the Dutch forces that were resisting and the Achehnese who seemed on the point of winning. The Acheh War—it was "the Dutch War" for the Achehnese, of course—nearly bankrupted Batavia and tied up much of its small army, and in this way it prevented any rapid expansion of Batavia's authority elsewhere in the archipelago in the period.

Outside Java, change was not general or uniform in the last decades of the nineteenth century but instead was confined to particular areas, such as North Sumatra. Much of the outer circle of *Kumpeni* influence remained essentially as it had been in 1870 or even in the seventeenth century. Meanwhile, on Java, the process of defeudalization, begun prematurely in the time of Daendels and Raffles and then reversed in the early years of Van den Bosch's Culture System, resumed in earnest.[16] In a setting of booming export industries (lowland sugar, now in private hands, and upland tea, coffee, and cinchona plantations), of railroad building (150 miles in 1873, 1,200 in 1900), of newspapers, the telegraph, and modern banks, the comfortable old feudal association between the *priyayi* and the Dutch began to lose its meaning. In the world into which Achmad Djajadiningrat was born in 1877, the Regency of Serang, in Bantam, was conceived of as a *negeri;* as a boy, he served as a page in the court of his uncle, the regent, and was trained in the feudal ethics of the Javan *priyayi.* By 1901, he had been ushered through a Dutch-language education and was himself installed as one of the first of a modern class of regents, no longer lords of *negeri,* except perhaps to their peasant subjects, but members of an elite, Java-wide corps of Javan officials.[17] Djajadiningrat was ahead of his time, but in the 1860's regents and Dutch officials lost their "cultivation percentages"; in 1874, the parallel European and native administrative services were reorganized and rationalized; and in 1882 regents were deprived of their rights to levy peasant labor for personal services. Dutch residents and other officials maintained their outward signs of feudal status for a time, but they increasingly plunged into paperwork and developed new specialist services, such as those for irrigation and forestry. The old-style regents and *priyayi* increasingly became decorative fixtures, while Dutch officials carried on an ever more modern administration.

A new wave of change began on Java after the turn of the century, in the first triumphant years of the "Ethical Policy." Among other things, the period saw the beginning of Dutch-language education for all *priyayi* and the penetration of modern administrative innovations to the village level. Several of the factors that contributed to the changes on Java also facilitated a new imperial movement in the islands beyond, where Dutch advances of the late nineteenth century, blocked by the Acheh War, were quickly brought to conclusion. The "Ethical Policy," a Dutch version of the "white man's burden," provided a convincing rationale for reorganizing and not merely presiding over the political affairs of the archipelago. The acute budgetary pinch beginning in the mid-1870's was eased by new taxes at the end of the century; government revenue doubled between 1899 and 1912. Other factors were peculiar to the situation outside Java. The KPM (Koninklijk Paketvaart Maatschappij, or Royal Steamship Company) began operations in 1891 in order to break the virtual British monopoly of steam shipping and to lessen the tendency of archipelago trade to flow through Singapore rather than Batavia. As a semiofficial line, it provided mail service and troop ships for the government, operating at a loss, if necessary, in marginal areas. Its growing net of routes and services drew together the Dutch-controlled islands as never before.

The Acheh War, too, was finally ended. After 1896, Dutch forces had shifted to a new strategy of ceaseless attack and patrol, and, by 1902, the Achehnese were at last fairly well subdued, in practice if not in spirit. The effects were many. The financial drain was finally ended, and troops were released for service elsewhere. Acheh produced, in the person of the army commander who had developed and applied the new policy, a classic example of an imperial governor-general, J. B. van Heutz (1904–9). The *marechaussee*, the lightly armed, highly mobile special force so decisive in harrying the resistance in Acheh, proved a powerful tool for achieving the same results elsewhere in the islands.

By a series of quick thrusts, the remaining *negeri* and societies of Batavia's old outer sphere were brought under effective administrative control. When van Heutz retired in 1909, more than 200 such states and chiefdoms had signed the Short Declaration introduced in 1898, which specified simply that they acknowledged Dutch rule and undertook to obey all Dutch orders concerning their lands. In those same years, the Dutch tariff law of 1873, originally applied only to Java and directly administered areas outside, was rapidly extended over most of the archipelago. Dutch currency steadily supplanted the great variety of coins customary in the different island areas and built up yet another uniformity, as did the ever spreading services of the KPM. Thus, by 1910, in the "outer islands" as well as on Java, the *Kumpeni* was dead. In its place had arisen a new, comprehensive, and increasingly uniform Netherlands East Indies.

British Malaya. In January, 1874, following an arranged appeal to the British by Raja Abdullah, one of the unsuccessful claimants to the disputed throne of the west-coast Malay *negeri* of Perak, three small groups of men met on the island of Pangkor, off the Perak coast. One of the groups was Malay, consisting principally of a number of the more important chiefs in the state, including Abdullah, but not the *de facto* sultan, Ismail, nor the remaining possible contender. The second group was Chinese, principally the leaders of the two rival secret societies that had been fighting over the tin fields of the Larut District of Perak. The third was British, led by the newly appointed governor of the Straits Settlements, Sir Andrew Clarke. Clarke had arrived in Singapore only a few weeks earlier, with instructions from the Colonial Office to inquire into and report on the current disturbances in the west-coast *negeri* and, in particular, to say whether or not he considered it advisable to appoint a British officer to reside in any of the states. In his brief acquaintance with the Straits, Clarke had come easily to share the view of the mercantile community there, which wanted intervention. Not one to waste time making recommendations to London, he arranged the Pangkor meeting to accomplish three things: to settle once and for all the disputed Perak succession, preferably in favor of Abdullah; to end the fighting among the Chinese miners; and to install a British officer with sufficient powers to bring order to the *negeri* in the interests of economic exploitation of its resources by aliens.

Within a week, these ends had been achieved, and the assembled Malay chiefs signed before the governor what became known as the Pangkor Engagement, a document providing that Raja Abdullah be recognized as sultan by the signatories; that the Perak court receive a British officer to be styled Resident, "whose advice must be asked and acted upon on all questions other than those touching Malay Religion and Custom"; and that the collection and control of all revenues and the general administration of the state be regulated under the advice of the Resident.

Certain of the fictions embodied in the document, and in the circumstances in which it was signed, were later to provide a continuing theoretical justification for the arrogation by the British of all effective power and authority not merely in Perak but in most of the remaining *negeri* of the peninsula. The "inability of the Malays to govern themselves," a cardinal clause in the arguments put forward to warrant the initial acts of intervention (though it was increasingly difficult to sustain for later episodes), was happily testified to by Abdullah's letter to Clarke—inspired by Clarke and drafted by a Singapore lawyer in touch with Abdullah—which asked for "advice and assistance" in the running of the state. For Abdullah, who certainly assented to the letter even if he did not write it, the request was probably a ritual one, part of the traditional pattern of seeking help from stronger powers in the course of a contest for succession. Yet even if it were to be taken seriously, the best advice, in view of the admitted problems of exercising effective central authority in a Malay *negeri* in circumstances of disparate district wealth and mass immigration of warring Chinese miners, might well have been, "Get rid of the Chinese." But getting rid of the Chinese was the last thing the British had in mind. On the contrary, the key to any understanding of the agreement reached at Pangkor between the two principal groups—British officials and a section of the Malay ruling class—is supplied by the silent presence of the third, the Chinese miners and merchants. Thus emerged the creation myth of the British presence: That intervention was undertaken in the interests of the Malays themselves, which interests, it was said, would naturally remain paramount.

If that was the first and largest fiction during the creation of what became known as "British Malaya," a series of smaller enabling fictions followed. In Perak, and later in Selangor, Negri Sembilan, and Pahang, the fiction of the Resident's "advice" failed to obscure the reality that it was the Resident and his English bureaucracy who ruled, the sultan and his chiefs who advised and, occasionally, assisted. When federation of the four states was pushed through in 1895, in the interests not of the Malays but of British administrative convenience, the sultans were assured that in signing the new agreement they would not "in the slightest degree . . . be curtailing the right of self-government which they at present enjoy." A cynic might observe, of course, that these words described the situation exactly. Later still, in 1909, when a Federal Council was created as a supra-state legislative body, largely at the instance of the burgeoning European rubber interests and in order to curb the authority of the Resident-General of the Federated States, the argument was that the Council would restore to the sultans some of the authority they had lost at federation. But they sat merely as ordinary members, listening to proceedings conducted in a language they did not understand.

The Malay ruling class in the Federated States accepted the steady extension of British control over their affairs after 1874 for a variety of reasons. In the first place, in the early stages of intervention, those who rebelled were put down by force, as in Perak in 1875 and Pahang in the early 1890's. In the atmosphere of acceptance so engendered, it made sense to settle for what one could get—a political pension commensurate with previous income from tax and toll, subordinate office in the administration as a "superintendent of *penghulus*," or a seat in the early state councils, the appointive legislative assemblies of the separate states and advisory bodies to the Residents. For a sultan, acceptance of British rule entailed a reasonable income from the civil list, new and more elaborate palaces and other proud appurtenances, and, perhaps most important of all, the sort of respect and recognition for his position as head of state that would render *de facto* within Malay society itself the authority that had in the past so often been merely *de jure*. What the protectorate system protected most of all was the shape and structure of the traditional society, from the top down.

All this resembled what was going on in Kengtung, Banjarmasin, and dozens of other sparsely populated areas of Southeast Asia in this period. What set it off and gave it a fateful significance was the development in west-coast Malaya of a distinct new society, created by Chinese and British entrepreneurship, alongside the traditional Malay one. The two decades before the 1901 census saw an increase in the combined population of Perak and Selangor alone from about 130,000 to nearly 600,000, the larger part of it representing alien, predominantly Chinese, immigration. Though the process resembled patterns of development prior to 1874, which had, in fact, contributed to British intervention, the magnitude of the resulting demographic change marked it as an innovation in kind rather than degree. Immigration grew with the booming export economy; the value of exports, mainly tin, from the protected states rose from less than half a million Straits dollars in 1875 to more than 60 million in 1900. This in turn required and stimulated the building of railroads, roads, and other communications, which penetrated the western side of the peninsula and tied it together in ways impossible before. Finally, the establishment of a single European administrative service for the Malay States and the Straits Settlements as a whole produced an overlying uniformity in such diverse matters as public education, land legislation, and fiscal organization. Most of the changes had little to do with either peasant or prince, though it is true that the Malays reaped incidental benefits both from the *Pax Britannica* and from the rise in the general level of prosperity.

Between 1909 and 1914, British control over the remainder of the Malay *negeri* of the peninsula (save the territories to the north, still administered as provinces of Thailand) was completed by the acquisition of Kedah, Perlis, Kelantan, and Trengganu in the north, and Johore in the south. All of them in due course accepted "advisers" on the pattern of the residents of the Federated States, but with slightly reduced powers, which (reflecting the strength of the ruling elites in Kedah and Johore, and the unattractiveness of Kelantan and Trengganu to the export economy) left Malay participation in the governance of the state somewhat more intact. These states became known collectively as the Unfederated States, for they resisted all blandishments to join the federation. In an important sense, however, the peninsula of Malaya, "British Malaya," formed a unity after 1914, bounded by British political control.

British Borneo. About the same time that the British were extending control in the peninsula, there was a similar forward movement in northern Borneo, a movement not wholly British but ultimately under British auspices. Already in the 1840's the leading coastal state of the area, Brunei, had granted the district of Sarawak to "Raja" James Brooke, an English adventurer, in return for assistance in putting down a Dayak revolt against overbearing Brunei Malays. During the next thirty years, Brooke absorbed other pieces of Brunei territory, moving northward up the coast, and he sought in vain to get formal British protectorate status for his domain. His nephew, Charles Brooke, who succeeded him in 1868, was at first no more successful in the latter quest. Eager to improve Sarawak's trading prospects and to continue the extension of its dominion at the expense of Brunei, Brooke tried to persuade the British to countenance his own absorption of the Sultanate. Irritated at his attempts at territorial aggrandizement, the British Foreign Office refused to concur, continuing to insist on Brunei's integrity.

Meanwhile, the Sultan of Sulu, plagued by increasingly heavy intrusions by Spanish and other Europeans and by falling profits from the Borneo parts of his loose naval and trading domain, was open to persuasion, as the Sultan of Brunei had been earlier in dealing with James Brooke. In 1865, he entered into the first of a series of engagements by which he leased, sold, ceded, or otherwise transferred his claims to the northern part of Borneo to Western entrepreneurs. The precise form of the transactions has been a matter of international dispute in recent years, but the sultan's overriding interest throughout was the promise of annual payments for what was by now, for him, a lost cause. His Western counterparts—Americans, an Austro-Hungarian consul, and Englishmen—followed one another in untidy succession, but eventually, in 1881, the situation stabilized. The British Government granted a royal charter to a newly-created North Borneo Company for the exploitation of the part of northern Borneo now known as Sabah under certain conditions, including the supervision of its foreign relations by Britain.

The grant of the charter made it difficult for the British Government to continue to oppose further acquisition of territory by Sarawak, but the growing rivalry between Brooke and the company for the rest of Brunei's territories threatened to extinguish the sultanate, and in 1888 Whitehall finally extended formal British protection to all three states. Though some erosion of Brunei on both the north and the south continued, it finally came to an end in 1906, when the sultan accepted a British resident, on the pattern of those already established in the peninsular states.

From that time forward, though all three territories in Borneo were administered separately, they were linked in some degree at the top by the governor of the Straits Settlements, who functioned as high commissioner for Borneo as well as the Malay states. Supervision of administration in Borneo was, however, considerably less than in the peninsula, and Sabah and Sarawak in particular developed along somewhat different lines. The governor of North Borneo ruled unhampered by all but a small advisory council consisting of five officials, a European planter, and a Chinese (later, a wholly appointed legislative council). In Sarawak, Brooke, who prided himself on his enlightened principles of government, did in fact do something to draw the peoples of the state into consultation by means of the Council Negri (most of whose Sarawak members, however, were Malays, very much a minority community in the state), and the General Council, which, held less frequently, was attended by upriver Dayak leaders as well. Both states were characterized by the kind of paternalism that does not hasten to see its children grow up.

The Philippines. Developments in the Philippines in the same decades were in some ways atypical. By 1870, Luzon and the Bisayas had already been ruled as a Spanish colony for three centuries, but Spain was in eclipse in Europe, and the economy in the Philippines was dominated by the British and Chinese. The islands were attractive to the rising imperial powers—Germany, Japan, and the United States. Moreover, Philippine society at the time was undergoing rapid change of a sort unknown elsewhere in Southeast Asia until the early twentieth century, which meant that Spanish rule was threatened internally by the prospect of a nationalist revolution. At the close of the century, both dangers materialized. In 1896, a revolution broke out, and two years later the United States went to war with Spain, defeating the Spanish forces at Manila and compelling Spain to surrender the Philippines for the price of $20 million.

In other respects, however, developments in the Philippines did resemble those elsewhere in Southeast Asia. Internal reorganization after 1870 proceeded much as in Java, the other old and locally ingrown European domain. The fiscal structure of the colony was reorganized with the abolition of the tobacco monopoly in 1881 and with a general tax reform in 1884. In 1886, there was an attempt at modernization of provincial administration with the appointment of provincial comptrollers and with the rearrangement of provincial governorships. The Spanish penal, civil, and commercial codes were extended to cover all inhabitants in the colony; the Becerra Law of 1889 established town councils (*ayuntamientos*) similar to those in Spain itself; and, in 1893, the Maura Law modernized municipal organization. In general, then, the quasi-feudal patterns of an earlier age were modified as the Spanish attempted the shift from a loose, indirect rule to a centralized, nonecclesiastical, direct rule.

Spanish expansion southward from Luzon and the Bisayas paralleled attempts at internal reorganization. Manila had long claimed Mindanao and the Sulu Islands as part of its domain, but, apart from the northern shore of Mindanao and an outpost at Zamboanga, it had never been able to validate its claim against the Muslim sultanates and peoples there. In the mid-nineteenth century, spurred on by the fear that those areas would fall to other European powers and buttressed by superior technology in the form of the steamship, the Spanish pushed south. In 1847, they permitted a Basque soldier of fortune, Oyanguren, "last of the *conquistadores*," to mount a private expedition against the Muslims on the Gulf of Davao. He did, in fact, succeed in bringing that area under Spanish control. In 1859, the Jesuits were permitted to return to their missionary work in Mindanao, and for the next four decades they encouraged the Spanish Government to subdue the remaining Muslim strongholds, especially the Sulu sultanate.

The southward advance secured Manila's claims to the south against potential European rivals, but it still fell far short of effective administrative control. Not until the Americans replaced the Spanish in the Philippines was the Muslim south finally "pacified" and integrated into the colony. The Americans, full of imperial vigor, had a more efficient army and, as Protestants representing a secular state, aroused much less religious hostility than the Spanish had in three centuries of holy war. In August, 1899, an American general, John Bates, negotiated an agreement with the Sultan of Sulu, promising stipends, religious liberty, and protection in return for allegiance and for an end to the slave trade and marauding. The Bates Treaty with the sultanate seemed too lenient to men like Leonard Wood, who became commander of the "Moro" Province. He viewed the Muslim leadership as "corrupt, licentious, and cruel . . . nothing more or less than an unimportant collec-

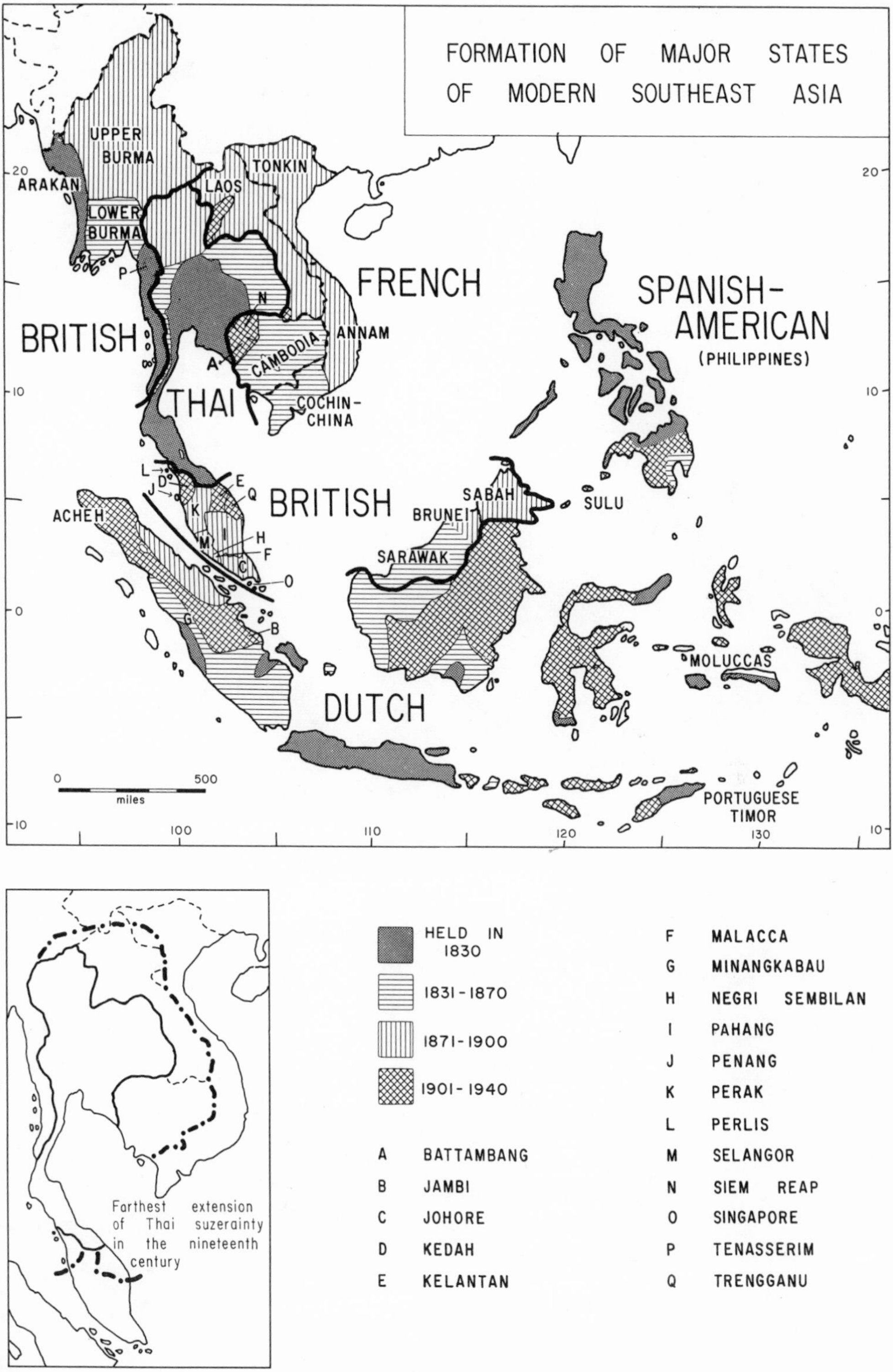

FORMATION OF MAJOR STATES OF MODERN SOUTHEAST ASIA

UPPER BURMA
ARAKAN
LOWER BURMA
TONKIN
LAOS
FRENCH
SPANISH-AMERICAN (PHILIPPINES)
BRITISH
ANNAM
CAMBODIA
THAI
COCHIN-CHINA
BRITISH
SABAH
SULU
ACHEH
BRUNEI
SARAWAK
MOLUCCAS
DUTCH
PORTUGUESE TIMOR
0 500 miles
20 10 0 10
100 110 120 130

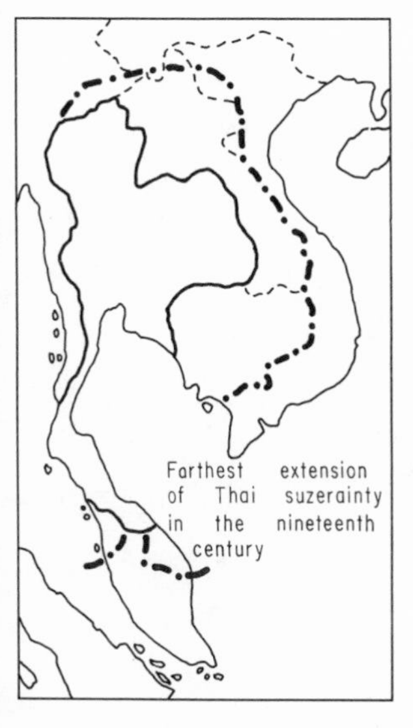

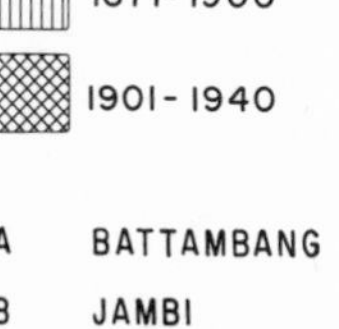

A BATTAMBANG
B JAMBI
C JOHORE
D KEDAH
E KELANTAN
F MALACCA
G MINANGKABAU
H NEGRI SEMBILAN
I PAHANG
J PENANG
K PERAK
L PERLIS
M SELANGOR
N SIEM REAP
O SINGAPORE
P TENASSERIM
Q TRENGGANU

tion of pirates and highwaymen" and imposed a much harder line.[18] Diplomacy and leniency were replaced by military pressure: In 1906, for example, 600 Muslims were killed at the massacre of Bud Dajo on Jolo Island. The Americans, however, never threatened the legitimacy of the sultan, calling him "the titular spiritual head of the Mohammedan Church in the Sulu Archipelago."[19] A Muslim south was thus incorporated into what became in time the Philippine Republic.

21

BUREAUCRATIC AND ECONOMIC FRAMEWORKS

It might seem surprising, in view of the political turmoil in Southeast Asia after 1941, that the often quite arbitrary boundaries imposed on the political map of the area by about 1910 should be virtually identical with those of today. Even the obvious exception, French Indochina, which has fallen apart again into its three cultural components of Vietnam, Cambodia, and Laos, bears out the rule, for those components still retain the boundaries drawn for them by the French. It might also seem surprising, in view of the intensity of anticolonial feelings since 1941, that great old capitals such as Mandalay, Hue, Surakarta, and Jogjakarta have remained the secondary towns they became in the colonial period, while the capitals of independent Burma, Indonesia, and Malaysia are the upstart colonial capitals of Rangoon, Jakarta, and Kuala Lumpur.

Such curious details show how deep a reorganization took place within the political units created at first by mere conquest. Rangoon remained the capital of independent Burma because during the high colonial period it became the seat of a modern administrative network, a new judicial system, and ultimately a Legislative Council, as well as the hub of a modern sea, rail, and river transport network and the focus of a ramifying tax, banking, and credit system. The Union of Burma retained the same boundaries as British Burma because these interlocking bureaucratic and economic structures had created a new interdependence for all who lived within those boundaries and, by the same token, increasingly separated them from all who lived beyond.

At the same time, the growing bureaucratic and economic frameworks both built upon and hastened the pervasive economic transformations of the period. Growing bureaucracies became possible because of rapid economic growth, and at the same time they served to further it. Export taxes on Thai rice and Malayan tin did much to finance the railway systems built in those countries, while the railways in turn facilitated further rapid increases in exports. Rising receipts from taxes on peasants helped to pay for irrigation works in Java and Cochinchina, and newly irrigated areas accommodated new hundreds of thousands of peasant taxpayers. In these ways, conquest, new frameworks, and sweeping economic movements reinforced each other in a cycle of revolutionary change.

BUREAUCRATIC FRAMEWORKS

To understand the origins of modern bureaucratic government in late-nineteenth-century Southeast Asia, one should begin not with charts in the offices of power but with the cultural milieu in which new experiments in organization were first carried out. One should look at the photographs of the time: Achehnese chiefs posed proudly and somewhat menacingly in front of a thatched hut, Thai court ladies in the crew-cut hair style of the time, Chinese with pigtails, Vietnamese mandarins in their long robes, and, alongside them, beefy Europeans in field boots or covered with sashes and medals. One should read the reports of such European visitors as Crawfurd, Pavie, and the governess Anna Leonowens and the autobiographies of Achmad Djajadiningrat and Munshi Abdullah—all, in their ways, explorers of strange lands. One should read the last section of Joseph Conrad's novel, in which Jim comes to Patusan and there finds his vocation, bringing peace and order to the small valley and becoming its Lord Jim.

Gunboats and uniformed troops established physical power—that was not new to Southeast Asians—but had nothing to say about how it would be exercised afterward. The building of modern administrations was above all a great cultural achievement—in the minds of the aliens holding the new power, who came to envision a net of administration cast over these variegated lands with their old familiar ways of government; in the meeting of these men and older indigenous elites, and the accommodations they came to; and eventually, most significant of all, in the minds of Southeast Asians themselves.

The process began with, and within, the colonial administrative elites holding power in 1870 or acquiring it soon after, and the modernizing Thai elite grouped around Chulalongkorn and his brothers. They were tiny minorities—tinier, perhaps, than most ruling elites. But what was fundamental to their situation was the degree to which they differed culturally from their subjects. Most, of course, were Christian conquerers among Buddhists, Muslims, and Confucians, speaking foreign languages and wearing trousers. More important yet—for Chulalongkorn was Thai, and the Spanish were Catholic like the Filipinos—they were separated from those they ruled by their modern education. Most, therefore, believed in progress and saw power primarily as a means to effect change. Sharing basic attitudes that set them strikingly apart, and themselves mostly civil servants in bureaucratic harness, they formed tightly knit groups with what might fairly be called revolutionary goals, though the description would have horrified them.

At the beginning of the high colonial period the goals were still largely potential. The new administrations, even where they were not newly inaugurated or politically precarious, still did not reach very far outward or downward. Communications were poor, and both colonial governors and their subordinates in the field operated very much on their own initiative. Field officers lived far apart in their separate districts and, at a time when few European women came to Southeast Asia, took Southeast Asian mistresses and wives. In such conditions, accommodation to local practice—in way of life and style of rule—was almost universal. In the older European-ruled areas, like the Christian Philippines and Java, such accommodation had become systematized and had the inertia of tradition. In newer colonial areas, the same circumstances led to wide variations in practice and highly personal systems of government. Conrad's Lord Jim had dozens of counterparts in real life, such as the well-known late-nineteenth-century Malayan district officer Humphrey Berkeley, the "King of Grik."

But the solidarity of the administrative elites was strong, and the germ of change was deeply planted in them. Berkeley's "kingdom," like the loose supervision exercised by the first of Chulalongkorn's royal commissioners over Lao principalities like Chiangmai in the 1870's and 1880's, was a frontier institution in an expanding bureaucratic system. In the last decades of the nineteenth century, as administrations gained greater revenues, better communications, and more staff, the older accommodations began to give way. A new generation of colonial officers came out imbued with a stronger sense of mission and of superiority. In a series of circulars issued in the years after 1900, the Netherlands Indies Government discouraged its officials from using the ceremonial appurtenances by which they had symbolized their Javan-style rule. Colonial officials more often married European wives, creating tensions revealed in Somerset Maugham's Malayan short stories, which return obsessively to the theme of wives, "native" mistresses, and Eurasian children. In noncolonial Thailand, the new elite around Chulalongkorn was Thai to begin with, remaining so in many of its essential values. But in the 1880's, "Young Siam" was in some ways so different from the conservative bureaucratic nobility it was replacing that its representatives were like foreigners. They consciously followed European administrative organization and behavior, kept regular office hours, dressed in modified European fashion, and began to conduct business in a pattern of paperwork quite unlike the personal administration of their elders.

Such changes in life style reflected the growing self-confidence and broadening vision of change among the small groups in the upper echelons of the new administrations. Such men were often more earnest and idealistic than their predecessors, who in the pioneer days had had a well-founded skepticism about the degree of change they could bring about. As a group, though, they lacked the personal charm of so many of the older generation, spoke local languages less fluently or not at all, and often misunderstood the societies they thought they were improving. By about 1900, almost everywhere in Southeast Asia, they had become bureaucrats in fully routinized general administrative services, which governed the countries of the area with an increasingly efficient but cold hand.

In the last decades of the nineteenth century, while the colonial and Thai elites were being thus transformed, other changes were taking place in the relations between them and the subordinate Southeast Asian elites with which they dealt. From their first arrival, the tiny minorities of European rulers had found it prudent, convenient, and, in fact, absolutely necessary to leave direct governance of the masses of the population to whatever traditional Southeast Asian leaders and classes would cooperate with them. Such groups varied enormously among themselves, in the nature of their ties to particular European regimes, and in the changes in these ties, but there were three main patterns in the period.

The numerous small states and societies of the Shan/Lao and Malayo-Muslim zones were in general the last to be brought under firm imperial (or Thai) control, mostly in the years around 1900. In those areas, as generally elsewhere, the colonial powers began with forms of indirect rule, recognizing kings, sultans, chiefs, and other traditional leaders, harnessing them with separate treaties or agreements, and posting political agents to supervise and instruct them. Throughout those areas, with a few notable exceptions, the comparatively loose administrative arrangements continued in effect until quite recent times. Before 1900, much the same was true, for quite different reasons, of overseas Chinese communities, which largely governed themselves through "secret societies" and other institutions of their own, dealing with the ruling powers through leaders generally called—in the Malay world at least —*Kapitan China*.

A much swifter and further-reaching pattern of change in the relations between central administrations and traditional elites characterized a second group of areas, including the west coast Malay States, Sumatra's East Coast Residency, Java, Thailand, northern and central Vietnam, and, to some extent, Cambodia. All were originally governed under formulas of indirect rule, but in the course of the late nineteenth century the growing power of the colonial and Thai governments overtook that form of political insurance. Moreover, the rapid economic change or large populations of these areas called for increasingly complex administrative methods. The central administrative elites that extended and manned these systems, eager to run things their own way and increasingly confident of their ability to do so, became less tolerant of the formalities of indirect rule. The traditional rulers, for their part, ill-equipped to govern in the new style and generally unsympathetic to what it stood for, became increasingly irrelevant in the daily administration of their own lands. In most cases, rather like European monarchs, they were bought off with substantial emoluments and encapsulated in ceremonial roles, while the colonial elites bypassed them to deal directly with traditional officials at lower levels. Javan regents continued to be treated with great deference, although, increasingly, Dutch Residents gave the orders and young Dutch *controleurs* supervised Javan district and subdistrict officers in the field. The Nguyen court was infiltrated with French officials in key positions, while mandarins throughout northern and central Vietnam came under the control of French *résidents supérieurs*. The west coast Malay sultanates were amalgamated in 1895, and a unified (British) Malayan Civil Service under a Resident-General dropped all but the pretense of "advising" sultans, while British district officers, governing at an unusually low level of administration, dealt directly with Malay *penghulu*, themselves well on the way to becoming British-style functionaries. By 1910, the old Thai bureaucratic nobility in the center and subordinate kings and provincial elites in the outer regions were being pensioned off, so that, from Bangkok to the district level, Thailand was coming to be governed by a single national administrative elite.

The third and most thoroughgoing pattern of change was found in Cochinchina and the main Burman-populated area. The French severed Cochinchina from the rest of Vietnam; similarly, the British first cut off sections of the Burman Kingdom and then, after the final war in 1885, abolished the monarchy altogether. In these two areas, therefore, the Europeans never governed by indirect rule but instead dealt from the beginning with lower-level traditional leaders or, as in Cochinchina for a time, experimented with direct local rule themselves. In both cases, moreover, new nontraditional indigenous administrative classes emerged before 1900—the "interpreters" of Cochinchina and the *a-so-ya-min* in Burma. The latter were recruited through an examination system testing knowledge of English, surveying, and administrative procedures. Beginning at the bottom, they were able to rise through the ranks of the modern administrative hierarchy—the first Burman deputy commissioner, a quite high post, was appointed in 1908. The *a-so-ya-min* class, evolving its own mixed Anglo-Burman life style, described in Mi Mi Khaing's delightful family history,[20] was fully formed by 1900.

The early years of the twentieth century were a watershed in the administrative history of Southeast Asia. The last corners of the area were being incorporated into the six large states that had been constructed, and the basic administrative grids covering the six countries had been laid down. The European and Thai central administrative services were in full running order—with graded hierarchies, regular recruitment and promotion procedures, and paperwork up to international standards. They kept a careful eye on the still indirectly ruled outlying areas and fairly closely supervised the general affairs of the major concentrations of population. By then, they had reached down below the traditional rulers in most areas to work through Southeast Asian chiefs and traditional leaders at regional and local levels of administration. There was thus a characteristic joint in the administrative systems where the lower European officials (or, for that matter, Bangkok Thai) dealt with Southeast Asian local elites across a cultural and historical gap symbolized by the need for bilingualism or interpreters. Beyond lay the mass of the folk who still rarely dealt with a European official on any kind of business. It was here—across the bureaucratic joint, and in relations between the modern state and the peasants—that the administrative developments of the decades before World War II were most striking.

The cultural gap between the Europeans and Southeast Asians in government service had appreciably widened in the decades before 1900, as the European sections of the bureaucracies had modernized themselves. That gap was largely closed during the early decades of the twentieth century, as Southeast Asian civil servants acquired a modern education. Whereas in 1900 most Southeast Asians in government service—apart from Bangkok Thai, of course—were educated in traditional modes and held office because of traditional status, by 1940 virtually all had had a modern education, and many had achieved their positions on that basis, rather than through inherited status.

There were many reasons for the change. In the twentieth century, with larger revenues and larger goals, administrations grew enormously, as whole new specialist services—government school systems, agricultural research stations, archaeological departments—were created, to join the older and more basic general administrative services. To save money, as well as to be true to self-imposed ideas of tutelage, colonial governments aimed to fill many of the new jobs with Southeast Asians. To do so, they needed men educated in the modern way, not only for the specialist services (which was obvious) but for the general administrative services as well (by this time even village headmen were beginning to be required to keep various written records). The colonial and Thai governments, therefore, opened an increasingly wide range of modern educational opportunities. The general European-language (or Thai-language) government schools, which burgeoned in the early twentieth century, produced a large proportion of the Southeast Asian civil servants of the period. It was characteristic, though, that governments from the beginning provided modern schooling specifically intended for such jobs. The beginnings may be seen in the small schools founded in late-nineteenth-century Java for training vaccinators, teachers, and future administrators. Such education spread rapidly in the early years of the twentieth century, as, for example, in the schools for training district officers, police, agricultural officers, and others, which came to be established within virtually every Bangkok ministry and government department.

New schools and the bureaucratic jobs for which they prepared people proved increasingly attractive to Southeast Asians. Many were the sons of the old ruling elites, which were increasingly bypassed in the late nineteenth century. The regent class on Java was restored to relevance by the 1920's on a new basis, wearing neckties, speaking Dutch, and merging fully into the modern administration. The sons of Chiangmai and Lao princes loosened their connections to their home areas, as they were coopted into the national Thai elite. Others—most often, perhaps, in Java—were the sons of lesser officials or provincial or local elite families. For them, a civil service position obtained on the basis of training and merit rather than birth represented a step toward higher status, which had been largely closed to them under the traditional order. Yet others, like many of the nineteenth-century *a-so-ya-min* in Burma, came out of still more humble or even peasant families. This was perhaps most common in the Philippines, because of the mainly English-language education system and the swift Filipinization of the bureaucracy by the Americans. But it was possible elsewhere and was the rule rather than the exception among the Minangkabau of West Sumatra, for example, where the higher-status families tended to look down on modern education and civil service jobs, while large numbers of poorer boys got their start in this way. In the early decades of the twentieth century, everywhere but in the Philippines, jobs in the expanding civil services were the single most important avenue of upward social mobility. Families scraped deeply to finance the education that could make a son into a forest officer or a postal clerk.

It would be a mistake, though, to see the phenomenon simply in terms of social ambition. The government training schools and civil service positions were opening up, but nothing compelled Southeast Asians to enter them. There is, in fact, considerable evidence from various parts of the area around the turn of the century to indicate strong family resistance to such paths. One is struck by the cultural vitality and, indeed, by the plain courage of many Southeast Asians in the early twentieth century who were willing to recast their lives to the requirements of modern civil service careers and who accepted the premises of modern bureaucratic government—so alien to their own political culture—as their own. In time, nationalists were to criticize colonial government service—accurately enough—as collaboration, but they too rejected traditional political structure in favor of a modern conception of the state.

Three broader consequences of the process require special notice. First, almost everywhere in Southeast Asia in the years after 1900, a civil service career became the dominant ambition of the new "middle sector." In this way, deep-rooted conceptions of a hierarchically graded society, with status defined in terms of relative distance from the apex of political authority, were translated into modern terms and carried forward. Such ambitions, with their wide political implications, constitute one of the most prominent features of Southeast Asian societies today.

The second consequence had more immediate political significance. By 1940, the cultural gap in the governing hierarchy had been more or less closed. Now, from governor-general to just above the village level, most of Southeast Asia was administered by bureaucratic elites, European and Southeast Asian, which shared most of the same operating assumptions about government, used one main (or sole) language of administration, and maintained similar life styles. Nevertheless, in sharp contrast, the bureaucratic joint retained its racial aspect: Europeans on top, Southeast Asians below. Appreciation of the contrast did much to stimulate nationalist movements.

The third consequence was deeply ironical. The process described above tended inevitably to pull modern-educated Southeast Asian civil servants away from the life of the peasant. A new cultural joint had appeared, in some ways as wide as the earlier one, but now it was between the folk and the Southeast Asian bureaucratic classes that, along with Europeans, ruled over them. The implications of that development are only now beginning to be worked out in the history of the area.

While the above changes were proceeding, mainly within the growing Southeast Asian bureaucratic classes, administrative development was generating important effects outside as well, among the population at large. The general administrative services that developed in the late nineteenth century confined themselves mainly to the fundamentals of government—maintaining order, administering the law, and collecting taxes. In this—though they differed markedly in other respects—they certainly resembled their predecessor governments and could thus, for example, incorporate traditional local elites more or less unchanged, appearing to peasants as not much more than new dynasties.

The rapid expansion of government activities after 1900, however, implied quite new relations between the state and its subjects, especially in the case of the specialist services. With few exceptions, they were established precisely to perform functions that had no local precedents. Unlike the earlier general administrative services, they rarely incorporated traditional leaders into their ranks; from the beginning, they were staffed almost exclusively with modern-educated men—Europeans, local Southeast Asians, and a characteristically high proportion of Indians, Chinese, and nonlocal Southeast Asians. Born out of the needs of European and other economic interests for various facilities, but also out of paternalist ideals, however confused, of serving the public welfare, the specialist services were dedicated by their very nature to change.

The same came increasingly to be true of the general administrative services. While they continued in the twentieth century to perform the basic functions of government, they also became much more deeply involved in programs of change, if only in coordinating the activities of the specialist services at the local level and in enforcing the latters' policies. Their ability to effect change, moreover, was greatly increased by the replacement of traditional-minded Southeast Asian administrative officials at local levels by a new generation of modern-educated men who cherished many of the same ideas of progress.

While some of these new government programs had nothing to do with the mass of the population (e.g., geological services) or affected them only indirectly (e.g., postal, telegraph, and telephone services, railroads, censuses), many were directed specifically at improving village life—a wide variety of public health programs, forest reserves to check erosion, village schools, rural credit services, cooperatives, agricultural extension services, the reorganization of village structure. The list seems estimable, and so it seemed to the zealous European district officers or Southeast Asian schoolteachers who introduced—not to say imposed—the measures in the villages. But peasants seldom shared the assumptions and goals of the agents of progress, and they judged the new programs by their own well-tested standards of efficiency and purpose. A few of the programs, such as public health nurses and village schools in some areas, gained wide approval. Others, such as rural credit services and agricultural extension, were well received by at least the minority who made use of them. Virtually all were at least acceptable in most villages most of the time. But all, too, aroused discontent or passive resistance in many areas, in some cases contributing directly to rebellious movements. Governments, to save money, often made villagers pay for changes they had not wanted in the first place. Forest reserves were universally disliked because they hampered the collection of firewood. The slaughter of cattle to prevent the spread of rinderpest could bring ruin to individuals whose animals were killed. The rearrangement or amalgamation of hamlets and villages, mainly for administrative convenience, broke up natural communities or submerged them in arbitrary groupings. New rules for the appointment or choice of village headmen—such as a series of village elections in northern Vietnam, which caused most of the notables to withdraw from public life—often disturbed village social structure. Everywhere new duties and closer supervision tended to draw headmen apart from village life, making them as much the lowest agents of government as leaders and members of their communities.

Well-intended programs of village welfare—not to speak of policies followed for other reasons and often quite callously applied—represented an unprecedented assault upon the ways of village life. Older rulers had extracted all the taxes and forced labor they could, but, except in time of war, they had not been able, nor had they wanted, to intrude directly upon village affairs. Twentieth-century colonial and Thai governments were both able and eager to do so, and they drew the peasants willy-nilly into the new frameworks they were driven to create.

ECONOMIC FRAMEWORKS

Few changes in the economic apparatus of the area in the three-quarters of a century before 1941 were more striking than those in transportation. In the land areas of Southeast Asia, transport had always been slow, expensive, and difficult. The Nguyen emperors constructed the Mandarin Road from Hanoi to Saigon, but they built and used it mainly for political communications; goods, such as tax rice to the court at Hue, went by sea. It took three months to go upriver from Rangoon to Mandalay, a month and a half by ox cart from Nongkhai on the Mekong to Bangkok, several weeks from Semarang to Surakarta. Transport difficulties, in themselves, set strict limits to the intensity of governance in the circles of influence more remote from the capitals and restricted trade by land. Movement along the coasts, and particularly throughout island Southeast Asia, was much easier, and trade played a much more important economic role generally in that region. But in an age of *perahu*, junks, and European square-rigged vessels, the long seaways and scattered coastal settlements of the archipelago dictated a politics of raid and vassalage rather than steady administration, and such vessels had a limited capacity for bulk shipments.

The Irrawaddy Flotilla Company, founded in the 1860's, was the first and largest inland steamship service in Southeast Asia. By the end of the century it dominated inland water traffic with its large fleet, dockyards, warehouses, rice mills, and sawmills. It carried migrant laborers between Upper Burma and the delta rice frontier and hundreds of thousands of tons of paddy to the mills at Rangoon and Bassein. It permitted British troops to steam upriver in a few days in order to overthrow Thibaw's kingdom in 1885. Steam launches and barges played an important but lesser role on other rivers, such as the Čhaophraya, lower Mekong, and Solo. But the Irrawaddy, navigable from Bhamo to the sea, had always been the most important of the inland waterways of the area, and it remained so in the age of steam.

Elsewhere, in the land areas, it was the railroad that inaugurated the transport revolution. The backbone line of the Burmese system ran up the Sittang valley from Rangoon, reaching Toungoo in 1885, Mandalay in 1889, and Lashio in the Shan hills in 1902, while a later branch connected Mandalay with Myitkyina, in the far north. The Rangoon-Prome line opened up large areas to export rice cultivation in 1877, as did later lines to Bassein and Moulmein. By the 1920's, Burma was crisscrossed with a 2,000-mile railway network, with no outside connections, defining in its way a distinct economic domain. Other areas where economic life was powerfully affected by railway systems were Java, with its particularly rugged terrain for so heavily settled an area, and Luzon, where the line from Manila north across the central plain opened up rich areas in the twentieth century for rice and, especially, sugar production.

It was in Thailand, however, that the railway was most decisive. The Thai Government, pressed between dangerous colonial neighbors, kept political considerations always foremost in framing its policy. It gave the Germans a major role in the Railway Department because Germany was no threat to Thailand. Ever mindful of the survival value of fiscal conservatism and financial self-sufficiency, it paid for all of its early railway projects from current revenue rather than foreign loans. The first of the three major lines, begun in 1892 and reaching Khorat in 1900, was intended to help counter the French advance through Laos. From Khorat (Nakhọn Ratchasima), lines were extended toward the Mekong in the 1920's and 1930's, north to Udon and Nongkhai opposite Vientiane, and east to Ubon. The second major line ran north, reaching Uttaradit in the foothills in 1909 and pausing before pushing through to Chiangmai in 1921. The third line was begun in 1909—with a British loan accompanying the final division of the Malay states between the British and Thai—and connected Bangkok to Penang by 1922.

The economic effects of Thai railways were impressive. The northern and northeastern lines permitted, for the first time, major rice exports from those areas. The Chinese moved outward to each new railhead in turn, reinforcing the railway network with their own commercial one. The political-economic effects were fully as significant. By 1930, a national system of 1,875 miles, centered on Bangkok, greatly enhanced the primacy of that city and the government located there. It was only after the railroad reached Chiangmai (though not entirely because of that) that Bangkok began in earnest to collect taxes throughout the north, and it was only then that the *baht* replaced the rupee as the basic currency there. Much the same was true in the northeast, and it is clear that the railroad has been particularly important in binding modern Thailand together. At the same time, the Thai railways, unlike the Burmese, have provided important links to the outside as well. The southward line reinforced an earlier tendency for parts of southern Thailand to orient themselves economically toward Penang; in the nineteenth century, most Chinese tin miners had reached southern Thailand via Penang, and in the twentieth century the area's tin went there for smelting—a reduction of Bangkok's economic suzerainty not effectively challenged until the 1960's. On the other hand, the northeastern lines toward the Mekong, not counteracted by any French railways into Laos, strongly reinforced a long-standing tendency of the Mekong Lao to orient themselves toward Bangkok.

By contrast, the grandiose French railway system in Indochina was of limited significance. Two lines led off into China, reflecting (rather faintly) old nineteenth-century dreams of "tapping the China market." The major line, completed just before World War II, ran along the coastal route of the Mandarin Road and, like it, was of little economic use where ships could do the job. The French were more successful with roads, opening up several new passages into the mountainous spine and along the Mekong, though not decisively enough to overcome the natural cleavages within Indochina. It was Java, which had a fine road system for its time as early as 1850, along with the Philippines and Burma, that developed the most significant road networks before World War II.

Steamships played a less revolutionary role in the sea transport of Southeast Asia than railroads and modern roads with motor vehicles did on land, for the latter were altogether new, while the steamship was simply a better version, for many purposes, of a familiar means of transport. Sailing vessels, in fact, predominated in coastal traffic until the 1890's and have continued to play an important economic role to this day. Nor did steamship lines have quite as direct and powerful an integrative effect in island Southeast Asia as railroads in Thailand and railroads and roads in Burma. The newly emerging political units in island Southeast Asia incorporated great expanses of an established maritime world whose trade could move at will on the open seas. Throughout the nineteenth and into the twentieth century, in fact, the general trade of most of what became the Netherlands Indies and the southern Philippines was focused on Singapore, which belonged to another political jurisdiction.

Nevertheless, steam did bring important changes. The steamship was an important weapon in the successful piracy suppression campaigns, which in time made the region safe for other kinds of economic exploitation and political intrusion. The growing export economy of the Philippines gave rise to a busy interisland shipping, dominated by Chinese *mestizos;* and this, in turn, facilitated economic development, creating much closer and more regular ties among the islands and peoples of that country. In the Netherlands Indies, a single far-flung shipping enterprise, the KPM, had the same kind of influence, though under much more difficult circumstances.

Unlike rail and road, of course, the steamship greatly strengthened connections with the world outside Southeast Asia as well. In this period, the numerous small, local economies that had characterized traditional Southeast Asia were not only being tied together in new "national" economic structures but also were being brought into touch with the world economy. British steam shipping lines serving Southeast Asia, at first mainly in passing, on the way to the China coast, began to appear in the 1860's. They were joined in the following decades by increasing numbers of French, Dutch, German, American, Japanese, and other lines, along with privately owned tramp shipping. The major lines often served the larger Southeast Asian ports as part of their global routes. But others provided shorter-range services, from India across the Bay of Bengal and from the China coast and Japan to the smaller ports on the Southeast Asian coasts.

International shipping, steadily increasing in tonnage, frequency, and scope of service, provided perhaps the most fundamental link between Southeast Asia and the world economy and became one of the major agents of economic change within the area. Steamships carried out the hundreds of thousands and then millions of tons of sugar and rice, bringing in textiles, canned goods, and heavy machinery. Steamships, not junks, carried most of the rising numbers of Chinese immigrants in the half-century before 1930 and almost all of the Indians to Burma and Malaya. They brought in European soldiers, colonial officials, and ambitious young men to run the plantations and, in the twentieth century, their wives and families, along with increasing numbers of tourists.

The transportation systems were the most obvious of the new economic structures, because they impinged physically on the landscape, because they carried people and bulk goods, and because—visible in a different way—they could be drawn on maps. Economic machinery of many other sorts was no less important for being less obtrusive to the eye and invisible on the map. Not the least of the preconditions for a more highly structured and efficient economic life was a standardized currency system. In Thailand in 1850, to take an extreme case, the largest unit of traditional currency was the *chang,* equal to 20 *tamlüng,* or 80 *baht,* or 320 *salüng,* or 640 *füang,* or 1280 *sik,* or 2560 *siao,* or 5120 *at,* or 10,240 *solot,* or 512,000 cowrie shells. In addition, Indian rupees circulated in the teak areas around Chiangmai, and Mexican and other dollars circulated elsewhere, especially in the south. Minted coins, which circulated early in Mongkut's reign at 64 *at* to the *baht,* simplified matters somewhat, but it was not until foreign coins were made legal tender in 1857, at 5 *baht* to $3 Mexican, that the difficulties occasioned by foreign commerce and exchange were rendered manageable.

In a somewhat different case, the comparatively well-developed Vietnamese currency system was not modified but replaced, starting in Cochinchina, by a new French colonial system using the piaster as its basic unit. Colonial Burma did not even get its own currency; it got instead the Indian rupee and was thus annexed financially, as well as politically and administratively, to the Indian empire. In island Southeast Asia, which for centuries had done most of its business through a whole family of different silver dollars, the political partition completed about 1910 had its counterpart in the field of currency. In the Philippines, the silver peso carried on, tied 2 to 1 to the U.S. dollar after 1903; the guilder spread rapidly over the new Netherlands Indies after 1900; and the British sphere got its first Straits dollar notes in 1906, pegged to sterling at the rate of two shillings and fourpence.

The introduction and spread of new currency systems illustrate three types of economic linkages: to the world economy in general; to the economies of the various metropolitan powers; and among the different parts of the new colonies themselves, as economic activities within each "national" unit were increasingly expressed in terms of a single medium of exchange. New tariff systems had more limited effects. While everywhere they marked off the new political units as distinct economic domains, the most powerful consequences came where colonial policy dictated tight tariff links with the metropolitan country. This was particularly true of the Philippines and of Indochina. France enclosed Indochina in its own highly protectionist tariff system, thus forcefully cutting Vietnam's close economic association with China, just as it had also cut Vietnam's ancient but loose political subservience to China. Vietnamese were thereby forced to buy higher-priced French textiles and other goods, while large quantities of Cochinchinese rice went to France, spurred by a program of popularization that brought rice, for the first time, to an important place in the French cuisine. In the Philippines, the effects were similar and far more profound in the long run. Spanish restrictive tariffs had had little impact on Anglo-Chinese domination of Philippine foreign trade. But when virtual free trade within the United States tariff walls was established in 1913, the Philippine economy was shaped to conform to the needs of the American market. This comfortable dependence, while providing fortunes for Filipino sugar barons, among others, encouraged inefficient production methods, which priced Philippine sugar and other products out of the world market.

By contrast, the chief significance of the modern banking systems was the way they integrated the emerging export economies of Southeast Asia into the world market rather than merely into those of the metropolitan countries. The official Bank of Indochina dominated the economy of that colony, but, in general, colonial central banks, such as the Java Bank, developed rather slowly, and in most of Southeast Asia, private banks with worldwide connections dominated the field. The British ones, notably the Chartered Bank of India, Australia, and China, and the Hong Kong and Shanghai Banking Corporation, came first, establishing major branches in most of the Southeast Asian countries. They were soon followed by Dutch, American, French, Japanese, and, shortly before World War II, Nationalist Chinese banks. In individual countries, however, Europeans, a few overseas Chinese and Indians, and even fewer Southeast Asians, founded a number of banks that confined their operations within "national" spheres.

Banks, insurance firms, and all-purpose service institutions, such as the agency houses of the Straits Settlements, which dominated the export-import business, managed plantations, and did much else, were most significant as mediating institutions through which Southeast Asian economies were incorporated into the world economic system. Nevertheless, they also played a crucial role in shaping and tying together the separate economies. Banks, concentrated in the major city of each country, stood at the center of ever more complex financial systems and, alongside the more informal Chinese and Indian networks, presided over "national" credit systems. European, Chinese, and Indian chambers of commerce, while often representing export-oriented interests, represented business communities whose primary frame of reference was the colony in which they operated.

Much of the economic policy of the colonial (and Thai) governments had the same effect of reinforcing the growing "national" economic frameworks. Banking, currency, and contract laws, for example, facilitated and shaped the development of new institutions. New land laws—the issuance of title deeds and regular cadastral surveys in nineteenth-century Philippines or twentieth-century Thailand, standardized seventy-five-year plantation leases in the Netherlands Indies, new mortgage provisions in Burma or the Malay Reservation areas—created types of access to land and strongly affected the peasant's relation to the soil. The most profound consequences of these and other land laws were socio-economic, but they had other effects as well. They systematized traditional land tenure customs hitherto marked by all sorts of local variations, and they brought the mass of the population into much more direct and regular contact with the emerging administrative systems. More generally, new laws helped shape a distinct set of economic practices within each "national" system.

While government tax policy, similarly, was most important for its socio-economic impact, it also contributed to the creation of "national" economic structures. Periodic "land settlements" in British Burma, for the purpose of reviewing land productivity and ownership and of re-assessing taxes, made possible a Burma-wide, impersonal system of taxation, probably heavier in its incidence but fairer and more uniform in its application than those which had preceded it. Everywhere in Southeast Asia in the high colonial period there was a trend away from the more diverse, local, and personal forms of taxation: in goods, levied on a great variety of products; in different kinds of labor services owed to, or through the intermediary of, patrons; and in the form of tax farms on opium, gambling, road and river tolls, sold to the highest bidder or granted to a king's favorite in appanage. In their place came a new range of taxes: excise taxes on salt and alcohol in Vietnam and on other consumer goods elsewhere; head, land, and produce taxes in cash; export and import taxes. From them emerged increasingly uniform and efficiently enforced colonywide tax systems, expressed in the standard and impersonal medium of "national" currencies.

One thing that stands out in the administrative and economic re-organizations of the high colonial era is the unprecedented role played by government. In traditional Southeast Asia, the main function of the ruler was to *be*, symbolizing in his person an agreed-on social order, a cultural ideal, and a state of harmony with the cosmos. The new colonial and Thai governments existed primarily to *do*, providing themselves with a permanently crowded agenda of specific tasks to accomplish. They felt, by older Southeast Asian standards, a peculiar need to tidy up casual and irregular old customs, to bring uniformity to the numerous small, local societies in their jurisdictions, to clear paths for economic "progress," to organize, reform, and control. To do these things, the new governments also possessed unprecedented powers: overwhelming military superiority, new technological tools, larger revenues, and, in the colonies at least, a freedom to innovate conferred by conquest and by an external base of political authority and cultural reference.

The result, although by no means due entirely to government action, was a striking historical reversal. Societies that had been rather loosely organized politically and economically were pressed within steadily tightening bureaucratic and economic frameworks. The same process, however, profoundly disrupted the formerly secure social and cultural order of those societies, generating new ambitions and visions as well as social plurality, cultural alienation, degradation, and despair. One of the basic appeals of modern nationalism, when it appeared, was the solution it offered to the disorder resulting from the historical reversal: to preserve the tightening frameworks, but within them, as nations, to recreate lost social and cultural harmony.

22

ECONOMIC TRANSFORMATION, 1870–1940

It was said extravagantly of Java in the time of the Culture System that the island was one vast government plantation. In the same way, there has been a widespread impression that the whole of Southeast Asia's economy was given over to export production in the high colonial period. The impression is far from true. Peasant subsistence cultivation, especially of rice, remained the largest single sector of the economy. Commercial agriculture for domestic consumption, small-scale domestic industry, transportation, and credit systems all grew steadily in the period. Rapid population increase set in motion a very different train of economic events, especially among peasants. Nevertheless, the burgeoning export industries were the dominant economic force of the age and thus a major influence on developments in the other economic sectors, and indeed in society generally. The rise of export industries can therefore serve as a major theme around which one can survey the vast, complex, and as yet barely studied subject of the economic transformation that took place between 1870 and 1940.

The impetus for the export boom came from rising world market demand, felt ever more strongly in Southeast Asia after the arrival of the steamship, with its cheap bulk transport, in the 1860's. The world market, however, exerted its attraction impartially on every part of the globe. The particular way in which the Southeast Asian export industries developed was determined by conditions in the region itself; certain general features of the premodern Southeast Asian economic landscape were crucial. The area as a whole was sparsely and unevenly populated. Transportation was slow and difficult. Economic transactions were conducted mainly by barter; taxes were mostly in kind and labor; there was very little currency in circulation or use of credit. It was a landscape of small, local, and largely self-sufficient economies only loosely associated in provinces and kingdoms whose common bonds were more cultural and social than economic.

Southeast Asia, to be sure, had always had some export trade, particularly from the island area, where it was often locally very important. It is significant that, apart from some minerals, such as tin and gold, the exports were all tropical or subtropical agricultural commodities: cloves and nutmeg from the Moluccas, pepper from Sumatra, coffee from West Java, to mention a few of the most important. There were good reasons for this. Southeast Asia exported raw materials, not manufactured goods, because basic economic conditions in the area precluded any but small-scale domestic industries, such as hand looms and court crafts. Instead, over the centuries, it imported large quantities of Indian textiles and Chinese ceramic wares.

This pattern of trade—tropical agricultural raw materials and some minerals for imported manufactured goods—continued through the export boom of the late nineteenth and early twentieth centuries. Modern critics of colonialism attribute its continuation to the policies of the colonial powers, and the latter in their day were glad to take the credit, for they easily confused the selfish interests of the West and Westerners with the cause of advancing civilization. There is ample evidence to show the importance of colonial policy in promoting this pattern of trade. The French enclosed Indochina in a net of tariffs designed to assure a complementary flow of French manufactures and Indochinese raw materials, and similar though less thoroughgoing arrangements were made in the other colonies. Colonial governments zealously fostered the development of export agriculture and did little or nothing to help the development of local industry. Similar attitudes and policies still govern the economic relations of the developed countries with the now politically independent countries of Southeast Asia, with results at best dubious for the latter.

But everywhere in the modern world governments have had only a limited capacity to influence the fundamental economic changes set in motion by the scientific and industrial revolution. Economic and social conditions in late-nineteenth-century Southeast Asia itself made industrialization, in the short run at least, quite impossible. Meanwhile, the developing industries of the West, and later Japan, offered inexpensive machine-made textiles and locomotives. Growing and increasingly prosperous populations in Europe and elsewhere demanded more sugar, tea, and coffee; canning and electrical industries required tin; automobiles and bicycles needed rubber tires. It was above all the impersonal forces of the world market that determined that Southeast Asia would enter the emerging world economy of the late nineteenth century as an exporter of tropical raw materials.

The tug of outside markets for such products created a great potential for economic change within Southeast Asia. The shape of the various new export industries which grew so rapidly there after 1870 was very largely determined by the particular responses of various social and ethnic groups to the available possibilities.

On the eve of the export boom, the economic mobility—the willingness and ability to assume new economic roles—of Southeast Asians was in many ways limited. Most peasants, to begin with, were settled in a subsistence way of life. They had enough land, produced most of what they needed, bartered for a few necessities like salt and fish, and bargained on fairly even terms against the demands of the elites in their societies. All this, confirmed by the experience of generations, was deeply entrenched in their values and beliefs. Most of them, too, were subject to *corvée* labor or were attached to patrons as clients or debt-bondsmen, which restricted their economic mobility in other ways. None of this prevented peasants from responding to the possibilities of export production; quite the contrary. But it did dictate the ways in which they would do so and set limits on how far and how fast they would go in adapting to the stimulus of the world market.

Throughout Southeast Asia, their first and greatest response was smallholder production of export crops, sometimes in their home villages but more often on forest land in the vicinity or in new holdings on a nearby agricultural frontier. There was ample precedent. Some of the larger export industries of earlier centuries had started in the same way: Moluccan smallholders in the fifteenth and sixteenth centuries had traded cloves and nutmeg for textiles and rice, and peasants in Upper Burma from the seventeenth century onward grew cotton for the caravans to China. The same occurred on a larger scale in the nineteenth and twentieth centuries: Hundreds of thousands of Burman, Thai, and southern Vietnamese peasants moved steadily out over the deltas to grow rice in exchange for cash and imports; hundreds of thousands of peasants in Sumatra, Malaya, and Borneo planted stands of rubber trees on the edge of the forests near their settlements; more tens of thousands produced many other export crops in other places.

It was a swift and massive response, a great change made easy precisely because it required so little change in peasant practices and economic values. Growing familiar crops like rice and coconuts, or new crops like rubber and tea, whose market value had been demonstrated by European plantations, was a natural extension of the peasants' established subsistence agriculture. Those who produced millions of tons of export rice remained peasants. They readily opened new land, increased production, grew new crops, adopted kerosene lamps and made greater use of cash, but their economic mobility did not as yet extend much farther. They continued to be small-scale growers, almost always leaving it to others to get the goods to the market. In 1870, very few were willing to leave their villages to work for wages in plantations or in the cities, and this was still true of many in 1940.

The established economic values of the comparatively few Southeast Asians who were not peasants—the merchants, religious leaders, aristocrats, and king—similarly restricted their response to the possibilities of export agriculture. In traditional Southeast Asia, prestige could lead to wealth but rarely the reverse. None of the societies, except that of the Philippines, had a clear social image of an indigenous rich man risen to high status merely by an accumulation of wealth. The avenues to high status were those of birth, personal connections, Confucian study, Buddhist piety, or Islamic learning. The majesty of kings was revealed by plenitude of manpower—the retainers, craftsmen, officials, and concubines of the palace cities—rather than by riches in goods or money.

In the Southeast Asian societies, indigenous merchants were usually small traders operating on the fringes of the subsistence economies and pinched in the narrow social space between lord and peasant. Almost everywhere but in the Islamic islands they remained small traders under the shadow of growing immigrant commercial communities, and they took little part in the export industries.

Merchants had played a much more important role in the widespread communities of the Malayo-Muslim world over the centuries. Trade was more important in many areas there, and, as Muslims, the merchants had a religious motive to make money—in order to be able to go on the *haj* to Mecca and when they returned, as *haji*, to enjoy high prestige. Such merchants continued in the years of the export boom to play a large part in the older miscellaneous export trades of the islands, collecting small quantities of a great variety of special forest and sea products and bringing them to entrepôts like Singapore. In central Sumatra and southern Borneo, they competed successfully against Chinese as middlemen in the smallholder rubber trade. On Java, they dominated domestic trade at the lower levels and also pioneered in many lines of domestic industry, notably the manufacture of *batik* cloth and *kretek* cigarettes.

But everywhere in the area these *santri* merchants operated at the outer end of commercial channels that led inward to larger and stronger Chinese businesses in the trading centers. Forest products and smallholder rubber were assembled and shipped in bulk by Chinese (if not European) firms, *batik*-makers and *kretek* manufacturers bought their raw materials from Chinese wholesalers, *santri* traders in the rural areas of Java sold their onions and soybeans to Chinese wholesalers. Various reasons have been offered for the phenomenon. *Santri* merchants, accustomed to a less consuming struggle for existence, were not so highly motivated. They lacked the experience of the Chinese in credit, international marketing, and other aspects of large-scale trade. Above all, their commercial ethic was highly individualist, whereas Chinese commerce operated through a whole range of kinship connections, secret societies, and speech-group associations. The young Minangkabau man off with a bit of trading capital to make some money, the Palembang peddler walking through the hills of West Java, the Bugis trader on his *perahu* always came in the end to deal with the wider and stronger networks that grew from Chinese shops in the towns and great ports.

Finally, the aristocrats and kings of Southeast Asia had always interested themselves to some extent in the export trade, though for all but archipelago sultans and chiefs it was generally only a sideline to their basic business of extracting rice and labor from their peasant subjects. Even the Thai kings and nobles who had extensive interests in the export trade from the seventeenth to the mid-nineteenth century seldom took a direct part in the trade itself. In effect, they rented out political rights over the peasant—and later provided some capital—to Chinese merchants, who collected the goods and did the actual trading. For rulers and province chiefs to squeeze as much as they could from traders in their jurisdictions was very much in accord with elite values in those sharply stratified societies. But for the Vietnamese mandarin, the Javanese *priyayi*, and most of their counterparts, trade itself was an occupation for lesser men. Conquest by the Europeans brought an end to their accustomed exploitation of merchants, and the unequal treaties did the same to the more active and creative participation of the Thai elite. It did not, given their attitudes, incline them to take up new, more direct roles in the growing export industries. It was not until several generations later, with independence, that their descendants and heirs were once again in a position to levy tribute on export trade.

There were thus definite limits to the willingness or ability of Southeast Asians of all classes and regions to respond to the opportunities opened by the growing market for tropical export commodities. Their limited economic mobility in the face of a world economic revolution was of fundamental importance, for it opened room for immigrant entrepreneurs—Chinese, Indians, and Europeans—to play roles of unprecedented importance in the societies of Southeast Asia.

The Chinese who were drawn to Southeast Asia came almost exclusively from the coastal areas of the provinces of Kwangtung and Fukien. Though all were Chinese, they belonged to many speech-groups—especially Cantonese, Hokkien, Hakka, Teochieu, and Hainanese—whose spoken languages were unintelligible to each other, whose customs and economic specializations were often different, and who were frequently hostile to each other. But they shared certain important characteristics and attitudes. The Chinese had long had a complex economy marked by general use of money and credit, considerable manufacturing, and substantial regional and longer-distance trade. This was even more the case with the South China coast, with its thousand-year history as a region dominated economically by trade with Nanyang and beyond. On the South China coast, a distinct seafaring and trading tradition had grown up over the centuries, the merchant's way of life was more highly honored, commercial skills were more highly developed, and wealth was more seriously pursued than elsewhere in China.

In earlier times, merchants from the region had traded along the shores of most of Southeast Asia, normally staying over in port towns for months waiting for the monsoon to change, but few had settled, even in the ports. In the seventeenth and eighteenth centuries, as the trade of Southeast Asia continued to grow, Chinese had begun to settle in larger numbers, especially at those places where economic opportunities were particularly good: in Thailand around Bangkok and in the south, where they collaborated in royal trading enterprises and mined tin; on Java, where they organized the pepper business of Bantam in the seventeenth century and flourished under the regime of the VOC, growing sugar and farming taxes; in Manila, to which they were drawn by the silver of the galleons. In the course of the nineteenth century, their numbers steadily increased. After 1870, the influx became a flood, rising each decade to 1930—tens of millions moving back and forth, and several million ending up permanently in Southeast Asia. The migration was greatly facilitated by the rapid growth of steamship services. It was pushed from behind by the massive population growth of China in the eighteenth century, followed by the widespread disruption of the Taiping Rebellion in the mid-nineteenth century and the chaos that followed it. But above all, the Chinese were pulled by conditions in Southeast Asia, an open frontier of opportunity.

In a few places, Chinese settled down as peasants—near Bangkok and Batavia, on the lower Rejang River in Sarawak, at the northeastern corner of northern Vietnam. Some came as merchants from the beginning, simply moving outward along their commercial channels from China coast cities. But the great majority came, packed in the steerage of the coolie ships, as simple laborers, owing passage money to those for whom they first worked. They came to work on the European plantations of Sumatra's East Coast Residency, to build the 2,000 miles of Thai railways, to work the tin deposits of southern Thailand, Malaya, Bangka, and Billiton, and to work in a variety of new jobs in the port cities and towns of Southeast Asia, as labor for the docks, hand sawmills, rice mills, and building trades. Those few who settled and remained as peasants were finding only a frontier of empty land and showing only a geographical mobility. But the rest were economically as well as geographically mobile, moving into newly opening slots that Southeast Asians were not filling. The mobility of many led them little further; almost all intended to stay only a few years, save up some cash, and return home; and the majority did just that. The remainder, however, sooner or later took a further step, becoming shopkeepers in the towns and villages and middlemen in the growing export trades and at the same time settling down and marrying in what became their new home.

Like the Chinese, the Indians came from an overcrowded land with a long history of manufacturing, of extensive and sophisticated commerce, and of a monetized economy. Their late-nineteenth-century migration, however, did not unfold as naturally from a long history as that of the Chinese. Merchants from many parts of India had been trading with Southeast Asia, mostly selling Indian-made textiles, for much longer than the Chinese, and Indian textile shops have remained a characteristic feature of many of the larger Southeast Asian cities. But it was quite new groups of Indians who formed the bulk of the immigrants in the high colonial age, and they went almost entirely to British Burma and Malaya, following the lines of a new imperial connection rather than those of their older maritime expansion. Indian migrants, too, were more rigid in their economic specialization than Chinese.

The most important groups were the Chettyars—a South Indian money-lending caste, which played a decisive role in the Lower Burman rice export industry—and Telugus and Tamils, who went to Burma and Malaya as laborers and, unlike their Chinese counterparts, seldom became shopkeepers. Finally, substantial numbers of Indians went to Burma and Malaya as lawyers, clerks, and civil servants already familiar with British ways and with the English language—a white-collar movement entirely without a Chinese equivalent.

A final major group of immigrants to respond to the new economic possibilities in Southeast Asia were the Westerners. The background of their migration, which was worldwide in the period, is a familiar story. It is enough to remark that they had considerably greater freedom of action in their economic enterprises than their Chinese and Indian counterparts, since they came without liens on their labor, had more capital and scientific knowledge at their disposal, and enjoyed excellent connections with the colonial regimes after they arrived.

The export industries that grew up in the different parts of Southeast Asia, particularly in the sixty years after 1870, took a great variety of forms. They were based on many kinds of soil, land rights, and crops; used widely varying amounts of capital and machinery; and were conducted by members of many different ethnic groups—combining all the elements in a host of different ways. Still, just as the hundreds of different commodities exported in the period consisted principally of agricultural raw materials and minerals, so the great variety of ways in which those commodities were produced and marketed can be reduced to a number of basic patterns. The four most important were the Chinese small capitalist, the Western capitalist, the peasant and middleman patterns, and a variant of the Western capitalist pattern in which labor was local rather than immigrant.

CHINESE SMALL CAPITALISTS

The economic preferences of Southeast Asian peasants—their willingness to respond to new incentives inside the village but not to accept regular wage labor outside it—made it natural that Chinese immigrants should take up complementary economic roles. Thus, Chinese merchants served as middlemen for peasant-produced export crops, while Chinese labor was generally concentrated in the service industries, on the docks, and in the processing mills and railway construction crews, which for a long time held no appeal for Southeast Asians. The only exceptions to the rule were found in areas where the original population was very sparse. In a number of such places, there developed small Chinese frontier societies organized on *hui*, or lineage lines, and based economically on their own all-Chinese export industries. Many of the early industries —Chinese pepper plantations in Kampot and Singapore Island, gold mines in western Borneo, and sugar plantations in southeastern Thailand—declined in the course of time. But Chinese tin-mining in the belt of deposits running from Phuket in southern Thailand to Negri Sembilan in the southern part of the peninsula continued vigorously through the years of the export boom and beyond.

After 1870, Chinese tin-mining in Thailand and Malaya continued in an established pattern—many small units of production organized in partnerships or small companies and labor-intensive methods made possible by large supplies of cheap immigrant labor. Chinese miners made some changes—in Malaya, most of them went over to the much more effective European steam pump at the end of the century—but only changes that were compatible with the established many-unit, labor-intensive pattern. Their unwillingness or inability to accommodate larger change became significant when heavily capitalized European firms entered the tin business in the late nineteenth and early twentieth centuries. They built large modern tin-smelters in Penang and Singapore, driving small-scale Chinese smelters in southern Thailand out of business by 1920 and forcing all tin to be shipped south thereafter. More important, the Chinese miners did not take up the tin-dredge when it was introduced by English and Australian companies after 1900. In the beginning, at least, they could not have raised the capital for the enormous and expensive machines, but it seems clear that the more basic reason for their not adopting the dredges was that these required an entirely different industrial pattern: a few large firms using a great deal of capital and very little labor. Between the mid-1920's and mid-1930's, in both Thailand and Malaya, production from European dredges jumped from about one-third to about two-thirds of total tin production. Chinese production in those years was still well above nineteenth-century levels, but the industry had divided into two sharply different sectors, one Chinese and small capitalist, the other European and big capitalist.

WESTERN CAPITALISTS

The Western capitalist mode of production, characterized by large units under a single management, wage labor, investment of money capital, and scientific methods, was in all respects quite different from prevailing methods of production in Southeast Asia. For that reason, in most parts of the area where it became established in the decades after 1870, it was not a natural outgrowth from local economic activity but imported from outside and run entirely by Westerners.

By the early twentieth century, practically all of the substantial mineral exports of Southeast Asia were being produced by Western firms using fully capitalist methods. Chinese tin from Malaya and Thailand was the outstanding exception. Against it must be set Western capitalist production of tin in those countries and also in the islands of Bangka and Billiton off Sumatra; oil in Burma, Sumatra, and Borneo; coal from the Hong Gai mines in northern Vietnam; gold from Luzon; and various minerals from the Mawchi and Bawdwin mines in Burma. Though many of the deposits had been worked on a smaller scale before by Southeast Asians or Chinese, the modern, large-scale production of the minerals was dominated by European enterprises. Large-scale production of almost all minerals requires heavy equipment and advanced technology, which in turn require capital-intensive methods. It is more interesting, therefore, that the same methods were also used extensively for agricultural export production, to which no such economic imperatives apply and which was in fact carried on vigorously by millions of peasants in the same period.

To understand the place that capitalist agriculture—chiefly plantations—acquired in Southeast Asia, one must examine where it developed.[21] Leaving aside sugar, which was always a special case, plantations were not established in the more heavily settled parts of Southeast Asia. There, the land was already occupied by peasants practicing subsistence agriculture and in many cases developing their own export production. Western entrepreneurs accommodated themselves to this reality as readily as did the Chinese. They therefore located virtually all of their plantations in areas of sparse population—particularly on west-coast Malaya, east-coast Sumatra, the interior of West and East Java, in Mindanao, and in the hilly interior of Vietnam and Cambodia.

The history of what became the East Coast Residency of Sumatra, a rectangle about 150 miles long and 50 miles deep centered on the modern city of Medan, is a classic example of the growth of a plantation system. In 1863, when an errant Dutch tobacco planter, Jacobus Nienhuys, arrived there, it resembled its coastal neighbors on both sides of the Straits of Malacca: an area of small riverine sultanates and chiefdoms set over a sparse, Malay-speaking population cultivating dry rice as a staple and exporting small quantities of pepper and other forest products. But the soil was unusually good, and the local sultans were well content, in exchange for large annual payments, to sign over great stretches of land to Nienhuys and to the planters who followed him. The plantations, prospering from the sale of what turned out to be unusually fine cigar tobacco, spread out around the new town of Medan. In the 1890's and after, new crops were added—coffee, tea, palm oil, and, above all, rubber—and the half-empty land gradually filled up with new belts of plantations. Medan became a city, and through its port, Belawan Deli, passed a quarter or more of all Netherlands Indies exports in the decades before World War II.

In the plantation system of the East Coast Residency, everything but the soil and the complaisant sultans was imported: the planters (Dutch, English, American, and Belgian), their capital ($250 million invested by 1929), their scientific technique, and, most important perhaps, their labor along with most of its food. The original inhabitants numbered only some tens of thousands and in any case were making a perfectly adequate living; they were not interested in wage labor. The planters therefore imported their labor, first Chinese and, after about 1890, as the Chinese began to move into shopkeeping and other urban occupations, increasingly Javanese. By 1930, the population had risen to 1.8 million, of whom 645,000 were Javanese (225,000 then working on the plantations) and 195,000 were Chinese (11,000 on plantations). The various laborers lived on plantations averaging 8,000 acres in size—almost complete societies in themselves, with their own housing, staff doctors, processing plants, and, in effect, their own law and government. The East Coast Residency, made up of hundreds of enclaves, was itself an enclave, though one that exerted an increasingly strong influence on the neighboring parts of Sumatra and Malaya.

Nowhere else in Southeast Asia did plantations produce quite so great a change as in the East Coast Residency, where a whole new society, half the size of Cambodia in population, was created in sixty years. But everywhere they brought similar changes because, settling in areas of sparse population, they served as frontier institutions, creating new and much larger economic bases and importing or attracting whole new populations. In some cases, moreover—most notably in the East Coast Residency and on the western coast of Malaya, where the imported labor was alien to the area—plantation regimes contributed significantly to the development of plural societies and, in this way, to long-lasting social tensions.

Plantations began to play a decisive role in Malaya later than they did across the Straits in the East Coast Residency, and they built on an economic foundation already laid by Chinese tin-mining. It was Malayan plantations that first responded to the suddenly rising world demand for rubber after 1900. In the boom years of the first three decades of the twentieth century, rubber came to dominate Malaya's agriculture and indeed its whole economy. Between 1905 and 1929, rubber acreage in Malaya increased from 50,000 to 3 million (about three times the acreage of rice, the next largest crop); rubber exports rose from 6,000 tons in 1910, as trees came into production, to 446,000 tons in 1929. Around 1914, rubber passed tin as Malaya's largest export, producing 27 per cent of Malaya's export income in 1916 and 60 per cent by 1929. Though smallholdings produced an increasing proportion of the totals after about 1915, it was the plantations that contributed a whole new element to the Malayan population in those years. As in the East Coast Residency, the Malays had no need or desire for wage labor; their response to the rubber boom, when they found the way, was smallholding. Chinese, though they provided some plantation labor and owned a handful of plantations, stayed mainly in their own businesses of tin and commerce; and when they, in turn, took up rubber, it was characteristically on medium-sized holdings. The English rubber planters therefore turned to the readily available supply of unskilled labor in southern India. Like the Chinese, the Indians intended to come for only a few years, sending cash home to their impoverished villages and returning later with some savings, and most followed that program. Also like the Chinese, however, some stayed on. During the first decade of the Indian Immigration Committee, established in 1907 by government and planters to organize and supervise the migration,

700,000 Indian laborers entered Malaya, and 480,000 departed. By such steady net additions, the third major element of the Malayan plural society was built up.

PEASANTS AND MIDDLEMEN

European-run plantations in Malaya, followed shortly by those in the Netherlands Indies, led the way in rubber-growing, as late as 1929 still producing about 50 per cent of all world rubber. But smallholders in those two countries, beginning large-scale planting about a decade after the plantations, were catching up rapidly. In 1929, they were already exporting almost 40 per cent of world rubber. A decade later, roughly 1 million smallholders in Sumatra, Malaya, and Borneo had more than 4 million acres of mature trees capable of supplying most of world demand at prices that few plantations could meet. Only gross discrimination under colonial commodity control programs prevented them in the 1930's from dominating production of one of the world's most important export products.[22]

The above figures show the magnitude of the swing to smallholder rubber, but contemporary sources provide little information on the history of this peasant movement and its meaning to the societies it swept over.[23] Word of the fabulous prices and of the success of both plantations and smallholders spread rapidly, and peasants soon saw rubber as an ideal crop for their purposes. In the boom years—1910–20 in Malaya and the 1920's in Sumatra—they followed their conclusions with action. Rubber was ideal in many different ways. Ecologically, the rubber tree—a great success in its wild state in tropical Brazil—was very well adapted to the poor soils and fierce botanical competition of Southeast Asian forests. It required little effort to plant rubber seedlings on an already cleared and used swidden plot before moving on in the swidden cycle, or to plant an acre or two on permanently cultivated land. Once planted, the rubber trees grew just like any other secondary forest, requiring little tending. Tapping techniques were easily learned.

Rubber was also ideal in economic terms. While waiting for their seedlings to mature, and in bad times when rubber prices were low, peasants could live as before on their wet rice or swidden. In good times, a few acres of trees, tapped by the owner himself, provided cash for buying more rice than a one-family rice farm yielded with much harder work, and also for taxes and imported goods. Peasant export production, of course, required middlemen to move the rubber to the market, and that part of the industry grew up as quickly and naturally as the peasant side: Chinese merchants (and some Sumatrans) moved readily to perform their complementary role. At assembly points in the rubber districts, dealers set up the inexpensive equipment necessary to prepare rubber for shipment, and from there the smoked rubber sheets moved down to the larger ports, such as Singapore, from which 300,000 or 400,000 tons of smallholder rubber were shipped each year.

Finally, rubber was ideal in social terms for subsistence peasants venturing into a cash economy. Though some peasants hired share-tappers to help them at peak periods, and others had large enough stands to require regular share-tapping, nearly all the million or so smallholders of the 1930's owned just a few acres of trees, which they operated themselves with the help of their relatives.[24] Owning a few such plots near his village, and usually continuing to cultivate rice or other crops, the peasant could enjoy the advantages of a prime cash crop without risk and without leaving village society. It was an irresistible prospect and led quickly to a classic peasant-middleman export industry.

Rubber—plantation and smallholder—was the most spectacular export industry in early-twentieth-century Southeast Asia. Virtually none was exported in 1900, but by the 1930's it had become the most important export generally from Malaya and the Netherlands Indies and by far the most important peasant export from those countries. Its world significance was even greater: In the first four decades of the twentieth century, Malaya and the Netherlands Indies consistently supplied 75 per cent or more, and all of Southeast Asia 90 per cent or more, of all world rubber consumption.

Rice, the other major peasant export crop of Southeast Asia, had a much plainer record. In world terms, for example, Southeast Asia produced 70 per cent or more of world exports, but they represented only a tiny fraction of world consumption. The long-term significance of rice in the economic history of Southeast Asia, however, was considerably greater than that of rubber. It was not rubber, but tin, sugar and other products, that had inaugurated the export economies of Malaya and the Netherlands Indies. Rice, however, was the first major export of Burma, Thailand, Cambodia, and Vietnam, and it remained their leading export earner through almost the whole colonial period. It was also, throughout the period, a wholly peasant-produced crop and therefore the most important of the peasant-middleman industries.

The large-scale rice export industries which grew up in Lower Burma, Cochinchina, and central Thailand (Cambodian exports were much smaller) from around 1870 had much in common. They were made possible in the first place by the fact that the deltas of the Irrawaddy, Mekong, and Čhaophraya rivers, soggy alluvial plains very suitable for rice-growing, had never been heavily settled because the incentive to drain them had not previously existed. Unlike the Red River delta and Java, which produced large quantities of rice in the same period but also supported heavy populations and therefore could not yield an export surplus, those three deltas were able to produce large exports without any major change of growing technique. When worldwide demand increased, around 1870, peasants in or near the delta zones responded readily, moving out over the uncultivated stretches to practice a somewhat more extensive agriculture, which yielded a salable surplus. Middlemen—Chinese, Indian, and some indigenous—moved in to supply credit and imports and to assemble the rice in larger quantities for eventual milling and export.

Such was the common pattern of the industry. But the elements were mixed very differently, and the historical development and consequences diverged even more markedly, in the several countries. Since the Lower Burma rice industry was the earliest, largest, and most complex, it will serve as the type case here.[25] In 1855, just after the second Anglo-Burman War, in which the British seized the delta, there was an estimated total of 1 million acres under rice in Lower Burma.[26] By 1873, a second million had been added, and thereafter the amount of land under rice increased by 1 million acres every seven years, reaching 10 million in 1930. In the same period (1855–1931), the population of Lower Burma increased from about 1.5 million to about 8 million, more than twice as fast as the population of Upper Burma (which suggests the social effects of the rice export industry), but half as fast as rice acreage (which yielded an ever-increasing surplus for export).

The complex social history of the Burmese rice export industry from 1870 to 1940 may be divided into three phases: 1870–1900, the open frontier; 1900–29, maturity and internal change; 1930–40, depression and social collapse. The first phase was given its character by the vast amounts of good rice land readily available throughout the delta. It was dominated socially by the independent Burman smallholder. World demand led European shippers and millers in the major ports to pay steadily rising cash prices for rice. That exciting prospect drew pioneers from the settled areas of the delta and down from Upper Burma to clear and plant fifty-acre holdings. The holdings were much larger than traditional peasant subsistence plots and therefore required sizable amounts of seasonal labor, which came mostly from Upper Burma. From the beginning, too, the whole rice industry was lubricated by an elaborate system of credit. Big mills in Rangoon and Bassein gave cash advances to the larger rice brokers, and they in turn gave advances to smaller brokers. Chettyars made mortgage loans to cultivators needing capital to pay for clearing and plow animals. Burman and Chinese shopkeepers and Burman moneylenders made short-term loans to cultivators to pay for migrant labor, marriage ceremonies, or *pwe* performances. At the heart of the credit system stood the Chettyar firms, a tightly knit fraternity of honest and efficient bankers who asked lower interest rates than those customary in Burma, because they confined themselves mainly to well-secured loans. It is not clear whether it was the extraordinarily rapid growth of the industry that required so vast a use of credit or the extraordinary services of the Chettyars that made possible the rapid growth. But there is no doubt that credit, especially Chettyar loans, was fundamental to the industry as it grew.

Some of the special features of the Burmese rice industry are already evident from the list of participants given above. Indigenous smallholders, immigrant Asian moneylenders, and European shippers are familiar from other Southeast Asian peasant-middleman industries. But in Lower Burma, the peasant cultivators from the beginning hired migrant labor not only for harvesting help, as in quite a few other cases, but for such jobs as clearing forest and plowing—labor long ahead of harvest and therefore usually requiring cash payment. There were also three quite distinct immigrant Asian groups occupying particular slots that elsewhere were usually all occupied by the Chinese. First were the Chettyars, who specialized in rural banking and played virtually no part in commerce. Second were the Indian (mostly Telugu) seasonal laborers, who in this phase largely confined themselves to wage labor jobs in the cities—in rice mills and on the docks—which Burmans would not take. Third were the Chinese shopkeepers, who played the more familiar role of advancing goods and cash against repayment in rice at harvest time, but on a much smaller scale than elsewhere.

The most atypical feature, however, was the vigorous thrust of Burmans into middleman functions elsewhere left almost entirely to Chinese. From the beginning, Burman shopkeepers and moneylenders played a major role throughout the delta. Above all, Burmans did much of the brokerage by which a few dozen baskets of rice here, 100 baskets there, were assembled into the hundreds of thousands of tons that flowed into the mills in the ports. Burmans certainly made up the great majority of the "jungle-brokers," who acquired the rice directly from the cultivators, but they apparently played a considerable part as well in larger-scale brokerage farther down the veins of the system. It is not clear why. Perhaps the reluctance of Chettyars to deal in rice, coupled with the paucity of Chinese, left a gap in the chain, which Burmans came to fill. Perhaps Burman peasant values allowed for more risk-taking and entrepreneurship than is considered "normal" for Southeast Asian peasants. Certainly, there was a land-rush atmosphere on the delta at the time, and Burmans engaged in all sorts of speculations.

In its second phase, from around 1900 to the onset of the Depression, the Lower Burma rice industry reached full maturity, at the same time changing markedly in its internal organization. Rice acreage rose from 7 million in 1904 to 10 million in 1930; exports rose from about 2 million to 3 million tons; export income, compounded by rising prices, doubled between 1906 and 1926; annual totals of Indian labor migration into and out of Burma rose from 284,000 in 1900 to 777,000 in 1929.

The internal changes that accompanied the flowering were ominous, particularly for the characteristic figure of the previous phase, the peasant pioneer. Having committed himself in the days of the open frontier to a more thoroughly commercial mode of agriculture than most Southeast Asian peasant producers of export crops, the Burman smallholder now faced directly the inevitable risks of this economic system. A fluctuation in the world price for rice, the death of a costly plow animal, or an impulsive extravagance could suddenly turn his precariously balanced load of credit into an unpayable debt. The same had often happened in the pioneer phase, too, but then there was plenty of land, and the peasant could simply move on deeper into the delta and start again. Now population was rising and the land was filling up; insolvent peasants slid swiftly down to tenancy or landlessness.

Tenancy had begun earlier—25 per cent of the land in the thirteen main rice-producing districts of Lower Burma was already operated by cash tenants in the early twentieth century—but rents and conditions were still comparatively good. By 1928, however, the figure had risen to 42 per cent; rents were much higher, tenants were more liable to eviction, and increasingly land was rented annually to the highest bidder. Some of the land that Burman smallholders were losing passed into the hands of Chettyars and Chinese shopkeepers, but the bulk of it went to Burmans. The emerging Burman landlord class had very heterogeneous origins, including moneylenders, former smallholders, government officials from the towns, and the owners of the hundreds of smaller Burman-run local rice mills, which were established in the delta after 1900. Most landlords, alien or Burman, were absentee, living in the towns or Rangoon.

In those years, moreover, the character of delta society was strongly affected by a growing influx of Indians. In the late nineteenth century, Indians had largely confined themselves to urban jobs. At that time, the typical landless laborer in Lower Burma was a seasonal migrant from Upper Burma who came down river to earn some cash before returning home. After 1900, few Upper Burmans came south. Their place was partly taken by Lower Burman peasants—former smallholders or tenants. But more and more of the field labor was now done by organized Indian work gangs, under *maistry* (crew bosses), which circulated through the rice districts, contracting for a job, doing it, and moving on to the next. Indians, too, provided a steadily increasing proportion of tenants in the rice districts, where their competition helped drive up the rents.

In the early decades of the twentieth century, the above trends had not yet reached their limits. More than half the land was still owned by smallholder cultivators. Burman landlords, especially those who lived on their properties, could have close relations with their tenants. But the social context of rice production was steadily loosening. The one-family holding of the traditional subsistence pattern was a sharply defined institution, the basic building block of a village community. The commercial smallholding of the late-nineteenth-century rice frontier—though penetrated by market forces, credit, and outside labor—was still a meaningful social unit. Now, however, the edges of even that unit were blurring; men were becoming mere factors of production, pushed about by economic forces across the expanses of an increasingly shapeless delta society.

This curious and unpleasant social machine continued to operate, producing huge exports and profits, until the Depression. Then, suddenly, it broke down, and since no one knew how to fix it properly it was allowed to carry on improperly, doing damage to almost all concerned, until the Japanese invasion wiped it out. It seems clear in retrospect that by about 1930 the system had come to the end of its rope. It had been made possible, to begin with, by the sparse population and abundance of uncultivated land in the delta. That frontier was now almost closed—rice land in Lower Burma stayed steady at just short of 10 million acres from 1931 to 1941, while population continued to rise. Pressure on the land, compounded by the peculiarly commercial character of the industry, had already been undermining established social patterns for decades. The Depression, which manifested itself in Burma by steeply falling rice prices and a sharp drop in rice export earnings, disintegrated the pyramid of credit on which the whole system was based. The Depression precipitated the crisis, but it fell on a house of cards.

The symptoms of social collapse were many. Labor gangs and annual renting of land to the highest bidder grew more common. The amount of land owned by landlords in the thirteen main rice-producing districts of Lower Burma rose sharply from 43 per cent in 1928 to 58 per cent in 1935, and many of the remaining smallholders were by that time little more than debt-bondsmen on their own land. One very clear sign of crisis was the rapid increase in foreclosures by Chettyars. As late as 1930, they owned only 500,000 acres (6 per cent) in the thirteen districts; by 1935, they had acquired 1.5 million acres more, holding 24 per cent of the land there. Chettyars wanted land as little as mortgage bankers want houses; only catastrophic insolvency among their debtors could force them to accumulate land, and they spent the rest of the decade trying (at some profit) to extricate themselves from their Lower Burma quagmire.

A more obvious symptom of social collapse was the cycle of anti-Indian and anti-Chinese riots in Lower Burma between 1930 and 1932 —the later stages of which were mixed up with the Saya San Rebellion —and the further anti-Indian riots of 1938. Partly as a result of this, and partly because of the general stagnation of the rice business, the volume of Indian migration into and out of Burma fell off sharply from 777,000 in 1929 to an annual average of 483,000 in the years 1933–38. After 1931, moreover, almost the same number left as entered Burma each year, so that the Indian minority in Burma, which had almost doubled to 1 million (7 per cent) between 1901 and 1931, stayed level.

The third phase ended with serious efforts by home-rule Burman governments to solve the delta problem, but war proved more efficient. The Japanese invasion drove several hundred thousand Indian refugees to India, and the Japanese occupation quite simply made rice exports impossible. It was left to the independent nationalist governments after the war to pick up the pieces and to try to construct a new society in Lower Burma.

The other two major rice exporting areas in Southeast Asia were the Čhaophraya and Mekong deltas, each of which consistently produced about one-half as much export rice as Lower Burma. They followed the same general pattern as in Burma, but the differences—especially in Thailand—are well worth noting.

In the mid-nineteenth century the Mekong delta was even more sparsely populated than the Irrawaddy delta. In the course of their thousand-year drive to the south (*Nam Tien*), the Vietnamese had first reached the open delta in the seventeenth century, but two and a half centuries later their settlements were still comparatively small and were mainly confined to the eastern region around Saigon. It was that area which the French first conquered in 1858–67, and one of the first things they did was redirect its small rice surplus from Hue to overseas markets. In the next two or three decades, there developed a peasant rice frontier moving southwest from the settled area deeper into the delta, a movement rather similar to that of Lower Burma but considerably smaller and slower. Beginning in the late nineteenth century, however, vast canal and drainage projects undertaken by the colonial government brought a much more rapid expansion of the industry, and by the mid-1930's the population of Cochinchina had increased three times (to 4.5 million), rice acreage four times (to 5.5 million acres) and rice exports about five times (to 1.2 million tons).

The social and ethnic structure of the Cochinchinese rice industry was considerably simpler than in Burma, mainly because the Chinese dominated marketing and processing to the virtual exclusion of other aliens and of Vietnamese. French citizens who owned a handful of mills in Saigon did much of the shipping, but otherwise the rice business was almost entirely in Chinese hands—from the big millers and exporters in Saigon, through the large rice dealers in Saigon and their agents in the rural market towns, down to the thousands of Chinese shopkeepers and small-boat traders who sold goods on credit to the Vietnamese producers and acquired their crops in return. Like their compatriots in Thailand, the Chinese in Cochinchina acquired rice-growing peasant debtors but not rice land—quite unlike the Chinese, and especially the Chettyars, in Lower Burma.

The pattern of moneylending and peasant landlessness was rather like that of Burma by the 1930's, but its process of development was quite different. In the eastern delta around Saigon, the longer-established peasant society drifted under the influence of commercial export production into a pattern of medium-sized landlord holdings, built up mostly by local moneylending, of a sort more or less familiar in Vietnam. Farther west, especially in the area beyond the Bassac, the westernmost branch of the Mekong in the delta, much larger properties predominated from the beginning, as the colonial government sold off great blocks of land after completing its drainage projects there. Those estates, cheaply acquired by Saigon Vietnamese closely associated with the French regime and by French individuals, were called "plantations" but were operated like Philippine *haciendas*, with the land parcelled out among tenants. Rice was grown in small peasant units, with heavy use of seasonal labor by landless peasants living nearby or coming from the eastern delta or northern Vietnam. Since the rice itself passed through Chinese channels, the profits to the absentee landlords came from rent and moneylending to tenants. As in Lower Burma, the peasants had moved out onto an almost empty frontier to clear and plant the land, but in the Mekong delta they began in a state of tenancy and landlessness that in the Irrawaddy delta took half a century to evolve. In the long run, however, Vietnamese peasants were no more willing to accept such conditions than were the Burmans. The political significance of their growing resentment was to become fully apparent after 1945.

The Thai rice industry, by contrast, had a straightforward, steady, and serene history up to 1940. One reason is that Thailand was opened to world commerce not by conquest, like Lower Burma and Cochinchina, but by the relatively conservative formula of the 1855 treaty, which entrenched the authority of the pragmatic and cautious modernizers of the Mongkut-Bunnag school, supported by like-minded English advisers to the court. The regime moved steadily but slowly to abolish *corvée* and slavery (both of which inhibited the free movement of the Thai peasant and therefore the pace of the rice industry's growth) and refused, for fiscal reasons, to invest more than small sums in irrigation and drainage (which again slowed the pace and tended to keep rice land in peasant hands). More generally, much less outside capital—from government investment and alien moneylenders—seems to have gone into the agricultural side of Thai rice than in Lower Burma and Cochinchina. For these and other reasons, the rice industry in the Čhaophraya delta, from which virtually all exports came until the 1920's, grew more slowly than in Lower Burma and was always far less commercial than in both Lower Burma and Cochinchina. As Thai peasants moved into the open lands of the delta, they cleared smaller cultivating units, used less seasonal labor, and above all financed the expansion very largely by themselves. The rice frontier was a great movement, as in Lower Burma and Cochinchina, but it was much more a peasant movement. The central Thai peasant remained throughout the period an independent subsistence farmer who also grew large amounts of rice as a cash crop with which to pay money taxes and to buy such imported goods as textiles, kerosene lamps, and kerosene.

Since there were few landlords—and those few mainly Thai—and since European-owned mills in Bangkok quickly gave way to Chinese competition after the 1890's, the only real partners of the peasants in the rice industry were the Chinese. In Bangkok, large Chinese mills, using Chinese labor, dominated the rice business. In the rural areas Chinese middlemen circulated in their small boats, dealing with a familiar clientele, bringing news, selling imported goods, advancing supplies, loaning money, and taking out the surplus rice at harvest time. By the 1930's, the Thai elite in Bangkok was much exercised about Chinese commercial dominance, but the peasants found the Chinese middleman indispensable and easy to deal with. So did the Cambodian peasants in their much smaller rice industry, so closely resembling the Thai one.

Rubber and rice were the most important peasant-middleman export crops in Southeast Asia in the period and played decisive roles in the social and political as well as the economic history of large parts of the area. But peasants and foreign middlemen brought a wide variety of other crops to the world market, including rubber from Burma and Thailand, abaca and copra from the Philippines, and copra from the eastern islands of the Netherlands Indies. Nor, of course, did peasant producers or middlemen confine themselves to export products and markets. There had always been a certain amount of local and regional trade, particularly in essential foodstuffs like fish and salt, and with rapidly increasing populations, improving transportation, increasing economic specialization of certain areas, and above all the growth of cities and towns throughout the area, the volume of internal trade increased enormously. In the early twentieth century, various parts of Upper Burma sent almost 100,000 draft animals a year to the rice areas of Lower Burma; the Chinese fishing villages at Bagan Si-Api-Api in East Sumatra shipped 80,000 tons of fish a year to markets in Malaya and Sumatra; the Hindu-Buddhist Balinese sent shiploads of pigs stacked noisily in wicker baskets to feed the Chinese and Europeans in most of Islamic Indonesia and Malaya. Except for some Chinese market gardening near the larger cities and the unique Bagan Si-Api-Api fisheries, the agricultural and sea products, baskets, hats, and the like were all produced by peasant smallholders, often as a cash sideline to their subsistence farming. And except for short-distance trading of foodstuffs to markets, which peasant growers often conducted for themselves, and some of the wider activities of *santri* traders in the archipelago, the commercial side of the internal trade was largely incorporated into the Chinese middleman networks. Even rice—as urban demand grew, smaller local mills spread through the countryside, and peasants developed a taste for the white milled product—ceased in many areas to be something peasants grew, stored, milled and ate themselves. It became a major item in trade, serving as one of the main levers of Chinese commercial dominance in non-rice-exporting areas such as northern and central Vietnam, Java, and the Philippines.

WESTERN CAPITALISTS WITH LOCAL LABOR

The final group of export industries comprised those Western capitalist enterprises that for one reason or another used locally resident labor rather than immigrants housed on the premises. The distinction between them and the other capitalist industries already discussed is not always clear-cut and may even be insignificant from the point of view of economic organization, but it tells a great deal about the social history of Southeast Asia. One example was the teak industry of Burma and northern Thailand—the second or third largest export earner in those countries for much of the period. On the management side, it was fully a capitalist industry, dominated by a handful of European-run firms that mobilized the large amounts of capital required by the cost of elephants and by the long waiting period between the first girdling of a teak tree and its sale as board-feet in India or Europe six or more years later. Teak labor—a gaudy mixture of Burmans, Shan and Lao, Karens and hill tribesmen—was vastly different from the company-housed, -doctored, and -schooled Tamils of a Malayan rubber plantation. The teak companies acquired labor by bringing employment to their employees rather than vice versa, just as they cut wild teak rather than grow it. For those reasons, their vast operations had very little effect (except ecologically) on the areas they moved through, while plantations were nodes of settlement and permanent economic activity in their sparsely settled areas, around which new societies grew.

The latter point is illustrated by the second set of cases, the considerable number of plantations in the hilly and previously sparsely settled interior of East and West Java, which in the early twentieth century began to rely more and more on local peasants for labor, after having done much to build up the local population and economy themselves in the nineteenth century. In this respect, the Java plantations were only anticipating what was to become a general change in the character of plantation labor in later decades. Plantations in Malaya and the East Coast Residency of Sumatra, for example, began to hire local labor on a considerable scale in the 1950's, as population built up and local peasants began to change their economic attitudes and to accept wage labor. The plantation in Southeast Asia was a frontier institution of the high colonial period, a transplant from the industrial West, run by Westerners, set down in the emptier parts of Southeast Asia where at first no other methods were possible. As such, it was necessarily transitory. In time, Chinese and Southeast Asians, individuals, companies, and governments, were to begin taking over the management of those enterprises, and labor came more and more from local sources. The plantation began to be absorbed into its local economic environment—which it had often largely created—and lost its special historical character. In place of the sharp discontinuities of the pioneer phase (plantations utterly different from peasant subsistence at the other extreme) came a more evenly graduated spectrum (more and less capital-intensive, large- and smaller-scale) on a more homogeneous economic landscape.

The sugar industries of Java and the Philippines were much the largest and most important of the capitalist enterprises using peasant rather than imported labor. Between 1870 and 1930, the Java sugar industry grew enormously, shipping 100,000 tons in 1865, 750,000 in 1900, 3 million in 1930, and becoming far and away the leading earner and premier export industry of the Netherlands Indies in that period. A small but substantial sugar industry developed on the Philippine island of Negros in the second half of the nineteenth century (90,000 tons by 1893), but it stagnated after that. The real growth of the Philippine sugar industry came when the Philippines was granted a sizable quota in the protected high-price U.S. market. Sugar quickly became and remained the Philippines' leading export industry, recovering its vigor on Negros and developing a second main focus on the central plain of Luzon.

Throughout its long history, sugar has almost always been a capitalist industry, if only because of the heavy costs of mill equipment (a modern Philippine centrifugal central cost about $1 million in 1920). Sugar all over the world in the past few centuries has almost always been grown on plantations with imported (often slave) labor. It was, therefore, particularly significant that in Java and the Philippines the sugar labor consisted of local settled peasants or at most seasonal migrants. In the Javanese case, the reason was that the sugar mills were built in already populated areas, where irrigated rice land highly suitable for sugar was already available. Javanese peasants in the early nineteenth century were no more interested in wage labor than other Southeast Asian peasants, but the older tradition of *corvée* could be modified to produce a suitable labor force.

The use of peasant labor in Philippine sugar had a somewhat different background. On Luzon, sugar became a major crop in a landscape already largely occupied by peasant cultivators. The sugar centrals, therefore, rarely had their own fields and full-time wage labor force, and they did not need them. Instead, they worked through the *hacienda* with its many tenants, contracting for certain amounts of cane and dividing the proceeds with the *hacendero* for further division down the line to his tenants, who actually grew the cane. The industry flourished under that arrangement, but it created a characteristic tension between *hacenderos* and *centralistas* over the division of the profits, a dispute that, given the great economic power of those concerned, expressed itself regularly in Philippine party politics.[27] More important, sugar-growing under that formula exacerbated relations between *hacenderos* and tenants, contributing to the political and revolutionary movements there in the 1930's and thereafter.

Sugar began to be grown on Negros in important quantities after 1855, when the port of Iloilo, across the strait on the island of Panay, was opened to world trade. At that time, Negros was very lightly populated, but the land was highly suitable for sugar cane. With the encouragement of British export-import firms, Chinese *mestizos* from Iloilo crossed to Negros and set up small but up-to-date mills. Elsewhere that might have led quickly to plantations, but since the *mestizos* lacked the capital, and since they were more at home with the *hacienda* as a type of landowner-labor relation, the Negros sugar industry developed with millers normally owning *haciendas* and tenants growing most of the cane. With some difficulty, therefore—eased by heavy use of seasonal labor from the nearby islands—the millers of Negros managed to create on the open frontier of their island a land and labor pattern like that of the older and more densely populated areas of Luzon. Negros, however, saw much less tension between *centralistas* and *hacenderos* and between *hacenderos* and tenants, and its social and political history at least for the first half of the twentieth century was considerably calmer than that of central Luzon.

The importance of the export industries that grew so rapidly between 1870 and 1940 went far beyond the statistics by which their progress is often measured. They stood near the center of the economic and social history of the high colonial age, powerfully influencing—and also influenced by—developments in other spheres. The export industries both gained from and served to reinforce the new "national" frameworks that were developing in the same period. Their growth created in the economic life of Southeast Asia a dependence on world markets whose real long-term significance was only suggested by the painful episode of the Depression. They provided the economic base and much of the impetus for the growth of the modern urban areas and also did much to create a demand for modern-educated Southeast Asians—developments that themselves were prime determinants of twentieth-century Southeast Asian history. They also attracted large numbers of alien immigrants, thus contributing directly to the growth of the plural societies that were so typical of the area in the period and that brought such severe conflicts in the 1940's and afterward.

The export boom, nevertheless, was not the only driving force behind economic change in the period, and there were major economic movements that cannot be fully dealt with in terms of the rise of the export industries alone. This was particularly true of the changes that took place in the economic life of the great mass of the peasant population.

In 1940, after seventy years of rapid change that had created export-dominated economies through Southeast Asia, it was doubtful whether as many as half of the peasants played any direct part in export production. A considerably smaller proportion were anything more than part-time export growers. Even fewer had replaced the fundamental goal of subsistence with the goal of personal advancement, which so fiercely drove the Europeans, the Chinese, and some Indians. Nevertheless, the economic life of almost all Southeast Asian peasants had been profoundly altered in the previous three-quarters of a century. Economic change among the peasant millions was gradual, often almost invisible, but cumulatively massive. Within this tidal movement, peasant export production was simply one of many types of response to a variety of new forces impinging on village economic life.

There were three major determinants of economic change among peasants in the period. One was increasing exposure to the world economy—to world market demand for export products but also to imported consumer goods. As such goods became available, flowing inward from the great ports through improving transport and market networks, peasant families looked them over with the same shrewd eye they used for new opportunities for earning income, rejecting shoes as they did wage labor, accepting undershorts as they did export rubber or rice. Southeast Asian peasants had long accepted sizable quantities of

Indian textiles and Chinese ceramics, and they responded as readily, and often remarkably fast, to new imports. By the turn of the century, imported soap, for example, had already replaced homemade varieties in rural Thailand; Milkmaid Brand condensed milk was so widely used in Lower Burma that its tins became a standard of measurement in country rice transactions; kerosene, first introduced in the 1860's, was already selling in the millions of gallons a decade later, and by the end of the century the kerosene lamp was well on the way to ousting coconut oil and wick all over rural Southeast Asia. Machine-made textiles, matches, and, in the twentieth century, sewing machines and bicycles all gained wide and easy acceptance.

A second major determinant of peasant economic change was colonial government policy. British land policy in Burma made it possible for landlords and moneylenders to gain control of most Lower Burma land by 1940, while the Malay Reservations Enactment of 1913 and the Netherlands Indies Land Law of 1870 helped preserve peasant smallholdings throughout the period—a situation not necessarily more advantageous for the peasant, but certainly very different. The more efficient collection of land, harvest, and head taxes throughout the area, particularly because they were increasingly levied in cash, required peasants to seek cash incomes in various ways. Irrigation and drainage works, disease-prevention measures, government grants of land to Europeans, salt and other monopolies, increased use or gradual abandonment of *corvée* levies—all had strong effects on peasant economic life.

A third major determinant was the rather sudden and very large increase in the population of Southeast Asia from about 55 million in 1870 to about 145 million in 1940. While immigration, particularly of Chinese, played an appreciable part in the increase, most of it came from slowly falling death rates and stable or slightly rising birth rates among the great mass of peasants. In 1940, as throughout history, most of the area was still lightly populated by the standards of its neighbors, India and China, but there were ample signs of the coming demographic crisis. Java, to take the extreme case, had a population of 17.5 million and a good portion of empty land in 1870; by 1940, it had 48 million, and, for practical purposes, all cultivable land was occupied. Even in less crowded areas—such as Thailand, whose population rose from 6 to 15 million in the period—the rapid increase itself had powerful effects on the economic life of the peasantry.

In speaking of the effects of these strong new forces, there is a tendency to depict the peasants as objects rather than subjects, as passive beneficiaries of health measures or agricultural extension work, or as helpless victims relentlessly milked by the Indochinese salt and alcohol monopolies, losing their land in Lower Burma, squeezed onto smaller and smaller plots on Java or Luzon. All that is true enough; in many ways, peasants were swept along by economic forces that they could hardly hope to deflect and never fully understood. But if the historian sees the people of a society as simply the objects of policies, the locus of problems, and the occasion for revealing his own ideas of right and wrong, he denies those people the right to enact their own history. Much of the effect of the economic changes of the period on Southeast Asian peasants can be understood only in terms of their active response to new dangers and opportunities. To simplify again, there were at least three broad types of peasant response.

One form of peasant response was adoption of the habits and assumptions of a cash economy, not necessarily the same as those of townspeople and aliens, but adapted to their own economic context. In general, Southeast Asian peasants seem to have thought of money not as an absolute standard of value but as an additional medium—just like land, rice, and socially-prescribed labor obligations, for example—for use in economic transactions. As such, money had the virtue of flexibility—it was easily handled, free of social meanings that might restrict its use, and valued outside as well as inside the village. Peasants readily added it to their economic repertoire for use in an increasing number of cases where such flexibility was needed, but they did not rely on it exclusively.

They also responded in various ways to the extra-village money economy, which required them to pay taxes in cash and offered them attractive imports, which had to be bought with cash or its equivalent. Smallholder export production was one of the ways, but in many areas peasants also took up domestic cash crops and home industries in the same spirit: sesame oil and other food crops in Upper Burma for sale in Lower Burma, sleeping mats and rattan chairs in northern Vietnam, all sorts of vegetables in Java, tobacco in northern Luzon after the end of the government monopoly. In time, too, peasants became more willing to take up wage labor outside the village.

A second major type of peasant response to the various new economic forces impinging on peasant life was migration, much of it, but not all, in the search for cash pay. Socially, the easiest form was seasonal migration, usually in the harvest season, a pattern found in the Burman and Cochinchinese rice industries and Negros sugar but not confined to them. It was more significant when, around the turn of the century, large numbers of contract laborers from certain areas began to go to plantations: Javanese to the East Coast Residency of Sumatra and as far away as Surinam; northern Vietnamese to rubber plantations in Cochinchina and to New Caledonia and elsewhere in the Pacific; Filipinos to Hawaii, Guam, and the continental United States. The migration was partly coerced and thoroughly controlled by one-sided devices like penal sanctions to enforce labor contracts. But it was essentially voluntary, a peasant solution, in areas that had particularly dense populations, to the problem of increasing pressure on the land. In the twentieth century, another form of labor migration was to the rapidly growing areas all over Southeast Asia. In the early twentieth century, immigrant peasants in the towns conformed to the plural patterns of the time: They were primarily servants, trishaw drivers, office messengers, and street vendors, leaving other occupations, such as dock and factory work, to Chinese and Indians. It was only subsequently that Southeast Asians—new arrivals or by now permanent city dwellers—began to move into those latter occupations, either competing with the aliens, as in Rangoon in the 1930's, or replacing them as they moved upward socially.

The peasants, particularly in the decade or two before 1940, gradually lost their earlier reluctance to leave their villages to seek wage labor. Meanwhile, other peasants were engaged in a quite different, and socially more conservative, form of migration, spreading out more evenly on the land and filling up unoccupied areas with peasant villages. The peasant rice frontiers of the Irrawaddy, Čhaophraya, and Mekong deltas have already been mentioned, but there were other important cases as well. Some were extensions of much older historical movements. The Vietnamese who pushed into the western delta and northward across the Cambodian border were carrying forward the thousand-year-old drive to the south. The Javanese who moved into the interior of West Java, to the Lampung area at the southern tip of Sumatra, and to parts of Borneo, Celebes, and Malaya were following predecessors who had spilled outward from the relatively heavily populated Javanese core areas, for example to the north coast of West Java in the sixteenth and seventeenth centuries. Other such migrations were newer: Ilocanos, in the nineteenth and twentieth centuries, spread widely over northern Luzon from their overcrowded coastal lands; Bisayans began to settle heavily on the northern coast and major river valleys of Mindanao in the same period; Madurese came to occupy much of the eastern coast of Java.

A third type of peasant response, agricultural intensification, was due primarily to population pressure and manifested itself mainly inside the village. Peasants adopted crops new to Southeast Asia, or to their areas, such as peanuts, cassava, maize, and dozens of others. They began to grow cash crops on rice fields in the dry season, or double-cropped rice, or made more use of flooded fields to grow fish; they cultivated more intensely, pregerminating rice in their houses before planting and then transplanting; they grew cassava on the dikes between the paddies, and they harrowed and weeded more thoroughly. In such ways, by raising productivity per acre while the population was rising, they managed to keep per capita productivity more or less constant—a greater number of people treading water in the same pool.[28] Throughout the area—but most of all in the extreme Javanese case of agricultural involution—intensification affected not only agricultural practices but all aspects of village life. Increasingly elaborate patterns of tenancy and subtenancy, of land-renting and crop- and labor-sharing grew up in order to accommodate more and more people on limited amounts of land. Java was and is exceptional. But even the desperate expedients of its involution—undertaken so calmly by Javanese villagers—demonstrate the creativity of peasants in devising the patterns by which their own history was lived, while they were carried along by a flood they could not hope to control.

PART FOUR

Social Change and the Emergence of Nationalism

23

PRELUDES

As the author of a distinguished study of peasant revolt in colonial West Java has remarked, the history of the peasantry, however obscured by the activities of the great and powerful, contains currents that flow straight into modern times.[1] No phenomenon more frequently accompanied the intensification of Western rule than sporadic, localized, and usually short-lived episodes of peasant unrest. Because the voice of the peasant is too often submerged in the roar of high affairs, such episodes have seldom received the attention they deserve, either from contemporary colonial observers—who tended to regard them as, in the main, aberrations of the misled and the fanatical—or from historians. Peasant risings, in modern times as in the past, were seldom, if ever, "nationalist." The use of this term obscures many of the more important characteristics of peasant movements. If a sense of proportion is to be maintained, they are perhaps best seen as part of a long historical continuum in which peasant discontent has at all times and in all places manifested itself, where leadership was forthcoming, in outbreaks of opposition against authority. One historian has described those occasions as the "revolution of rising irritations."[2] In the nineteenth and early twentieth centuries the irritations sprang, for the most part, from the increasing irksomeness of Western colonial rule—administrative, economic, and other interference in peasant welfare and social values. Peasant rebellion tended to reflect revolt *against* changing times, rather than forward-looking desire for social reconstruction. Though directed in some sense at colonial authority, peasant movements seldom had far-reaching aims beyond the improvement of the peasants' own immediate situation, the removal of the irritant. Though they are, accordingly, different in character and intent from urban-based nationalism, they have an important place alongside the latter, which they often paralleled and sometimes fed, and into which they were eventually absorbed.

Though the countless manifestations of peasant discontent in Southeast Asia resulting directly or indirectly from Western intrusion were of many different kinds, it is possible to detect features that, if not always held in common, seem to be fairly characteristic. Most obviously, all were, by definition, agrarian—that is to say, they took place in rural areas among persons engaged in agricultural occupations of a traditional kind. They tended also to be highly localized, for, although on occasion movements amassed some thousands of followers, organization and leadership seldom extended beyond the immediate region. Generalized peasant discontent, which was as often a response to paternalistic interference and officious welfare policies as to calculated or careless harshness, may be assumed to have been somewhat more widespread than actual revolt. Where the latter crystallized out of the former, it was usually in response to leadership beyond the ordinary. The leaders of peasant revolts came less often from the rank and file of the peasantry than from what is sometimes called the rural elite—the better-off landholders, minor government functionaries at the village level, or religious leaders. In general, leadership was characterized by an emphasis on the traditional rather than the modern and offered a return to previously known (or imagined) patterns of stability. Many revolts had strong religious overtones or were explicitly religious, and some sought by puritanism and reform, or reformulation, to create the conditions for a millenarian return to or quest for the perfect state.

A few examples may serve to illustrate the variety as well as the similarities of peasant movements. In the Blora District of Central Java around 1890, the ideas and beliefs of an unlettered but tolerably well-off villager called Surontiko Samin began to attract followers from his own and neighboring villages.[3] Though later stages of the Samin movement were certainly associated with early-twentieth-century Dutch administrative efforts at village reorganization and alterations in the tax structure, its initial impetus remains obscure. From about 1905 onward, the Saminists came increasingly to Dutch attention as a result of their explicit withdrawal from the existing social and bureaucratic order by refusing to contribute to village rice banks and other communal agricultural institutions, by rejection of Islamic marriage forms, and by their insistence that taxes, if paid, were to be regarded as donations, not obligations. At the height of the first phase of Saminism in 1907, the movement was credited with only some 3,000 members, but the Dutch, always on the lookout for "fanaticism" and rebellion, and despite the careful nonviolence of the movement, feared a more general rising. Samin and his immediate followers were banished to the Outer Islands. Though it is possible that some peasants saw in Samin the expected *ratu adil,* or just prince, of Javanese-messianic expectations, there is little real evidence that the movement was millenarian in character. Samin's exile did not put an end to the movement, which continued sporadically in the district until the 1920's and beyond, usually associated with what were seen as the harassments of new taxes, new restrictions on forest product collection under revised forestry laws, and the like.

Newly imposed land taxes were also the immediate cause of the "To' Janggut" peasant rebellion in the Pasir Puteh district of Kelantan in 1915, a localized rising that nevertheless prompted nervous British administrators to see signs of a more general revolt in the state, and possibly throughout the Malay peninsula.[4] There is no evidence that such a revolt was imminent. The peasant rebellion appears to have taken its origin from a combination of circumstances. At a time when the traditional territorial chief was chafing at the loss of authority that had attended the introduction of the British-inspired administrative system, a fixed land rent was substituted for an earlier tax on crop production during the incumbency of a Malay assistant district officer from another state. Haji Mat Hassan, known as To' Janggut, an elderly peasant landowner and peddling trader with considerable personal charisma who had the clandestine encouragement of the territorial chief, raised a peasant following to attack and burn the district office as a protest against the new tax, and, it was rumored, to lead an army downriver and toward the capital of Kota Bharu. In fact, fewer than 200 men were directly involved, and, though there is no doubt that other peasants in the state disliked the new tax, evidence of anything like a general rising is lacking. Alarmed by a recent troop mutiny in Singapore and by confused reports from Kelantan, the British sent a detachment of the Shropshire Light Infantry and a gunboat to the state, where they rapidly succeeded in putting the peasant rebels to rout. Within the month, To' Janggut and a number of others had been killed, and an end had been put, if not to the discontent, at least to its open expression.

Saya San, leader of the 1930 peasant revolt in Lower Burma, unlike Samin and To' Janggut, was not a peasant but a former monk who in the late 1920's had conducted a survey of peasant grievances for a branch of the Rangoon-centered General Council of Burmese Associations. Retreating, symbolically, from the town, Saya San collected around himself in the Tharrawaddy District a peasant following, organizing a rebellion not along modern but on traditional lines. Saya San, as self-proclaimed heir to the Buddhist Burman kings—complete with the appurtenances of royalty and a forest "capital"—gave reality to the peasantry's desire not merely to rid itself of the ills of the present (born in part of the Great Depression), but to recreate an ideal past. Attacks on police stations, forestry headquarters, and the homes of village functionaries caught up in the colonial administration began a revolt that took the British more than a year and a half to stamp out.

At much the same time, on the headwaters of the Rejang River in Sarawak, a Dayak leader, Asun, who had for some years been a *penghulu* in the Brooke administration, was organizing another armed rising. The immediate cause of the unrest was the falling price of forest produce (on which the Iban economy in some important respects depended), along with the increasing incidence of administrative control in the form of restrictions on shifting cultivation, introduction of gun licenses, and the setting up of Forest Reserves, which trespassed on traditional rights to wood and water.[5] The revolt was scarcely a major one from the point of view of the colonial administration—a few dozen longhouses burned, a handful of people killed—but it kept the administration occupied until 1940, eight years after Asun himself had surrendered and been banished to another part of the state.

Movements of yet another kind, with large peasant followings, but originally of urban, Western-influenced beginnings, were exemplified by the *Guardia de Honor* in the Philippines and Cao Dai in Vietnam. The *Guardia de Honor*, founded in the 1880's by the Dominicans on Luzon as a confraternity devoted to the Virgin Mary and used by the friars as a paramilitary force to combat anti-Spanish revolutionaries in 1896, transformed itself in the last years of the century into a Filipino-inspired messianic sect.[6] Centered in the *barrio* of Cabaruan, it attracted many thousands of peasants to settle there, bringing with them their rice, which they gave to communal granaries. The leader of the sect, Baltazar, and his principal aides, were worshipped as the Trinity, the Virgin Mary, and the Apostles, and ruled the *barrio* as a theocracy. Though the movement had economic overtones—landlords were regarded as sinners, and the virtues of communal economic organization were emphasized—it appears to have been primarily religious in character, offering to its adherents revitalization of their own society and salvation through faith. At the height of the movement, some 25,000 people lived in Cabaruan, but in 1901 the Americans arrested the leaders on charges of banditry and murder, and the community dispersed—only to reappear briefly thirty years later in modified form at Tayug, twenty miles away, where the Colorum Rebellion took place.

Cao Dai, which took root in southern Vietnam in the 1920's, was perhaps less a peasant movement than any of the others discussed, though it had a large peasant following. On the borderline between religious reform and nationalist movement, Cao Dai attempted at one and the same time to outmodernize the West by presenting to its adherents an ideological synthesis of several of the major world religions—Buddhism, Taoism, Confucianism, Islam, and Christianity—and to restore the traditional values of Vietnamese civilization. Ngo Van Chieu, a middle-aged civil servant in the Cochinchina colonial government, was perhaps its principal founder, though the eventual result was an amalgam with systems other than his own. Attracting hundreds of thousands of peasant adherents, as well as townsmen, Cao Dai offered a restatement of traditional values in the context of manifest needs to combat Western influence in terms the West itself employed. Anticolonial in a conservative way, many Cao Dai leaders later became monarchical nationalists, retaining the allegiance of large numbers of peasants.

But if peasant, or peasant-based, movements of a variety of kinds were in the long run to lend substance to—if not always to find common cause with—the rising nationalisms of the region, it was chiefly in the new towns that political organizations with programs directed at independent nationhood and at the substitution of indigenous for alien rulers had their origin and their being. Many of the traditional elites of Southeast Asian societies, as we have seen, were pushed aside under the impact of intensive Western rule in the nineteenth century and thereafter, leaving a vacuum which was now to be filled either by elements of the old elite made over or more commonly by the new urban intelligentsia, whose aims and ideas owed much to the West itself and to its organizational forms. The new urban elites were influenced not only by the phenomena of urbanization and Western education but also by the presence in almost all Southeast Asian societies of powerful alien mercantile communities, principally Chinese, and by the presence in the air, as it were, of a range of new ideas, some alien in origin, others less so, which did much to determine some of the patterns that nationalist movements assumed.

It has been a persistent feature of the history and society of Southeast Asian states that many of their commercial and trading functions have been in the hands of foreigners, particularly Chinese. The earliest Chinese communities in the region—apart from the few river-based colonies in the remoter parts of Borneo and South Sumatra—were for the most part small settlements, ghettos (one writer has called them) outside the pale of the walled port towns or inland capitals.[7] From that vantage point, in strict subordination to court or harbor officials or to the local nobility, they conducted all manner of trade and commerce, within the country and without. Many of the communities probably varied seasonally in size; where they were larger and more permanent, they usually had a form of internal self-government, whereby the leading resident merchant (known subsequently in Malay as the *Kapitan China*) ordered the affairs of the Chinese populace and answered for them to the local ruler. Though there was some intensification of Chinese trading relationships with Southeast Asia after the European powers entered the maritime commercial scene, it was not until the onset of the high colonial era in the nineteenth century that major changes took place. Then, in response to the protection afforded and to the opportunities arising for participation in wholesale economic exploitation of the hinterland, much larger numbers of Chinese took up residence in the interstices of the colonial society as entrepreneurs, middlemen, retail merchants, domestics, and unskilled labor.

Early Chinese immigrants into the area, in the port settlement days, often married local women. In some societies—that of Thailand for example—the resulting offspring were regarded as indigenous quite as much as Chinese. Elsewhere, as with the *mestizos* of the Philippines, the *baba* Chinese of Malacca, or the *peranakan* of Java, the mixed community acquired a distinct identity of its own, although it was highly acculturated to the local society and was often regarded as a related part of it. With the greatly increased immigrations of the nineteenth century, all this began to change. Large, almost entirely male, Chinese communities appeared, frontier in character, and unassimilable by local societies. As physical and economic circumstances improved in the early twentieth century, women were brought from China to join the men, sex ratios began to stabilize, and the resulting Chinese communities became biologically as well as culturally a great deal more distinct from their neighbors (as well as much more numerous) than they had been before.

Some parts of Southeast Asia saw a much greater influx of Chinese than others. The outstanding example, of course, was peninsular Malaya, which, with a total population in 1850 of perhaps 500,000, mainly Malay, saw no fewer than 19 million Chinese arrive between the early nineteenth century and World War II. Most stayed only for a time, but the residue in 1931 accounted for 39 per cent of the total population. In the western coastal states, where they were most strongly concentrated, they far outnumbered the Malays. The Netherlands Indies had a much smaller Chinese component—less than 3 per cent of the total population in 1931. In both areas, ethnic Chinese, because of religious and other important cultural differences, remained quite distinct from the local population, and relatively easy to count. In many of the mainland states, where past assimilation had proceeded more rapidly even if, as in Thailand, a strong anti-Chinese reaction had set in in the twentieth century, it was less easy to determine who was Chinese and who was not. At a conservative estimate, some 12.2 per cent of Thailand's population in 1932 was ethnically Chinese;[8] the comparable figure for French Indochina was about 1.6 per cent, as it was for Burma.

But neither absolute numbers nor relative proportion were as significant as was economic role (except perhaps in Malaya, where a demographic revolution had occurred). Subject only to a bigger European share of major enterprises, the Chinese in all cases enjoyed a virtually complete ascendancy in business and commerce, from rice-milling and marketing (it has been estimated that in the 1930's nearly 90 per cent of the mills in Thailand, more than 80 per cent in Indochina, and 75 per cent in the Philippines were owned by Chinese)[9] to urban-based wholesale and retail trade, which penetrated right into the village heart of the countryside. Their astonishing predominance had been built on the trading experience and connections of the past, on family and lineage networks that transcended state boundaries, on specifically Chinese "training" institutions (like loan associations), and on industry and thrift.[10] It was—and in many cases remains—an unbeatable combination, and the result was the virtual exclusion from commercial or trading activity of indigenous Southeast Asians and the corresponding absence of any growth of an economic middle class based on those activities. Attention has already been drawn to the way in which the "middle class," the new bourgeoisie, in most Southeast Asian societies has been largely composed of bureaucrats and government servants.

The majority of Chinese lived in the towns. Correspondingly, a great many urban societies in Southeast Asia were substantially Chinese. It was characteristically in the towns, therefore, that modern Chinese political and cultural activity found its most lively expression. During the first three decades of the twentieth century, Chinese nationalism on the mainland—and its eventual polarization between the Kuomintang (KMT) and the Chinese Communist Party (CCP)—generated a strong response in overseas Chinese communities. Sun Yat-sen, who visited the area more than once, was largely financed by overseas Chinese capital, and the Chinese Revolution of 1911 was accompanied—in Singapore, Bangkok, Manila, and elsewhere—by growing enthusiasm for modern education (in schools staffed mainly by teachers brought from China), by study and reading clubs with political overtones, and by a flourishing popular press. Such activities, strengthened again by the politicization that followed the KMT-CCP split in 1927, greatly fostered internal Chinese cohesion and knowledge of distinctness and helped to retard further assimilation in the host societies—a process aided in turn by suspicion and sometimes hostility on the other side. More than that, however, the material success of the overseas Chinese; their ability to organize, educate, and otherwise improve themselves; and the fervid nationalism and anti-imperialism of mainland Chinese politics as reflected in Southeast Asia acted as irritants, stimulants, and sometimes models, providing an important part of the environment in which Southeast Asian nationalism grew.

Chinese nationalism and its associated phenomena made up only one among a wide range of constellations of ideas that impinged on the intellectual world of Southeast Asia in the first part of the twentieth century. Japan's success in avoiding colonialism and becoming the first industrial power in Asia, an achievement sealed by its victory over Tsarist Russia in 1905, was much admired and later held up for emulation. The upheaval in ideas that followed World War I in Europe had many repercussions in Southeast Asia. The spread of socialism and Communism, though difficult to generalize about and not yet sufficiently studied, dated from that time. Western radicalism was propagated both by the activities of European socialists in the area (like Hendricus Sneevliet and Adolf Baars in Java, engaged in trade-unionism) and by the international wanderings of such Comintern leaders as Tan Malaka and Ho Chi Minh. But the influence of Marxist-Leninist ideas concerning colonialism, and theories of finance capital and surplus value, went much wider than their immediate standard-bearers, becoming a tone, an influence, in the thinking of many educated and self-educating Southeast Asians. The same can be said of the ideas associated with the gradualist doctrines of trusteeship and mandate, which, under the auspices of the League of Nations, came to afford new rationalizations and new motivations for the activities of the colonial powers. Indian nationalism, based on ideas of *swaraj* (self-rule) and Gandhian passive resistance, though not directly reflected in Southeast Asia except within the Indian communities of Burma and Malaya, nevertheless contributed its own coloration to the *mélange* of ideas characteristic of the time.

The locus of new ideas was the town, the vehicle was modern education of a variety of kinds, and the recipients were the new urban elites.

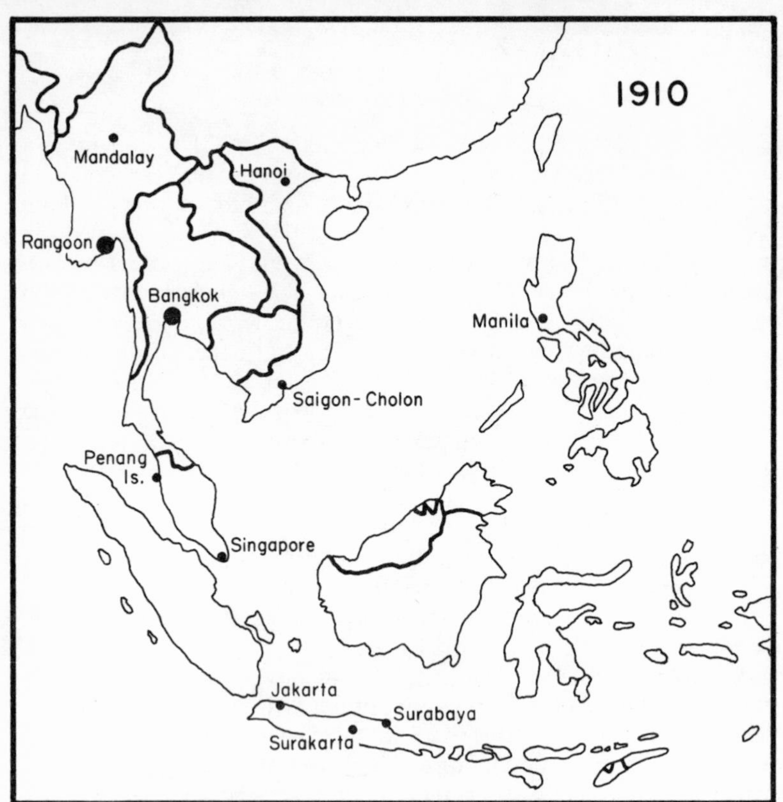
1910
Mandalay
Hanoi
Rangoon
Bangkok
Manila
Saigon-Cholon
Penang Is.
Singapore
Jakarta
Surabaya
Surakarta

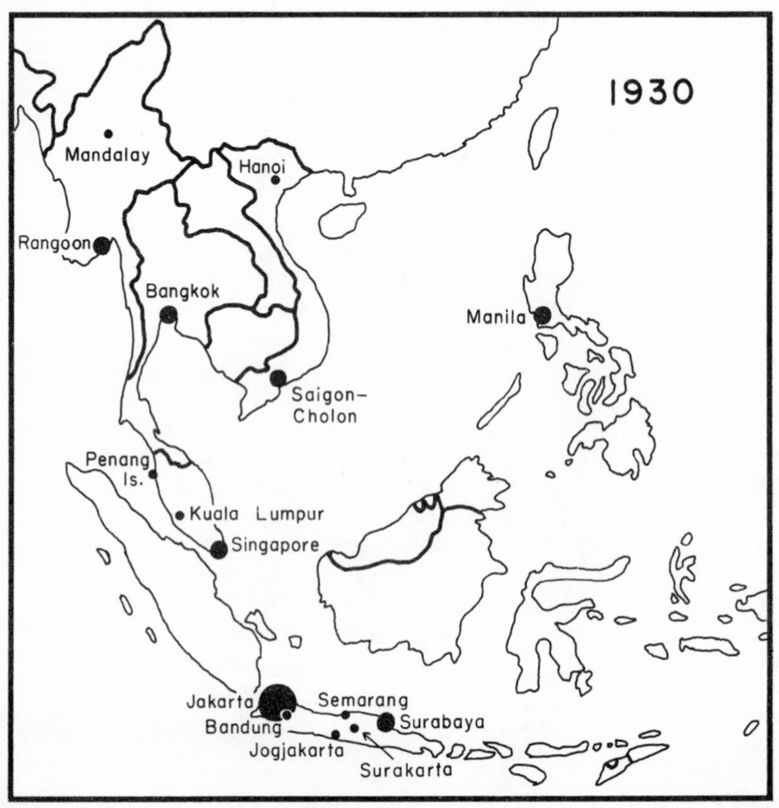
1930
Mandalay
Hanoi
Rangoon
Bangkok
Manila
Saigon-Cholon
Penang Is.
Kuala Lumpur
Singapore
Jakarta
Semarang
Bandung
Surabaya
Jogjakarta
Surakarta

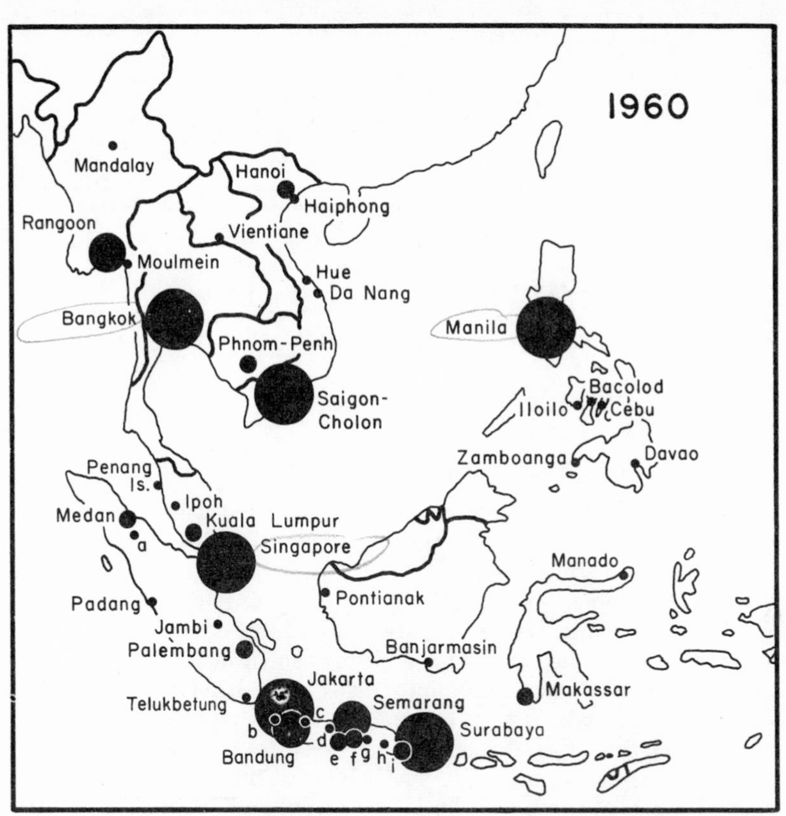

a.	Pematangsiantar	f.	Surakarta
b.	Bogor	g.	Madiun
c.	Cheribon	h.	Kediri
d.	Pekalongan	i	Malang
e.	Jogjakarta		

CITY POPULATIONS

- 100,000 - 300,000
- 300,000 - 500,000
- 500,000 - 1,000,000
- over 1,000,000

24

CHANNELS OF CHANGE

URBANIZATION

If the degree of creative confusion associated with urbanization in Southeast Asia in modern times was new, the cities and towns themselves were not. Precolonial Southeast Asia had many urban communities—autonomous societies, centers of government and officials, of religious and intellectual activity, and of commerce, inhabited by a population detached from the land, townsmen rather than countrymen. The largest and most important towns, and therefore the best known, were state capitals, but there were many smaller provincial towns too. Of the bigger cities, one of the best examples is the Malacca of the fifteenth century, center of a great Malay commercial empire. The wide paved streets of the town's business section, lined with tiled or thatched wooden dwellings and warehouses and thronged with residents and traders from all over Asia, sat across the narrow canal-like river (spanned by a bridge of booths) from the fortified precinct that overlooked and commanded it, and within which were the palace of the Malay sultan, the court and its environs, and the houses of the Malay nobility and its retinue.

Another example is Bangkok, which, like its predecessor Ayudhya, was laid out in concentric circles. The innermost circle was dominated by the palaces of the king and later by the massive buildings that served as the headquarters of the major ministries. The next ring of settlements comprised the Thai portion of the city, the homes of princes and government officers and their households, retainers, and families. And beyond that was the Chinese mercantile quarter, surrounding the inner core and edging off into the countryside.

Nineteenth-century Hue, headquarters of the Nguyen court and bureaucracy, was in some respects similar. Like other major precolonial Vietnamese cities, it was rigidly divided. The principal part was the walled *thanh*, or citadel, where the court, officials, and soldiers lived. The subordinate part was the *thi*, or market, where the ordinary Vietnamese lived and where the traders hawked their wares. Observing Confucian forms of social hierarchy, in which merchants ranked below scholars and peasants, Hue confined its merchants and its bazaars to the outskirts of the city.

One of the most obvious things that colonialism and European domination did was to turn the new towns it created inside out, so that at their heart lay not the monarchy but money—the counting houses of the Chinese and other traders, the shophouses full of consumer goods from Manchester, Marseilles, Bombay, and Hong Kong. The citadel was forced to give way to the market, as mammon became king; economic gain was both the *raison d'être* of the new towns themselves and the motive of most of those who came to them, peasant or profiteer. Though some of the old towns also were transformed by this process, many were simply bypassed, receding in political and cultural importance like Hue and its court, which lost place in the 1880's to the colonially dominated and economically burgeoning areas of Saigon-Cholon and Hanoi-Haiphong, or like the small royal town of Kuala Kangsar in Perak in the same years, residence still of the sultan but not of the new state administration springing up on the Chinese tin fields at Taiping. In 1872, the population of Rangoon was less than 99,000, that of Mandalay at least double; thirty years later, Rangoon had swollen to nearly a quarter of a million and Mandalay had not merely stopped growing, it had begun to shrink.

Most of the new towns, then, were the focus for new or intensified economic energies and new or changing social groups. Some were frontier towns associated with rapidly developing extractive industries. In Thailand, for example, as in Malaya, a number of new towns sprang up with the opening of the tin mines. An example is Phuket, probably the first town in the country to have paved roads and automobiles, toward 1910. Like Taiping and Seremban in the Malay states, it was substantially a Chinese town, with its lines of communication running mainly to Singapore and Penang. In the north of Thailand, where the major extractive industry was teak logging, towns such as Paknampho arose for the collection and milling of timber. Kuala Lumpur, which began in 1858 as a huddle of Chinese huts at the confluence of the Klang and Gombak rivers, was built from tin revenues. By 1896, it was the capital not only of Selangor but of the Federated Malay States as a whole. It had a population of more than 32,000, of whom 23,000 were Chinese and only 3,700 Malays.

Virtually all these towns produced for export, not for local consumption. To facilitate their trade, great seaports arose, funneling tin, rubber, rice, and other primary products into world markets. Some of the ports, like Manila and Batavia, were old towns transformed; others, like Haiphong and Penang, were essentially creations of the nineteenth century. But the archetype, perhaps, was Singapore, founded in 1819 to participate in older patterns of archipelago trade; it became in the course of the nineteenth century a vast export market for the produce of its immediate region as well as a transshipment port of the old kind. Singapore at the close of the nineteenth century was perhaps the most polyglot city in Asia. With nearly three-quarters of its 228,000 inhabitants Chinese, it can in one sense be described as a Chinese city run by the British for the benefit of both. But it was also a meeting place for 23,000 Malays from the peninsular states, more than 12,000 assorted Javanese, Sumatrans, Bugis, Filipinos, Baweans, and other Southeast Asians, numerous Muslim and non-Muslim Indians, and at least 1,000 Arabs. It thus exemplified something that was true of all the new cities of Southeast Asia, whether or not they were dominated by aliens—the bringing together of large numbers of people from many different social backgrounds and varieties of experience to share a common, or at least contiguous, life.

Finally, in listing the kinds of economic activity that gave rise to the new cities, mention should perhaps be made of industrialization, the force behind so much urbanization elsewhere. Because the economies of colonial Southeast Asia were primarily, if not quite entirely, extractive, few of the new towns could be called manufacturing or industrial towns. The few that existed were mainly in Vietnam, where French economic policy differed in marginal respects from that of the other colonial powers. Textile mills were built in Hanoi and Nam Dinh in the early 1890's, and the important Haiphong cement factory dated from 1899. Railway workshops (as also in Kuala Lumpur and at Semarang in Java) made their appearance, as did plants (as in Manila or Singapore) for the manufacture of carbonated waters and cigarettes. But industrialization everywhere was minimal, and even in Vietnam the bulk of the labor force in the 1930's remained outside the cities—on the big plantations of Cochinchina or in the coal mines in the north.

The main function of the cities and towns was to serve the ends of alien trade and commerce by draining out primary products and pumping in consumer goods. As an adjunct to that, however, most urban areas developed as important communications and administrative centers for the surrounding countryside. Towns like Kuala Lumpur in Malaya, Saigon in Cochinchina, and Medan in Sumatra, became junctions for networks of road, rail, and other communications, which transported not merely rubber, tin, and powdered milk but people and ideas. At the same time, improved communications assisted and were indeed part of the building up of the increasingly elaborate administrative systems (ranging from land survey and police to schools and traveling dispensaries), which were regarded by colonial governments as necessary aids to economic development and proper government in rural areas. Though the interactions between town, communications and administrative systems, and countryside were complex, they can for simplicity be represented as a two-way flow. From the town moved carriers of metropolitan values and urban culture, performing integrative and dissemination functions similar to but much more intense than those performed by the town in the precolonial past. In the other direction, large numbers of people from village and rural society poured into the town, carrying with them not merely the mixture of hope and fear that approach to the city arouses in all travelers, but their own values, ideas, and habits to throw into the urban crucible. Each side of the transaction fed and reinforced the other, making the city one of the most important single agents of change in modern times.

Most people who came to the city did so for economic reasons. The truth of that statement is most obvious in the case of the immigrant aliens, like the Chinese, who predominated in most Southeast Asian towns, and certainly in the larger ones. But it tended to be true also for the Malay, Filipino, or Javanese peasant who came to Kuala Lumpur, Manila, or Jakarta. By no means all forays into the town were permanent. Quite apart from the one-day visitors, who by definition could come from only a few miles away, perhaps to sell vegetables or eggs, there were seasonal workers (taking up agricultural slack times at home), those who left families behind for periodic spells to make a bit on the side as house servants, rickshaw pullers and casual laborers, and at all times hosts of young men who wanted to try their luck in the metropolis and might or might not go back to the village to settle down. Like the Chinese *towkay,* who, it was always said, just wanted to make his fortune and go home to die among his ancestors, the "urban peasant" usually retained close emotional (and, indeed, physical) links with his village, returning to celebrate religious festivals and hoping to make enough to buy retirement land there.

In most of the new cities, as in their older counterparts, people of one ethnic or territorial origin, or one language group, tended to live together in the same part of town. Though initially the "quartering" of towns was sometimes the result of administrative decision, people themselves tended to prefer it, for it assured them neighbors whose speech, religion and habits of life they shared and understood, helping to perpetuate community. Sometimes, as in Manila until the late Spanish period, they even had their own form of district governing council, there known as the *gremio.* Localized patterns of residence of this kind were often found in association with specialization of occupation. The two practices together assisted newcomers to find both a place to live and work to do. Singapore, although too variegated to be altogether typical, nevertheless offers many examples of situations in some degree found everywhere. In the principal "Malay quarter" of downtown Singapore, Bugis Street was the merchandizing center for Bugis maritime traders from the eastern archipelago, and Kampong Jawa contained many of the quarter's eating houses, coffee shops, and flower stalls kept by the Javanese womenfolk. Bawean *pondok*—single houses or groups of houses in which people from the same village lived together in a semblance of the village community itself, complete with traditional institutions in microcosm—were the base from which Bawean immigrants fared forth into the city at large, mainly to become grooms and coachmen and, later, chauffeurs.

As cities grew bigger, by natural population increase and by continued immigration, and as rising land values and house rents combined with the decay of older areas to encourage commercial pre-emption and urban renewal, original patterns of residence and occupation became diversified and confused. Transitional institutions, such as the urban *kampong* or village, which, like the Bawean *pondok*, had eased peasant movement onto the labor markets of Jakarta, Kuala Lumpur, and Rangoon, were pushed farther out of town or became overcrowded and unsanitary urban slums. Traditional forms of social organization, or replicas of them, became more vulnerable to the disintegrative effects of urban individualism and, more importantly, less relevant to the new quest for status and prestige in the totality of the urban social structure. But, though there were many casualties along the way, the process was by no means a wholly negative one. While it is true that urban life tended to weaken traditional social ties and loosen the hold of traditional beliefs and values, it also offered much that was positive—new opportunities for specialization and skills, new relationships with others of differing social background and experience, affording new points of contact and common interest, and, in the most general way, new and enlarged liberty of thought and action. For many, particularly the young, urban life offered not the breakdown of the known, the familiar, and the secure that is so often described, but an opportunity to rid themselves of parental and other authoritarian constraints and to make life anew.

One product of the evolution of traditional institutions in the city, of the need to seek new forms of social security, of the discovery of new interest groups, and of the desire for self-improvement in a competitive environment was the emergence of "voluntary associations." Individuals joined or helped to form such clubs and societies out of choice, rather than belonging ascriptively, by accident of birth. Associations blossomed throughout Southeast Asian urban societies in the late nineteenth and early twentieth centuries. Their enormous variety reflects the complexity of city life itself, but it is possible to distinguish a few general categories. Many of the first clubs were purely recreational—especially football clubs, which in Singapore, for example, were taken to task by the more serious sections of the Malay press as time-wasting frivolities. Another early and very common form of voluntary association was the burial society, established to ensure that, by common subscription, members and the immediate families of members would be assured of a properly conducted funeral. One of the largest and, to the social historian, one of the most interesting categories was what one might call the "cultural welfare and progress" societies—debating clubs, literary circles, study groups, religious reform societies, language improvement associations. All alike, whether led by Western-educated government servants, vernacular or religious schoolteachers, or occasional members of the traditional elite, were endowed with their own private vision, each setting out to create a new and better version of its own society.

In the circumstances of colonial rule and foreign economic dominance, which, in one way or another, afflicted all of Southeast Asia, associations of the kind just described, embodying the strivings of urban Burmese, Javanese, or Filipinos to enter and compete in the modern world on their own terms, could scarcely fail to find themselves at odds with the assumptions on which colonial rule was based. The fact of their organization, let alone the content of the largely ephemeral newspapers and journals by means of which they so frequently propounded their ideas, brought them under the surveillance of the colonial authorities, and on occasion they were suppressed—most often, perhaps, in French-controlled Vietnam. The relevance of the first associations, however, lay less in what they accomplished by means of a political confrontation seldom attempted than in the training ground they afforded for wrestling with new problems and shaping a new generation of leaders and followers—training in organizing clubs, running meetings, keeping accounts, operating elective institutions, handling information from outside, and transmitting it within. The cities of Southeast Asia were essentially foreign bodies to the societies in which they were embedded—fewer than 5 per cent of all Malays, for example, lived in the towns, where they made up only 10 per cent of the total population—but the importance of the city lay outside the realm of numbers or proportion. It lay in its ability to give birth to new elites.

EDUCATION AND LANGUAGE

A nineteenth-century Malay writer once observed that the founding of Singapore had made "dragons out of worms and worms out of dragons."[11] Nothing contributed more to the metamorphosis, which was in one sense or another a general phenomenon in Southeast Asia, than the education systems of the colonial powers. But "the knowledge that is given to people under foreign influence," argued another Malay in 1927, "has no purpose other than to impoverish the intellect and teach them to lick the soles of their masters' boots."[12] Between those two remarks, the first sociological and dispassionate, the second political and heated, both pointing to change, lie the problems and complexities of understanding the incidence, the impact, and the intent of the process often known contemporaneously as "public instruction."

European systems of colonial rule were imposed on Southeast Asian societies with varying degrees of intensity, but most had one common purpose, the organization of the state in such a way as to maximize its potentialities, first as a producer of raw materials and foodstuffs for export to the West, and second as a market for Western manufacturers. The type of control and the extent of direct interference in the administration of the state necessary to accomplish that purpose varied with the state's economic importance and promise, on the one hand, and, on the other, with the extent to which indigenous elites and systems of administration could be, or were willing to allow themselves to be, adapted to Western organizational purpose. In the so-called indirectly ruled, economic low-pressure states—like some of those in the Malay peninsula, for example, and Cambodia, or for a time the outer edges of the Dutch Indies—traditional elites continued in some measure to play an active part in the administration, even while it was being reshaped to meet Western needs. In many other states, however, in spite of initial efforts to retain or work through indigenous administrative institutions, the urgency of Western demands prompted the growth of very complex bureaucracies that set a high premium on efficiency and technical competence of a kind either not available or not forthcoming from within the traditional social order. In many cases, as in Burma, the indigenous administrative hierarchy came merely to be ignored; in others, as in Vietnam, it preferred retreat into political isolation to collaboration.

In the directly ruled states in particular, and to a lesser extent in those more indirectly ruled, the main need of the colonial authorities, as economic development gathered speed, was for what one might call an administrative labor force—the overseers, deputy supervisors, clerks, accountants, and technical subordinates, who could be provided from the West itself only at prohibitive cost, if at all. Occasionally—especially in British Malaya and Burma—that kind of trained assistance was available from either resident or imported nonindigenous Asians, mainly Indian or Chinese. In most cases, it was not and had to be created locally.

This, then, provided the first and most obvious motive for Western-style training of segments of the population of Southeast Asian colonies—and an adequate explanation of why it was often called instruction rather than education, a process usually understood to have a nobler purpose than mere equipment to earn a living on someone else's behalf. But many other motives were at work, too, some of them clear and some confused or contradictory. None of the Western powers assumed territorial responsibilities in nineteenth-century Southeast Asia without at the same time taking upon themselves in some degree the tasks of the *mission civilisatrice*, or civilizing mission. Many Europeans (and Americans) really did see themselves as, in the words of Kipling's poem "The White Man's Burden," waiting in heavy harness "on fluttered folk and wild/Your new-caught sullen peoples, half-devil and half-child." Children existed to be educated, or at least toilet-trained. Intoxicated not only by their own power and inventiveness but by currently fashionable theories of evolution, Westerners readily accepted justifications of colonial rule based on tutelage. Notions of bringing backward peoples into the world by teaching and example were never wholly absent from ideas of colonial governance—except when the results of teaching seemed likely to render colonial rule superfluous.

For all the above reasons, then, colonial authority found itself engaged in providing a variety of forms of educational institution for the peoples it ruled. Earlier in the nineteenth century, during the liberal era of free trade in ideas as well as goods, the British in particular, who were relatively untrammeled as yet by the need to direct labor, had made some attempt to sustain or adapt indigenous educational institutions, especially in Burma. Simple literacy in the Buddhist countries of mainland Southeast Asia was far more widespread in the mid-nineteenth century than it was in Europe. In the 1860's, Sir Arthur Phayre, Governor of Burma, proposed to leave the bulk of the educational task in the hands of the monastery schools, encouraging them, however, by means of the provision of books on Western subjects such as arithmetic and land-measurement, to enlarge their curricula. At the same time, the growth of lay schools of a wholly Western kind was to be restricted. Failure on each side to understand the intentions of the other rendered the policy nugatory. In Vietnam (though not in Cambodia, where traditional systems persisted), early French policies regarding education, combined with the action of the Nguyen emperor in withdrawing educational as well as other officials from the directly controlled French areas in the south, spelled the end of the Confucian examination system in Cochinchina in the 1860's. Under the sway of cultural expansionism, and in need of greater linguistic access to the society themselves, the French then attempted, by means of interpreters' schools that trained teachers as well as interpreters, to spread knowledge of at least elementary French for limited Franco-vernacular education, adopting at the same time the *quoc ngu* romanization of the Vietnamese language, which eventually became the mode of instruction in the peasant village schools. In Java, Dutch attitudes toward education in the nineteenth century were inconsistent but mainly illiberal, and by the 1860's they had clearly embarked on educational policies directed solely toward the production of a suitable range of officials and subordinates. It was partly against this wholly self-interested approach to education that the Ethical Policy was to react at the beginning of the new century.

As the twentieth century opened, then, several distinct features of colonial education had emerged, which were to do much to determine the shape of the new society then also emerging. At the base was the vernacular education offered to some proportion of the rural peasantry. Though in a few places, such as Burma and Cambodia, vernacular education was still largely supplied by traditional institutions, the colonial powers accepted at least some responsibility for financial aid or direct, government-run schemes. Answering probable critics of the small amount spent on vernacular education in the Malay states, an official remarked in 1908 that "the Government has never desired to give the children a smattering, or even a larger quantity, of knowledge which will not help them to more useful and happy lives than they now lead. To the Malay, the principal value of school attendance is to teach him habits of order, punctuality, and obedience."[13] Similar arguments were employed elsewhere; vernacular education was intended merely to make the peasant a better peasant, to reconcile him to his lot. The important thing was to avoid what was often called "overeducation," by which was meant taking people off the land and disturbing the even tenor of village life, or producing people who, unsatisfied with the dignity conferred upon them by manual labor, acquired aspirations that could not be satisfied under colonial rule. If this was true of colonial mass education in the vernacular, even more was it held to be true of education in Western languages. Too rapid an extension of English education, Malayan administrators were wont to say, would bring about "economic dislocation and social unrest."

The only colonial power seriously to dissent was the United States in the Philippines, where it was held, to the contrary, that a greater risk of social unrest lay in "a vast mass of ignorant people easily and blindly led by the comparatively few."[14] Between 1901 and 1902, more than 1,000 American teachers were recruited to teach in Philippine schools, and by 1920 there were nearly 1 million children receiving English-language education at all levels. Elsewhere in Southeast Asia, ironically enough, it was the restricted nature of vernacular education (invariably limited to little more than the rudiments of drilling in the three R's), rather than the relatively small proportion of the peasantry granted it, that led to serious dissatisfaction among its recipients at their exclusion from the more rewarding paths of Western education.

Above the level of vernacular education, colonial administrations and Western economic enterprise alike were increasingly demanding trained subordinates. Pressures from both quarters fused with policies based on ethical recognition of past injustices and on a new desire for cultural association (as in the Dutch Indies), on the transmission to a select few of an allegedly superior culture (as in French Indochina, and less systematically elsewhere), on slightly aloof notions of trust and tutelage (as in British Burma and Malaya), or on slightly apologetic fulfillment of promises to introduce democratic institutions in return for the imposition of colonial rule (as in the American Philippines) to make available increasing amounts of Western-language education. In some areas, notably in the Malay states, in other indirectly ruled territories, and, to begin with, in Java, the principal beneficiaries were the existing traditional elites. Everywhere, in some degree, the already socially and economically advantaged were in the best position to obtain the Western education through which, it seemed clear, all future advantage lay. But gradually, in response to two factors in particular—the leveling effect of impartially applied academic standards and the virtually exclusive location of Western educational opportunity in the towns—the product became diversified, and the new elites who emerged from the system did so as a heterogeneous group, drawn from no one social class, and finding identity in a common interest in the future rather than a common relationship with the past.

As systems of Western education became thoroughly established, so did they grow in complexity and in internal stratification, which they imposed upon those who passed through the various meshes of the sieve. One of the more complex examples of this was found in Vietnam, where, by the end of World War I (and after the final destruction of the Confucian examination system in the north and center, as well as the south), entry into the civil service required not merely completion of "horizontal plane" vernacular education (a graphic term) in the village, but ten years of "vertical plane" education through the three formal stages of French education. Following that, a handful of students might go on to French education overseas or to the university in Hanoi, where specialized schools gave additional training for the public service to students drawn from all of Indochina. Talented or fortunate Javanese followed a similar pattern, ending up in the engineering, law, or medical schools formed between 1919 and 1926. At each stage of the process, many fell by the wayside, and it must be recalled in any case that the total numbers affected (and even more their proportion to the populace at large) were small. Around 1937, with a population of some 23 million, Indochina had only about 500,000 children being educated, the vast bulk of them being in the first two grades of elementary school; it had only about 600 university students. In the Netherlands Indies, with a population of 68 million, 93,000 Indonesian children were receiving Dutch-language education, the vast majority in elementary schools, and there were a mere 496 students at university level. Though the Indonesian figures were probably the smallest in Southeast Asia, the general proportions were much the same throughout, save for the two important exceptions of the Philippines and Thailand. In the Philippines, where mass education in English had been embarked upon early in the century, there were, by 1938, more than 2 million pupils attending schools of all levels, and more than 7,000 at local universities. In Thailand, vernacular education did not have the disadvantages or colonially imposed limitations it possessed elsewhere, and in the mid-1930's there were some 45,000 students at Thai secondary schools, out of a population of 14 million, and 800 or so more at universities in the country. Both the Philippines and Thailand also had considerable numbers of students studying at universities overseas, more, at any rate, than any other country in the area.

Education outside the colonial society, though intended as merely an extension rung on the ladder already described, was actually, for most of the handful of people who achieved it, an educational experience qualitatively so different as to set it quite apart. Probably the first thing that metropolitan education did was to cut the colonial powers, and Westerners in general, down to size. For Indonesians, that was literally the effect. Many have recorded their astonishment and incredulity at discovering Holland so small geographically. It had always loomed so large, appearing in schoolbooks in enormous scale maps so that they could study every rock and rill. In addition, it was a liberating experience to be treated as a human being and not as a member, however "evolved," of an inherently inferior people. It was instructive, even when it was only a matter of having one's luggage carried by an English porter, to learn at first hand that Western societies themselves were highly stratified. And finally, many of the students met Westerners who were not merely critics of the existing social order in their own societies, but who argued fiercely against colonial subjugation and held theories of economic exploitation that both explained it and forecast its eventual termination. Overseas students returned to Southeast Asia not only to take up senior positions in the indigenous levels of the public service, but also to provide leadership in nationalist struggles for independence.

For the Muslim societies of Southeast Asia, in which (as elsewhere except Thailand) the channels opened by strictly vernacular education were blocked at a point not very far downstream from their origins—where the most one could hope for was a poorly paid teaching post in the same system or a precarious life as a journalist—there was a side-stream opening to the outside world, an opportunity similar to that afforded to a section of the Westernized elite. Following the great improvements in communications with the Middle East (which, it is sometimes forgotten, is also "West" from another point of view) at the end of the nineteenth century, greater numbers of people from the Dutch East Indies and Malaya were able to make the pilgrimage to Mecca. Though the majority spent only a few weeks there, rising cash incomes from participation as smallholders in the lower levels of the export economy made it possible for many more than in the past to stay on in Mecca or Cairo for some years, primarily to study religion. The advantage of Cairo, as one young man remarked, was that there one could study politics as well. Amid the intellectual and political ferment that possessed the Arab world at the time—engaged both in the renovation of Islam and in nationalist struggles for freedom from the West—students from Indonesia and Malaya acquired new language and new ideas with which to combat the colonial rule that possessed their own society and determined their disadvantaged position within it.

The urban intelligentsias of the mid-1920's had as vessels for their strivings and instruments of their discontent the wide range of voluntary associations already referred to—culminating in the actively nationalist political parties of Burma, the Netherlands Indies, and Vietnam, and nascent movements of a similar kind elsewhere. They also had the written word, and though some had made an extremely thorough job of assimilating Western language and culture, it was to their own in the last resort that both they and the vernacular-educated turned. Language has a peculiarly intimate relationship with cultural identity, both as the most expressive vehicle for a society's beliefs, values, and sentiments —for its innermost spirit—and as a means of self-recognition. The travail of the early twentieth century, which saw the birth of anti-colonialist nationalist movements, crystallized, for many, first and foremost around concern for the language of the people, or, where there was no single language, around the need to adopt one as a symbol and expression of unity in the face of cultural as well as political imperialism.

In Malaya, the first known lexicographical work by a Malay, Raja Haji Ali's *Kitab Pengetahuan Bahasa*, was compiled in the late 1850's, though it was not published until 1928. A kind of Johnsonian dictionary, in which definition is made the occasion for comment, it dwelt critically on the ways in which Malay life and language were changing under the impact of the West. One of the earliest of Malay cultural-welfare societies was started in Johore in 1888 in order to modernize Malay and make it an independent vehicle for modern systems of administration. In southern Vietnam, Huynh Tinh Cua's two-volume dictionary of the Vietnamese language, published in 1896, standardized meanings in a fashion that was to give real impetus to uniform linguistic usages throughout the country. Later, the language issue tended to center on the schools, where French cultural aggressiveness punished even the informal use of Vietnamese in institutions of higher education.

In the Netherlands Indies, the Dutch had, since the nineteenth century, used Malay as the language of "native administration" and, in contradistinction to the French, discouraged or forbade the use of Dutch by indigenous civil servants. Such attitudes, along with the almost universal use of the language in the press and organizational life of the early twentieth century, helped modernize and entrench Malay—already for centuries the lingua franca of the archipelago—and led eventually to its adoption in the 1920's as the national language, thereafter called Indonesian. In the Philippines, where the mass education policies of the American administration were doing so much to spread a knowledge of English, the desire felt by nationalists to have an indigenous national language finally led in 1936 to the establishment of an Institute of National Language and to the eventual adoption of "Pilipino," based on Tagalog, a Manila-dominated compromise among the possible alternatives. Even in Thailand, fears were expressed about the purity of the language, and a special commission, which later became the Thai Royal Academy, was set up to nurture it.

Much of the force given to national language growth was expressed through the vernacular press, which everywhere in Southeast Asia played an increasingly prominent role in cultural and political life. No other medium or expression of social change is as easily accessible to study; the files of old newspapers and journals constitute an invaluable repository of the inner history of the times. Throughout the area, the first newspapers in the vernacular tended to be wholly or partly translations from the foreign language press. By the 1890's, however, and certainly in the twentieth century, most of the principal cities had at least one vernacular newspaper appearing with fair regularity and usually a host of smaller and more ephemeral weeklies and monthlies, often the product of the new voluntary associations. With the increase in basic literacy, which was fairly general in Southeast Asia, despite the unsatisfactoriness of education programs, the press became a vitally important influence in the dissemination and discussion of new ideas and in shaping the intelligentsia, training its leaders, and extending their influence. Few coffee shops or tea houses, even in the village, did not possess a newspaper from time to time, which could be read to the illiterate and argued over by budding politicians. In 1906, one of the most important of the early Malay journals listed no fewer than twenty-six different virtues of newspapers, among them that they were "the light of the mind, the talisman of the thoughts, the mirror of events, the servant of the wise, the prompter of the forgetful, a guide to those who stray, a prop to the weak, the guardian of the community, and the forum for all discussion."[15] In the hands of the new elites, that was scarcely an exaggeration.

25

THE PHILIPPINES

Modern nationalism emerged first in the Philippines. The Spanish responded to the increasing pace of change by repression, pursuing a policy that one Spaniard saw as "suspicious and unenlightened but still useful for preserving the colony."[16] Endemic domestic instability in Spain and political, economic, and military weakness in the Philippines produced indecisiveness, which the Spanish hoped to hide by bravura. Nationalist sentiment found focus in 1872 as a result of Spanish repression. The *ilustrados* blamed the friars for the evils of the Spanish colonial system, because the friars were the most visible, most conservative, most able, and most permanent segment of the Spanish community. During the last quarter of the nineteenth century, the congruence of wealth, awareness, education, and discontent among these *ilustrados* led them into direct conflict with Spanish authority.

The first expression of Philippine nationalism occurred not in the Philippines itself, where censorship was rigidly imposed, but in Spain. After the mutiny at the Cavite Arsenal in 1872, many *ilustrados* were arrested; they, or their sons, subsequently went abroad to escape repression and to improve their education. The Filipino emigrés organized what became known as the Propaganda Movement. Meliorist and evolutionary in approach, it advocated equality for Filipinos, representation in the Cortes in Spain, freedom of speech and assembly, nonrepressive taxation, and staffing of the clergy with Filipinos. It contained a marked element of cultural nationalism, including emphasis on Tagalog literature and the arts, pre-Spanish Philippine history, and a self-conscious effort to search out and identify the national character. The movement was permeated with youthful moralism and romanticism, censuring unenlightened Filipino institutions like the *cacique* system, as well as Spanish repression. Its major vehicle became a newspaper called *La Solidaridad,* which began publication in 1889 in Barcelona and then moved to Madrid. Its two most famous spokesmen were Marcelo H. del Pilar (Plaridel) and José Rizal. Both men had become politicized by the Spanish suppression of the Cavite Mutiny. Rizal, a wealthy fifth-generation Chinese *mestizo,* wrote about himself that had it not been for 1872, he would have become a Jesuit, and instead of writing *Noli me tángere*—his first and most famous novel—he would have written the opposite.

The *ilustrados* were profoundly influenced by the anticlerical traditions of nineteenth-century Europe, especially the Spanish Masonic movement. Freemasonry served as the institutional and ideological link between Spanish Liberals and these Filipino propagandists. In particular, del Pilar saw Masonic lodges as a vehicle for political action both within Spain and in the archipelago. The growth in Spain of the Filipino lodge "Revolucion" and later of its successor, "Solidaridad," led to the establishment of Masonic lodges in the Philippines itself.

As the Propaganda Movement matured, it increased its demands, especially after del Pilar took over control of *La Solidaridad.* His attack on the friars for "monastic exploitation," along with Rizal's fictional but pointed criticism of friar abuses, alarmed the Spanish. The University of Santo Tomas rector, for example, castigated Rizal's novel as "heretical, impious, and scandalous in the religious order and antipatriotic, subversive of public order," and offensive in the temporal sphere.[17] The issue of friar landholdings, in particular, became a point of controversy. In 1887, as a result of a government tax questionnaire, Rizal and his family organized a petition requesting formal and just contracts for the sale of land to the tenants. The petition became a test case for all parties: A rent strike was organized, the Dominicans instituted eviction proceedings, and the issue went to court. The governor-general, aware of the political character of the issue, sided with the Dominicans. He sent in troops, suspended the court hearings, gave 400 tenants twenty-four hours to leave, and then burned their homes. Twenty-five people, including Rizal's father and three sisters, were deported.

By the early 1890's, the Propagandists were becoming disillusioned and bitter. The goal of assimilation within the Spanish empire was abandoned, and the emigrés came to realize that their influence on events was negligible as long as they remained abroad. Propaganda and lobbying proved only marginally effective. Del Pilar abandoned all hope of peaceful change and before his death in 1896 was already contemplating revolution.

Rizal, on his return home in 1892, had at once organized La Liga Filipina. The Liga had a nonradical program, largely concerned with economic and educational advancement. Even that, however, was too much for jittery Spanish officials, who arrested Rizal and deported him to Mindanao. Spanish intransigence prompted Andrés Bonifacio, a clerk in Manila, to organize the Katipunan, a Tagalog acronym for the "Highest and Most Respectable Association of the Sons of the People." The organization was neo-Masonic and very secretive. Operating through cells, it pursued avowedly revolutionary aims. Bonifacio, acutely aware of his own educational limitations, attempted to attract *ilustrados* into the Katipunan. His revolutionary goals, however, frightened many away, including Apolinario Mabini, Antonio Luna, Rafael Palma, and, most importantly, José Rizal himself. Bonifacio eventually despaired of winning their support; instead, he plotted to implicate them through forgery in the hope that Spanish repression would radicalize them for him. The Spanish learned about the Katipunan, and on August 26, 1896, Bonifacio and his supporters had to flee to the Manila suburb of Balintawak, where he issued a call to open rebellion. Bonifacio's rebellion spread throughout the Manila area, but his tactics to win over the Manila *ilustrados* failed despite Spanish arrest and torture of many of their number.

Bonifacio needed to mobilize the *ilustrados* to succeed. Though *ilustrado* status was primarily defined by educational attainment, the sons of rich *inquilinos* or *caciques* had much greater access to educational opportunity. Bonifacio was poor, urban, and, most importantly, uneducated by *ilustrado* standards. He therefore lacked access to money, to power, and to groups beyond the Tagalog region around Manila. Only the *ilustrados* could claim a national constituency. That newly emergent intelligentsia, however, refused to accept Bonifacio's leadership, because it had already arrogated to itself the right to speak for Philippine nationalism. Rizal had noted some years earlier that "a numerous educated class, both in the archipelago and outside it, must now be reckoned with . . . . This educated elite grows steadily. It is in continuous contact with the rest of the population. And if it is no more today than the brains of the nation, it will become in a few years its whole nervous system. Then we shall see what it will do."[18]

Spanish clumsiness, however, achieved what Bonifacio could not accomplish by cajolery or forgery. Spanish officials, well aware that it was the *ilustrados* who had developed nationalist consciousness, put Rizal on trial as the principal organizer and the very soul of the Philippine insurrection. From prison, Rizal wrote a "Manifesto to Certain Filipinos," in which he reiterated that the education of the people was a prerequisite to liberty. Noting that without study and the civic virtues the Philippines could not find redemption, he stressed that "reforms, if they are to bear fruit, must come *from above*, for reforms that come *from below* are upheavals both violent and transitory." Rizal condemned "this ridiculous and barbarous uprising," but the Spanish failed to see their opportunity to isolate Bonifacio from the group he most needed.[19] Instead, they did the one thing likely to unite the *ilustrados* with the Katipunan—they executed Rizal publicly and conducted a reign of terror against his fellows. Many years earlier Rizal had written that "the day they [the Spanish] inflict martyrdom . . . farewell, pro-friar government, and perhaps, farewell, Spanish Government."[20]

Increases in population, dissemination of the ideas of the Propaganda Movement, rising rice prices, a business recession that lingered after 1893, a plague of locusts, an increasingly unfair tax burden, the Cuban Revolution, and the chronic inefficiency of the Spanish bureaucracy all helped the Katipunan. Bonifacio himself proved to be a very poor general, however. Indeed, it was only in Cavite, across the bay from

Manila, where the friars owned half the rice land, that a young *gobernadorcillo* of Chinese-*mestizo* stock named Emilio Aguinaldo was able to win a significant battle against Spanish troops. His victory gave the Filipino revolutionaries new heart and made Aguinaldo a hero overnight. He moved quickly to challenge Bonifacio for leadership.

Kinship ties played a central part in the complex struggle that ensued. After a confused period of political friction, Aguinaldo, who had managed to gain election as leader of the movement, had Bonifacio arrested for treason in April, 1897. The charge and the subsequent trial by Aguinaldo supporters were a farce. Bonifacio was not guilty of treason to Philippine nationalism; he had merely lost the struggle to retain control of the revolution. Aguinaldo's aides found him guilty, however, and condemned him to death. Aguinaldo himself issued an amnesty but was neither surprised nor upset when it failed to be delivered, and Bonifacio was shot. Though Aguinaldo emerged as the unquestioned leader, the revolution had been badly shaken by the contest for power.

The early failure of the Katipunan to mobilize the *ilustrados*, the divisive leadership struggle, the Spanish reign of terror, and Aguinaldo's reliance on friends and kinsmen from Cavite limited his ability to spark the revolution across the archipelago. The Spanish responded to armed revolt by recruiting volunteers from linguistic and geographic areas outside Manila—Pampanga, Bicol, Cagayan, Ilocos, Pangasinan, and the Bisayan Islands—and by bringing in troops from Spain. By 1897, they had increased their forces to the point where superior military technology and communications permitted them to gain the upper hand. Aguinaldo was driven out of his home province of Cavite and into the mountains of Bulacan, where he set up temporary headquarters at a small *barrio* called Biyák-na-bató. In November, one of his aides wrote what has since been known as the Biyák-na-bató Constitution in an attempt to legitimize Aguinaldo's claim to government. Despite the patriotic rhetoric contained in the document, however, it was clear that the revolution was in serious trouble.

Fortunately for Aguinaldo and the Filipinos, the Spanish had serious problems of their own. The war of national liberation in Cuba during the same years had forced them to commit most of their army and national treasure to suppress it. They knew that they could not afford to fight a similar war in the Philippines. From the Spanish point of view, it was imperative to gain time, to reduce costs, and to restore peace. From Aguinaldo's point of view, the obvious tactic was to maintain pressure. Instead, he agreed to discuss terms through a self-appointed *ilustrado* intermediary, Pedro Paterno. Aguinaldo asked for the expulsion of the friars, representation in the Cortes, equality in justice, participation in government, adjustment of property taxes, parish assignments for Filipino priests, and a bill of rights. The terms finally accepted, however, included none of those provisions. Instead, the revolutionaries were promised an amnesty, a chance to go without harm into enforced exile, and 800,000 pesos, to be paid in three installments.

While Aguinaldo subsequently claimed that the Spanish had promised much more, the only things written into the three-stage agreement concerned amnesty and money. The Spanish thereby achieved a major victory, since for a relatively small sum they had gotten Aguinaldo to end resistance and to leave the country. Though he, if not his supporters, apparently intended to use the initial payment of 400,000 pesos to buy arms in Hong Kong, the Spanish had good reason to order a *Te Deum* sung in the Manila Cathedral.

Aguinaldo's place in history was salvaged by the accident of American intervention in the Cuban revolution. The Spanish-American War that resulted suddenly altered the balance of power as Commodore Dewey, under orders to destroy the enemy's navy in the Pacific, sailed into Manila Bay and obliterated the Spanish squadron. Though his continued presence there was ostensibly in order to await, and destroy, the Spanish relief column, Americans had already begun to realize that they had gained a Far Eastern base for expansion. The Spanish, equally aware of changed circumstances, attempted to recover Filipino loyalty by offering various concessions, including a consultative assembly to be composed of *ilustrados*. Their efforts failed both because of the residue of *ilustrado* hostility and because of the American Navy's return of Aguinaldo from Singapore via Hong Kong.

His repatriation re-established the revolution, but with a significant difference: Aguinaldo got widespread support from the *ilustrados* by surrendering his power to them. Although he continued to surround himself with relatives and Cavite supporters, he felt out of his depth and abdicated political decisions to the *ilustrados*, especially to his new adviser, Apolinario Mabini. *Ilustrados* outside the Tagalog areas were induced to join the movement out of allegiance to and confidence in their Tagalog compatriots. The radical, as opposed to the nationalist, goals of the Katipunan were abandoned as private property was guaranteed and as the suffrage was limited to those "distinguished for high character, social position, and honorable conduct." Aguinaldo's initially clumsy announcement of a "dictatorial government" was rapidly altered to the declaration of a "Philippine Republic" by Mabini, who also persuaded Aguinaldo to declare national independence on June 12, 1898.

The new government quickly took control of the countryside from the Spanish, establishing its capital at the provincial city of Malolos. Under Mabini's direction, it moved to fill the void created by the collapse of Spanish power. Throughout Mabini's writings, including his *True Decalogue* and *Constitutional Program*, runs the theme that the country required a simultaneous external and internal revolution. He was romantic, authoritarian, and nationalistic. He saw unity and discipline as essential to any social regeneration, hence he favored a strong executive and a weak, consultative legislature. The great majority of the *ilustrados*, however, were suspicious of Aguinaldo's power and favored a strong legislature as a means of insuring their control. Felipe Calderón, for example, afraid that the "military element, which was ignorant in almost its entirety, would predominate," wanted to see the military neutralized "by the oligarchy of intelligence, seeing that congress would be composed of the most intelligent elements of the nation."[21]

The question turned on whether the *ilustrados* summoned by Aguinaldo to act as a legislature at Malolos had the mandate to draft a constitution. Among the delegates were forty-three lawyers, eighteen physicians, and numerous other professional people. Mabini himself was an *ilustrado* of humble origins, a fact, together with his close association with Aguinaldo and his philosophical outlook, that put him at variance with the majority. As a result, the draft constitution that emerged made the legislature supreme. Under suasion from Mabini, Aguinaldo refused at first to sign the draft, but, faced with disaffection of the congressional *ilustrados,* he reversed this decision despite warnings from Mabini, who threatened to resign. Mabini, who knew he was beaten, reluctantly accepted the compromise draft, which was promulgated on January 21, 1899.

During the six months in which the Filipinos were establishing a government, the Americans were debating whether or not to demand final possession of the Philippines in future peace negotiations with Spain. Captain Mahan's theories, Social Darwinism, the lure of the China market, and missionary zeal encouraged the Republicans in Washington to advocate retention of what had been won. While Kipling urged America to take up the white man's burden, Mr. Dooley, less reverently, noted that it was less than two months since most Americans had learned whether the Philippines were islands or canned goods. After testing the mood of the country, President McKinley announced that he had no choice but "to educate the Filipinos, and uplift and civilize and Christianize them, and by God's grace do the very best we could by them. . . ."[22] Maintaining that "the march of events rules and overrules" his actions, he strengthened Dewey's flotilla until the Americans had more than 10,000 troops around Manila Bay. The Spanish in Manila, preferring to surrender to the Americans rather than to Aguinaldo's Filipino troops, conducted a sham battle which ended on August 13 with capitulation to Dewey. The Philippine forces that had been blockading the city were prevented from entering, and the tenuous alliance between Americans and Filipinos collapsed as their joint enemy, Spain, surrendered.

McKinley's selection of delegates to the Paris Peace Conference with Spain, his refusal to see Aguinaldo's representative, and the actions of his field commanders made it clear to those in Malolos that a strong colonial power was about to replace a weak one. Unexpectedly, however, the Filipinos found support in rising anti-imperialist sentiment in America. The debate in Congress and in the country created strange alliances. Combining idealism with racism, the anti-imperialists polarized much of American society in a way that took the Republican leadership by surprise. McKinley, suddenly on the defensive and not sure of getting the necessary two-thirds vote for ratification of the peace treaty in the United States Senate, ordered his commander in the Philippines to promise the Filipinos a regime of "benevolent assimilation." To the Filipinos, however, that merely made clear McKinley's annexationist intentions. On February 4, 1899, under circumstances that have long been disputed, fighting broke out; the Americans made no real effort to re-establish a truce. Two days later, after narrowly defeating a number of anti-imperial and Democratic amendments, the United States Senate decided to retain possession of the Philippines by ratifying the peace treaty with Spain. The imperialist margin of victory was one vote.

Translating that decision into reality proved both costly and embarrassing. The alliance between *ilustrados* and Aguinaldo mobilized a much larger segment of the nation than had participated in the 1896 Revolution. While the Americans could win set battles against Filipino troops, they were frustrated by the guerrilla techniques of a war of national liberation. As the Americans bogged down literally and figuratively on the battlefield, the Republican administration became concerned for its own political fortunes, aware that the Democrats planned to use anti-imperialism as a central campaign issue in the coming presidential election.

The Americans broke the back of Filipino resistance by splitting the tenuous alliance between the *ilustrados* and the provincial followers of Aguinaldo. Jacob Schurman, head of the newly arrived Presidential Commission, promised that America would satisfy the views and aspirations of educated Filipinos in creating a new government. The message was clearly understood. While it is far too simple to claim that all *ilustrados* became *Americanistas*, it is true that the American offer weakened the consensus forged by Aguinaldo's capitulation to the *ilustrados*. The Americans called for negotiations; Mabini, as *de facto* foreign and prime minister, took a hard bargaining position. When his negotiator proved too sympathetic to the Americans, he was arrested. The *ilustrados*, from their dominant position in the legislature, forced Aguinaldo to dismiss Mabini and to replace him with their candidate, Pedro Paterno, who advocated compromise. The generals around Aguinaldo, most importantly Antonio Luna, called Paterno a traitor. As American military power increased, and as the Government of the Philippine Republic was hounded from place to place, *ilustrados* began to slip away quietly and return to Manila. General Luna, an implacable foe of appeasement and one of the few *ilustrados* in the military, emerged as the alternative leader of the republican movement. He constituted a threat Aguinaldo could not tolerate; in circumstances that are still not clear, Luna was shot by Aguinaldo's followers. Mabini openly accused Aguinaldo of ordering Luna's death. Whatever the truth of the matter, his death ended the revolution. Aguinaldo, though not captured for some time, became a harried fugitive, isolated from power.

The tension between the *ilustrados* and Aguinaldo was not simply a class struggle. It was, among other things, a contest between two world views—the urban, cosmopolitan, and educated versus the rural, unsophisticated, and innocent. Aguinaldo lost control because he lacked the range of experience needed; the *ilustrados* talked circles around him, and yet they seemed to him city slickers, men who had become so Westernized that they had lost touch with the people and with the traditional verities. The *ilustrados*, for their part, saw Aguinaldo as a bumpkin, a peasant. They recognized his hold on the imaginations of the common folk but, from their urbanized and internationalized perspective, thought it foolish to continue struggling against the Americans when the opportunities were so great not only for themselves but for what they saw as the best interests of the country. In effect, the Americans made a deal with the *ilustrados*. At the price of collaboration and allegiance, they were offered the chance to fill the vacuum created by the Spanish withdrawal. The Americans ended all friar power, agreed to limit the franchise, guaranteed private property, and acknowledged the social and economic realities of Philippine life. The Americans needed the *ilustrados* to end the war, break the resistance, and demonstrate America's altruism. The *ilustrados* turned to the Americans to achieve hegemony politically, dominance socially, and security economically. Both groups had much to gain; neither was to be disappointed.[23]

The Filipino-American War and the anti-imperialist debate combined to alter rapidly American objectives in the archipelago. Whatever the dreams of the early expansionists, the Republicans had by 1900 arrived at a policy of self-liquidating imperialism. The Americans saw their mission as providing tutelage and protection so that, in due time, the Philippines could become self-governing and independent. Whether out of guilt or by shrewdness, America rationalized its imperialist adventure by conferring upon it the benefits of American-style democracy. "The destiny of the Philippine Islands," wrote Schurman, was "not to be a State or territory . . . but a daughter republic of ours—a new birth of liberty on the other side of the Pacific," which would stand as a monument of progress and "a beacon of hope to all the oppressed and benighted millions" of Asia.[24] Implicit in Taft's condescending phrase "little brown brother" was the eventual maturation of the ward. The Americans, arguing that the colonial government had to conform to the Filipinos' customs, habits, and even prejudices, supported a strong, centralized government, dominated by educated and conservative Filipinos, to whom would be permitted increasing power as the nation developed.

By 1900, therefore, the basic pattern of Philippine national development had been established. For the next twelve years, William Howard Taft—first as Governor-General, later as Secretary of War, and finally as President—shaped that policy. He not only moved to minimize "the bitterness and distrust" by getting "Filipinos of education, intelligence, and property" to cooperate, but he also encouraged the *ilustrados* to alter the character of Philippine society from "the medieval-religious type" to one in which "the modern lawyer-politician" dominated.[25] Establishing civil government on July 4, 1901, Taft modeled Philippine governmental structures on American examples. Noting with satisfaction that the Filipino people, especially those he felt were of the better class, were happy with the Philippine Act of 1902, Taft went on to hold municipal and local elections and, subsequently, provincial and national ones. He encouraged *ilustrados* to hold office on the premise that no American should be appointed to any office in the Philippines for which a reasonably qualified Filipino could be found. As early as September, 1901, three ranking *ilustrados* had been appointed to the seven-man ruling Commission.

The emergence of Philippine nationalism was closely related to religious developments. Roman Catholicism in the islands dramatically changed as a result of antifriar hostility and the American occupation. A concomitant to the revolt against Spain had been a religious nationalist movement against Rome. During the war, a young Filipino priest named Gregorio Aglipay split the clergy along ethnic lines. Aglipay, appointed chaplain-general of the revolutionary troops by Aguinaldo, was excommunicated by the Spanish hierarchy. Although he did not at first intend to break with Rome, the intransigence of the Vatican and the seeming alliance between Madrid and Rome drove Aglipay and many others toward the creation of a Philippine national church. By 1902, the movement had become the Iglesia Filipina Independiente, with Aglipay as Archbishop. Aglipayanism filled the religious vacuum created by the withdrawal of the Spanish friars. Many Filipino priests took over parishes formerly held by the Spanish and joined the new church. Within a few years, it was able to claim 1.5 million adherents, about 25 per cent of the Christian population.

The Roman Church, clearly on the defensive, sought to restore its position. The Vatican agreed to Filipinize and Americanize the hierarchy, recalled the friars, bowed to the reality of separation of church and state, agreed to limit the activities of priests to ecclesiastical and charitable work, and, most significantly, accepted Taft's offer to buy the large *haciendas* of the friars and sell them out in small holdings to the present tenants—a land reform that the Americans never did see to completion. By withdrawing in some degree from its exposed position as a hated landlord, the Church freed itself from a heavy liability. During the same years, it managed to regain some of its former adherents from the Aglipayan movement. In 1906, the conservative Philippine Supreme Court—composed of Americans and *ilustrados*—ruled that all Roman Catholic properties taken over by the Aglipayans had to be returned to the Church. As a result, the Aglipayans had to find makeshift quarters, while Roman Catholic priests regained imposing stone churches. Though many Filipinos followed the Aglipayan priests, many others continued to worship where they always had, thus returning to Roman Catholicism. By 1918, the Aglipayan share of the Christian population had slipped to about 13 per cent. Aglipay himself attempted to translate his position into political power—but, like Aguinaldo, he was unable to compete against the urbanized and sophisticated lawyers, politicians, bureaucrats, and professional men of the temporal *ilustrado* community. The power of the ecclesiastical world decreased, and the Philippines became a secular polity.

The seeming success of American policies in the Philippines obscured their fundamental contradiction. In order to end nationalist resistance to American rule and to extricate itself from an ideologically embarrassing situation, the Republican leadership had promised to shape colonial policy to comply with *ilustrado* aspirations and prejudices. By 1908, Taft realized that America had paid a high price to gain *ilustrado* collaboration. While theoretically committed to "popular self-government" and to the extension to the masses of sufficient education "to know . . . civil rights and maintain them against a more powerful class and safely to exercise the political franchise," Taft was alarmed that American policy might actually be "merely to await the organization of a Philippine oligarchy or aristocracy competent to administer government and then turn the Islands over to it."[26] In offering the *ilustrados* power, the Americans also accepted a particular social system and pattern of land tenure. Education, it was hoped, would in time redress the balance of economic and political power. Taft noted that the "work of instruction in individual rights will require many years before the country is rid of the feudal relation of dependence which so many of the common people now feel toward their wealthy or educated leaders. . . ."[27] Consequently, though independence might be the goal of American policy, it could scarcely come rapidly if early pragmatic expedients were to be reconciled with idealistic commitments.

The Republicans lacked the necessary luxury of time. They had been able to blunt the fighting only by reversing Clausewitz's maxim—by making politics an extension of war by other means. Under the exigencies of war, they had actively encouraged the *ilustrados* to form, in late 1900, the Federalista party, which advocated collaboration with the Americans and eventual statehood within the American union. Pedro Paterno and others very quickly split off to form their own parties, both to establish their individual power bases and to place themselves on record as supporting eventual complete independence. During the first few years, the Americans prohibited any open advocacy of independence, but by 1907, during the National Assembly elections, politicians campaigned as Inmediatistas and Urgentistas. The two groups fused into the Union Nacionalista and won fifty-nine out of eighty seats. The new Nacionalista party, moreover, quickly turned to a group of young leaders, relegating the older *ilustrados* to positions of ceremonial impotence. Sergio Osmeña, at the age of twenty-nine, was elected Speaker of the new Assembly over Paterno, who was seen as "too Spanish." A new generation of younger men—led by Osmeña and Manuel Quezon—gained control of the nationalist movement and dominated it for the next forty years.

The key issue in both the United States and the Philippines was the timing of independence. The Nacionalistas, aware of the political value of the call for immediate independence, advocated it publicly. The opposition, eventually led by Juan Sumulong, came out for a more gradual approach. Like Taft, Sumulong believed that premature independence would establish an oligarchy rather than a democracy. His voice went unheeded, however, as nationalist rhetoric made independence the all-embracing goal. The issue became even more pressing after Wilson's victory in the American Presidential election of 1912, since the Democratic party had consistently advocated rapid independence. Under the influence of former Democratic colleagues with a record of anti-imperialism, Wilson appointed F. B. Harrison Governor-General with instructions to increase the tempo of decolonization. Harrison established a Filipino majority on the Commission and increased the Filipino representation in the bureaucracy from 71 per cent to 96 per cent. In Washington in 1916, the Democrats passed the Jones Act, which promised independence as soon as a "stable government" could be established. The Clarke Amendment, which specified the time limit as four years, was passed in the Senate and only narrowly defeated by the Republicans in the House. Since independence seemed imminent, especially after Wilson's advocacy at Versailles in 1919 of worldwide self-determination, Harrison abdicated his supervisory functions and permitted the Filipinos to modify American institutions to satisfy indigenous desires.

Harrison actively supported the independence mission that went to the United States in 1919. Quezon and Osmeña, despite their political rhetoric, were far less eager for immediate independence than Harrison, since what they privately wanted was the benefits of self-rule without the liabilities of ultimate authority. Quezon secretly was willing to accept a twenty-five-year Commonwealth. Such an arrangement would have left problems of defense, currency, and free trade to the Americans while placing political, social, and economic power securely in the hands of the Manila elite. Quezon was spared the embarrassment of publicly admitting his plan, however, by the accident of the American election returns. Just as the fate of the archipelago had been shaped by the 1900 election, so too was its independence delayed by the Republican victory in 1920. The Harding Administration, unhappy about the lax quality of the Harrison era and about a series of economic scandals, dispatched Leonard Wood and William C. Forbes to investigate. Their mission concluded that "it would be a betrayal of the Philippine people . . . and a discreditable neglect" of national duty to withdraw "without giving the Filipinos the best chance possible to have an orderly and permanently stable government."[28] Recommending that the office of governor-general be strengthened, the Wood-Forbes mission postponed the independence that had seemed so near.

Harding's appointment of Wood as Governor-General guaranteed a confrontation between the Filipino leadership and the American administration. An authoritarian, Wood served as a magnet to attract Filipino hostility. Quezon shrewdly saw great personal opportunity in the situation, using Wood's unpopularity to establish himself as the most important Filipino leader. Attacking Osmeña's allegedly dictatorial and autocratic tendencies, Quezon split the Nacionalista party in two. He then magnified the tensions with Wood and summoned the nation to form a united front. Osmeña, caught by Quezon's appeal for a transcendental nationalism, found himself forced to accept second place in the reformed Nacionalista party. Having established his own position, Quezon then whipsawed the opposition parties into forming an even broader coalition, which the Nacionalistas dominated. Through a whole series of incidents, including the Fairfield Bill, the Conley affair, Wood's abolition of the Council of State, and the Plebiscite Bill, Quezon exploited nationalist fervor by making Wood a foil for his own leadership. By the time Wood died in 1927, Quezon had projected himself as the embodiment of the Philippine nation.

Quezon and the Nacionalistas dominated Philippine nationalism up to World War II. Opposition critics like Sumulong were relegated to a peripheral position. The one major challenge to Quezon's position came in 1930–33, when a concatenation of factors, including Democratic victories in the American Congress and for Franklin Roosevelt, the rise of Japanese militarism, growing opposition to retention of the Philippines by American labor and farming groups, and racial hostility toward Filipino immigrants, combined to make the American Congress again receptive to Philippine independence. The Hare-Hawes-Cutting Bill, advocating independence after a further ten-year Commonwealth period, was passed by the American Congress after Osmeña and Manuel Roxas had lobbied in Washington for it. It was vetoed by President Hoover, passed despite his veto, and then blocked in the Philippines by Quezon, who was afraid that Osmeña might regain his earlier position as the architect of independence. During the bitter pro- versus anti-independence fight in the Philippines, the Nacionalista party again split. Quezon, the master politician, used his patronage and leverage to block the Hare-Hawes-Cutting Bill and then negotiated (as he had known he could) a slightly more favorable bill from the newly elected President Roosevelt. The measure was known as the Tydings-McDuffie Act. Osmeña, much to Sumulong's disgust, again decided not to establish himself as an opposition leader and ran as Quezon's vice-presidential candidate in the elections for the new Commonwealth government.[29]

In summary, the forty years from 1901 to 1941 contrast sharply with the last decades of the nineteenth century. Whereas in the earlier period the political structure of society was undergoing profound reorganization, later it remained relatively stable. On the other hand, the twentieth century saw striking increases in the numbers of people involved in urbanization, in education, in the franchise, and in modernization. In the late nineteenth century, the *ilustrados* represented a minute percentage of the nation; by 1941, the actual number and the relative proportions of the educated had dramatically increased. Geographic, linguistic, and ethnic distinctions became less important as local patterns were replaced by national ones. People of every economic class and social category came to identify with Philippine nationalism—the flag, the anthem, and the abstraction. Thus, while the dichotomies of tenant and landlord, urban and rural, rich and poor, elite and peasant increased rather than decreased, all strata found a common locus of loyalty in the Commonwealth. Nationalism could supply cohesion, even though it left unanswered substantive questions of direction and identity. The success of Philippine nationalism led one Filipino to write that they were "an Oriental people standing at the portals of Asia, in deep sympathy with its kindred neighbors yet with hands outstretched to the cultures of Spain and America."[30] In the prewar period, Filipinos took great pride that their nation could offer a model for other Southeast Asians to emulate. The optimism of the period was to be tempered by the problems of independence.

26

BURMA

British control over all Burma lasted for less than sixty years. It began and ended in near chaos, and most of the interim was troubled. The politics of colonial rule operated within narrow constraints, imposed in a worldwide imperial framework dominated by nearby India. Economic and social change resulting from or accompanying colonial rule created within Burman society an unanswerable demand for independence and a leadership capable of exercising independence in a world that by traditional standards was harsh. The colonial situation required drastic adjustments in structure and attitude; the painful working out of the adjustments gave to the country an exciting and often perilous political life.

The resistance the British encountered in extending their control in Burma at the end of the nineteenth century reflects both the strengths and the weaknesses of Burman society. Extended conflict had undermined that state long before Mandalay fell in 1885. Lower Burma had never been totally integrated into the kingdom, for Mon separatism, which had rendered brittle the delta's ties with the capital, lessened its susceptibility to central control. British insistence on making village and township headmen the arms of their authority had greatly compromised traditional village leadership. In the absence of alternative leadership, it was easy for monks to assume a stronger role than their vows ordinarily would have permitted, especially when the British refused to give legal sanction to central ecclesiastical authority.

Dacoity was well established as a political pattern in traditional Burma, occurring in response to official abuses or to the absence of clear governmental authority. A number of prominent officials at the Burman court in the nineteenth century began their careers as dacoit leaders, challenging local authority by the only means available to them. Acts of violence and robbery proved their qualities of leadership and the rightness of their cause when the formal hierarchy of authority failed, much as the piracy of the Malay world stemmed from similar circumstances. It was natural that such protests should continue under British rule, especially where, as in Lower Burma, new villages were founded by immigrants from the north, and where leadership, slow to develop from within, was defined artificially by British administrative fiat.

Another sort of resistance to the British in the late nineteenth century came from the ethnic minorities—the Shans, Kachins, Chins, Wa, and other peoples who only with great difficulty had maintained some degree of autonomy within the traditional tributary framework. As Mindon and Thibaw attempted to strengthen their control over the minorities, they provoked a resistance that outlived the Konbaung Dynasty, as with the Limbin Confederacy in the Shan hills. The Shans can only have seen the collapse of the Mandalay monarchy as a release from a relationship they increasingly resented; the British did not, in their eyes, automatically succeed to the suzerain's rights.

All those elements—village headmen, monks, dacoits, and, in outlying areas, the ethnic minorities—actively resisted the imposition of British control throughout Burma. The resistance and rebellion that swept the country in 1886–88 was unquestionably political in motivation. Whether those involved were "nationalists," however, is another question. It is too easy to dismiss them as merely xenophobic or romantic or opportunely lawless, though to some extent they were all three and though the British usually regarded them in this light. They naturally looked backward to an earlier state of things, in order to preserve their traditional values. They could not have succeeded in repulsing British authority, because British power was too strong, and because the rebels were themselves symptomatic of Burman weakness born of a century of turmoil—particularistic, localized, nativistic, and hostile to the changes already irresistibly set in motion from the coast.

In a fundamental manner, the changes deliberately and unconsciously introduced in Burma under colonial rule divided the country even more profoundly than it had been divided before. Among the most important forces for change were modern education and rural economic development, which worked in an unpredictable and impersonal fashion. Both were promoted by the colonial government for practical—if narrow—ends, but both had wider effects on the country as a whole.

Education was an integral part of colonial rule in Burma. It was geared to providing the civil service and modern economic enterprise with English-speaking clerks and other functionaries and providing the state with the skills a modern state was held to require. The cities and towns of British Burma became the centers of such schooling; the homes, shops, and offices the repositories of values communicated in the schools. Recruits into government service came primarily from the towns (especially those of Lower Burma) rather than from the villages, or from the north; the gradual colonization of Burma from the coast inward encouraged the process, at least for the period up to World War I. The British trained a bureaucracy that was nonhereditary and did not come from the old official elite; social development under British rule thus built upon patterns established prior to the fall of Mandalay. Non-official families that remained in or emigrated to Lower Burma before 1885 and took up new land, or who went into business in the towns, or who took up service under the British, were likely to send their sons to

English schools; and those young men, grown up under British rule, had both established connections with economic interests in the towns and an acquired bureaucratic position to defend against latecomers from the north after 1885.

The education of urban dwellers in government-aided schools, through curricula emphasizing the English language and Western arts and sciences, defined their outlook and way of life in sharp distinction to the culture of the villages, and their life apart in cities and towns accentuated the divergence. It was characteristic of this group that some of its younger members, in 1906, should express their desire to identify with indigenous Buddhist values by founding the Young Men's Buddhist Association (YMBA), an association based on an obvious Western model (the YMCA), and that they should engage educated laymen, rather than monks, as teachers of Buddhism. The YMBA and similar groups formed at the turn of the century attempted to assert a cultural identity distinct from the Western culture all about them, one in which they could find security while at the same time establishing their legitimacy as leaders of their own society. Such sentiments still fell far short of political expression. The colonial government, however, was suspicious of the YMBA's political potential and forbade membership in it to its civil employees. Few of the educated elite were willing to jeopardize their careers by engaging openly in political activity.

World War I and associated events in British India rapidly widened the horizons of the urban elite. Burma's direct involvement in the war was less even than that of Thailand and Vietnam, as only a few thousand (mainly Indian) police volunteered for service in Europe and 8,000 Burmans for labor service in Iraq. Even rice exports were only temporarily disturbed by shipping shortages. The indirect effects, however, strongly influenced the new elite and made it both politically aware and active. The YMBA was raising an ostensibly religious and cultural issue in 1916, when it protested the manner in which Europeans (and non-Buddhist Asians) persisted in wearing shoes when visiting Buddhist monasteries, but, of course, the matter went straight to the heart of the colonial situation. It was a question not merely of careless scuffing by foreigners of floors and courtyards polished by countless bare feet but rather of implicit assumptions of cultural superiority and defiant disdain for Buddhist culture, no less contemptuous than if Burman men had insisted on visiting British cathedrals in bare feet, wearing hats, and smoking. The 1916 "footwear controversy," like that of half a century earlier, was really a political issue—a challenge to the British right to rule in a manner defined only by themselves. This time, after all fifty YMBA branches had mounted agitation in every town, the Burmans won. In 1918, the government ruled that abbots had the right to determine the dress appropriate in their monasteries. The importance of this victory can be gauged from the self-assurance and organization with which the YMBA tackled issues more directly political in the following year.

As late as 1916, despite these straws in the wind, a committee appointed by the colonial government to consider political reform saw little need for change. When changes began in India, however, the Burmans were quick to see possibilities for themselves. In 1917, the British Government in London announced its intention of moving toward a greater measure of self-government in India. The YMBA responded by requesting Burma's separation from India. The unrestricted immigration of Indians, the inappropriateness of Indian legislation and administration, the employment of Burma's revenue surpluses to support the Indian Government, and the prospect that the rule of Burma might pass into the hands of Indian politicians were among the many grievances for which the Burmans felt they deserved redress. The Joint Committee on Indian Constitutional Reform, reporting in 1918, recognized the justice of such representations: "Burma is not India," it decided and stated that "the problem of political evolution of Burma must be left for separate and future consideration."[31] This consideration was apparent in the tentative scheme of reform put forward by the British governor in Rangoon later in 1918, advocating only that local self-government be strengthened at the district level by the setting up of elective governing boards, while the legislative council (61 per cent indirectly elected and overwhelmingly weighted in favor of urban interests) was to remain purely advisory. Those proposals were, however, overtaken by developments in India.

Alarmed that separation from India might mean missing out on the greater measure of self-rule to be granted to India, younger and more forward-looking elements in the YMBA, joined by other associations, attacked the proposed reforms. In 1919 and 1920, they sent delegations to London, which gained from the British similar concessions—constitutional diarchy under which some limited government functions would be transferred to Burman ministers responsible to a more representative legislative council. While the Burma delegation members talked in London, however, their compatriots were shouting in the streets at home, and the views they came to express were much more radical than could be contained within the political structure slowly being put together by the colonial government.

The agitation in Burma centered first on the recently founded (1916) University of Rangoon, where new and stiffer standards were put into operation at the end of 1920. The YMBA, after changing its name to the General Council of Burmese Associations (GCBA) in a bid to attract Christian and Indian support, led a boycott of the university, which grew to embrace all government schools. At issue were the standards required of Burmese students, which the leaders felt were unfair and irrelevant; the use of the educational system to inculcate Western (and Christian) values; and the question of who should control education. The agitation that ensued was essentially youthful and urban-centered. Careers were at stake. The degree of self-sacrifice required inhibited participation in the boycott by all but a very few. However, in the short run it did prove the effectiveness of the technique, giving to its leaders a sense of their own power.

The political activity that began with the university strike and boycott in 1921 and continued through the 1920's witnessed increasing public involvement. The GCBA encouraged organization at the village level, giving impetus to the creation of *wunthanu athin* (Own Race Societies), which attempted to bring peasant support to agitation otherwise exclusively urban. Village headmen were denied participation in the societies, because they were regarded as public servants (and indeed were excluded by law from holding higher elective office for the same reason). Both within these groups and outside them, Buddhist monks took an increasingly prominent role in political agitation, creating in 1922 the General Council of Monkhood Associations to direct such work. The monks who were thus active in the 1920's—attacking foreign rule, village headmen, the police and courts, tax collectors, and Indians—were in many respects little different from those who had resisted the British in the 1880's and earlier: Theirs was still a defensive position, which rested on the values of traditional society. Their organization, tactics, and issues were new, but they were traditional in their outlook and had only a frail connection with the educated townsmen.

The introduction of the diarchy constitution in 1923 tested and strained the alliance of urban politicians and rural leadership, whether religious or secular. Under that arrangement, a legislative council was installed with 80 elected members in a total membership of 103. Of the 80, 15 were elected from communal constituencies (8 Indians, 5 Karens, 1 Anglo-Indian, and 1 British), recognizing Burma's ethnic diversity. Three members of the governor's council were put in charge of agriculture, excise, health, public works, forestry, and education and were made responsible to the legislative council. Still reserved to the governor was control over the central administration, the courts, police, land revenue, labor, and finance, as well as the "excluded areas" (Karenni, the Shan states, and the Kachin and Chin hill areas), while the British Government in India kept control of defense, foreign relations, communications, immigration, income tax, and civil and criminal legislation.[32] The elections to the Legislative Council held in November, 1922, split the Burmese elite over the issue of participation or collaboration in what some regarded as an unacceptable constitution. A majority of the GCBA, led by U Chit Hlaing, boycotted the elections, while a minority faction led by U Ba Pe formed the "21 Party" to contest the elections, winning just under half the noncommunal seats. Their split was reflected in GCBA branches and the *wunthanu athin*. The net result was political fragmentation, in which opportunism, generational differences, ethnic and regional origins, educational background, economic concerns, and numerous other forces played a part, dividing both urban elite and village society. All agreed on the necessity of change, but many differed, often violently, on its likelihood, its nature, and the tactics by which it might be mastered. The vast majority saw the electoral process as irrelevant to its concerns; indeed, less than 7 per cent of the eligible electorate voted in 1922, 16.26 per cent in 1925, and 18 per cent in 1928.[33]

Nationalism in Burma prior to 1942 was a minority matter, the political expression of the interests, hopes, and ideas primarily of an educated elite. The issues that moved the elite, though ultimately relevant to the peasant cultivator's daily life and livelihood, were largely incomprehensible to him. Despite the efforts of politicized monks and *wunthanu athin* in the villages, the urban elite was able only slowly to communicate its concerns and ideas to the whole population. Its members thought of themselves primarily as leaders and seldom questioned their own right to the traditional prerogatives of leadership. Although by the mid-1920's a few had begun to conceive of Burma as a single, multi-ethnic nation, with a leadership that would properly be legitimized only by responsibility for and responsiveness to public welfare, most politicians seem to have thought in more private or partisan terms.

This is not to say that Burma was politically quiet in the 1920's. The elite rapidly split still further into at least six parties. In the Legislative Council, increasing representation of the nationalist parties at successive elections served only to swing the communal representatives into the government ranks and to bring about a majority vote against the Burmans. Because they voted with the government, it was the communal representatives and independents who were given cabinet posts. The nationalists' ranks were broken by defections and recrimination as their position worsened. Rural political activity increased substantially as a result of the large number of parties—and independent candidates—competing for votes. Given the lack of popular understanding of the powers and limitations of the legislature under diarchy, violence in both action and language became prevalent under pressure of electioneering, worsening as economic conditions in the countryside deteriorated.

Political activity was inflamed by the local effects of the world depression. Rice prices fell by more than one-half between 1928 and 1931, while land rents, payments on indebtedness, taxes, and the prices of many imported necessities dropped more slowly, if at all. The foreclosure of mortgages on some 2 million acres of agricultural land between 1929 and 1934—almost 20 per cent of the total agricultural land in Lower Burma—was but the most striking symptom of a major agrarian crisis. Tensions exploded in anti-Indian riots, beginning in Rangoon in May, 1930, and moving out into the countryside to create, a year later, general disorder of an openly anticolonial kind.

The most serious of the explosions was the rebellion led by Saya San, which broke out in Lower Burma in December, 1930. Its leader was a former monk, a country "doctor" and seller of folk medicines, and a member of the executive committee of one of the splinter GCBA parties that had been advocating full independence for Burma. For that group, he had undertaken in 1927–28 an extensive survey of agrarian conditions and peasant grievances against colonial rule. His background suggests, as does the way in which his rebellion was organized, that the village organizations of the GCBA and the *wunthanu athin* by the late 1920's had become relevant to the peasant and that rural leadership—though not always coordinated with urban politics—was beginning to give local or personal grievances a larger meaning. Taxation, crime, rice prices, land alienation, and employment were now seen as direct products of colonial rule. Moreover, the new village organizations succeeded in some areas in constructing a hierarchy of leadership based on real peasant leaders—monks, headmen, dacoit leaders, and local politicians—defined in more traditional ways.

Just as peasants earlier had greeted U Chit Hlaing, the GCBA leader, with a royally caparisoned elephant to give him the dignity that, in traditional terms, set him symbolically above other men as a leader, Saya San was surrounded with the trappings and symbolism of royalty—the white umbrella and a capital. The peasants who followed him provided themselves with tattoos and magical amulets to secure the physical protection of Buddhist and animistic powers. Over a period of two years, Saya San carefully prepared his rebellion, drilling and indoctrinating his poorly armed troops and enlisting support. They began their rebellion with attacks on police posts, the forestry service (which denied peasants their customary access to firewood and lumber), uncooperative village headmen, and any Indians and Chinese they came upon. The rebellion moved swiftly through Lower Burma, until nearly 12,000 troops were engaged in the government effort to suppress it. With the capture of its leaders toward the end of 1931, the rebellion began to wane. It was broken by mid-1932.

The Saya San Rebellion proved the futility of peasant rebellion to any who might have been tempted to mount one. Weapons were hard to get, and government Indian and Karen forces were vastly superior in firepower and mobility (the rebels suffered 3,000 casualties, the government 138).[34] It was not, however, a total failure. It awakened public opinion, setting an example of sacrifice and anticolonial zeal that few could ignore and many romanticized. Government prestige was shaken as the seriousness of grievances was emphasized and as its own negativism and indifference were demonstrated.

When the British had begun to re-examine the Indian constitutions in 1929, the issue of separation of Burma from India was also revived. The Simon Commission, which reported on the subject, recommended separation. Many Burmans distrusted British intentions, still fearful that India might be granted more autonomy than Burma and suspicious that the prominence given to the views of Karen and Shan leaders in the Commission's report foreshadowed British manipulation of the minorities as an excuse for maintaining strong legislative and administrative control. Most of the GCBA, therefore, denounced separation. The "separationists" took a broader view of the problem, but they were in a minority, put on the defensive against their rivals by continued British refusal to specify in advance the terms on which separation might be granted. The issue was tested in the general elections of 1932, in which the "antiseparationists" won an important victory on the basis of GCBA, *wunthanu athin*, and monkhood support, gaining forty-two of eighty elective seats. The newly elected Legislative Council, perhaps hopeful that the Indian Congress Party would grant Burma separation on terms more favorable than the British would allow, voted for federation with India, on condition that Burma retain the right to secede. When federation on such terms proved impossible, opinion grew more divided and uncertain, until in 1934 the Council reversed its decision and voted in favor of separation.

The constitution of 1935 provided for a cabinet of nine ministers responsible to a fully elected House of Representatives, with thirty-three additional general and seven additional Karen constituencies, against which was balanced a Senate of thirty-six members, of whom half were to be elected from among men of substantial property and income. Still reserved to the governor were control over the "excluded areas," defense, foreign relations, and monetary policy. Political activity approaching the 1936 elections, which were to inaugurate the new order, seemed sluggish—less meaningful and more confused than in 1932. Politicians who had campaigned in 1932 against separation returned to constituencies holding precisely the opposite view, and since little was seen to have been done to alleviate rural conditions in the meantime, they appeared to many as self-serving office-seekers.

Increasingly, established politicians were challenged by younger men, the more effectively as older parties were split by the prospects of increased power and spoils. A movement centered in the university student union in Rangoon and influenced by radical European Marxism took formal shape as the Dobama Asi-ayone (We Burmans Society) in 1936. The leaders called each other *thakin* (lord, master) to emphasize their assertion of the right of Burmans to rule themselves. They organized labor and student unions and, within the same year, mounted a major educational strike led by Thakin Nu and Thakin Kyaw Nyein and joined by Thakin Aung San, which essentially was a gesture of defiance against school authorities and the colonial educational system. It was called off only when the university and legislature agreed to investigate student demands, ultimately bringing to the university more political independence. Though the Thakin went on to win three seats in the elections of 1936, the principal importance of the movement lay in the political experience that Burma's postwar leadership gained from it.

The parties that contested and won seats in the 1936 elections were badly divided, more by personalities than by issues. The five-party alliance that won the largest bloc of seats in the legislature was unable to agree on the distribution of cabinet posts, and so, in 1937, Dr. Ba Maw —who had defended Saya San at his trial for treason and had led antiseparationist campaigning in 1932—formed a coalition of minor parties, minority leaders, and defectors from other parties to lead the first government of separated Burma. Party divisions, bitter personal feuds, and some self-seeking did not make ruling easy, but the government did at least begin to attack problems unsolved or ignored through the whole period of British domination. Agrarian issues, taxation, university reform, and agricultural credit were all subjects of careful study and legislation, although the reservation of some areas of governmental authority to the governor tied the hands of the legislature, inhibiting reform.

On the eve of World War II, politics reflected the structure of society in its division, its uncertain articulation of national aspirations, and its imperfect joining of urban and rural forces and ethnic minorities. The older leadership, men like Dr. Ba Maw, U Saw, and U Ba Pe, had become more than urban politicians—yet they remained less than national leaders. Having come to maturity during the heyday of Western values in Burma, they hesitated at too strong an affirmation of national values, frightened of a younger radicalism they could not understand. The Japanese invasion of 1942 brought the Burma they had known crashing about their feet.

27

INDONESIA

On January 12, 1900, as the new century was dawning, a Javanese girl called Raden Adjeng Kartini wrote, in Dutch, in a letter to a friend, "Oh, it is splendid just to live in this age; the transition of the old into the new!"[35] The exclamation point was Kartini's, but the vision was true for her time; a new age was opening in the Netherlands Indies. In the early years of the century, the many societies of the archipelago, including her Javanese one, were coalescing in a new and more comprehensive Indies society. The export economy was booming, new investment capital was pouring in, muddy-streeted towns were becoming modern cities. The government, fortified by a freshly proclaimed colonial ethos, the "Ethical Policy," was beginning to penetrate the life of the village with a host of new development programs. A new sense of change and purpose was in the air.

Kartini was aware of all this. But for her the new age was first of all in her own mind; she had needed new eyes to see the society now taking shape so rapidly around her. Her life story, as it is recorded in her published correspondence, was a voyage of self-discovery. Its special quality came not from her earliest childhood in the *priyayi* establishment of her father, the regent of Japara, but from her education in the local European primary school. There she learned Dutch, thus gaining access to all that modern European thinking had to offer. It made her voyage difficult and often painful, for she remained deeply attached to her Javanese heritage. But it enabled her to see the new Indies around her and at least to begin the task of defining a place for herself in it.

What happened to Kartini happened in many different ways to many others in the early twentieth-century Indies: not only to Javanese, Sundanese, Makassarese, and Achehnese but also to Eurasians, Chinese, and the Dutch themselves. The outer political history of the period was the story of how, at the height of Dutch colonial rule, the initiative passed to its subjects, who, developing a nationalist movement, challenged that rule and prepared for its demise. The inner political history of those years consisted of a series of self-transformations by all who came to play roles in that outer history. In the older Java and in the islands beyond it, numerous different societies, indigenous and immigrant, lived side by side, either having little to do with each other or, where they did interact, accommodating fairly easily to each others' cultures. After 1900, the tightening frame of modern Indies society pressed them more closely together, dissolving the old accommodations and challenging the established culture of each separate group. All came under strong pressure to redefine their cultural identities and find places for themselves in the emerging social order. Before politics, therefore, came education, both in the narrow sense of schooling and in the more fundamental sense of self-discovery.

Of all the social groups in the Netherlands Indies, it was the *totok* Dutch who found their transformation the easiest, though it went deep and was to have fateful consequences.[36] In part, the ease of this process was due simply to heavy immigration from Holland, as government and especially business expanded rapidly. *Trekkers,* as they were called, came out to the Indies, usually with Dutch wives, for a career of specified length, went home periodically on leave, and planned to retire there. Their cultural identity was already formed before they came; as their numbers increased, they found little reason to accommodate to local cultures. Thus, they differed markedly from the older, smaller group of Dutch *blijvers* (stayers), who thought of the Indies as their home. The great influx swamped the *blijvers,* and, after 1900, it was *trekkers* who set the style for the *totok* Dutch community. In the cafés, department stores, and comfortable bungalows of the European quarters of the new cities, an all-Dutch life established itself.

As Dutch *totok* in their private life drew apart into a closed community, a parallel development was taking place in the *totok*-run government. The change began in the time of the "Ethical Policy," a nickname given to the new attitudes toward colonial rule that came to the fore at the turn of the century. The leaders of the Ethical movement were high-minded men, troubled by reports of the declining welfare of the Javanese and determined to create a new class of modern-educated indigenous people to take some part in governance with themselves. To those ends, they developed a substantial Dutch-language school system and launched a series of welfare programs that thrust the government into much more direct involvement with the affairs of its subjects.

Closer involvement, however, led to greater dissociation between ruler and ruled. The Ethical Policy was a thoroughly European conception of the role of government, without roots in local political tradition. Ambitious welfare programs were necessarily administered in a bureaucratic way, through government departments and regulations rather than in the personal *priyayi* style of older Dutch officials on Java. Most of all, the Ethical Policy was founded on the cultural arrogance of *totok* Dutch. "But how glorious is the aim that we pursue!" wrote one. "It is the formation out there . . . of a social entity which is indebted to the Netherlands for its prosperity and higher Culture, and thankfully recognizes this fact."[37] Like the *totok* community in which it was rooted, *totok* government had drawn apart from its subjects to become a private club of aliens at the remote pinnacle of a bureaucratic machine.

Totok Dutch, for all their prominence, were only a minority among those classified as "European" by Indies law. The majority were *peranakan,* or Eurasians.[38] In the nineteenth century, all Eurasians shared in the mixed *Indisch* (Indies) culture, but they did not form so distinct and tightly knit a social community as did Chinese *peranakan.* The poorest, such as the enlisted men in the Royal Netherlands Indies Army, lived much as their Ambonese and Javanese counterparts did, using the common Malay of the barracks and back quarters of Batavia.[39] Planters' assistants, petty clerks, and the wives and mistresses of Dutch officials spoke more Dutch and lived a petit-bourgeois life. At the top, Eurasians overlapped with Dutch *blijvers,* occupying high positions in the government, speaking mainly Dutch, and exemplifying the *Indisch* style of life at its most expansive. All, however, enjoyed the prestige of being European and the security of established social roles and cultural patterns.

Around 1900, the situation began to change. As *blijvers* gave way to *trekkers,* and as the *totok* Dutch as a group began to withdraw into a new all-European community, the social and cultural meaning of being European became more restricted, whatever the law said. An increasingly racist white community came to look on a darker skin as a sign of shame, jeered at fractured Dutch, and rejected *Indisch* culture as "native." Eurasians found it painfully necessary to redefine their cultural identity. Some merged into the poorer Malay-speaking population of the cities, ceasing for all practical purposes to be "Dutch." The majority, however, chose to define themselves culturally in *totok* Dutch terms, going to European primary schools and procuring whatever further Dutch-language education they could, abandoning *Indisch* ways, and speaking Malay only to their servants. This movement implied social and political, as well as cultural, pursuit of the fast-receding *totok* Dutch in the early decades of the century. For a brief period after 1912, however, one group of Eurasians attempted a different definition of themselves. In that year, E. F. E. Douwes Dekker founded the Indies Party, an avowedly revolutionary movement whose slogan was "the Indies for those who make their home there." Though his cofounders were Javanese, most of the party's few hundred members were Eurasians, like Douwes Dekker. In turning against *totok* Dutch, they were trying to establish a specifically Indies nationalism that would be broad enough to encompass Eurasians as well as modern-educated Javanese and other indigenous people.

Somewhat similar social groups had succeeded in just the same enterprise in the late-nineteenth-century Philippines, but it failed in the Indies. Mild government repression was hardly necessary; the movement limped on under a variety of names until the end of the decade and then collapsed. In the troubled year 1919, Eurasian opinion moved decisively in another direction, symbolized by the name of their major organization, the Indo-European Union, founded in that year. They had now defined themselves—as a distinct and lesser kind of Dutch, wedded to continued *totok* rule—and, like the *totok* Dutch, had withdrawn into a clearly demarcated community of their own.

There were many more Chinese than Dutch in the Indies, but they numbered only about a quarter of a million (1 per cent) in 1870, a million and a quarter (2 per cent) in 1930. Like the Dutch, they too were divided into *totok* and *peranaken,* and the historical development of the two elements in the early twentieth century in some ways paralleled that of their Dutch counterparts. But their internal social divisions were more elaborate, the routes of cultural change open to them were longer and more numerous, and their minority position in an alien-dominated society did not permit the kind of political allegiance to both homeland and colony simultaneously that *totok* Dutch and even Eurasians achieved easily. In all respects, then, the self-transformations of Chinese in the early twentieth century were more complex, dangerous, and exciting than those of the Dutch.

Before 1900, almost all established Chinese communities in the Indies were *peranakan,* formed originally by the intermarriage of male Chinese immigrants and local women, stabilized by the formation of all-*peranakan* families, and marked by varying degrees of accommodation to their host societies and cultures. By far the largest and most important of these was the *peranakan* community of Java. Compelled by Indies law to live in special quarters of the towns, dominated by a wealthy and often hereditary hierarchy of Dutch-appointed majors, captains, and lieutenants, organized in families whose kinship patterns were more Javan than Chinese, and originating almost exclusively from just one of the many South China speech groups, the Hokkiens, Java *peranakan* formed a clearly demarcated community. At the same time, they had a secure and important place in the larger society, for *peranakan* middlemen and shopkeepers were indispensable to peasants and townsmen, while the majors and captains ran the opium monopoly and other tax farms for the government.

In the first decade of the twentieth century, this comfortable and well-established community was rather suddenly faced with a series of converging pressures and new opportunities, and its members set forth on a quest for new cultural and social identities that is not yet concluded today. On one side, the pressures came from the establishment by *totok* Dutch, in the cities where *peranakan* lived, of a modern European way of life and a new standard of social status. On the other side, pressure came from events in China itself, as new revolutionary movements gathered strength after 1900. Emerging Chinese nationalism provided a second and more emotionally powerful model of cultural and political identification, which, like the Dutch one, made *perana-*

kan feel ashamed of what had a decade earlier been so satisfying a style of life.

The opportunities, as for all groups, were first of all in new schools. In the late nineteenth century, small but increasing numbers of Java *peranakan* began to go to new Christian missionary schools. It was mostly missionary-educated *peranakan* who founded the first modern pan-Chinese association, the Tiong Hoa Hwe Koan, in March, 1900, and it was the THHK a year later that opened the first modern Chinese school in the Indies, in Batavia, an example quickly followed in the other major cities of Java. In such schools, *peranakan* were taught by young nationalist teachers imported from China, and they used textbooks from China. Above all, *peranakan*—who spoke only Hokkien and Malay and who were fully literate only in Malay in the Latin script—were taught in *Kuo-yü*, the Chinese national language, and they became literate in Chinese characters. They thus garbed themselves in a new cultural identity—modern, nationalist, and Chinese in the fullest sense.

The section of the *peranakan* community that set out on this route was first accompanied and then overtaken by Chinese *totok*. Rapid economic growth after 1870 brought ever increasing numbers of Chinese immigrants to Java, as elsewhere in the Indies. In areas like East Sumatra, with no previously established *peranakan* communities, the immigrant society was *totok* in character from the beginning. On Java the established process of absorption into the *peranakan* community continued until the turn of the century and then broke down. One reason was the steadily increasing weight of new immigrants, accompanied for the first time by substantial numbers of *totok* women, who now formed all-*totok* families more resistant to incorporation. More important, in a time of rising Chinese nationalism, *totok* had every reason to hold on to their Chineseness and to see *peranakan* ways as an ignoble compromise. Enrolling their children in the growing Chinese school system, they could in fact do more than hold fast, for, through education in *Kuo-yü*, they could begin to submerge their own particularisms as Hakka, Cantonese, or Teochieu in modern pan-Chinese culture.

From that process, there had emerged by about 1915 a new and specifically Chinese community in the Indies, dominated by *totok* but also incorporating substantial numbers of Chinese-educated *peranakan*. The members of this community oriented themselves politically not to the Indies but to China. They contributed to famine relief there and, at times of threat, organized boycotts against Japanese, British, or other imperialists. Even more than *totok* Dutch and Eurasians, *totok* Chinese had drawn themselves into a tight little cell in one corner of the larger Indies society.

Many *peranakan*, like Eurasians, followed the lead of their *totok* into a new national identity focused on the homeland outside the Indies.

But *peranakan* were long-established residents of the Indies with deep roots there. In the twentieth century, one large group of them went to missionary schools, acquiring the knowledge of Dutch and English, and often the Christianity, which opened the way to a modern identity on European cultural grounds. A still larger group went to the government Dutch-Chinese Schools launched in 1908.[40] In the following years, Indies law was revised to give *peranakan* a legal position closer to Europeans, and they gained access to higher Dutch-language education, the civil service, and the various advisory legislative bodies, such as the Volksraad. Most of the new leaders of the *peranakan* community took that route, and Dutch-educated *peranakan* showed a strong tendency in the following decades to move toward white-collar occupations, government service, and the professions, while *totok* remained overwhelmingly in commerce. As the majors and captains faded away, a new *peranakan* social order appeared, headed by the best-educated—doctors, professors, and lawyers.

In a sense, these *peranakan* were perpetuating their old special community in new cultural dress. But the *peranakan* community never closed in upon itself as the *totok* Dutch, Eurasians, and *totok* Chinese did; it could still contain Dutch-educated doctors, Chinese-educated shopkeepers, and Malay-speaking traders within its broad net of family ties. A man like Kwee Kek Beng, the editor of the newspaper *Sin Po*, had had a Dutch education, was active in Chinese nationalist causes, and wrote his autobiography in *peranakan* Malay. And, in East Java in the 1930's, a small group of *peranakan* founded the Partai Tionghoa Indonesia (Chinese Indonesian Party), which supported the Indonesian nationalist cause—a portent of new *peranakan* movements to come.

The transformations among the Dutch and Chinese showed how general and powerful were the social forces at work in the Netherlands Indies in the early years of the twentieth century. They also illustrate a striking paradox, for, as these groups became more tightly interlocked within an ever more complex Indies economy, they tended to draw apart into their own private compartments. That was eventually to prove a fatal weakness, but, in the age of high colonialism, it had a more immediate significance. These dominant minorities, by thus isolating themselves from the subject population, were abdicating their power to influence developments within that population and to absorb whatever new movements and elites might emerge from it. Compelled, and freed, to seek their own new cultural identities and social roles, the weak in time found ways to be strong.

But it was a stupendous task. The Indies of the early twentieth century incorporated a whole world of indigenous societies: large and small; Islamic, Hindu-Buddhist, Christian, and pagan; wet-rice growers, swidden cultivators, and traders; kingdoms and kin-groups; literate and nonliterate. There were certain commonalities in the historical experience, artistic traditions, and religious assumptions of those societies.

But each had its own integrity, a distinct cultural tradition defined and enforced by its own language and shared by aristocrats and commoners alike. Members of those societies, as they sought to come to terms with modernity, had models to use, but they were foreign and difficult to translate. There were no pre-existing versions of modernity for any of the indigenous societies of the Indies, let alone for all of them in common. This was something that members of those societies had to do for themselves, if they chose to, an immense job of creating and re-creating their identities.

In a population that counted 40 million in 1905 and was divided into dozens of distinct societies, the range of choices offered and paths of change to be followed were innumerable. Different societies varied widely in their need for change. The Balinese, for example, remained emphatically Balinese. Left entirely alone by Dutch planters and sugar-growers, and well satisfied with their uncommonly intricate cultural order, they reacted in quite their own way, by appropriating a handful of admiring Western artists as a catalyst to bring forth new schools of Balinese painting and sculpture, an artistic revolution unparalleled in the Indies at the time.[41] Elsewhere, Bugis and Makassarese, for example, were less bold in their experiments than their fellow Muslims on Sumatra. In general, peasants, particularly in the larger and more stratified societies, moved more slowly than the small elites, which obtained modern schooling and ventured into self-change.

Such transformations led off in many different directions, but for virtually all they began in one of three modes of education—in the deeper sense as well as the narrower one of schooling. One was Christian, the second Islamic, and the third was in the classrooms of modern Dutch-language schools.

Christianity had very little influence in the archipelago before 1800, but the worldwide missionary movement of the nineteenth and twentieth centuries spread out widely among the societies of the Indies. Missions had their greatest impact in non-Islamic areas outside Java. Many of these regions were inhabited by scattered swidden-cultivating populations like the numerous groups in the interior of Borneo, in central Celebes, and on the island of Flores. The missions provided the peoples there with their first opportunity to acquire literacy and the wider vision opened by a world religion—experiences that most Southeast Asians had undergone centuries or millennia earlier. Before 1940, most were fully occupied with developing the possibilities of this kind of transformation: creating new and larger communal identities as Dayak, Toradja, and Florinese or building new religious and, in effect, political bulwarks against their historically exploitative Muslim neighbors.

The effects were more far-reaching among the Toba Batak in north-central Sumatra.[42] The Toba, though preliterate, formed a large, compact, wet-rice–growing society with a strong tradition of territorial expansion. After the 1860's, this dynamic found new expression in the channels opened up by the German Protestants of the Rhenish Mission. Younger Toba, in particular, quickly sought a newly created prestige as evangelists and school teachers in mission schools. By 1917, the process had reached one climax with the founding of the Hatopan Kristen Batak (HKB), or Batak Christian Association, which gave concrete form to their new identity as modern Christian Bataks, and which took the lead in a quarter-century struggle against the old-fashioned and authoritarian rule of the Rhenish Mission. But the HKB proved just a way-station, in the political sense at least, for it represented only a Toba Christian "nationalism" directed against an equally parochial "colonialism" of the mission. Even as it was being founded, Toba were pressing eagerly into newly established Dutch-language schools in the vicinity and spreading out in increasing numbers to the nearby Medan plantation region and to Batavia and other cities on Java. On those new frontiers, they gained jobs as civil servants, schoolteachers, and doctors and took an active part in creating wider identities.

The Islamic mode of education and self-change was far more important, if only because so many of the peoples of the Indies were at least nominally Muslim. Before 1900, with few exceptions, Islam was practiced throughout the islands as a traditional folk religion. Boys went to Kuranic classes to learn the established practices of the adult Muslim community; for this purpose, it did not matter at all that they learned to recite in a language—Arabic—that they could not understand, for that very fact assured the sanctity of the mysteries whose outward forms they were memorizing. Muslim scholars found intellectual challenge and enlightenment in their study of an immense religious literature and served in an indispensable role as legal experts and spiritual leaders. Everywhere Islam had gracefully united with local beliefs.

Life in the Indies of the early twentieth century, however, brought new experiences that became increasingly difficult to comprehend within the frame of thought provided by the traditional versions of Islam. It was not only that the more direct intrusion of a Christian government threatened or challenged the old ways. There were new opportunities as well, and, to seize them, men needed new images of who they were and what they were doing. Increasing numbers of Muslims began to doubt the adequacy of what had been perfectly satisfactory identities; in their need, they were presented with an outside model of modernity—Reform Islam, which had risen in the Middle East in the last years of the nineteenth century as a response to precisely the same urgent needs. Reform Islam stood for a return to what it called the fundamental truths of the Kuran, discarding both the accretions of medieval scholasticism and the compromises with local animism, thus clearing the way for a thoroughgoing modernization of Islam. It offered self-respect and a guide for new times without a denial of one's identity, a way to become modern while remaining Muslim. This gave it great appeal and roused strong resistance in the Islamic societies of the Indies.

These Islamic societies were diverse, and the Reform movement took very different forms in different areas. Among most of the Muslim peoples of Sumatra, for example, its development was closely associated with the old and powerful *rantau* pattern. *Rantau* has many meanings: It can refer to movement out to a frontier of settlement, to traders off seeking their fortunes in distant lands, and also to men who set out on the road to deeper religious knowledge. In all its meanings, it connotes a drive outward from one's present situation to embrace new opportunities.

In such societies, Reform Islam provided not only its general program for a Muslim modernity but also a new and wide channel for the *rantau* drive. Reform ideas supplied the base for the most important Achehnese movement of modern times, the PUSA, founded in 1939 by Daud Beureueh, which embodied a singularly intense drive to reformulate Achehnese Islam and to remake the whole of Achehnese society in that image.[43]

A Reform movement also dominated the life of Minangkabau after 1900, vigorously attacking both Minangkabau matrilineal custom and traditional Islamic practice, and arousing strong counterattacks in turn. The movement produced notable figures, such as the novelist and controversialist Hamka and Hadji Agus Salim, the leading national exponent of Reform Islam in the political sphere.[44] While with PUSA, the *rantau* drive was turned inward; among the Minangkabau, Reform Islam was associated with expansive movements: the rubber-planting boom of the early twentieth century and a remarkable migration of Dutch-educated intellectuals to Batavia and other cities on Java.[45]

The religious pattern of the Javanese was different from those on Sumatra—and, for that matter, those of other peoples on the island—and consequently Reform ideas had a different role to play there. Virtually all Javanese professed themselves Muslims, but within that unity there were two distinct variants whose roots went back to the sixteenth century. The great majority of Javanese, peasants and *priyayi* alike, were *abangan*, who had responded to the coming of Islam by absorbing it, along with much that was Hindu, Buddhist, or animist in origin, into a larger complex of belief—the "Javanese religion," as it is often called. The minority, the *santri*, took their self-identification as Muslims more seriously, distinguishing themselves from *abangan* by their more exacting performance of such requirements as the five daily prayers and abstinence from food and water during the daylight hours of the fasting month.[46]

Javanese, however, place a high value on harmony; *santri* and *abangan* had lived comfortably together for centuries. *Abangan*, after all, were Muslims too, while *santri* Islam, as taught in the *pesantren* scattered about the countryside, was a folk religion containing many pre-Islamic elements. That social harmony, like so many others, was destroyed by the relentless quest for new identities and social roles in the twentieth century.

The process began quietly enough, in the changing economic conditions of the late nineteenth century. After 1870, the steamship made it possible for much greater numbers of *santri* to make the pilgrimage to Mecca, and they returned more conscious of their Islam and wearing a modified version of Arab dress. In the rural areas, from which most came, returned *haji* often established new *pesantren*, and around them the rural *santri* community grew in numbers and piety. Some also grew in wealth: rural traders, peasants saving for the pilgrimage, *pesantren* heads using the labor of their students in fields they accumulated. While the great majority of rural *santri* remained no better off than other peasants, the accumulative ethic of the minority gave rise in time to the hostile *abangan* image of all *santri* as rich, stingy, sanctimonious "Arabs." Rural *santri*'s religious beliefs changed little in the process; they were not so much seeking a new identity as expanding the scope of an old one. But their increasing consciousness of themselves as members of a distinctly Muslim community had the same effect as the economic behavior of the richer few. Rural *santri* as a group drew slowly apart from their *abangan* neighbors.

In the longer run, this slowly expanding gap was to have profound consequences in Javanese rural society. But after 1900 it was overtaken for a time by a more dramatic development, an altogether new and deep cleavage inside the Javanese *santri* community itself. The economic changes of the late nineteenth century had affected urban *santri* more deeply than rural ones. Urban traders expanded their businesses, moving into new lines. *Santri* groups built up substantial *batik* cloth and *kretek* cigarette industries in towns like Jogjakarta, Surakarta, and Kudus. In the towns, they felt the pressure of Chinese competition; at the same time, they saw at first hand the transformations of the Chinese and the Dutch communities. By around 1900, many had come to feel the need for a new image of the world and their place in it. It was they who welcomed Reform Islam and claimed it as their own.

Most urban *santri*, particularly in the larger towns and cities, went over quickly to Reform Islam in the first two decades of the century. As they did so, they spread out from commerce and small industry to a wider range of urban occupations—as journalists, schoolteachers, and white-collar workers—laying the base for a self-confident, modern, and specifically Muslim urban community. The community's character was exemplified by the activities of its most important organization, Muhammadiyah, founded in Jogjakarta in 1912, which grew very rapidly in the following decades. Muhammadiyah was modern by its very nature, for Indies Muslims had not previously organized themselves in associations with boards of directors, branches, and the like. It carried on its work through further organizations: youth and women's associations, clinics, orphanages, and above all a large school system, which presented academic subjects along the lines of the contemporary government Dutch-language schools and taught Islam not by recital and exegesis but as a basic system of religious, ethical, and social beliefs. Most important, perhaps, Muhammadiyah soon developed branches in the non-Javanese areas of the island, in Sumatra, and elsewhere. From the beginning it was not a Javanese organization but a specifically Muslim one; the new identity it embodied transcended ethnic particularism—and traditional local variants of Islam—in the various societies of the Indies.

It also inevitably opened a wide gap within the Javanese *santri* community, as in Minangkabau and elsewhere. Everywhere in the smaller towns, and sometimes in the countryside itself, small but militant groups of modernists attacked what they called the meaningless ritual of Kuranic chanting and the quibbles of traditional scholasticism, and they demanded that Javanese Islam be purged of its non-Islamic "superstitions." Such attacks threatened the identity of rural *santri* for the first time and, in particular, challenged the leadership of *pesantren* heads and traditional scholars. They responded in kind, calling the modernists Christians and unbelievers.

The battle raged through the 1910's and 1920's; half a century later the wounds still had not fully healed. But in time traditionalists founded modern Islamic schools and modern organizations—the first and greatest of the latter, the Nahdatul Ulama, being established in 1926 precisely to use the modernists' own methods against them. For their part, modernists drew back from the more extreme of their views. Together, too, they felt the increasing pressures of new movements among *abangan*—both peasants in the countryside and the rising Dutch-educated intelligentsia in the cities.

It was the third major mode of education, in Dutch-language secular schools, that was most significant for the depth, and especially the breadth, of the transformations it engendered among the peoples of the Indies. The beginnings were slow. In the nineteenth century, the government developed a small but good system for its European nationals, but before 1900 only a handful of high-ranking "natives," such as Kartini, were allowed to attend European Primary Schools. The number increased in the years of the Ethical Policy, reaching 4,000 in 1905 and 6,000 in 1920.[47] Those privileged students, still largely from the traditional elite classes in the different Indies societies, also predominated among the very small numbers of indigenous people who went on through the new European secondary schools and colleges (Engineering School, 1920; Law School, 1924; Medical School, 1927) or to study in Holland.

Meanwhile—alongside this European school system always intended primarily for the Dutch themselves—a separate government system of Native schools was growing. Most of the Native schools of the nineteenth century, as well as the very large system of village schools developed after 1907, used local languages as the medium of instruction and hence had much less cultural impact. But the "Dokter Djawa" School, which came in time to graduate fairly completely trained "native doctors," used Dutch as the language of instruction after 1875. For that reason, its few hundred students played a disproportionately large role in the political and cultural movements of the first two decades of the twentieth century. It was after 1900, however, that the government Dutch-language Native system really developed. Between 1907 and 1914, the existing Native primary-level schools evolved into Dutch-Native Schools (DNS), which provided primary education for "natives" entirely in the Dutch language. During the following decade, a latticework of new schools was built above the DNS to provide higher education for a few "natives" and transfer routes to advanced training in the parallel European system. But it was the government Dutch-Native Schools, with 20,000 students in 1915 and 45,000 in 1940, that were decisive—perhaps the most important single institution in twentieth-century Indies history.

Dutch-language secular education had many consequences. Most obviously it opened a new route for upward social mobility into urban positions as civil servants, teachers, white-collar workers in private business, journalists, lawyers, and doctors. It also provided a new criterion of social status, which had a double effect. On the one hand, Dutch education placed all those who had it above those who did not, graduates from the European system above those from the Native system, and so on upward to the handful who had advanced degrees from the Netherlands. It was a new, easily calculated hierarchy of standing, which put those lower down in an often painful position and left the peasant an outcaste. On the other hand, this criterion necessarily challenged the old status hierarchy, which was based, within each indigenous society, mainly on birth. A lower *priyayi* official who had an education as good as, or better than, that of the hereditary Regent he served under found it difficult or unpleasant to use the humble "high" Javanese when speaking to him, as required by traditional status ranking. Virtually all of the modern movements of the early twentieth century, therefore, had a strong anti-"feudal" aspect. By the same token, the new criterion increasingly called into question the high status the Dutch inherited with their skin. The engineer Sukarno was fully as well educated as the lawyer governor-general who exiled him in 1933, but he could not possibly have attained that office. Dutch education, finally, gave easy access to the self-proving truths of modern science, to new and conflicting political visions, to whole schools of literature not necessarily better but certainly different and stimulating. More deeply, the very fact of thinking in a foreign language, as several tens of thousands came to do, imposed a new geometry on what they thought.

The experience of these changes defined, in both social and cultural terms, a new group that rose in the early-twentieth-century Indies, the secular urban intelligentsia of indigenous origin. But that educational experience did not of itself provide them with a new identity. They were no longer traditional Bugis, Minangkabau, or Javanese—though they continued to think in those languages too, with all that that implied. Nor, evidently, in a racist Indies, were they Dutch or Eurasians or *peranakan* Chinese—though they shared a language and much else with them. Their predicament gave rise to a whole series of efforts in the early decades of the century to create new identities. This quest was not in origin a political one, but the politics of the time was very largely determined by it.

One avenue that many groups explored was that of ethnic identity redefined on a modern basis. The first and most important of the organizations formed on this basis was the Budi Utomo, founded in 1908 on the initiative of a group of Javanese students in the "Dokter Djawa" School.[48] Throughout its twenty-seven years, Budi Utomo stood for an effort by Dutch-educated Javanese *priyayi* to create a modernized Javanese cultural foundation on which they could base a more secure self-respect and from which they could, somehow, claim a greater say in affairs. But the difficulties inherent in this project were reflected in a complicated history marked by persistent difficulty in deciding between a purely cultural program and experiments with various political postures. Budi Utomo was moderate in tone, for many of its *priyayi* members were reluctant to go too far in abandoning their traditional culture, which, among other things, assured them a high status. It often showed uncertainty in defining the identity it represented; thus it spoke frequently of "Greater Java," a notion that Sundanese and Madurese, understandably, found not at all attractive.

In all these respects, Budi Utomo was typical of numerous similar organizations established by other ethnic groups in the 1910's. Student organizations, beginning somewhat later, tended to be more militant. It is revealing that, while they continued to organize along ethnic lines, their names almost all began with the Dutch word "Jong" (Young), thus neatly symbolizing the poles of their cultural and political dilemma: Jong Java, Jong Sumatranen Bond, Jong Minahassa, Jong Celebes. The Jong Islamieten Bond of the same period represented the same phase in the thinking of Dutch-educated Reform Muslims.

The Indies Party and its successor organizations represented a second avenue explored by some of the Dutch-educated. Two important members of the intelligentsia, Suwardi Suryaningrat and Tjipto Mangunkusumo, were cofounders of the party, playing a major role in its early life. Few other non-Eurasians ever joined the party, but it exerted a wide influence nevertheless, for, at a time when other organizations were speaking of self-improvement and a greater degree of autonomy, it came boldly forth with a demand for the end of Dutch rule. What was for Eurasians their last chance, in effect, to escape a cultural and political second place was for Javanese and others their first chance to experiment with a much broader definition of their political identity. "Indies" nationalism—which included Eurasians and in principle Dutch *blijvers* and Chinese *peranakan*—did not long survive, but the idea of nationalism did.

Unlike the Indies Party and such ethnic associations as Budi Utomo, the Sarekat Islam (Islamic Union) did not stand for any single identity, however loosely defined. Its significance was precisely the opposite. It was the first mass movement in Indies history (the only one before 1945), and, at one time or another in its fourteen years, groups of almost every persuasion enrolled under its banner. The extraordinary confusion and excitement of its career reflected the confusion and venturesome spirit of the times.

Sarekat Islam (SI) was founded in 1912, the same year as Muhammadiyah, and by members of the same social group, the urban Reformist *santri*. Both were influenced by the new winds blowing through the Chinese community at the collapse of the Manchu dynasty in 1911; urban *santri*, who had close contacts with Chinese, felt both a threat and a stimulus to their own growing sense of community. But while Muhammadiyah stood for the religious interests of such *santri*, the Sarekat Islam—founded by a prominent Surakarta *batik* merchant, Hadji Samanhudi—stood mainly for their economic interests at a time of increasing pressure from Chinese wholesalers and competitors.

But the SI did not long remain confined to its original economic aims and to the particular social group those aims served. In a Muslim Java and a predominantly Muslim Indies, "Sarekat Islam" was a rallying cry, implying a wider movement for change. The organization quickly attracted members of a second group, disaffected intelligentsia, which within a year had taken over leadership. The most important of them was Umar Said Tjokroaminoto, a Dutch-educated *priyayi* and an extraordinarily eloquent orator who was largely responsible for the mass following that SI quickly acquired.

Two other important groups soon emerged within the SI's leadership. One was a small group of Dutch-educated Reformist Muslims around Hadji Agus Salim, who became Tjokroaminoto's right-hand man and the leader of the organization's specifically Muslim wing. The other was an equally small and able group of socialists. A handful of *totok* Dutch immigrants had established an Indies Social-Democratic Association (ISDA) in Semarang in 1914, and their views—Western but anti-colonial and anti-capitalist—had the same formative influence on some Dutch-educated Javanese and others as Reformist doctrines from Cairo had on urban *santri*. Some, such as Alimin Prawirodirdjo, Darsono, and a young railway employee, Semaun, joined the ISDA. Semaun and others were active in the radical wing of the growing trade-union movement of the late 1910's. From that organizational base, working mainly through the Semarang branch of the Sarekat Islam, they came to play an increasingly important role in the central SI after 1916.

The SI's mass following, which was what attracted these and other disparate and often hostile groups to the SI leadership, was not created by their efforts. It developed, instead, out of a curious interplay among three elements: government policy, inchoate folk feeling, and Sarekat Islam, acting not as an organization with a program but as a symbol and a voice—especially the voice of Tjokroaminoto himself. The Ethical government of those years was inclined to look indulgently on "native" movements for self-improvement, and despite strong pressure from Dutch opinion, it gave the SI wide latitude. Tjokroaminoto spoke of wrongs to be righted, and millions flocked to follow his charismatic lead: urban *santri* in Kudus, traditional rural *santri* in West Java, *abangan* peasants, Muslims throughout Sumatra, the Celebes, and elsewhere, even Toba Christians.[49] They had grievances—a greater number than usual, because those were rapidly changing times—and they reported them to local SI branches in a great flood, expecting redress. Moreover, the Sarekat Islam took on a messianic significance. Tjokroaminoto's name, by what appeared to be more than coincidence, was one of the traditional Javanese names of the expected deliverer, Prabu Heru Tjokro. SI membership cards were widely believed to guarantee salvation. Tjokroaminoto criticized *priyayi* officials, even the regents and the remote Dutch Government itself, and they appeared too weak to stop him. That could mean only one thing: The *wahyu*, the magical potency of rule, was passing to new hands.

Sarekat Islam membership grew to more than 2 million in 1919, but the figures meant little, since only a few tens of thousands were members in the sense of joining an organization, while many more than 2 million felt the pull of what was a great folk movement. Tjokroaminoto and other members of the leadership felt that pull too; SI propaganda became steadily more militant between 1916 and 1919. So, by the same token, did the government. A number of local rebellious incidents in 1919 broke its tolerance forever. In short order, some members of the central SI and the ISDA were brought to trial or exiled. Local officials, both Dutch and indigenous, harassed SI branches and repressed strikes everywhere.

The year 1919 marked the end of the Ethical Policy. Some of its slogans and programs remained, but from then until the end of colonial rule in 1942, the government never hesitated to suppress whatever it considered subversive native movements. That year also marked the end of the Sarekat Islam as a mass movement. Its founders, the non-Dutch-educated urban *santri*, had already largely gone back to Muhammadiyah. Now the secular intelligentsia also withdrew to join other organizations and to look in other directions. And much of the folk following simply looked the other way, not really leaving because they had never really joined.

What was left was the organization's symbolic name, its leader Tjokroaminoto, and the more deeply committed fraction of its original mass following—mostly local leaders and vernacular-educated men who could no longer be content with village life but lacked the credentials for good urban jobs. The two remaining wings—Muslim and socialist—of the central leadership immediately fell into bitter dispute. As they did so, each found it necessary to define its political identity more clearly. The socialists were more successful. As non-Dutch members of what had been a Dutch-founded organization with a Dutch name (the ISDA), and likewise at best nominal Muslims in an organization called Sarekat Islam, they had good reason to sharpen their self-image. Meanwhile, the Russian Revolution provided an attractive new model and the Comintern a strong framework in which to reorient themselves. In 1920, the socialists, still including a few not yet exiled Dutch, changed the name of their organization to the Perserikatan Komunis di India (PKI, Indies Communist Party) and joined the Comintern. They thus defined for themselves a new and explicitly international identity. Hadji Agus Salim's Muslim wing also moved in an internationalist direction during the early 1920's. It needed an ideological counterweight to the PKI and found it in the worldwide pan-Islamic movement of the time, focused on the idea of restoring Kemal Ataturk as the Caliph of all Islam.

The Muslim wing soon won Tjokroaminoto and control over the name Sarekat Islam, forcing the PKI out of the central SI in 1921. In the course of the next few years, on the other hand, the PKI gradually gained the support of the great majority of the remaining branches and followers. But the cost of the intense struggle was high for all concerned. In many Javanese areas, the dispute, expressed in new ideological terms, gave a new and bitter meaning to the slowly growing gap between rural *santri* and *abangan*—a focusing of opposed identities that was to bear terrible fruit after 1945. And elsewhere the tension kept alive the fervor of the remaining faithful, who stumbled on toward the final disaster. A scattered and easily suppressed revolt broke out in December, 1926, led in most areas by local PKI members. In the repression that followed, the government rounded up 13,000 "subversives" of various political colors, exiling 1,000 to the malarial swamps of New Guinea. The PKI was broken for a generation. Sarekat Islam was left holding the by now dead cause of the Califate. It was the end of the great folk movement of the SI and the end of a political era.

Over the wreckage of the old movement, the idea of Indonesia rose suddenly and, within a few quick years, implanted itself forever in the minds of men who now became Indonesians. In July, 1927, a small group led by Sukarno founded the Partai Nasional Indonesia (PNI, Indonesian National Party). As its name made clear, the PNI stood for a new political identity that on the one hand transcended and encompassed the many societies of the Indies, and on the other declared the end of waiting for "an airplane from Moscow or a Caliph from Istanbul." In October, 1928, a congress of youth organizations brought the idea forth in one echoing phrase, "one nation—Indonesia, one people—Indonesian, one language—Indonesian." The congress also adopted the red over white national flag as its own and sang for the first time the newly composed national anthem, "Indonesia Raya." The wave spread swiftly through public life: The SI became the Partai Sarekat Islam Indonesia, Budi Utomo merged into a new Partai Indonesia Raya, hundreds of new organizations with "Indonesia" in their titles were established in the next few years. More deeply, in the privacy of their own thoughts, virtually all modern-educated men and women came in those years to identify themselves as Indonesians.

The idea of Indonesia spread so easily, once launched, that it seemed to later historians as if it had always existed, if not actually explicitly then inchoate in the hearts of the people. But it was, in fact, a new creation, the product of a great and difficult leap of the imagination. The idea of Indonesia required the denial of the political meaning of the societies into which the first Indonesians had been born. It required also the acceptance of the new reality of the Dutch Indies, and then the transmuting of that into "Indonesia."[50] In the first decades of the century, in effect, only the Dutch-educated had the kind of experience that made this creative leap possible and ultimately necessary. In Dutch-language schools, members of all ethnic groups underwent the same transforming education together and came out with as much in common as any had with the non-Dutch-educated of their own ethnic background. The jobs they took were mostly unknown to the traditional societies, with meaning only in an Indies-wide frame of reference. The modern cities where they studied and worked were in many ways closer to each other than to their respective hinterlands.

Even so, up to the mid-1920's, the politically active few among them joined organizations such as Budi Utomo, Sarekat Islam, and Jong Minahassa, which were certainly not Indonesian. It was a tiny minority of a minority, students in Holland, who actually took the lead in creating the idea of Indonesia. In Holland, they were liberated from the daily reality of the Dutch-run Indies and enabled to view it as a whole but not necessarily as the Indies. They were also liberated more fully from ethnic ties; it was inconceivable for their dozens, among millions of Dutch, to divide up into Jong Java, Jong Celebes, and the rest. Their first organization, founded in 1908, was called the Indies Association, itself an early and clear indication of a common identity. The decision in 1922 to reconstitute that organization as the Perhimpunan Indonesia (PI), or Indonesian Association, was the first unambiguous declaration of the birth of the Indonesian identity.

The term "Indonesia" was beginning to be used in discussion at home as well, but it took several years for the implications to sink in and for the PI's program to be widely accepted. Students, with less stake in established organizations and identities, responded more quickly; two youth groups with "Indonesia" in their titles and straight nationalist programs were founded in 1927 before the PNI. But it was the PNI—catching the growing trend at the right moment and riding on the remarkable personality of Sukarno—that brought Indonesian nationalism into the open in the Indies and did most to ensure its success.

Indonesian political life in the 1930's took place in a context of rigorous police surveillance and infrequent but effective repression, which made mass movements impossible and helped to keep a majority of civil servants and others out of public activity. Within that narrow political space, great numbers of different organizations grew, split, merged, and quarreled among themselves, but not on fundamentals. Some ethnic associations continued actively, but, with few exceptions, they came to see themselves as representing parts of a larger Indonesian whole rather than separate entities. Muslim organizations, insofar as their activities were political, had given up the pan-Islamic movement, seeking instead to define Indonesia in Islamic terms. The small minority of "non's" (noncooperators), who refused to work within colonial institutions, such as the largely powerless electoral bodies of the time, fiercely attacked the great majority of "co's," who were willing to do so. But the controversy concerned only tactics. When the Japanese arrived in 1942, the members of the urban elite—and to a great degree the hereditary elites most closely attached to the Dutch—shared a common and by then well-established Indonesian national identity.

During the same two decades in which the political idea of Indonesia arose and gained general acceptance among the modern-educated elite, a parallel process of creating an Indonesian national culture was under way. The major symbol of the movement was the transmutation of the universal Malay of the islands into the national language, Indonesian—an act of re-creation strikingly similar to the political one and quite as significant. But in other respects there were greater differences. The political idea of Indonesia had emerged in the minds of men who had their roots in one or another of the many regional societies and who through education—primarily in Dutch—had grasped the reality of the modern Indies. At that point, they were bipolitical, for they were at home in two different political worlds—fairly comfortably in the case of the Ambonese and Minahassans and the traditional elites close to the Dutch, uncomfortably in the case of the new urban intelligentsia. But when the leap had been made and the Netherlands Indies redefined as Indonesia, it was quite easy for the intelligentsia to commit themselves unambiguously to that new political identity. The Indies as a working system was already there; they needed only to appropriate it as their own, first symbolically and later actually. In so doing, they also directly served their own political interests, since they would be the ones who would have the best opportunity of rising to political leadership in an independent Indonesia.

The same education had also made them bicultural, specifically bilingual, in their home languages and in Dutch. This tension, however, was not so easily surmounted: On the one side, they could not simply decide to stop thinking in Javanese or Madurese or to erase the cultural assumptions of their childhood, as they could change their political commitments; on the other side, they could not simply rename Dutch

"Indonesian," nor could they ever take over Dutch culture from its original possessors to make it theirs only, as they could hope to do with the political unit, the Dutch Indies.

It was out of this tension that the Indonesian language was born, what one writer has aptly called "Revolutionary Malay" and "an enterprise for the mastery of a gigantic cultural crisis."[51] Malay was in many ways highly appropriate for the role it was to play. It was the home language of only a few scattered peoples in the Indies, and thus it had the great political advantage of belonging to no one. In another sense, Malay belonged to all, for it had been the lingua franca of commerce and Islam in the whole archipelago for centuries. As such it had many virtues: flexibility, a "democratic" character marked by the absence of elaborate status distinctions, a simplicity that left it open to the infusion of modern terms and concepts.

Those attributes had already given Malay wide currency in the century or so before 1920. The Dutch had used it for convenience as a secondary language of administration; *peranakan* Chinese used it for commerce and also in their homes, and so did most Eurasians; from the very beginning, around 1900, the indigenous press had used it almost exclusively. It was quite natural, therefore, for the emerging Indonesians of the 1920's to adopt it as their national language and to rename it Indonesian—a vessel into which to pour their discontents and their hopes.

The very qualities that made Malay so suitable for transformation to Indonesian, however, also made this a precarious enterprise in its first two decades, and in some ways long after. A modern literature in Indonesian began to appear from the 1920's, mainly from writers connected with the government-run popular publishing house, Balai Pustaka, and from the Indonesian literary journal *Pudjangga Baru* of the 1930's. But it is remarkable how many of the authors were Sumatrans, especially Minangkabau, whose language is closely related to Malay; it proved difficult for Javanese and others to do creative work in the national language. The public life of Indonesian organizations was conducted almost entirely in Indonesian, but few thought in it; committee meetings, draft writings, and most of the private life of the intelligentsia continued to be carried on in Dutch, or a regional language. Moreover, only a very small part of the Indies school system of the time used Indonesian as the language of instruction. Indeed, before 1942, it was only the Taman Siswa school system, founded by Ki Hadjar Dewantoro in 1922, and some of the informal and quasi-political "wild schools" of the 1930's, which might qualify as the beginnings of a fourth major mode of education for modern Indonesians.[52] Meanwhile, students who were Indonesian by political conviction and committed to the ideal of an Indonesian national culture, continued like their elders to be educated largely in Dutch. By the end of colonial rule, the Indonesian cultural identity, unlike the political one, had only been sketched in principle, and was as yet fully practiced only in limited circles.

In a larger sense, however, the same was true of both. The idea of

Indonesia, in both the political and the cultural sense, had been achieved and had set down its roots. But it was still confined to a very small proportion of the population, those who had themselves been transformed in one of the modes of modern education: Dutch, Muslim, Christian for a few, and Indonesian for even fewer. Beyond and around them remained the mass of the peasants, still living mainly in the traditional political and cultural worlds defined by the languages of the many societies of the islands. In fact, one of the chief consequences of the remarkable changes of the previous forty years had been to open up a new and dangerously wide gulf between the Indonesian elite and the folk of the land, whom they also called Indonesians.

28

VIETNAM

Radical absorption of Western institutions and philosophies, a growing individualism among the elite, and the appearance of strains between old values and new ones were not really prominent features of Vietnamese life before 1900. If nationalism in the Southeast Asian context means ideologies that simultaneously stress the rediscovery and preservation of a distinctly non-Western cultural identity and the assimilation of modern Western material techniques and revolutionary ideas, then Vietnamese resistance to French colonialism before the 1900's was not nationalistic but a compound of xenophobia and Confucian loyalism. It was nonetheless a vital forerunner of Vietnamese nationalism. It is desirable, perhaps, to distinguish between prenationalistic *traditionalist* ideologies of resistance and *change-absorbing* ideologies of resistance in modern Vietnamese history.

Southern resistance to the French conquest of "Cochinchina" in the 1860's had been led by men of different backgrounds: sons of court military commanders (Truong Cong Dinh), scholars (Nguyen Huu Huan), and fishermen (Nguyen Trung Truc). By the summer of 1861, the most famous of these leaders, Truong Cong Dinh, had recruited a volunteer army of perhaps 10,000 men to fight the French. Southern political self-consciousness was also stimulated in the 1860's by the celebrated "writing-brush war" between two southern scholars, Ton Tho Tuong and Phan Van Tri. Tuong collaborated with the French, serving them as a provincial official and political middleman. Tri, on the other hand, invoked the Confucian tradition that "the loyal minister does not serve two princes," declining French invitations to serve in the Cochinchina colonial government. The two men exchanged brilliant, heavily allegorical poems justifying their respective positions of collaboration and resistance in a savage polemical battle that was designed not as private correspondence but as an appeal to the public opinion of the southern scholar class as a whole. The outstanding southern apologist of collaboration with the French, Tuong went so far as to compare himself to a woman (Sun Fu-jen) in the medieval Chinese novel *Romance of the Three Kingdoms* (*San kuo chih yen i*) who must live with her husband (the French) even though he is the arch-enemy of her own father (the Vietnamese court). Tri, in turn, argued in a poetic response that the obligations of a woman to her husband and of a man to his political morality were intrinsically incomparable, and that Tuong's use of *Three Kingdoms* political mythology to objectify—or give an artificial historicity to—transparent time-serving was unconvincing.[53]

From the 1870's to the 1890's in northern and central Vietnam, the provincial intelligentsia swung between philosophic disillusionment and militant anti-Catholic xenophobia. A provincial governor-general who was also one of the most sensitive writers in Vietnam in the 1880's, Nguyen Khuyen, saw the Vietnamese court's collapse not so much in terms of technological inferiority as in terms of a strange moral paradox: namely, that until 1885 France had conquered separate regions of Vietnam while outflanking, rather than attacking, the traditional structure of political loyalties, which remained oddly untouched at the very moment that the state was losing its sovereignty. For until 1885, active resistance to the French had often meant disloyalty to the negotiation-prone court. Analyzing the conquest, Khuyen focused upon the growing discrepancy between forms (the mandarin class was still intact, with its books, gowns, and seals) and realities (it had lost its power and supposed moral invulnerability). As Khuyen put it of himself, in a famous "self-satire" written perhaps about 1885: "When I open my mouth, I speak strongly and with a bookish authority. Yet my soft, flaccid lips can also drink me into drunken stupors. When I think of myself I am disgusted with myself, yet even with all this . . . my name has appeared upon the gold examination list."[54]

After the death of the Tu-duc Emperor in 1883, an anti-French "war party" of officials led by a strongman regent named Ton That Thuyet became the masters of Vietnamese court politics. Thuyet and his allies disposed of a succession of youthful emperors (Duc-duc, Hiep-hoa, Kien-phuc) in 1883–84 but were unable to block the establishment of the French protectorate over northern and central Vietnam. In July, 1885, however, after launching an unsuccessful surprise attack against the first French *résident supérieur* for central Vietnam, Thuyet fled from Hue, taking the Ham-nghi boy emperor with him. He now had Ham-nghi issue a decree calling for general insurrection in the provinces. Although the French captured Ham-nghi in 1888, transported him to exile in Algeria, and found another prince to serve as emperor at Hue (Dong-khanh, 1885–89), the decree finally galvanized the provincial elite into action. Their movements of resistance to the French, which began in 1885 and merged eventually with the newer nationalist struggle, rallied initially under the slogan "aid the king" (*can vuong*), a Sino-Vietnamese adaptation of a Chinese concept more than twenty centuries old.

The two most celebrated leaders of the provincial resistance movements were Phan Dinh Phung in the Ha Tinh area and Hoang Hoa Tham in the northern mountains. "Aid the king" partisanship had a character both ideological and racial-political. Its theme was to "exterminate the religion and drive out the French," the former objective being accomplished by the indiscriminate slaughter of Vietnamese Catholics. The movements, heavily dependent upon their leaders, were fragmented by region. High-ranking provincial officials were often less responsive to "aid the king" sentiments than were notables on the outer fringes of the bureaucracy—village chiefs, former officials, examination system students. In at least five provinces, the governors and financial and judicial commissioners fled, were imprisoned, or were murdered by "aid the king" bands. One consequence of the royalist movement of 1885 was, therefore, the near-collapse of the indigenous provincial bureaucracy, which French colonialists were never completely able to restore qualitatively. A second fateful consequence of the movement was its aggravation of Vietnamese Catholics' traditions and feelings of separateness.

The "aid the king" movement was ethnocentric without having any real concept of Vietnam as a nation-state in competition with other nation-states. Authentic nationalism, however, emerged after 1900, receiving its inspiration by way of China. By 1900, the works of Rousseau, Voltaire, and Montesquieu and of social Darwinists like Herbert Spencer had begun to appear in China in classical Chinese translations. Since Vietnamese scholars could still easily read classical Chinese but rarely any European languages, they first became familiar with European ideas as translated by Chinese intellectuals like Yen Fu. Two Chinese ideologues in particular enjoyed a tremendous popularity in Vietnam in the early 1900's through their writings—K'ang Yu-wei and Liang Ch'i-ch'ao, leaders of the abortive 1898 reform movement in Peking. Liang's works were certainly sources from which a few Vietnamese scholars at this time gained an awareness that the world was not, as they had thought, a place of harmony governed by a hierarchy of the unequal, but rather a battleground of competition between strong and weak but legally equal nations. Liang's example helped Vietnamese reformers to discard some of their Confucian outlook and to adopt social Darwinist concepts instead. Here was the beginning of an important change in values.

The two giants of early nationalist politics were Phan Boi Chau (1867–1940) and Phan Chau Trinh (1871–1926). The two men came from different regions and further diverged in that Chau flirted with revolutionary monarchism while Trinh became an antimonarchical democrat. Chau, born into a Confucian scholar family, organized an "aid the king" military company in 1885 and was, in a sense, a bridge to the later nationalistic age. Although he entered the examination system and passed the regional examinations in 1900, he fell under the spell of Liang Ch'i-ch'ao, embarking upon a lifetime of anticolonial activities. In 1902–1903 he wrote a tract entitled "A New Book about the Tears of Blood of the Ryukyu Islands," perhaps the first book ever written in Vietnam expressing the nationalistic idea that all Vietnamese were fellow countrymen who should be united in love of country. At the same time, the indirect model of the Ryukyus, recently annexed by Japan, was used to persuade other members of the mandarin class of the evils of the loss of independence. In another tract, "Idolizing Beautiful Personages," Chau exalted the story of George Washington, arguing that Washington had become a soldier in the British army so that he could acquire the proper methods and background for fighting it. One moral was that Vietnamese revolutionaries should attempt to infiltrate the Indochina colonial militia in order to enlighten Vietnamese militiamen ignorantly serving the French.

After the Japanese victory in the Russo-Japanese War, from 1905 until about 1912, the encouraging Meiji Japanese example of progressive, modernizing monarchism became paramount in Vietnamese revolutionary politics. The most consistent Vietnamese admirer of the Japanese model—of nationalism and modernization combined with a "restored" monarchy—was probably Prince Cuong De (1882–1951), a descendant of Prince Canh, the eldest son of Gia-long, who had visited Paris in 1787. In a polemic he wrote in classical Chinese, Cuong De proclaimed that French rule in Vietnam was impermanent and that the Japanese army would help him recover the country. By 1908, 200 Vietnamese students had gone to Japan to study at Japanese universities. Phan Boi Chau himself, by this time the leader of a political group known as the "Renovation Society" (Duy Tan Hoi) initiated this so-called Eastern Travel (Dong Du) Movement, arriving in Japan in 1905. He immediately came under the tutelage of Liang Ch'i-ch'ao, who was living in exile in Japan as the editor of a Chinese newspaper published there, and wrote, with help from Liang, a history of Vietnam's recent loss of independence. Copies of the book were smuggled back to Vietnam by returning Vietnamese students, who formed, in Saigon, Hanoi, My-Tho, and other places, secret regional organizations of the "Renovation Society" that went by the names of hotels, business cooperatives, and village associations. The disguises were intended to fool the colonial secret police, for whom liberty, equality, and fraternity were not adoptable ideals in Vietnam.

The Dong Du Movement itself lost its momentum in 1908–1909 when the Japanese Government, responding to French diplomatic pressure, formally expelled the Vietnamese students. But the real climax of those early stirrings of Vietnamese nationalism had come not in Japan but in Hanoi, with the opening there of the famous Dong Kinh Free School in March, 1907. Indeed, the Dong Kinh Free School marks one of the major watersheds of the modern Vietnamese revolution. As an institution, it was a Vietnamese imitation of Keio School, later Keio University, in Tokyo, founded in 1868. It was Vietnam's first university. Education was free to all comers, the expenses of the school being paid by patriotic elite families in northern Vietnam. At its height, it attracted about 1,000 students. It had a number of divisions specializing in "education," "literature," "economics," and, significantly, "propaganda." It remained open for less than a year, since French colonial authorities suppressed it in November, 1907, arresting some of its leaders and banishing them to the prison island of Poulo Condore.

Expressing the dogmatism of cultural revolutionaries in its most fastidious form, teachers at the Dong Kinh Free School commenced their mission by attacking the use of Chinese characters in Vietnam. They demanded the use of romanized Vietnamese instead, because it would allow the elite to teach literacy to, and communicate with, Vietnamese peasants, and thus win the mass support that eluded them as long as they isolated themselves by writing esoterically in classical Chinese. Dong Kinh teachers also attacked the Confucian civil service examinations, which perpetuated an anachronistic elite culture and produced mandarins, untainted by nationalism, who would serve the puppet court and thus the colonialists. Since the traditional institutions had been captured by the French, they had to be undermined. Yet the sudden reversal of values was indicated by the fact that the school's principal, Luong Van Can, held a degree from the very examination system he was attacking. Although the examinations survived until 1918–19, they received their death blow in 1907 from the Dong Kinh scholars, who now molded the opinion of the more enterprising students. The program of the Dong Kinh School did not exclude anticolonial activism: Its vice-principal, Nguyen Quyen, and some of his colleagues were implicated in a plot to poison French army officers as a means of seizing Hanoi. Above all, the Dong Kinh School pioneered the teaching in Vietnam of all the newest Western theories of the nation, of the social contract and the general will, of evolution. It even called for the adoption of Western clothing as a means of losing old-fashioned appearances. One of the jingles that students at the school recited, the "Cut Your Hair Now Song," suggested: "Your left hand should clasp a comb, your right hand should clutch a pair of scissors. Cut off your bun of hair at the back now. . . . Do it leisurely so that your haircut will be skillful. Cast away your stupidities, throw away your foolishness. Today we'll have a haircut, tomorrow we'll have a shave."[55]

After the expulsion of Vietnamese students from Japan, and after the October, 1911, revolution in China, the Chinese model of revolutionary change became more attractive to Vietnamese nationalists. In February, 1912, Phan Boi Chau and more than 100 other Vietnamese, in exile in China, replaced the "Renovation Society" with a new organization called the Vietnamese "Revival Society" (Quang Phuc Hoi). The purpose of the organization, it was decided after a vote (and despite Chau's own monarchism), was to create a democratic republic in Vietnam similar to the one Sun Yat-sen was trying to achieve in China. South China Kuomintang leaders like Hu Han-min gave financial aid to the "Revival Society." More important, the society decided to create its own army in order to liberate Vietnam, drawing its military cadres from Vietnamese graduates of cadet schools in China and Japan. The strategy of reconquering Vietnam from China border bases, crucial to nationalist history, was born at this time. But despite a windfall the army received in 1915, when the German consul in Siam supplied it with 10,000 piasters, it remained bedeviled by a lack of funds. Chau decided that a premature uprising in Vietnam, even if it were unsuccessful, would garner enough publicity to improve the movement's financial prospects. The attacks the army did launch in 1915, from South China, against seemingly vulnerable centers in the north (Mong Cai, Lang Son) were badly defeated. It was typical of the lack of power of the "Revival Society" army—a far-flung, tenuous organization with cells scattered from Yunnan to Hanoi—that its own internal circumstances and needs as an organization, and not Vietnam's inviting revolutionary potentialities, had dictated its 1915 insurrectionism.

Furthermore, Phan Boi Chau himself was a Confucian revolutionary, more at home with Mencius than with Montesquieu. As he wrote in his book, *Khong hoc dang* (*The Lamp of Confucian Scholarship*), he admired the unhurried mythological "democracy" of the Chinese sage-emperors, who acknowledged that their throne belonged to the people, not to themselves. What was wrong with colonial Vietnam, in his eyes, was not just its inability to modernize itself but its loss as well of the self-regulating moral education and social rituals of its classical past. It now had the worst of both worlds: Its residual Eastern spirit of "government by men" had long since disappeared, yet the colonial regime had not given it all the requisite institutions of "government by law"—habeas corpus, labor codes, taxation through genuine representation, and others. With its ossified Confucian education, its corruption, and its arbitrary political controls, it was a society neither of perfectly preserved cultural obsolescences nor of freely acquired constitutional modernities, but an eccentric half-way house between two civilizations.

The other father of early Vietnamese nationalism, Phan Chau Trinh, was a more straightforward advocate of a Western-style written constitution and of a republican presidency whose incumbent could be impeached. After being active as the sponsor of a celebrated tax resistance movement in central Vietnam in 1908, Trinh spent the 1911–25 period in France, sometimes in prison. He was especially famous in the 1920's, both in France and in Vietnam, for his attacks upon the concept of monarchy in general ("the emperor is the man who takes other people's rights and makes them his own, who takes public powers and makes them private powers") and upon the Khai-dinh Emperor (who reigned from 1916 to 1925) in particular. When Trinh died in the spring of 1926, his funeral in Saigon turned into an unprecedented mass demonstration, with Vietnamese students striking their classes all over the country in order to attend memorial gatherings. A new phase of nationalism, involving greater popular participation than that of the Phan Boi Chau–Phan Chau Trinh era, was now at hand.

Before 1926, Vietnamese nationalism had faced two significant limitations. First, the surviving Confucian mystique of public service, the desire of literate Vietnamese not to rebel but to acquire government positions, perfectly suited the purposes of the French. Nationalists had to prove that the colonial regime was using educated Vietnamese, in the words of Phan Boi Chau, as "bottles for storing French wine in, as clotheshangers for hanging French clothes on, as puppets for sitting in French cars and living in French buildings,"[56] and that entering the civil service was not, as in the past, a legitimate means of social advancement but rather a form of enslavement to an alien colonial power. The absence of many occupational opportunities for Vietnamese youth outside the civil service and the failure of industry and commerce to develop extensively under indigenous control further undermined their cause.

Second, the decline of the monarchy as the unifying symbol of Vietnamese society, the administrative fragmentation of Vietnam into three regions and sixty provinces, and the efficiency of the French secret police combined to make it difficult for Vietnamese politicians to build nationwide associations or movements of any kind. It was characteristic of a situation in which patriotic mass mobilization seemed hardly possible that the term "socialism" (*chu nghia xa hoi*) became very popular among nationalists by the 1920's; instead of suggesting specific policies, like state control of economic enterprises or expropriation of land owned by landlords, to them the term simply represented a gospel of togetherness, an ideal of collective action. Phan Chau Trinh noted in 1925:

> In Europe, socialism is so extremely popular and so greatly developed, yet people over here are indifferent to it like sleepers who do not know anything. . . . If you have understood how to live, then you must protect each other—in the old days even our forefathers understood it. Only through that did the expressions arise: "Nobody breaks chopsticks which are in a bundle," and "many hands make a big repercussion."

He commented that in the ancient period "the Vietnamese people knew group action and . . . their situation was not like the current deplorable one of mutual abandonment. . . . In a village today, there may be 100 people, but the relationships of people on this side of the village with people on the other side are all magnetized by considerations of power." He concluded that "if we want the Vietnamese nation one day to achieve freedom and independence, then before all else the Vietnamese people must have community spirit and action. But if we want to have community spirit and action, is there anything better than to preach socialism among the Vietnamese people?"[57]

By the late 1920's and early 1930's, Confucian familism had begun to dissolve, and the individual had begun to be less dependent upon his elders and other relatives. While such a development temporarily increased that fragility of social relationships which Trinh had condemned, it also reduced the attractions of the civil service career as a means of satisfying traditional family (rather than individual) ambitions. In his controversial novel, *Doan tuyet* (*A Severance of Ties*), the brilliant writer Nhat Linh, founder of the influential Self-Reliance Literary Group (Tu luc van doan), attacked the passivity created in other family members by the absolute authority of the traditional family head and warned that Vietnam was falling behind, that "in all the Far Eastern countries, Japan, China, and Siam, the scope of the family now is no longer what it was in the past."[58]

In 1927, the Nationalist Party (Kuomintang) came to power in China as a result of Chiang Kai-shek's "Northern Expedition." The Chinese Revolution seemed finally to have supplied Vietnamese political ideologues with a definitive, conclusive model of a revolutionary party suitable to East and Southeast Asia. In December, 1927, a Vietnamese Nationalist Party (known as the Quoc dan dang, the Sino-Vietnamese equivalent of the Chinese term *kuo-min-tang,* and hereafter referred to as the VNQDD) was secretly created in Hanoi. It grew out of a small Hanoi book club, whose purpose had been to write and translate, and above all to publish, books that could be cheaply purchased by a wide audience. As of 1927, the VNQDD had a secret society cast, using the traditional method of sworn brotherhood, including a ritual act before an altar, to cement its membership.[59] A new recruit had to be introduced by two party members, who guaranteed him. Many of its idealistic but inexperienced founding members were students from higher-level commercial schools of the Hanoi area, like the party chairman himself, Nguyen Thai Hoc (1901–30). A feature of the VNQDD, from the very beginning, seems to have been the immobility of its borrowed political symbols. Although it held discussions with other revolutionary groups, including the early Communists, in attempts to unify the Vietnamese nationalist movement, agreement foundered upon two issues. First, the VNQDD rather incautiously insisted that the central committee of any unified party should operate *inside* colonial Vietnam, whereas the Communists, in Canton, Hong Kong, and Thailand, preferred to operate *outside.* Second, the VNQDD's deference to the prestige of its Chinese model was so literal-minded that it balked at entering any amalgamation of nationalist groups that would force it to sacrifice its name.

The structure of the VNQDD was a secondhand copy of Leninist democratic centralism (collective discussions of party policy at many levels, combined with the hierarchical imperative that the lower ranks of the party obey the higher ranks), an imitation of the Chinese Kuomintang's own incomplete reflection of Russian Communist organization. There were, on paper, local cells, provincial committees, regional committees, and a central committee at the summit. A party rule insisted that the executive of each group, from local cells to the central committee, be elected or re-elected every six months—a utopian organizational requirement for a secret, illegal revolutionary party under police surveillance. Unlike its Chinese namesake, the VNQDD lacked the support of a large treaty-port merchant class, of a group like the

Shanghai bankers who could combine nationalism with specific, pragmatically defined non-Communist political objectives. Perhaps partly for this reason, the VNQDD also lacked any specific image of what future Vietnamese society should be like after colonialism had been overthrown. In its three-stage revolutionary program of the late 1920's, stage one was the "embryo period" when new members were recruited, stage two was the "strategy preparation period," and stage three, the final stage, was the "destruction period" of the colonial regime. The very idea of violent revolution had become an end in itself. The party newspaper was called *The Soul of Revolution* (*Hon cach mang*), and a whole subcommittee of the party central committee was charged with "assassinations," the murders of key colonial authorities. The ghost of Blanqui reigned with that of Sun Yat-sen.

By the 1920's and 1930's, the Vietnamese reaction to French colonialism exhibited a dichotomy of form between northern political parties and southern religious movements. Of the latter, the Cao Dai religion, claiming converts at the rate of 1,000 a day by 1926–27 and preaching the virtues of spiritualism, Confucian piety, and vegetarianism, displayed an anticolonial bias of a conservative kind. (The term *Cao Dai* means "high platform," a platform so high that it has no roof; above it exists the Supreme Being, which cannot be designated by any one name and which expresses itself in this world only through a medium.) Many Cao Dai leaders soon became monarchical nationalists, willing to collaborate loosely with the Japanese army when it arrived in the early 1940's. Another southern religious movement, Hoa Hao Buddhism, founded in 1939 and dedicated to the elimination of idol worship and expensive ceremonies in Vietnamese temples, had for its founder a charismatic faith-healer (Huynh Phu So, 1919–47) who deliberately grew his hair long in the nineteenth-century manner to demonstrate that he was not under Western influences. Yet for the leaders of political parties more dependent upon Western political theories than upon the cultural mystique of the past to resist Western imperialism, political recruitment possibilities in the south did nonetheless exist. The development of plantations in the south, for example, had created a landless agricultural worker class that was more mobile and slightly more likely to support revolution than parochial landholding peasants. Circulating through the south, rural wage laborers might serve a number of employers, less commonly owing noneconomic, particularistic loyalties to one employer or one village. Their circumstances were miserable, yet they were free of the domination of the notables of their native villages back in the north.

The VNQDD was weak in southern Vietnam. In 1928, it had twenty-two cells in the south, with a total of 256 armed members.[60] Nonetheless, in early 1929, attempting to win the allegiance of the agricultural workers there, party members in Hanoi assassinated a Frenchman named Bazin who was the chief labor recruiter throughout

Indochina for the southern plantations. The French response was a reign of terror, which saw the arrest and brutal liquidation or maltreatment of 225 VNQDD members and the destruction of most of the party's cells. Hoc, the VNQDD leader, escaped but decided to launch armed uprisings immediately, even against hopeless odds, in order not to lose whatever resources he still controlled. In February, 1930, the VNQDD briefly seized the northern town of Yen Bai, engineering an uprising of the Vietnamese garrison. In the repression that followed, the French captured and guillotined the VNQDD leaders, including Nguyen Thai Hoc. That was possibly a turning point in Vietnamese history, for with the liquidation of so many non-Communist revolutionaries, the Communists were in a favorable position to regroup the forces of Vietnamese nationalism under their own banner.

The man who always had the clearest title to wave that banner learned his Marxism in France during World War I. Born in 1890 in a Nghe An village that was a hotbed of "aid the king" and subsequent scholarly resistance to the French, Ho Chi Minh (to use his best known pseudonym, in vogue since the early 1940's) had traveled to Europe as a messboy on a French ship. First reading the works of Lenin in the French Communist Party newspaper *L'Humanité*, he went as a convert to Moscow in 1923 and then to Canton in 1925, to serve in South China as a Comintern agent. At Canton, he founded an organization known as the Vietnamese Revolutionary Youth League, whose newspaper *Thanh Nien* (*Youth*) translated Marxist terminology into Vietnamese and some of whose members, drawn from Vietnamese exiles, enrolled in the Chinese Whampoa Military Academy. And in 1930, while in Hong Kong, Ho persuaded the leaders of several other Vietnamese Communist-oriented political parties to join him in founding the Indochina Communist Party. From then until the early 1940's, in and out of jail, Ho spent his time in exile in Russia or organizing Vietnamese revolutionaries in areas like South China and northeastern Siam. In its early stages, his work should be seen as contributing not merely to the evolution of Vietnamese nationalism but also to an international plan to foster Communism throughout all of Southeast Asia—among Malays, for example, as well as among Vietnamese.

In some respects, Ho Chi Minh differed remarkably from Mao Tse-tung, his Chinese counterpart. While the Chinese Communist revolution seems ultimately to have called for the leadership of a provincial radical from inland China sensitive to the moods of the peasantry and antagonistic to all forms of treaty-port intellectuality, the Vietnamese one drew instead on the leadership of a peripatetic, cosmopolitan master of the coordination of geographically scattered anticolonial enterprises. Yet Ho became a Communist for the same nationalistic reasons as Mao. The Leninist doctrine of imperialism offered a convincing explanation of French behavior in Vietnam and suggested at the same time that colonialism was ultimately doomed. And Leninist elitist organizational theory supplied a methodology capable of confounding even the secret police. In the 1930's, however, all orthodox Communists in Vietnam had to coexist or compete with so-called Trotskyist Communists. The Trotskyists were a group of radical teachers, students, and journalists, strong in the south, who claimed a following of some 3,000 enthusiasts in Vietnam by 1939. They attacked the Indochina Communist Party for its acceptance of the patronage of the French Communists, whom the Trotskyists correctly believed did not entirely yearn for the disintegration of the French colonial empire. The Trotskyists also denounced the gradualism of the regular Party's two-stage blueprint for a limited bourgeois-democratic revolution for national independence, involving a broad coalition of social classes, as the appropriate precursor of the proletarian socialist revolution. Profiting by the accession to power of a left-wing government in France, which relaxed political controls in the colony briefly, Trotskyists and Communist regulars fought each other in municipal council and colonial council elections in southern Vietnam in the middle and late 1930's. The Trotskyists, who functioned far better in the towns than in the countryside, where the Vietnamese revolutionary struggle was to be transferred in the 1940's, usually won these contests. *La Lutte*, a Saigon French-language newspaper, commonly presented the Trotskyist viewpoint.

Except during this strange interlude (roughly, 1936–39) when, as a result of domestic politics in France, legal political activity could be carried on through front groups, the Indochina Communist Party expected and received the savage repression of the colonial government. In 1930, at the height of the world Depression and upon the collapse of the price of rice, it made its first violent bid for power—the creation of rural "soviets" in the north-central provinces of Nghe An and Ha Tinh. Communist sources claim that in 1930–31, 535 peasant demonstrations, involving 500,000 people in twenty-five provinces, took place in Vietnam.[61] The soviets, created in the vacuum left by local administrators fleeing from Party-organized intimidation, published their own clandestine newspapers—for example, *Nghe An Do* (*Nghe An the Red*)—and began the domestication of international Communist symbols in Vietnam, like May Day and red flags. More important, they informally promised the peasants land redistribution, the land issue being one the VNQDD had neglected. Preaching the solidarity of urban workers and rural peasants, Party committees transported Communist workers of factories in the city of Vinh to rural areas to augment the ranks of politically active peasants. By the summer of 1931, however, French troops had crushed the soviets. It was only in 1941, ten years later, that the Party's prospects, more closely than ever associated with those of Vietnamese nationalism in general, began meaningfully to improve.

Up until the 1940's, in fact, nationalism was more or less confined to the intelligentsia. It could be plausibly argued that the socio-economic condition of the Vietnamese peasant was worse in 1935 than it had been a century before—because of the new and unprecedented taxes, especially those on salt and rice wine; because of the collapse of dynastic restraints, however ineffective, on landlordism; because of the unprecedented export of rice that in precolonial days had been consumed entirely in Vietnam; because of the pressure of a rising peasant population on the land in the north; and because of the new vulnerability of the peasant to world price changes in rice and other commodities. Yet the situation in the countryside remained so peaceful as late as World War I that almost 100,000 Vietnamese were transported, with little significant resistance, to France to serve as soldiers and war workers, while the French military garrison in Indochina itself dwindled to less than 3,000 men. Even in the late 1930's, the Vietnamese proletariat—including miners and plantation workers—could not have numbered more than 200,000 people, its modest size forcing the Communists to devise at the time of the soviets the sociologically expansive but doctrinally questionable slogan, "poor people are proletarians."

29

THAILAND

The history of Thailand between the death of King Chulalongkorn in 1910 and the outbreak of World War II in 1941 is essentially the political working out of the social consequences of the reforms of Chulalongkorn's reign. Chulalongkorn and his ministers fundamentally changed the structure of the kingdom. They revived royal authority as against that of the old nobility, directed a thoroughgoing formalization and depersonalization of the administration, and created a new class of civil servants whose status was legitimized by education and by function within a hierarchical bureaucracy. They reduced the power of local ruling families in the provinces and of the noble families in the capital. Ironically, however, the system had come nearly full circle; the stability and effectiveness of government still rested heavily on the king's personal control over the bureaucracy. The king had partially freed himself of the wickerwork of ceremony that had enveloped his person, engaging directly in the day-to-day workings of the government. While his personal authority was thereby enhanced, it was also more exposed to challenge. The extension and elaboration of the bureaucracy made it more directly responsive to the royal will, but its Westernized ideals and functions also made it, in the long run, virtually impossible to control within the traditional framework of royal authority.

It is useful to conceive of modern Thai history in generational terms, according to which the successive groups of men who come to prominence in Thai public life may be defined in relation to changes in ideas and experience. The intellectual and psychological distance separating successive generations is particularly important in such times of great change as the century following the Burney Treaty of 1826. The generation of Mongkut and Suriyawong, which came to power in the 1850's, was the first to experience the West and to adjust to it. It did so primarily in terms of traditional values. Chulalongkorn's generation, on the other hand, was a modernizing one. It fell to Chulalongkorn, Damrong, and Devawongse to found a modern state on Western lines, selecting from the West whole institutions and sets of ideas, the value of which they did not question, but which they knew only from a distance, secondhand. It was within the framework they constructed that the third generation grew up, to face the problems of reconciling the contradictions Chulalongkorn never quite recognized. The contradictions were the consequences of modernization begun from the top down, a superstructure of modern administrative bureaucracy and economic institutions set atop a society and state whose lower portions no longer fitted comfortably within the old mold of the absolute monarchy. The cabinet ministers and department heads of 1910 wore European suits, lived amidst grand pianos and printed books in modern houses with indoor plumbing, drank iced beverages and ate with European silver, worked with modern law codes and administrative regulations, and invested their personal savings in modern banks or businesses. At the same time, Thai peasants still lived much as they had a century earlier, in rude houses on piles with no conveniences, growing their rice and marketing their surpluses. The discontinuity between the two realms of experience was most evident to those in the middle—junior army officers, schoolteachers, doctors, and merchants—who could see both sides of the modern-traditional division within Thai society. Theirs was the first generation of Thai who in substantial numbers were trained abroad. However enlightened their bureaucratic superiors, there was a deep gulf in ideas and experience between them. By virtue of their trained skills, their modes of thought, and their generally liberal political commitments, the members of the foreign-trained group felt they deserved a greater share of power than the existing order granted them. Their "nationalism" was, essentially, the sets of ideas—and the rhetoric—in which they expressed that demand, in both positive and negative terms. Positively, they expressed their commitment to modernity, to keeping up with the rest of the world, against which they constantly measured Thailand and found it wanting, or at best too slow. They thought, too, in terms of a unified Thai nation enclosed within defined frontiers and peopled by Thai speaking a single language and pledging their loyalty to a single monarch and state. Negatively, they thought their power should be directed against economic, political, and social divisions remaining—and growing—within the nation, and against the injustice they felt their country had suffered and continued to suffer at the hands of the imperialist West.

The ideas and experience of the "new men" of the 1910's were shaped by the general acceptance of the West that King Chulalongkorn and his brothers had forced upon the nation, and they saw more clearly than either their royal patrons or the peasantry the fundamental problems of unfinished business and incomplete change—political, economic, and intellectual or cultural—that still faced their nation. Politically, they felt Thailand's most serious problem to be the distribution of political power, and specifically the relationship of the absolute monarchy to increasingly aware political interests in the bureaucracy, which could not be contained within the narrow channels of the administrative hierarchy. Economically, Thailand's Chinese minority, which occupied a commanding position in the economic life of the country by 1910, was increasingly felt to be alien in its life and methods. The power of the

Chinese was demonstrated forcefully to the Thai in the course of a short Chinese strike in 1910 against a tax rate the same as that imposed on the Thai. The ensuing reaction against the Chinese was to a considerable extent negative, directed against the supposed materialism of the Chinese and their un-Thai behavior, but it was also positive, affirming the younger generation's commitment to Thai values.

One important bridge across generational and class lines that helped to hold society together was Buddhism. Religious modernism in Thailand was shaped only in part by contact with the West. Whereas in Burma the refusal of the colonial government to sanction authority in the monkhood meant that no modernist sects could organize and gain recognition, though some monks—like the Ledi Sayadaw—were influential exponents of modern religious and social ideas, the case was quite different in Thailand. There, Buddhist modernism even antedated the influence of Western ideas. The prince-monk Mongkut, in his personal quest for a meaningful religious experience, founded in 1829 an intellectual movement within Buddhism based upon a critical rationalism, universalism, and careful textual study of the Buddhist scriptures. Its effect was to create a tradition that advocated a self-conscious, living religion composed of the essential values and ideas of Buddhism and unencumbered by inherited local tradition.[62] Here was an intellectual framework within which Mongkut and his fellow monks could accommodate Western science and a world broader than that encompassed by traditional cosmology and morality. For reasons essentially political, the brotherhood of monks Mongkut established in the 1830's did not gain formal status as a separate sect, the Dhammayut, until Chulalongkorn's reign, by which time it had expanded into the provinces, Laos, and Cambodia. Though it remained a minority within Thai Buddhism, the Dhammayut Sect was disproportionately active and influential from the 1880's on. Under the leadership of Prince Wachirayan Warorot (King Chulalongkorn's younger brother), it was an extremely important force for educational and ecclesiastical modernization, as Prince Wachirayan and his brother monks organized provincial schools and created a national ecclesiastical hierarchy in the decade following 1898. It was a Dhammayut monk, Phra Thammathiraratchamahamuni (Čhan), who spoke out against Thai entry into World War I. Others, in sermons and writings, were influential in giving Thai Buddhism an intellectual strength that weathered the general acceptance of modern science and Western ideas. The vigor of the Thai monkhood (Sangha) was a product not only of the Dhammayut Sect's activities but also of a religious institution that could tolerate dissent and divergence and could serve the whole of a population increasingly disparate in education and daily concerns.

Thai secular culture, however, remained threatened by the widespread influence of European ideas. It was some decades, for example, before the elite could be certain that its language might retain its vitality in the face of foreign words (new words were coined from

Sanskrit roots) or that Thai literature could hold its rightful place in the intellectual firmament of the Thai gentleman. It was only in the reign of King Vajiravudh, Chulalongkorn's son, that such problems and fears were tackled head-on.

Vajiravudh (r. 1910–25) was one of the younger generation—educated abroad at Oxford University and committed to the same ideas as others of his generation. He did more than any other individual to make such national sentiments a part of the ideas of every educated Thai. A prolific writer and ardent dramatist and actor, he promoted those ideas on the stage and in the public press through voluminous writings, numbering well over 200 pieces, which ranged from translations of Shakespeare and Molière and trenchant bits of romanticized Thai history to political essays directed against the Chinese ("The Jews of the East") or Germany during World War I ("Freedom of the Seas"). Through several organizations he founded and headed, the Wild Tiger Corps (an adult paramilitary movement), the Boy Scouts, the Royal Navy League, and his dramatic and literary groups, the king was the nation's most vocal advocate of cultural nationalism, its most effective propagandist, and the creator of organizations of lasting social and political importance.

Vajiravudh, however, was a poor politician. Anxious to escape the domination of his father's generation, he had forced all but one of Chulalongkorn's ministers from office by 1915 and surrounded himself with a government made up of his personal favorites, most of them from nonroyal families and many of them younger men educated abroad. Personal alliances and favorites shaped many of his choices, and his lack of interest in administration left them beyond his direct control. He thereby alienated many. The Wild Tiger Corps in particular was, in effect, the king's private army, and it sorely antagonized, among other groups, the regular army.

An early reaction against Vajiravudh came in 1912, when a group of junior military officers in their early twenties planned a coup against the king. They claimed to have been reacting against the incomplete modernization of the administration, against its unfinished business in the countryside, against the degree to which personal relationships still governed administrative acts, and against the low moral caliber of many they saw about them. Their ideas had been shaped in part by the Russo-Japanese War of 1905 and by the Chinese Revolution of 1911, from which they gained both a sense of their own national identity and a sense of shame in comparing their country with what they knew of more advanced Asian and Western nations. Quietly subverting military posts in the Bangkok area and upcountry, they planned to carry out a revolution at the annual oath of allegiance ceremony in April, 1912. Their activities were, however, uncovered in February, and ninety-one men were given prison sentences ranging from twelve years to life.[63]

It is possible that another military coup was forestalled in mid-1917, when there was a wave of arrests in the army at the time Thailand entered World War I on the side of the Allies, but it is more likely that those events reflected simply internal army politics. In any case, by participating in World War I, the kingdom gained a voice at Versailles and sufficient diplomatic momentum to end, by 1925–26, extraterritoriality and all but a few clauses of the unequal treaties.

Vajiravudh died without an heir in 1925. He was succeeded by a much younger brother, Prajadhipok (r. 1925–35), who had never expected to become king and was unprepared for his new tasks. While he had strong liberal-democratic sentiments, he had neither the personal nor the political power to put them into action. His government was one in which Chulalongkorn's generation and the royal family enjoyed a return to power at the expense of the younger nonroyal men Vajiravudh had favored. Unlike his elder brother, Prajadhipok made regular use of advisory councils composed of princes and high officials, and it is likely that he seriously considered turning them gradually into a parliament. He was dissuaded by his uncles, the senior princes, the more easily because popular demand for representative government was not strong.

The demand for political change did exist, however, even though there were no well-defined channels for its expression. Over the course of the preceding forty years, the kingdom had been building a new elite of civil administrators, professionals, and soldiers. For some time, their upward movement in society and government was continual and satisfying, but it was checked and even reversed during Prajadhipok's reign, when many princes were returned to high office, and when promotions and salary increases were held back at a time of retrenchment in the late 1920's.

The world Depression also helped to reawaken the sentiments expressed, and afterwards muted, in the unsuccessful rebellion of 1912. A small group of radicals had been quietly organizing for some years, beginning with meetings when they were studying in Europe. The royalist tone of Prajadhipok's reign, together with retrenchment, made many more receptive to the idea of revolution against the absolute monarchy —young military officers deprived of promotions, students returned from training abroad to find jobs not up to their expectations, and older men no longer so certain about the dignity and generosity of the monarchy. Younger radicals and older moderates joined together to plan and execute the bloodless revolution of 1932.

After the tanks rolled out on June 24, 1932, and after the government had been taken over by what the challengers called the "People's Party," they asserted their Western political ideas in a letter to the king asking that he submit to a constitution and in another to the general public explaining their actions. Both were written in terms strongly condemning absolute monarchy and the previous reign and proclaiming the party's own intention to rule for the good of the people. The initial republican radicalism of some civilian members of the group was soon toned down so that the group's leaders might bring in senior civil officials from the old regime favorable to their cause for the purpose of heading the new provisional government, thereby reducing the chances of any immediate conflict. The balance of power remained, however, unmistakably in the hands of the People's Party when a constitution was inaugurated in December, 1932. The radical civilian wing of the party, the leader of which was the university law lecturer, Luang Pradit Manutham (Pridi Phanomyong), made a brief attempt to carry out the early ideals of the coup in an economic plan of March, 1933, but the king and the conservative nobles who had continued in government moved against them, forcing Pridi from office and muting the voice of the radicals. A few months later, in June, the military staged another coup to install their own man as Prime Minister, Phraya Phahon (Phot Phahonyothin). When a royalist countercoup led by Prince Boworadet failed in October, the military group was left firmly in control, having defeated all its rivals, left and right—Pridi's civilian radicals, the conservative civilians carried over from the prerevolutionary regime, and the royalists. Their success was confirmed with the abdication of King Prajadhipok in 1935 and with the accession of a boy-king, Ananda, still at school in Switzerland.

The constitutional regime then inaugurated was not a great advance on the previous period in democratic terms. Power was still concentrated in the hands of a few, the members of the People's Party, who, in the initial stages of constitutional development, maintained their primacy through an appointive monopoly of seats in the Assembly and the Cabinet, although appointees were supposed to be replaced gradually by elected representatives when educational levels permitted or ten years had passed. Indirect elections in 1933 and 1937 gave the Assembly a membership of which half was elected, keeping the pressure on the government to fulfill its liberal program and to maintain its expressed democratic ideals. Despite a shortage of funds during the period, the government was able to make considerable progress in social welfare, particularly in the area of education and public health, and, to a lesser extent, in economic affairs. Universal and compulsory primary education finally was extended throughout the kingdom. The government was particularly alert to the impact of its taxation policies on the village, making efforts to reduce taxes when economic conditions were poor. The *quid pro quo* for those programs was the support of the elected members for continued strong military budgets, which the army justified first in terms of internal threats and later by external ambitions and fears. From mid-1933 to the end of 1938, Phraya Phahon, as Prime Minister, steered the government along a course that by Thai standards was moderate and certainly progressive. His government finally fell in December, 1938, when strong questioning of the budget by the elected members of the Assembly resulted in a vote of no confidence. Luang Phibun Songkhram, a colonel popular in the army for his strong championing of its cause and more widely for his role in breaking the royalist forces in 1933, came to power. He was a vigorous exponent of Thai nationalism and the logical choice of the ruling group.

Phibun's first government (1938–44) is understandable principally in terms of the world environment in which it was set. At a time when the prestige of the Western democracies was low and when the capacity of Western ideas and values to solve grave economic crises and to survive international strife seemed spent, assertive, ultranationalist, and militarized states such as Japan were attractive to the Thai. And so Thai politics took a turn to the right, with open glorification of the army, assertion of national values, and strong attacks upon Western culture, Western imperialism, the Chinese position in the Thai economy, and the regime's own critics. Thailand carefully cultivated relations with the Japanese Government, establishing strong economic and political ties. Once France had fallen to German armies in June, 1940, Phibun stepped up pressure on French Indochina with irredentist territorial claims, associated with a more general pan-Thai movement. This led to full-scale war with France in 1940–41. The war was popular in Thailand but ended with Japanese mediation and with the cession to the Thai of western Cambodian provinces and some Lao territories. Phibun's government was undoubtedly strengthened by the outcome of the war, but he had found himself more heavily dependent on Japanese aid than he could have anticipated. The limits of Thai military power were now as clear as the real predominance of Japan in Southeast Asia. When Japanese forces suddenly disembarked at six points along the coast of peninsular Thailand, crossed into the country from Cambodia, and landed at the airfield near Bangkok, they met with the automatic resistance of local Thai garrisons. But Phibun, informed of the landings, could see no alternative but to capitulate and join the Japanese.[64] There were, after all, some Thai goals that could be served in the process. Although, at Japanese urgings, he agreed to declare war on the American and British governments, it was not a Thai affair: The war was between Japan and the West. With two such ponderous elephants fighting, the ant of Thailand scurried to avoid being crushed.

The increasing prominence of the military in the Thai elite stemmed primarily from the unique advantages of military organization, which helped the army to maintain strong hierarchical and personal (patron-client) relationships while inculcating cohesive and modern values. They were much better organized than their competitors, they had had less exposure to the West, and they were somewhat more conservative and formalistic in their approach. The civilians, who were disorganized to the point of inability to function consistently as a unity and who lacked physical force, were more willing to see radical change. Their numbers were small, and they were distributed in small pockets through the society of the capital, while the military was neatly organized in a single hierarchy. Together, the two elements were the young elite of the society, their status clearly defined in the public view. Peasants and townsmen expected them to act as "big men"—government was their business, not the public's. When these men began to talk directly to the peasant in the language of equality, on new radios and through the press, it took time for some people to realize that the game of politics had really changed—that it was now about "us" and not simply "them."

30

MALAYA

Though the protectorate control established by the British in the peninsular Malay *negeri* was based on earlier patterns of suzerain relationship and was seen by some of the Malay rulers as a means of obtaining powerful and knowledgeable assistance in the profitable governance of their territories, it rapidly came to entail a great deal more than that and to introduce radical changes in the life of the states. On the west coast in particular, with the Federated Malay States (FMS) in the lead, there took place large-scale development of European and Chinese entrepreneurial and extractive economic activity, with a startling increase in alien immigration. In the FMS, population rose from 218,000 in 1891 (at the time of the first full census) to 1.7 million in 1931. Already, by 1891, as the result of accelerating Chinese (and to a lesser extent Indian) immigration during the previous two decades, Malays, including immigrants of Malay stock from elsewhere in the archipelago, could muster only 53 per cent of the total population. By 1931, a mere 34.7 per cent of the population was of Malay stock, while the Chinese had risen to 41.5 per cent, and there were, in addition, 22.2 per cent of Indians. Though the census-taker in 1931 argued that most Chinese remained transient, which may well have been true, there was already a substantial residue who regarded the peninsula as their permanent home, as well as many thousands who had been born there. Even in the Unfederated Malay States (UMS), Johore, the state most developed in relation to the export economy, was by 1931 very similar in racial composition to the FMS, and Kedah, too, had a large alien component. Down the whole of the west coast, with Penang and Singapore as the northern and southern nodal points and Kuala Lumpur as the federal capital in the center (all three demographically Chinese cities), stretched a complex system of roads, railways, telephones, and telegraphs, which provided the bones and sinews for an export economy whose earnings had risen from 10 million Straits dollars in the late 1880's to more than 300 million dollars just before the depression of 1930.

Much of the change, however, despite its revolutionary and lasting character, did not immediately or directly affect the Malays. Not that Malay life continued in uninterrupted tranquility—for, manifestly, much happened to shift the peasant view of the world—but the changes that did take place did not coincide with or take their direction solely from the incidents of British rule, and change occurred within (or coexisted with) a remarkable persistence of traditional patterns of social organization. The relative sparseness of the Malay population and its involvement in a traditional social order based on the village and cultivation of the land meant that few Malays were available or willing to engage in the wage labor needed for rapid development of export industries and their ancillary facilities. British policy in the peninsula was, accordingly, based on a mutually profitable alliance with the Malay ruling class, by which, in return for the right to develop a modern extractive economy within the *negeri* by means of alien immigrant labor, the British undertook to maintain intact the position and prestige of the ruling class and to refrain from catapulting the Malay people into the modern world. This symbiotic relationship certainly deprived the Malay sultans and territorial chiefs of most of their decision-making or policy-making powers, but it was furthered with a tact that carefully preserved the fiction that the sultans were autonomous rulers acting under advice from Residents, who were in some sense their servants. Though this fiction wore threadbare less rapidly in the UMS than in the FMS (where mild protests at procrustean amalgamation were to result in a measure of decentralization in the 1920's), it nowhere completely concealed the fact that the rulers, in direct proportion to the value of their states to the export economy, were bound hand and foot to British policies.

To say that the sultans lost all substantial powers of decision and control, however, is to take something of a Western view. Within Malay society itself, they not only remained paramount but had their position considerably strengthened by the improvement, under the aegis of the British, of the centralized apparatus of government, by the reduction of previously competitive territorial chiefs to the status of titled courtiers and pensioners or government-salaried bureaucrats, and by the strengthening of their customary but previously unexercised control over religion. The saving clause in the protectorate agreements concluded between the Malays and the British, excluding from residential "advice" matters touching upon "Malay religion and custom," encouraged both a turning to the ceremonial trappings of Malay life and, more importantly, the creation in most states, in one form or another, of elaborate administrative and judicial establishments for the governance of Islam. Known generically as Councils of Muslim Religion and Malay Custom, the establishments were largely appointed by, dependent on, and answerable to the rulers. They became important repositories of traditional and usually conservative authority in relation to Malay society as a whole.

Nor were the effects of British rule seriously disruptive of the role played in Malay society by the aristocracy, once the initial period of adjustment to deprivation of taxation rights and other privileges of territorial independence had passed. It is true that, for the most part, they ceased to be politicians, and the importance of this should not be discounted. But senior chiefs in particular, who stood to lose most, played a deliberative role in the State Councils (a more meaningful task in the unfederated states than in the federated), and the territorial structure of the traditional Malay aristocratic establishment was maintained alongside the new centralized bureaucracy in sufficient degree to afford district chiefs some continuing responsibility for Malay customary life. In return, they were rewarded with state pensions or salaries and had, by reason of their position and influence, other economic advantages, such as access to the disposal or acquisition of land, of mining rights, and the like.

In the FMS after the turn of the century, the Malay aristocrats of the younger generation received special education and training, reserved largely for the sons of the traditional elite, and were recruited into the colonial bureaucracy. Though the positions they occupied were subordinate in relation to the European civil service, the Malay administrative cadre thus created had a dual advantage—over their fellow Malays of peasant origin, who had not had the same educational opportunities, and over all non-Malays, who were by policy barred from the administrative or executive ranks of the public service. Malay Officers, as they were styled, were almost invariably employed in rural administration among their own people, where the tasks they performed, though different in detail, were at least comparable to those of the territorial Malay administration of an earlier time, insofar as the nexus between peasant and prince was concerned. The prestige and authority conferred by traditional social status was thus re-emphasized by administrative authority derived from the colonial regime. The pattern was repeated, and indeed intensified, in the UMS, where the incidence of direct British participation in local administration was less. Only in Kedah was there something like a truly autonomous Malay administration of a modern kind acting under British advice, though in Johore the strong Malay aristocratic establishment retained a firm hold on Malay affairs, even as the direction of administrative matters in general came to rest only nominally in their hands. In the east-coast states of Kelantan and Trengganu, which approached the modern world only slowly, the Malay aristocracy remained largely untouched.

The maintenance of the traditional Malay elite throughout the peninsula, either in its customary form or as the new bureaucracy, was paralleled by a striking absence of Malay peasant involvement in the mushrooming export economy, either as part of the work force or as entrepreneurs. The British sought actively to shield Malay peasant society from the disruptive effects of the new economic order, partly in the interests of the protectorate relationship and of a sentimental view of the idylls of village life, partly as a means of ensuring continued food production, and partly in order to avoid the political consequences thought likely to follow any substantial disorganization of the peasant economy. The traditional Malay ruling class actively concurred in the measures that resulted. The problem of providing the work force (clerical and technical as well as manual) for expanding export industries and burgeoning government services was met by the wholesale importation of immigrant workers from South China, British India, and Ceylon. Relative abundance of unoccupied land made it possible to allot large tracts to European and Chinese plantation enterprises without trespassing seriously on Malay holdings. Land policies were framed to give the Malay individual title to his land, to keep the peasant in possession of his patrimony, and to encourage his continuing cultivation of traditional crops, in particular wet rice. Such measures were reinforced by a system of elementary vernacular education (in Malay, and, effectively, for Malays only) which, though fairly widespread in incidence, at least in the FMS, had as its principal objective the creation of a "vigorous and self-respecting agricultural peasantry," conscious of the dignity that attaches to hewing wood and drawing water.

Though the effect in general of these policies and practices was to reduce the impact and the rate of socio-economic change at the village level, this is not to say that changes did not occur, but rather that they were neither radical in extent nor structural in implication. Individual land title tended to encourage both the sale and the mortgaging of peasant lands, though the government attempted, in the interests of prevention and reduction of rural indebtedness, to curtail transactions in certain types of land by the creation of Malay Reservations, within which land could be disposed of only to other Malays. One effect was to hold down the price of Malay land and to encourage Malay at the expense of non-Malay landlordism, economic developments of doubtful value to the peasant. The only substantial participation of the Malay in the export economy—the adoption by large numbers of peasants after 1910 of rubber smallholding as a means of earning cash income—led to more intensive monetization of the peasant sector of the economy. But after some years, the government, in the interests of food production and later of plantation-biased rubber restriction schemes, introduced legislation that drastically limited new Malay rubber planting. In addition, the presence of non-Malay middlemen, in control of preparation, marketing, and profit-taking, seriously reduced the stimulant effect that rubber-growing might otherwise have had upon Malay economic life. Despite this, rubber incomes (until the slump in the late 1920's) did enable some Malays from the first generation of smallholders to purchase for their sons a better education than was possible in the village and thus a chance to enter the upwardly mobile ranks of the government civil service.

One of the principal results of the wholesale retention of the Malay peasant within the matrix of the traditional agricultural society was the small part played by the Malay in the urban life of the developed western states or the Straits Settlements and his consequent isolation from social change arising within the urban environment. In numerical terms, Malays constituted in 1921 only some 10 per cent of the urban population of the peninsula, a figure corresponding to perhaps 4 or 5 per cent of the total Malay population. Those proportions rose only very slowly in the course of the next two decades, despite the eventual introduction of policies designed to lessen non-Malay predominance in the urban-centered subordinate ranks of government employment. Though the small Malay component of urban society was to be of great significance for eventual nationalist movements, the great majority of Malays continued to find the town alien and strange, if indeed they had any acquaintance with it at all.

Despite the slow pace and limited extent of social change among the peninsular Malays, in comparison with peoples more rudely embroiled in colonial economic development, the relatively brief period of British rule before 1941 witnessed the appearance of a nascent Malay nationalism, appealing at first to loyalties to religion, race, and language and seldom effectively transcending traditional state boundaries, but coming ultimately to seek a specifically political community that would safeguard Malay interests against those of the culturally alien myriads who now claimed residence in the peninsula. In the course of this process of growing self-recognition, it is possible to discern the emergence of three new elite groups in Malay society, each associated with a particular educational environment and each in turn offering its own vision, based on interest and background, of what Malay society must become to survive and prosper in the modern world. The first of the groups was grounded in the Islamic-educated religious reform movement; the second was the largely Malay-educated radical intelligentsia; and the third was the English-educated bureaucracy, its upper echelons drawn from within the traditional elite itself.

The religious reform movement had its ideological origins in the Islamic renaissance, which took place in the Middle East around the end of the nineteenth century. Malaya-born Muslims, sometimes of Arab or Sumatran descent, returning from sojourns in Cairo or the Hejaz, brought with them a burning desire to renovate Islam in their own society and to make it a fit instrument with which to respond to the social and economic challenges posed by alien domination. In propagating doctrines of the essential unity of the Islamic community without regard to potentates and powers, of the need to cleanse local Islam of accretions of custom standing in the way of progress, and of the essential equality of all Muslims before God, they came into immediate conflict with well-entrenched elements in Malay society, especially the separate state rulers and their religious establishments, newly developed under British rule. Though the strength of the movement lay in the urban centers, particularly Singapore and Penang (where its individualistic ethic proved attractive to those engaged in modern economic competition), it found adherents also among religious teachers and others in rural village society. The contest between the reformers and the traditional establishment was essentially unequal, but its many-sided and protracted argument acted as an important modernizing force within Malay society. In the long run, the religious reform movement failed to create or to lead a mass movement among the Malays, primarily because of opposition from the traditional establishment (religious and secular), which still held the loyalty of the great majority of the people, but also to a considerable extent because the issues on which it fought were being overtaken—or taken over—by a secular nationalism more concerned with pragmatics than piety.

Already, in the mid-1920's, a number of young Malays who had had their introduction to anticolonialist ideas in Egyptian Islamic reform circles were voicing overtly political, pan-Indonesian nationalist sentiments with little religious content in two journals published in Cairo. On their return to Malaya, they joined forces with the more numerous, secular, Malay-educated intelligentsia, which formed the second of the three new elite groups in Malay society. In large part teachers and journalists, products of the Sultan Idris Training College for vernacular schoolteachers and of two similar institutions for technical and agricultural education, the radical Malay intelligentsia was strongly influenced by the left wing of the Indonesian nationalist movement and looked to the creation of a Greater Malaysia or Greater Indonesia, which would embrace both the British and the Dutch colonial territories. With few exceptions, the radical intelligentsia was drawn from the peasant class, and though its ideology was in many ways confused, it criticized alike, mainly by way of the flourishing town-based vernacular press, the traditional elite and the new English-educated bourgeoisie (whose privileges it often envied), as well as British colonialism. It attracted to its cause some English-educated journalists and public servants, but its program was unformed and never really achieved organizational coherence. The Kesatuan Melayu Muda (Young Malay Union), an embryo political organization formed by the radicals late in 1938, spent the last year or two before the war under cautious surveillance by the British. It was mistrusted or feared by the majority of Malays who came into contact with it for its radical social views and its pan-Indonesian political aims. Though it served as a valuable training ground for left-wing nationalists later active during the Japanese occupation and after the war in radical Malay political movements, it failed utterly before the war to gain anything like a mass or solidly peasant-based following.

The leadership of the third new elite group in modern Malay society sprang for the most part from within the traditional ruling class itself, among the English-educated administrators and public servants. Essentially, this group was reacting against increasingly vociferous claims in the 1930's from the local-born elements of the Chinese and Indian communities (in 1931, 31 per cent and 21 per cent, respectively) for a larger share in government and administration and in the public life of a unitarily conceived British Malaya. The economic depression of the early 1930's, coming on the heels of revised policies aimed at increasing the Malay share of urban-based subordinate government employment, placed great strain on the neat plural society formulae by which Malaya had lived up to then. Many Chinese and Indian mine and estate workers, thrown out of employment, sought to settle on the land as agriculturalists, previously an entirely Malay preserve. Aspiring Malays in the towns, in receipt of slightly increased measures of English education, were vying with local-born Indians and Chinese for government clerical and technical posts at a time of general retrenchment of staff. The leaders of both the Straits Chinese and the local-born Indian communities were arguing strongly that, in the new Malaya, non-Malay residents must be afforded equal rights with Malays, at least in proportion to their contribution to the economy—to which a frequent Malay response was: "If you get someone in to build a house, you don't ask him to live with you afterward." Simultaneously, other Chinese, looking more obviously to metropolitan China for political satisfactions, were engaged in Kuomintang politics in the peninsula (despite the proscription of the KMT in 1930), or in the founding of the Malayan Communist Party (1930), an almost wholly Chinese organization with links nevertheless to Indonesia and Vietnam.

From the late 1920's onward, the traditional Malay ruling class—both those who, like the rulers and their immediate establishments, were still part of the old structure and those who had become absorbed in the new colonial bureaucracy—showed concern at the obviously disadvantaged position of the Malay in the modern world. Periodic gatherings of rulers (*durbars*), begun in 1927 as part of a token devolution of federal authority to the states, became the occasion, especially toward the end of the 1930's, for proposals by the rulers to encourage Javanese and to limit Chinese immigration, to strengthen Malay rights to the soil, and similar measures. In the Federal and State councils, the Malay members—all of high status within the traditional establishment—argued civilly for more jobs in the administrative apparatus for English-educated Malays or for more Malay Reservations for the peasants, but they were hampered in expressing (or perhaps holding) views directly critical of government policies by reason of the fact that most were also in the upper ranks of the bureaucracy. It was in part to meet that situation, to provide alternative forums for Malay opinion, and to organize "constituency support" for council representatives that elements of the English-educated elite began in 1938 to form avowedly political Malay Associations on a state basis. Conservative in bias, loyal to the rulers (who in most states had given their blessing to the enterprise), and displaying an almost equal enthusiasm for British colonial rule—bulwark for the time being against the clamorous demands of Malaya-born and domiciled aliens—the Malay Associations movement, linked as it was with the traditional leadership to which the bulk of the Malays still gave their loyalty, was the only prewar movement that showed real signs of gaining anything like mass support. Though little success attended efforts, made at national conferences in 1939 and 1940, to unite the associations in a single organization, and though state loyalties remained powerful, the growth of a genuine Malay nationalism after the war owed much in both ideology and structure to the Malay Associations movement and its leadership.

31

LAOS AND CAMBODIA

In the years preceding World War II, French administrators in Laos and Cambodia, gratified by the apparent docility of the kings and people under their protection, hinted that both kingdoms were approaching an unspecified kind of renaissance. To assist in bringing it about, the French concentrated their resources on public works, primarily the extension of all-weather roads, and on cultural projects like the restoration and maintenance of Angkor Wat. In both protectorates, the French worked through princely families and bureaucratic elites. The generation of Lao and Cambodian leaders that matured under the French worked comfortably with them, seldom urging any modifications of French control. Because they lacked enough power to alienate anyone, and because the largely rural population was politically passive and geographically dispersed, the leaders themselves were unchallenged. Moreover, the rudimentary condition of the French-controlled educational system delayed the appearance of qualified rivals. Finally, the mechanisms through which French and elite rule could have been challenged, such as a vernacular press, elected assemblies, and voluntary associations, barely existed among the Cambodians and Lao.

In both protectorates, the events of World War II played a crucial part in the emergence of nationalist sentiment and organizations. French policy toward Laos and Cambodia was forced into a more positive stance by the Indochina War of 1940–41, when the loss of sizable portions of territory to Thailand forced the French to renegotiate the loyalties of the protected monarchs. In Laos, the renegotiation took the form of strengthening and expanding the powers of the king of Luang Prabang; in Cambodia, where the newly installed King Sihanouk was considered more malleable than King Sisavangvong of Laos, the new policy took the form of increasing the king's visibility to his people.

LAOS

In any formal sense, Laos was swamped within the larger unity of French Indochina—it contained only 4.3 per cent of the population, generated only 1 per cent of its foreign trade, and employed only 162 French administrators. Moreover, much of its economic and administrative activity was carried on by foreigners—mainly Vietnamese immigrants, who constituted three-fifths of its urban population of 50,000 in 1943. However, the French political and emotional commitment to Laos was much stronger than such quantitative indices would suggest. It was based upon the situation of helplessness that beset the divided Lao elite in the later years of the nineteenth century and, perhaps, on some French feeling that more was owed to the Lao than the French could do for them with limited colonial budgets and, eventually, limited power.

There was no Lao society as such, apart from local societies in each *müang*, when the French took control in 1893. At the vortex of a tributary system in the extreme north was the ruling family of Luang Prabang, trying with difficulty to fend off bands of marauding Chinese in order to maintain its suzerainty over nearby vassals and to sustain its autonomy in the face of increasing Thai interference. In the far south, at Čhampassak, was a ruling family recognized as governors by the Bangkok monarchy, similarly maintaining a weak hold over nearby *müang* to the north and east. With their officers and vassals, they constituted a clearly defined ruling class of royalty and nobility. The French position of rule in Laos was founded upon the personal relationship between King Oun Kham (r. 1872–94) of Luang Prabang and Consul Auguste Pavie and on the Franco-Thai Treaty of 1893, by which Thailand gave up its "pretensions" to the east bank of the Mekong River. No written agreements between the French and Lao regulated their relations. The French had little difficulty working on the basis of such an ephemeral legal situation, because they simply assumed the role of a suzerain power—in this case, making real their claim to act in the name of the court of Hue. For their part, the Lao elite could enjoy an order, security, and prosperity denied them since the end of the seventeenth century, accepting French rule because they derived "modern" benefits from it, such as education and heightened administrative authority.

In a sense, the French froze Laos in the *status quo*—particularly by maintaining the powers and prerogatives of the ruling families of Luang Prabang and its provinces. But they did more than that: The French declared their mission to be "to create . . . a sufficiently numerous and aware elite . . . so as to form a national consciousness."[65] The effort involved the delicate task of selective education of the princely and governing elite to French values and the neglect of Lao traditions. Its political effect was to strengthen the monarchy as an institution and to fortify the existing distribution of political power in Laos, while working to increase the elite's dependence on French power.

The political history of Laos under French rule up to the Japanese *coup de force* of March, 1945, is primarily constitutional. French rule was extended in the south with the posting of French commissioners to seven chief provinces to superintend the administration, while six more were posted in the major provinces of Luang Prabang. The indigenous administration, however, remained intact and indeed was strengthened by the creation of a unified Laos in 1899 (to which the Lao territories opposite Luang Prabang and the remainder of Čhampassak were added by treaty with Thailand in 1902 and 1904), under the authority of a *résident supérieur* in Vientiane. Gradually, the continuing participation of the Lao elite in government was regularized by the formal creation in 1920 of provincial consultative councils to advise the French Government on "all questions of economic and social interest . . . which were submitted to them, and especially the program of public works . . . for the succeeding year."[66] Shortly thereafter, the Royal Council in Luang Prabang, which the French had attempted unsuccessfully to abolish in 1915, was reorganized along functional lines, three high dignitaries being put in charge of interior; justice, education, and religion; and finance, public works, commerce, and agriculture.

For such executive functions, various members of the Lao elite—the royal family of Luang Prabang and the provincial ruling families—were provided with full French education, beginning in Vientiane and continuing in high school in Hanoi, Saigon, or Paris before university or technical education in France. King Sisavangvong (r. 1904–59) of Luang Prabang spent a year in France as early as 1900–1901, and many of his sons and nephews followed him there. One indication of the size and composition of the Lao elite might be gained from the fact that nearly all of Laos's educated political leaders as late as 1945 could be represented on a single genealogical chart, composed of the direct male line of the kings of Luang Prabang and the line of the *upahat* (viceroy) Boun Khong (whose son Phetsarath was refused succession to that office in 1914). Trained as engineers and lawyers, these young men were employed in technical positions—less frequently in administration—throughout the French colony. Prince Souvanna Phouma, as a young engineer, for example, superintended the restoration of Vientiane's most important religious center, Vat Phra Keo, between 1937 and 1940, and Prince Souphanouvong was put to work building bridges in Vietnam.

The French attitude toward Lao culture was ambivalent. Both traditional and modern cultural interests made natural the resort of the Lao elite to Thai newspapers, books, and radio, all in a language they could understand, and many Lao monks sought Buddhist higher education in Thailand. To counter that attraction, the Kingdom of Laos participated in the founding of the Buddhist Institute in Phnom Penh in 1930 (Laos later had its own institute, in 1937), and the French started a weekly newspaper and radio broadcasts in Lao in 1941. It was on the initiative of the Lao elite, however, that the critical break with Thai culture was attempted in 1941, with the introduction of romanized script for the Lao language to replace the Thai-style script previously employed. The attempts, none of which endured, had their immediate origins in circumstances directly political.

After the fall of France in 1940, the French and Lao were virtually helpless in the face of the pan-Thai pretensions and irredentist claims of Phibun's government in Thailand. At the conclusion of the Indochina War of 1940–41, France was forced to cede to Thailand the Lao provinces on the west bank of the Mekong opposite Luang Prabang and Pakse. The former territory, the province of Sayaburi, was a particularly painful loss, as the mausoleum of the Luang Prabang royal family was situated there. For those territorial losses, France—as Laos's protecting power—was held responsible. A reaction against Thai culture followed, as did an attempt by France to repair the damage done to its reputation. The present-day provinces of Xieng Khouang, Vientiane, and Nam Tha—areas the monarchy had not controlled since the seventeenth century—were transferred from direct French administration to the king. Furthermore, a formal treaty establishing the French protectorate was finally concluded, replacing the informal agreement with Pavie and a nondiplomatic agreement with the governor-general of Indochina concluded at the beginning of the French period. The king was given a new cabinet with five functional posts. Prince Savang Vatthana was named heir-apparent, and Prince Phetsarat finally succeeded to his father's post as viceroy, as well as becoming prime minister. The two main branches of the royal family—the line of the king and that of the viceroy—were brought back together. The elite, however, small as it was, was still divided by the uncertain position of the house of Čhampassak in the south, just as both royal and French authority were administratively divided. Some members of the elite were so awakened politically by the events of 1940–41 and their consequences that they began to envisage a future for Laos of which the French would not be a part. One French official in Luang Prabang warned his government to "watch this prince [Phetsarath] carefully at the end of the war: He will join with Thailand to seize [Lao] independence."[67]

CAMBODIA

In terms of Cambodian nationalism, the most significant institutional innovation of the years preceding World War II was the Buddhist Institute, founded in Phnom Penh in 1930 under the joint patronage of the Cambodian monarchy, the king at Luang Prabang in Laos, and the French. The Institute was intended to focus and encourage Buddhist studies throughout Cambodia and Laos; it had the effect of intensifying the relationship between the Cambodian monarch and his people. Using printing equipment supplied it by the French, the Institute soon began to issue editions of Buddhist texts in Pali and Cambodian, collating material sent to it from provincial monastic libraries. The Institute's output of printed matter, although not large by absolute standards, far exceeded what had been previously available. As the Institute's reputation grew, enhanced by frequent conferences, it became a rallying point for an emerging intelligentsia. The Institute's librarian, Son Ngoc Thanh, who had been born in southern Vietnam of Vietnamese-Cambodian parents, founded a Cambodian-language newspaper, *Nagaravatta* (*Angkor Wat*) in 1936. The pressure of events, like the war with Thailand in 1940–41 and the coronation of Prince Sihanouk as king soon afterward, obscured but failed to extinguish the kinds of ideas that the paper set in motion.

The brief war with Thailand and the subsequent losses of Cambodian territory coincided with the final illness of the sixty-five-year-old Cambodian monarch, Sisowath Monivong, who had reigned since 1927. The French were eager, as in Laos, to arrange the succession in a way that would strengthen their hand vis-à-vis the Thai, seeking a candidate for the throne whom they could manipulate. For these reasons, when Monivong died in April, 1941, French officials had already successfully proposed to the colonial office in Paris that Monivong's thirty-two-year-old son, Monireth, be passed over in favor of Prince Norodom Sihanouk, the eighteen-year-old son of Monivong's eldest daughter and, on his father's side, the great-grandson of King Norodom. The young prince, then in his last year at the French lycée in Saigon, was totally untrained for his new position. In October, 1941, he received his crown from the Governor-General of Indochina, Admiral Decoux, who took pains to note that Sihanouk's great-grandfather had also been crowned by a French naval officer. Sihanouk's reply, probably written by the French *résident*, was suitably humble about himself and grateful to the French.[68]

Over the next few months, as war spread across most of Southeast Asia, the components of Indochina remained isolated from their neighbors and from the war itself, for French policy was formulated in France by the neutralist Vichy government. The French maintained day-to-day control over Indochinese affairs until March, 1945. Internal disturbances in the meantime were severely dealt with. The most important of them, in Cambodian terms, took place in July, 1942, shortly after the French had arrested two monks on charges of "spreading discord" among members of the Cambodian militia. Approximately 1,000 people, roughly half of whom were monks, assembled outside the headquarters of the French *résident supérieur* to demand that the monks be released. When the French authorities temporized, elements of the crowd (including a large number of monks) stormed up the steps of the building, hitting out at the French with sticks, umbrellas, and sandals. More than twenty people were injured before order was restored.[69] Lay spokesmen for the demonstration were arrested, accused of treason, and shipped to the penal colony France maintained off the coast of southern Vietnam. Son Ngoc Thanh, a friend of the detained monks and of the lay spokesmen for the demonstration, later denied any involvement in the disturbance. Nonetheless, he left Cambodia for Thailand soon afterward, gaining asylum in Bangkok at the Japanese Embassy, which arranged for him to be flown to Tokyo, where he remained until the spring of 1945.

The demonstration probably surprised the French, accustomed since Norodom's death to treating Cambodia with a drowsy kind of paternalism that took for granted Cambodian acquiescence to French rule. The French were aware, of course, that religious movements, such as the Cao

Dai in Vietnam, contained a potential for subversion and, in the 1920's, had prohibited proselytization in Cambodia by heterodox religious sects. They had also assumed, however, that the Cambodian Sangha's loyalty to the monarch was indistinguishable from the monarch's loyalty to the French. The idea that the Buddhist Institute might provide a platform for Cambodian nationalism seems to have been overlooked. In any case, the French now believed, rightly as it turned out, that the platform provided by the Institute was not very wide and that discontent among the Sangha as a whole did not run very deep. As a result, under a vigorous young *résident* appointed in 1943, the French moved to reduce the generally conservative influence of the Sangha while integrating Cambodia more closely with other components of Indochina and enhancing the public role of the young Cambodian king. A royal decree of 1943 made the use of a romanized Cambodian script mandatory for official documents; another regulation replaced the Buddhist calendar with the Gregorian. Both moves were deeply resented by the Sangha, however, and never took full effect.

Another facet of French policy at the time was to make King Sihanouk more visible throughout the protectorate than his forebears had been and to bring him in touch with the similarly protected monarchs of Vietnam and Laos. Within Cambodia, Sihanouk's increased activity consisted largely of sponsoring the paramilitary youth organizations encouraged throughout Indochina by the Vichy regime. The groupings, the first of their kind in Cambodia, gave Sihanouk ideas about political organizations that he used after the kingdom gained independence. Under the policy that brought him face-to-face with his people, the young king's self-confidence increased. Although he was still hemmed in by protocol and by French and pro-French advisors, it is likely that in those years Sihanouk glimpsed the kinds of power and prestige the French had allowed to reside in the institution of the monarchy.[70]

The liberation of Paris in late August, 1944, further isolated the Vichy-oriented French administration in Indochina, which had been physically cut off from France for more than two years. On March 9, 1945, the Japanese throughout Indochina moved to imprison all French military and civilian personnel, turning day-to-day administration over to the largely unprepared Cambodians, Lao, and Vietnamese. On March 10, the Japanese commander in Phnom Penh informed King Sihanouk that Cambodia was independent. The monarch cautiously replied by requesting diplomatic recognition from Tokyo (which never arrived) before proclaiming Cambodia's independence himself on March 12. At this point began a new phase, in many senses the first, in the development of Cambodian nationalism.

PART FIVE

The Preoccupations of Independence

32

AN OVERVIEW

World War II combined with the intrusion of Japanese military power into Southeast Asia to shatter both the mystique and the institutions of Western colonialism. The expansion of the Japanese empire dramatized the vulnerability of the West, proving that Western hegemony was not, after all, eternal. The war years constituted an important break in the historical continuum, as ideas, institutions and people held in check by the colonial governments were liberated. World War II greatly accelerated the process of change and the fruition of nationalism in Southeast Asia. During and immediately after the war, a new generation of Southeast Asians gained power. Intent on freeing their societies and leading them toward a new era, these nationalists did not intend to surrender their newly achieved authority. In that sense, the Japanese claims of "a new dawn for Asia" and an "Asia for the Asiatics" were true.

Despite the widely varying impact of the Japanese occupation in different parts of Southeast Asia, certain common features stand out. Thus, between 1941 and 1945 a number of indigenous military forces emerged in Southeast Asian countries. In Indonesia, the Japanese developed a military force (Pembela Tanah Air, or PETA) of about 100 well-trained battalions under their own officers, which formed the core of the Indonesian army after 1945. Equally important, the Japanese military administration of the Dutch colony effectively demonstrated a principle of army participation in politics that would be remembered in postwar Indonesia. In Burma, the Burma Independence Army (BIA), which emerged in December, 1941, participated with the Japanese in the conquest. The BIA diffused *thakin* revolutionary leadership throughout the countryside, fostered the development of a cohesive army officer corps that could impose its ideas upon national politics after the war, and overthrew the established colonial pattern of an army recruited mainly from minority groups rather than from ethnic Burmans. In Indochina, the Liberation Army of the Viet Minh, created in the northern borderlands and in southern China during the Japanese occupation, became the first Vietnamese political-military force capable of avenging the defeats the nineteenth-century Tu-duc court had suffered at the hands of the early French colonialists.

The revival of indigenous military traditions and the violent exorcism of the illusion of the indestructibility of Western colonial regimes were two of the legacies of the Japanese occupation. Intentionally or not, the occupation policies of the Japanese in a number of Southeast Asian countries also provided nursing grounds for the expansion of popular participation in politics. The leaders of the revolutionary "generation of 1945" in Indonesia obtained public offices under the Japanese that would have been beyond their reach in the normal circumstances of Dutch colonial rule. At a lower social level and in a different way, the Burman peasant, rudely forced by the Japanese army to abandon his village and join the "Sweat Army" of conscripts toiling on the construction of the Burma-Thailand railway, did at least meet other villagers drawn from all over Burma. Maung Tin's novel *Nga Ba* (*To All Peasants*), published in Burma in 1947, examines the positive consequences of this encounter. It suggests that the wartime mobility of "Sweat Army" peasant labor made it easier for the peasants to accept the modern concept of nationhood after the war.

Japanese patronage of Southeast Asian nationalism, where it existed, was hardly disinterested. To many Southeast Asians, it seemed to be as much a profanation of their desires for emancipation from colonialism as an international legitimization of them. Kamei Katsuichiro, a postwar Japanese critic of Japanese expansion into Southeast Asia, argued that Japanese contempt for other Asian countries, a psychological by-product of Japan's more rapid modernization than its neighbors, had been his country's great modern tragedy. For although Japanese wartime propaganda in Southeast Asia belittled the West and its colonialist political mythology, many Japanese occupation officials shared the Western spiritual disease of condescension to the Southeast Asians they governed. Japanese military men in Indonesia, for example, publicly called Indonesians *genjumin*—"natives," the same word that they would have used to designate Australian bushmen. Furthermore, the period of the Japanese occupation in Southeast Asia proved to be ruinous economically. The decline of exports, the increasing unemployment of plantation labor, the requisitioning of rice and other commodities by the Japanese army, the recurrence of serious rice shortages, and brutal programs of forced labor were factors contributing to an environment of extreme social and economic distress. Rampant wartime inflation further exacerbated the situation.

The securing of political independence from the Western colonial powers after the war represented a fundamental historical achievement. But by itself it could not immediately eliminate such obstacles to progress as insufficient food production for expanding populations, bureaucratic inefficiencies, ethnic disharmonies, the persistence of economies based on the export of raw materials, and those patterns of societywide privation that the Japanese army had left behind. Nor could the achievement of independence repress the memory or prevent the continuing influence of prewar colonial institutional frameworks.

As one important example, the educational systems the colonial period had brought to Southeast Asia engendered both academic underdevelopment and linguistic imperialism. In Burma, a Burmese who did not graduate from an English-language school had poor professional prospects in his own society, and at Judson College in Rangoon, Indians outnumbered Burmese four to one. The exiguous group of some 600 university students in all of French Indochina in 1939 was forced to speak and write French even during their study of Vietnamese literature. The result was that within those educational systems before 1945 ("slave education" as Burmese and Vietnamese nationalists independently called it), no attempt was made to develop necessities of modernization like scientific dictionaries and agrarian technology textbooks written in the indigenous languages. Before 1945, higher education had existed largely to train indigenous administrative elites who would be subservient to the colonial rulers. It had not produced an adequate number of scientists and engineers or an adequate supply of educational tools for the successful domestication of modern science.

Such colonialist conditioning of Southeast Asian educational systems has been all the more serious for the postcolonial history of the region because of the relative paucity of opportunities for formal education—and entry into government service—the major institutionalized channels of upward mobility in Southeast Asia. Historically speaking, there have been fewer systems of apprenticeship or opportunities to open small business enterprises in postcolonial Southeast Asia than in early modern Europe, for example. And because colonial education failed to bring widespread modernization to Southeast Asia, after 1945 urgent needs for accelerated modernization remained to compete with the equally powerful needs of decolonization. Postcolonial Southeast Asian societies have consequently found themselves drawn inexorably into expensive, sometimes quixotic crusades to institutionalize Western scientific education in their schools and universities and yet at the same time to satisfy nationalist feeling by reducing the use of Western (colonial) languages as classroom media of instruction.

Since 1945, international great-power conflicts have distorted Southeast Asian social, economic, political, and military developments, preventing Southeast Asian societies from evolving independently and even forcing new postcolonial patterns of dependency upon them. Sukarno was merely the most prominent among Southeast Asian postwar leaders to call this "neocolonialism." International mass communications media in Southeast Asia have publicized "modern" norms of behavior, making Southeast Asian leaders acutely sensitive to opinion outside their national boundaries. At the same time, the cultural traditions of their own societies have imposed limitations upon the nature of the revolutionary change that these leaders can induce from the top downward. It is not unimportant that the "Red Dragon" party song of Burma's *thakin* nationalist revolutionaries of the late

1930's demanded prosperity and independence "so that the poor will be enabled to build monasteries," or that Viet Cong ideological novels like Anh Duc's *Hon Dat* (*Mound of Earth*) could, in 1967, preach to Vietnamese women the traditional Confucian virtues of feminine loyalty and purity. The exoteric traditions of the Southeast Asian peoples have always circumscribed the esoteric innovations of their leaders. And so, denied any natural cultural autonomy both by the colonialist intrusion before 1945 and by the communications revolution since 1945, but denied also sufficient freedom to experiment with innovative ideas, Southeast Asian leaders have become the world's most embattled cultural middlemen. They have been forced to live in the spotlight of worldwide publicity, which magnifies even the smallest intrigue among them, while they grapple with timeless problems in a context of unpredictable cultural change.

By Western standards—that is, by the standards of a minority of the world's population—Southeast Asian societies lack cohesion. Nationalism by itself could not be a total belief system, a new political religion, able to supply Southeast Asian societies with ideological direction. It could not by itself suggest a specific political program, once its principal targets, the alien colonial regimes, were overthrown.

Elite groups in each of the societies have often lacked any firm consensus, partly because of the deadly paradox that cultural modernization has made national cohesion more rather than less difficult to achieve. "Westernization" has undermined unity by increasing the range of cultural choices that Southeast Asian leaders enjoy, thereby multiplying the opportunities for factionalism and disagreement among them. The few instances in which the ruling elites apparently achieved consensus have still found them faced with the challenge of communicating their concept of "progress" to the rural masses. For if the period since 1945 in Southeast Asia has been an age of urbanization, or of calamitous "pseudo-urbanization," in which the need to improve the lot of unstable agglomerations of peasants living in cities has been acute, it has also been, ironically, an age in which urban-based elites have belatedly discovered the countryside. But the irrevocable expansion of perspective has had a tragic side: The elites have simultaneously discovered their own potentially crippling social isolation.

Stability in any nation anywhere in the world is dependent upon a proper balance between the willing compliance of the individual citizen and the coercive power of the state. The balance can exist only where the individual feels that he has a stake in the government, and such a sense of allegiance can exist only where there is a set of values, however crudely expressed, that is widely shared across the lines of the society in question. In those societies that have an easily discernible historical continuity, established terminology can be used to portray these values. In societies that have lost the images and momentum of historical continuity, there is a greater need for a new symbolism. In all cases, the process of inculcating elite values in the habits of thought of the people at large is a slow one, requiring the skillful use of communications media, the emergence of transitional intermediaries to bridge the gaps in society, and the demonstration of political and cultural sensitivity by the elite groups. In the postindependence period, some Southeast Asian elite groups have shown a tendency to monopolize the formulation and expression of their nations' values. Populists in theory but oligarchs in fact, they have often detached themselves from the people in whose name they justified their claim to power, to the point where their decisions had little relevance to the lives of the populations they ruled.

Within the politically conscious classes themselves, the generation gap was an important source of strain. Leaders who came to maturity during the colonial era continued to fight the battles of independence after freedom had been won. Younger men, for whom direct colonial rule was more of a historical fact than a personal ordeal, viewed the world differently. To some extent, the older group retained a sense of inferiority, the so-called colonial mentality, with deleterious results. The older men, most of whom held power in the first decade of independence, sometimes merely created nationalized versions of the social and political worlds of the colonial period. Even Sukarno, who was exceptionally skillful in synthesizing the traditional and the modern, dressed rather as if he were a European field marshal. Other leaders became Southeast Asian copies of a Queen's Counsel or of a senator from Ohio. They took over the former European clubs, played Western sports, and maintained the life style of a bygone age. The younger men, to whom all the trappings of former European rulers seemed anachronistic and alien rather than prestigious, developed a different life style.

The tension between the generations frequently expressed itself in terms of priorities. The older group, of whom Sukarno was one example, attributed greater importance to the cause of national unity than to that of economic development. Aware that they were responsible, in large measure, for redefining the meaning of the nation, they were afraid that the nation itself would not survive unless it received prime attention. To the younger, more technocratic generation, for whom the nation-state was a living reality and not a utopian abstraction, the "integrative revolution" has required emphasis not upon constitutional democracy or political religion but rather upon economic development and bureaucratic mobilization as the method of ensuring cohesion. The younger men were perhaps correct in their belief that integrated nation-states remotely approximating the deservedly or undeservedly orthodox Western kind could never be established permanently without the creation of integrated national economics to support them. Only in such national economies would the social relationships become so diversified, involving membership in so many overlapping groups, that each member of the society would recognize his dependence upon his compatriots.

Southeast Asian countries have drifted away from democracy because, to the younger generation, democracy has seemed too divisive, too slow, and too wasteful. That tendency has marked a change from the immediate postcolonial period, when many Southeast Asian countries adopted the institutions of the Western democracies that had colonized them partly because those institutions still possessed the residual prestige of Southeast Asia's military conquerors. As problems have mounted and as the younger generation has gained power, these countries have moved toward what might be called "participatory authoritarianism." The mass-based militarized party of the left or right has offered one means of social organization and mobilization, the politicized army another. Both the party and the army offer democratic centralism, organizational discipline, and upward social mobility for the individual. Each permits tight allocation of resources and gives to the ruling elite representation as the voice of the nation.

That the history of modern Southeast Asia has revolved about the basic need of Southeast Asian societies to reconcile the cultural predispositions of their long, sophisticated historical pasts with the exigencies of modern institutional development is not surprising. Internally, the new and the old must be harmonized. Externally, cultural and technological borrowing from stronger foreign powers is tolerable only if it is not converted into political dependency. The problems of balance are enormous. Most Westerners are ignorant of and behave irresponsibly toward contemporary Southeast Asian history and the peoples who make it. Even uninformed sympathy directed toward "underdeveloped" nations, which in fact are "underdeveloped" only in economic and scientific organization, is no longer enough.

33

THE EVOLUTION OF NEW POLITICAL SOCIETIES

It is ironic that the Japanese brought the high colonial era to an end. Japan's massive gamble to establish a Greater East Asia Co-Prosperity Sphere and to substitute Japanese power for Western hegemony was predicated on the assumption that Japan could and should be "the light of Asia." The Japanese militarists did not challenge the assumptions of high imperialism. They believed that they knew better than the West what had to be done and that under the banner of "Asia for the Asiatics" they could rally support from Asians everywhere. Japan—the last of the nineteenth-century imperialist powers—ended the imperial age by attempting to reshape it. Though they were able to shatter Western authority, they were not able to sustain the momentum initially achieved by their victories at Pearl Harbor, Bataan, and Singapore. In the ensuing struggle with the West, both the European powers and the Japanese were exhausted; the resultant power vacuum in Southeast Asia offered Southeast Asian nationalists an opportunity they were quick to seize. Though some Western powers, with varying degrees of intensity, tried to resurrect the prewar imperial structure, they discovered that they could not put colonial Southeast Asia, like Humpty-Dumpty, back together again.

THE UNION OF BURMA

The Japanese invasion of Burma in January, 1942, six weeks after the landings on the east coast of the Malay peninsula, was not unexpected, but British forces were still too weak to mount any serious resistance. Rangoon fell to the Japanese on March 7, and almost all of Burma was in Japanese hands by the end of the month. The ease with which the British were defeated surprised the people of Burma, to whom British power had seemed invincible. The Japanese were accompanied by a small group of young Burmans, the "Thirty Heroes," led by Thakin Aung San and including others of the prewar *thakin,* who recruited men in Thailand, entering Burma as a force of 1,000 and soon swelling to 30,000 men—the Burma Independence Army (BIA). Though their actual engagement in combat was limited, their participation in the victory gave it a Burman aspect, and initially they were given some responsibility for local administration, especially in rural areas. Soon, however, the Japanese pushed them aside in favor of an older and more experienced group of prewar politicians led by Dr. Ba Maw. The Japanese granted Ba Maw's government a limited measure of administrative authority and then, in August, 1943, nominal independence as an ally. Beneath the surface of the difficult and delicate rule of Ba Maw's government, a deadly struggle for power went on between the older politicians and civil servants and the *thakin*, who were more radical and had, through Aung San's continued control over the BIA, a militant following in a good position to mobilize popular support in the rural areas.[1] The *thakin* position was strengthened by two parallel developments. First, Ba Maw's government was gradually discredited by its association with the Japanese and by wartime hardships, as popular resentment grew against Japanese outrages, labor conscription (from which many never returned), and severe economic distress and dislocation. Second, the British wartime government steadfastly refused to give assurances that Burma would move rapidly to independence in the postwar period. Thus, the secret formation of the Anti-Fascist People's Freedom League (AFPFL) by the *thakin* late in 1944, though directed initially against the Japanese, committed them equally to an independence denied them by the British.

As British troops rapidly reconquered Burma in the early months of 1945, they were joined by elements of the army under Aung San's command. Prior to the actual reconquest, Admiral Louis Mountbatten, Supreme Allied Commander in Southeast Asia, had chosen to acknowledge their strength and political power in Burma, as well as their potential threat to the re-establishment of British authority. Overriding the advice of civilians, largely on military grounds at a time when the end of the war was not yet in sight, Mountbatten decided to incorporate Aung San's force into the British armies, thereby avoiding the clash that almost certainly would have followed any attempt to arrest Aung San and his men as "collaborators." Despite later British attempts to disband that force, Bo-gyok (General) Aung San retained control over the military arm of the AFPFL in the difficult period that followed the end of the war in August, 1945, and Burma's return to civil government in October.

The British refused to give the AFPFL a majority on the governor's reconstituted Executive Council, postponed consideration of political change until "more settled conditions" had been established, and embarked upon policies designed to revive the prewar economic order by bringing in Indian labor and reinstating Indian and British business interests. When Governor Dorman-Smith encouraged the formation of political parties other than the AFPFL, he placed that party clearly in the opposition. Well-disciplined demonstrations and strikes with massive public support were staged throughout Burma until they forced Dorman-Smith's resignation, making his successor and the British Government realize that governing Burma was impossible without the

AFPFL and without more rapid progress toward independence. Accordingly, in September, 1946, the 1937 constitution was restored, with a cabinet in which the AFPFL held six of eleven seats. Aung San became Prime Minister. Negotiations were soon begun, resulting in January, 1947, in an agreement that elections would be held for a Constituent Assembly, which would draw up the constitution of an independent Burma as rapidly as possible. In April, the AFPFL won 171 of the 182 seats up for election, demonstrating the strength of its position in Burma's political life.

The most serious constitutional problem facing the assembly was the status of the "excluded areas" and of Burma's substantial minorities. Burman-Karen conflict had been growing rapidly since the early days of the war, and the majority of the Karens were seeking separate administration for Karen areas. With some difficulty, the assembly drew up a constitution in the latter half of 1947 which provided for the complete union of Burma. Subordinate states were granted to the Shans, Kachins, and Karen-ni which were to have limited legislative and administrative autonomy. The Shan and Karen-ni states were given the right to secede from the Union after ten years. Many of the Karens, however, lived in Burman areas where they were a minority, and separate administration for them was held to be unworkable. Such success as was achieved in conciliating Burma's minorities was largely attributable to the care Aung San had taken as early as 1944 to gain their good will and cooperation. However, Aung San did not live to see his work and policies brought to fruition with independence. On July 19, 1947 he and seven associates were assassinated at the behest of former Prime Minister U Saw in an unsuccessful bid for power. The Vice President of the AFPFL, U Nu, was named to succeed the fallen leader. Preparations for independence proceeded unchecked.

At 4:20 A.M. on January 7, 1948—an auspicious moment chosen by Burmese astrologers—the independent Union of Burma came into existence. Almost immediately, it was forced to fight for its survival as a nation. Serious divisions within the country were expressed in open rebellion against the authority of the new government. Insurrections had begun with the "Red Flag" wing of the Communist Party as early as 1946. Then, in March, 1948, after Soviet policy had shifted to a revolutionary strategy, the "White Flag" Communists, led by Aung San's erstwhile colleague, Than Tun, took the offensive. They were joined by the remnants of Aung San's army, the People's Volunteer Organization (PVO) in July. Scarcely had the government countered the most severe threats of these rebellions when militant Karens went into rebellion at the end of 1948. The year 1949 was as dark as any in Burma's history, as the country was torn by civil war and the government found itself in control of only a few urban islands awash in a sea of rebellion. Gradually the government regained ascendancy, although the intrusion into the Shan hills of defeated Kuomintang troops at the end of China's Civil War complicated the conflict and prolonged it until 1951. Only then was security sufficiently established to permit the holding of elections. The government, and the Union, had survived that difficult period because of the particularism and poor leadership of the several insurgent groups, the creation of a strong national army, the popularity and flexible leadership of U Nu, and the cohesiveness of the AFPFL and government as long as the threat to their rule lasted. Once the rebellions had collapsed, however, both the effectiveness of U Nu's leadership and AFPFL internal cohesiveness declined.

The AFPFL originated as a coalition of forces—mass organizations, ethnic groups, political parties, and independent members—bound together mainly by their opposition to the Japanese and British and by their common goal of independence. It began to split with the expulsion of the "Red Flag" and "White Flag" Communists in 1946–47 and unraveled still more with the expulsion of the pro-Soviet Burma Workers' and Peasants' Party (BWPP) for disputing the government's approval of the United Nations' entry into the Korean War in 1950. Although the AFPFL and its affiliates won about 200 of the 239 seats contested in the 1951–52 elections, the opposition parties drew large votes. The prestige of the AFPFL declined further as pre-independence hopes remained unfulfilled, as the economy failed to recover rapidly, and as internal unrest continued. Sharp policy divergences worked further to divide the ruling coalition. To maintain his position as the 1956 elections approached, U Nu was increasingly under pressure to satisfy one special interest or another, to tackle unresolved problems, and to raise sagging morale. One notable government effort was sponsorship of a world Buddhist Council in 1954–56, only the sixth held since the days of the Buddha, which summoned Buddhists from all over the world to examine critically the texts of the scriptures. At the same time, U Nu and his colleagues strove to combine Buddhist and Marxist values in a new national ideology. Buddhist Socialism, as it was named, represented a return to fundamental ethical principles and an attempt to avoid the abuses of international capitalism, while embarking on rapid economic development.

The 1956 elections revealed the continuing erosion of AFPFL popularity. The AFPFL and its affiliates won 173 of 230 seats, while the largest opposition party, the National Unity Front (NUF, successor to the BWPP) gained only 47; but the AFPFL had only 48 per cent of the total vote while the NUF had 30 per cent. U Nu recognized the dangers to which the AFPFL was subject and retired from office for a period "to undertake the reorganization of the AFPFL and the elimination of corrupt elements."[2] Shortly after his return to office in 1958, however, the party split completely in two: U Kyaw Nyein, leader of the small Socialist Party, led a substantial proportion of the AFPFL in breaking with U Nu and in contesting his control of the government in the Chamber of Deputies. The split was partly a matter of personalities, but it also involved serious issues of policy and a natural tension between men oriented to policy and politics and those more inclined toward administration. To maintain himself in power, U Nu yielded substantial concessions to the minorities, the NUF, the Shans, and Arakanese nationalists. But when total amnesty was promised all insurgents and when U Nu stated his willingness to consider the formation of separate Arakanese and Mon states, the army became alarmed about such an alliance of essentially contradictory elements. Hampered by bureaucratic paralysis, by the disaffection of ethnic minorities, and by increasing army opposition, U Nu voluntarily handed over the government to the army and to General Ne Win in October, 1958, for a period of six months (later extended to eighteen months) of caretaker rule, while order and stability were restored and preparations made for new elections, held in February, 1960.

U Nu's faction of the AFPFL returned to power with a strong parliamentary majority, buttressed by the support of the ethnic minorities. The policies on which his party won the election, however, and which they proceeded to implement, again endangered national unity. The ruling party began to divide over membership questions, and Shan insurgency broke out in the east. U Nu antagonized religious minorities by the establishment of Buddhism as the state religion. And when U Nu announced his intention to resign as party leader in 1962 (and as prime minister in 1964), his party began to fight over the succession. U Nu had lost his touch for effective leadership, but none of his civilian rivals could fill his necessary role. To the army, it appeared that Burma was heading back to the bitter conflicts of 1958. Because its period of rule as a caretaker government had been marked by some success in combating corruption and inflation, in bringing back law and order, and in promoting economic growth, the army and General Ne Win could not ignore what they felt to be a clear call to reimpose military rule: They considered themselves the heirs of Aung San. They staged a *coup d'état* on March 2, 1962, imprisoned most civilian politicians, suspended the constitution, and again set about building the new Burma, which had been so long desired and had remained so elusive.

Turning inward upon itself and avoiding the intensity of foreign contact and involvement that has so disturbed its neighbors, Burma in the 1960's began again to seek political structures that could bind together a precarious unity, economic progress that could bring prosperity without disparities in wealth or exploitation, and symbols for nationhood that could have meaning for all Burmese.

THE KINGDOM OF THAILAND

Thailand's wartime policy of collaboration with the Japanese was useful to the Thai only so long as Japan's power was paramount. It spared Thailand extensive damage and left the power of its government unimpaired. When the course of the war turned against the Japanese, however, Thai policy had to change. Accordingly, in August, 1944, the National Assembly forced Phibun's government to resign and installed a new government led by a civilian politician, Khuang Aphaiwong, and directed from behind the scenes by Pridi Phanomyong. Since early in the war, Pridi had acted as regent for the absent boy-king Ananda, organizing from the regent's palace an underground movement of resistance against the Japanese, the Free Thai Movement, which was in contact with the British Force 136 operating from Ceylon and with the American Office of Strategic Services through Yunnan. Those connections were used in an attempt to gain the good graces of the allies, especially when some Thai offered to mount an armed uprising against the Japanese in May, 1945, an offer later rejected.

At the end of the war in August, the gravity of Thailand's international position was exposed by the victorious Allies. At that time, Thailand still held Lao and Cambodian territories annexed after the Indochinese War of 1940–41, as well as the four states of northern Malaya and two Shan states of Burma granted them by the Japanese in 1943, in an attempt to elicit Thailand's more thorough complicity and participation in the war. Britain attempted to impose what amounted to a protectorate over Thailand by advancing eighteen demands, requiring that Thailand participate in international tin and rubber regulation, that it "accept allied military control . . . and an allied military mission," that it "accept an allied rice unit to control the production and export of Thai rice, and accept allied controls over exports of tin, rubber, and teak." Furthermore, Thailand was to be compelled to furnish the Allies 1.5 million tons of free rice "as a special measure of reconcilement and aid by Thailand toward those who had suffered because of Thai denial of rice exports during the war years."[3] With the assistance of strong American diplomatic pressure hastily mobilized by the new Prime Minister, Seni Pramoj (the wartime Thai Ambassador to the United States, who had decided on his own not to inform the American Government officially of Thailand's declaration of war against the United States), the most extreme demands were moderated, and Thailand had to agree only to furnish the Allies rice at low fixed prices. French demands for the retrocession of Lao and Cambodian territories were even more strongly resisted, but it was the minimum price the French charged for allowing Thailand admission to the United Nations, a symbol of international respectability that the Thai felt they needed to secure. After the signature of treaties with Britain and France in January and November, 1946, Thailand was admitted to the United Nations in December, expressing from the first a strongly pro-Western foreign policy.

Postwar politics in Thailand were influenced heavily by considerations of external affairs; the period immediately following the war set patterns that persisted. The army, whose prewar predominance reflected the coherence of the military elite and the weakness of its divided rivals, was at least temporarily discredited by its association with the Japanese (although it had never fought the Allies). The willingness of the Allies to settle their claims on terms favorable to the Thai was due in part to an apparent resurgence of parliamentary democracy. A new constitution providing for a fully elective legislature came into force early in 1946, when Pridi left his protected position as regent to become Prime Minister. He soon encountered a number of political problems in making the new parliamentary system work. Postwar economic dislocation and the attendant problems of inflation and corruption were more than he or his successors could manage without jeopardizing their parliamentary position. Pridi was forced from office in the aftermath of the violent death of King Ananda on June 9, 1946—an event never satisfactorily explained—and Luang Thamrong Nawasawat, who succeeded him, lacked the strong following that would have made effective government possible. The politicians drifted in indecision until an army conspiracy seized power late in 1947 to establish a nominally independent civil government under Khuang. The army was reluctant to show its full presence as long as Western disapproval threatened, but Western distrust of military rule began to lessen in mid-1948, when other countries of the region were beset by Communist insurrection. At that point, Khuang was forced from office, and Field Marshal Phibun again became Prime Minister.

For the first three years of Phibun's rule, the army temporized, and a semblance of parliamentary government remained. The civilian politicians, however, were divided. The radicals, led by Pridi, were in disrepute as the investigation of Ananda's death dragged on, while the Democrat party led by Khuang resented its exclusion from real power. The armed forces were split on service lines, while the army itself was divided, and younger officers were still distrustful of Phibun. The government needed foreign support and aid, but it was anxious not to incur American disapproval by establishing an avowedly military government. Phibun gradually won a substantial measure of American support when he committed Thai troops in Korea and kept Thailand relatively stable. Four abortive military coups between 1948 and 1951 reduced Phibun's rivals to two men: General Phao Siyanon, Director-General of the paramilitary police force, and General Sarit Thanarat, who commanded the First Army in Bangkok. Caught between the two rivals, as well as between them and the parliament, Phibun saw his grip on power begin to loosen in the early 1950's.

The successes of the Viet Minh in Indochina in 1953 and early 1954 and the possibility of Communist-dominated regimes in Cambodia and Laos made the government receptive to the efforts of the American Secretary of State, John Foster Dulles, to bolster the region's military security by organizing the Southeast Asia Treaty Organization (SEATO) in 1954. In addition, American military and economic aid to Thailand was increased. The civilian politicians were worried by the advantage this gave the army; General Phao's arbitrary acts of imprisoning government opponents, together with rampant official corruption, brought the government under increasing attack. Phibun visited Europe and America in 1955 and returned enthusiastic about the possibilities of strengthening his own position by democratization.

He legalized political parties and lifted press censorship in preparation for general elections early in 1957. A massive government party pledged to Phibun conducted an intense campaign managed by Phao, while the major opposition came from the weak Democrat party and smaller leftist parties in the poor Northeast. Despite flagrant electoral corruption, however, the government party was able to win no more than a bare majority of the seats in the election. Sarit, who avoided full participation in the campaign and election, became the focal point of agitation against the conduct of the elections, and, on September 16, 1957, he led a bloodless *coup d'état,* which ended the long political career of Phibun.

The new parliamentary government inaugurated after new elections, in December, 1957, had but a short life. The parliament reflected the grave divisions stemming from personal feuds, disparate ideological and economic interests, and the clash of traditional and modern political styles and outlooks within Thailand's urban elite. When the new government proved in the army's eyes incapable of acting decisively on the many local and international policy problems facing it, Sarit returned from medical treatment abroad to restore military rule in October, 1958. Sarit still commanded strong political support on a national base much broader than that of any of his predecessors. He was respected throughout the armed forces, as well as by the older conservatives of the civil service and the royal family, and he raised many professional civil servants to prominent positions in the government. He moved firmly against the most extreme of the radical opposition and attempted at the same time to isolate it by embarking on strong policies of economic development, public welfare, and education. He enhanced the authority of the government by encouraging King Phumiphon Adunyadet to play a stronger role in the public life of the nation. Promulgating an authoritarian interim constitution based on those of Gaullist France and Nasser's United Arab Republic, he appointed a Constituent Assembly composed of representatives of all wings of public opinion to draft a "permanent constitution."

Thailand's problems and policies in the years since 1958 derive their meaning from the context of international relations within which they are set. Since the end of World War II, Thailand's security concerns have focused primarily on the states of former French Indochina. The resurgence of Vietnam has awakened Thai fears for the country's eastern frontiers, especially as the Viet Minh and its successor in Hanoi have been seen by the Thai consistently to fight and to think in terms of Indochina, not Vietnam alone. Naturally, the Thai army, which was the main proponent of pan-Thai sentiment in the Indochinese War of 1940–41, is most consciously aware of the dangers of Vietnamese encroachments on the sovereignty and territory of Laos and Cambodia, particularly as Thailand's natural defense perimeter (as opposed to its borders) is not the Mekong River, which is a highway, but rather the chain of mountains that divides Vietnam from the rest of the Southeast Asian mainland. Thus, the Thai Government was long anxious about the delicate balancing game played by Prince Sihanouk in Cambodia, and it has taken a strong interest in events in Laos, where the Thai on several occasions have supported rightist military factions. Thai disquiet over the inability of SEATO to act in the Lao crisis of 1960–62 and over the outcome of the Geneva Conference of 1962, which established a neutralist government in Laos, led to quiet agreements that same year with the American Government providing for a direct commitment by the United States to come to Thailand's defense, should its security be seriously threatened.[4]

Internal developments have reflected the same concerns. In the late 1940's and early 1950's, Thailand's Chinese minority, numbering in excess of 2 million, was held to be a source of considerable potential danger, particularly when Pridi took up exile in Communist China and became the leader in exile of a Thai Patriotic Front. More recently, the impoverished Northeast, with an ethnic minority akin to the Lao approaching 10 million, has drawn increasing government attention as a potential source of agrarian unrest. The government of Sarit—himself a northeasterner—and that of his successor, Thanom Kittikachorn, following Sarit's death in 1963, mounted a considerable program of economic development in the Northeast, which by the late 1960's had brought a dramatic improvement in living standards there, with an overall rate of economic growth in excess of 7 per cent per year. In the late 1960's the government's attention turned to its political vulnerability in the cities, where economic growth and expanded educational opportunities had dramatically enlarged the middle class. Under increasing pressure to justify itself and to share political power, the government promulgated a new constitution in 1968, providing for an elected lower house of parliament. Elections held early in 1969 worked to the regime's advantage. Support for the government party was strongest in the Northeast, where its efforts at economic development were appreciated. The opposition, led by Seni Pramoj, took its main strength from the urban centers, especially in Bangkok. The relationship between the government, still backed by the military and still strongly in control of internal security, and the civilian politicians was beginning on a new plane of watchful cooperation as the 1970's began.

THE KINGDOM OF LAOS

The political history of Laos since 1945 has been dominated by the efforts of various Lao and foreign groups to construct a political entity named "Laos" where none had existed before. The Lao and the outsiders have been thwarted by deeply embedded habits of regionalism and family rivalries among the Lao elite and by the pressures of the war in Vietnam. The royal government at Luang Prabang, the civil administration at Vientiane, and both "rightist"-controlled areas (generally in the south) and "leftist" areas (in the north and east) have often operated to split the country four ways, a process hastened by intense foreign interference.

In March, 1945, when the Japanese informed Sisavangvong, the Lao king at Luang Prabang, of his country's independence, his heir, Prince Savang Vatthana, rejected the offer, proclaimed that Laos would always remain a protectorate of France, and was arrested. The viceroy, Prince Phetsarath (1890–1959) then gathered a nucleus of independence-minded members of the elite and made the old king declare independence. In the confusion that followed—the French did not reoccupy Vientiane until April, 1946—Phetsarath and his entourage, calling themselves the Lao Issara (Free Lao), took control of much of central and northern Laos. In the south, the hereditary prince of Čhampassak, Boun Oum (born in 1900), aided the French. When French administration resumed in 1946, the king at Luang Prabang was rewarded by being named the ruler of the "Kingdom of Laos"—an invented entity—encompassing all of the French-controlled areas, including Čhampassak. Phetsarath then fled with his full brother, Souvanna Phouma, and their half-brother, Souphanouvong, to exile in Thailand.

Over the next four years, French willingness to negotiate the issue of independence gradually drew many Lao Issara, including Souvanna Phouma, back from Thailand. Phetsarath, in disfavor with Luang Prabang, remained in Bangkok until 1957. Souphanouvong also refused to return home peacefully, preferring to take to the hills and to ally his military following, the Pathet Lao (Lao Nation), with Vietnamese troops fighting the French in eastern Laos and in northwestern Vietnam. In October, 1953, France granted Laos its independence within the framework of the French Union, promising to defend it militarily. France was forced to honor its pledge almost at once, after a Vietnamese–Pathet Lao feint into central Laos late in 1953 threatened to cut the kingdom in two. The French then hastened to fortify the valley of Dien Bien Phu in northwestern Vietnam, hoping to withstand a Vietnamese–Pathet Lao attack on Luang Prabang, which never came. Instead, Dien Bien Phu itself fell, after a long siege and heavy losses, in May, 1954, just as the Geneva Conference on the Far East turned its attention to Indochinese affairs.

Under terms agreed upon at Geneva, the Pathet Lao were allowed to "regroup temporarily" in two northern provinces of Laos, over which they have continued to exercise administrative control. In 1955, a pro-Western government in Vientiane attempted unsuccessfully to force the Pathet Lao to disarm. "Neutralist" governments between 1956 and 1958, often headed by Souvanna Phouma, then sought, with moderate success, to integrate the Pathet Lao into the national army and to bring its leadership, including Souphanouvong, into the central government. The "neutralist" solution ran counter to policies of the United

States, which had poured money and advisers into Laos since its independence, viewing it as an essential bulwark for the containment of China. In 1959, a rightist regime, backed by the United States, replaced Souvanna, stiffened the terms for a coalition, and jailed Souphanouvong, who escaped (in a thunderstorm, accompanied by his jailers) a few months later. By the end of 1960, a neutralist *coup* led by a Lao army captain, Kong Le, provoked a rightist attack on Vientiane by troops financed by the United States and Thailand, and led by a Lao general, Phoumi Nosavan, who was a relative of the Thai premier. The inauguration of a rightist government under Prince Boun Oum, backed by Phoumi, took place early in 1961, provoking Pathet Lao feints toward the Mekong and (so the Thai leadership thought) at Thailand and culminating in the "battle" of Nam Tha, where rightist Lao forces disintegrated and fled into Thailand. Such was the situation when the newly installed Kennedy Administration in the United States, acting through Savang Vatthana, who had succeeded as King of Laos in 1959, persuaded Boun Oum to attend a second Geneva Conference, specifically concerned with Laos, which convened in May, 1961.

The conference lasted until March, 1962, when the powers that attended it were able to persuade the three Lao factions—represented by three princes—to coalesce around a neutralist government. The powers agreed in theory to guarantee Lao neutrality. The restructured Lao Government, or series of governments, presided over by Souvanna Phouma, was rapidly overtaken by events, especially the intensification of the conflict in Vietnam. It soon fell back upon the United States, provoking violent responses from Hanoi and the Pathet Lao. The kingdom's geographic position has made it a seemingly natural theater of intrigue for outside powers, particularly Russia and the United States, as well as a bone of contention between the Vietnamese and the Thai. At the same time, communications difficulties and patterns of history have encouraged regional fragmentation rather than national integration among the ethnic Lao elite. "If we sit in a boat," the neutralist Kong Le has said, "we must sit in the middle."[5] One problem has been that the Lao are not alone in the boat; another has been that the fictive nation of Laos, built up out of a succession of French sentimental gestures, probably cannot by itself withstand the pressures put against it, outside of a cold war context, by Thailand and Vietnam.

THE KINGDOM OF CAMBODIA

In May, 1945, two months after Sihanouk had unilaterally declared Cambodia's independence from France, the nationalist leader Son Ngoc Thanh returned to Phnom Penh from Tokyo. A month later, Sihanouk named him Foreign Minister, presumably to negotiate with the Japanese authorities in Phnom Penh, and in August, after an abortive coup in which Thanh may have been involved, Sihanouk appointed him Prime Minister. As French authorities began filtering back into Indochina, Thanh attempted to strengthen his position by organizing a plebiscite in which only 2 out of 500,000 votes cast rejected his five-point anti-French program. The French returned to Phnom Penh in force in early October and arrested Thanh, whom they tried for treason and then exiled to the south of France.

French administrators resumed work in Cambodia under terms that were formally defined in a *modus vivendi* signed by representatives of both powers in January, 1946. Under the agreement, Cambodia became an autonomous state within the French Union, and France promised, for its part, to regain from Thailand the areas wrested from Cambodia in 1941. While the agreement provided Cambodia with nothing larger than nominal independence, French control over provincial administration was somewhat loosened.

In April, 1946, permission was granted by the French for the formation of political parties. Three parties, led by members of the royal family, swiftly took shape. Two of them favored continued association with France; the third, the Democratic party, favored negotiations leading toward total independence. Many of its adherents admired the principles of Son Ngoc Thanh. Its leadership included a small group of administrators educated in France during World War II. The Democrats dominated the Consultative Assembly, which convened at Phnom Penh in September, 1946, and effectively supervised the drafting of Cambodia's constitution, promulgated early in the following year. That document, modeled on the French Constitution of 1946, featured a strong legislative body, the National Assembly, which was to be balanced, theoretically, by the newly defined—and sharply reduced—powers of the king. The first elections for the National Assembly were held late in 1947, and the Democrats captured an overwhelming number of seats.

Over the next four years, the French war in Indochina deepened concomitantly with the recovery of Europe, the collapse of Nationalist China, and the institutionalization of the cold war. Inside Cambodia, where there was little military action, Sihanouk and his assembly fought a running battle for control over the mechanisms of power and for credit in gaining independence from France. Initially, Sihanouk had generally respected the members of the bureaucratic elite who had framed the constitution and who spoke so fervently of the need to modernize the kingdom. His enthusiasm faded, however, as his own self-confidence increased, as he began to form a private set of advisers, and as the Democrats began to speak out in favor of a nonmonarchic system of government. In late 1951, Son Ngoc Thanh was brought back to Cambodia at Sihanouk's request after pledging not to indulge in political activities. He promptly broke his word, founded a newspaper, and began touring the country, making anti-French and antiroyalist speeches. In the spring of 1952, Thanh was forced into hiding, and he remained a fugitive thereafter as leader of an anti-Sihanouk "liberation" movement, allegedly financed by the Vietnamese and the Thai, with its headquarters located frequently in Saigon.

Shortly after Thanh's disappearance, Sihanouk staged a showdown with the Democrats by dismissing the cabinet, calling for emergency powers, and pledging to obtain complete independence by 1955. The assembly's failure to approve his plan led Sihanouk to dissolve that body *sine die* in early 1953, when he embarked on a world tour to publicize his cause. That voyage, later known as the Royal Crusade for Independence, took the young king—he had just turned thirty—to Paris, Washington, Tokyo, and Bangkok. Everywhere, by mixing private talks with public statements, Sihanouk strove to shake his country loose from France. The trip embarrassed the French, whose war in Indochina was going badly and who had been content until then to feed out relatively meaningless tidbits of autonomy to the Cambodian Government, such as the right to be recognized diplomatically without the capacity to send ambassadors abroad. In November, 1953, Sihanouk returned from "exile," and the French acceded to his request for total independence.

The Cambodian delegation thus reached the Geneva Conference convened in May, 1954, to settle the Indochina War with a relatively strong hand. The delegation played its hand well by stubbornly resisting pressures and blandishments from representatives of the great powers who were eager to save their own faces and ideologies by manipulating the future of the components of Indochina. Cambodia came away from the conference as perhaps its only "winner"; unlike Laos or Vietnam, Cambodia was free to form military alliances and released from enforced adjustment of its territory or its politics.

In keeping with his promise of 1953, Sihanouk organized a national referendum early in 1955 in which the populace was asked to express an opinion about his crusade for independence. One ballot bore his picture and the word for "Yes." The other, colored black, had the word for "No" inscribed on it. Nearly a million "yes" votes were cast, and only 1,800 black ones. Perhaps dazzled by the dimensions of his popularity, but more probably following a scenario plotted in advance, Sihanouk abdicated the kingship in April, 1955, to free himself from the pressures of traditional protocol and the assembly, turning the crown over to his father, Norodom Suramarit, who reigned until his death in 1960. Later in the summer of 1955, Sihanouk launched a national political movement, the Sangkum Reastr Niyum (People's Socialist Community), membership in which was limited to people with no other political affiliation. In elections for the National Assembly in the fall of 1955, Sangkum candidates—many of them bureaucrats who had deserted the Democratic party—won all the seats and 82 per cent of the vote. The Sangkum remained in power under Sihanouk, claiming in 1967 more than 2 million members.

In the months that followed, Sihanouk further reduced the power of the political parties, setting up in their place a National Congress of the Sangkum, which was to meet twice a year in Phnom Penh, just outside the royal palace, to discuss and approve, *en masse*, government policy and practice. Following his father's death in 1960, Sihanouk held a referendum in which the electorate was asked to choose among him, Son Ngoc Thanh, the Communists, and a blank ballot. More than 99 per cent of the voters requested that Sihanouk continue in office, and he assumed power as Chief of State. He placed the ceremonial functions of the monarchy in the hands of his mother, Queen Kossamak.

From 1945 until 1970, Cambodian history was dominated by one man and to a large extent shaped by his personal style. The style itself, especially to unfriendly observers, frequently obscured the substance and consistency of Sihanouk's overriding concerns, which had to do with Cambodia's survival as a state, especially in relation to Thailand and Vietnam. These concerns also dominated Cambodia's foreign policy, finding expression through a bewildering array of public mechanisms, which Sihanouk personally directed, including newspapers, magazines, films, speeches, conferences, interviews, visits with chiefs of state, and the political process itself. Informally titled *Samdec ou*—literally, Prince Daddy—throughout the kingdom since 1961, Sihanouk was long successful in manipulating Cambodia's institutions largely by means of his charisma, even though he inhibited institutional development. Throughout the late 1960's, the economic and military situation in Cambodia, so long neutralized and manipulated by Sihanouk's charismatic rule, provoked increasingly bitter protests from the Cambodian "right," whose leadership was middle-aged, middle-of-the-road, and generally loyal to the Prince. In March, 1970, when Sihanouk was vacationing in France, the National Assembly—to a large extent purged of leftists in the preceding years—voted unanimously to remove Sihanouk from office as Chief of State. A caretaker regime under a military premier, Lieut. General Lon Nol, assumed power and moved to get military aid from the United States, among others, with which to disperse north Vietnamese and National Liberation Front forces inside Cambodia. The outlook for these efforts and the future of Sihanouk himself, who called from Peking for the formation of a liberation army (supported also by Hanoi) to help him regain power, remained unclear. Moreover, during its first few months in office, the Cambodian Government seemed to have exerted no strong hold on the Cambodian people who in turn were apparently reluctant to resist it. Whatever the eventual outcome of this struggle, the peace so carefully guarded by Sihanouk has been brutally shattered.

VIETNAM: THE DEMOCRATIC REPUBLIC AND THE REPUBLIC

The Japanese occupation of Vietnam from 1941 to 1945 transformed the unpromising revolutionary prospects there as completely as did Japanese occupying armies elsewhere in Southeast Asia. In addition to undermining the reputation of French military power in Vietnamese eyes, the Japanese invasion gave the Vietnamese Communists an opportunity to blend their Marxist dogmas with the more easily understood nationalist cause of resistance to both the French and the Japanese. In 1939, Vietnamese Communists had suffered from factionalism. In the northern areas, where the Party was dominated by leaders like Vo Nguyen Giap and Pham Van Dong, Trotskyism—meaning hostility to Russia, little interest in contact with other Communists like the Chinese, and insistence upon immediate social revolution almost at the same time as the achievement of political independence—was relatively weak. In the southern part of the country, Trotskyists like Ta Thu Thau dominated revolutionary politics, having been far more successful than orthodox Party members in "democratic front" political activities in Saigon. In November, 1939, in an effort to overcome such factionalism, a Party conference established the "People's Anti-Imperialist Front of Indochina," in which the emphasis was placed not upon class warfare but upon a nationalistic military crusade. In the autumn of 1940, the new policy crystallized with a series of abortive armed uprisings by Party-sponsored guerrillas, first at Bac Son in the northern border province of Lang Son, and later in the south as well.

Ho Chi Minh left Russia in 1938, and traveled to South China by way of Yenan, and convened a meeting of the Party's central committee in a Kwangsi village in May, 1941, founding the Vietnamese Independence Brotherhood League, more popularly known as the Viet Minh. Putting a new face on the Vietnamese Communist movement for domestic consumption, the Viet Minh sought to circumvent Japanese schemes of manipulating Vietnamese patriotic groups by creating its own heterogeneous coalition of patriots—peasants, teachers, merchants, priests—dedicated to the winning of independence. Through such reorganization and limitation of objectives, the newly christened Viet Minh also hoped to obtain aid from Chiang Kai-shek and his anti-Communist Kuomintang by playing upon their desire to defeat the Japanese. The period 1941–44 is justly famous for its intrigues and counterintrigues, for Ho's picaresque but deadly serious attempts to extract aid from both Chinese and American sources, and for his poetry-writing sojourns in Chinese jails.

In December, 1944, with local administration in northern Vietnam collapsing, the Viet Minh officially formed its own army, a more ambitious enterprise than the scattered guerrilla units of 1940. Japanese fortunes in the Pacific war were waning, and the French were unable to reassert themselves. On March 9, 1945, the Japanese army in Vietnam dramatically revoked and suppressed French rule. Its intention behind the coup was to substitute its own puppet regime and protectorate for that of the French, capitalizing upon anti-French, pro-Japanese sentiments among conservative nationalists like the Cao Dai.

But while one façade of authority was being exchanged for another in the towns, the countryside was experiencing more portentous upheavals. The worst health disaster of the entire colonial period in Indochina, the great famine of 1944–45 in northern Vietnam, claimed the lives of between 400,000 and 2 million people (French and Vietnamese statistics, respectively). The French suggested that the mass starvation had been caused by the collapse of northern dikes during the Japanese occupation, which in turn had allowed the rice fields to be flooded and the crops destroyed; southern rice could not be imported in compensation because of a breakdown in transportation. Vietnamese eyewitness accounts of the famine, especially Tran Van Mai's shocking book, *Ai Gay Nen Toi* (*Who Committed This Crime?*), contended instead that both the French and the Japanese had systematically hoarded rice since October, 1943, partly to feed their own soldiers and brutally to weaken the morale of local Vietnamese resistance leaders. Against that background, the Viet Minh army was the only indigenous political force capable of moderating the famine and lesser troubles through more efficient organization of available resources. It swept to power quickly. By June, 1945, it had carved out a "liberated area" embracing six northern border provinces. By late August, 1945, soon after the Japanese surrender, most of the major cities of Vietnam, including Hanoi and Hue, were in Viet Minh hands. Bao Dai, Emperor since 1925, abdicated, recognizing the new Viet Minh–dominated regime at Hanoi as the one provisional but legitimate government for all Vietnam. Having received the blessings of the last representative of the Nguyen Dynasty, the "Democratic Republic of Vietnam" was proclaimed at Hanoi on September 2, 1945, with Ho Chi Minh as President. Twenty years later, one former Viet Minh soldier could still remember ecstatically the apocalyptic transition he and others had made from the rural borderlands to the strangely urban life of Hanoi: "Those summer nights of 'forty-five,' the very first nights of sleeping in rooms in the high upper storeys of buildings . . . people were going about in crowds more merry than those of village gatherings at home."[6]

All the above events constituted the "August Revolution," a sacramental date in Vietnamese Communist history. But the August Revolution was a revolution of administrative structures, not a socio-economic revolution; it was a battle for control of the instruments of rule rather than an ideological confrontation between well-defined rival groups. Designed to win the sympathy of non-Communist nationalists and foreigners, it was a "bourgeois democratic" revolution with a moderate program: the creation of a democratic republic, the abolition of the special colonial taxes, the promulgation of labor laws providing for an eight-hour day and a minimum wage, the reduction of land rents and the equitable redivision of village public lands, the nationalization of the property of "Vietnamese traitors." The methods of the August Revolution were diverse. Printing presses and radio stations were requisitioned; population and land records were transferred to the custody of people's committees; police stations, post offices, railway stations, and government treasuries were seized; and the bureaucratic appurtenances of the colonial regime (seals, documents, commissions of office) were destroyed.

The August Revolution was not a minor preview of the Maoist takeover in China in 1949. The Vietnamese Communists pride themselves on the fact that their movement has usually had a greater dimension of urban political action than that of the Chinese Communists. Diverging from the Maoist strategy of "the countryside encircling the cities," in which the cities were supposed to fall like overripe plums under external pressure, the Viet Minh in 1945 (and the Viet Cong in southern Vietnam in 1968, in their famous "Tet offensive") preferred a scheme in which revolutionary movements were organized and revolutionary disorder stimulated in rural and urban areas simultaneously. Although Hanoi had fallen to the Viet Minh only in August, 1945, Viet Minh agents had been active in the city since March, holding market-place demonstrations, disseminating revolutionary handbills among students, and selling "letters of credit" to Hanoi merchants.[7] The army's role in ultimately seizing the city from without supplemented and climaxed those activities but did not begin them. It is an error to look at Vietnamese Communism entirely as if it were an imitation of the Chinese variety: As the theorist Le Quoc Su has suggested, the Vietnamese Party, operating in a smaller country, could not afford the Chinese plan of conducting formal military campaigns from a fixed territorial base like Yenan. Throughout its history it was compelled to attempt a tactically more diversified revolution: semilegal campaigns for tax reduction, shifting guerrilla movements, far-flung small-scale violence, or even, as in the 1930's, participation through front groups in municipal council elections.[8]

Between September, 1945, and December, 1946, one ambition uppermost in the minds of the men who carried out the August Revolution—the ambition of obtaining independence from France peacefully—was irretrievably lost. The French Army, heavily dependent on British military support, recaptured Saigon on September 23, 1945, and then attempted to regain control of the southern countryside. The Viet Minh, weak in the south and checkmated there by a "united national front" of Cao Dai, Hoa Hao, and Trotskyist partisans, could not by itself prevent them. The region north of the sixteenth parallel, meanwhile, was being occupied by some 180,000 Chinese troops nominally exploiting Kuomintang China's right, as one of the Allied Powers, to receive the Japanese surrender, but actually seeking to replace the hegemony of the Vietnamese Communists in Hanoi with that of surviving, second-rank VNQDD leaders brought back to Vietnam from their exile since 1930 in China.

Before the Kuomintang armies withdrew in 1946, unsuccessful in the latter task for a variety of reasons, Ho Chi Minh, needing a counterweight to the Chinese, adopted a conciliatory posture toward the French. In March, 1946, he agreed to the return of French soldiers to the north. In the summer of 1946, he visited Paris to negotiate a new, less colonial basis for Vietnamese participation in the French Union. But the French, while recognizing the Viet Minh government at Hanoi, refused to relinquish any of their authority over their colony in the south. By promoting in Saigon the slogan "Cochinchina for the Cochinchinese," they attempted to transform the real issue of a continued French presence in Vietnam versus independence into the artificial issue of southern Vietnam versus northern Vietnam. Fighting broke out between Viet Minh and French soldiers in Haiphong and Hanoi in December, 1946, and almost immediately became a full-scale war. The Viet Minh withdrew from, or camouflaged its presence in, the cities it had captured during the August Revolution and mounted rural guerrilla campaigns.

The war lasted seven and a half years. Its climax, which startled the world, came in the spring of 1954, when the Viet Minh army surrounded a French garrison at Dien Bien Phu in northwestern Vietnam and won a crushing victory. The war in the countryside was extremely complex. The Viet Minh faced two threats: the French army, and its own shortage of food, clothing, weapons, and ammunition. Under the slogan "a decimeter of soil is a decimeter of gold" (*tac dat tac vang*), the Viet Minh expanded agricultural production in areas it controlled by fining landlords who did not cultivate all their lands, by reducing land rents by 25 per cent (Viet Minh rent reduction councils were functioning in most northern provinces by 1949), by employing women more comprehensively in agriculture, and by organizing cooperatives and labor exchange groups. Although the French air force replied by bombing crop lands in Viet Minh territory, the Viet Minh proved itself capable of mounting the formidable economic organization any military victory would require by mobilizing the peasants under its rule to spend an estimated total of 14 million man-days of labor between 1946 and 1954 reinforcing the dikes of northern Vietnam.[9]

Viet Minh rifles, grenades, and mines were manufactured in small rural factories organized along handicraft-industry lines. By early 1949, the Viet Minh claimed to have some 100,000 workers in the factories, scattered as they were in the hinterlands. Other weapons were, of course, received from the Chinese Communists after 1949. True to their program of simultaneous urban and rural action, Viet Minh agents encouraged the segments of the labor movement loyal to their cause to slow down the urban economy by strikes and sabotage: 9,950 men participated in thirteen strikes in the Saigon-Cholon area alone in 1949. Goods and machinery were systematically stolen from urban areas. "His face swollen and black with grit . . . he was wearing nothing but American clothing" is the way Nguyen Dinh Thi described a Viet Minh soldier in his novel, *Xung kich* (*The Assault*), to which the Party awarded its second prize for literature in 1951–52.[10]

From the French side, the politics of the war focused upon the search for a Vietnamese alternative to Ho Chi Minh who could command popular support. In 1949, the French constructed the so-called Associated State of Vietnam within the French Union, whose chief of state was none other than the ex-Emperor Bao Dai. To Bao Dai, they made a concession they had not been willing to make to Ho Chi Minh:

Cochinchina could become a part of the new state, which still remained divided, however, into three regions with separate governors, and which suffered French control of its foreign and defense policies. Almost bankrupt politically from the beginning, the Bao Dai regime was nonetheless transformed rather than liquidated by France's military defeat in Vietnam in 1954.

The Geneva Agreement of 1954, one of the most controversial diplomatic settlements of modern history, provided for the withdrawal of French military forces from Indochina and set its seal upon the legitimacy of the Viet Minh government of Vietnam north of the seventeenth parallel. Meanwhile, however, on the other side of the seventeenth parallel, the Bao Dai regime evolved into an independent southern Vietnamese polity, centered at Saigon, led no longer by Bao Dai but by an energetic Catholic nationalist from central Vietnam, Ngo Dinh Diem (1901–63). The Diem regime, in company with its leading foreign patron, the United States, announced that it would not adhere to the Geneva Agreement, which had included the stipulation that pan-Vietnamese general elections be held in July, 1956. As prospects for the peaceful reunification of Vietnam, after its century of colonial administrative divisions, dimmed, it was certain that civil war threatened.

After 1954, the northern Vietnamese state was governed from Hanoi by three hierarchies—those of the army, the civil administration, and the Communist Party, known after 1951 as the Vietnam Labor Party (Dang Lao Dong). The three hierarchies really expressed the multifaceted nature of the authority exercised by an oligarchy of revolutionaries. Party cells existed at all levels of the army, and political commissars functioned as army members. At the top, the same people tended to occupy positions in both the Party and the civil administration: Ho Chi Minh, for example, served as Chairman of the Party Central Committee and as President of the Republic. Each of the three hierarchies linked the village to the capital. In civil administration, there were people's councils in the villages, district committees, provincial people's councils, and a National Assembly; the Party, in addition to having cells in villages, factories, schools, and hospitals, moved upward with its own district committees, provincial committees, and its National Party Congress. Chinese-style mass organizations were also adopted: cultural associations, women's groups, young workers' organizations, and religious association fronts. In fact, the mass organizations were spread thin at the village level, and Party membership (760,000 people in 1966) was not extensive enough to cover or control the entire rural population. In 1966, for example, the regime revealed that in one village in Thai Binh Province, village notables were masquerading as hierarchs of the Catholic Church in order "to restrain the villagers from studying" the new dogmas and to win extra submissiveness from their peasants, long after the Communists had come to power.[11]

Before the American bombing of northern Vietnam began in 1965, inducing a patriotic rallying to the government, the loyalty of all the members of the northern intelligentsia to the Hanoi regime could not be taken for granted. In the mid-1950's, famous writers like Truong Tuu and Phan Khoi publicly attacked the government through an influential journal, published in Hanoi, entitled *Nhan Van* (*Humanistic Writings*). Criticizing the Party for its "dogmatism" and advising it to sever its relations with Russia and China, Truong Tuu and his friends advanced the slogan "the independence of the intellectuals." As Phan Khoi put it in the compilation *Giai pham mua thu* (*Belletristic Jewels of Autumn*), literature does not require the political leadership of the Party, but instead "literature and political administration tap each other on the shoulder, enjoy the advantages of mixing with each other, and both sides receive the profit." The *Nhan Van* intellectuals proposed that the function of writers in the north was to serve as "umpires" between the Party and the masses.[12]

Ultimately suppressed, the revolt of the intelligentsia attested the fact that the Viet Minh, when it had come to power in 1954, had been a loose coalition of anticolonial nationalists controlled by the Communists but not completely Communist in its membership. Moreover, not having enjoyed the advantage of operating from a fixed territorial base for more than a decade, as the Chinese Communists had, the Viet Minh had lacked equivalent opportunities for carrying out programs of thought reform and ideological purification among its supporters.

Agricultural modernization and reorganization, completely neglected in the colonial period, were among the chief concerns of the Hanoi regime. Between 1953 and 1957, its land reform campaign, reminiscent of the one in China, redistributed more than 800,000 hectares of land among 9 million people in thousands of villages. In 1958, declaring formal war against what it called the "individualistic" peasant economy and its exaltation of private property, the government began the conversion of village agriculture, handicraft industries, and other forms of economic life into cooperatives. Whole villages might constitute cooperatives, or there might be several cooperatives to one large village. Cooperatives might range in size and function from one of, say, 450 families (about 2,000 people) devoted entirely to wet-rice agriculture to one of, say, fifty-four families (300 people plus) devoted to the management of water resources and flood control. This was the most politically ambitious (and perhaps the harshest) attempt at agricultural reform in all of Southeast Asia. Not only had the traditional Vietnamese village enjoyed more autonomy with regard to the central government than the new cooperative now did, but facilities like paddy barns and drying yards that had been found in the old villages only on the estates of landlords, where peasants had to pay fees to use them, now were government-owned. Families living in the cooperatives, however, were still allowed to tend private gardens.

Ngo Dinh Diem transformed his status from Premier of the new southern state at Saigon to that of its President in 1955 by means of stage-managed elections aimed at the political destruction of Bao Dai. Diem was probably the last upholder of an important tradition in Vietnam, which went back to the mid-1800's. It was the tradition, represented at the Tu-duc court by Nguyen Truong To, of nonideological modernization by maverick Catholic politicians devoted to their country but alienated from many of its prevailing ideological trends. Anti-colonial but also anti-Communist, Diem ruled the south from 1954 to 1963 as an aloof dictator whose power was conditioned less by formally acknowledged accountability to the Vietnamese people than by his success or lack of it in manipulating his American allies and in surviving the opposition of military and religious leaders. Surrounded by his ambitious brothers (one of whom was his senior adviser, another the Catholic Archbishop of Hue, a third a kind of deputy ruler in central Vietnam, a fourth Ambassador to Great Britain), he promulgated a constitution in 1956 that allowed him to suspend laws and to rule by decree in emergencies, which he himself defined. Lacking an adequate administrative structure to carry out a land revolution, the Diem regime, whose vice-president was a major landlord, also depended for its political power upon the preservation of at least certain segments of the landlord class.

Diem was overthrown and assassinated in November, 1963, by members of his own armed forces, following a crisis involving the confrontation between his largely Catholic regime and a renascent Buddhist religio-political movement. But the real opposition to his government was that furnished by Communist guerrillas, known to their enemies as the Viet Cong. Through the activities of the guerrillas, vast tracts of the countryside soon fell under the influence of the National Liberation Front, officially created in December, 1960, whose Chairman, Nguyen Huu Tho (born in 1910), the son of a rubber plantation manager, had been a Viet Minh leader. The Front itself was a kind of southern resurrection of the Viet Minh, a coalition of nationalists organized by the Communists, whose purpose was to win power in Saigon and create a "national democratic coalition" government capable of carrying out land redistribution and negotiating the reunification of the country. The Diem government's proposed antidote to the guerrillas, the "strategic hamlets" of 1962–63, which required the arbitrary relocation of thousands of villagers away from their ancestral homes, was a failure.

American intervention in the civil war, reflecting a mixture of misapplied advanced technology, ignorance of Vietnamese history, and often self-defeating political instincts, increased after Diem's overthrow. Militarily, one conspicuous form it took was the sustained bombing of northern Vietnam from 1965 to 1968, carried out in an attempt to suppress northern assistance to the National Liberation Front. Politically, it involved an alliance with Diem's successors, the military elite who had overthrown him. After 1963, military officers alternated with civilians in presiding over a succession of precariously balanced governments.

American intervention also involved the promotion of American-style political development, specifically the two-house legislature and presidential executive enshrined in the new constitution promulgated in Saigon in April, 1967. But if it were true, as the shrewd commentator The Uyen wrote, that the Americans had originally been invited to Vietnam by a colonial-minded Vietnamese urban middle class that did not understand its own peasantry, by 1967 the same urban middle class desired nothing but an end to the civil war.[13] A military officer, Nguyen Van Thieu, won the presidential elections of September, 1967. But he did not run first in such major cities as Saigon, Hue, and Da Nang; a "peace candidate," Truong Dinh Dzu, who was subsequently jailed, received more than 800,000 votes, and the Saigon General Students' Association, among others, charged that the elections had been arranged "by the hands of a foreign power."

Some Vietnamese intellectuals subscribed to the pessimistic opinion of Hoang Trung, a Catholic priest, that importing wholesale into Vietnam the institutions produced by Western revolutionary traditions was like attaching a pair of very large wings to the body of a sparrow: The sparrow lacked the power to flap the wings to raise itself from the ground.[14] To the Vietnamese peasant, domestic politicians who imported foreign soldiers who in turn destroyed village property were conspirators who "brought elephants back through the ancestors' graves." Even lavish American aid to villagers conferred unwanted obligations upon them almost as often as it stimulated their gratitude, because of their belief in the moral necessity of reciprocity: "If one piece of cake is received, a larger piece of cake must be given." The scope of the tragedy had become so vast, by the end of the 1960's, that a whole generation of Americans, as well as most Vietnamese, had become its scarcely believing prisoners.

MALAYSIA AND SINGAPORE

When the British returned to Malaya in September, 1945, some of its people looked forward to, while others were fearful of, an early release from colonial rule. The Japanese interregnum, though it had loosened many of the psychological bonds that had permitted the continuance of Western domination, had done nothing to bring the people together. On the contrary, the occupation had greatly exacerbated tensions only latent in the 1930's. Toward the Malays, the Japanese, if scarcely paternalistic, had been at least conciliatory, pursuing as the British had done policies directed to the minimal disturbance of the indigenous society in the interests of economic control. Toward the Chinese, the invaders had been initially brutal, in memory of Nanyang assistance to China during the Sino-Japanese war, and subsequently mistrustful and harassing. The Chinese, in turn, had provided the only active guerrilla resistance to Japanese rule, organized through the Malayan Peoples' Anti-Japanese Army (MPAJA), the nucleus of which was the prewar Malayan Communist Party (MCP). Some Indians had found themselves caught up in the enthusiasms of the Indian National

Army, but thousands of others were carried off to work, and die, on the Burma railway. Many Malays had, at least for a time, filled positions in the occupation administration to which they had not been able to aspire under the British. Those of all ranks of society who had "collaborated" with the new rulers found themselves the targets of MPAJA hostility, and the eventual Japanese surrender was followed by a settling of old scores on both sides. Throughout the latter part of the occupation, the only common experience was of hunger, sickness, misery, and demoralization, with a marked decrease in standards of personal trust and an increase in corruption.

Malaya's gradual achievement of independence during the decade that followed the British return, though sometimes derogated as nonrevolutionary, was the product of new and hard-won understandings between the then accepted leaders of the peoples of Malaya. The nature of the compact arrived at in the early 1950's was to underlie not merely the forms the new state would take but the manner of its politics (and much else) during the early years of independence. It was a compact reached between two groups: on the one hand, the Western-educated Malay leadership, composed largely of administrators drawn from the traditional elite or its fringes, and on the other, a small group of Western-educated Chinese, drawn mainly from among wealthy, Malaya-born businessmen. In essence, the understanding reached was that, in the interests of both leadership groups and, it was argued, of the society as a whole, the Malay right to political and administrative authority (premised on their better claim to be the original owners of the land) should be accepted unchallenged, at least for the time being, in return for noninterference in Chinese control of the economy. With those understandings as a starting point, a process of reconciliation of interests would be embarked upon, aimed explicitly, for the Malays, at measures intended to redress the balance of economic power, and implicitly, for the Chinese, by gradual admission to the franchise and a consequent adjustment of the balance of political power. Subsequent problems have centered upon two issues—the extent to which the two leadership groups have continued to be acceptable to the communities for which they professed to speak, and the fact that one side of the bargain (the increment of political power for the Chinese) operated largely by effluxion of time, while the other (the increment of economic power for the Malays) did not.

During the war years, while Malays and Chinese alike had been coming to a new appreciation of the problems of their continued relationship, the British—prompted by administrative considerations, probably by recognition of the need to move toward organized and independent nationhood, and by a combination of wartime disillusionment with the Malays and a sense of indebtedness to the Chinese—had been planning a reorganized version of the Malayan polity. Unveiled in a government White Paper in January, 1946, the intention was to create a unified Malayan state (excluding only Singapore, which was to remain a separate colony) by cession of all separate jurisdiction from the sultans to the British Crown, and to confer citizenship within the new state to all born there or resident for ten out of (effectively) the preceding nineteen years.

As one writer has said, it was "annexation after all,"[15] and Malay opinion was grievously affronted, both by the loss of Malay sovereignty and by the extension of full participatory rights in the state to hundreds of thousands who were still regarded as resident sojourners with external loyalties—though in fact, out of the 2.5 million Chinese in Malaya at the time (comprising 38 per cent of the total population) some 64 per cent were locally born and presumably intended to stay. What had been viewed by its Whitehall originators as a sensible administrative rearrangement elicited from the Malays a remarkable political response, far outshadowing any demonstration of feeling manifested before the war. Resurrecting and building upon prewar state Malay Associations and similar organizations, Malay leaders—pre-eminent among them Onn b. Jaafar of Johore—brought into being within a few weeks a mass Malay movement, the United Malays National Organization (UMNO), to fight the Union scheme. UMNO's protests were in part directed at the Malays' own rulers (many of whom, however, had signed the cession agreements under duress and now rapidly disowned them), but principally at the British Government, in which latter activity they were joined by many "old Malaya hands" among retired administrators in London, who saw the Union as a betrayal of past promises to protect the Malays and the Malay political system.

The effect of these pressures was to inhibit full implementation of the scheme and, within eighteen months, to force its abandonment. Talks among the British Government, the sultans, and UMNO were begun as early as mid-1946 with the object of devising an alternative. Non-Malay response to the Union, initially largely indifferent (a fact that appeared to lend credence to Malay arguments that the Chinese were less interested in local than in overseas political concerns), was somewhat stirred by the exclusively Malay-British composition of the talks and by the likely outcome not merely in terms of deference to Malay interests but in a retreat from some of the more liberal provisions of the Union constitution. In the absence of any coherent, specifically Chinese view, opposition to those probabilities took the form of a broad and rather unstable coalition of mainly left-wing groups, led by the multiracial and socialist Malayan Democratic Union (MDU) and joined by both Chinese Communists and Malay pan-Indonesianists. This popular front was unable to exercise much influence on the course of events, and the consensus that emerged from the official talks (and subsequent taking of evidence from a variety of non-Malays) was for a return to a federal system of government based on the traditional state structure, greatly restricted citizenship, and the introduction of a nonelective legislative council with an appointive unofficial majority, which would, however, be a majority only by virtue of the inclusion of the nine Malay rulers. The new Federation of Malaya was inaugurated on those terms on February 1, 1948. Singapore remained a separate state.

When, at the end of the war, the MPAJA had disbanded itself (though with some safeguarding of arms and internal structure), it appeared that the Malayan Communist Party was, at least for the moment, prepared to pursue by constitutional means its opposition to the restoration of colonial rule. In the circumstances of economic dislocation and social unrest then prevalent, the MCP was able to work most effectively through the industrial labor unions, and in the course of 1946 and early 1947 it established a convincing hold over the labor movement, expressed in the Pan-Malayan Federation of Trades Unions.[16] Though not all industrial labor was Chinese, a large proportion was, and thus, as before the war, the MCP became primarily identified with the Chinese community. Notwithstanding the considerable success that for many months attended MCP attempts to create industrial disorder, British repressive measures, combined with encouragement for non-Communist unionism, proved unproductive. By 1948, faced with a political situation in the peninsula in which conservatism had clearly regained the upper hand and Chinese interests appeared to be losing by default, the Party turned, with the encouragement (if not necessarily at the instigation) of the international Communist movement, to armed revolt. The resulting "Emergency," as it became known, lasted for twelve years, though the back of the revolt was broken by the mid-1950's.

The initial aim of the MCP, and of the Malayan Races Liberation Army (MRLA) it shortly set up, was to subvert the economy by disrupting the rubber plantations and tin mines that provided most of Malaya's wealth, to destroy authority by attacking and defeating government security forces, to win mass local support, and, by these conjoint means, to overthrow the colonial government. Though some early successes were recorded in assassinating European and capitalist Chinese rubber planters and tin miners and in isolated acts of sabotage, the MRLA by 1949 was forced to retire to the jungle, where it engaged in a sporadic guerrilla war, the essence of which was a struggle for the loyalty of the Malayan peoples. Protracted though the struggle was, it early proved an unequal one. Although, through a combination of disaffection and fear of reprisals, numbers of Chinese were prepared to give aid and encouragement to the MRLA, the Malays—comprising nearly half the total, and the larger part of the rural, population—saw the war as pre-eminently a Chinese attempt to gain control of the state, and consequently not only remained loyal to the colonial power but also fought actively against the MRLA. Even where the bulk of the Chinese was concerned, government successes in the field, coupled with evidence of both the intention and the ability to protect most of the populace most of the time, encouraged resistance to MCP demands, and the so-called Briggs' plan of forcibly regrouping in "New Villages" vulnerable Chinese peasant squatting communities from the jungle fringes did much to restrict support for the Communists. Between 1950 and 1952, no fewer than 500,000 Chinese were resettled, in more than 400 areas. During the same period, nearly 10,000 Chinese were deported to metropolitan China.

But the war was above all a political one, and it became increasingly clear to Malays, non-Communist Chinese, and British alike that the only ultimate way to repudiate the MRLA's claim to be a liberation army was by moving toward self-government and independence. At the same time, the British refused to consider self-government until greater national unity of purpose had been achieved by the rival Malay and Chinese communities. The onset of the Emergency in 1948 and the stringent detention and other security measures that accompanied it had engendered something of a moratorium in overt political activity. Leading Chinese, in particular, became increasingly concerned that the Chinese community lacked any politically acceptable organization, comparable to UMNO, to speak for it, and in February, 1949, with the encouragement of the British, a number of well-to-do, Western-educated Chinese (led by the millionaires Tan Cheng Lock and H. S. Lee) were successful in forming a Malayan Chinese Association (MCA). While the MCA's constitution described the association's first aim as "the promotion and maintenance of interracial harmony in Malaya," Tan Cheng Lock, in an inaugural address at Malacca, said that its chief task would be to work to secure justice for the Chinese community.[17] Though the two objectives were not necessarily incompatible, simultaneous pursuit of them created considerable problems of accommodation.

Paradoxically, the existence of two strong communal groupings (UMNO could claim a much more extensive popular base than the MCA, but the leadership of the latter had no effective rival save from the outlawed Communist Party) was greatly to assist the process of compromise. Already, early in 1949, shortly before the formation of the MCA, a British-sponsored Communities Liaison Committee had taken the first steps toward a reconciliation of interests, formulating somewhat more liberal citizenship proposals for the Chinese in return for promises of special economic assistance for the Malays, which were later to bear some fruit in the Rural and Industrial Development Authority. In 1952, with the first democratic elections under the Federation constitution approaching—for the municipality of Kuala Lumpur—the Selangor state branches of UMNO and the MCA agreed to form a temporary pact in the elections, largely in the joint interest of defeating the Independence of Malaya Party (IMP), a noncommunal party formed by Onn b. Jaafar after his break with UMNO over communal questions the previous year. The electoral pact was highly successful—UMNO and the MCA between them took all but two of the contested seats—and despite some misgivings on the part of both strenuous communalists (who tended to see it as a traitorous compromise) and dedicated multiracialists (who saw it as institutionalized separatism), the arrangement rapidly proved so politically productive (at similar elections in Johore Bahru, Muar, and Malacca) that its continuance was assured. In August, 1953, the National Alliance was formally constituted, and, in September a year later, the makeshift "Round Table Conference" that had assisted internal bargaining gave way to a thirty-member National Executive Council. Finally, in October, 1954, the Malayan Indian Congress agreed to join the alliance, thus completing the Malayan communal spectrum.

During 1953, Alliance leaders had become increasingly critical of British tardiness in accepting elective institutions at state and federal levels as a step to independence. They threatened to boycott the existing Legislative Council, in which some of its members held ministerial-level portfolios. Partly as a result of their pressure, the government announced that elections would be held in July, 1955, for fifty-two out of ninety-eight seats in a reorganized Legislative Council. The majority principle and responsible self-government had, in effect, been conceded, though the Alliance complained bitterly at the slenderness of the margin, which, its leaders said, would make it virtually impossible for a single political interest to command a majority in the house. In fact, their anxieties proved unnecessary, for Alliance candidates, campaigning on a platform of immediate self-government and early independence, took fifty-one out of the fifty-two seats—thirty-four of them going to Malays, fifteen to Chinese, and two to Indians. It is noteworthy that, even under the revised (1952) citizenship regulations, the electorate was 80 per cent Malay, for of the 600,000 Chinese eligible to vote (about half the adult population) fewer than one-fourth chose to register. Though the proportions of Chinese enfranchised and registered was to rise markedly in the years to come, many MCA members would continue to depend largely on Malay votes.

The way was now open for *merdeka* (independence), for if the British had initially been reluctant to hand over power to purely communal parties, the success of the Alliance at the polls, and subsequently in government, made it a strong contender for national leadership. Certainly no other was evident. In addition, the character and interest of its leaders—moderate, administration-minded, often aristocratic Malays and well-to-do Chinese and Indian businessmen—seemed to the British to offer future political and economic stability and a reasonable insurance for their own investments. During the long series of constitutional talks that ensued, there was considerable difference of opinion among the communities on certain crucial issues relating to citizenship, language, the status of the Malays, and other questions—issues that illustrated clearly the enormous problems in nation-building that faced the Malayan peoples. UMNO and the MCA, recognizing that neither community could successfully go it alone, finally presented to the British a joint set of Alliance proposals embodying compromises made by both sides. With little further demur, the

British accepted them, and on August 31, 1957, the independent Federation of Malaya came into being. Insofar as they can be briefly summarized, the essential elements of the constitutional compact arrived at were these: continuance of the Malay sultans in each state, acting as constitutional monarchs on the advice of ministers chosen from the majority party in fully elected state legislative assemblies; quinquennial appointment by the rulers from among themselves of a paramount ruler who likewise would act on the advice of ministers responsible to a fully elected national parliament; establishment of Islam as the state religion, within the framework of individual freedom of religion; extension of citizenship to all thenceforward born in Malaya and increasingly, by registration or naturalization, to much larger numbers of Chinese and Indians resident there; determination of Malay as the sole national language at a date to be fixed after the elapse of ten years, while Malay and English continued as the national languages in the interim; and recognition of the special position and needs of the Malays by reservation to them of quotas of entry into the public services, of scholarships, and of certain sorts of economic opportunity.

Meanwhile, the colony of Singapore was also moving toward independence, though more slowly. The principal hindrance in the overwhelmingly Chinese island-city was the British fear that Singapore (and consequently its military base) would succumb to Communist subversion. After a very limited introduction of representative institutions in 1951, a constitutional commission in 1954 recommended a greater measure of democracy (twenty-five out of the thirty-two seats in the Legislative Assembly to be directly elected, the leader of the majority party to be chief minister). At elections in 1955, the moderate left-wing Labour Front, led by the Singapore Jewish lawyer David Marshall, was able to form a coalition government with UMNO and MCA members. Following upon Tengku Abdul Rahman's successful visit to London early in 1956, during which he obtained the assurance of independence, Marshall went on a similar mission in December. He was offered, he complained, only "Christmas pudding with arsenic sauce"—limited independence subject to continued colonial control of defense and internal security. His case had not been helped by widespread Chinese middle school and labor disorders toward the end of the year. Marshall resigned and was replaced by the colony's first Chinese Chief Minister, the Straits-born trade unionist Lim Yew Hock, who in the course of the next year, by pursuing policies of rigor toward dissidents and reassurance toward the British, was able to get a firm promise of independence for 1959. When the 1959 elections for a fully elected Assembly were held, the Labour Front lost the support of the Chinese-educated, and victory went overwhelmingly to the Peoples' Action Party (PAP). Led by an intellectually brilliant Cambridge-educated lawyer, Lee Kuan Yew, the PAP, though essentially a pragmatic socialist party, had gained wide support from the Chinese proletariat by working with more doctrinaire left-wing and Communist groups. Though the party moved, after the election, to subdue its own far left, the possibility of ultimate Communist control of Singapore remained to alarm both the British and the government of the Federation of Malaya.

It was partly for this reason that, in May, 1961, Tengku Abdul Rahman, with British knowledge (but not necessarily at British instigation), proposed the federation of the existing Federation of Malaya with Singapore and the three remaining British-controlled territories in Borneo—Sarawak, Sabah, and Brunei—to form a united Malaysia. The "merger" of Singapore and Malaya alone, in recognition of their long economic interdependence, had often been urged by Singapore politicians and others, although it was unattractive to Malay opinion in the peninsula because of the great increase it would have meant in Chinese population. In the proposed federation of Malaysia, that would be counterbalanced demographically by the indigenous tribal and Malay peoples of the Borneo territories. At the same time, both the Malayan and the British governments probably felt that what they considered dangerous left-wing elements in Singapore might be controlled more successfully if the state were to come within the security ambit of the central government in Kuala Lumpur. The two years following Tengku Abdul Rahman's Malaysia proposals were marked by much confused international politicking, notably Indonesia's armed "confrontation" of the Malaysian states. Though in large part confrontation related as much to Indonesia's troubled domestic politics as to the facts of the case, it also reflected, in part, a genuine belief that Malaysia was a "neocolonial" creation. Ironically, the opposition expressed by confrontation (in which the Philippines also joined for a time) probably did more to weld the new federation together and to create a feeling of national unity in peninsular Malaya than it did to accomplish the reverse. The new state came into being in September, 1963, minus, however, Brunei, which had opted to stay out.

The internal politics of peninsular Malaya were at once affected by the new arrangements, for Lee Kuan Yew's PAP not only decided to take part in the March, 1964, elections there, but did so on the basis of the slogan, "a Malaysian Malaysia"—by which was meant a Malaysia in which no one community (the Malays were clearly intended) should have a monopoly in nation-building and its prerogatives. This struck at the heart of the largely implicit understanding existing between Malay and Chinese partners in the Alliance, threatening the principle of "democracy in camera," by which differences between the two communities were discussed in private by UMNO and MCA leaders and a united front presented to the electorate. The Malay response to the PAP's (and Singapore's) emphatically multiracial style of politics was hostile, and even after the 1964 election (which, fought in the circumstances of Indonesia's confrontation, was won handsomely by the Alliance), tempers remained high. In the fear that Malaysia's (principally peninsular Malaya's) delicate communal balance would be irremediably upset if matters continued in that fashion, in August, 1965, Kuala Lumpur asked Singapore to leave the federation, and the island was thereafter an independent city-state. The PAP government, which continued to exercise unchallenged political sway in Singapore, adopted the view that the two territories were "separated but not divorced," and many on both sides of the causeway hoped for eventual reunification.

Singapore's expulsion from Malaysia led to disquiet in Sarawak and Sabah, the remaining "new members." In those areas, some real resentment remained on the part of the politically very lively Ibans and Kadazans at what was seen as Kuala Lumpur's insistence on the export of the Alliance pattern of politics, which was held to favor the relatively much smaller Malay communities in the two territories. In Sarawak, Chinese unrest also gave the central government cause for anxiety. There was, however, no sign that the federation of Malaysia was about to break up further.

In the peninsula itself, political life after *merdeka* in 1957 continued to be dominated by the working out of the Alliance compact between Malays and Chinese; in this respect, the three general elections held in 1959, 1964, and 1969 are instructive. Both the 1959 and 1969 elections showed a pattern—broken only by the 1964 election, fought in the heightened nationalistic climate of confrontation, when a vote against the Alliance could be represented as a vote for the enemy—of a steady loss of confidence of the Chinese in the capitalist leadership of the MCA. This proved mainly to benefit a rather chauvinist left, and there was a slower drift of Malay opinion away from UMNO's politics of compromise toward the communalism represented by the Pan-Malayan Islamic Party (PMIP).[18] As more and more Chinese came to exercise the vote and to expect a larger share of political power, increasing numbers of Malays came to recognize that language, education, and economic policies were affecting only slowly their generally disadvantaged position. In May, 1969, after a bitterly contested election that demonstrated once and for all the loss of MCA support and the power of the Chinese vote in the cities, communal riots in Kuala Lumpur led to the suspension of parliament and of the democratic process. Though many hoped that democracy and communal partnership could be restored, it was clear that all Malaysians faced an agonizing reassessment of the legacies, and of the challenges, left them by the past.

THE REPUBLIC OF THE PHILIPPINES

At the outbreak of World War II, Commonwealth President Quezon summoned his nation to fight against the Japanese, noting that "no nation is worth anything unless it has learned how to suffer and how to die."[19] The Filipinos rallied to his appeal and to General Douglas MacArthur's charismatic leadership, in part because they felt a debt of obligation (*utang na loob*) to the United States, and in part because they saw the struggle as their war rather than as a confrontation between two imperial powers. The Fil-American forces were driven to the redoubt of Corregidor across Manila Bay. Rapid Japanese victories doomed MacArthur's defense; the American relief fleet was rusting at Pearl Harbor. Just prior to the surrender of the Fil-American forces and the Bataan Death March, MacArthur, Quezon, and Osmeña were evacuated—MacArthur to plan the reconquest, Quezon and Osmeña to maintain a government in exile. The Japanese, who had in the meantime occupied the city of Manila on January 2, 1942, persuaded most of the prewar Manila elite left behind to collaborate with them. With the notable exceptions of Chief Justice José Abad Santos, the opposition leader Juan Sumulong, and a few others, the elite saw it as its duty to rally to Jorge Vargas, Quezon's former Executive Secretary, and join the Philippine Executive Commission. The same elite subsequently served under the successor government, the Japanese-sponsored Philippine Republic led by José P. Laurel. A great many Filipinos, however, did not follow its leadership. Hundreds of thousands actively joined the guerrilla movement to fight for MacArthur's and Quezon's promised return. While individual motivation for joining the guerrillas varied, the fact of continued resistance opened a serious gap between the decisions of the elite and those of the common man.

Human carnage, physical destruction, and the confusion over wartime behavior combined to leave the country divided and uncertain. Many Filipinos felt cheated, despite their sacrifice, by history. In the process of reconquest, the country was ravaged. Manila was, with Warsaw, one of the most-damaged cities of World War II. Since the modern sector of the nation was almost exclusively within that urban environment, the precious resources of universities, hospitals, port facilities, banks, libraries, and, most important, trained citizenry were lost. The physical suffering exacerbated the crisis in human values. Japanese propagandists had consistently argued to the Filipinos that "regardless of whether you like it or not, you are Filipinos and belong to the Oriental race. No matter how hard you try, you cannot become white people."[20] The appeal for an "Asia for the Asiatics" touched an exposed nerve, for it challenged the initial decision to fight and die. Moreover, the war opened cracks in the society that might never have appeared in peace. The exigencies of the occupation polarized the community between urban and rural, elite and mass, landlord and tenant, guerrilla and collaborator.

Since the Japanese were concentrated in population centers, urban Filipinos lived under constraints not felt by those in remote areas. The collaboration issue touched the political, economic, diplomatic, social, and moral aspects of postwar national development, creating dissonance in all of them. In a colonial milieu, collaboration was a concomitant of foreign rule; the decision of the Filipino elite to cooperate with the Japanese was in some ways similar to earlier collaboration with the Spanish and American regimes. The question, however, was whether in the intervening forty years Philippine nationalism had rendered such action not only anachronous but treasonable. If the elite were thought of as having ignored a national consensus expressed in the guerrilla movement and in the anti-Japanese sentiment of the populace, then "collaboration" had pejorative connotations. Had the Philippine elite, by a stroke of irony, having created and articulated the national code of values, been guilty of violating it through collaboration? The wartime leaders vehemently denied that they had. They argued that they "should be credited with the highest sense of patriotism," since the suffering of the people, great as it was, would have been worse if the elite had forsaken the nation "in that grave hour of peril for the Filipino race." They defended collaboration by arguing that "during those moments of confusion and bewilderment, it was possible to entertain different conceptions of how best to serve one's country."[21] The question of whether or not such a claim was valid divided the country.

Sergio Osmeña, who had become President when Quezon died in exile in 1944, was in a difficult situation, since he returned as prosecutor rather than as leader of his peer group. MacArthur had initially arrested all the collaborators except Quezon's heir presumptive, Manuel Roxas. Roxas became their leader, split the dominant Nacionalista party by creating his own Liberal party, attracted to himself key wartime officials now on bail, and forced Osmeña to accept support from fringe groups like the Huks, who had hitherto been denied access to political power. Roxas was younger than Osmeña, seemed far more dynamic, had the open support of MacArthur, and gained the backing of powerful elements in the society. Osmeña, exhausted, refused to campaign and was defeated by Roxas in the Presidential election. The collaboration issue was left to the specially created People's Court, although Roxas and his supporters claimed that the electorate had vindicated them. Of the many political collaborators initially arrested, only the very first one indicted was ever convicted prior to Roxas's amnesty proclamation in 1948.

The nation elected Roxas because it felt that it had to have its prewar elite at the helm at independence. The reality of continuing control, however, had both tangible and intangible consequences. The ability of the prewar elite to retain office made it seem that there was no crime, not even the most serious social crime of treason, that could keep these men from power. Although José Laurel had stated during the war that "public office is a public trust. The beneficiaries of an established government are the people and the people only,"[22] the rewards of office rather than its duties seemed paramount. The prewar elite's retention of power also led many former guerrillas, including the Hukbalahap, to see their sacrifice as wasted. On the eve of independence on July 4, 1946, therefore, many in the nation were bitter rather than ecstatic, bruised rather than vigorous, cynical and callous rather than idealistic and hopeful. The war had drained away much of the romanticism and youthfulness that had been present in Philippine nationalism, and what was left was at the same time more strident and more uncertain.

Despite Roxas's close friendship with MacArthur, the Philippine-American relationship also soured. Filipinos felt they had given their national treasure to the American cause. The American debt of gratitude, therefore, should have been enormous. Instead, Filipinos were bitter that America had turned its attention to other areas of the world, all but forgetting the "spirit of Bataan." While American aid was forthcoming, it was less generous than the Filipinos felt they deserved and was subject to conditions that were demeaning and neocolonial. The Americans imposed economic and military restrictions on the Philippines, using aid as a lever to gain concessions. The dream of independence had become something of a nightmare.

In this highly unstable situation, therefore, it is not surprising that the Hukbalahap turned against the government. The problems of tenancy, poverty, demography, and frustrated expectations had plagued the central Luzon rice provinces for decades. The radical right-wing Sakdalista uprising of the Commonwealth era demonstrated the explosive potential in that region. Socialist and Communist organizers had moved into the area in the late 1930's, but it was the phenomena of the worldwide united front and the anti-Japanese guerrilla movement that gave shape to the Hukbalahap (the People's Anti-Japanese Army). The degree of external influence upon this movement remains unclear to this day; while Communists were active in organization and in supplying an ideological umbrella, the core of the movement was provincial and indigenous—a reaction against tenancy abuse, absentee landlordism, and grinding poverty. Led by a charismatic peasant, Luis Taruc, the movement also was anti-elite and anti-urban. There were sharp differences between the intelligentsia in the Manila Politburo and Taruc. The resultant tension inhibited the Hukbalahap from moving out of its regional, rural base and becoming a national movement.

Corruption, low morale, inflation, and economic exhaustion prevented the Manila government from defeating the Huks, however. Roxas, prior to his death in office in 1948, and his successor, Elpidio Quirino, simply lacked the strength or appeal to break the agrarian uprising, even though the United States was channeling increasing amounts of aid both for rehabilitation and to prevent "America's showcase of democracy" from going Communist. The 1949 Presidential election, in which Quirino defeated the wartime President, José Laurel, through bribery, fraud, and violence, shook people's confidence in the democratic procedure. In 1950, the country went through an economic, moral, political, and military crisis. In October of that year, the Central Bank had to borrow $50 million in order to meet government payrolls. Production levels remained low; the country's economy suffered inflation as a result of American aid; the sense of malaise was growing; and the Huks were predicting victory.

The emergence of Ramón Magsaysay altered the history of the Philippines. Magsaysay, a guerrilla leader during the war and thus free of the taint of collaboration, became Quirino's Secretary of Defense.

He made three great contributions in his years as Secretary. First, he infused a corrupt and demoralized army with a new sense of purpose and *esprit de corps*, so that the army became a relatively effective weapon against the Huk military units. Second, Magsaysay's intelligence network enabled him to arrest en masse the Communist Party Politburo and to seize documents that listed sympathizers. Third, and most important, he called out the army to guarantee that the 1951 congressional elections would be honest. By protecting the ballot box he restored a degree of confidence in the electoral process that kept many loyal to the system of government. His flair, his relatively humble origins, his wartime record, and his accessibility to the masses made him an easy victor in the Presidential election of 1953. Gathering a brain trust of bright young men, he broke the Hukbalahap uprising by a combination of heavy military pressure against those who refused to surrender, amnesty for those who did, and a series of resettlement schemes to ease tenancy in the Huk areas. He was only partially able to translate his popularity into a legislative program, both because Congress remained the bastion of the prewar group and because he lacked the temperament and political sophistication to get his measures, such as nationwide land reform, passed undiluted. By the time of his death in a plane crash in 1957, however, he had done much to restore vitality and cohesiveness to the nation.

In the years since his death, there has been a treadmill succession. There is almost no difference between the two political parties. Politicians shift party allegiance whenever there seems to be any personal advantage in doing so. Magsaysay's Vice President, Carlos Garcia, was elected to a full term in office in 1957. He was, in turn, defeated by Diosdado Macapagal in 1961, who, in turn, was defeated by Ferdinand Marcos in 1965. In 1969, Marcos became the first man since independence to win a second full term, defeating Sergio Osmeña Jr. in a bloody and corrupt election. Interestingly, Osmeña was hampered by the accusation that he had been a collaborator during the war, whereas Marcos was a famous guerrilla leader.

In one way, the succession of presidents may demonstrate that the Philippines has been a working democracy: Men in power have yielded office peacefully if defeated. However, to take another view, the government has been controlled by a single oligarchy, which shares power, a fact that the interchangeability of party affiliation has tended to confirm. Since a man can fulfill his obligations to kith and kin in one full term of office, there seems to have been a tacit understanding that he must not indulge greed by seeking to overextend his tenure. Marcos's retention of power has interrupted the system, sapping some of the optimism of those who have always believed that the next administration would solve the nation's problems and lead the people to their elusive dream of freedom, prosperity, and equality.

The stability of the oligarchic system has been increasingly challenged by those who see it as a neocolonial inheritance and as a self-seeking device for the perpetuation of an entrenched elite. Urban and rural blight, tenancy abuses, blatant corruption, and gross violations of social justice are among the complaints of those out of power, especially the students. To misquote Marx, the rich have got richer and the poor have begotten children. Violence and the potential for revolution have rapidly increased as the quality of life has deteriorated for all but the rich. Philippine society must now either restructure its priorities and redistribute its wealth through evolutionary means or be prepared to encounter revolution. One hundred years after the *ilustrados,* under the leadership of idealistic students like Rizal, began the Filipino revolution and arrogated to themselves the national leadership, another generation of students has turned against the direct lineal heirs of the original *ilustrados,* the present elite. The nation now stands at a critically important crossroads; it will not be able to linger there for long. The Constitutional Convention, scheduled to convene in 1971 to redraft the Philippine Constitution (promulgated in 1935), and the renegotiation by 1974 of many major agreements with the United States will mark the direction of the nation.

THE REPUBLIC OF INDONESIA

At the outbreak of war in 1941, the Netherlands Indies was in a nearly perfect state of what the Dutch called *rust en orde,* calm and order. The rapid changes of the previous decades, while creating deep social tensions, had not shattered colonial stability. Dutch rule, occasionally disturbed earlier in the century, was secure and nowhere effectively challenged from within. Indies society—a mosaic of numerous folk societies and small, ethnically defined urban communities—was intact in its complex order. The small, mainly Dutch-educated elite of "Indonesians" was itself just another such urban community embedded—alongside similar Dutch, Eurasian, and *totok* and *peranakan* Chinese ones—within the frame of the plural Indies structure.

The Japanese occupation ended the old order, overturning the politically and economically dominant elites, herding the *totok* Dutch into concentration camps, and harassing Chinese and Eurasians in various ways. By hasty improvisation, the Japanese drastically simplified the Indies' plural legal structure and, more important, the plural education system, which it replaced with a unitary system using Indonesian as the medium of instruction. The export industries collapsed, unbacked occupation currency caused a huge inflation, and rationing led to black markets and widespread corruption. Hundreds of thousands of peasants were marched off as slave labor to die in various parts of Southeast Asia.

In one sense Japanese rule simply exchanged one externally based colonial power for another. The Japanese maintained the basic Dutch administrative system, continuing to rule through established elites like the Javan *priyayi.* But their political style was fundamentally different: Where the Dutch were conservative and aimed to keep their subjects quiet, the Japanese were totalitarian and sought to stir them up. They mounted a relentless, provocative propaganda campaign designed to enlist the energies of their new subjects in their own desperate war effort. On Java, where the occupation had its strongest impact, the Japanese set out to enlist the Muslim and secular nationalist elites in their cause. In particular, a series of Japanese-run, essentially powerless but widely publicized mass organizations gave the nationalist intelligentsia opportunities (inconceivable in the Dutch era) to build networks and to gain access to a broad public. Established prewar leaders, such as Sukarno and Mohammed Hatta, publicly supported Japan in order to spread the nationalist idea of Indonesia. The Japanese actively indoctrinated young people in schools and a host of special organizations. In PETA (Pembela Tanah Air: Defenders of the Fatherland), finally, the Japanese built up a well-trained military force of 65,000, officered up to the battalion level by Indonesians—a development quite without colonial precedent.

Japanese rule ended in August, 1945, as abruptly as it had begun and before most of the Indies had been reconquered by the Allies. Competing forces moved quickly to fill the vacuum of power thus created. The first to act were the older-generation nationalists who had built up a momentum of leadership during the Japanese occupation. In Jakarta on August 17, two days after the Japanese surrender, Sukarno and Hatta proclaimed the independence of Indonesia. In the next two weeks, a small committee quickly sketched the outlines of the new Indonesian state: a constitution, a cabinet, Sukarno as President, and Hatta as Vice-President. The colonial response came soon enough; on September 29, the first British army units began landing at Jakarta. Representing the victorious Allies and, in particular, the Dutch Government, they supported Dutch administrators whose task was to restore Dutch colonial rule.

The ensuing collision opened a long and bitter struggle, which lasted until the achievement of Indonesian political independence in December, 1949. More important, it precipitated a mass movement, a violent upheaval that completed the destruction of prewar Indies society and deeply influenced the character of the emerging Indonesian society. It was this social upheaval, and not simply the political fight for independence, that made the Indonesian Revolution the central event and experience in modern Indonesian history.

The mass movement rose first because of the sudden disappearance of effective government. The Japanese administration had collapsed overnight; the British had few troops available and were only marginally interested; the Dutch had the motive and a precedent for rule but, until 1947, few troops; the Republic, finally, was at first only an idea, with almost no machinery for enforcing its will. In any society, absence of government stirs deep fears and generates powerful impulses aimed at recovering the lost commonwealth. In Indonesia, in September, 1945, those emotions were fixed most immediately and massively on the symbol of the Indonesian Republic, and the mass movement, which arose with startling suddenness, was founded on an impassioned Indonesian nationalism.

It was mostly men and women between fifteen and thirty who responded in this way, and hence the outpouring is called the *pemuda* movement.[23] The movement swept over *pemuda* of all classes and ethnic groups, uniting them in a common commitment to the cause of independence and a powerful sense of liberation and idealism. *Priyayi pemuda* dropped their titles and abbreviated their aristocratic names; men vowed not to cut their hair until freedom had been achieved; girls left home to work in the Indonesian Red Cross; a cult of heroes sprang up. The primarily political energies, moreover, spilled over into other domains, producing a flowering of specifically Indonesian painting, fiction, and poetry inconceivable a few years earlier and as yet unsurpassed.

The other side of idealism, of course, is fanaticism. The political significance of the *pemuda* movement lay in the violence it mobilized and sanctioned. It began in late September with attacks on Japanese posts in many areas, progressed to fighting the British, and reached one climax in the battle of Surabaya in early November, in which the larger part of a British division would have been destroyed had Sukarno not intervened. The movement's domestic political impact, however, was more significant. In the extreme disorder it created throughout Java and Sumatra, all established claims to political and social leadership were subject to a drastic test. Those unable to justify themselves, to adapt to revolutionary conditions, or to defend themselves were abused, driven out, or killed. Minority groups—Dutch, Chinese, Eurasians, and Ambonese—suffered particularly heavily from looting and atrocities. A wave of local "social revolutions" spread over the whole area between Acheh and Surakarta between late 1945 and mid-1946, overturning the traditional elites on which Dutch, Japanese, and now Republican rule rested.

The most violent, and politically significant, phase of the *pemuda* movement lasted from September, 1945, to mid-1946. During that period, and long after, *pemuda* associated themselves loosely in what were called *badan perdjuangan,* spontaneous local groupings usually formed around a leader with charismatic qualities.[24] Hundreds, perhaps thousands, of groups emerged, dissolved, and combined in the tumult; the *badan perdjuangan,* one of the key institutions of the revolutionary years, was the most characteristic manifestation of the *pemuda* movement. During the same period, however, certain *pemuda* leaders and groups began to build a national army. In some cases PETA companies —which had all been disbanded by the Japanese immediately after the surrender—reconstituted themselves; in others, PETA officers or others organized their own units. Over the years, as the local units aggregated into battalions and divisions and the hierarchical military routine slowly established itself, the army developed as a major independent political force.

The enormous but unchanneled power of the *pemuda* movement

decisively influenced political developments at the national level. It brought what was from one viewpoint a struggle between two small elite groups—the Dutch and the Dutch-educated Indonesian intelligentsia—out into the arena of mass politics. In particular, it greatly complicated the affairs of the small group of older nationalists who had founded the Republic. These men had declared independence and created the Republic, but they lacked a mass organization like the Viet Minh because they had been isolated from the masses both by Dutch and Japanese design and by their own precocious cultural and political development. Nor did they have much taste or aptitude for military organization. During the first months of the revolution, they made no serious effort to establish a national army, which left the field wide open for *pemuda*. As a group, the founders and leaders of the Republic were urban politicians—committee men and orators. Characteristically, they organized themselves in terms of political parties, which grew in great profusion in late 1945 and after. Few if any of their parties gained mass followings during the revolution; like their predecessors, the prewar parties, they were mainly vehicles of intra-elite politics. During the revolution, cabinets rose and fell regularly without changing the basic policy of the Republic.

That policy was *diplomasi*, a program for attaining independence by negotiating with the Dutch and by mobilizing international opinion. *Diplomasi* was the antithesis of the *pemuda* ideal of *perdjuangan*, an uncompromising armed struggle for total independence. The question of *diplomasi* or *perdjuangan* became the overriding issue of domestic politics throughout the revolution. Each of the five cabinets that fell during the revolution resigned because of a public outcry against the concessions it had made to the Dutch—a protest always supported by parties and factions out of power. Each of the succeeding cabinets carried on the same basic *diplomasi*, with the support of former advocates of *perdjuangan* currently in power and, always, of Hatta and Sukarno.

Until mid-1947, the Dutch were quite as willing as the Republicans to negotiate. Holland was exhausted by the German occupation. Moreover, the Dutch were lucky, with the help of the British and the Republic, to be able to hold out against the *pemuda* in their enclaves in the major cities of Java and Sumatra. The negotiations themselves dragged on until November, 1946, when they produced a compromise satisfactory to neither party. Meanwhile, the Dutch had reoccupied the more sparsely populated islands outside Java and Sumatra with little resistance. In December, 1946, they established the state of East Indonesia, comprising the Celebes, Bali, and the rest of the eastern archipelago, as the first in a series of regional member states in a projected federal system, which they could expect to control from the center.

By July, 1947, the Dutch had assembled enough divisions to launch a

"Police Action" in which they easily seized West and East Java and the plantation and oil areas of East and South Sumatra. Though the United Nations began to intervene at that point, the Dutch were able, in January, 1948, to compel the government of the Republic to accept those conquests. In the occupied areas, they quickly established new federal member states based politically on more conservative social groups—hereditary elites, former cooperating nationalists, Chinese, Eurasians and others—which were badly shaken by the *pemuda* movement. The next step was logical: In December, 1948, the Dutch began their second "Police Action," quickly occupying virtually all the remaining Republican territory and capturing Sukarno, Hatta and other major leaders.

The success of the campaign proved fatal, however. The Indonesian army, released from the restraints of *diplomasi*, began guerrilla war; the United Nations turned strongly against Dutch policy; the leaders of many of the new federal states, nationalists too, took a more independent political line. The Dutch were forced to give way; the Republican leaders, as always, were ready to negotiate. The Hague Agreement of November 2 brought a settlement: a sovereign Republic of the United States of Indonesia, in which the revolutionary Republic was one of sixteen member states; temporary retention of western New Guinea by the Dutch; and guarantees for Dutch investments in Indonesia. On December 27, 1949, the Dutch flag was hauled down for the last time, and Indonesia became free.

Political independence was only the most tangible of the legacies of the struggle. In the course of the revolutionary upheaval, the Indonesian language had acquired a new emotional significance and the unitary Indonesian school system had been permanently rooted; the base for a common national culture had been laid. By translating the political idea of Indonesia into a cause, the *pemuda* movement had broadened the political base. Many vestiges of the old order remained, however. The great majority of Indonesians still lived in a cultural universe dominated by the traditional regional languages they spoke, while the national elite still thought mainly in Dutch. And, although in the early months of 1950 a popular movement quickly overthrew the Dutch-made federal states, and although on August 17, 1950, Indonesia was formally proclaimed a unitary state, the economic provisions of the compromise settlement reached in the Hague Agreement were more deeply entrenched. The guarantees to foreign investment and other provisions implied a continuation of colonial economic patterns, and, indeed, in 1950 Dutch, Chinese, and other aliens still dominated the economy of a now politically Indonesian country. The large Chinese minority, *totok* and *peranakan* alike, stirred by the emergence of a strong and united China in 1949, was more Chinese than ever. Nevertheless, the context in which those features persisted was now unambiguously Indonesian. The mood was confident: These were problems to be solved on the way to building a modern Indonesia. In 1950, no one anticipated how difficult and painful these tasks were to be.

The politics of the postindependence period were dominated by two basic factors. The first was economic, and beneath that, ecological. Indonesia was an agrarian country, dependent on export for foreign exchange, and its peasant labor force was ill-prepared for industrialization. More fundamentally, its population was growing, overwhelming the land: 70 million in 1940, 27 million more by 1961, 120 million in 1970. The second basic factor was more immediately apparent. The revolutionary upheaval had accelerated the making of a nation, but it had also created greater expectations among greater numbers of people. The veterans of the *perdjuangan* expected personal prosperity with the independence they felt they had assured. The graduates of the rapidly expanding school system of the 1950's pressed into an equally rapidly expanding bureaucracy. At the same time, the revolution had sharply accentuated internal divisions. Chinese and Indonesians each had much stronger grounds for mistrust than they had had five years earlier. New Indonesian institutions—the army, political parties, government departments—had emerged, but their interests often clashed. In some areas, such as East Sumatra, ethnic differences had become open ethnic hostilities after clashes in the revolution. In West Java, South Celebes, and Acheh, Islamic groups, stirred up by the revolution and hostile to the triumphant secular state, launched rebellions in the cause of an Islamic state. The Communist Madiun Rebellion in 1948, rising mainly out of party politics at the national level, had led to savage fighting between Javanese *santri* and *abangan* in the villages.

The two sets of conditions—economic and ecological, on the one hand, and social and psychological, on the other—combined to determine the main line of political events after 1950. Individuals and groups struggled fiercely for a share of the small surplus yielded by the agrarian economy, or just for a place in the overcrowded landscape. This struggle, in turn, exacerbated not only group hostilities but also deep psychological and ideological tensions. A spirit of national unity had created an independent Indonesia, but Indonesia was more divided than ever. The more bitterly men clashed, the more deeply they yearned to restore the lost sense of community.

During the first three years of independence, a series of conservative cabinets, working through the provisional parliament, which appointed and dismissed them, concentrated on the practical jobs of repairing the ravages of a decade of chaos and on restoring the economy to something resembling its prewar condition. Their task was eased by the national mood of optimism, the patronage they commanded in establishing the organs of a new state, and the Korean War boom for Indonesian export products.

Those favorable circumstances came to an end in late 1952, and the intensity of conflict grew steadily over the next three years. Party politics became more bitter and divisive; Muslim Reformists and traditionalists split into two separate parties, while the PKI (Communist Party) made a remarkable recovery from its debacle at Madiun. More important, the political parties, up to that point representing mainly small urban elites, made their first serious efforts to build up mass support in preparation for the elections to be held in 1955; they thus introduced the conflicts of urban politics directly into village life. Meanwhile, governments and parties, faced by falling export revenues and rising demands from their urban constituents, developed devices that were to be used more and more heavily up to 1965. One was deficit financing, which started a cycle of rapid inflation. The other was antiforeign, especially anti-Chinese, economic nationalism.

The elections of 1955, though a great success as an act of popular franchise, ended parliamentary democracy; the election of the old politicians to parliament belied the hopes that new groups would find new solutions. Between 1956 and 1958, the parties, parliament, and the cabinet collapsed as major political institutions, and new political forces rose in their stead. In Sumatra and Celebes, export areas whose foreign exchange went primarily to feed Java and to support urban elites concentrated there, local army commanders asserted local autonomy in a series of coups beginning in December, 1956. By early 1958, the movement had proclaimed a rebel Indonesian government, which took several years to suppress. Meanwhile, the PKI grew rapidly, and the army gained wide administrative powers with the declaration of martial law in March, 1957. After December, 1957, when, following a United Nations rebuff to Indonesia's claims to western New Guinea, all Dutch enterprises in Indonesia were seized, the army gained control of a large new pool of patronage. Finally, President Sukarno, as the one intact symbol of Indonesian unity, played an increasingly active role in national politics.

In mid-1959, Sukarno abrogated the provisional constitution and inaugurated Guided Democracy. During the next six years, political power rested in a stable though competitive alliance between the army and Sukarno, who was supported by a lesser third partner, the PKI. To foreigners, the policies of Guided Democracy seemed irrational in the face of falling exports, insufficient food supplies, and an epic inflation. The government launched two major "confrontations"—the first (1960–62) against Holland for recovery of New Guinea, which it successfully negotiated in 1962, the second (begun in 1963) against the newly formed state of Malaysia. For the purpose it imported great quantities of expensive military equipment from Russia. It also built a large sports stadium complex and many monuments it could equally ill afford. It disrupted commerce with a ban on Chinese trading in rural areas and expropriated British and Indian enterprises. Sukarno himself propagated an unending stream of new slogans, which became part of an official ideology in which all civil servants and students were indoctrinated. Westerners were concerned at a steady movement toward diplomatic association with China, at Sukarno's ever more frequent use of Communist ideas, and at his public support of the PKI.

Guided Democracy, however, was a natural and logical extension of the political trend of the previous nine years. The large budget deficits, the expropriations, and the arms imports were all devices to provide reserves of patronage with which to placate the bureaucracy, the army, and the urban elite in general, and thus to prevent the kind of slide toward civil war that had begun in the late 1950's. The aggressive foreign policy and the building projects were efforts to restore a sunken national morale. Sukarno's empty slogans, as they seemed to outsiders, were a serious effort to re-create political and ideological unity, a new "language" through which to master reality. In the face of virtually insoluble economic and ecological problems and deepening internal divisions, they were desperate attempts to preserve Indonesia.

In the longer run, it may turn out that those six extraordinary years did in fact preserve and deepen the union. But in the short run, they led, amid mounting excitation, to a crisis. On October 1, 1965, a group of junior army officers assassinated some of the leading generals and proclaimed their assumption of power under Sukarno. The origins of the coup are still obscure, but it was soon widely believed—as may have been the case—that the PKI was behind it. At any rate, it was the aftermath of the coup—suppressed within a day by forces under General Suharto—that was decisive. Suharto's leadership in the moment of crisis gave him momentum and authority. In the following months, he led the army in a campaign against the PKI, while Sukarno, his program and leadership threatened, exerted his immense prestige in counterattack. The struggle paralyzed the urban elite and government, creating a growing vacuum of power like that of 1945, and generated terrible consequences. During late 1965 and early 1966, throughout the rural areas of Central and East Java, Bali, and several other regions, hundreds of thousands of peasant members of the PKI were massacred, systematically and almost without resistance, by their neighbors. In the Javanese areas, where the numbers of victims were greatest, it was Muslim youth groups that took the lead in the slaughter, acting out the latest chapter in the conflict between *santri* and *abangan*.[25]

Amid those horrors, in March, 1966, Sukarno was pushed from power by the army and by an urban *pemuda* movement consciously modeled on that of 1945. A new regime under General Suharto consolidated its power cautiously, taking care to absorb as much of the legitimacy of its predecessor—and especially of Sukarno himself—as it could and, at the same time, gradually staking out a new image. In many respects, it returned to the policies and style of the cabinets of the first three years of independence: practical, problem-oriented, seeking economic stability and development, and accepting a major role for Western economic interests and influence. Whether the cycle would continue in the same way again, only time could tell.

34

THE POSTWAR ARENA: DOMESTIC AND INTERNATIONAL THEMES

The political histories of Southeast Asian countries after the Pacific war were heavily conditioned by a mixture of socio-economic and international factors as complex as they were apparent. Continuing population growth was the most outstanding and pervasive of them.

DEMOGRAPHY

The population of Southeast Asia in 1940 was approximately 145 million; by the mid-1960's it had swollen to 250 million and was continuing to grow at an annual rate somewhere between 2.5 and 3.5 per cent. The Philippines, which is perhaps the fastest growing nation, grew from 19 million in 1948 to about 38 million in 1970; it is now the fifteenth largest country in the world and faces the prospect of perhaps 100 million citizens by the century's end. Indonesia, one of the slowest growing, added 27 million between 1940 and the 1961 census. Java, if it were a separate country, would be the eighth largest in the world. Indonesia, with about 120 million people, is now the world's fifth most populous state. Even war-torn Vietnam has undergone a population explosion, which has kept Vietnam the largest society on the mainland. The upward population curve is constant everywhere throughout Southeast Asia.

Such demographic growth not only threatened the prospects of any revolutionary economic gains in Southeast Asia but also challenged whatever traditional capacities Southeast Asian societies possessed for feeding their own people. Equally important, in many areas, Southeast Asia's population problem was intimately connected to its economic subordination to the West during the colonial period. To the historian, the experience of Java is especially enlightening. The Dutch made Java a prodigious exporter of sugar, coffee, and other raw materials. The economic logic behind their development policy was significant: The age of political imperialism was also the age of ecological interdependence, in which the expanding Western industry of the nineteenth and early twentieth centuries required such ancillary raw materials as rubber, as well as vast amounts of tropical labor to produce them. In the postcolonial period, however, more sophisticated industrial processes, capable of dispensing with tropical raw materials like rubber, became general in the West, as scientists learned how to synthesize nearly all the materials Western machines needed.

But the short-lived age of ecological interdependence had been responsible in part for Java's population boom. And the population kept rising as the Western demand for Javanese products first grew, then leveled off, and finally declined. This is an oversimplified summary of a very complex pattern, for other factors—including medical progress—also contributed to population growth. But population expansion was Dutch colonialism's most durable monument in Indonesia.[26] As a consequence, people on Java by 1940 had begun cultivating land that should have been left uncleared. In such a situation, land reform as a solution was almost irrelevant, for the problem was lack of enough land in general, not how it was distributed.

Population pressures nonetheless helped to make the issue of land reform an unprecedented storm center for postwar politicians through most of the region. It was not certain that land reform by itself would unequivocally guarantee agricultural development. Improvements in rural transportation, marketing, farm technology, education, and production credit facilities were also needed, although they were less popular as revolutionary slogans. On the other hand, land reform at the very least promised the peasant social and psychological emancipation, prefiguring a society in which the sum of the existing wealth, no matter how inadequate, would be more evenly distributed. In the Philippines, population pressure and the impossibility of reviving the American policy of resettlement on the Mindanao frontier made land reform in the face of increases in absentee landlordism a crucial issue. However, land ownership remained the most desired form of economic investment for the rich. The political elite had become an indistinguishable part of the landlord class. Under these circumstances, land reform legislation, like that of 1955 and 1963, was not made effective enough to improve the situation. American specialists who visited the Philippines in 1951 concluded that the unreformed land tenure system thwarted all efforts for technological improvement in agriculture. The Filipino elite was greatly angered at the bluntness with which that view was expressed.

Colonial and postcolonial population growth in Vietnam required an end to the stagnation of traditional agriculture there. Such stagnation was caused more by the nature of the peasant's position in the traditional rural social structure—a position in which he owed continuing economic debts to his landlord and social debts to a swarm of relatives—than it was by deficient agricultural instruction in the schools or by the academically oriented values of the Vietnamese elite, although they were factors too. The revolutionary regime at Hanoi, seeking also to increase state tax revenues from rural Vietnam in order to finance immediate industrialization, reduced land rents and established rent controls, confiscated the lands of "reactionaries" and gave them to landless peasants, and created special "people's tribunals" to judge those who had broken the new land laws. Sophisticated as that land reform blueprint might have been, its potential effectiveness was reduced by the disorganized radicalism of poorly trained Communist cadres in the villages themselves. According to Pham Van Dong, the Prime Minister, the land reform program had called for reliance upon the poor peasants, unity with the middle peasants, and a coalition with rich peasants for the sake of a concerted attack upon large landlords who opposed the Communist Party. In fact, the Party cadres who carried out the program behaved not like social engineers but like a conspiratorial oligarchy, causing poor peasants to "suffer losses" in certain places, attacking middle peasants, treating rich peasants like landlords rather than entering a coalition with them, and treating all landlords as enemies instead of giving special recognition to landlords who had contributed sons to the army or to the Party itself.[27]

Even if it had not attempted such a highly political redistribution of resources at the same time, land reform in the Red River delta, involving as it did an assault against centuries-old landholding patterns, was a complex proposition. As a result of the "errors" in the program described by Pham Van Dong, rural uprisings against the Hanoi regime occurred; the most famous, at Quynh Luu in Nghe An Province in 1956, reportedly was spearheaded by Catholic dissidents and included assaults upon public security offices. In southern Vietnam, where landlordism was more severe, much more limited land reform schemes proved failures in the 1950's. Although the Diem government registered some 700,000 rent contracts in order to provide security of tenure to tenant farmers and even, on paper, expropriated about 1 million acres of privately owned rice lands, many large landowners evaded redistribution of land merely by transferring portions of their holdings to other members of their family.

The situation also remained grave but unresolved in Malaya, where between one-half and two-thirds of all rice planters were tenant farmers. Incomes were extremely low, rent varied from one-third to two-thirds of the crop, and between the landlord (Malay) and the middleman (Chinese), the Malay peasant was becoming proletarianized. Rural development programs, framed with an awareness that Malaya was still importing about 50 per cent of its needs in rice, stressed seed improvement, drainage and irrigation, double cropping (in Kuala Kedah, for example), credit provision, cooperative marketing, and price supports. But fragmentation of landholdings, called for by customary and Islamic law, was one important obstacle to land reform, and the association of political power with landholding another. Despite the general prosperity of the Malayan economy, the trend of productivity in the peasant sector was downward rather than upward. Insofar as this affected the Malays in the rural areas (and about 70 per cent of the total rural population is Malay), it meant that in 1958 probably nearly 20 per cent more people were living off the same, or possibly slightly less, total production than had been ten years before.[28]

Prospects of landlessness and near-landlessness were less common and less oppressive among Thai peasants. In Thailand of the late 1960's, pressures on the land and inequitable landholding patterns were not a serious problem, except in certain limited areas. Overall, 82 per cent of all peasants owned the land that they worked, although landlordism was especially common in areas where double-cropping was possible: 90 per cent of all peasants owned their land in the northeast, 74 per cent in the north, 75 per cent in the central region, and 84 per cent in the south. Government efforts to improve the lot of the peasant took the form of extending agricultural credit through a new (1966) Bank for Agriculture and Cooperatives capitalized at 1 billion baht ($50 million).

Apart from the fact that at least some Southeast Asian societies, like Thailand, are not required to eliminate, almost overnight, productivity-limiting economic inequities originally called into existence by outmoded social structures, technology itself may assist in the short run to preserve a balance between population and supporting resources. For example, in addition to remedies like improved chemical fertilizers, breakthroughs have been made by the International Rice Research Institute in the Philippines. This internationally sponsored organization, located at Los Baños in Luzon, has developed a rice seed bank in which new, faster-growing, disease-resistant hybrid rice strains have been bred. Different strains of this "miracle rice" are now growing commercially all over Southeast Asia. The most promising aspect of that development is that the use of such rice strains means larger yields per unit of land, even in the context of traditional agricultural techniques, lack of water and poor soils.

Thus, the significance of the contemporary Southeast Asian struggle to feed growing populations is not that a historically determined disaster is inevitable and is already in sight, although one may come, but that economic modernization must occur, if at all, in circumstances very different from those of North America and early modern Europe. Environments of increasingly dense populations, rather than of free lands and easy access to a bountiful nature, must somehow stimulate entrepreneurial ambitions and initiatives on the part of both governments and individual men.

THE POLITICAL-ADMINISTRATIVE SETTING

With the end of the colonial period in those Southeast Asian societies that had known colonization, indigenous elites assumed control over colonially created bureaucracies. Having inherited the machinery, they then set out to make it serve what they saw as the goals of their revitalized societies. But in those countries, and also in Thailand, rapid social change, including the population growth described, meant troubled political-administrative settings. An increasing flow of graduates from new educational systems clamorously demanded places of their own in the elite. The inability of the first postwar generation of leaders to define systems of power-holding that would be accepted by everyone also contributed to the recurrence of administrative instabilities.

Actually, in some postcolonial societies, the new elites were more prepared to break with the past than their Western colonial predecessors had been. To take an example from the history of the Indonesian legal system, the Dutch had applied Indonesian *adat* law in an anthropological spirit, relativistic and detached. When a legal elite of Indonesian judges inherited their positions, they showed an inclination to move away from *adat;* their nationalistic pride would not allow them to apply too often a law the rest of the world might regard as "primitive" and old-fashioned. But despite the unquestioned appetite for political modernity—or at least for effective nation-building—on the part of many of the members of the new ruling groups, the new bureaucracies remained too circumscribed by culture, economics, and history always to play the dynamic developmental roles that their more optimistic constituents had so hopefully assigned to them. At least, it would be fair to say that in most prewar Southeast Asian societies, civil administrative systems had developed more extensively than had legislative assemblies, political parties, or judicial institutions. The marked predominance of the bureaucracy after the war made its weaknesses all the more serious, even if some of the weaknesses—resistance to change, distortion of information, organizational biases—could be found in Western bureaucracies too.

Disunities caused by ethnic divisions and the gulf between rural culture and that of bureaucratized cities have induced many Southeast Asian administrations to avoid radical changes, to introduce small changes only gradually, if at all, and to seek all the while to buy off (or win over) potential opponents. That description, for example, fits the Thai bureaucracy. Like others in Southeast Asia, it has seemed top-heavy by Western standards, mainly because it embraces virtually all the upper levels of Thai society. It numbers at least 250,000 officials, including all the armed forces and all the nation's schoolteachers, and employs most of the doctors and lawyers and other professionals in Thailand. Social status generally becomes a function of bureaucratic position, in a finely graded system of ranks and salaries. The continuity in Thai social history has been impressive, for today, just as a century ago, political society and administration are virtually synonymous. Most political activity takes place within a framework of ministerial and departmental divisions, as well as of military units. Nonetheless, Thailand outside the central plain (which comprises some two-thirds of the kingdom), is a society of minority groups, only relatively recently integrated into the nation and still weakly bound to the central authority by loyalties of any kind. The government follows conservative fiscal and economic policies, in the interests of preserving a far from secure *status quo,* rewarding those who seek economic benefits (Chinese businessmen or high bureaucrats) and attempting to avoid the creation of pretexts for dissent.

Unencumbered by the legacies of colonialism, the Thai bureaucracy historically has enjoyed the luxury of being able to preside over the rate of change in its society. But bureaucratic stability of this highly purposeful type will hardly continue forever. Having roughly tripled in size since 1932, the bureaucracy is no longer as susceptible as it was to the old-style personal controls of its senior members. Restless subordinates, moreover, the postwar generation of bureaucrats, have been far more widely educated abroad than their superiors, who were trained almost entirely in Thailand in the 1930's and 1940's. Yet the younger challengers must confront the fragility of Thai unity and the limits to the rate of political development that the kingdom in its present form is capable of tolerating.

Even the most effective bureaucracy in Southeast Asia—one secure in its relationship to the social forces around it, stable in its lines of authority and communication, and homogeneous in its view of its own role as an organization—cannot afford to take initiative into its own hands so exclusively that it loses its capacity to interact with the culture of the peasant society it is in danger of leaving behind. Yet decentralization means surrender of much of the power required to introduce structural change. In northern Vietnam in 1965, during the movement to reform the management of the cooperatives, Communist Party theorists debated the issue of increasing "democracy" in those institutions. There were some heavily Westernized Party members who conceived of democracy "as being merely a matter of protecting individual freedoms, like freedom to come and go, freedom of the person, the inviolability of a man's household residence and of his correspondence."[29] In fact, democracy in the cooperatives was seen entirely in a non-Western context as a populist antidote to the arbitrary, omnipotent bureaucracy rapid political development had summoned into being. It specifically meant such things as holding regular plenary meetings of all cooperative members to discuss problems of finances, harvesting, and income distribution, rather than ruling the cooperatives without plenary meetings through the decisions of committees. It meant attacking the phenomenon of "commandism" among the cadres, their arbitrary use of power demonstrated, for example, in their refusal to issue rice or cloth rations to people they disliked. Democracy meant popular participation, not control. On the other hand, plenary meetings of rural cooperative members are significant in a society where traditional decision-making in the villages was the prerogative of a small elite of notables and where imperial edicts were read by Confucian scholars at the communal meeting house but never discussed.

In some postwar Southeast Asian societies, indigenous control of the civil service after years of colonialism has made the civil service a more socially and politically meaningful part of the national life. But its loss of detachment has sometimes resulted in a decline in its professional effectiveness. "Corruption" represents many different things in Southeast Asia. It indicates nepotism and patronage, in which the values of serving real and putative kinship or ethnic group interests take precedence over those of universalistic recruitment. It indicates income adjustment to counteract inflation; in Indonesia in the 1960's, for example, civil servant salaries and allowances fell far behind prices, leading to the private sale of bureaucratic services. It signifies the flexible circumvention of laws originally made to serve the purposes of nationalism. To take a second Indonesian example, regulations in 1959 prohibited alien Chinese from trading in rural areas; by adroit recourse to corruption, the Chinese evaded the prohibition, an evasion beneficial to Indonesian society as well as to themselves, since non-Chinese were not always capable of providing the service of Chinese merchants. "Corruption" may even serve as a mode of informal taxation. Chinese bribery of government officials represented a revenue more easily collected than that provided by more formal systems for taxing Chinese commerce.

Bureaucratic corruption through nepotism is present throughout Southeast Asia, but perhaps it is most extensive in the Philippine civil service. The obligations of real and fictive kinship, a sensitivity to reciprocity in relationships, and the high social value placed upon wealth all stand behind it. In this context, only a shadow line exists between being a bureaucrat and being a politician; and the interpenetration of political and administrative functions that has prevailed is a departure from the American-imposed concept of a civil service removed from the political arena. Factors that have led to corruption among Philippine politicians include the collapse of law and order during the Japanese occupation, the crisis of elite collaboration, the privations of the early postwar period, and the opportunities for making private profit from the manipulation of American aid and Japanese reparations. Since the possession of public office has meant power and therefore wealth, elections often include fraud, murder, and bribery.

The difficulties of civil government in Southeast Asia have been compounded by extraordinary bureaucratic growth. There has been a discrepancy between the gross rate of school output of graduates and the slower, less impressive expansion of occupational opportunities within the private sector of the economy. In fact, most Southeast Asian economies offer few well-paid, high-status employment opportunities outside the government and its agencies, and government positions, moreover, enjoy the greatest prestige among job-seekers. But the new indigenous elites, as opposed to their colonial predecessors, have lacked the political strength to deny access to government posts to the thousands of graduates of the new schools who have wanted them. Colonial governments, with their myth of racial superiority and their rather vicariously derived stability (as extensions of centers of power located outside Southeast Asia altogether), were less vulnerable to that kind of inefficiency. They lacked a sense of responsibility to indigenous power-seekers, and their socially restricted educational systems ensured that such power-seekers would be few in number.

In Indonesia in particular, the government in the period of Guided

Democracy (1959–65) became less and less able to resist the pressure for expansion of the bureaucracy. One reason, in fact, for the durability and seemingly unchallengeable power of the Sukarno "dictatorship" was its skill at buying off elite interests by abandoning tight control of government expenditures in order to absorb large numbers of civil service candidates.

In southern Vietnam, it is estimated that the number of government servants expanded from 120,000 in 1963 to 300,000 by 1968.[30] One reason was that a single autocrat—the emperor in the old days, or Ngo Dinh Diem until 1963—was more likely to restrict the bureaucracy's numbers, in order to ensure his own control, than the post-1963 unstable mixed government in Saigon was capable of doing. But government agencies themselves in southern Vietnam expanded in size only by about 50 per cent between 1963 and 1968. The greater proliferation of personnel than of agencies reflected a deterioration of performance by the civil service as a whole. More men were needed to do the tasks fewer men had done earlier. Because prices in southern Vietnam rose by something like 250 per cent between 1965 and 1968, while salaries rose by only 30 per cent, civil servants were forced to take additional jobs either in their regular working hours or outside them. Additional employment fatigued them and reduced their competence as civil servants. Since raising their salaries would have encouraged further inflation, the government simply hired more officials, aggravating its budgetary deficiencies. The deadly progression from price inflation to "moonlighting" civil servants to an oversized bureaucracy to administrative stagnation was also present elsewhere.

URBAN TRENDS

One of the legacies of Western colonialism in Southeast Asia was undoubtedly the "primate city." The populations of gigantic urban centers like Singapore, Bangkok, Manila, or Saigon-Cholon were at least five times as large as the populations of the next largest cities in their societies. The process by which those cities grew has been called "pseudo-urbanization," since their populations in certain instances multiplied not because they were industrializing and attracting migrants from the countryside with the promise of expanding employment opportunities, like cities in early modern Europe, but because the rural society around them was afflicted by war, disorder, or overpopulation. Use of such a term, though apt in some degree, is also dangerous. It implies that there is only one historically valid form of urbanization—the European form—and that contemporary Southeast Asian cities, by deviating from that model, have somehow fallen from sociological grace.

Most Southeast Asian cities grew in population without acquiring all the cultural properties of industrial urban civilization as it has been known in the West: secularization, economic specialization, the emergence of highly impersonal human relations, the decline of kinship obligations. But it would be parochial to assume that the emergence of such features is inevitable. As in the colonial period, Southeast Asian cities could dominate their societies as vital centers of social, cultural, and economic change. Their difficulties stemmed in part from the fact that they remained the homes of plural societies in which racial-ethnic memberships predetermined economic roles and political identities, with the result that socio-economic or political controversies in them characteristically degenerated into conflicts among ethnic groups. And because there was comparatively little industrial employment in the cities, vast numbers of people were either chronically jobless or crowded into menial service occupations as casual laborers, watchmen, taxi and trishaw drivers, hawkers, and vendors.

Civil war, the appearance of mammoth, short-run, American-financed military industries, and the systematic destruction of the countryside, which forced peasants to find refuge in the towns, make the application of the negative term "pseudo-urbanization" to the situation in southern Vietnam perhaps more appropriate than elsewhere. Between 1956 and 1967, the population of Saigon rose from 1.7 million to 2.2 million, that of Da Nang from 99,000 to 237,000, that of Dalat from 25,000 to 77,000, and that of Hue from 93,000 to 140,000. Urban administrative structures varied from city to city, bearing little correspondence to the size of the populations. Dalat, whose population was largely engaged in such rural pursuits as vegetable-planting, was subdivided into counties, street districts, and hamlets, and it enjoyed a relatively specialized administration. Qui Nhon (105,000 people) and Nha Trang (110,000), which were more complicated urban areas, were still merely subdivided into hamlets, as if they were small villages. Congestion, the American presence, and moral decay made Saigon the "desert of youth," to invoke the title of a 1967 novel by Duyen Anh. Although the population of the Saigon–Gia Dinh area was advancing at a rate of 4.7 per cent per annum in 1967, lack of capital, of materials, of facilities, and above all of land were keeping construction down to about 2,000 residential units a year. As of 1967, all but about 12 per cent of the Saigon population lived in flimsy shacks, in houses on piles above the river, or in small apartment dwellings.[31]

Urban growth was less of a problem for Vietnam's neighbors, Cambodia and Laos, although in 1967 the population of Phnom Penh (600,000) was roughly equal to 10 per cent of the total population of Cambodia, only 11 per cent of whose population was "urban" at all. Before 1950, Phnom Penh was largely a city of Chinese and Vietnamese minorities. But between 1950 and 1965 enough Cambodians migrated to the city, at a time when Phnom Penh's population increased by 400 per cent, for Cambodians to make up 58 per cent of the people of Phnom Penh by 1965. As for Laos, in 1966 it possessed only five towns with more than 5,000 people.

Laos was the least urbanized country in Southeast Asia. Malaysia, as long as it included Singapore (which accounted for 40 per cent of the total urban population), was the most urbanized. Furthermore, its rate of urbanization had gone up since the war. Between 1947 and the late 1950's, the total population of Malaya and Singapore rose by 32.8 per cent, the urban population by 76.2 per cent. In 1957, 66.9 per cent of the Chinese in Malaya lived in towns, compared with only 22.8 per cent of the non-Chinese. Here, however, matching the postwar influx of Cambodians into Phnom Penh, a new trend was emerging: Most new migrants to towns in western Malaysia were Malays, partly because the numbers of potential Chinese immigrants remaining in rural areas had dwindled to insignificance. The prospect that loomed for the 1980's, which could revolutionize Malaysian politics, was that the Malays might form one-third of the urban population, instead of one-fifth as in the 1960's.[32] It seemed just possible that the increasing urbanization of the Malays might encourage the growth of economic rather than communal stratification of the society, with the urban Malay and Chinese proletariats recognizing a common interest.

In Burma, the pace of urbanization was comparatively slow. In 1957, 16 per cent of the population was living in some 252 towns, of which the largest, Rangoon, contained no more than an estimated 740,000 people by 1963. Rigorous government control of economic development throughout Burma was unable to transcend political instability outside the major towns. Consequently, most of the enterprises connected with the 1951 Burma industrial plan had to be concentrated in Rangoon: a cement factory, a sawmill, a textile factory, and a steel mill. Yet because of improved manufacturing methods requiring less labor, and because of the flow of rural refugees into the wholesale and retail commercial sectors of the Rangoon economy, the percentage of the Rangoon population actually employed in manufacturing declined from 24 per cent in 1931 to 18 per cent in 1953.[33] As in other Southeast Asian cities, the Rangoon black market—known ironically as "trading corporation number twenty-three" in Burma—recurrently raised its head, especially after the nationalized people's stores failed to supply a satisfactory quantity and quality of daily commodities at controlled prices.

The Bangkok-Thonburi urban colossus offered yet another spectacular example of a "primate city." Its population rose from 781,670 in 1947 to 2 million by 1967, while the next largest town, Chiangmai, so far down the scale as to be almost out of sight, moved from 38,211 to about 80,000 in the same period. However, in the late 1960's, Thai provincial towns were showing new upsurges in population, with centers like Khorat expanding remarkably, partly because of American military bases in the area. There was a relatively more positive explanation for urban growth in Thailand, at least in the Bangkok area: The Thai Government had succeeded in strengthening the nonagricultural sector of the economy, creating new employment in industrial and commercial enterprises. In the Philippines, it was the growth of the private sector that helped explain the speed of urbanization. With a population of 1.3 million in 1948 and 2.1 million in 1960, Manila in the twentieth century had grown at twice the speed of the rest of the Philippines. More than half its contemporary residents were born outside the city. Its elegant suburbs, like Forbes Park, were jostled by slums of shacks without water and sanitation, and nowhere in Southeast Asia was there a more startling juxtaposition of rich and poor, of color television and lack of electricity, of supermarkets and ramshackle outdoor bazaars.

An outrage to social revolutionaries, the spectacular differences in life styles between the upper and lower classes in certain Southeast Asian cities could nonetheless strengthen as much as dispel the general belief of the rural population that the cities were places of opportunity. Urban life meant the possibility of higher incomes and better educational facilities. Sometimes Southeast Asian elites, who had been educated abroad and were more comfortable in the "modern" environment of the primate cities, were reluctant to leave them to serve in official positions in the provinces. There they felt removed from the political and economic centers of their societies. In southern Vietnam, where that situation was most acute in the late 1960's, the lowly provincial official's lack of contact with his superiors in Saigon was summarized in the comment that the voice of the assistant district chief concerning his fate and his problems was like a thin trail of smoke, which became increasingly dissipated the higher it rose. To compensate, the Vietnamese civil service offered faster promotions to government servants holding provincial posts than to those holding posts in Saigon. Outside the context of the civil service, however, peasants who went to the cities to serve as transient labor took back to their villages new ideas, new gadgets, and a new sense of nationhood. In all Southeast Asian societies, the provenance of most cultural innovation continued to be the cities and towns.

SOUTHEAST ASIAN REACTIONS TO ALIEN ECONOMIC INFLUENCE

Of all the alien or supposedly alien influences at work in Southeast Asian economies, none has been more heavily canvassed academically or more strongly suspected politically than that of the overseas Chinese. Yet to be a "Chinese" in Southeast Asia is largely a matter of self-identification, the preservation of a surname inherited patrilineally from a Chinese ancestor or retention of the ability to speak some form of the Chinese language. Numerous Southeast Asians of Chinese origin can neither speak nor understand Chinese, and widespread assimilation, contrary to popular belief, has taken place in the past. In postwar Southeast Asia, where the largest clusters of overseas Chinese live in Malaya, Thailand, Indonesia, and southern Vietnam, the era of mass immigrations of Chinese has ended. Yet assimilation is less rapid than it was in the early 1800's, when Chinese nationalism did not exist, when the number of women who came from China to live in the Chinese communities was too small to allow the communities to become biologically self-contained, and when Chinese-language schools were still in the future.

In postwar Southeast Asia, moreover, the commonest form of reaction to the entrepreneurial superiority of the overseas Chinese has been discriminatory legislation. In the Philippines, for example, at the achievement of independence, Chinese merchants controlled between 70 and 80 per cent of the retail trade and rice-milling. But in May, 1954, the retail trade was nationalized, with aliens forbidden to engage directly or indirectly in it. The legislation apparently affected some 15,000 to 20,000 Chinese retail establishments, at the very least by forcing them to find Filipino fronts. In southern Vietnam, the Ngo Dinh Diem regime in 1956 blocked Chinese nationals (though not, it must be said, ethnic Chinese) from entering eleven important occupational categories and threatened to force aliens to divest themselves of all their existing interests in rice-milling, the cereals trade, transport enterprises, and commission agencies. Had the law been enforced, it would have seriously undermined the Vietnamese economy.

In Thailand, legislation of 1949, 1951, and 1952 reserved some eighteen industrial and service occupations for Thai citizens. A 1956 law provided that any class of business employing ten or more people might be required by royal decree to fill half its roster of employees with Thai nationals. Of the new factories and businesses that began in Thailand in the 1960's, by far the greatest number were joint Sino-Thai enterprises, and it is possible to claim that the Chinese are becoming less distinct as a separate group in Thailand both economically and socially. On the other hand, while major firms have Thai participation in capitalization and on their boards of directors, the managers who run the firms are still mainly Chinese.

In Indonesia, government action sought formally to exclude alien Chinese and completely alien corporations from importing large categories of goods, from establishing new banks, and from owning rice mills and types of transport agencies. Ministerial regulations and decrees were not as formidable as they seemed, however, there or elsewhere, and bribery was one way of circumventing them.

In Malaya, government policy has been concerned with the task of redressing the economic imbalance between the two sectors of a dual economy—the developed, urban, non-Malay sector and the underdeveloped, largely Malay rural sector. The political importance of the task was indicated by the fact that, although Malays constituted a majority of the electorate, the average income of Malay rural households about 1960 was between 60 and 120 Malayan dollars a month, whereas that of Chinese urban households was some 275 dollars a month, or more than double. Severe restrictions upon immigration into Malaya after the war were largely the product of Malay fears of the Chinese. Echoes of those fears could be found in neighboring countries; despite a population growth of 3.4 per cent per annum, for example, one reason why the Thai Government has hesitated to embark upon a birth control program is that it fears the Chinese population would disdain birth control and increase faster than the Thai.

The measures described indicate the depth of Southeast Asian anxieties about Chinese entrepreneurial domination. Yet most of the overseas Chinese who lived in Bangkok, Rangoon, and Cholon were really Southeast Asians themselves, in that they were born and had lived all their lives there. Domination of Southeast Asian economies by culturally much more alien influences, wielded by people who did little more than sojourn in the region, are at least as evident. Declining to give the Philippines full economic independence along with political freedom in 1946, for example, the United States offered the Filipinos rehabilitation payments for their war-shattered economy only on condition that they revise their constitution in order to allow Americans equal rights with Filipinos in the economic exploitation of Philippine natural resources. The United States also tied the Philippine peso to the American dollar at a ratio of two to one, initially preventing the Filipinos from gaining control of their own currency. Before 1941, American free trade policies had created a favorable balance of trade for the Philippines, but only by encouraging the Philippine economy to emphasize export crops that would be well received in the American market. An imposition of such trade arrangements perpetuated undiversified colonial production patterns and also stimulated considerable economic nationalism.

SOUTHEAST ASIA AND INTERNATIONAL POLITICS

To Southeast Asians, questions of international relations cannot be dissociated from considerations of the vulnerabilities of their economies to foreign control and foreign pressures. A fundamental if not immediately attainable goal of the foreign policies of most Southeast Asian states since the war has been the reduction of the importance of economic and cultural links to former colonial metropolises. One consequence of that objective has been the rediscovery of long-lost neighbors. International relations in Southeast Asia in the 1950's and 1960's showed a steady increase in the intensity of relationships between countries like Indonesia and Malaysia, the Philippines and Malaysia, Cambodia and Thailand, and Vietnam and Laos. Combined with this was a fear of "neocolonialism"—a belief that old metropolitan ties were too intractably rooted in important trading patterns to vanish completely and a frustrated awareness that nationalism as it had developed in Southeast Asia could effectively attack only visible targets. The invisible, indirect controls of the postcolonial era were less easily fought. The Vietnamese political theorist Nguyen Van Trung, writing at the height of American participation in the Vietnamese civil war, dissected the situation candidly for other Southeast Asian countries, as well as for his own:

> Because the new-model policy of intervention of the strong democratic powers does not directly control and govern its victims, the masses of the people do not feel resentment of it. Not only does it not produce feelings of nationalism, it makes those feelings disappear. Even among those revolutionaries who fought against the old colonialism, now because they hold power they receive the aid of "advisers" and enjoy it. Precisely be-

> cause of that, the new-model policy of intervention is more dangerous than the old colonialism, because the new style does not create conditions which give rise to opposition to it. But the real substance is still domination, domination in a manner subtle, scientific, and courteous, through the forms of advisers and aid.[34]

With the relative decline of Europe, the number of non–Southeast Asian powers capable or desirous of significant intervention in Southeast Asian affairs has dwindled at the very time when the actual methods of interference have become more subtle. The Japanese are certain to play an increasingly vigorous role in the region in the future. In the late 1960's, their reviving interest was shown by such diverse activities as their commercial investments in Thailand (nearly half the sum of $233 million invested in Thailand by foreigners in the year 1967, for example, appears to have come from Japanese sources), or their academic study, centered in Kyoto, of many facets of contemporary Southeast Asian life. The Japanese historical model of industrialization and economic modernization is probably too idiosyncratic to be imitated very closely by Southeast Asians—Meiji educational reforms, for example, were carried out within a framework of administrative and financial stability that most Southeast Asian societies would find difficult to reproduce. But its pan-Asian inspirational values should not be underestimated. A Russian interest in Southeast Asia also exists, as is attested by the very extensive Soviet assistance to both the Vietnamese Communists and the Indonesian army, which suppressed the Indonesian Communists. But through most of the postwar era, only two countries have possessed the resources and the interest to intervene very dramatically in Southeast Asian affairs: China and the United States.

From 1949 through the 1960's, the policy of the Chinese Communist regime toward Southeast Asia moved through three discernible stages. During the initial stage of militance (1949–54), China gave support to Vietnamese, Malayan Chinese, and Filipino Huk insurgents. During the "peaceful coexistence" stage (1954–58), celebrated most notably by the Bandung Conference in Indonesia in 1955, China approved of Southeast Asian "neutralism" toward great powers, fostered anticolonialist associations and fronts throughout the region, and worked harmoniously with as many existing Southeast Asian governments as it could. During the revolutionary "people's war" stage after 1959, China encouraged Southeast Asian revolutionaries to attack certain existing Southeast Asian governments by using the Chinese example of the 1940's: rural guerrilla armies surrounding cities and towns and strangling vulnerable urban-based elites. However, certain themes remained constant throughout all three stages: a genuine belief, going back to the days of Sun Yat-sen, that China had at least a moral mission to obstruct Western colonialism as much as possible in Southeast Asia, and a more general theory that the revolutionary potentialities of the "middle world" of Asia, Africa, and Latin America would ultimately confound the plots of the industrial powers (the United States, the Soviet Union, and Japan), which were supposedly encircling China.

Southeast Asian fears of Chinese ethnocentrism, however, were amply demonstrated by a passage in a 1967 Vietnamese novel, published in Saigon, in which a character argued that the Maoist-Marxist dogma that all history is struggle benefited China only because China was so populous, and that in Southeast Asia the dogma was a shield for Chinese neocolonialism.[35] Between 1949 and 1957, some 45,000 overseas Chinese students went to China to study. Although Peking initially encouraged other overseas Chinese in Southeast Asia to invest in China, it modified its policy later: No attempt was made to hold elections among the Southeast Asian Chinese for the seats reserved for their representatives in the Chinese National People's Congress. Moderation alternated with militance. With Burma, for example, China negotiated a generous border treaty in 1960 and a ten-year treaty of friendship and nonaggression, advertising a "cousinly relationship" between Peking and Rangoon. But in 1967, China exported its "cultural revolution" to Burma, encouraging Chinese students in Rangoon to hold Maoist demonstrations, against which the Burmese rioted, and maintaining a training camp for Burmese Communist Party cadres at Kunming. Other Southeast Asian regimes, like Cambodia, could tell a similar tale of unpredictable relations.

The emergence of Communist China, wedded as it seemed to be to an expansionist Soviet Union in 1949, stimulated American political and military interests in Southeast Asia. Mao Tse-tung's triumph hastened a re-evaluation of American foreign policy, one almost more instinctive than rational. Whereas in 1944 President Roosevelt had condemned French colonialism in Vietnam in the strongest terms, by the outbreak of the Korean war in 1950, his successor had decided to finance the French-Vietnamese struggle, then entering its final stages. Tragedy resulted, the product of two different circles of comprehension that had failed to intersect. Americans had learned to fear Stalinism after witnessing the successive Russian-sponsored subversion of Eastern European states in the late 1940's, and now they saw it cast a shadow, East European-style, over Southeast Asia. Southeast Asians had learned to fear colonialism after experiencing at least a century of it, and now they saw a new Western power possibly resurrecting it in a different guise.

The United States not only failed to adhere formally to the Geneva Agreement of 1954 but also sought to form politically and militarily asymmetrical alliances with a number of Southeast Asian states in order to prevent them from falling like "a row of dominoes" into Communist hands. By September, 1954, John Foster Dulles, American Secretary of State, had constructed the Southeast Asia Treaty Organization (SEATO), with headquarters in Bangkok. But Thailand and the Philippines were the only genuine Southeast Asian powers to become members of that organization. Fashioned in the image of the European collective defense community (NATO), the Southeast Asia Treaty Organization had a striking preponderance of non-Southeast Asian members—the United States, Australia, Pakistan, New Zealand, France, and the United Kingdom—that demonstrated its lack of congruence with the needs of the region as most Southeast Asians saw them. In the absence, outside the Philippines, of much long-established sharing of cultural, economic, or social interests between the United States and Southeast Asia, American "national interest" in the region was usually defined in terms of a professedly temporary military commitment and in terms, too, of geopolitical theories aimed against Peking. Bureaucratic inertia in policy-planning circles and psychological needs for policy continuity may have contributed more substantially to the maintenance of such a posture than did the actual wishes of the American people. Another theme of the American approach to Southeast Asia was the determination to disseminate the benefits of the "American way of life," expressed through the activities in the region of the Peace Corps and of the Agency for International Development. Those organizations might be regarded as secularized equivalents of American missionary enterprises in Southeast Asia, which ranged from the support of urban hospitals to the scientific translation of the Bible into the languages of the various hill peoples.

Southeast Asians naturally brought their own psychological and cultural predispositions to bear in their participation in the international politics of their region. For example, one reason why many Indonesians supported Sukarno in his "confrontation" (from 1963 until his downfall) of the new state of Malaysia was that Malaysians seemed a recognizably kindred people who had nonetheless shamefully omitted waging a proper revolution against colonialism. The new Malaysian Government could be plausibly depicted in the same light as the Indonesian conservative elites and sultans who had sided with the Dutch against the Indonesian revolution.

The precolonial past has also made its presence felt in Southeast Asian diplomacy. The dicta of the Asian counterpart of Machiavelli, the *Arthasastra* of Kautila, continue to be pertinent in Southeast Asian capitals like Bangkok. The *Arthasastra* counsels a ruler to consider his state a center of successive concentric circles. His immediate neighbors in the innermost ring are his enemies. Those of the next ring are potential allies. And those neighbors of the ring beyond are, as his allies' enemies, his own enemies. In 1969, the Thai Foreign Minister, Thanat Khoman, could express Thailand's perception of its immediate international situation in such terms. Looking forward to a day when the local threats to Thailand's security had disappeared, he envisaged a time when the whole of Southeast Asia would constitute a diplomatic core, when future allies of Thailand like Korea, Japan, India, and Pakistan would compose the outer ring, and when China, of course, would remain the long-term enemy in the ring between.[36]

The theoretical preconceptions of the Vietnamese in dealing with the Cambodians, the Indonesians in dealing with the Malaysians, or the Thai in dealing with the Chinese or the Americans, are important to the future of Southeast Asia. But the search by Southeast Asian diplomats for more modern applications for such long-descended preconceptions is just one aspect of a larger process that might be called, with some accuracy, cultural reconstruction: the quest for a modern world view that will at the same time accommodate and define with pride the heritages received from history.

35

CULTURAL RECONSTRUCTION AND POSTWAR NATIONALISM

THE EXPANSION OF EDUCATION

Many Southeast Asian nationalists have tended to be advocates of mass popular culture in their societies, regarding the court-centeredness of the aristocratic traditions of the past not as a paradise lost but as a liability in effective nation-building. In 1945, Ho Chi Minh spoke for many nationalists elsewhere in the region when he associated the classical court "high" cultures with excessive dependence upon sources of culture outside Southeast Asia. He went on to say: "We can imitate the good things of any country in Europe or America, but the essential thing is to be creative. . . . We mustn't go on borrowing and not make repayments."[37] His position hardly did justice to the creativity inherent in Southeast Asian reinterpretations of borrowed cultural elements. It also implicitly denied the very real transforming interaction of court and village cultures in traditional Southeast Asia. But it was symptomatic of the Southeast Asian nationalist's strong self-consciousness.

The Southeast Asian nationalist, often the possessor of a modern outlook of foreign origin in a peasant society whose overall culture had not changed as rapidly as his own, was aware of the ways in which his cultural distinctiveness from most members of his national group was compromising his populist predilections. In order to overcome that isolation and distinctiveness, he was determined to reduce the degree of the previously acceptable cultural distance between elite and peasantry. One of the things that has made elite culture more popular in some Southeast Asian countries has been the educational revolution.

The Thai educational system, admittedly, entered the postwar period comparatively well developed, for universal primary education was offered virtually throughout the kingdom. By the late 1950's, the government was ambitious enough to begin to extend compulsory primary schooling from four to seven years, a measure that would take years to implement. Thailand's eight universities (as of 1969) had an enrollment of more than 45,000 students, and the creation of regional universities in the 1960's—at Khonkaen in the northeast, Chiangmai in the north, and Patani in the south—removed higher education somewhat from its elitist confinement to the capital. Moreover, literacy rates in

Thailand revealed how recently the impact of educational modernization upon society had occurred. According to the 1960 census, fewer than a quarter of all Thai sixty-five years of age or over were literate, compared to 88.5 per cent of those between the ages of fifteen and nineteen.

The educational revolution in Indonesia, which began in the period of the Japanese occupation, has been far more dramatic. With a few brisk strokes, the Japanese abolished the complex, ethnically plural, multi-track government school system of the Dutch. In its place, they installed a single, uniform twelve-year system (six years of primary, three of lower secondary, three of upper secondary) in which Indonesian, not Dutch, was the language of instruction. The Indonesians themselves preserved the system after independence, and on the whole the transition from the small, plural colonial educational program to its larger homogeneous replacement was accomplished comfortably. Expansion was the keynote, even though the legal enforcement of a compulsory six years of primary education was never complete. Whereas there were about 2 million students in government schools in Indonesia in 1938, there were about 9 million in 1960. But expansion occurred much more rapidly at the higher levels of the system. The number of students in secondary schools in 1960 had multiplied about ten times since the late prewar years, and the number of students in universities had multiplied in the same period about a hundred times.

The greater pressure for expansion here was hardly inexplicable, for only graduates of secondary schools and universities could win admittance to the governing class and its concomitant high status. Even in the prewar period, nationalists had been more inclined to complain about the absence of enough Dutch-language education for their elite-oriented sons than about the lack of village schools. In postindependence Indonesian government schools, local languages might be used for the first three years of primary school, but after that all education was in Indonesian. Such institutionalized universal use of this one language in a vast, multi-ethnic society "nationalized" the generation that was going to school; their own local culture and language continued to be transmitted to them, but now the process occurred within a national cultural framework. Needless to say, Indonesian-language newspapers and radio broadcasting contributed to such nationalistic acculturation or linguistic socialization outside the schools.

To be fair to the colonial regimes of Southeast Asia, which have often been charged with being more interested in building railways than in building schools, the discovery that an abundant, constantly increasing supply of highly educated people was necessary to economic growth has come only recently in human history. Until the early twentieth century, few societies, even in Europe, could afford more than a tiny elite of educated people: Education meant unproductive time, separation from manual labor, "idleness." But by the postwar period, in the Western world and then in Southeast Asia, the acquisition of knowledge not only carried social prestige as before but also was seen in a new light as being productive of goods and services, through its entrepreneurial, managerial, and scientific applications. Thus, in the societies once subsumed under the title French Indochina, as elsewhere, educational growth was a particularly pressing necessity, in view of the inadequacy for modern purposes of colonial educational facilities, especially in Vietnam. Laos saw few changes. In 1965, not more than 30 per cent of its eligible children attended school. Surviving colonial influences could be found in such places as the Lycée Pavie in Vientiane, the only full-scale secondary school in the country, where, as of 1966, fifty-four members of the faculty of sixty-five were French citizens. In Cambodia, however, the number of primary school students increased from 144,510 in 1953 to 942,000 in 1967, while university students increased from a scant 116 in 1955 to 7,400 in 1967.

Educational reform in northern Vietnam began in Viet Minh–held areas long before 1954. It involved an expansion of facilities; an emphasis upon the production of doctors, engineers, teachers, and technical cadres; and the use of Vietnamese rather than French language textbooks. Expansion took place at all levels but was perhaps most dramatic, as in Indonesia, at the higher levels. In the academic year 1966–67, according to Hanoi statistics, there were 46,429 university students in the north—some seventy-seven times as many as there had been in all of Indochina in 1939. The purpose of village schools in the north was to create "a new rural people." Teachers were supposed not merely to teach academic subjects but also to solve the problems of village families by serving as the custodians of new crop seeds in the village, by introducing new plants to their localities, and by popularizing them among the villagers. In that way, a historically prestigious occupation was firmly linked to the revolution in agricultural technology. And the village school of the past, representing "the vase of precious flowers" (*bình hoa quī*) tradition in Vietnamese education, was condemned for having been an insensitive, untouchable outpost of the Confucian elite tradition.

Because it had gone relatively unscathed by the 1946–54 war for independence and had then received a flow of educated refugees from the north, southern Vietnam enjoyed a superiority over northern Vietnam in educational facilities in 1954. But after 1954, the south failed to attack less desirable legacies of the colonial period as decisively as the north. French-language private schools remained in business, the multiple-level examinations and diplomas which had fragmented the colonial system were preserved into the late 1960's, and only in 1967 was a committee organized to compile terminology in the Vietnamese language for use in university classrooms in teaching science and engineering. However, one common postwar Southeast Asian pattern that extended to southern Vietnam was the rise of the university. Of the five universities in the south in the late 1960's, the largest, Saigon University, saw its student population multiply more than five times in less than a decade, from 4,315 students in 1958 to 22,619 students in 1966. The students were more likely to become journalists, civil servants, teachers, and unemployed Saigon street politicians than technocrats. More than half of them were enrolled in 1966 in the colleges of law and letters, where educational methods were highly literary and where many students sought to find an atmosphere of "carefree elegance" (*bay buom,* literally "butterfly flights").

In the Philippines, on the other hand, educational expansion was a direct force for political democratization. Since a literacy test existed as the qualification for the right to vote, the growth of the electorate depended on the spread of literacy. A census of 1960 testified that 72 per cent of the population over ten years old was literate. Education is conducted primarily in Pilipino and English. Since universal education had been a goal of the American colonial administration, the Philippines inherited a more broadly diffused educational system than any other country in the region. In the 1960's, more than 50,000 students were attending state colleges and universities in a given year, while approximately a quarter of a million more attended private colleges. In quantitative terms, this was as close as any Southeast Asian society had come to mass education, even if many of the private schools were diploma mills, schools run for profit. Like other Southeast Asians, Filipinos preferred education in law and the humanities to education in science, partly because of the connection between the law degree and upward social mobility into the governing class. Thus, while vocational schools in the late 1960's had a total annual enrollment of more than 100,000 students, most Filipinos continued to covet liberal arts degrees. The society could not absorb the number of lawyers it was training. Manila had become the home of an underemployed intelligentsia.

In Western eyes, the popularity and pre-eminence of humanistic curricula in Southeast Asia educational systems (with the exception of that of northern Vietnam) seemed self-defeating, in view of the fact that economic development required many graduates with greater technical training and skills. But the need in those societies for technically trained graduates was more obvious to social scientists studying development models than it was to the indigenous job-seeker looking for immediate employment in a struggling economy in Jakarta, Manila, Saigon, or Rangoon. Truly flourishing, socially accepted technical education was more likely to accompany economic growth than it was to precede it. Furthermore, the general feeling that access to the political elite was open rather than closed was important to societies attempting to encourage various formerly isolated groups to accept a common national identity. Such a politics of egalitarianism revolved around the socially enlarged search for status in neotraditional terms.

RELIGION, POLITICS, AND SOCIOCULTURAL CHANGE

Religious leaders and religiously minded politicians in Southeast Asia have been particularly concerned with the adaptation to modernity of inherited institutions, attitudes, and world views. In one of a collection of short stories published in Saigon in 1967, *Nguoi Giet Nguoi* (*People Killing People*), the Vietnamese writer Ly Hoang Phong described an elderly woman, originally a Catholic, who had married a Buddhist. When she was dying, she called upon a priest for absolution, but her husband forbade him to give it to her, and she died without knowing whether her soul would have a Catholic or a Buddhist fate. In Southeast Asian societies like Vietnam, where the colonial period had encouraged the development of a religious plural society, it was important that members of diverse religious groups become involved together more regularly in political, social, and occupational relationships and that differences in religious values not be made grounds for the exclusion of any group from certain spheres of secular activity. In the words of Ly Chanh Trung, a Vietnamese Catholic intellectual, "all the ways of looking at things in terms of dichotomies, of dividing people unambiguously into two groups, one of which is completely ugly and one completely good," must be abandoned in favor of social unity, in favor of a "harmonizing oneness" but not a "conforming oneness."[38]

In Southeast Asian countries with more homogeneous religious backgrounds, religious predispositions exercised a strong influence over political and cultural change in general. Political monks in Burma of the 1920's like U Ottama had invoked the bodhisattva ideal of renouncing personal liberation until all beings are liberated from suffering as a discipline of selflessness for their anticolonial struggles. Postwar Burmese politicians like U Nu saw the problems of capitalism and community economic development through the powerful but non-Western lens created for them by a centuries-old ecclesiastical moral imagination. In U Nu's socialist outlook, the construction of a welfare state represented a salutary denial of the illusion of self, through the denial of the high value placed upon the accumulation of private property, which sprang from that illusion. And the welfare state, by providing everyone with the leisure to meditate, was merely designed as a means to the more considerable end of enlightenment and of release from the ties of attachment to an evanescent existence.[39]

If Southeast Asia's Buddhist heritage shaped the intellectual evolution of major political leaders, it hardly remained excluded from the institutional development that followed. In Thailand, for example, the large number of Buddhist monks who wrote to such periodicals as the *Social Science Review*, an important organ of the younger, urban-educated elite, suggested that they considered themselves a part of the modern, assertive Thai culture for which that journal stood. Traditional role-playing could be broadened to suit modern contexts, as the village monk who preached a sermon in Thai on the implications of Darwin for Buddhism proved. The Thai monkhood was divided on the issues of whether they should play an active part in government development efforts and whether they should be trained for this role. These issues were raised by a general recognition of the critical role of the monks' leadership in the village. The two major ecclesiastical universities made pilot efforts to send monks into the countryside as teachers and as leaders. One ecclesiastical school mounted a health education project in Chiangmai in cooperation with the medical faculty of Chiangmai University.[40]

The point, however, is that just as elite culture in Southeast Asia has been affected by mass education and is no longer quite so court-centered, so too the perspectives of the monkhood are no longer necessarily limited to the environs of their own village temples. Social, geographical, and cultural mobility are much more extensive than they were in the early nineteenth century in the sometimes intermingled worlds of politics and religion. The renascence of Vietnamese Buddhism dates from 1931–34, with the founding of Buddhist studies associations and of a Buddhist vernacular press, which for the first time translated extracts from the sutras into colloquial Vietnamese, in order to compete with Vietnamese translations of the Christian Bible and to free traditional Vietnamese religion from its anachronistic linguistic matrix of classical Chinese. The climax of the renascence came with the first nationwide Buddhist meeting in Vietnamese history, the national Buddhist congress at the Tu Dam temple in Hue in 1951. The legal representative organ that the congress created, the General Association of Vietnamese Buddhism, became one of the chief adversaries of the Catholic-dominated Ngo Dinh Diem regime in Saigon from 1954 to 1963. But it also constructed an unprecedented supra-village institutional framework within which Vietnamese Buddhists could operate, organizing Buddhist "cells" (a Marxist-Leninist organizational term) in every provincial capital and district town, opening an academy for monks to train "men of talent" (a Confucian phrase) for the clergy, and establishing youth education groups, like the Buddhist Youth, Buddhist Families, Buddhist Elementary School Students, Buddhist University Students, and Buddhist Guides. In competitive imitation of Catholic private schools, the Association sponsored *bodhi* (*bo de*) or "great awakening" middle and elementary schools to educate the children of Buddhist families. This deliberate postwar expansion of horizons did not merely consist of taking a formerly village-centered religion and giving it pan-Vietnamese outlets. For the first time in history, Vietnamese Buddhists participated in Buddhist conferences held in Ceylon, Thailand, and Burma. Saigon Buddhist politicians like Thich Tam Chau wrote poetry in Chinese, as in the past, but now often wore the saffron robes common to Theravada Buddhists elsewhere in Southeast Asia, rather than their own brown Mahayana robes, as a public demonstration of a new cosmopolitan spirit.

The greater postwar involvement of Southeast Asian religious traditions with the symbolism or content of national and international political and social movements was sometimes as likely to magnify existing disunities as it was to give Southeast Asian societies greater cohesion. Parts of rural Java, after 1940, saw a deepening of the dichotomy between *santri* (devout Muslims who prayed five times a day, fasted in the fasting month, and for whom Islam was very much a part of their self-identification) and *abangan* (Javanese who were first and foremost Javanese and only nominal Muslims). In the period of the revolution, when all claims to cultural authority and social power were brought out into the open and tested, *santri* Islam became militant in the rural areas, arousing a strong reaction on the part of the threatened *abangan*. It would not be too grotesque an exaggeration to claim that many *abangan* became Communists in part because they were seeking a useful counter-ideology. The triumph of the government over the Communist Party in the Madiun Rebellion of 1948 at the national level meant that locally the *santri* had won out over the *abangan* in a bloody rural Javanese civil war. Deeply resentful of the *santri*, whom they were inclined to caricature as hypocritical, penny-pinching, religiously ostentatious "Arabs," the *abangan* provided many recruits when D. N. Aidit reorganized the Communist Party in the 1950's. It is worth noting that *santri* tended to be the richer peasants or traders who accumulated money and, therefore, land. *Abangan* tended to be poorer peasants. After the upheavals of 1965–66, when *santri* at the local level massacred the Communist *abangan*, Communism became a hazardous belief in Java, but the success of Christian missionaries in Java in the late 1960's possibly indicates that *abangan* have discovered Christianity as their new counter-ideology against a bloody-handed *santri* Islam. Strife of the same kind overshadowed religious conflicts elsewhere in the region. But what was particularly noticeable here was the way in which local religious differences, often reflecting differences in socio-economic status, borrowed the pretexts and the ammunition for their destructive confrontations from national and international sources. Religious systems had expanded their political and social consciousness, but their greater cosmopolitanism had not brought peace to the Javanese village.

According to the 1960 Philippine census, about 84 per cent of the total Filipino population was Catholic. The Church was a national organization reaching into every nook of the country. Although the friar lands had been sold at the beginning of the American era, the diocesan church retained its landholdings, and the Church remained a major landlord. In the late 1960's, the Filipinized Church could boast of having two Filipino cardinals, but, ironically, some Filipino prelates voted in the Vatican councils as if they were part of the Spanish hierarchy. Being a very conservative element in Philippine society, the Catholic Church openly opposed divorce legislation and quietly opposed land reform. More significantly, it has prevented the adoption of effective birth control measures, despite the fact that the annual rate of population growth of the Philippines was 3.5 per cent. To make the irony complete, it was now the Jesuits and the other orders who were proposing welfare programs, simplification of ritual, liquidation of excessive Church wealth, and other relevant social action programs. The willingness of the Church to become actively involved in the solution of social problems may be vital in determining the future of the Philippines. Perhaps only the government itself could mobilize as many resources or as much authority and prestige in any attack on the questions of tenancy, urbanization, and poverty.

NATIONALISM AND ITS PARTICIPANTS IN THE POSTWAR PERIOD

While the number of active nationalists in postwar Southeast Asia has often been exaggerated, nationalism itself has grown strong indigenous roots. Few revolutions have been the work of majorities, and irrevocable societywide changes have been caused historically by the occurrence of very small changes in the level of a society's political mobilization. Life styles in northern Vietnam today, for example, have changed drastically from what they were in 1939, yet the membership of the Indochina Communist Party in 1945, on the eve of the August Revolution, could not have been more than 5,000 people. But if the programs of numerically small elite groups are the engines of change in the region, it is not necessarily true that nationalistic elites themselves are united or consistent in their views of the past, in which they must find the symbols to legitimize both themselves and their nationalist doctrines. Cultural change creates mythologies of the past: To conservative nationalists who dislike such change, the past represents a golden age, yet to those less conservative it seems a time of "feudalism" or misery. Public memory of the past becomes a battleground.

The ways in which Southeast Asian nationalists rewrite the histories of their societies illuminate both the progress of the battle and the consolidation of nationalism in its vulnerable peasant-society context. In Indonesia, for example, one leading nationalist myth-maker, Muhammad Yamin, wrote a history entitled *Tiga Ribu Tahun Sang Merah Putih* (*3,000 Years of the Red and White*, referring to the colors of the Indonesian flag) in which he contended that "Indonesians" had used the red and white flag as their national symbol for thirty centuries. Ironically, however, in rewriting the history of the colonial period itself, Indonesian history schoolbooks altered the interpretations but preserved the structure of the original Dutch colonial histories. A consequence was that, although in reality the Netherlands East Indies had only dated from about 1900, Indonesian historians accepted the picture painted by Dutch colonial historians of the 1920's and 1930's, in which Dutch rule was presumed to stretch back over the Netherlands East Indies for some 350 years. Their own texts diverged merely by stressing that they had been 350 years of exploitation.

In some instances, trends in elite self-conceptions in Southeast Asia had fluctuated dramatically over a century and a half. In the early nineteenth century, the Vietnamese court saw itself as a proudly independent bastion of East Asian classical civilization, the "imperial south" of an unparalleled culture area, in which China was publicly acknowledged to be only the slightly senior, slightly more powerful "northern court."

But by the late 1960's, one prominent Vietnamese intellectual could even see Vietnam's successful historical struggle to resist Chinese invasions not as proof of the justice of Vietnam's claim to be creating its own independent variant of the one classical culture, but as a costly diversion from the work of producing more visible national heirlooms like those of its Southeast Asian neighbors. "Why do we not have an Angkor Wat, or towering gilded and silvered pagodas as exist in Burma?" asked Nguyen Van Trung in 1966. "The essential nature of monarchical and feudal systems is the love of squandering resources lavishly; but the feudalism of Vietnamese emperors was . . . of necessity concerned with hoarding foodstuffs . . . with building dikes and drilling armies . . . because of constantly living under the obsession of threats of invasion. . . . An Angkor Wat requires several decades of peace before it can be created."[41] Nonetheless, the more common theme was the unashamed popularization of historical monuments about which peasants of the prenationalistic age had known or cared very little. Sihanouk traced the origin of Khmer Buddhist socialism back to the reign of Jayavarman VII, whose public works projects, like those of modern Cambodia, required the use of extensive peasant labor; and as Cambodia's national anthem, written by a Buddhist monk, declared: "The temples sleep in the forest, recalling the grandeur of the Moha Nokor [the great city]. The Khmer race is as eternal as the rocks."

Possessing a nationalist psychology, governing elites could now reach unprecedented mass audiences through newspapers, radio, and even television. In Cambodia, the number of radios multiplied from 20,000 in 1957 to an estimated 400,000 in 1967. The one radio station was controlled by the government. In Thailand, the 1960's saw a strong growth of provincial presses in such centers as Khonkaen (for the northeast), Songkhla (for the south), and Chiangmai (in the north). In northern Vietnam, where the Hanoi elite was making the most dedicated effort of any in the region to institutionalize science, and to "Vietnamicize" its teachings, the Vietnamese mathematics society was certain of a large enough constituency to publish a journal entitled "Mathematics and Youth" (*Toan hoc va tuoi tre*)—100,000 copies at a time. In the Philippines, elite ownership of newspapers, television, and radio stations was indispensable to political power. The circulation of daily newspapers was more than half a million; the *Philippine Free Press,* a national news weekly, enjoyed an audience of more than 100,000 readers. By 1970, chains of television networks extended across the archipelago, reaching millions of viewers. The dissemination of urban values in the countryside could be predicted from these statistics, for Manila was the center of all mass communications media, no matter what the language of any publication or broadcast.

In Indonesia, the content of the *ludrug* theater of East Java implied and depicted a social universe that was emphatically not the circumscribed village world but the Indonesian nation itself, with national slogans, causes, and figures. Loyalty to the nation was a very definite part of the ideology of the theater, and its urban proletarian audiences understood that they were not the only people concerned with offering such loyalty. *Ludrug* plays emphasized the values of modernity as being the most admirable, portraying social goals that were not those of harmony inside an unchanging village community but rather those of acquiring wealth and moving toward elite status. *Ludrug* audiences may in part have accepted those basic views, for the actors in the plays were of the same social class as the audiences, audience responses echoed the ideas, and *ludrug* was undeniably popular.[42] But the manners of modernity were advertised even more conspicuously in Indonesia (and elsewhere) by American movies, which were very popular in the postwar period and which provided new behavioral models, desirable and undesirable. Many militant youth activists in the Indonesian revolution cultivated a *koboi* ("cowboy") style, including the wearing of pistols.

Despite the undeniable impact of such institutions as the *ludrug* theater, it was not at all certain that the peasants to whom nationalist elites appealed with such diversified ingenuity were willing to be embraced by the age of modernization. The assault upon traditional rural values did not proceed without awakening important reactions. A good example of such a reaction was the resurgence of millennialism among Filipino peasants in the 1960's. The *Rizalista* sects, for example, combined folk Christianity with folk nationalism. The *Rizalistas* endowed Filipino nationalists with occult, supernatural, religious powers and properties; Rizal and Christ were fused into one deity. In 1967, a group of fanatic *Rizalistas* attempted to destroy the Philippine Government by attacking the city of Manila. Believing they were immune to death, and wearing amulets, they marched along Taft Avenue in downtown Manila, eventually forcing a confrontation with the police in which thirty-three were killed. The violence of their resentment of urbanization and Westernization was clear evidence of tensions among the peasantry.

Industrialization, the sacred goal of many Southeast Asian nationalists, meant factory discipline and the acceptance by the peasant worker of a more scientifically measured, less elastic consciousness of time than that to which he was accustomed—a form of loss of freedom. As a Vietnamese factory official serving in a northern provincial railway factory commented in 1965, "Regarding the problem of organizing labor more rationally, there were people who said there was no way in which we could have more rational organization, principally because they feared that if there were more rational organization, there could not be the same freedom as before. Regarding the problem of employing machines in production, there were people who proposed that the difficulty would exist of our not having any experience, but they said this chiefly because they feared manning machines would mean more tension."[43]

Much of the audience to which nationalist elites preached feared or suspected cultural change. In many societies, that audience was also divided by its own cultural plurality. The extreme example is the one most worth discussing: that of Malaysia. The question of language use and language instruction has been central to the politics of Malaysia. There was a general consensus that a common language was required if the separate communities were to become in the fullest sense a nation, and there was no serious dissent from the view that the "national language" could only be Malay. Yet the immigrant communities desired to preserve their own cultural heritage and feared that propagation of Malay as the sole official language was an integral part of specifically Malay nationalism, or of a design to ensure continued Malay political dominance. When the Federation of Malaya gained independence in 1957, the constitution stated categorically that "the national language shall be the Malay language," but it accorded to English concurrent official status for ten years "and thereafter until Parliament otherwise provides."

Although the major questions concerning the use of Malay were thereby postponed, the two years between 1957 and the first fully independent elections in 1959 saw growing tension within the Alliance of communal parties, and especially within the Malayan Chinese Association (MCA), concerning the languages of education. In 1959, the Chinese President of the MCA, Lim Chong Eu, was placed in a politically untenable position within the Alliance by the pressure from Chinese-language schoolteachers and Chinese guilds and associations to give party endorsement to their campaign to have Chinese recognized as an additional official language. He led a substantial section of the party out of the Alliance, later starting a United Democratic Party based on one of the Chinese strongholds of power, Penang. Malays, meanwhile, were concerned about the initially extremely slow development of Malay-language secondary education and felt unhappy, too, about the low "economic value" attached to Malay education in a world in which the languages of government and business alike tended still to be alien. The principal provisions of the National Language Bill enacted in March, 1967, were that the national language should be used "for all official purposes," but that the federal and state governments would retain the right "to use any translation of official documents or communications in the language of any other community in the Federation for such purposes as may be deemed necessary in the public interest." An additional clause empowered the king to permit the continued use of English for official purposes when necessary. The bill satisfied no one. The language issue remained a potent force for divisiveness in a society that was still struggling to reach some kind of consensus not based solely on the interests of one community or another.[44]

Contemporary Southeast Asian history has been distinguished not merely by the existence of such disunities and parochialisms but also by the ways in which many of these seemingly intractable problems have been imaginatively and courageously overcome. The numerous official language commissions of the area did not always help with their bulky lists of often rather stilted new words. But in the Philippines, Tagalog (the basis of the national language Pilipino) spread through the islands by means of radio, movies, and comic books. In Indonesia, the brilliant stroke of the imagination by which nationalists in the 1920's rechristened the Malay lingua franca as "Indonesian" paid off in the 1940's and after. In the stirring days of the postwar revolution against the Dutch, the language acquired a deep psychological resonance, and after independence a new generation of Indonesians emerged from an entirely Indonesian-language mass education system.

The complexities of the processes of change at work in the different nations and localities of Southeast Asia are so formidable, by any general synoptic reckoning, that only a foolhardy scholar would attempt to give a final schematic exposition of them. Attainment of an understanding of the developments in education, communications, religion, and language discussed above is only a prelude to the gaining of greater wisdom. Because of this, it would be artificial to draw up a balance sheet of the supposed successes and failures that all Southeast Asian countries have experienced in their efforts to reconstruct their political and social systems for the purpose of reducing their vulnerabilities in the shrinking world community. Confronted with any temptation to make far-wandering judgments about the future of the region, historians are probably best served by remembering how recently they and other scholars have begun to study Southeast Asia, and by invoking for a time the Vietnamese proverb: "If you know something, speak, but if you don't know, lean against the pillar and listen."

ASSAM
MANIPUR
Kunming
Bhamo
Kaungton
YUNNAN
Hsenwi
Shwebo
Lashio
Black R.
Red R.
Mandalay
KYAUKSE
Ava
Amarapura
Irrawaddy R.
Dien
Bien
Phu
Yen
Bai
Bac Son
Lang Son
Pagan
Kengtung
ARAKAN
20°
Salween R.
Mong Cai
Chiangsaen
Nam Tha
Hanoi
Haiphong
Thai Binh
Nam Dinh
Luang Prabang
Toungoo
Chiangmai
Sayaburi
Nan
NGHE AN
Prome
Sittang R.
Xieng
Khouang
Tharrawaddy
Lamphun
Lampang
Vinh
Ha Tinh
Pegu
Vientiane
Bassein
Rangoon
Uttaradit
Nongkhai
Martaban
Tak
KHORAT
Moulmein
Phitsanulok
Khonkaen
PLATEAU
Hue
THUA THIEN
Da Nang (Tourane)
Quang Nam
Paknampho
Chao Phraya R.
Nakhon Ratchasima
(Khorat)
Ubon
Pakse
Ayudhya
Champassak
TENASSERIM
Bangkok-Thonburi
Binh Dinh
Qui Nhon
Paknam
Angkor
Battambang
Mekong R.
Chanthaburi
Dalat
Nha Trang
Wa Ko
Udong
Bay of
Kompong Som
Phnom Penh
Gia
Dinh
Bien Hoa
10°
Kampot
Sihanoukville
Ha Tien
Saigon-Cholon
DING TU'O'NG
My-Tho
AN GIANG
Vinh Long
Rach Gia
Ca Mau
Nakhon Si
Thammarat
Poulo Condore Is.
Phuket Is.
Phatthalung
Songkhla
Patani
Kuala Kedah
Kota Bharu
ACHEH
Penang Is.
Taiping
Kuala Kangsar
Pangkor Is.
Medan
Kuala Lumpur
SUNGEI UJONG
EAST COAST
RESIDENCY
Seremban
NANING
Malacca
Muar
Rajang R.
Lupar R.
Sambas
R.
Singapore
RIAU
ARCHIPELAGO
Kapuas
0°
Pontianak
Jambi
Bangka Is.
Palembang
Billiton
Is.
Benkulen
Bantam
Jakarta (Batavia)
Kudus
Cheribon
Demak
Blora
Semarang
Surabaya
Bandung
Surakarta
Solo R.
Brantas R.
Jogjakarta
(Mataram)
* This map includes only places mentioned in the text. For a present-day map, see the end-paper map.
10°
100°
110°

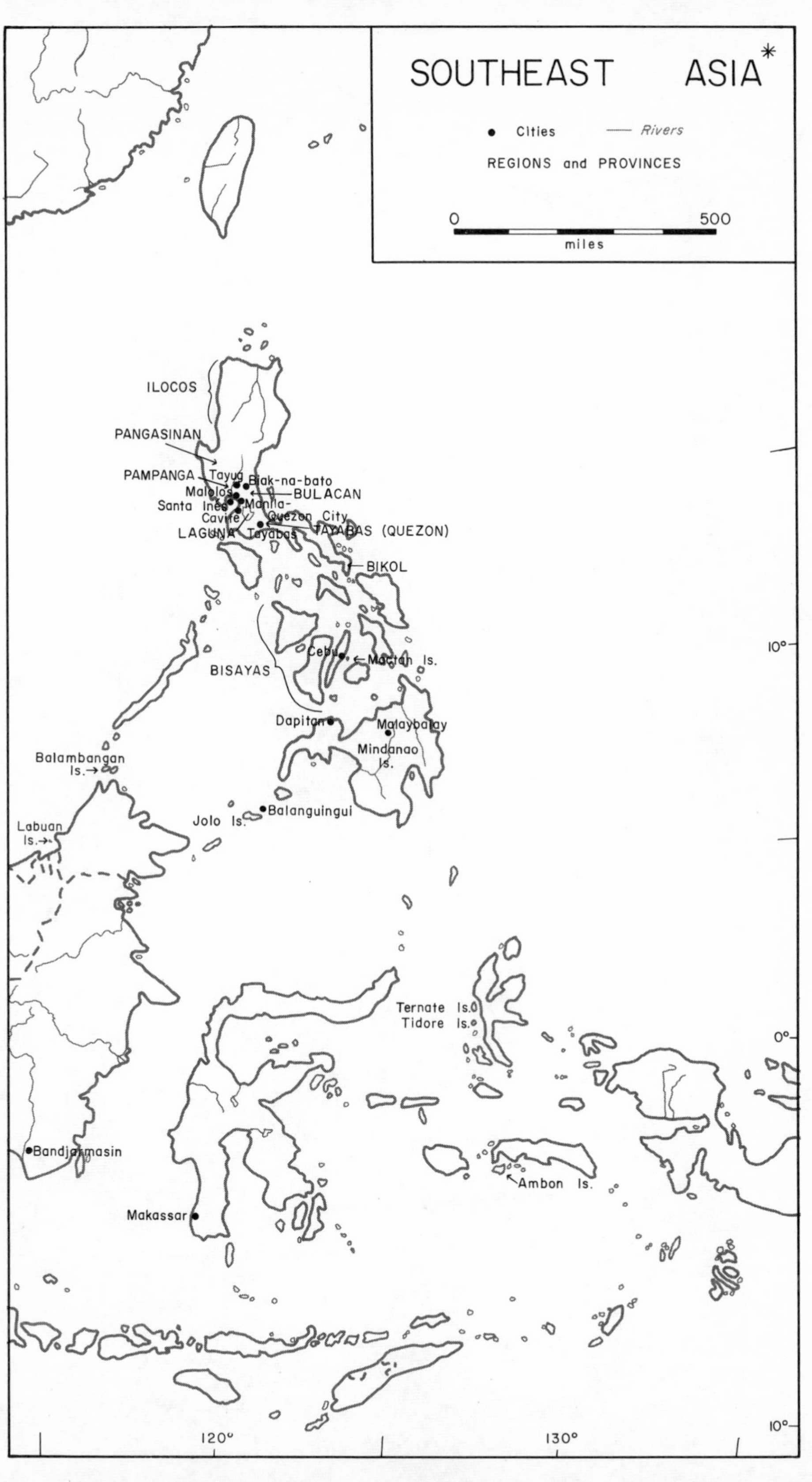

SOUTHEAST ASIA*
Cities
Rivers
REGIONS and PROVINCES
0
500
miles
ILOCOS
PANGASINAN
PAMPANGA
Tayug
Biak-na-bato
Malolos
BULACAN
Santa Ines
Manila-
Cavite
Quezon City
LAGUNA
Tayabas
TAYABAS (QUEZON)
BIKOL
Cebu
Mactan Is.
BISAYAS
Dapitan
Malaybalay
Mindanao Is.
Balambangan Is.
Jolo Is.
Balanguingui
Labuan Is.
Ternate Is.
Tidore Is.
Bandjarmasin
Ambon Is.
Makassar
10°
0°
10°
120°
130°

APPENDIX

SOUTHEAST ASIAN LANGUAGES

BURMESE

The phonetic system of transcription that has been used for Burmese should be in most respects pronounceable to English-speaking readers without comment. Note, however, that *gy* is pronounced as English *j* (*gyi* is pronounced *jee*), in all final *-n*, *-m*, and *-ng* are pronounced as the final nasal *-n* in the French *vin*, and final *-t* and *-k* are not aspirated (being sounded like the *-t* of *set* in the phrase *set to* and the *-k* in *talk clearly*). In the interest of making pronounciation easier, words like *myo-za* (often rendered *myosa*) and *bo-gyok* (often *bogyoke*) have been divided.

CAMBODIAN

The most recent transliteration system for the Cambodian language is that proposed by Mme. Saveros Lewitz in the *Bulletin de l'École Française d'Extrême Orient*, LV (1969). Not enough Khmer words appear in this book to warrant a discussion of pronunciation, although the rules for Thai governing *ph* and *th* (e.g., in the Cambodian word *phnom*) generally apply. The language itself is most closely related to those spoken in the upland regions of southern Vietnam, southern Laos, and eastern Thailand. Unlike the other non-Malay national languages of Southeast Asia, Cambodian has no tones.

LAO

The only Lao words that appear in this book are proper names which are so well known in French transcription as to resist any attempt to make them more amenable to English pronunciation. Note, however, that Vientiane and Luang Prabang are pronounced as if transcribed (following the system employed for a similar language, Thai) Viang Čhan and Luang Phrabang. As demanded by conventional English usage, plurality is not formed by adding *-s* when the language from which the word is taken does not add *-s*. We have used *Lao* instead of *Laotian* to follow Lao usage.

MALAY/INDONESIAN

Malay is a member of the Indonesian or western branch of the Malayo-Polynesian language family, which is geographically one of the most widespread of language families, second only to the Indo-European. Malay is spoken as the mother tongue in Malaya and certain parts of southern Thailand, Sumatra, and Borneo. It has for centuries, however, performed the role of lingua franca throughout a major portion of the Indonesian archipelago and has functioned as the medium of communication for traders, itinerants, and immigrants of all races and creeds.

The earliest records of Malay are found in inscriptions written in an Indian script and dating from the seventh century A.D. The language of these inscriptions is often termed "old Malay." The language of most Malay literary works prior to the twentieth century is generally termed "classical Malay." These works emanated mainly from the sphere of the palace, forming what is sometimes called a court literature. The term "classical" is, however, somewhat misleading and should not be understood to mean that there existed one standard form of literary Malay, for, although "classical" Malay is usually identified with Riau-Johore Malay, the language of the literary works of various regions—for example, Acheh, Kutai, and Brunei—all possessed distinctive features.

In Malaysia today, Malay is spoken as mother tongue in a number of dialects, delimited by isoglosses that to some extent coincide with state boundaries. Throughout the country, there is one form of speech that is understood by most Malays and is the language of school instruction, of the radio, and in general of formal occasions. This form of speech may be termed "standard Malay." Most educated Malays speak both standard Malay and their own dialect. Since 1957, standard Malay has been the national language, termed (since 1968) *Bahasa Malaysia*, and government policy encourages its widespread adoption and use by all sections of the population.

The national language of Indonesia is *Bahasa Indonesia* (or Indonesian). This is not a distinct language, for *Bahasa Malaysia* and *Bahasa Indonesia* are dialects of the same language, Malay. Standard Malay and Indonesian grew apart in the twentieth century as the former slowly absorbed English loan words and the latter more rapidly added Dutch (or, after 1945, English) ones. Each, however, is still easily intelligible to speakers of the other. Although Indonesian is the mother tongue of only a small minority of Indonesians, Dutch colonial practice, Indonesian nationalist adoption, and present policy have had the result that virtually all everyday public affairs are conducted in this language. Almost all Indonesians speak a regional language in the home, such as Javanese, Sundanese, Madurese, Batak, or one of many others.

For most of the early and much of the colonial period, Malay in the mother-tongue areas of Malaya, Thailand, Sumatra, and Borneo was written in the *jawi*, or modified Arabic, script, though in Indonesia, and increasingly in Malaysia since independence, the latin script has tended to displace it. As one of the products of colonialism, the spelling systems adopted in the latin script in Indonesia and Malaysia differed in certain respects, but agreement has now been reached on a unified system. A variant of it is used in this book, except in the case of a number of well-established proper names. Malay/Indonesian spelling is, in general, closely phonemic, but the following points may be noted:

MALAY	INDONESIAN	PHONETIC EQUIVALENT
e	e	ə
k (final)	k (final)	ʔ
ny	nj	ɲ
ng	ng	ŋ
ch	tj	tʃ
j	dj	dʒ
sh	sj	ʃ
kh	ch	ɣ
y	j	j

PILIPINO

The national language of the Philippines is a modern effort to create an indigenous lingua franca. Tagalog, the language of the area around Manila, has been broadened to include words and idioms both from the scores of other vernaculars and from Chinese, Spanish, and English.

Many Filipinos acquired Spanish names over the long colonial period, even though they had no Spanish blood and could not speak Spanish; thus, a Spanish name is today no guarantee of *mestizo* parentage. Some Chinese chose to adopt Spanish names, while others merely continued to use their Chinese ones, for example, Teehankee or Locsin. The only difficulty readers of this book may have in pronouncing Filipino names is in those which have a tilde [ñ]. The name Osmeña, for example, should be pronounced *Oz-main-ya.*

THAI

The "General System of Phonetic Transcription of Thai Characters into Roman" of Thailand's Royal Institute has been employed here. It contains a number of pitfalls for English readers. First, note that *h* following a consonant means that that consonant is aspirated. *Kh-* is pronounced like the *c* in *car,* while *k* alone is pronounced like the *g* in *glockenspiel.* Similarly, *th* and *ph* are pronounced like the *t* in *table* and the *p* in *power. Čh* is pronounced as if written *tj,* while *ch* is pronounced as the *ch* in *chair.*

To avoid confusion, "Thai" and "Thailand" have been used throughout to refer, respectively, to the people and kingdom of today. Note, however, that "Siamese" and "Siam" were in general use before 1939, though used officially only in the century preceding World War II. The continued (and retrospective) use of "Siam" and "Siamese" has been rejected by those who view these terms as having narrower ethnic connotations than "Thai" and as having been used primarily by foreigners, and who translate "Thai" to mean "free."

Most Thai names appearing in this book are prefixed by a bureaucratic rank, which ascends from *luang to čhaophraya.* The main name by which a person was known was the bureaucratic title which follows; but as many different individuals were known by the same title at different times, the personal (given and family) names of the individual are inserted after rank and title in parentheses. Thus, Čhaophraya (rank) Si Suriyawong (title) is followed by (Chuang Bunnag), the man's personal name. In modern times, men generally are called by their given names, rather than their family names—thus Pridi rather than Mr. Phanomyong.

VIETNAMESE

Because of the unreasonable cost, it has not been possible for us to write Vietnamese names and terms in this book in the full glory of their diacritical marks. It is necessary to apologize for this omission, because those marks indicate the tones of words and the correct pronunciation of their vowels, and tones and vowel pronunciations are crucial to an understanding of the meanings of Vietnamese words. Even when the vowel pronunciation of a word is obvious, and no tone marks are required, the romanized Vietnamese language requires special markings for it to be intelligible. To take a simple example, when the word *dinh* is written without a stroke through the stem of the "d," it is pronounced *zinh* and means "military camp" or "palace of an official." Only when *dinh* is written with a special stroke through the "d," is it pronounced the way it looks without the stroke to a Western reader, and it then means "adult male taxpayer" or "nail."

Vietnamese names are complicated. The first word in a three-word sequence like Cao Ba Quat indicates the family or lineage to which the person belongs. The second word, known as a "cushion" or "lining" word, may indicate the sex of the person and may also be used for all the male members of one family or, less commonly, may designate one generation of the male members of a family. The third and final word in the sequence is the given name of a Vietnamese individual. But unlike Western usage, and even unlike Chinese usage, a Vietnamese person is ordinarily cited by his given name, not by his family name. Thus Ngo Dinh Diem is referred to in these pages as Diem, Nguyen Truong To as To. Very rarely are there exceptions to this rule. The most famous exception is the bearer of the artificial Sino-Vietnamese pseudonym Ho Chi Minh, who is referred to as Ho.

NOTES

Introduction

1. For a pioneering study of the relationship between ecology and history in Southeast Asia, see Clifford Geertz, *Agricultural Involution: The Processes of Ecological Change in Indonesia* (Berkeley, Cal., 1963).

Part One

1. Dao Duy Anh, *Viet-Nam Van Hoa Su Cuong* (*A General History of Vietnamese Culture*) (Hanoi, 1938), p. 43.
2. Akin Rabibhadana, *The Organization of Thai Society in the Early Bangkok Period, 1782–1873* (Ithaca, 1969).
3. Alexander Woodside, *Vietnam and the Chinese Model* (Cambridge, 1970), Ch. 5.
4. Charles Archaimbault, "Religious Structures in Laos," *Journal of the Siam Society* [hereafter *JSS*], 52:1 (April, 1964), 57–74.
5. Ch. XXXVIII of the Malacca Code, as given in T. J. Newbold, *Political and Statistical Account of the British Settlements in the Straits of Malacca* (London, 1839), II:275–76.
6. *Indio*: literally, Indian. The Spanish applied the term, first used in Latin America, to all natives of the archipelago.
7. Yi Yi, "Kon-hpaung khet sit-tan mya" ("Records of the Konbaung Era"), *Journal of the Burma Research Society*, 49:1 (1966), 71–128.
8. *Dai Nam thuc luc chinh bien* (*Primary Compilation of the Veritable Records of Imperial Vietnam*), I, 43:15.
9. "Thamniap kharatchakan nakhǫn si thammarat khrang ratchakan thi 2" ("Directory of the Officials of Nakhǫn Si Thammarat in the Second Reign"), in *Ruam ruang muang nakhǫn si thammarat* (Bangkok, 1962), pp. 96–149.
10. Pierre Bitard, "Le Manuscript 145 des fonds indochinois de la Bibliothèque Nationale," *Bulletin de la Société des Études Indochinoises*, XXI (1956), 314.
11. Minh Hanh in *Phat-giao Viet-Nam* (*Vietnamese Buddhism*) (Saigon, n.d.), pp. 8, 22.
12. From Vietnamese texts in Pham Van Dieu, "Viet Nam Van Hoc," *Giang Binh* (*Lectures on Vietnamese Literature*) (Saigon, 1960), pp. 74, 77–78.
13. Thich Thanh Tu, *Phat giao trong mach song dan toc* (*Buddhism in the Life Pulse of the People*) (Saigon, 1966), pp. 58–63.
14. H. de la Costa, "The Development of the Native Clergy in the Philippines," in *Studies in Philippine Church History* (Ithaca, 1969), pp. 69–72; *idem*, "Patronato Real and Recurso de Fuerza," in *Asia and the Philippines* (Manila, 1967), pp. 39–48.
15. H. de la Costa, *Readings in Philippine History* (Manila, 1965), pp. 87–91.
16. A. H. Johns, "Sufism as a Category in Indonesian Literature and History," *Journal of Southeast Asian History* (hereafter *JSEAH*) 2:2 (July, 1961), 10–23.

17. Wong Lin Ken, *The Malayan Tin Industry to 1914* (Tucson, 1965), pp. 2–4.
18. T'ien Ju-k'ang, *17–19 shih-chi chung-yeh Chung-kuo fan-ch'uan tsai Tung-nan Ya-chou* (*Chinese Sailing Junks in Southeast Asia from the Seventeenth to the Nineteenth Century*) (Shanghai, 1957), pp. 29, 33.
19. *Konbaungzet mahayazawin dawgyi* (*Royal Chronicle of the Konbaung Dynasty*) (3 vols., Mandalay, 1922–23), 1:574–75.
20. E. H. S. Simmonds, "Thai Narrative Poetry: Palace and Provincial Texts of an Episode from Khun Chang Khun Phaen," *Asia Major*, n.s. 10:2 (1964), 279–99.
21. Edgar Wickberg, "The Chinese Mestizo in Philippine History," *JSEAH*, V:1 (March, 1964), 68 and *passim*.

Part Two

1. Daw Yi Yi, "Additional Burmese Historical Sources (1752–76)," *Guardian*, 15:11 (November, 1968), 33–35 *et seq*.
2. *Konbaungzet mahayazawin dawgyi* (*Royal Chronicle of the Konbaung Dynasty*) (3 vols., Mandalay, 1922–23), I, 529.
3. W. S. Desai, "Events at the Capital and Court of Ava During the First Anglo-Burmese War," *Journal of the Burma Research Society*, XXVII (1937), 3–4.
4. J. Crawfurd, *Journal of an Embassy . . . to the Court of Ava* (2d ed., London, 1834), I:342.
5. Ma Kyan, "King Mindon's Councillors," *Journal of the Burma Research Society*, 44:1 (June, 1961), 43–60.
6. Dorothy Woodman, *The Making of Burma* (London, 1962), p. 139.
7. Henry Yule, A *Narrative of the Mission Sent by the Governor-General of India to the Court of Ava in 1855* (London, 1858; reprinted Kuala Lumpur, 1968), p. 109.
8. D. G. E. Hall, *Burma* (3rd ed., London, 1960), p. 105.
9. The official chronicles state that Taksin was executed shortly thereafter, although persistent legends insist that he escaped to the region of Nakhǫn Si Thammarat and lived there until his death in 1825.
10. See Akin Rabibhadana, *The Organization of Thai Society in the Early Bangkok Period, 1782–1873* (Ithaca, 1969); and David K. Wyatt, "Family Politics in Nineteenth-Century Thailand," *JSEAH*, 9:2 (September, 1968), 208–28.
11. Čhaophraya Thiphakorawong (Kham Bunnag), *Phraratchaphongsawadan krung rattanakosin ratchakan thi 3–4* (*Royal Chronicles of the Third and Fourth Reigns of the Bangkok Era*) (Bangkok, 1963), pp. 369–70; and William L. Bradley, "The Accession of King Mongkut," *JSS*, 57:1 (January, 1969), 148–62.
12. Sir John Bowring, *The Kingdom and People of Siam* (London, 1857), I:226.
13. "Europeans in Siamese Employ," *Siam Repository* (1870), pp. 401–403.
14. This subject remains obscure by default. For example, the Vietnamese diplomatic records dealing with this problem—especially correspondence exchanged between the Bangkok and Hue courts about Cambodia in the 1820's—have survived and may be found in the Nguyen Dynasty *thuc luc* (veritable records) and *chau ban* (vermilion books). See Alexander Woodside, *Vietnam and the Chinese Model*, (Cambridge, 1970), Ch. 5.
15. J. H. Moor, *Notices of the Indian Archipelago* (Singapore 1838: reprinted London 1968), p. 238, quoting *Calcutta Journal*, February 11, 1823.
16. Charles Meyniard, *Le Second Empire en Indo-Chine* (Paris, 1891), p. 461.
17. G. Finlayson, *Mission to Siam and Hue, the Capital of Cochinchina, in the Years 1821–1822* (London, 1826), p. 366.
18. *Nghien cuu lich su* (*Historical Researches*) (Hanoi), LXXVIII (1965):13.
19. Do Thuc Vinh, *Ho Xuan Huong: tac gia the ky XIX* (*Ho Xuan Huong: Nineteenth-Century Writer*) (Saigon, 1956), p. 63.
20. *Dai Nam thuc luc chinh bien*, II, 168:1 ff.
21. *Dai Nam thuc luc chinh bien*, II, 79:29b ff.

22. Nguyen Khoa, *Khao luan Doan Truong Tan Thanh* (*A Study of the* Doan Truong Tan Thanh) (Saigon, 1960), p. 309.

23. Phan Phat Huon, *Viet Nam Giao Su* (*A Religious History of Vietnam*) (Saigon, 1962), II, 231–33.

24. *Dai Nam thuc luc chinh bien*, II, 205:12b ff.

25. *Dai Nam thuc luc chinh bien*, II, 122:8–8b.

26. Nguyen The Anh, *Kinh te va xa hoi Viet Nam duoi cac vua trieu Nguyen* (*The Vietnamese Economy and Society under the Rulers of the Nguyen Court*) (Saigon, 1968), p. 178.

27. Raja Ali Haji, *Tuhfat al-Nafis* (romanized ed., Singapore, 1965), pp. 188–190. The *jawi* (Arabic script) text from which this edition was transliterated appears, edited and with a summary in English by R. O. Winstedt, in the *Journal of the Malayan Branch of the Royal Asiatic Society*, X (1932).

28. Quoted in Rupert Emerson, *Malaysia, A Study in Direct and Indirect Rule* (New York, 1937), p. 81.

29. J. D. Vaughan, *Manners and Customs of the Chinese of the Straits Settlements* (Singapore, 1879), p. 16.

30. Emily Sadka, *The Protected Malay States, 1874–1895* (Kuala Lumpur, 1968), p. 23.

31. It is G. J. Resink who has called attention to the historical value of Conrad's writings as pictures of archipelago conditions in the late nineteenth century. See his *Indonesia's History between the Myths: Essays in Legal History and Historical Theory* (The Hague, 1968), pp. 305–24.

32. J. J. M. de Groot, *Het Kongsiwezen van Borneo* (The Hague, 1885).

33. For a list of some of the others, see Resink, *op. cit.*, pp. 312–13. Conrad was much taken with this theme; *Lord Jim* was one of several explorations of it.

34. The best of the Europocentric versions of Sarawak history is Steven Runciman, *The White Rajahs: A History of Sarawak from 1841 to 1946* (Cambridge, 1960). For the early history of the Iban, see Benedict Sandin's *Sea Dayaks of Borneo Before White Rajah Rule* (East Lansing, 1968). Robert Pringle's *Rajahs and Rebels: The Ibans of Sarawak Under Brooke Rule, 1841–1941* (Ithaca, 1970) puts the two perspectives together in the finest social history of nineteenth- and early-twentieth-century Sarawak.

35. Anne L. Reber, "The Sulu World in the Eighteenth and Early Nineteenth Centuries: A Historiographical Problem in British Writings on Malay Piracy," unpublished M.A. thesis, Cornell University, 1966. John Keith Reynolds, "Towards an Account of Sulu and Its Borneo Dependencies, 1700–1878," unpublished M.A. thesis, University of Wisconsin, 1970.

36. Jeanne Cuisinier, "La guerre des Padri," *Archives de Sociologie des Religions* (January–June, 1959), pp. 70–88; Taufik Abdullah, "Adat and Islam: An Examination of Conflict in Minangkabau," *Indonesia*, II (October, 1966), 1–24.

37. There were and are three major ethnic groups on Java: the Javanese (much the largest), Sundanese, and Madurese. Although the term "Javan" is sometimes used to refer to all of them together, so, more often, if less correctly, is "Javanese."

38. Traditional appanage was the free grant to officials of the sovereign's tax rights over village land and, especially, labor, in lieu of salary. The "leasing of villages" was the renting of appanage rights for cash to private individuals for short terms and for new commercial purposes. "Private lands" differed from village leases only in being permanent or for very long terms.

39. Soepomo Poedjosoedarmo and M. C. Ricklefs, "The Establishment of Surakarta, a Translation from the *Babad Gianti*," *Indonesia*, IV (October, 1967), 94. The original and translation are in verse, rendered here in prose format.

40. The most convenient description of the language is in Clifford Geertz, *The Religion of Java* (Glencoe, 1964), pp. 248–60. On the cultural movement in general see D. H. Burger, *Structural Changes in Javanese Society: the Supra-Village Sphere* (Ithaca, 1956).

41. In 1808, about 60 per cent of Java was under direct Dutch rule; by 1830,

93 per cent. Conversely, in 1757 and up to 1808 the Central Java principalities contained about 40 per cent of the population of the island; after 1830, less than 10 per cent.

42. This administrative pattern has persisted to the present day. In modern Indonesian: *keresidenan* (headed by a *residen*), *kabupaten* (*bupati*), *kewedanan* (*wedana*).

43. On the Java War, see Justus Van der Kroef, "Prince Diponegoro, Progenitor of Indonesian Nationalism," *Far Eastern Quarterly*, VIII:4 (August, 1949), 424–450.

44. María Lourdes Díaz-Trechuelo, "The Economic Development of the Philippines in the Second Half of the Eighteenth Century," *Philippine Studies*, XI:2 (April, 1963), 228.

45. In the late eighteenth century, the friars were made "irremovable parish priests." In 1804, the control over the friars in Spanish dominions was placed in the hands of a special Vicar General who lived in Spain rather than Rome. The papal bull *Inter Graviores* created a very narrow and exclusive character for the Spanish Orders. John N. Schumacher, "The Filipino Nationalists' Propaganda Campaign in Europe, 1880–1895," unpublished Ph.D. dissertation, Georgetown University, 1965, pp. 28–29.

46. Nicholas Loney to Consul W. Farren, July 10, 1861 (PRO FO, 72/1017), and April 12, 1857 (PRO FO, 72/927) cited in Robert MacMicking, *Recollections of Manilla and the Philippines* (Manila, 1967), pp. 245, 250.

47. Reliable census figures are hard to find, but there were approximately 4,000 Europeans in the Philippines at the beginning of the nineteenth century. In 1850, there were about 5,000 *peninsulares* or creoles, 20,000 Spanish *mestizos*, 5,000 Chinese, 240,000 Chinese *mestizos*, and 4,750,000 *indios*. According to the 1876 figures of the Archdiocese of Manila, there were 13,265 Spaniards with no official capacity, plus an additional 24,983 clergy, bureaucrats, and military personnel. Between 1834 and 1862, Spain had four constitutions, twenty-eight parliaments, forty-seven Presidents of the Council of Ministers, and 529 ministers with portfolios. James A. LeRoy, *The Americans in the Philippines* (Boston, 1914), I:52.

48. Edgar Wickberg, *The Chinese in Philippine Life, 1850–1898* (New Haven, 1965), p. 52.

49. Cited in Edgar Wickberg, "The Chinese Mestizo in the Philippines," *JSEAH*, V:1 (March, 1964), 75.

50. Sinibaldo de Mas, *Secret Report of Sinibaldo de Mas* (Manila, 1963), p. 133.

51. Quoted in H. de la Costa, "Development of the Native Clergy in the Philippines," *Studies in Philippine Church History* (Ithaca, 1969), pp. 99–100.

52. As the French consul, Fabre, noted, "This whole affair in which the Spanish Government, in effect, told the creoles, 'You are our enemies,' has added hatred to the jealousy that already existed between Spaniards and creoles. With an unbelievable lack of prudence, the Spanish themselves encourage this hatred and jealousy by arrogantly assuming an attitude of supreme contempt toward the colonial-born. The authorities are at present seriously considering an ordinance which would permit only Spaniards to reside in the walled city, the creoles being sent out to live in the suburbs." Fabre to Minister of Foreign Affairs, Manila, May 29, 1842, *AMAE Corr. comm. Manille,* II:32, cited in H. de la Costa, *Readings in Philippine History* (Manila, 1965), p. 215.

53. Austin Craig, *The Filipinos' Fight for Freedom* (Manila, 1933), p. 400.

Part Three

1. N. J. Brailey, "The Origins of the Siamese Forward Movement in Western Laos," Unpublished Ph.D. dissertation, University of London, 1968, pp. 165–69.

2. *Phongsawadan muang songkhla lae phatthalung* (*Chronicles of Songkhla and Phatthalung*) (Bangkok, 1962), Chart 1 at end.

3. Philippe Preschez, "Les relations Franco-Birmanes aux XVIIIe et XIXe siècles," *France-Asie*, 21:3 (September, 1967), 275–425.

4. Whether he was really a "second king," like his father in Mongkut's reign, or just an heir-apparent was a major issue in the conflict.

5. See David K. Wyatt, *The Politics of Reform in Thailand* (New Haven, 1969), pp. 35–62.

6. *Ibid.*, pp. 84–93.

7. But a French researcher sent into the Vietnamese imperial archives to find justification for these claims returned empty-handed. Pensri Suvanij Duke, *Les relations entre la France et la Thaïlande (Siam) au XIXᵉ siècle, d'après les archives des Affaires Étrangères* (Bangkok, 1962), pp. 129–30.

8. Tej Bunnag, "Khabot phu mi bun phak isan" ("The Holy Men's Revolt in the Northeast"), *Sangkhomsat parithat*, 5:1 (June, 1967), 78–86; and "Khabot ngiao müang phrae" ("The Shan Revolt of Phrae"), *ibid.*, 6:2 (September, 1968), 67–80.

9. The remaining areas of predominantly Malay population, just to the north of these four states, continued as part of Thailand.

10. Trinh Van Thanh, *Giang luan Viet Van* (*An Exposition of Vietnamese Literature*), (Saigon, 1962), p. 687.

11. *Receuil de traités Conclus par la France en Extrême Orient: 1648–1902* (Paris, 1902–7), I:209.

12. For a full discussion of this rebellion, see Milton E. Osborne, *The French Presence in Cochinchina and Cambodia: Rule and Response, 1859–1905* (Ithaca, 1969), pp. 206–230.

13. *The Times* (London), May 11, 1927 (obituary for Sisowath).

14. See, for example, Roland Meyer, *Komlah: Visions d'Asie* (Paris, 1927), and Jean Ajalbert, *Sao van Di* (Paris, 1905).

15. "Melayu," the indigenous root of the modern invention "Malaysia," referred to a language and an Islamic people, not to a state.

16. D. H. Burger, *Structural Changes in Javanese Society* (two parts, Ithaca, 1956–57).

17. See his autobiography, *Kenang2an* (Batavia, 1936). The photographs in this volume show the transformation very clearly.

18. Report of General Wood as to Abrogation Bates Treaty, Zamboanga, Mindanao, December 16, 1903, cited in *Report of the Philippine Commission* (1903), I:489–90.

19. William Cameron Forbes, *The Philippine Islands* (New York, 1928), II:31.

20. Mi Mi Khaing, *Burmese Family* (Bloomington, Ind., 1962).

21. The term plantation, in the narrow sense used here, refers only to large units under a single management using wage labor. What the literature often refers to as Cochinchinese rice "plantations" and Javan and Philippine sugar "plantations" are discussed below. In Malaya, what are called plantations in this book are always referred to as "estates."

22. Colonial legislation and administrative pressure made it very difficult for Malays to plant new rubber areas all through the 1920's and 1930's; quotas assigned to Malayan smallholders under the restriction schemes of 1922–29 and 1934–42 were palpably unfair. In the Netherlands Indies, the most flagrant measure taken against smallholders was the special surtax, levied between 1934 and 1938 on smallholder rubber only, which took as much as 95 per cent of the net proceeds from these growers. P. T. Bauer, *The Rubber Industry* (London, 1948).

23. The exception is the sections of B. J. O. Schrieke's "West Coast Report" in his *Indonesian Sociological Studies* (The Hague, 1955), I:95–143, which catches the excitement of the swing to the cash economy with the planting of coffee and rubber in the 1910's and 1920's.

24. About a third of "smallholder" rubber in Malayan statistics of this period consisted of medium-sized commercial holdings of 25–100 acres owned mostly by Chinese. Although this type of enterprise was unknown in the Netherlands Indies, it was also common in Sarawak and South Thailand. These holdings, operated like

the small capitalist Chinese tin mines, were thus an intermediate form of production between the very large, highly capitalized English plantations and the Malay peasant plots of a few acres each.

25. The following pages are based mainly on the new research (as yet unpublished) of Michael Adas.

26. The administrative unit of Lower Burma included Arakan and Tenasserim as well as the delta proper. The Burmese rice trade had begun in the 1820's from these areas, after the British acquired them at the end of the first Anglo-Burman War. In 1855, they had about as much land under rice as the whole delta and produced virtually all the relatively small exports of that time. But they had much less land suitable for rice and, as the delta opened up, became less and less important in the statistics.

27. Owners of sugar *centrals* were a thorough mixture of Americans and Spanish (both almost all Philippine residents) and *mestizos*. *Hacenderos* were almost all *mestizo* or *indio*. The ethnic factor was not important in these political disputes.

28. Clifford Geertz, *Agricultural Involution* (Berkeley, Cal., 1963), p. 78.

Part Four

1. Sartono Kartodirdjo, *The Peasants' Revolt of Banten in 1888* (Verhandelingen van het Koninklijk Instituut voor Taal-, Land- en Volkenkunde, No. 50, The Hague, 1966), p. 5.

2. Harry J. Benda, "Peasant Movements in Colonial Southeast Asia," *Asian Studies* (Manila), III:3 (December, 1965), 433–34.

3. The most recent discussion of the Samin movement is contained in Harry J. Benda and Lance Castles, "The Samin Movement," *Bijdragen tot de Taal-, Land- en Volkenkunde,* Deel 125 (1969), 207–40.

4. For a similar hypothesis by a recent historian, see J. de V. Allen, "The Kelantan Rising of 1915: Some Thoughts on the Concept of Resistance in British Malayan History," *JSEAH,* IX:2 (September, 1968), 241–57.

5. Robert M. Pringle, "Asun's 'Rebellion': The Political Growing Pains of a Tribal Society in Brooke Sarawak, 1929–1940," Paper delivered to the International Conference on Asian History, Kuala Lumpur, 1968.

6. David R. Sturtevant, "Guardia de Honor: Revitalization Within the Revolution," *Asian Studies* (Manila), IV:2 (1966), 342–52.

7. Victor Purcell, *The Chinese in Southeast Asia* (2d ed., London, 1965), Introduction.

8. G. William Skinner, *Chinese Society in Thailand: An Analytical History* (Ithaca, 1957), p. 183.

9. W. Gordon East and O. H. K. Spate, eds. *The Changing Map of Asia,* 4th ed. (New York, 1950), p. 214.

10. For a discussion of Chinese economic expertise, see Maurice Freedman, "The Handling of Money: A Note on the Background to the Economic Sophistication of the Overseas Chinese," *Man,* LIX (1959), 64–65.

11. Quoted by R. J. Wilkinson, "The Education of Asiatics," *Special Reports on Educational Subjects,* Vol. 8, published as Cd. 835, Great Britain Parliamentary Papers, 1902, 687.

12. Tengku Abdullah Ahmad, "Apa-Kah Faedah Merdeka?" ("What is the Advantage of Freedom?"), *Seruan Azhar,* 3 (Cairo, October, 1927), 492–93.

13. Frank Swettenham, *British Malaya* (London, 1907), p. 248.

14. *Report of the Philippine Commission,* 1903, I:59.

15. *Al-Imam* (Singapore), 1:6 (November, 1906).

16. Sinibaldo de Mas, *Report on the Condition of the Philippines in 1842* (Manila, 1963), p. 169.

17. John N. Schumacher, "The Filipino Nationalists' Propaganda Campaign in Europe, 1880–1895," unpublished Ph.D. dissertation, Georgetown University, 1965,

p. 191. See, for example, Marcelo H. del Pilar, *Monastic Supremacy in the Philippines* (Quezon City, 1958).

18. José Rizal, "Filipinas dentro de cien años," (1890), cited in H. de la Costa, *Readings in Philippine History* (Manila, 1965), p. 229.

19. W. E. Retana's transcription of *The Trial of José Rizal*, translated and edited by H. de la Costa (Manila, 1961), pp. 102–3.

20. José Rizal to Mariano Ponce, April 1889, cited in Schumacher, p. 547.

21. Maximo M. Kalaw, *The Development of Philippine Politics, 1872–1920* (Manila, 1926), p. 128.

22. Richard Hofstadter, "Manifest Destiny and the Philippines," in Theodore P. Greene, ed., *American Imperialism in 1898* (Boston, 1955), p. 91.

23. As the Schurman Commission noted, "These picked Filipinos will be of infinite value to the United States in the work of establishing and maintaining civil government throughout the archipelago. As leaders of the people, they must be the chief agents in securing their people's loyal obedience to which, therefore, the dictates of policy, as well as plain common sense and justice, require us to secure their cordial attachment." *Report of the Philippine Commission to the President, January 31, 1900* (Washington, 1900), I:120, 183.

24. Garel A. Grunder and William E. Livezey, *The Philippines and the United States* (Norman, Okla., 1951), p. 2.

25. *Report of the Philippine Commission, 1904*, I:3–4; Rōyama Masamichi and Takéuchi Tatsuji, *The Philippine Polity: A Japanese View* (Yale University, Monograph No. 12, 1967), p. 77.

26. *Special Report of the Secretary of War, William H. Taft to President Theodore Roosevelt, January 23, 1908*, III:238–39.

27. *Report of the Philippine Commission*, 1902, I:4.

28. William Cameron Forbes, *The Philippine Islands* (Boston, 1928), II:520–44.

29. Sumulong noted that "any reunion of the followers of Quezon and Osmeña—call it fusion, coalition, cooperation, or conjunction—would mean the restoration, inexcusable from all angles, of the feared and detested oligarchy. Such a reunion would undo a transcendental political reform, providentially or accidentally effected through our own dissensions over the Hare-Hawes-Cutting Law. . . . It would be a step backward, contrary to the general interest, and especially destructive of the future of a sane and genuine democracy in this country." Juan Sumulong, *Philippine Free Press*, May 11, 1935, p. 30.

30. Maximo M. Kalaw, *Introduction to Philippine Social Science* (Manila, 1937), p. 185.

31. The Report was published as Cmd. 9109, Great Britain Parliamentary Papers, 1918, Vol. 8.

32. John F. Cady, *A History of Modern Burma* (Ithaca, 1958), pp. 242–43.

33. Lest these figures be held to show the effectiveness of electoral boycott, it might be noted that similar statistics hold for the first elections in Thailand.

34. Cady, *A History of Modern Burma*, p. 317*n*.

35. *Letters of a Javanese Princess* (New York, 1964), p. 63.

36. *Totok* is an Indonesian term for foreign-born immigrants. As used in this chapter it refers to (in principle) pure-blooded individuals identifying themselves, and identified by others, as Dutch and Chinese, respectively.

37. Quoted in Robert Van Niel, *The Emergence of the Modern Indonesian Elite* (The Hague, 1960), pp. 38–39. It was a prominent Ethical official who collected and published Kartini's correspondence under the revealing title "Through Darkness to Light."

38. The Indonesian term *peranakan* (from the root *anak*, child) means local-born foreigner. As used in this chapter, it refers to Dutch or Chinese *mestizos* of mixed blood and, before their transformations at least, of mixed culture. The 1930 census recorded about 40,000 *totok* Dutch and 200,000 Eurasians. They constituted only .4 per cent of the total population but were much the largest such groups in Southeast Asia, except for the special case of the Philippines.

39. In 1900, out of a large group of legally defined "European" children, mostly Eurasians, entering primary school, 70 per cent could speak little or no Dutch. I. J. Brugmans, *Geschiedenis van het Onderwijs in Nederlandsch-Indie* (Groningen, 1938), p. 295.

40. The "Dutch" in the name of these schools referred to the language of instruction, not the pupils' nationality. They were intended solely for Chinese.

41. For the best survey of this movement, see Claire Holt, *Art in Indonesia: Continuities and Change* (Ithaca, 1967), pp. 168–87. New developments occurred in Balinese dance and other art forms in the same period without as direct a Western stimulus. See Beryl de Zoete and Walter Spies, *Dance and Drama in Bali* (London, 1938).

42. A. J. van Zanen, *Voorwaarden voor Maatschappelijke Ontwikkeling in het Centrale Batakland* (Leiden, 1934).

43. For a fuller treatment of this theme, see James Siegel, *The Rope of God* (Berkeley, 1969). PUSA stands for Pusat Ulama Seluruh Acheh, Central Association of the Ulama of all Acheh.

44. See Hamka's autobiography, *Kenang2an Hidup* (Kuala Lumpur, 1966) and his biography of his father, *Ajahku* (Djakarta, 1950).

45. Among the best known were the political leaders Mohammad Hatta and Sutan Sjahrir and the literary figures Takdir Alisjahbana and Mohammad Radjab.

46. The literal meaning of *santri* is student (of religion), and the term forms the root of the word *pesantren*, traditional religious school.

47. These and figures on the following pages are drawn from the useful tables in S. L. van der Wal, *Het Onderwijsbeleid in Nederlands-Indie, 1900–1940* (Groningen, 1963), 693–700.

48. Akira Nagazumi, "The Origin and the Earlier Years of the Budi Utomo, 1908–1918," unpublished Ph.D. dissertation, Cornell University, 1967. Budi Utomo is conventionally translated as "Noble Endeavor," which conveys the original spirit of the enterprise very well.

49. On Kudus, see The Siauw Giap, "Group Conflict in a Plural Society," *Revue du Sud-Est Asiatique* (1966), 1 & 2. On West Java, see W. A. Oates, "The Afdeeling B: an Indonesian Case Study," *JSEAH*, IX:1 (1968), 107–16. On the Toba (who only listened), see Zanen, p, 75.

50. The word "Indonesia" (Latin: island India) was not commonly used at the time. It was a technical term coined by nineteenth-century anthropologists to refer to island Southeast Asia in general.

51. Benedict Anderson, "The Languages of Indonesian Politics," *Indonesia*, I (1966):89.

52. For the complex and creative mixture of ideas behind Taman Siswa, see Ruth McVey, "Taman Siswa and the Indonesian National Awakening," *Indonesia*, IV (1967):128–49. It was a very early effort to create a national philosophy of education and had strong influence on the government school system after independence. Ki Hadjar Dewantoro was the name taken by Suwardi Suryaningrat after his Indies Party phase had ended and his educational career begun.

53. See Ta Van Ru, *Luan de ve Ton Tho Tuong va Phan Van Tri* (*A Discussion of Ton Tho Tuong and Phan Van Tri*), (Saigon, 1960), pp. 18–22.

54. Trinh Van Thanh, *Giang luan Viet Van* (*An Exposition of Vietnamese Literature*), (Saigon, 1962), p. 375.

55. Nguyen Hien Le, *Dong Kinh Nghia Thuc* (*The Dong Kinh Free School*), (Saigon, 1956, 1968), p. 83.

56. Lam Giang, *Giang luan ve Phan Boi Chau* (*A Disquisition on Phan Boi Chau*), (Saigon, 1959), pp. 96–97.

57. Translated from the text in Pham Van Dieu, *Viet Nam van hoc giang binh* (*Lectures on Vietnamese Literature*), (Saigon, 1960), pp. 474–76.

58. Nhat Linh, *Doan tuyet* (*A Severance of Ties*), (Saigon, 1967 edition), p. 187. First published in 1935.

59. Hoang Van Dao, *Viet Nam Quoc Dan Dang, lich su dau tranh can dai*

1927–1954 (*The Vietnamese Nationalist Party: A History of its Modern Struggle, 1927–1954*), (Saigon, 1964), p. 33.

60. Hoang Van Dao, p. 44.

61. Tran Van Giau, *Giai cap cong nhan Viet Nam* (*The Vietnamese Labor Class*), (Hanoi, 1962), I:117.

62. King Mongkut, *Prachum phraratchaniphon phasa thai* (*Collected Royal Writings in the Thai Language*), Part One (Bangkok, 1968), pp. 378–82. See also Henry Alabaster, *The Wheel of the Law: Buddhism Illustrated, from Siamese sources* (London, 1871).

63. Rian Sichan and Net Phunwiwat, *Prawat patiwat khrang raek khong thai r.s. 130* (*History of the First Revolution in Thailand, 1911–12*) (2d ed., Bangkok, 1960).

64. Direk Chainam, *Thai kap songkhram lok khrang thi 2* (*Thailand and World War II*) (2 vols., Bangkok; 1966), I, esp. 184–203.

65. *Indochina*, September 2, 1943.

66. Jean B. Alberti, *L'Indochine d'autrefois et d'aujourd'hui* (Paris, 1934), p. 447.

67. "3349" (pseud.), *Chao Phetsarath, burut lek haeng ratcha-anachak lao* (*Prince Phetsarath, Iron Man of the Kingdom of Laos*) (Bangkok, 1956), p. 79. This book is written in the first person, as though it were the autobiography of Phetsarath.

68. *Preah reac pii thii rechea pisek* (*Coronation Ceremonies*) (Phnom Penh, 1942), 29 ff.

69. Information regarding the demonstration was provided by Mr. Leonard Overton, who has studied the trial records of the civil spokesmen involved. See also Claude Fillieux, *Merveilleux Cambodge* (Paris, 1962), p. 166.

70. Norodom Sihanouk, "La Monarchie Khmère," in *Le Sangkum*, No. 9 (April, 1966), p. 22, note 2.

Part Five

1. Ba Maw, *Breakthrough in Burma: Memoirs of a Revolution, 1939–1946* (New Haven, 1968).

2. Hugh Tinker, *The Union of Burma* (3d ed.; London, 1961), pp. 90–91.

3. Herbert A. Fine, "The Liquidation of World War II in Thailand," *Pacific Historical Review*, 34:1 (February, 1965), 65–82.

4. *New York Times*, July 9, 1969.

5. Noted in Hugh Toye, *Laos: Buffer State or Battleground* (London, 1968), p. 204.

6. Thu Son in *Van Nghe* (*Literature and the Arts*) (Hanoi), No. 73, September 18, 1964.

7. Tran Huy Lieu, Van Tao, *Tong Khoi Nghia Thang Tam* (*The August General Uprising*) (Hanoi, 1957), pp. 43–45.

8. *Nghien cuu lich su* (*Historical Researches*) (Hanoi), No. 50, May, 1963, pp. 11 ff.

9. *Ibid.*, No. 80, November, 1965, p. 61.

10. Hoang Nhu Mai, *Van hoc Viet Nam hien dai 1945–1960* (*Contemporary Vietnamese Literature, 1945–1960*) (Hanoi, 1961), p. 263.

11. *Hoc Tap* (*Learning and Practice*) (Hanoi), No. 9, 1966, p. 57.

12. Hoang Nhu Mai, *op. cit.*, pp. 492–502.

13. The Uyen, *Nghi trong mot xa hoi tan ra* (*Thoughts from Within a Disintegrating Society*) (Saigon, 1967), pp. 81–82.

14. Tran Van Tuyen, et al., *Nghi ve cach mang, chien tranh, va hoa binh* (*Reflections on Revolution, War and Peace*) (Saigon, 1967), p. 61.

15. James de V. Allen, *The Malayan Union* (Yale Southeast Asia Studies, New Haven, 1967), p. 19.

16. See Michael R. Stenson, *Repression and Revolt: The Origins of the 1948*

Communist Insurrection in Malaya and Singapore (Papers in International Studies, Southeast Asia Series, Ohio University, Athens, 1969).

17. Margaret Roff, "The Malayan Chinese Association, 1948–1965," *Journal of Southeast Asian History*, VI:2 (September, 1965), 42.

18. On the earlier stages of this process, see R. K. Vasil, "The 1964 General Elections in Malaya," *International Studies*, VII:1 (July, 1965), 20–65.

19. Carlos P. Romulo, *I Saw the Fall of the Philippines* (New York, 1942), pp. 59–60.

20. *Official Journal of the Japanese Military Administration*, VII (Manila, n.d.): viii.

21. Letter of José Yulo, *et al.*, to Douglas MacArthur, May 20, 1945, cited in *Documents on the Japanese Occupation of the Philippines*, Mauro Garcia (ed.) (Manila, 1965), pp. 179–183.

22. José P. Laurel, *Forces that Make a Nation Great* (Manila, 1943), p. 32.

23. *Pemuda* means literally youth, but in the revolution it took on a deeper connotation of activism, militance, and patriotism. The theme of the *pemuda* movement is developed in John R. W. Smail, *Bandung in the Early Revolution, 1945–1946* (Ithaca, 1964) and especially in Benedict Anderson, "The *Pemuda* Revolution: Indonesian politics, 1945–1946," unpublished Ph.D. dissertation, Cornell University, 1967.

24. *Badan* means organization, group. *Perdjuangan*, one of the key emotive words of the revolution, means struggle for the cause.

25. In Acheh, and later in West Borneo, considerable numbers of Chinese were massacred as well.

26. Nathan Keyfitz, in *Asian Survey*, V:10 (October, 1965), 503 ff.

27. Pham Van Dong, *Bao Cao cua chinh phu . . . Ngay 2-1-1957* (*Government Report of January 2, 1957*) (Hanoi, 1957), p. 31.

28. E. K. Fisk, "Features of the Rural Economy," in T. H. Silcock and E. K. Fisk, eds., *The Political Economy of Independent Malaya* (Berkeley, 1963), p. 165.

29. *Hoc Tap* (*Learning and Practice*), (Hanoi), 9, 1966, p. 57.

30. Tran Van Qua in *Chinh Luan* (Saigon), December 9, 1968.

31. Ton That Dong in *Chinh Luan* (Saigon), October 30–31, 1967.

32. Caldwell, in Silcock and Fisk, eds., *op. cit.*

33. T. G. McGee, *The Southeast Asian City* (New York, 1967), pp. 87–88.

34. Nguyen Van Trung, *Nhan Dinh IV: Chien tranh, cach mang, hoa binh* (*Realizations, Fourth Volume: Conflict, Revolution, Peace*) (Saigon, 1966), p. 129.

35. Ho Huu Tuong, *Hoa dinh cam tran* (*Flower Camps and Brocade Battle Lines*) (Saigon, 1967), p. 254.

36. Interview with the *Times* of India, January 31, 1969; in Permanent Mission of Thailand to the United Nations, Press Release No. 9, February 19, 1969.

37. Hoang Nhu Mai, *Van hoc Viet Nam hien dai 1945–1960* (*Contemporary Vietnamese Literature, 1945–1960*) (Hanoi, 1961), pp. 45–46.

38. *Chanh Dao* (Saigon), September 12–13, 1968.

39. E. Sarkisyanz, "The Place of U Nu's Buddhist Socialism in Burma's History of Ideas," *Studies on Asia*, II, 1962.

40. "The Sangha and Social Activities," *Sangkhomsat parithat* (*Social Science Review*), spec. no. 4 (August, 1966), pp. 15–17.

41. Nguyen Van Trung, *Nhan Dinh IV*, pp. 120–21.

42. James L. Peacock, *Rites of Modernization* (Chicago, 1968).

43. *Nhan dan* (Hanoi), June 27, 1965, p. 2.

44. Margaret Roff, "The Politics of Language in Malaya," *Asian Survey*, No. 7 (May, 1967), pp. 316–28.

GLOSSARY

a-so-ya-min: Burman bureaucratic class in the colonial period, whose members evolved their own mixed Anglo-Burman life style

abangan: the variant of Javanese religion characterized by an eclectic blend of Islamic, Hindu-Buddhist, and earlier beliefs and practices. Used in contrast to the *santri* variant.

adat: custom in the widest sense, and customary law in general, in Malaysia and Indonesia

ahmudan: that portion of the population in monarchical Burma which rendered labor service to the king and his officers and were bound personally to the king by virtue of their hereditary status and occupancy of royal lands, usually in Upper Burma

alcalde-mayor: a Spanish provincial governor in the Philippines

alun-alun: the central square of a Javan royal capital or other town, on which the court of a king or *bupati* looks out

amphoe: Thai term for the administrative districts into which a province is divided

atap: the Malay term for roof thatch, usually made from the leaves of the nipa palm

athi: the portion of the population in monarchical Burma that rendered labor service impersonally to local officers rather than to the king

atwin-wun: the "inside ministers" or palace privy councilors who presided over the Burman king's privy council (*byè-daik*), and who directed the service corps at the palace

audiencia: the highest tribunal of justice, and the advisory council to the governor of the Spanish Philippines

baba: colonial-born; the community of Chinese in the Malay peninsula (especially Malacca) who, through intermarriage with Malays and long residence, have acquired a distinct identity of their own. Also used for the analogous group of *peranakan* Chinese on Java.

bach lang: "blank coins," a traditional Vietnamese term for inflation

badan perdjuangan: "struggle groups,"–a term from the Indonesian Revolution–armed groups spontaneously formed in the post-1945 struggle for independence

baht: the basic unit of the Thai currency

balai: the audience hall of a Malay raja's palace

barangay: a kinship unit in the pre-Spanish Philippines that consisted of from 30 to 100 families, which the Spanish preserved as the basic unit of local administration in the Philippines

barong tagalog: a loose-fitting embroidered shirt worn without neck ornaments in the Philippines

barrio: a village in the Philippines

batik: a type of Indonesian or Malay dyed cloth

bay buom: "butterfly flights," an atmosphere of carefree elegance and freedom sought by some Vietnamese higher-education students

bekel: "tax farmer," the individual who did the actual tax collecting for the princes or officials granted appanages by the Mataram king

bendahara: the "treasurer" of a Malay raja; honorific given to one of the most senior of Malay chiefs

bilal: the Muslim officer who makes the daily calls to prayer

binh hoa qui: "vase of precious flowers," a tradition in Vietnamese education—attacked by revolutionaries—in which the village school is considered an outpost of the Confucian elite, not an agency for mass education

blijvers: "stayers," those Dutch who thought of the Indies as their home (used in contrast to *trekkers*)

Bo-gyok: a Burmese term meaning commander-in-chief

bodhi: "great awakening," part of the name of middle and elementary schools sponsored by the General Association of Vietnamese Buddhism for the children of Buddhist families in Vietnam

bodhisattva: men, lay or ecclesiastical, who have become Buddhas-to-be and who compassionately help others to reach Nirvana before entering it themselves

budak-budak raja: the "bully boys," or armed retainers of a Malay raja

bundok: Tagalog for "mountain"

bupati: Javan local lord or leading territorial official, called "regent" in Dutch and English

byè-daik: the Burman king's privy council

cabecilla: "boss," "foreman," or "ringleader"—a system of distributing and purchasing goods in the Spanish Philippines in which a Chinese central agent with his provincial factors provided a link between the *indio* producer and the foreign export community

cabeza de barangay: the Spanish term for the hereditary headmen (formerly *datu*) of the smallest unit of local administration in the Philippines

cacique: a member of the privileged landholding elite in the Spanish Philippines

central: a sugar refinery in the Philippines

cetiya: a tower-like Buddhist monument usually containing relics

chang: the largest unit of premodern Thai currency; 80 *baht*
čhangwat: province, in twentieth-century Thailand
čhaomüang: the "lord" of a town and its territory. Used throughout the Thai-Lao world.
Chettyar: a caste of Indian money-lenders, originating near Madras, who played a particularly important role in nineteenth- and twentieth-century Lower Burma
chu nghia xa hoi: "socialism"–the Vietnamese term
co mat vien: the Vietnamese Privy Council created by the Emperor Minh-mang
cofradía: a term for a religious brotherhood in the Philippines
consulado: "consulate," or "guild." Such a guild was established in the Philippines in 1769. It consisted of Spanish merchants in Manila who supervised the galleon trade, subject only to the control of the governor.
controleur: subordinate Dutch administrative official in the Indies
Cortes: the Spanish parliament in Madrid
creoles: a term for Spaniards born in the Spanish empire, in contrast to those born on the Iberian Peninsula (*peninsulares*)
dacoit: an armed brigand in Burma
dalang: the puppeteer for the Javanese shadow-play (*wayang kulit*)
dalem: the court of a *bupati* on Java
datu: (also spelled *dato*) aristocratic title used throughout island Southeast Asia
daulat: the mystical powers conferred by kingship on a Malay raja
devaraja: "god-king"
Dhamma: Pali term for the teachings of Buddha; *Dharma* to Mahayana Buddhists
diplomasi: In Indonesian literally "diplomacy." In political disputes of the Indonesian Revolution, the term stood for a policy of negotiating for independence, in contrast to *perdjuangan.*
djago: an Indonesian term for bandit
Do sat vien: the Censorate in traditional Vietnam; a body of officials who scrutinized the conduct of other mandarins, and sometimes that of the emperor himself
Dong Du: "eastern travel," a movement of Vietnamese who went to Japan to study between 1905 and 1908
filipino: prior to the nineteenth century, a term applied to Caucasians born in the Philippines (*creoles*), as opposed to Caucasians born in the Iberian Peninsula. During the nineteenth century it came to include *mestizos* and *indios* born in the Philippines as well.
genjumin: "native," a condescending term used by the Japanese in World War II to refer to Indonesians
gobernadorcillo: "petty governor," the chief magistrate of a municipality in the Spanish Philippines, and the highest *indio* official in the Spanish bureaucracy

gremio: a district governing council in Manila during the late Spanish period
guru: a teacher in Indonesia and Malaysia
hacienda: an estate in the Philippines
haj: the pilgrimage to Mecca
haji: a Muslim who has performed the *haj*
hakim: Malay-Indonesian word for "judge," one of the principal officials of a Malay raja, sometimes also his chief religious dignitary
halus: "refined" or "polished," a Javanese concept defining one polar type of life style and behavior, particularly for *priyayi*. The opposite is *kasar*.
hlutdaw: the supreme council of state in traditional Burma
hoi chu ba: associations of temple nuns in Vietnam
hoi dong hao muc: the village council of notables in Vietnam
hui: "secret society," a type of social organization common among overseas Chinese in Southeast Asia
hukum adat (an Arabic term referring to Muslim religious life): Malay custom and customary law
hukum akl (an Arabic term): Malay principles of natural justice based on the intellect
hukum faal (an Arabic term): Malay principles of right conduct
hukum shera: *shar'ia* law; the canon law of Islam
ilustrado: "enlightened one," a member of the indigenous intelligentsia in the late-nineteenth-century Philippines, which spoke for the emerging Filipino community
imam: the leader of a mosque congregation and, by extension, of any Muslim community
indio: a Spanish term for the Malays of the Philippines
Indisch culture: literally "Indies" culture; the mixed Dutch-Javan culture pattern adopted by most Eurasians and *blijver* Dutch on Java in the nineteenth century
indulto de comercio: a fine paid in advance by the Spanish provincial governors of the Philippines who expected to transgress the legal proscription on commercial activity
inquilino: "lessee," an *indio* or *mestizo* to whom was given a concession to clear and improve church land in the Philippines. The land remained the property of the church, and the lessee would sublet it to tenants for a percentage of their crop yield.
istana: Malay/Indonesian word for "palace." In particular, the palace of the *raja* of a Malayo-Muslim *negeri*.
jawi: a Malay (modified Arabic) script
Jawi Peranakan: a Muslim of mixed Indian-Malay descent born in Malaysia
kalahom: originally the ministry of military affairs in fifteenth-century Thailand, it came to denote the ministry of the southern provinces in the eighteenth and nineteenth

centuries, and became the modern ministry of defense in 1894

kamma (Pali) or *karma* (Sanskrit): the Buddhist law of deed, which affirms that deeds in one's existence determine one's situation in a later incarnation

kampong: a Malay/Indonesian term for village, used in Indonesia to describe an urban neighborhood

kanmüang: "the business of the province," a Thai word for politics in general

Kapitan China: a Malay/Indonesian term for the leading resident Chinese merchant

kasamahan: the landholding system in the Spanish Philippines whereby an *inquilino* leased land from the church and sublet it to tenants for a percentage of their crop yield

kasar: "coarse," or "unrefined"; a Javanese concept defining one polar type of life style and behavior, typical for peasants or uneducated people generally. The opposite is *halus.*

kathi: an Islamic magistrate in Malaysia and Indonesia

Kempeitai: the Japanese military police in World War II

kerah: a Malay term for tribute labor (*corvée*)

kha: "savage," or "slave"; a term sometimes used in Laos and Thailand to refer to upland peoples whose linguistic affiliation is Mon-Khmer (the Lamet, Khmu, P'u Noi, and others)

khao tich: the triennial rating reports on Vietnamese officials, a device by which the emperor kept watch over his provincial officials

khatib: the reciter of the *khutbah* (address) at the Friday mosque service

khau phan dien: "allotment lands," lands given to local officers of Emperor Gia-long's armed following

kongsi: generically, an association of any sort. Used especially for working communities of Chinese miners in the Malay peninsula and Indonesia.

kraton: the sacral palace-city of the Javanese kings

kretek: Indonesian cigarette, with cloves mixed into the tobacco

krom müang: the ministry in charge of the districts around the capital, and of metropolitan law and order, in Thailand through the nineteenth century

krom na: the ministry of lands in Thailand, superseded in 1892 by the ministry of agriculture

kuasa: the supreme temporal authority embodied in a Malay raja

Kuo-yü: Mandarin Chinese, the official "national speech" of China

kyaung: a Buddhist monastery in Burma

laksamana: "warden of the seas," honorific given to one of the most senior of Malay chiefs

langgar: a small prayer house in Java, sometimes attached to the home of one of the wealthier peasants in a village

luc bo: the Six Boards, which crowned the traditional Vietnamese administrative structure

ludrug: a popular dramatic genre of East Java

lukčhin: a term for Chinese born in Thailand

mahatthai: originally the ministry of civil affairs in fifteenth-century Thailand, it came to denote the ministry of northern and eastern provinces in the eighteenth and nineteenth centuries and became the ministry of the interior in 1894

maistry: boss of an Indian work gang in Burma

mantja negara: the third administrative circle of Mataram, which consisted of most of Java outside the palace city and the core administrative area

Marechaussee: the mobile Dutch armed force, which was effective against Indonesian resistance to the Dutch regime

Marhaenisme: a term created by Sukarno to express a concern for the interests of the common man

menteri: "minister," officer of state in the Malay *negeri*

merdeka: "freedom" or "independence" in Malay and Indonesian

mestizo: a Spanish term for people of mixed blood

monthon: the "circles into which King Chaulalongkorn grouped Thai provinces in an effort to expand the control of the central administration over the provinces

müang: in Thailand, a town or city, and by extension the area administered or controlled by it

myei-taing: see *ywa thu-gyi.*

myo: in Burma, a town or city, and by extension the area controlled or administered by it

myo-thu-gyi: a township chief in Burma

myo-wun: a provincial governor in pre-British Burma. Unlike the *myo-thu-gyi,* the *myo-wun* derived his authority from the royal court rather than from local allegiance.

myo-za: a province or town "eater" in pre-British Burma; a prince or high official to whom was awarded the revenue from a designated town or province

nam giao: the "southern altar" of the Vietnamese emperor

Nam Tien: the 1,000-year Vietnamese drive from the Red River delta to present-day central and southern Vietnam

Nanyang: "the southern region," a Chinese term for Southeast Asia

nat: term for animist spirit in Burma

negara: Sanskrit for "kingdom" or "capital." *See kraton.*

negara agung: the second administrative circle in the kingdom of Mataram. It consisted of the core area immediately outside of the palace-city.

negeri: A Malay/Indonesian word for "state." In particular, a riverine or coastal principality in the Malayo-Muslim world.

nhap the: "participation" in worldly affairs as a course of action in Vietnamese Buddhism. Used in contrast to *xuat the.*

Nirvana: the final transcendence of the self, which is the goal of Buddhists

noi cac: the Grand Secretariat created by Emperor Minh-mang in

1829 in order to improve the coordination of the central Vietnamese administrative structure

noi vu phu: the Vietnamese Household Affairs Office, which served as the private treasury of the imperial household

nom: the indigenous Vietnamese writing system

pactos de retro: a system in the Spanish Philippines used by money-lenders to gain ownership of land. A Chinese *mestizo* would buy land from an *indio* owner, granting him the option to repurchase later. Because the original owner rarely was able to repurchase, the money-lender usually kept the land.

pantja sila: the five basic principles of an independent Indonesia as outlined by Sukarno in 1945: nationalism, internationalism, democracy, social justice, belief in one God

pasisir: "coast"; in particular, the north coast of Java and the historical complex based on Islam and trade that developed there in the fifteenth and sixteenth centuries

patih: the chief minister of the Kingdom of Mataram or, later, of a Javan *bupati*

payung: the Javanese ceremonial parasol, which symbolized high rank

pemuda: Malay/Indonesian word for "a youth," "youths." In the Indonesian Revolution, the term acquired powerful overtones of militance and patriotism.

penghulu: a Malay village headman

peninsulares: a term for Spaniards born on the Iberian Peninsula, in contrast to those born in the Spanish empire (*creoles*)

perahu: a small Malay sailing vessel

peranakan: "locally born foreigner," a Malay/Indonesian term for people of mixed Malay and foreign blood, born in the region

perdjuangan: Malay/Indonesian word for "struggle." In the Indonesian Revolution the term acquired a deeper significance: struggle for the revolutionary cause. In the political disputes of the time it stood for uncompromising armed struggle, as opposed to *diplomasi*.

pesantren: the Javanese term for a community of students formed around an Islamic scholar and holy man

phi: animist spirits in Thailand and Laos

phrai luang: those in premodern Thailand who rendered labor service impersonally to the king and his designated representatives, rather than personally to local officials

phrai som: those in premodern Thailand who rendered labor service personally to local officials, rather than to "the government"

phrakhlang: the Thai ministry, and minister, responsible for finance and foreign affairs (and also, in the nineteenth century, for the administration of the provinces at the head of the Gulf of Siam). Its functions were divided at the beginning of King Chulalongkorn's reign.

picul: a variable unit of weight, usually about 60 kg. (132 lbs.)

piezas: the shares into which the Manila galleon space was divided. Each galleon was supposed to be divided into 4,000 shares.

polo: a term for draft labor (*corvée*) in the Spanish Philippines

pondok: literally "hut" or "shanty," a Malay-Indonesian term for a community of scholars formed around an Islamic teacher

pongyi: "great glory," a Buddhist monk in Burma

principalía: the village elite in the Spanish Philippines

priyayi: the Javanese and Sundanese hereditary aristocracy or gentry; also, a member of the same

proconsul: a paternalistic colonial administrator who defined his role as being the protector of the common people against their anticolonialist leaders

pueblo: an administrative unit in the Spanish Philippines which consisted of a church and several *barrios* with a combined total of at least 500 tribute-tax–payers, centered on a plaza

pwe: a popular dramatic performance in Burma

quan lo: the "mandarin road" in nineteenth-century Vietnam

quoc ngu: the Vietnamese "national language," written in romanized form rather than in Chinese and Vietnamese characters

Quoc tu giam: the National College in traditional Vietnam

raja: the ruler of a Malay *negeri*.

Ramakian: Thai versions of the *Ramayana*

rantau: a term for a strong outward drive—for trade or for settlement, for example—typical of many Sumatran societies

ratu adil: the "just prince" of Javanese messianic expectations

regent: see *bupati*

regulares: the friars, those ecclesiastics in the Spanish Philippines who belonged to a religious order, as opposed to the *seculares,* or diocesan priests

residencia: the judicial and public review faced by all Spanish officials in the Philippines at the termination of their service and prior to their departure from the colony

Resident: title of a high Dutch or English territorial official in the Netherlands Indies or Malaya

rijsttafel: the Dutch term for a Javan meal of rice with many side dishes

Sangha: Pali term for the Buddhist monkhood

Sangharaja: the supreme patriarch of Buddhism in Burma, and also in Thailand, whose decisions and injunctions on affairs respecting the Sangha were enforced by civil authority

sangley: the Spanish term for Chinese immigrants to the Philippines

santri: the variant of Javanese religion characterized by more self-conscious identification as a Muslim and stricter observance of Islamic requirements such as the daily prayers and the fasting month. Used in contrast to *abangan*.

sawah: Malay-Indonesian term for the wet-rice paddy field and, by extension, for the whole wet-rice pattern

sawbwa: Shan rulers of principalities

seculares: diocesan priests in the Spanish Philippines, in contradistinction to the friars (*regulares*) who belonged to religious orders

senabodi: ministers of state in Thailand

shahbandar: an officer of trade who acted as liason between a Malay raja of a *negeri* and the foreign traders in his port

shaykh: an honorific given to (or assumed by) many Malayan Hadrami Arabs other than *sayyids* (those tracing their descent back to the Prophet Muhammad), and to men of unusual religious learning

situado: the annual subsidy sent to the Philippines from the Spanish treasury in Mexico

Straits Settlements: Singapore Island, Penang and Province Wellesley, and the territory of Malacca, including Naning

sultan: honorific given to the raja (ruler) of a Malay state

surau: a building in Malaya that is not a mosque of general assembly but is otherwise devoted to religious or quasi-religious purposes

Susuhunan: the title of the ruling prince of Central Java

swaraj: a Hindi term for "self-rule," hence, independence

swidden: an anthropological term for the worldwide agricultural pattern characterized by slash-and-burn, shifting cultivation. Used in contrast to the wet-rice pattern

tam cuong: the "three principles" or "three bonds" that were the operative ideal of traditional Vietnamese life: a subject's loyalty to his ruler, a son's obedience to his father, and a wife's submission to her husband

tam giao: "the three religions," a formula describing the syncretistic existence of Buddhism, Taoism, and Confucianism in traditional Vietnam

tanah sabrang: the fourth administrative circle of Mataram, consisting of the coastal states overseas that acknowledged the suzerainty of Mataram and sent tribute

tarekat: literally (Arabic), "path" or "way"; used to denote Sufi mystic orders

temenggong: a Malay chief of high rank

thakin: "lord, master"; a word originally used by Burmese when addressing an Englishman. It was adopted in the 1930's by Burmese student nationalists as a way of addressing each other.

thanh: "walled citadel," the walled part of a traditional Vietnamese city, where officials lived

thi: the market area of Hue, where the ordinary Vietnamese lived

Tipitaka: the Pali scriptures of Theravada Buddhism: *Tripitaka* in Sanskrit Buddhism

tjatjah: the head of a peasant family in Java during the Mataram period *totok:* an Indonesian term for foreign-born, pure-blooded immigrants. Used in contrast to *peranakan.*

towkay: a Malay/Indonesian term for rich Chinese

Tran Tay: the province name given Cambodia by the Nguyen court during Cambodia's subjection by Vietnam, 1834–41

trekkers: Dutch who came out to the Indies, usually with Dutch wives, for a career of specified length, and who planned to retire in Holland. Used in contrast to *blijvers.*

trung quoc: "middle kingdom," a term for Vietnam used by the Vietnamese court to differentiate its society from the non-Sinicized societies of Indochina

tulisanes: bandits in the Philippines

ulama: those learned in Islam

ummat: the Islamic community

uposatha: a building for ordinations and rites in the Theravada Buddhist monastery

utang na loob: "debt of gratitude," a norm of social behavior in the Philippines. A recipient of a favor is obliged to return the favor with interest in order to discharge his debt of gratitude.

uy tin: a Vietnamese term meaning "prestige," a combination of *uy* (fearsomeness) and *tin* (capacity to inspire trust)

van te: a Vietnamese funeral oration, a particularly popular literary form in the 1790's and early 1800's

vihara: a small preaching hall in a Theravada Buddhist monastery

wahyu: the divine radiance, manifesting itself in various ways, which marks its possessor as a Javanese king, and whose departure signals his fall

wang: the ministry of the palace in traditional Thailand

wayang kulit: Javanese shadow-play, which uses puppets to dramatize stories from the Javanese versions of the *Mahabharata* and *Ramayana*

wayang orang: the Javanese dance drama derived from *wayang kulit*

wedana: a court official of Mataram. In the nineteenth and twentieth century, a Javan administrative official next in rank below a *bupati.*

wong tjilik: Javanese for the "little man," or peasant

wun-gyi: the chief royal ministers in Burma, members of the *hlutdaw*

wunthanu athin: "own race societies," village societies created in Burma in the 1920's, which attempted to gain peasant support for what had formerly been only urban agitation against colonial rule

xa: the Vietnamese village, the basic unit of peasant life in Vietnam, composed of a number of hamlets (*thon*)

xa truong: a village chief in Vietnam

xuat the: "abstention" from worldly affairs as a course of action in Vietnamese Buddhism. Used in contrast to *nhap the.*

Yam Tuan: short for *Yang di-Pertuan*

Yang di-Pertuan: "he who is made Lord"—the ceremonial title of a Malay ruler

ywa thu-gyi: a village headman in Upper Burma

BIBLIOGRAPHY

A NOTE OF EXPLANATION

Aside from the general works on Southeast Asia and the section on introductory works for Southeast Asian societies, the bibliography follows the format of the book itself, beginning with Part I, "The Eighteenth-Century World," and continuing through Part V, "The Preoccupations of Independence." Individual monographs, when considered useful for more than one topic or chapter, have been cited more than once. Although this makes for a bulkier bibliography, it is hoped that re-citing important studies wherever they apply will make the bibliography easier to use.

The bibliography has been compiled primarily from English-language materials. Only a very few works in the languages indigenous to Southeast Asia, such as Vietnamese, Burmese, Thai, Malay, Indonesian, or Tagalog, have been included, and the literature in Dutch and Spanish has also been largely omitted. The absence of such works here does not mean that there are not important materials in those languages. To the contrary, the reader is encouraged to carry his study beyond English-language monographs to the wealth of primary and secondary materials available in Western and Southeast Asian languages.

BIBLIOGRAPHIES OF SOUTHEAST ASIA

General Guides: Among the many bibliographic reference works, see G. Raymond Nunn, *South and Southeast Asia: A Bibliography of Bibliographies* (Honolulu, 1966); K. G. Tregonning, *Southeast Asia: A Critical Bibliography* (Tucson, Ariz., 1969); Stephen N. Hay, *A Guide to Books on Southeast Asian History, 1961–1966* (Santa Barbara, Calif., 1969); Cecil Hobbs, *Southeast Asia: An Annotated Bibliography* (Washington, 1964); Francis Carnell, *The Politics of the New States: A Select Annotated Bibliography with Special Reference to the Commonwealth* (London, 1961); John F. Embree and Lillian O. Dotson, *Bibliography of the Peoples and Cultures of Mainland Southeast Asia* (New Haven, Conn., 1950); Karl J. Pelzer, *Selected Bibliography on the Geography of Southeast Asia*, Volume I (3 vols., New Haven, Conn., 1949–56); Kenneth L. Neff, *Selected Bibliography on Education in Southeast Asia* (Washington, 1963); and Lian The and Paul W. van der Veur, *Treasures and Trivia: Doctoral Dissertations on Southeast Asia* (Athens, Ohio, 1968). The annual *Bibliography* published by the *Journal of Asian Studies* (*JAS*, known until September, 1956, as the *Far Eastern Quarterly*) is an essential cumulative source.

BIBLIOGRAPHIES FOR INDIVIDUAL COUNTRIES

Burma: The best available bibliography on Burma is Frank N. Trager, *Annotated Bibliography on Burma* (New Haven, Conn., 1956). The approximately 1,000 entries are annotated in detail, and there is an index of entries according to topic. Also useful is Trager's *Furnivall of Burma: An Annotated Bibliography of the Works of John S. Furnivall* (New Haven, Conn., 1963), valuable primarily because it lists all of Furnivall's many "minor" writings—articles, book reviews, and speeches. Cecil Hobbs's "Reading List on Burma," *Far Eastern Quarterly,* VI:1 (1945), 60–66, is a list of twenty-six books and articles designed to provide a general introduction to Burma.

Thailand: The most exhaustive bibliographies for Thailand are John Brown Mason and H. Carroll Parrish, *Thailand Bibliography* (Gainesville, Fla., 1958), and the *Bibliography of Material about Thailand in Western Languages* compiled by the Central Library of Chulalongkorn University (Bangkok, 1960). Also see Lauriston Sharp, *et al., Bibliography of Thailand* (Ithaca, N.Y., 1956), and David K. Wyatt and Constance M. Wilson, "Thai Historical Materials in Bangkok," *JAS,* XXV:1 (November, 1965), 105–18.

Vietnam: A great deal of bibliographical information about Vietnam, Laos, and Cambodia is contained in Henri Cordier's massive *Bibliotheca Indosinica* (4 vols., Paris, 1932). This work, originally completed before World War I, was carried forward by Paul Boudet and Rémy Bourgeois, *Bibliographie de l'Indochine française, 1913–1935* (4 vols., Hanoi and Paris, 1929–67). Also useful is Cecil C. Hobbs, *et al., Indochina: A Bibliography of the Land and the People* (Washington, 1950).

For the early period of Vietnamese history, see Émile Gaspardone's two articles, "Materiaux pour servir à l'histoire d'Annam" and "Bibliographie annamite," which appeared in the 1929 and 1934 issues, respectively, of the *Bulletin de l'École Française d'Extrême Orient.* Ralph B. Smith's "Sino-Vietnamese Sources for the Nguyen Period: an Introduction," in the *Bulletin of the School of Oriental and African Studies,* XXX:3 (1967), 600–621, is also useful. The history of Vietnamese-Western contacts is covered by Nguyen The Anh, *Bibliographie critique sur les relations entre le Viet-Nam et l'occident* (Paris, 1967). See also Roy Jumper, *Bibliography of the Political and Administrative History of Vietnam* (Saigon, 1962), and Tran Thi Kimsa, *Bibliography of Vietnam, 1954–1964* (Saigon, 1965), which includes a wide assortment of periodical literature.

Cambodia: In addition to Henri Cordier's *Bibliotheca Indosinica* and the Boudet/Bourgeois *Bibliographie de l'Indochine française,* the student of Cambodia should consult an accessible and thorough bibliography in the special issue of the French periodical *France-Asie,* entitled *Présence du Cambodge* (1955). For two excellent bibliographies of postwar developments, see Phillipe Preschez, "Le Cambodge depuis 1941," in *Revue française des sciences politiques* (December, 1961), pp. 906–35; and Mary L. Fisher, *Cambodia: An Annotated Bibliography of its History, Geography, Politics and Economy since 1954* (Cambridge, Mass., 1967).

Laos: The most comprehensive recent bibliography related to Laos is Bernard Lafont's *Bibliographie du Laos* (Paris, 1964). It fails, however, to gather up the extensive—and very largely ephemeral—periodical literature that has appeared since World War II. Cordier and Boudet/Bourgeois, mentioned above, should also be consulted.

Malaysia: There is as yet no good, comprehensive bibliography of Western language materials relating to Malaysia, although one about to be published by R. S. Karni will be more comprehensive than its predecessors, and a much revised and updated version of Karl J. Pelzer's *Selected Bibliography on the Geography of Southeast Asia: Part III, Malaya* (New Haven, Conn., 1956) is also due to appear. The principal bibliographies for the peninsula at present are H. R. Cheeseman, *Bibliography of Malaya* (London, 1959), and Beda Lim, "Malaya: A Background Bibliography," *Journal of the Malayan Branch Royal Asiatic Society,* XXV:2–3 (1962), 1–199. The former suffers principally from lack of completeness and the absence of pagination for articles; the latter from the absence of an author or title index. K. G. Tregonning, ed., *Malaysian Historical Sources* (Singapore, 1962), is a collection of bibliographical and descriptive articles, mainly relating to primary source materials. Two excellent bibliographies attached to other works merit special mention: Mary Turnbull's bibliography of writings in English on British Malaya from 1786 to 1867, in L. A. Mills, "British Malaya, 1824–67," *Journal of the Malayan Branch Royal Asiatic Society,* XXXIII:3 (1960), 327–424; and the bibliography of economic works appended to T. H. Silcock, *The Commonwealth Economy in Southeast Asia* (Durham, N.C., 1959), pp. 216–50.

Indonesia: The most useful English-language bibliographies with respect to Indonesia are W. Ph. Coolhaas, *A Critical Survey of Studies on Dutch Colonial History* (The Hague, 1960), and Raymond Kennedy, *Bibliography of Indonesian Peoples and Cultures,* (2d revised ed., New Haven, Conn., 1962).

The Philippines: Among the most useful bibliographies on the Philippines are Fred Eggan and Evett Hester, *Selected Bibliography of the Philippines: Topically Arranged and Annotated* (New Haven, Conn., 1956); Charles O. Houston, Jr., *Philippine Bibliography I: An Annotated Preliminary Bibliography of Philippine Bibliographies (Since 1900)* (Manila, 1960); A. P. C. Griffin, *A List of Books, with References to Periodicals, on the Philippine Islands* (Washington, 1903); and Gabriel A. Bernardo, comp., and Natividad P. Verzosa, ed., *Bibliography of Philippine Bibliographies, 1593–1961* (Manila, 1968). For Bibliographies on the Spanish era, see Wenceslao E. Retana, *Aparato bibliografico de la historia general de Filipinas* (Madrid, 1906); and James A. Robertson, *Bibliography of the Philippines* (vol. LIII of E. H. Blair and J. A. Robertson, *The Philippine Islands, 1493–1898*) (Cleveland, Ohio, 1903). Also helpful is Donn V. Hart's *An Annotated Guide to Current Philippine Periodicals* (New Haven, Conn., 1957), and Michael Onorato's *Philippine Bibliography, 1899–1946* (Santa Barbara, Calif., 1969).

HISTORIOGRAPHY

During the late colonial era, some European historians explained change in Southeast Asia in terms of a type of Hegelian dialectic in which the thesis was the European impact—as expressed in imperialism, capitalism, or socialism, in scientific technological rationalism, and in nationalism; the antithesis was the Southeast Asian response—as expressed in the drive for national independence, economic self-sufficiency, and a "modern" society;

and the synthesis would be the emergence of a Western-style Southeast Asian nation state, led by a foreign-educated elite and pursuing a blend of modern and traditional goals. In 1934, a young Dutch historian, Jacob Cornelius van Leur, was one of the first to call attention to this Europocentric bias in an essay entitled "On the Study of Indonesian History," reprinted in *Indonesian Trade and Society* (The Hague, 1955), pp. 145–56. Bothered by the way Asian factors were relegated to the background, he suggested the need for some historical revision. In effect, he advocated turning the European spyglass around, reducing what had previously loomed as significant to a lesser status. Subsequently known as Asiacentric history, this revision retained the dialectic but inverted it so that the thesis became the Southeast Asian state, the antithesis the European penetration, while the synthesis remained the Southeast Asian nation-state, pursuing a fusion of traditional and modern goals. Over the last decades this approach has enjoyed wide popularity, but, while it redresses Western condescension, it does retain a stress on polarities. By categorizing the last two centuries of Southeast Asian history as the interaction between the distinct elements of native and foreign, it has tended to perpetuate the debates and divisions of the colonial era.

Southeast Asian historiography is extraordinarily challenging. D. G. E. Hall has edited a stimulating volume of essays by many scholars entitled *Historians of South-East Asia* (London, 1961) and has written "Looking at Southeast Asian History," *JAS*, XIX:3 (May, 1960), 243–54. The collection of essays edited by Soedjatmoko, *An Introduction to Indonesian Historiography* (Ithaca, N.Y., 1965), has no equivalent for the other countries of the region, although K. Tregonning, *Malaysian Historical Sources* (Singapore, 1962), is frequently useful. The volume *Essays on Indonesian and Malayan History* (Singapore, 1961), by John Bastin, contains some of his most important thinking. In the early 1960's, a series of important pieces appeared in the *Journal of Southeast Asian History* (*JSEAH*), including D. P. Singhal's "Some Comments on 'The Western Element in Modern Southeast Asian History,'" I:2 (September, 1960), 118–23; John R. W. Smail's "On the Possibility of an Autonomous History of Modern Southeast Asia," II:2 (July, 1961), 72–102; F. J. West's "The Study of Colonial History," II:3 (October, 1961), 70–82; and Harry J. Benda's "The Structure of Southeast Asian History: Some Preliminary Observations," III:1 (March, 1962), 106–38. Two other important articles stand out: Lauriston Sharp's "Cultural Continuities and Discontinuities in Southeast Asia," *JAS*, XXII:1 (November, 1962), 3–11; and Harry J. Benda's "Political Elites in Colonial Southeast Asia," *Comparative Studies in Society and History*, VII:3 (April, 1965), 233–52. For an interesting debate on the problem of perspective, see Harry J. Benda, "Democracy in Indonesia" (a review of Herbert Feith's *Decline of Constitutional Democracy in Indonesia*) in *JAS*, XIII:3 (May, 1964), 449–56, and Herbert Feith, "History, Theory and Indonesian Politics: A Reply to Harry J. Benda," *JAS*, XIV:2 (February, 1965), 305–12.

GENERAL WORKS ON SOUTHEAST ASIA

General Histories: The single most complete history of Southeast Asia is D. G. E. Hall's *A History of Southeast Asia*, (3d ed., London, 1968). This remarkable *tour de force* by one of the region's greatest historians is especially valuable to the specialist. John Cady's *Southeast Asia: Its Historical Development* (New York, 1964) is a more easily read text. Brian Harrison's *Southeast Asia: A Short History* (New York, 1966) and Nicholas Tarling's *A Concise History of Southeast Asia* (New York, 1966) are more popular efforts. John Bastin and Harry J. Benda have collaborated to write a stimulating volume of interlocked essays entitled *A History of Modern Southeast Asia* (Englewood Cliffs, N.J., 1968). John Bastin has also edited a volume entitled *The Emergence of Modern Southeast Asia: 1511–1957* (Englewood Cliffs, N.J., 1967) in which Southeast Asian history is chronicled, from a persistently Western vantage point, through excerpts from the writings of other historians. For a shorter introduction to Southeast Asian history, W. F. Wertheim's essay entitled "Southeast Asia," in *International Encyclopedia of the Social Sciences*, I (New York, 1968), 423–38, is sinewy, shrewd, and full of ideas. Harry J. Benda and John A. Larkin have prepared a very useful book of readings based on primary sources—both Southeast Asian and foreign—called *The World of Southeast Asia* (New York, 1967). Jan M. Pluvier's *A Handbook and Chart of Southeast Asian History* (Kuala Lumpur, 1967) is a valuable compendium of chronology and succession.

Geography: Among the many Southeast Asian geographies, see Charles A. Fisher, *Southeast Asia: A Social, Economic and Political Geography* (London, 1964); Ernest H. G. Dobby, *Monsoon Asia* (Chicago, 1961); and Charles E. Robequain, *Malaya, Indonesia, Borneo and the Philippines* (New York, 1954). Karl J. Pelzer's *Pioneer Settlement in the Asiatic Tropics: Studies in Land Utilization and Agricultural Colonization in Southeast Asia* (New York, 1948) is also relevant.

A useful but by no means exhaustive atlas of Southeast Asia is Djambatan Uitgeversbedrijf, *Atlas of South-East Asia* (Amsterdam, 1962), with an introduction by D. G. E. Hall.

Ethnology: Two excellent specialized studies are: Frank LeBar, Gerald Hickey, and John Musgrave, *Ethnic Groups of Mainland Southeast Asia* (New Haven, Conn., 1964); and Peter Kunstadter, ed., *Southeast Asian Tribes, Minorities and Nations* (2 vols., Princeton, N.J., 1967).

Social and Economic Development: A good brief introduction to life in mainland Southeast Asia can be found in Robbins Burling, *Hill Farms and Paddy Fields* (Englewood Cliffs, N.J., 1965). As an introduction to the social forces at work in Southeast Asian history, Cora DuBois's three lectures first delivered in 1947 and republished under the title *Social Forces in Southeast Asia* (Cambridge, Mass., 1959) remain classics. See also the book edited by George P. Murdock, *Social Structure in Southeast Asia* (New York, 1960). John S. Furnivall's *Colonial Policy and Practice: A Comparative Study of Burma and Netherlands India* (Cambridge, England, 1948 [2d ed., New York, 1956]) has profoundly influenced subsequent thinking about Southeast Asia's economic and social development. Terence G. McGee's *The Southeast Asian City: A Social Geography of the Primate Cities of Southeast Asia* (London, 1967) makes a unique contribution to the literature. Robert O. Tilman has recently edited a major volume of essays by leading scholars in all fields of Southeast Asian studies entitled *Man, State, and Society in Contemporary Southeast Asia* (New York, 1969). Also see C. D. Cowan, ed., *The Economic Development of Southeast Asia: Studies in Economic History and Political Economy* (New York, 1964).

The best studies dealing with alien minorities in Southeast Asia are: Victor Purcell's *The Chinese in Southeast Asia* (London, 1951 [revised ed., 1965]); Virginia Thompson and Richard Adloff, *Minority Problems in Southeast Asia* (Stanford, Calif., 1955); and Lea E. Williams, *The Future of the Overseas Chinese in Southeast Asia* (New York, 1966).

A good introduction to Southeast Asian religions is Kenneth P. Landon's *Southeast Asia, Crossroad of Religions* (Chicago, 1949).

Politics: The literature dealing with Communism, nationalism, government, politics, and international relations in Southeast Asia is extensive. Of the books dealing with Communism, J. H. Brimmell's *Communism in Southeast Asia: A Political Analysis* (London, 1959); Charles B. McLane's *Soviet Strategies in Southeast Asia* (Princeton, N.J., 1966); and the four essays edited by Frank N. Trager under the title *Marxism in Southeast Asia* (Stanford, Calif., 1959), are among the best. For nationalism, see Rupert Emerson, *From Empire to Nation: The Rise to Self-Assertion of Asian and African Peoples* (Boston, 1960); Clifford Geertz, ed., *Old Societies and New States: The Quest for Modernity in Asia and Africa* (New York, 1963); and Philip W. Thayer, ed., *Nationalism and Progress in Free Asia* (Baltimore, 1956). George McT. Kahin has edited a monumental volume entitled *Governments and Politics of Southeast Asia* (Ithaca, N.Y., 1959 [2d ed., 1964]). For international relations in Southeast Asia, see Russell H. Fifield, *The Diplomacy of Southeast Asia: 1945–1958* (New York, 1958); and Bernard K. Gordon, *Toward Disengagement in Asia* (Englewood Cliffs, N.J., 1969). The *New Yorker* correspondent in Southeast Asia, Robert Shaplen, has compiled many of his most provocative pieces in *Time Out of Hand: Revolution and Reaction in Southeast Asia* (New York, 1969).

INDIVIDUAL SOCIETIES: GENERAL STUDIES

Thailand: John de Young, *Village Life in Modern Thailand* (Berkeley and Los Angeles, 1955), was among the first systematic studies of Thai village society. It has since been usefully elaborated upon by Michael Moerman, *Agricultural Change and Peasant Choice in a Thai Villlage* (Berkeley and Los Angeles, 1968); Howard Keva Kaufman, *Bangkhuad: A Community Study in Thailand* (Locust Valley, N.Y., 1960); and Herbert Phillips, *Thai Peasant Personality* (Berkeley and Los Angeles, 1965). The works of the late Phya Anuman Rajadhon, long the dean of scholarship in Thailand, are of enduring value: Some, like *Life and Ritual in Old Siam* (New Haven, Conn., 1961) and *Five Papers on Thai Custom* (Ithaca, N.Y., 1952), are available in translation, and others—surely his memorable *Chiwit chao thai samai kǫn (The Life of the Thai in the Past)* (Bangkok, 1967)—certainly should be. Thai religion is much more complicated than canonical Buddhism as such, to which Kenneth Wells's *Thai Buddhism: Its Rites and Activities* (Bangkok, 1960) is a useful introduction. An important forthcoming book by A. Thomas Kirsch will deal with the syncretism of Buddhism, animism, and Indic religious beliefs in Thailand.

The only general history of Thailand is W. A. R. Wood, *A History of Siam from the Earliest Times to the Year A.D. 1781* (London, 1924 [reprinted in Bangkok, 1959]) which is sadly outdated but still useful. The specialized studies of H. G. Quaritch Wales—*Ancient Siamese Government and Administration* (London, 1934 [reprinted in New York, 1965]) and

Siamese State Ceremonies (London, 1931)—remain useful. A great deal of important information first published in the *Journal of the Siam Society* (Bangkok, 1904–present) is made available in the *Selected Articles from the Siam Society Journal* (10 vols., Bangkok, 1954–59).

Burma: For Burma, perhaps the best introduction to village life might begin with Sir James George Scott (Shway Yoe), *The Burman: His Life and Notions* (London, 1882 [reprinted in New York, 1963]), proceed through Mi Mi Khaing's *Burmese Family* (Bombay, 1946 [reprinted in Bloomington, Ind., 1962]), to Manning Nash's *The Golden Road to Modernity: Village Life in Contemporary Burma* (New York, 1965). Closer to the ground is David E. Pfanner's Cornell University doctoral dissertation, "Rice and Religion in the Burmese Village" (1962). The numerous articles of E. Michael Mendelson on Burmese Buddhism are consistently stimulating, as is a more specialized work on *Burmese Supernaturalism* by Melford E. Spiro (Englewood Cliffs, N.J., 1967).

The best general histories of Burma are still the oldest: G. E. Harvey's *History of Burma* (London, 1925 [reprinted in London, 1967]), and Sir Arthur P. Phayre, *History of Burma* (London, 1883 [reprinted in London, 1967]). Htin Aung's *A History of Burma* (New York, 1967) is more readable but at times less rigorous. The best general history for the modern period is John F. Cady's *A History of Modern Burma* (Ithaca, N.Y., 1960).

Laos: The best introductions to Lao society are probably Joel Halpern's two studies, *Economy and Society of Laos* (New Haven, Conn., 1964), and *Government, Politics and Social Structure in Laos* (New Haven, Conn., 1964). A wide-ranging collection is René de Berval, ed., *The Kingdom of Laos* (Saigon, 1959).

The standard history of Laos is Paul le Boulanger, *Histoire du Laos français* (Paris, 1931), although the work of Maha Sila Viravong, a Lao scholar, entitled *History of Laos* (New York, 1964) puts Lao history in an altogether different perspective.

Cambodia: The best general view of Cambodian society is the sumptuously illustrated volume *Cambodge,* produced by the Cambodian Ministry of Information in 1964. Like most books about Cambodian life, it is in French, as are Solange Thierry's *Les Khmers* (Paris, 1964), and Simone Lacouture's *Cambodge* (Lausanne, 1963). Both are sensitive and useful. For the specialist, Eveline Porée Maspéro's *Rites agraires des Cambodgiens* (2 vols., Paris, 1962–66), and Jean Delvert's *Le Paysan Cambodgien* (Paris, 1961) are indispensable, as is Solange Thierry's "Contribution à une étude de la société cambodgienne," *L'Ethnographie* (1964–65), pp. 50–71.

Of the histories of Cambodia, the best study of the modern period is Achille Dauphin Meunier's *Histoire du Cambodge* (Paris, 1961), although it is based entirely on secondary sources. Martin Herz's *Short History of Cambodia* (New York, 1958), although essentially a cold war document, is valuable for its analysis of Cambodian politics in the 1940's and 1950's. For the earlier period, Adhémard Leclère's *Histoire du Cambodge* (Paris, 1914), despite some important errors, continues to dominate the field.

Vietnam: One outstanding summary of Vietnamese music, literature, social life, festivals, and other aspects of traditional Vietnamese civilization is that of Pierre Huard and Maurice Durand, *Connaissance du Vietnam* (Paris, 1954). Louis Bezacier, *L'Art Vietnamien* (Paris, 1955) brilliantly surveys the civil, military, and religious architecture of traditional Vietnam and also discusses the various periods of Vietnamese art. B. P. Groslier, *The Art of Indochina* (New York, 1962) is less useful but is written in English. On the subject of Vietnamese religion, the classical Western writings are those of Léopold Cadière, *Croyances et pratiques religieuses des Vietnamiens* (Saigon, 1958). See also Maurice Durand, *Technique et panthéon des médiums Vietnamiens* (Paris, 1959) and the fine general article by Durand, "Quelques éléments de l'univers moral des Vietnamiens," *Bulletin de la Société des Études Indochinoises*, XXVII:4 (1952). Surveys of Vietnamese literature include Maurice Durand and Nguyen Tran-Huan, *Introduction à la littérature vietnamienne* (Paris, 1969) and Duong Dinh Khue, *Les Chefs d'oeuvre de la littérature vietnamienne* (Saigon, 1966). As this paragraph should indicate, genuinely sophisticated English-language studies of the various aspects of premodern Vietnamese culture are still virtually nonexistent.

The most important general history of Vietnam written in a Western language is that of Le Thanh Khoi, *Le Viet-Nam: histoire et civilisation* (Paris, 1955). In English, the only serviceable survey is that of Joseph Buttinger, *The Smaller Dragon: A Political History of Vietnam* (New York, 1958), but it is not based upon a command of sufficient Vietnamese documentation. Ralph Smith, *Vietnam and the West* (London, 1968) is lucidly written and provides a brief introduction to tradition and change in Vietnam. Jean Chesneaux, *Contribution à l'histoire de la nation vietnamienne* (Paris, 1955) is a stimulating overview of the evolution of modern Vietnamese society.

Malaysia: A general introductory account of the peoples of peninsular Malaya is given by B. W. Hodder, *Man in Malaya* (London, 1959). Ooi Jin-Bee, *Land, People and Economy in Malaya* (London, 1963) contains substantial sections on population. N. J. Ryan, *The Cultural Background of the Peoples of Malaya* (Kuala Lumpur, 1962) is an unpretentious but attractive short account of the Malaysian scene. The standard demographic work for the Malay peninsula is T. E. Smith, *Population Growth in Malaya: An Analysis of Recent Trends* (London and New York, 1952), and for the remainder of Malaysia, L. W. Jones's *The Population of Borneo: A Study of the Peoples of Sarawak, Sabah and Brunei* (London, 1966). Also of interest are two collections of papers by the anthropologist I. H. N. Evans entitled *Studies in Religion, Folk-Lore and Custom in British North Borneo and the Malay Peninsula* (Cambridge, England, 1923), and *Papers on the Ethnology and Archeology of the Malay Peninsula* (Cambridge, England, 1927).

There are some useful studies of the different peoples of Malaysia. For the Malays, see R. O. Winstedt's *The Malays: A Cultural History* (5th ed., London, 1958) and *The Malay Magician* (revised ed., London, 1951). Both continue to be widely read, though they are increasingly regarded as old-fashioned in approach. J. M. Gullick's *Indigenous Political Systems of Western Malaya* (London, 1958), a pioneer examination by a sociologist of the workings of Malay society in the mid-nineteenth century, has become a standard reference work. For the Chinese in Malaysia, the most useful general account is probably Victor Purcell's *The Chinese in Malaya* (1st ed., London and New York, 1948 [reprinted in Kuala Lumpur, 1967]). C. S. Wong has published *A Cycle of Chinese Festivals* (Singapore, 1967) which describes many aspects of contemporary Chinese cultural life. There is very little descriptive material on the Indian communities of Malaysia, but Kernial Singh Sandhu's *Indians in Malaya, 1786–1957* (Cambridge, England, 1969) is a major work concerning Indian immigration and the peoples it affected. George Netto's *Indians in Malaya* (Singapore, n.d.) is an assemblage of facts and figures, mainly historical, while S. Arasaratnam's *Indian Festivals in Malaya* (Kuala Lumpur, 1966) gives a brief description of cultural life. C. H. Crabb, *Malaya's Eurasians: An Opinion* (Singapore, 1960) discusses some of the problems faced by this section of Malaysia's variegated population.

The fullest descriptive history of Malaya from early times to the twentieth century is R. O. Winstedt, *A History of Malaya* (London, 1935 [also published as a complete issue of the *Journal of the Malayan Branch Royal Asiatic Society*, XIII:1 (March, 1935), and in a revised ed., Singapore, 1962]). A more recent general introduction to Malayan history and society is J. M. Gullick's *Malaya* (1st ed., London and New York, 1963 [revised ed., entitled *Malaysia,* 1969]), which draws on the author's own sociological research. Useful histories of the individual peninsular Malay states have been published in the *Journal of the Malayan Branch Royal Asiatic Society* as follows: "A History of Perak," by R. O. Winstedt and R. J. Wilkinson, XII:1 (1934); "A History of Selangor," by R. O. Winstedt, XII:3 (1934); "Negri Sembilan: The History, Polity and Beliefs of the Nine States," by R. O. Winstedt, XII:3 (1934); "A History of Pahang," by W. Linehan, XIV:2 (1936); "A History of Johore," by R. O. Winstedt, X:3 (1932); "History of Kelantan," by Anker Rentse, XII:2 (1934); and "A Short History of Trengganu," by M. C. ff. Sheppard, XXII:3 (1949).

Indonesia: Indonesia's past contains many distinct cultural traditions and histories: those of the Hindu-Javanese-Islamic Javanese alongside those of the Protestant Toba Bataks, the Catholics of Flores, the Hindu-Buddhist Balinese, the pagan Dayaks, and a wide range of Malayo-Muslim coastal peoples who have more in common historically with the Malays of the peninsula than with any of the foregoing. Two works are particularly useful in surveying this multiplicity of cultures: Hildred Geertz's masterly essay, "Indonesian Cultures and Communities," in Ruth McVey, ed., *Indonesia* (New Haven, Conn., 1963), and Koentjaraningrat, ed., *Villages in Indonesia* (Ithaca, N.Y., 1967). Two basic ecological modes underlying this cultural diversity are brilliantly evoked by Clifford Geertz, *Agricultural Involution* (Berkeley, Calif., 1963).

A good introduction to Javanese society is available in two translated essays by D. H. Burger, *Structural Changes in Javanese Society: The Village Sphere/The Supra-Village Sphere* (Ithaca, N.Y., 1956–57), and in Clifford Geertz's germinal essay, *The Development of the Javanese Economy, a Socio-Cultural Approach* (Cambridge, Mass., 1956). The best introduction to the *wayang kulit,* the shadow drama which is the richest storehouse of Javanese cultural values, is Benedict Anderson's *Mythology and the Tolerance of the Javanese* (Ithaca, N.Y., 1965). See also R. L. Mellema, *Wayang Puppets: Carving, Colouring, Symbolism* (Amsterdam, 1954). The best way to approach the musical tradition of the *gamelan,* associated with the *wayang,* is through the record, *Music of the Venerable Dark Cloud* (University of California, Los Angeles: Institute of Ethnomusicology, 7501), and its accompanying forty-two-page booklet.

Among works on particular societies in the islands outside Java, a number stand out. J. M. Gullick's *Indigenous Political Systems of Western Malaya* (London, 1958) describes the general principles on which similar societies from Sumatra to the Moluccas were organized. Acheh is well represented with the classic by C. Snouck Hurgronje, *The Achehnese* (2 vols., Leiden, 1906), and the fine modern study by James Siegel, *The Rope of God* (Berkeley, Calif., 1969). Perhaps the best introduction to the remarkable culture of the Balinese is W. Van Hoeve, *Bali: Studies in Life, Thought, and Ritual* (The Hague, 1960), although the works of Jane Belo also merit attention.

There is no complete and fully satisfactory general history of Indonesia or of any of its constituent societies. Taken in conjunction, however, four distinguished works in English cover much of the ground. J. D. Legge's *Indonesia* (Englewood Cliffs, N.J., 1964) is a stimulating essay on the major themes and interpretations of Indonesian history. W. F. Wertheim's *Indonesian Society in Transition* (revised ed., The Hague, 1959) is a pioneer study of the social history of Indonesia, organized in topical rather than chronological chapters. J. S. Furnivall, *Netherlands India: A Study of Plural Economy* (Cambridge, England, 1944) surveys the dry details of administrative and economic history, particularly for the nineteenth and early twentieth centuries, in superb prose. Claire Holt's *Art in Indonesia: Continuities and Change* (Ithaca, N.Y., 1967), the first attempt at a general cultural history of Indonesia, encompasses both Java and the islands, both tradition and modernity, in a remarkable synthesis. Historical writings on Indonesia are admirably covered in Soedjatmoko and others, eds., *An Introduction to Indonesian Historiography* (Ithaca, N.Y., 1965). Major reference works include the still invaluable *Encyclopaedië van Nederlandsch Indië* (The Hague, 1917–32); the *Atlas van Tropisch Nederland* (Amsterdam, 1938); and the *Statistical Pocketbook of Indonesia 1962* (Djakarta, 1962).

The Philippines: A good introduction to Philippine society can be found in Fred Eggan, Evett Hester and Norton Ginsburg, eds., *Area Handbook on the Philippines* (Chicago, 1956 [preliminary edition]). The collection of articles compiled by Socorro C. Espiritu and Chester Hunt in *Social Foundations of Community Development: Readings on the Philippines* (Manila, 1964) is very uneven, although it contains some of the best articles written on the Philippines. Mario D. Zamora, ed., *Studies in Philippine Anthropology in Honor of H. Otley Beyer* (Quezon City, 1967), is also valuable. A good introduction to the geography and people is F. L. Wernstedt and J. E. Spencer's *The Philippine Island World, A Physical, Cultural and Regional Geography* (Berkeley, Calif., 1967). Jean Grossholtz's *Politics in the Philippines* (Boston, 1964) is a good introduction to the political system. For a more detailed analysis of the current political structure see Carl H. Landé's *Leaders, Factions and Parties: The Structure of Philippine Politics* (New Haven, Conn., 1964). Maximo M. Kalaw's primer entitled *Introduction to Philippine Social Science* (Manila, 1933) remains a useful reference volume, despite the fact that it is rather dated. George M. Guthrie and Fortunata M. Azores have published a fascinating study of "Philippine Interpersonal Behavior Patterns" in *Modernization: Its Impact in the Philippines,* III (Institute of Philippine Culture Paper No. 6, Quezon City, 1968), 3–63, a social science survey based on data gathered by a sentence-completion technique. One of the most creative and enjoyable articles on Philippine culture is Richard L. Stone's "Private Transitory ownership of Public Property: One Key to Understanding Public Behavior: I—The Driving Game," in *Modernization: Its Impact in the Philippines* (Institute of Philippine Culture Paper No. 4, Quezon City, 1967), pp. 53–63. Concerning religion in the Philippines, see Gerald H. Anderson, ed., *Studies in Philippine Church History* (Ithaca, N.Y., 1969). Also of value is Winfield Scott Smith, III, ed., *The Art of the Philippines, 1521–1957* (Manila, 1958).

For a general history of the Philippines, see Onofre D. Corpuz, *The Philippines* (Englewood Cliffs, N.J., 1965). This selective and nationalist account is complemented by the volume of readings edited and prepared by Horatio de la Costa and entitled *Readings in Philippine History* (Manila, 1965). The most important source for English language readers on the Spanish era is the fifty-five volumes of documents and footnotes prepared by E. H. Blair and J. A. Robertson, *The Philippine Islands, 1493–1898* (Cleveland, 1903). Nicholas P. Cushner's *Spain in the Philippines: From Conquest to Revolution* (Quezon City, 1970) brilliantly and succinctly describes the Spanish era. The book is especially valuable on the first two centuries of Spanish rule. E. A. Manuel's *Dictionary of Philippine Biography* (Quezon City, 1955), and the less scholarly but more broadly based volume by the National Historical Commission entitled *Eminent Filipinos* (Manila, 1965) offer valuable biographical information. See also Gregorio F. Zaide's *Great Filipinos in History* (Manila, 1970). A number of multivolume encyclopedias exist, including *The Encyclopedia of the Philippines* (Manila, 1950), but their quality is uneven.

PART ONE. THE EIGHTEENTH-CENTURY WORLD

There is very little material explicitly on Southeast Asian societies in the eighteenth century. The historian, therefore, is dependent in large part on studies of contemporary Southeast Asian societies and must use great care when drawing conclusions for the eighteenth century from these studies. Most of the works cited below on "The Peasant World," "The Upland Peoples," and "Religious Life and Leadership," are analyses of these subjects in contemporary Southeast Asia.

Chapter 1. The Peasant World

Perhaps the best general work on peasant society is Eric Wolf's *Peasants* (Englewood Cliffs, N.J., 1966). For analyses of lowland village life in Thailand, see John de Young's *Village Life in Modern Thailand* (Berkeley and Los Angeles, 1955); Michael Moerman's *Agricultural Change and Peasant Choice in a Thai Village* (Berkeley and Los Angeles, 1968); Howard Keva Kaufman's *Bangkhuad: A Community Study in Thailand* (Locust Valley, N.Y., 1960); and Lauriston Sharp and Lucien Hanks, Jr., *Bang Chan: A Social History of a Thai Farming Community* (Ithaca, N.Y., forthcoming). Lucien Hanks, Jr., has also written an important article entitled "Merit and Power in the Thai Social Order," in *American Anthropologist,* LXIV:6 (December, 1962), 1247–61. The numerous works of Robert Lingat, particularly his article "La Double crise de l'église bouddhique au Siam, 1767–1851," *Cahiers d'histoire mondiale,* IV (1958),

402–25, are immediately relevant. Herbert Phillips's volume *Thai Peasant Personality* (Berkeley and Los Angeles, 1965) also merits attention.

For village life in Burma, good introductions are to be found in Manning Nash, *The Golden Road to Modernity: Village Life in Contemporary Burma* (New York, 1965); and David E. Pfanner, "Rice and Religion in a Burmese Village" (unpublished Ph.D. dissertation, Cornell University, 1962). Sir James George Scott (Shway Yoe), *The Burman: His Life and Notions* (London, 1882 [reprinted, New York, 1963]); and Mi Mi Khaing, *Burmese Family* (Bombay, 1946 [reprinted, Bloomington, Ind., 1962]) are also useful. Yi Yi, in her monumental article on eighteenth-century Burmese records, "Kon-hpaung khet sit-tan mya" ("Records of the Konbaung Era"), *Journal of the Burma Research Society*, XLIX:1 (1966), 71–128, provides indispensable information on the premodern Burmese village.

Jean Delvert's *Le Paysan Cambodgien* (Paris, 1961) is a thorough and interesting study, covering all aspects of Cambodian rural life. It complements Henri Monod's more impressionistic *Le Cambodgien* (Paris, 1931) and René Morizon's *Monographie du Cambodge* (Hanoi, 1930). Guy Porée and Eveline Maspéro's *Moeurs et coûtumes des Cambodgiens* (Paris, 1938) is a good general work, as is Solange Thierry's *Les Khmers* (Paris, 1962). On housing in rural Cambodia, see Eveline Porée–Maspéro, "Kron Pali," *Anthropos*, LVI (1961), 179–251. On Cambodian village organization, see May Ebihara's contribution to Frank LeBar, Gerald Hickey, and John Musgrave, *Ethnic Groups of Mainland Southeast Asia* (New Haven, Conn., 1964).

One interesting investigation of Vietnamese peasant agriculture, which focuses upon twentieth-century landholding patterns but is still of great interest to historians, is Pierre Gourou, *L'Utilisation du sol en Indochine française* (Paris, 1940). Introductions to the organization of Vietnamese villages may be found in Paul Ory, *La Commune annamite au Tonkin* (Paris, 1894), and Nguyen Huu Khang, *La Commune annamite* (Paris, 1946). The best English-language study of the Vietnamese village deals with southern village life of the post–1954 period but contains themes of historical importance: Gerald G. Hickey, *Village in Vietnam* (New Haven, Conn., 1964). Also see Paul Mus, "The Role of the Village in Vietnamese Politics," *Pacific Affairs*, XXII (September, 1949), 265–72. On Vietnamese village organization in the traditional periods, an excellent survey is that of Phan Khoang, "Luoc su che do xa thon o Viet-Nam" ("A Brief History of the Village System in Vietnam"), in *Su Dia* (Saigon), I (1966), 34–51.

There have been a number of excellent studies of contemporary Malay peasant society by social anthropologists, among them Rosemary Firth, *Housekeeping Among Malay Peasants* (1st ed., 1943 [revised ed., London, 1966]); and Michael G. Swift, *Malay Peasant Society in Jelebu* (London, 1965). G. E. Shaw, "Rice Planting," in R. J. Wilkinson, ed., *Papers on Malay Subjects: Malay Industries*, III (Kuala Lumpur, 1911), gives some account of the traditional rice industry in the peninsula. Patterns of land ownership in the west-coast Malay states are examined in W. E. Maxwell, "The Law and Customs of the Malays with Reference to the Tenure of Land," *Journal of the Straits Branch Royal Asiatic Society*, XIII (June, 1884), 75–220. Although R. N. Hilton's article, "The Basic Malay House," *Journal of the Malayan Branch Royal Asiatic Society*, XXIX:3 (1956), 134–55, is of recent date, his detailed discussion of house types refers to many patterns of construction that were common in the eighteenth century.

For Indonesia, Clifford Geertz has provided an excellent general exposition of the contrast between wet-rice and swidden society in his book entitled *Agricultural Involution* (Berkeley, Calif., 1963). Another useful general study is Koentjaraningrat, ed., *Villages in Indonesia* (Ithaca, N.Y., 1967). The most comprehensive anthropological study of Javanese peasant life is found in the published works of a team that investigated the East-Central Javanese district of "Modjokuto" in the early 1950's. These include *The Religion of Java* (Glencoe, Ill., 1960) and the poignant essay "Ritual and Social Change: A Javanese Example," *American Anthropologist*, LIX:1 (1957), 32–54, by Clifford Geertz; *The Javanese Family* (Glencoe, Ill., 1961), by Hildred Geertz; Robert Jay's *Religion and Politics in Rural Central Java* (New Haven, Conn., 1963) and *Javanese Villagers: Social Relations in Rural Modjokuto* (Cambridge, Mass., 1969); and Alice Dewey's *Peasant Marketing in Java* (Glencoe, Ill., 1962). Several of the peasant societies in the islands outside Java are well described in the modern literature. For the Toba Batak see J. G. Vergouwen, *The Social Organization and Customary Law of the Toba-Batak of North Sumatra* (The Hague, 1964). Perhaps the best introduction to the Minangkabau of west central Sumatra are Taufik Abdullah, "Adat and Islam: An Examination of Conflict in Minangkabau," *Indonesia*, II (1966), 1–24; and B. J. O. Schrieke's well-known "West Coast Report" of 1927 published partly in Schrieke, *Indonesian Sociological Studies*, Part I (The Hague, 1955), and partly in Harry Benda and Ruth McVey, eds., *The Communist Uprisings of 1926–1927: Key Documents* (Ithaca, N.Y., 1960). See also Peter Goethals, *Aspects of Local Government in a Sumbawan Village* (*Eastern Indonesia*) (Ithaca, N.Y., 1961).

There is an extensive literature on lowland village life in the Philippines. For a good introduction, see Fred Eggan, Evett Hester, and Norton Ginsburg, eds., *Area Handbook on the Philippines* (preliminary edition, Chicago, 1956), and Socorro C. Espiritu and Chester Hunt, eds., *Social Foundations of Community Development: Readings on the Philippines* (Manila, 1964). One can get a sense of the traditional barrio in Mary R. Hollnsteiner's perceptive *The Dynamics of Power in a Philippine Municipality* (Manila, 1963). Among the many case studies recently completed are: James N. Anderson's "Kinship and Property in a Pangasinan Barrio" (unpublished Ph.D. dissertation, UCLA, 1964), Richard W. Lieban's *Cebuano Sorcery: Malign Magic in the Philippines* (Berkeley, Calif., 1967), Akira Takahashi's *Land and Peasants in Central Luzon: Socio-Economic Structure of a Bulacan Village* (Tokyo, 1969), and Ethel Nurge's *Life in a Leyte Village* (Seattle, Wash., 1965). Very little has been written about the principal minority group in the Philippines—the Muslims—but Najeeb M. Saleeby's *Studies in Moro History, Laws and Religion* (Manila, 1905), and Peter G. Gowing's more popular treatment entitled *Mosque and Moro: A Study of Muslims in the Philippines* (Manila, 1964), are helpful. Over the last few years there has been an intense debate attempting to define Philippine peasant values. A good introduction can be found in the articles by Fred Eggan and George Guthrie that appear in the book edited by George Guthrie entitled *Six Perspectives on the Philippines* (Manila, 1968). The *Four Readings on Philippine Values* (Quezon City, 1964), edited by Frank Lynch, are among the most brilliant and controversial. Other important pieces include: Charles Kaut, "Utang na loob: A System of Contractual Obligations Among Tagalogs," *Southwestern Journal of Anthropology*, XVII:3 (1961), 256–72; Jaime C. Bulatao, "Hiya," *Philippine Studies*, XXI:3 (July, 1964), 424–38; Sidney W. Mintz and Eric Wolf, "An Analysis of Ritual Co–parenthood (Compadrazgo)," *Southwestern Journal of Anthropology*, VI (1950), 341–68; George Forster, "Cofradía and Compadrazgo," *Southwestern Journal of Anthropology*, IX:1 (1953), 1–28.

The most instructive works about peasant fishermen describe Malay coastal fishermen, concerning whom one of the classics of social anthropology has been written, Raymond Firth's *Malay Fishermen: Their Peasant Economy* (1st ed., 1946 [revised and enlarged ed., London, 1966]). Thomas M. Fraser, *Rusembilan: A Malay Fishing Village in Southern Thailand* (Ithaca, N.Y., 1960), is more generally ethnographic.

A standard work on slaves and bondsmen is Bruno Lasker, *Human Bondage in Southeast Asia* (Chapel Hill, N.C., 1950). A classical study, with wide implications, is Robert Lingat's *L'Esclavage privé dans le vieux droit siamois* (Paris, 1931). It is amplified by Akin Rabibhadana, *The Organization of Thai Society in the Early Bangkok Period, 1782–1873* (Ithaca, N.Y., 1969). Also see Yvonne Bongert's "Note sur l'esclavage en droit khmer ancien," in *Études d'histoire du droit privé offertes à Pierre Petot* (Paris, 1959), 7–26. A rather theoretical account of debt–bondage in Malay society may be found in W. E. Maxwell, "The Law Relating to Slavery Among the Malays," *Journal of the Straits Branch Royal Asiatic Society*, XXII (December, 1890), 247–98. Dato' Mahmud b. Mat's article, "The Passing of Slavery in East Pahang," *Malayan Historical Journal*, I:1 (May, 1954), 8–10, reports on oral tradition concerning the practice of debt–bondage prior to British rule. One can get some sense of the slave trade in the Philippines through the writings of Antonio de Morga and Joaquín Martínez de Zúñiga. Morga's *Sucesos* has been translated by E. J. Stanley, retitled *The Philippine Islands*, and printed by the Hakluyt Society of London. Martínez de Zúñiga's *Historia de las islas Philippinas* (Sampaloc, 1803) focuses on the Spanish side. Few scholars, however, have examined this institution dispassionately.

In the area of folk religion, a forthcoming book by A. Thomas Kirsch will deal with the syncretism of Buddhism, animism, and Indic religious beliefs in Thailand. For Burma, Melford E. Spiro's book entitled *Burmese Supernaturalism* (Englewood Cliffs, N.J., 1967) is the best. Eveline Porée-Maspéro's *Les Rites agraires des Cambodgiens* (2 vols., Paris, 1962–66) is a good study of folk religion in Cambodia. W. W. Skeat's *Malay Magic* (1st ed., 1900 [reprinted in New York and London, 1967]) remains a classic account of Malay folklore and popular religion. Folk religion in Java is analyzed by Clifford Geertz in *The Religion of Java* (Glencoe, Ill., 1960). Léopold Cadière's *Croyances et pratiques religieuses des vietnamiens* (Paris, 1959) includes a description of family ancestor worship in Vietnam. Richard W. Lieban's *Cebuano Sorcery: Malign Magic in the Philippines* (Berkeley, Calif., 1967) is a vivid analysis of popular religion in lowland Philippines.

Chapter 2. The Upland Peoples

A good introduction to upland societies and their life is Robbins Burling's *Hill Farms and Paddy Fields* (Englewood Cliffs, N.J., 1965). J. E. Spencer's

Shifting Cultivation in Southeastern Asia (Berkeley, Calif., 1966) is an excellent analysis of upland agriculture, and is complemented by H. C. Conklin, "The Study of Shifting Cultivation," *Current Anthropology*, II (1961), 27–61, which contains a good bibliography. The best introductions to the study of individual upland groups are Peter Kunstadter, ed., *Southeast Asian Tribes, Minorities, and Nations* (2 vols., Princeton, N.J., 1967), and Frank LeBar, Gerald Hickey and John Musgrave, *Ethnic Groups of Mainland Southeast Asia* (New Haven, Conn., 1964).

Together with his stimulating essay, "The Frontiers of 'Burma,'" in *Comparative Studies in Society and History*, III:1 (October, 1960), 49–68, E. R. Leach's *Political Systems of Highland Burma* (2d ed., London, 1964) is the best analysis of upland groups in Burma. On the contacts between upland and lowland peoples, the best documentation for Burma, as far as the eighteenth and nineteenth centuries are concerned, is to be found in the monumental *Gazetteer of Upper Burma and the Shan States*, edited by J. G. Scott and J. P. Hardiman (5 vols., Rangoon, 1902–5). There is as yet but a single good study for Thailand: Kraisri Nimmanahaeminda, "An Inscribed Silver-Plate Grant to the Lawa of Boh Luang," *Felicitation Volumes of Southeast Asian Studies Presented to His Highness Prince Dhaninivat* (2 vols., Bangkok, 1965), II:233–38, although a forthcoming work by Charles F. Keyes is to make significant contributions to this field.

Materials dealing with the histories and cultures of the highland peoples of Indochina are scattered. Bernard Bourotte, "Essai d'Histoire des Populations Montagnardes du Sud-Indochinois jusqu'à 1945," *Bulletin de la Société des Études Indochinoises*, XXX:1 (1955), 5–116, analyzes the development of highland communities in south Vietnam and their relationship to Vietnamese political history. Gerald Hickey, *The Major Ethnic Groups of the South Vietnamese Highlands* (Santa Monica, Calif., 1964), gives an ethnographic survey. Note also Louis Malleret, *Ethnic Groups of French Indochina* (Washington, 1962), from an important French work originally published in Saigon in 1937, and Dam Bo (Jacques Dournes) "Les Populations Montagnardes du Sud Indochinois," *France-Asie*, V (spring, 1950), 49–50. Among the best studies of individual groups are those of the Mnong Gar of southern Vietnam by Georges Condominas, *Nous avons mangé la forêt* (Paris, 1957), and K. G. Izikowitz's study of a Laotian group, the Lamet, entitled *Hill Peasants in French Indo-China* (Goteborg, 1951). See also R. Baradat, *Les Samre ou Pear* (Hanoi, 1941); Charles Meyer, "Les Mystérieuses Relations entre le Roi du Cambodge et les 'Potao' des Jarai," *Études Cambodgiennes*, 4 (October–December, 1965), 14–26; J. Boulbet, *Pays des Maa'* (Paris, 1967); and Georges Condominas, *L'Exotique est quotidien* (Paris, 1967).

An early standard work on the aboriginal peoples of the Malay peninsula is W. W. Skeat and C. O. Blagden, *Pagan Races of the Malay Peninsula* (1st ed., 1906 [reprinted in London, 1967]). The anthropologist I. H. N. Evans, in addition to his study of one particular group in the peninsula, *The Negritos of Malaya* (Cambridge, England, 1937), published also two useful collections of papers, *Studies in Religion, Folk-Lore and Custom in British North Borneo and the Malay Peninsula* (Cambridge, England, 1923), and *Papers on the Ethnology and Archeology of the Malay Peninsula* (Cambridge, England, 1927). A brief and general *Introduction to the Malayan Aborigines* was published in 1952 by the then Protector of Aborigines, P. D. R. Williams-Hunt (Kuala Lumpur). Together, Benedict Sandin, *The Sea Dayaks of Borneo before White Rajah Rule* (London, 1968), based on oral tradition, and J. D. Freeman, *Iban Agriculture: A Report on the Shifting Cultivation of Hill Rice by the Iban of Sarawak* (London, 1955), give a good systematic description of the Iban swidden-cultivating society. For other descriptions of tribal life in Borneo, see Henry Ling Roth, *The Natives of Sarawak and British North Borneo* (1st ed., 1896 [reprinted in Kuala Lumpur, 1968]); C. Hose and W. McDougall, *The Pagan Tribes of Borneo* (London, 1912); and W. R. Geddes, *The Land Dayaks of Sarawak* (London, 1954). Geddes has also published a more popular account of Dayak life entitled *Nine Dayak Nights* (Melbourne, 1957). Alfred Hudson's "The Padju Epat Ma'anjan Dajak in Historical Perspective," *Indonesia*, IV (October, 1967), 8–42, is particularly useful in exploring the historical relationship between animists in the interior and coastal Muslims. Clark Cunningham's works on Timor, such as "Order and Change in an Atoni Dyarchy," *Southwestern Journal of Anthropology*, XXI (Winter, 1965), 359–82, are examples of the smaller number of good modern studies in English on societies in the islands eastward from Borneo and Bali. A useful and detailed account of the nomadic *orang laut* of the Malayan coast, the only one of its kind, has been published by David E. Sopher, *The Sea Nomads: A Study Based on the Literature of the Maritime Boat People of Southeast Asia* (Singapore, 1965).

Among the best studies of upland peoples on the island of Luzon in the Philippines are Felix M. Keesing's *The Ethnohistory of Northern Luzon* (Stanford, Calif., 1962); Roy F. Barton's *The Kalingas: Their Institutions and Custom Law* (Chicago, 1949); the *Autobiographies of Three Pagans in the Philippines* (New York, 1963) by the same author; and Edward Dozier's *Mountain Arbiters: The Changing Life of a Philippine Hill People* (Tucson, Ariz., 1966). Harold C. Conklin's *Ifugao Bibliography* (New Haven, Conn., 1968) contains references to more than 650 works on these upland people of Luzon. Conklin has also written a good case study of *Hanunoo Agriculture* (Mindoro: FAO, 1955). The literature about upland peoples in Mindanao is too extensive to cite here but see the writings of Charles O. Frake, Aram A. Yengoyan, and Stuart Schlegel.

Chapter 3. Authority and Village Society

(See bibliography for Chapter 1.)

Chapter 4. Provincial Powers

(See bibliography for Chapters 7–11.)

Chapter 5. Religious Life and Leadership

Mahayana Buddhism: In Western languages, perhaps the most useful introduction to Vietnamese Buddhism is Mai Tho Truyen, "Le Bouddhisme au Viet-Nam," published independently and in the special issue "Présence du Bouddhisme," of *France-Asie*, XVI (1959). Thich Nhat Hanh, *Vietnam: Lotus in a Sea of Fire* (New York, 1967), contains a very brief summary of Vietnamese Buddhism's history. For a discussion of the political potentialities of Buddhism in Vietnam, and methods of court control, see Alexander Woodside, "Vietnamese Buddhism, the Vietnamese Court and China in the 1800's," in Edgar Wickberg, ed., *Historical Interaction of China and Vietnam: Institutional and Cultural Themes* (Lawrence, Kan., 1969), 11–24. For readers with a rudimentary command of modern Vietnamese, a standard history of Vietnamese Buddhism is Mat The, *Viet Nam Phat giao su luoc* (*A Short History of Vietnamese Buddhism*) (Nha Trang, 1960).

Theravada Buddhism: Kenneth Wells, *Thai Buddhism: Its Rites and Activities* (Bangkok, 1960), and a forthcoming book by A. Thomas Kirsch are essential works for an understanding of Buddhism in Thailand. Simon de la Loubère, *A New Historical Relation of the Kingdom of Siam* (London, 1693 [reprinted in Kuala Lumpur, 1969]), includes an unbiased description of Thai Buddhism. Also see Robert Lingat's "La Double crise de l'église bouddhique au Siam, 1767–1851," *Cahiers d'histoire mondiale*, IV (1958), 402–25. Burmese Buddhism is analyzed in numerous articles by E. Michael Mendelson, including: "Buddhism and the Burmese Establishment," *Archives de sociologie des religions*, IX:17 (Jan/June, 1964), 85–95; and "A Messianic Buddhist Association in Upper Burma," *Bulletin of the London School of Oriental and African Studies*, XXIV, Part Three (1961). Useful information may also be found in Donald Eugene Smith, *Religion and Politics in Burma* (Princeton, N.J., 1965); and in E. Sarkisyanz's stimulating *Buddhist Backgrounds of the Burmese Revolution* (The Hague, 1965). Father Vincentius Sangermano's *Description of the Burmese Empire* (5th ed., London, 1966), while valuable, is understandably unsympathetic. Adhémard Leclère's *Le Bouddhisme au Cambodge* (Paris, 1899) is still useful, and for a more recent analysis of the monk's position in Cambodian society, see May Ebihara's contribution to Manning Nash, *et al.*, *Anthropological Studies in Theravada Buddhism* (New Haven, Conn., 1966).

Islam: A helpful historical introduction to Islam in Southeast Asia is provided in the appropriate chapters by H. J. de Graaf, William R. Roff, and Harry J. Benda in *The Cambridge History of Islam* (London, 1970). Surveys of interest that, though relating primarily to Indonesia, refer also to the remainder of the area, include P. A. Hoesin Djajadiningrat's "Islam in Indonesia," in Kenneth Morgan, ed., *Islam: The Straight Path* (London, 1958); and G. W. J. Drewes, "Indonesia: Mysticism and Activism," in G. E. von Grunebaum, ed., *Unity and Variety in Muslim Civilization* (Chicago, 1955). An important article on the pilgrimage to Mecca, as it affected Indonesians and Malays, is Jacob Vredenbregt's "The Hadj: Some of its Features and Functions in Indonesia," *Bijdragen tot de Taal-, Land- en Volkenkunde* (1962), 91–154. Most of the writings of the great Dutch Islamicist, C. Snouck Hurgronje, have not, unfortunately, been translated into English, but his classic description of Indonesian and Malay sojourners in *Mekka in the Latter Part of the 19th Century* (Leiden, 1931) is of great importance for any understanding of Southeast Asian Islam.

A number of useful works deal with particular parts of the region, though in this respect Malaysia has been much less well served than Indonesia. Among important works on the latter, see C. Snouck Hurgronje, *The Achehnese* (2 vols., London, 1906); Clifford Geertz, *The Religion of Java* (Glencoe, Ill., 1962); James Siegel, *The Rope of God* (Berkeley, Calif., 1969); and Taufik Abdullah, "Adat and Islam: An Examination of Conflict in Minangkabau," *Indonesia*, II (1966), 1–24. The small number of works that deal in some respect with Islam in Malaya include R. J. Wilkinson,

Malay Beliefs (1st ed., 1906 [reprinted in the *Journal of the Malayan Branch Royal Asiatic Society*, XXX:4 (1957), 1–40]); and R. J. Wilkinson and W. J. Rigby, *Malay Law*, in R. J. Wilkinson, ed., *Papers on Malay Subjects* (Kuala Lumpur, 1908); R. O. Winstedt, "Malaysia," in A. J. Arberry and Rom Landau, eds., *Islam Today* (London, 1943); Naguib al-Attas, *Some Aspects of Sufism as Understood and Practised Among the Malays* (Singapore, 1963); and two legal compilations, Ahmad Ibrahim, *Islamic Law in Malaya* (Singapore, 1965), and A. M. M. Mackeen, *Contemporary Islamic Legal Organization in Malaya* (New Haven, Conn., 1969). The Muslim population of the southern Philippines has been little described by scholars, but reference may be made to Peter G. Gowing, *Mosque and Moro: A Study of Muslims in the Philippines* (Manila, 1964); and Najeeb M. Saleeby, *Studies in Moro History, Law and Religion* (Manila, 1905). The best study of the Muslim minority in Cambodia and southern Vietnam is Marcel Ner's "Les Musulmans de l'Indochine Française," *Bulletin de l'École Française d'Extrême Orient*, XLI (1941), 156–200.

Christianity: The most important volume dealing with the Church in the Philippines is *Studies in Philippine Church History* (Ithaca, N.Y., 1969), edited by Gerald H. Anderson. Horatio de la Costa's *The Jesuits in the Philippines, 1581–1768* (Cambridge, Mass., 1961) is a classic. The casual reader, however, might prefer Gregorio F. Zaide's *Catholicism in the Philippines* (Manila, 1937), despite its pro-Church bias. The artistic and architectural impact of the Church can be studied in Richard Ahlborn's "The Spanish Churches of Central Luzon," *Philippine Studies*, VIII, 4 (October, 1960), 802–13; in Benito Legarda y Fernandez, "Colonial Churches in Ilocos," *Philippine Studies*, VIII:1 (January, 1960), 121–58; in Armengol P. Ortiz, *Intramuros de Manila de 1571 hasta su destruccion en 1945* (Madrid, 1958); and in Fernando Zobel de Ayala's *Philippine Religious Imagery* (Quezon City, 1963).

Concerning Catholicism in Indochina, volume one of Georges Taboulet's two-volume work entitled *La Geste française en Indochine: histoire par les textes de la France en Indochine des origines à 1914* (Paris, 1955–56) is a compendium of important documents, accompanied by analysis, revealing the evolution of missionary-sponsored Catholicism from the seventeenth century in Vietnam. A religious history of Vietnam written by a Vietnamese Catholic, Phan Phat Huon, *Viet Nam giao su* (2 vols., Saigon, 1962), explores Roman Catholic Community life in Vietnam in some detail. J. Pianet's "Histoire de la mission au Cambodge (1552–1852)," *Bulletin de la Société de Missions Étrangères*, 82–88 (1928), 90–94 (1929) is also valuable.

Chapter 6. Traders and Markets

Internal Trade: Late but extremely useful references to trade between lowlands and highlands in Burma are contained in Henry Yule's *A Narrative of the Mission to the Court of Ava in 1855* (London, 1968), first published in 1857. Probably the best treatment of goods produced in lieu of taxes in the eighteenth century is Wira Wimoniti, *Historical Patterns of Tax Administration in Thailand* (Bangkok, 1961). The doctoral dissertation of Constance M. Wilson at Cornell University (1970) promises to revolutionize our thinking on these problems. For information on the organization of internal trade within Vietnam, see Nguyen The Anh, *Kinh te va xa hoi Viet-nam duoi cac vua trieu Nguyen* (*The Vietnamese Economy and Society Under the Emperors of the Nguyen Court*) (Saigon, 1968). For cardamom production in Cambodia, see Réné Morizon, *La Province cambodgienne de Pursat* (Paris, 1936). The best short analysis of the economic structure of the Philippines is Benito Legarda y Fernandez, "The Philippine Economy under Spanish Rule," *Solidarity*, II:10 (November–December, 1967), 1–21. See also María Lourdes Díaz-Trechuelo, "Philippine Economic Development Plans, 1746–1779," *Philippine Studies*, XII:2 (April, 1964), 203–31; and "Eighteenth Century Philippine Economy: Commerce," *Philippine Studies*, XIV:2 (April, 1966), 252–79, by the same author. For a brief description of the tobacco monopoly in the Philippines see Eduardo Lachina's "The Tobacco Monopoly," *Historical Bulletin* (Philippine Historical Association), VIII:1 (March, 1964), 60–72. María Lourdes Díaz-Trechuelo's "Eighteenth Century Philippine Economy: Agriculture," *Philippine Studies*, XIV:1 (January, 1966), 65–126, is a study of commercial agriculture in the Philippines, and her "Eighteenth Century Philippine Economy: Mining," *Philippine Studies*, XIII:4 (October, 1965), 763–97, is an analysis of that aspect of the Philippine economy. See also María Luisa Rodríguez Baena's *La Sociedad ecónomica del Amigos des País de Manila en el siglo XVIII* (Seville, 1966).

Trading Networks: For information on the caravans that plied between Yunnan and Burma in the eighteenth century, Henry Yule's *A Narrative of the Mission to the Court of Ava in 1855* (London, 1968 [first published in 1857]) is a good source. Note also Kuo Tsung-fei, "A Brief History of the Trade Routes between Burma, Indochina and Yunnan," *T'ien Hsia Monthly*, XII:1 (1941), 9–32. Wira Wimoniti, *Historical Patterns of Tax Administration in Thailand* (Bangkok, 1961), includes some material relevant to royal trading monopolies. For the South China Sea network, Yi Yi's unpublished University of London dissertation on "English Trade in the South China Sea, 1670–1715" (1958) is of considerable interest, although it by no means exhausts the field, particularly on Chinese trade.

The classic study, *The Manila Galleon*, was written many years ago by William L. Schurz, and reissued in paper in 1959. Schurz wrote with verve and accuracy, and the book is fun to read. For shorter and more recent treatments of the Manila galleon trade, see Benito Legarda y Fernandez, "Two and a Half Centuries of the Galleon Trade," *Philippine Studies*, III:4 (December, 1955), 345–72; and María Lourdes Díaz-Trechuelo, "Dos Nuevos Derroteros del Galeon de Manila (1730–1773)," in Vol. XIII of *Anuario de Estudios Americanos* (1956), 1–83. Pierre Chaunu has edited and elaborated on the records pertaining to Spanish trade with the Philippines in the Archivos des Indes in Seville. His volume, entitled *Les Philippines et le Pacifique des Ibériques* (*XVI*^e^, *XVII*^e^, *XVIII*^e^ *siècles*) (Paris, 1960), is particularly relevant to trade in the sixteenth and early seventeenth centuries.

A book that is full of information on the Dutch East Indies Company trade is Kristoff Glamann's *Dutch-Asiatic Trade 1620–1740* (Copenhagen, 1958). C. N. Parkinson's *Trade in the Eastern Seas, 1793–1813* (Cambridge, England, 1937) is a good, readable survey. W. J. M. Buch's important study of the Dutch trade with Indochina is translated into French as "La Compagnie des Indes Néerlandaise et l'Indochine," *Bulletin de l'École*

Française d'Extrême Orient, XXXVI (1936), and XXXVII (1937). For British trade, see C. N. Parkinson's compilation entitled *The Trade Winds: A Study of British Overseas Trade during the French Wars, 1793–1815* (London, 1949). H. P. Clodd, *Malaya's First British Pioneer: The Life of Francis Light* (London, 1948), is a brief account of the founder of Penang; and K. G. Tregonning, *The British in Malaya: The First Forty Years* (Tucson, Ariz., 1965), also deals extensively with British trading at this time. D. G. E. Hall's *Early English Intercourse with Burma, 1587–1743* (rev. ed., London, 1968) merits attention, and the broader study of M. A. P. Meilink-Roelofsz, *Asian Trade and European Influence in the Indonesian Archipelago between 1500 and about 1630* (The Hague, 1962), though referring to an earlier period, certainly is applicable generally to the seventeenth and eighteenth centuries as well. J. A. E. Morley, "The Arabs and the Eastern Trade," *Journal of the Malayan Branch Royal Asiatic Society*, XX:1 (March, 1949), although concerned largely with later years, devotes considerable attention to the period before 1800. Recent scholarship has revealed that there was far more trade between the Philippines and the rest of Asia than earlier believed. See, for example, W. E. Cheong's "Anglo-Spanish-Portuguese Clandestine Trade between the Ports of British India and Manila, 1785–1790," *Philippine Historical Review*, I:1 (1965), 80–94; and Serafin D. Quiason's *English "Country Trade" with the Philippines, 1644–1765* (Quezon City, 1966). For a glimpse into the French trade with Manila, see H. de la Costa's "Early French Contact with the Philippines," in *Asia and the Philippines* (Manila, 1967).

Overseas Chinese: On the subject of the early history of the overseas Chinese in Vietnam, see Paul Boudet, "La Conquête de la Cochinchine par les Nguyen et le rôle des émigrés Chinois," *Bulletin de l'École Française d'Extrême Orient*, XLII (1942). For Thailand, the first chapter in G. William Skinner's *Chinese Society in Thailand: An Analytical History* (Ithaca, N.Y., 1957) is essential reading. *The Chinese in the Philippines, 1570–1770* edited by Alfonso Felix, Jr. (Manila, 1966), is important reading for anyone interested in this topic. Much information on the Chinese in early Batavia (Jakarta) may be gleaned from Joannes T. Vermeulen, "The Chinese in Batavia and the Troubles of 1740," *Journal of the South Seas Society*, IX:1 (1953), 1–68.

Chapter 7. The Buddhist Kings

A good introduction is Robert von Heine-Geldern's *Conceptions of State and Kingship in Southeast Asia* (Ithaca, N.Y., 1956 [first published in *Far Eastern Quarterly*, II (November, 1942), 15–30]), which gives a brief but important account of traditional ideas concerning monarchy and society, principally in the mainland states.

Ava: The best histories, which include analyses of Burma in the eighteenth century, are G. E. Harvey, *History of Burma* (London, 1925 [reprinted in London, 1967]); and Sir Arthur P. Phayre, *History of Burma* (London, 1883 [reprinted in London, 1967]). The classical Burman source for the period prior to 1752 is the *Glass Palace Chronicle, Hmannan yazawin daw gyi* (3 vols., Mandalay, 1921 [reprinted in Rangoon, 1960]). "The Nature of the Burman Chronicles," is discussed by U Tet Htoot in D. G. E. Hall, *Historians of South-East Asia* (London, 1961), pp. 50–62. Also see Yi Yi's article on eighteenth-century Burman records, "Kon-hpaung khet sit-tan mya" ("Records of the Konbaung Era"), *Journal of the Burma Research Society*, XLIX:1 (1966), 71–128. Such major sources as U Tin's *Myanma min okchok hpoun satan* (*Administration under the Burmese Kings*) (5 vols., Rangoon, 1963–) still would repay careful study, and one can hardly do better than J. G. Scott and J. P. Hardiman's *Gazetteer of Upper Burma and the Shan States* (5 vols., Rangoon, 1902–5).

Ayudhya: W. A. R. Wood's *A History of Siam from the Earliest Times to the Year A.D. 1781* (London, 1924 [reprinted in Bangkok, 1959]) is still useful, though outdated. H. G. Quaritch Wales has written two helpful studies: *Ancient Siamese Government and Administration* (1st ed., London, 1934 [reprinted in New York, 1965]) and *Siamese State Ceremonies* (London, 1931). Pertinent information first published in the *Journal of the Siam Society* (Bangkok, 1904–present) is made available in the *Selected Articles from the Siam Society Journal* (10 vols., Bangkok, 1954–59). The best of the contemporary accounts from the seventeenth century are Simon de la Loubère, *A New Historical Relation of the Kingdom of Siam* (London, 1693 [reprinted in Kuala Lumpur, 1969]); and E. W. Hutchinson, tr. and ed., *1688 Revolution in Siam: The Memoir of Father de Bèze* (Hong Kong, 1968). The latter author has provided us with the best description of that period in his *Adventurers in Siam in the Seventeenth Century* (London, 1940). Akin Rabibhadana, *The Organization of Thai Society in the Early Bangkok Period, 1782–1873* (Ithaca, N.Y., 1969), has some extremely important things to say about Thai society and the extent to which political struggles were affected by problems in the control of manpower. The chief Thai sources for the Ayudhya period are, of course, the multiple versions of the royal chronicles, *Phraratchaphongsawadan*. Other Thai sources are listed in David K. Wyatt, *Thai-Language Books: A Checklist* (London, 1967). Thai literature is surveyed by Paul Schweisguth, *Étude sur la littérature siamoise* (Paris, 1951). The role of the provincial town in pre-modern Thailand has only just begun to be studied. The chronicles of such provincial towns as Nakhọn Si Thammarat, Songkhla, Phatthalung and Nakhọn Ratchasima (Khorat) remain virtually untapped. Two such chronicles, however, are available in translation: *The Nan Chronicle*, edited by David K. Wyatt (Ithaca, N.Y., 1966), and *Hikayat Patani: The Story of Patani*, by A. Teeuw and David K. Wyatt (The Hague, 1970).

Phnom Penh: The best full treatment of this period in Cambodian history remains Jean Moura's *Le Royaume de Cambodge* (2 vols., Paris, 1884). Adhémard Leclère's *Histoire du Cambodge* (Paris, 1914) is less reliable, although his edition of *Les Codes Cambodgiens* (2 vols., Paris, 1898) is useful. Western visitors to Cambodia between the seventeenth century and the 1850's were infrequent and seldom recorded their impressions. For an excellent synopsis of Cambodian life two centuries before, see B. P. Groslier's *Angkor et le Cambodge au XVIe siècle* (Paris, 1958). Popular views of monarchy are discussed in Solange Thierry's "La Personne sacrée du roi dans la littérature populaire cambodgienne," in *Studies in the History of Religions:* Vol. IV, *The Sacral Kingship* (Leyden, 1959). See also Solange Bernard and François Martini, *Contes populaires inédits du Cambodge* (Paris, 1946). Although provincial power in Cambodia has rarely been studied, two articles by Milton E. Osborne are helpful: "Notes on Early Cambodian Provincial History," *France-Asie* (Summer, 1966), pp. 433–50, and "Regional Disunity in Cambodia," *Australian Outlook*, XXII:3 (December, 1968), 317–33.

The Lao and Shan World: Paul le Boulanger, *Histoire du Laos français* (Paris, 1931); and Maha Sila Viravong, *History of Laos* (New York, 1964), are general histories of Laos. The work of Charles Archaimbault in translating Lao chronicles is extremely important: "L'Histoire de Campasak," *Journal Asiatique*, CCXLIX:4 (1961), 519–95, and "Les Annales de l'ancien royaume de S'ieng Khwang," *Bulletin de l'École Française d'Extrême Orient*, LIII:2 (1967), 557–673. Chiangmai is the subject of the third volume of Camille Notton's translations of *Annales du Siam* (Paris, 1926–32), which will have to suffice until a more systematic study of the rich vernacular sources is undertaken. Some of these are delightfully exhibited in the late Georges Coedès's "Documents sur l'histoire politique et religieuse du Laos occidental," *Bulletin de l'École Française d'Extrême Orient*, XXV (1925), 1–202. Also see Nigel Brailey's Ph.D. dissertation for the University of London, "The Origins of the Siamese Forward Movement in Western Laos, 1850–92" (1968). The early history of the Shan states generally is known only through the *Gazetteer of Upper Burma and the Shan States*, edited by J. G. Scott and J. P. Hardiman.

Chapter 8. The Vietnamese Emperors

In the English language, a pioneering study of Vietnamese imperial politics of the pre–1800 period is that of John Whitmore, "The Development of Lê Government in Fifteenth Century Vietnam" (Ph.D. dissertation, Cornell University, 1968). A survey of latter Lê Dynasty political history is Charles Maybon's *Histoire moderne du pays d'Annam 1592–1820* (Paris, 1919), but it neglects all but the most narrow kind of political history. R. Deloustal, "La justice dans l'ancien Annam," *Bulletin de l'École Française d'Extrême Orient* (selected issues, 1908–23), presents translations of the controversial Hong Duc law code of the Lê period. Pierre Pasquier, *L'Annam d'autrefois* (Paris, 1907), describes the nineteenth-century political system (through the eyes of a colonialist who finds it quaint but useful), but the book's observations are not irrelevant to the previous centuries.

Chapter 9. The Malay Sultans

In his study of the *Indigenous Political Systems of Western Malaya* (London, 1958), J. M. Gullick examines Malay society in the mid-nineteenth century, but the book is relevant to the eighteenth century as well. Useful brief articles on the Sultanate as an institution may be found in R. O. Winstedt, "Kingship and Enthronement in Malaya," *Journal of the Malayan Branch Royal Asiatic Society*, XX (1947), and R. J. Wilkinson, "Some Malay Studies," in the same journal, X (1932). Winstedt's *A History of Malaya* (1st ed., 1935 [also published as a complete issue of the *Journal of the Malayan Branch Royal Asiatic Society*, XIII (1935), and revised ed., Singapore, 1962]) is markedly dynastic in approach. An excellent background to the eighteenth-century history of the peninsula is D. K. Bassett, "European Influence in the Malay Peninsula, 1511–1786," in L. A. Mills, *British Malaya, 1824–67* (Kuala Lumpur, 1967).

Chapter 10. The Javanese Kings

Theodore Pigeaud's *Java in the Fourteenth Century: a Study in Cultural History* (5 vols., The Hague, 1960–63) is an elegant reconstruction with much that is relevant to later centuries. B. J. O. Schrieke, "Ruler and Realm in Early Java," published as *Indonesian Sociological Studies*, Part Two (The Hague, 1957), is a pioneering effort to elucidate the ill-documented structure of Javanese political life using mainly seventeenth-century Dutch sources. The Javanese historian Soemarsaid Moertono uses hitherto untouched Javanese sources in his *State and Statecraft in Old Java: a Study of the Later Mataram Period, Sixteenth to Nineteenth Century* (Ithaca, N.Y., 1968) to comment on Schrieke and further develop the picture. C. C. Berg's "The Islamisation of Java," *Studia Islamica*, IV (1955), 111–42, provides a stimulating English-language introduction to that complex subject. A series of magisterial works by H. J. de Graaf surveys the political and other history of Mataram, for those who read Dutch.

Chapter 11. The Spanish Governors

For the Philippines, Onofre D. Corpuz's *The Bureaucracy in the Philippines* (Quezon City, 1957) is the most important and detailed analysis of the power structure in Spanish times. It should be read in conjunction with Nicholas P. Cushner's *Spain in the Philippines: From Conquest to Revolution* (Quezon City, 1970), since Cushner's scope is more broadly defined and not as narrowly bureaucratic as Corpuz's. A far more speculative analysis can be found in John Leddy Phelan, *The Hispanization of the Philippines: Spanish Aims and Filipino Responses, 1565–1700* (Madison, Wis., 1959). A detailed description of the tax structure of the Spanish colony can be found in the reprinted article of Carl Copping Plehn, "Taxation in the Philippines," *Journal of History* (Philippine National Historical Society), X:2 (June, 1962), 135–92.

Among the most important subjects in eighteenth-century Philippine history not already cited is the relationship between the Spanish and the Muslims. For sources dealing with the "Moros," see: H. de la Costa, "Muhammad Alimuddin I, Sultan of Sulu, 1735–1773," in *Asia and the Philippines* (Manila, 1967), pp. 81–114; Cesar A. Majul, "Political and Historical Notes on the Old Sulu Sultanate," *Philippine Historical Review*, I:1 (1965), 229–51; "Succession in the Old Sulu Sultanate," *Philippine Historical Review*, I:1 (1965), 252–71; and "Islamic and Arab Cultural Influences in the South of the Philippines," *Journal of Southeast Asian History*, VII:2 (September, 1966), 61–73. The early-twentieth-century works by Najeeb M. Saleeby, *The History of Sulu* (Manila, 1908), and *Studies in Moro History, Laws and Religion* (Manila, 1905), remain major scholarly sources. Two recent M.A. theses, Anne L. Reber's "The Sulu World in the Eighteenth and Early Nineteenth Centuries: An Historiographical Problem in British Writings on Malay Piracy" (Cornell University, 1966), and John Keith Reynolds's "Towards an Account of Sulu and Its Borneo Dependencies, 1700–1878" (University of Wisconsin, 1970), re-examine the Sultanate of Sulu.

PART TWO. NEW CHALLENGES TO OLD AUTHORITY

Chapter 12. Burma, 1752–1878

John F. Cady's *A History of Modern Burma* (Ithaca, N.Y., 1960) is less detailed for this than for the subsequent era. The period up to the first Anglo-Burman war is not easily followed, save in G. E. Harvey, *History of*

Burma, and Sir Arthur P. Phayre, *History of Burma*, although one can profit from a perusal of H. H. Wilson, *Narrative of the Burmese War in 1824–26 as Originally Compiled from Original Documents* (London, 1852), and J. J. Snodgrass, *Narrative of the Burmese War* (London, 1827). The subsequent period is better served with an excellent monograph, W. S. Desai, *History of the British Residency in Burma, 1826–1840* (Rangoon, 1939). The second war is best followed in the Parliamentary Papers published by the British Government to justify the actions they had taken—*Papers Relating to Hostilities with Burma* (House of Commons, Accounts and Papers, 1852, vol. 36), and *Further Papers* . . . (House of Commons, Accounts and Papers, 1852, vol. 69). These are usefully supplemented by Dorothy Woodman, *The Making of Burma* (London, 1962). D. G. E. Hall's *The Dalhousie-Phayre Correspondence, 1852–56* (London, 1932) has an excellent long introduction. From a growing list of important articles on King Mindon, one might single out the following in the *Journal of the Burma Research Society*: Thaung, "Burmese Kingship in Theory and Practice Under the Reign of King Mindon," XLII:2 (1959), 171–85; Ma Kyan, "King Mindon's Councillors," XLIV:1 (1961), 43–60, and Yi Yi, "The Judicial System of King Mindon," XLIV:2 (1961), 7–28.

The most useful of the contemporary accounts are the following: Father Vincentius Sangermano, *Description of the Burmese Empire* (5th ed., London, 1966 [first published in 1833]); D. G. E. Hall, ed., *Michael Symes: Journal of his Second Embassy to the Court of Ava in 1802* (London, 1955), which has a long introduction of great use; John Crawfurd, *Journal of an Embassy from the Governor General of India to the Court of Ava in the Year 1826* (1st ed., London, 1828); and Henry Yule, *A Narrative of the Mission to the Court of Ava in 1855* (Kuala Lumpur, 1968 [first published in 1857]). The Burman sources are discussed by Yi Yi in two articles: "Burmese Historical Sources, 1752–1885," *JSEAH*, VI:1 (1965), 48–66; and "Additional Burmese Historical Sources (1752–76)," *Guardian*, XV:11 (November, 1968), 33–35, and in subsequent numbers.

Chapter 13. Thailand, 1767–1868

Prince Chula Chakrabongse's *Lords of Life: The Paternal Monarchy of Bangkok, 1782–1932* (New York, 1960) is somewhat hagiographic, but is the single comprehensive treatment of modern Thai history. The monographic literature is more impressive. Klaus Wenk's *The Restoration of Thailand Under Rama I, 1782–1809* (Tucson, Ariz., 1968) might be interpretively weak, but it covers the reign in considerable detail. It by no means supersedes Prince Dhani Nivat's "The Reconstruction of King Rama I of the Chakri Dynasty," *Journal of the Siam Society*, XLIII:1 (1955), 21–47. Robert Lingat has written a number of important articles on the early Bangkok period, of which perhaps the most interesting is his "La double crise de l'Église bouddhique au Siam (1767–1851)," *Journal of World History*, IV:2 (1958), 402–25. David K. Wyatt's "Family Politics in Nineteenth Century Thailand," *JSEAH*, IX:2 (1968), 208–28, casts some new light on the politics of the period and is importantly supplemented by Akin Rabibhadana, *The Organization of Thai Society in the Early Bangkok Period, 1782–1873* (Ithaca, N.Y., 1969). Walter F. Vella's *Siam Under Rama III* (Locust Valley, N.Y., 1957) is the standard source for the period 1824–51.

The most important modern studies of King Mongkut are Alexander B. Griswold, *King Mongkut of Siam* (New York, 1961), and Abbot Low Moffat, *Mongkut, the King of Siam* (Ithaca, N.Y., 1961). The treaty of 1855 is discussed excellently by Nicholas Tarling, "The Mission of Sir John Bowring to Siam," *Journal of the Siam Society*, L:2 (1962), 91–118. Recent doctoral dissertations add a great deal to our knowledge of the period: particularly Neon Snidvongs, "The Development of Siamese Relations with Britain and France in the Reign of Maha Mongkut, 1851–1868" (University of London, 1961), and the just-completed dissertation of Constance M. Wilson, "State and Society in the Reign of Mongkut; 1851–1868: Thailand on the Eve of Modernization" (Cornell University, 1970).

The best of the contemporary sources of this period in Western languages are John Crawfurd's *Journal of an Embassy to the Courts of Siam and Cochin China* (reprinted in Kuala Lumpur, 1967); Vajiranana National Library, comps., *The Burney Papers* (5 vols., Bangkok, 1910–14 [reprinted in Farnborough, 1970]); Jean Baptiste Pallegoix, *Description du royaume thai ou Siam* (2 vols., Paris, 1854); and Sir John Bowring, *The Kingdom and People of Siam* (2 vols., London, 1857 [reprinted in Kuala Lumpur, 1969]). The standard Thai source for the period is available in translation, Čhaophraya Thiphakorawong (Kham Bunnag), *The Dynastic Chronicles, Bangkok Era, The Fourth Reign* (4 vols., Tokyo, 1965–70). The voluminous Thai documentation is discussed in David K. Wyatt and Constance M. Wilson, "Thai Historical Materials in Bangkok," *JAS*, XXV (1965), 105–18, and in David K. Wyatt, *Thai-Language Books: A Checklist* (London, 1967).

For Laos in this period, see David K. Wyatt, "Siam and Laos, 1767–1827," *JSEAH*, IV:2 (1963), 13–32; and Walter F. Vella, *Siam Under Rama III* (Locust Valley, N.Y., 1957). Also useful are Paul le Boulanger, *Histoire du Laos française* (Paris, 1931), and Maha Sila Viravong, *History of Laos* (New York, 1964).

Chapter 14. Cambodia, 1779–1863

For the early period, Jean Moura's *Royaume du Cambodge* (2 vols., Paris, 1883), and Étienne Aymonier's *Le Cambodge* (3 vols., Paris, 1901–5), are generally more reliable than a work that tries to synthesize them: Adhémard Leclère, *Histoire du Cambodge* (Paris, 1914). All these works rely heavily on Cambodian-language chronicle histories which still await comprehensive and comparative analysis. For the 1840's and after, these sources are supplemented by the recollections of Western travelers such as those of Émile Bouillevaux, *Voyage dans l'Indochine 1848–1856* (Paris, 1858), and Henri Mouhot, *Travels in the Central Part of Indochina* (2 vols., London, 1864), which has been reprinted in revised form and edited by Christopher Pym, as *Diary of Travels in Indochina* (London, 1966).

There is a good chapter on nineteenth-century Cambodia in Walter Vella's *Siam Under Rama III* (Locust Valley, N.Y., 1957). For the French efforts in the 1850's, the best published account is contained in Charles Meyniard, *Le Second Empire en Indochine* (2 vols., Paris, 1891); while Neon Snidvong's unpublished dissertation, "The Development of Siam's Relations with Britain and France in the Reign of King Mongkut" (University of London, 1961), is also good. The establishment of the protectorate is dealt with in P. Vial's *Les Premières Années de la Cochinchine française* (2 vols., Paris, 1874), and in A. B. de Villemerevil, ed., *Explorations et missions de Doudart de Lagrée* (Paris, 1883). G. Taboulet's *La Geste française en Indochine* (2 vols., Paris, 1955) is also important. English-language texts for the 1850's include L. V. Helms, "Narrative of an Overland Journey," *Journal of the Indian Archipelago*, IV (1851), 434–38; and a Madras officer's account, "Three Months in Cambodia," in the same journal, V (1854), 285–328. The French takeover has been analyzed by Stanley Thomson in "The Establishment of the French Protectorate over Cambodia," *Far Eastern Quarterly*, IV:4 (August, 1945), 313–40.

Chapter 15. Vietnam, 1802–67

English eyewitness accounts of Nguyen Vietnam in the early 1800's may be found in George Finlayson, *Mission to Siam and Hue, the Capital of Cochinchina, in the Years 1821–1822* (London, 1826), and John Crawfurd, *Journal of an Embassy to the Courts of Siam and Cochin China* (reprinted in Kuala Lumpur, 1967). A French eyewitness account, that of Michel Duc Chaigneau, *Souvenirs de Huê* (Paris, 1867), is an absorbing description of the courts of Gia-long and Minh-mang. P. L. F. Philastre, *Le Code anamite* (2 vols., Paris, 1909 [reprinted in Taipei, 1968]), translates the early-nineteenth-century Vietnamese law code. Another important translation is G. Aubaret's *Histoire et description de la Basse Cochinchine* (Paris, 1863 [reprint, Farnborough, England 1969]), an incomplete rendition into French of a guidebook to southern customs, markets, population distribution, and items of geographical interest written by Trinh Hoai Duc for the use of the Vietnamese court in the early 1800's.

Alexander Woodside, *Vietnam and the Chinese Model* (Cambridge, Mass., 1970), considers the politics and organization of the Nguyen state and bureaucracy from 1802 through 1847 and looks at Vietnamese institutions from a comparative point of view. For foreign relations, note Nguyen The Anh, *Bibliographie critique sur les relations entre le Viet Nam et l'Occident* (Paris, 1967). An appreciation of nineteenth-century literature is indispensable to an understanding of modern Vietnam. The reader should pay attention to Nguyen Du, *Kim Van Kieu*, translated into French by Nguyen Khac Vien (Hanoi, 1965); Nguyen Dinh Chieu, *Luc van tien, poème annamite* (Hanoi, 1927), translated into French by Nghiem Lien; and the translation of Bui Huu Nghia's "L'union merveilleuse de Kim et de Thach," *Bulletin de la Société des Études Indochinoises*, IX (1934). The pioneering French translation of the *Kim Van Kieu* is Abel des Michels, trans., *Kim Van Kieu* (Paris, 1884–85). See also Jean Chesneaux and Georges Boudarel, "Le Kim Van Kieu et l'esprit public vietnamien," *Publications de l'École Française d'Extrême Orient*, LIX (1966).

Vietnam's loss of sovereignty to French colonialists after 1858 is best studied from the Vietnamese side through the translations offered in Truong Buu Lam, *Patterns of Vietnamese Response to Foreign Intervention, 1858–1900* (New Haven, Conn., 1967), and from the French side through the documents presented in Taboulet, *La Geste française en Indochine* (2 vols., Paris, 1955). Joseph Buttinger, *Vietnam: A Dragon Embattled* (New York, 1967), surveys the politics of Vietnam from the loss of independence through the colonial period.

Chapter 16. The Malay Peninsula to 1874

L. A. Mills, *British Malaya, 1824–67* (1st ed., 1925 [reprinted in Kuala Lumpur, 1967, and also in the *Journal of the Malayan Branch Royal Asiatic Society*, XXXIII:3 (1960)]), is a good introductory study for this period. The principal Malay source for the period of British and Dutch rivalries, the *Tuhfat al-Nafis*, has not yet been translated, but an English summary by R. O. Winstedt appears in the *Journal of the Malayan Branch Royal Asiatic Society*, X:2 (1932); and English excerpts by H. Overbeck from a companion Malay work, the *Silsilah Melayu dan Bugis*, have been published in the same journal, IV:3 (1926), 339–81.

Perhaps the best of numerous studies of Raffles is C. E. Wurtzburg's *Raffles of the Eastern Isles* (London, 1954). A collection of Raffles's correspondence, with a commentary, was published by his widow, Lady Sophia Raffles, *Memoir of the Life and Public Services of Sir Thomas Stamford Raffles* (2 vols., London, 1830 and 1835). A Malay view of Raffles, and of a great deal else of importance in the British settlements and Malay states of the time, may be found in Abdullah b. Abdul Kadir, *Hikayat Abdullah*, of which an English translation by A. H. Hill appeared in the *Journal of the Malayan Branch Royal Asiatic Society*, XXVIII:3 (1955). An interesting account by Abdullah of a visit to the east coast peninsular states is contained in his *Kesah Pelayaran Abdullah*, translated into English by A. E. Coope as *The Voyage of Abdullah* (Singapore, 1949).

Descriptions of the settlements and the peninsular and Borneo states by European observers in the first half of the nineteenth century are numerous. Some of the more important are the following: John Anderson, *Political and Commercial Considerations relative to the Malayan Peninsula and the British Settlements in the Straits of Malacca* (1st ed., 1824 [facsimile reprint published in the *Journal of the Malayan Branch of the Royal Asiatic Society*, XXXV:4 (1962)]); P. J. Begbie, *The Malayan Peninsula* (1st ed., 1834 [reprinted in Kuala Lumpur, 1967); T. J. Newbold, *Political and Statistical Account of the British Settlements in the Straits of Malacca* (2 vols., London, 1839); Sherard Osborn, *Quedah, or Stray Leaves from a Journal in Malayan Waters* (London, 1857); Henry Keppel, *The Expedition to Borneo of H.M.S. Dido for the Suppression of Piracy* (2 vols., London, 1845); Hugh Low, *Sarawak: Its Inhabitants and Productions* (London, 1848); Spenser St. John, *Life in the Forests of the Far East* (2 vols., London, 1862); and Charles Brooke, *Ten Years in Sarawak* (2 vols., London, 1886). J. M. Gullicks's *Indigenous Political Systems of Western Malaya* has already been referred to.

Direct British intervention in the affairs of the western peninsular states in 1874 has been the subject of a number of studies, notably Nicholas Tarling's *British Policy in the Malay Peninsula and Archipelago, 1824–1871*, published in the *Journal of the Malayan Branch Royal Asiatic Society*, XXX:3 (1957); C. Northcote Parkinson, *British Intervention in Malaya, 1867–87* (Singapore, 1960); and C. D. Cowan, *Nineteenth Century Malaya: The Origins of British Political Control* (London, 1961). Recent research by two young Malaysian historians, Khoo Kay Kim and Rollins Bonney, dealing respectively with the economics of intervention in the west-coast states, and British relations with Kedah, are due to be published shortly in Kuala Lumpur.

Chapter 17. The Archipelago, 1785–1870

Scholars, particularly those writing in English, have largely ignored the nineteenth-century history of the island world reaching from Sumatra to Mindanao and the Moluccas. Much of G. J. Resink's pioneering work in defining and evoking this historical field can be found in his *Indonesia's History between the Myths: Essays in Legal History and Historical Theory* (The Hague, 1968). Most of Joseph Conrad's fiction, such as his novels *Lord Jim, Almayer's Folly,* and *The Rescue,* is located in the "Outer Islands," and provides an excellent introduction to this historical setting. See also Norman Sherry, *Conrad's Eastern World* (London, 1966). British and Dutch rivalries in maritime Southeast Asia have formed the subject of a number of studies, including: Nicholas Tarling, *Anglo-Dutch Rivalry in the Malay World, 1780–1924* (Brisbane, 1962); Harry J. Marks, *The First Contest for Singapore, 1819–1824,* no. 27 of *Verhandelingen van het Koninklijk Instituut voor Taal-, Land- en Volkenkunde* (The Hague, 1959); and Graham Irwin, *Nineteenth Century Borneo: A Study in Diplomatic Rivalry,* no. 15 of Verhandelingen van het Koninklijk Instituut voor Taal-, Land- en Volkenkunde (The Hague, 1955). Nicholas Tarling's *Piracy and Politics in the Malay World* (Melbourne, 1963) is an interesting attempt, within the framework of colonial diplomatic historiography, to explore a topic of great importance.

Chapter 18. Java, 1757–1875

Apart from sections of important broader works, such as D. H. Burger, *Structural Changes in Javanese Society: The Village Sphere/The Supra-Village Sphere* (Ithaca, N.Y., 1956–57); J. S. Furnivall, *Netherlands India: A Study of Plural Economy* (Cambridge, England, 1944); and Clifford Geertz, *Agricultural Involution* (Berkeley, Calif., 1963), listed elsewhere, there are a number of useful studies of Java during this period. On Raffles's administration, see John Bastin's *The Native Policies of Sir Stamford Raffles in Java and Sumatra: An Economic Interpretation* (Oxford, 1957), and *Raffles' Ideas on the Land Rent System in Java and the MacKenzie Land Tenure Commission* (The Hague, 1954). Justus Van der Kroef's "Prince Diponegoro: Progenitor of Indonesian Nationalism," *Far Eastern Quarterly,* VIII:4 (August, 1949), 424–50, provides a concise survey and interpretation of the Java War, 1825–30. In "The Function of Land Rent Under the Cultivation System in Java," *Journal of Asian Studies,* XXIII:3 (1964), 357–75, Robert Van Niel offers a picture of the early Culture System in actual operation. Sartono Kartodirdjo's *The Peasants' Revolt of Banten in 1888, Its Conditions, Course and Sequel: A Case Study of Social Movements in Indonesia* (The Hague, 1966) is a major contribution to the handful of studies on the social history of Java in the nineteenth century. The gorgeous photographs in E. Breton di Nijs, *Tempo Doeloe; Fotographische Documenten uit het Oude Indie 1870–1941* (Amsterdam, 1961), are invaluable for historical understanding.

Chapter 19. The Philippines, 1762–1872

In addition to the sources already cited, general surveys of Philippine history can be found in the "History" written by T. H. Pardo de Tavera for the *Census of the Philippine Islands,* 1903, I (Washington, 1905), 309–

410; and in José Montero y Vidal's *Historia General de Filipinas desde el Descubrimiento de Dichas Islas hasta Nuestras Dias* (Madrid, 1887). For a discussion of the changing economic environment, see: María Louisa Rodríguez Baena, *La Sociedad Ecónomica de Amigos del País de Manila en el Siglo XVIII* (Seville, 1966); Thomas R. and Mary C. McHale, *Early American-Philippine Trade: The Journal of Nathaniel Bowditch in Manila, 1796* (New Haven, Conn., 1962); and James F. Cloghessy, "The Philippines and the Royal Philippine Company," *Mid-America*, XLII (1960), 80–104. Austin Craig has edited a volume entitled *The Former Philippines Through Foreign Eyes* (Manila, 1916), in which he has brought together the observations of some of the visitors to the Philippines in the nineteenth century, and in which are included the writings of Tomás de Comyn–the Philippine Company agent in Manila—and of the German scholar Feodor Jagor. Also of value is Sir John Bowring's *A Visit to the Philippine Islands* (London, 1859). In recent years the Filipiniana Book Guild has done an outstanding job in reprinting many additional memoirs, including Paul P. de la Gironière's *Twenty Years in the Philippines*, and Robert MacMicking's *Recollections of Manilla and the Philippines, during 1848, 1849, and 1850*, among others.

The development of a Philippine political consciousness can be traced in Gregorio Y. Yabes, "The Philippine Representation in the Spanish Cortes," *Philippine Social Science Review*, VIII (1936), 36–67 and 140–60; and in Sinibaldo de Mas, *Report on the Condition of the Philippines in 1842*, vol. 3 (reprint, Manila, 1963). De Mas was both perceptive and blunt, and his report is essential to anyone studying the collapse of Spanish power in the Philippines. Austin Craig's *The Filipinos' Fight for Freedom* (Manila, 1933) is a useful, if limited, collection of documents in English. There has been very little good scholarship dealing with social change, but Edgar Wickberg's outstanding book, *The Chinese in Philippine Life, 1850–1898* (New Haven, Conn., 1965), and his article, "The Chinese Mestizo in Philippine History," *JSEAH*, V:1 (March, 1964), 62–100, are models for future historians. Wickberg has done seminal research on these key groups in Philippine life, and both works should be read carefully. The literature attacking and defending the friars is extensive and usually polemical. A good example of antifriar writing can be found in M. H. del Pilar, *Monastic Supremacy in the Philippines* (Barcelona, 1889 [reprint, Quezon City, 1958]). For a recent sympathetic defense of the friars, see Vicente R. Pilapil, "Nineteenth Century Philippines and the Friar Problem," *The Americas*, XVIII:2 (October, 1961), 127–48. Fathers John N. Schumacher and Nicholas P. Cushner have recently edited important "Documents Relating to Father Jose Burgos and the Cavite Mutiny of 1872," *Philippine Studies*, XVII:3 (July, 1969), 457–529. Carlos Quirino's *The Young Aguinaldo: From Kawit to Biyák-na-Bató* (Manila, 1969) is one of the first scholarly examinations of Aguinaldo's development.

PART THREE. FRAMEWORKS FOR NATIONS

Chapter 20. The Making of New States

The Province of Burma: The general background to the third Anglo-Burman war is treated in John F. Cady, *A History of Modern Burma*, and more elaborately, if not as reliably, in E. C. V. Foucar, *Mandalay the*

Golden (London, 1963). Such contemporary accounts as Horace Brown's *Reminiscences of the Court of Mandalay* (Woking, 1907), or Dr. Marks' *Forty Years in Burma* (London, 1917), tell us nearly as much about the British in Burma as about Burma and the Burmese. The war, its origins and course, are interpreted differently by D. P. Singhal, *The Annexation of Upper Burma* (Singapore, 1960), and Philippe Preschez, "Les relations franco-birmanes aux XVIIIe and XIXe siècles," *France-Asie*, XXI:3 (September, 1967), 275–425. Maung Htin Aung takes a broader approach, without close discussion of the evidence, in his *The Stricken Peacock: Anglo-Burmese Relations, 1752–1948* (The Hague, 1965). More specialized studies are Sao Saimong Mangrai, *The Shan States and the British Annexation* (Ithaca, N.Y., 1965), and Dorothy Woodman, *The Making of Burma* (London, 1962).

The Kingdom of Thailand: Thailand is very poorly covered in this period, the first book in the field being David K. Wyatt's *The Politics of Reform in Thailand* (New Haven, Conn., 1969), which deals with the domestic side of events. The only published study of Thailand's foreign relations during this period is Pensri Duke, *Les Relations entre la France et la Thaïlande (Siam)* (Bangkok, 1962), although Nigel Brailey, "The Origins of the Siamese Forward Movement in Western Laos, 1850–92" (unpublished Ph.D. dissertation, University of London, 1968), deals with some aspects of the problem.

French Indochina—Vietnam: Milton Osborne, *The French Presence in Cochinchina and Cambodia* (Ithaca, N.Y., 1969), traces the establishment of French rule in southern Vietnam, and compares French governmental techniques in southern Vietnam and Cambodia. The period of the French conquest of the north has so far been described only from the contemporary colonialist viewpoint, for example; André Masson, *Hanoi pendant la période héroïque, 1873–1888* (Paris, 1929). For the most part, the reader may conveniently follow the discussions in Le Thanh Khoi, *Le Viet-Nam: histoire et civilisation* (Paris, 1955); Joseph Buttinger, *Vietnam: A Dragon Embattled* (New York, 1967); and Jean Chesneaux, *Contribution à l'histoire de la nation vietnamienne* (Paris, 1955). The interested student should also read the translations given in the book by Truong Buu Lam, *Patterns of Vietnamese Response to Foreign Intervention, 1858–1900* (New Haven, Conn., 1967). S. H. Roberts, *A History of French Colonial Policy, 1870–1925* (London, 1929) is not yet out of date, and R. F. Betts, *Assimilation and Association in French Colonial Theory, 1890–1914* (New York, 1961) is worth reading.

French Indochina—Cambodia: Milton Osborne's excellent *The French Presence in Cochinchina and Cambodia* (Ithaca, N.Y., 1969) uses and, in many ways, surpasses such firsthand accounts as Paul Collard's *Cambodge et Cambodgiens* (Paris, 1925), and Edgar Boulanger, *Un Hiver au Cambodge* (Tours, 1888). An excellent study of Cambodia's borders with Vietnam and Laos is the monograph *Les Frontières du Cambodge*, by Sarin Chhak (Paris, 1966).

French Indochina—Laos: The various volumes issued under the auspices of the Mission Pavie (Paris, 1898–1919) are a rich source of data on Laos at the end of the nineteenth century. Étienne Aymonier's *Voyage dans le Laos* (2 vols., Paris, 1897) is also useful, and see Auguste Pavie's *À la Conquête des Coeurs* (Paris, 1947).

The Netherlands East Indies: Apart from sections of the broader works—D. H. Burger, *Structural Changes in Javanese Society: The Village Sphere/The Supra-Village Sphere* (Ithaca, N.Y., 1956–57); J. S. Furnivall, *Netherlands India: A Study of Plural Economy* (Cambridge, England, 1944); and G. J. Resink, *Indonesia's History between the Myths: Essays in Legal History and Historical Theory* (The Hague, 1968)—previously listed, there is virtually nothing in English on the making of the Netherlands Indies. The old-fashioned colonial history by E. S. De Klerck, *History of the Netherlands East Indies,* II (Rotterdam, 1938), is still valuable for factual information on the incorporation of the islands outside Java. Vicki Baum's excellent novel, *Tale of Bali* (New York, 1938), tells the story of the conquest of Bali from a Balinese point of view.

British Malaya and Borneo: Emily Sadka, *The Protected Malay States, 1874–1895* (Kuala Lumpur, 1968), gives an extremely detailed picture of the workings of the Resident system in the western peninsular states. See also her edited version of "The Journal of Sir Hugh Low, Perak, 1877," *Journal of the Malayan Branch Royal Asiatic Society,* XXVII:4 (1954). Sir Frank Swettenham, *British Malaya: An Account of the Origin and Progress of British Influence in Malaya* (London, 1907), gives the point of view of a participant; see also C. D. Cowan's edited version of "Sir Frank Swettenham's Perak Journals, 1874–1876," *Journal of the Malayan Branch Royal Asiatic Society,* XXIV:4 (1951). Of accounts by contemporary observers of the early Resident system, three are outstanding: J. F. A. McNair, *Perak and the Malays: "Sarong and Kris"* (London, 1882); Isabella L. Bird (Mrs. Bishop), *The Golden Chersonese* (London, 1883 [reprinted in Kuala Lumpur, 1967]); and Emily Innes, *The Chersonese with the Gilding Off* (2 vols., London, 1885). Two late-nineteenth-century administrators in Malaya, Hugh Clifford and Frank Swettenham, published a number of lively descriptions of Malay life at the time, of which Clifford's *In Court and Kampong* (London, 1897), and *Studies in Brown Humanity* (London, 1898), and Swettenham's *The Real Malay* (London, 1900) may be mentioned. Collections of their works have been compiled and introduced by William R. Roff: *Stories by Sir Hugh Clifford* (Kuala Lumpur, 1966), and *Stories and Sketches by Sir Frank Swettenham* (Kuala Lumpur, 1967). The further expansion of British control at the beginning of the twentieth century is discussed in detail in Eunice Thio, *British Policy in the Malay Peninsula, 1880–1910* (2 vols., Kuala Lumpur, 1969 and forthcoming). Chai Hon Chan's *The Development of British Malaya, 1896–1909* (Kuala Lumpur, 1964) is based largely on the Annual Reports of the several states.

For British rule in Borneo, K. G. Tregonning's *Under Chartered Company Rule* (1st ed., 1958 [2d ed., entitled *A History of Modern Sabah, 1881–1963* (Kuala Lumpur, 1965)]) deals with the politics and administration of the chartered Company, while Steven Runciman's *The White Rajahs: A History of Sarawak from 1841 to 1946* (Cambridge, England, 1960) performs a similar task for Brooke rule in Sarawak. Two contemporary accounts of real value and interest to the historian are Spenser St. John, *Life in the Forests of the Far East* (2 vols., London, 1862), and Charles Brooke, *Ten Years in Sarawak* (2 vols., London, 1866). Robert Pringle's *Rajas and Rebels: The Ibans of Sarawak under Brooke Rule, 1841–1941* (London, 1970) is the first social history of modern Sarawak. Two critical but balanced works by American scholars give an account of the processes and effects of British administration in the peninsula prior to World War II: Rupert Emerson, *Malaysia: A Study in Direct and Indirect Rule* (1st ed., 1937 [reprinted in Kuala Lumpur, 1964]); and Virginia Thompson, *Post-mortem on Malaya* (New York, 1943).

The Philippines: The story of how the Americans integrated the Muslim areas of Mindanao and Sulu into the Manila orbit is related in detail in the various reports filed by the American army. It is also described at some length by Dean C. Worcester, *The Philippine Islands* (1st ed., London, 1898 [revised edition, edited by J. R. Hayden, entitled *The Philippines Past and Present*, New York, 1930]), by William Cameron Forbes in his two-volume work, *The Philippine Islands* (Cambridge, Mass., 1945), and by numerous other participants. The Muslim side of the story has not yet been properly told, although the interested reader should note the references to the history of the southern Muslim groups in Part Two.

Chapter 21. Bureaucratic and Economic Frameworks

Bureaucratic: (NOTE: For more on bureaucratic development, see Part Five, Chapter 34)

Little systematic work has been done on bureaucratic penetration and elaboration in Burma, but James Guyot's "Bureaucratic Transformation in Burma," in Ralph Braibanti, ed., *Asian Bureaucratic Systems Emergent from the British Imperial Tradition* (Durham, N.C., 1966), pp. 354–443, is very useful. F. S. V. Donnison's *Public Administration in Burma* (London, 1953) is a good survey of the field, while J. S. Furnivall's *The Governance of Modern Burma* (London, 1959), and his *Colonial Policy and Practice* (Cambridge, England, 1948 [2d ed., New York, 1956]), have a quality of immediacy that renders them permanently useful. Hugh Tinker has treated *The Foundations of Local Self-Government in India, Pakistan, and Burma* (London, 1954).

For Thailand, the vitally important efforts at reform in the provincial administration are the subject of an unpublished doctoral dissertation by Tej Bunnag, "The Provincial Administration of Siam from 1892 to 1915" (Oxford University, 1968). Civil service reform is brilliantly handled by William J. Siffin, *The Thai Bureaucracy* (Honolulu, Hawaii, 1966). Fred W. Riggs's *Thailand: The Modernization of a Bureaucratic Polity* (Honolulu, Hawaii, 1966), is stimulating but historically unreliable. Also see David K. Wyatt, *The Politics of Reform in Thailand* (New Haven, Conn., 1969).

J. deGalembert, *Les Administrations et les services publics indochinois* (Hanoi, 1931), is an officially sponsored handbook expounding the ways in which colonial administrative, legislative, judicial, and educational processes were supposed to work in Indochina, especially in the 1920's. Astute students, aware of the regime's repressiveness and numerous fallibilities, will have little difficulty reading between the lines. Paul Doumer, *Situation de l'Indochine, 1897–1901* (Hanoi, 1902), is the report of the colony's most formidable early governor-general on his own handiwork and that of others. It gives the official picture of early colonial institutions. Robert Lingat, *Les Régimes matrimoniaux du sud-est de l'Asie: essai de droit comparé indochinois* (2 vols., Paris, 1952–55), discusses the construction of colonial civil law codes for different Vietnamese regions and shows how the codes were compromises between French and traditional Vietnamese law.

For Cambodia, see Jean Leclèr's *De l'Évolution et du développement des institutions annamites et cambodgiens* (Rennes, 1923), and Roger Pinto's *Aspects de l'évolution gouvernmentale de l'Indochine française* (Paris, 1946). Both are supplemented by Achille Silvestre's massive *Le Cambodge administratif* (Phnom Penh, 1924).

For the Netherlands Indies, the best work is still J. S. Furnivall's *Netherlands India: A Study of Plural Economy* (Cambridge, England, 1944). Furnivall's *Colonial Policy and Practice* (Cambridge, England, 1948 [2d ed., New York, 1956]) is a systematic comparison of the systems in British Burma and the Netherlands Indies. The official view is rendered in A. D. A. de Kat Angelino's *Colonial Policy* (2 vols., The Hague, 1931). See also Clive Day, *The Policy and Administration of the Dutch in Java* (New York, 1904 [reprinted in Kuala Lumpur, 1966]), and J. J. van Klavern, *The Dutch Colonial System in the East Indies* (The Hague, 1953).

For British Malaya, the principal studies are Rupert Emerson, *Malaysia: A Study in Direct and Indirect Rule* (New York, 1937); Emily Sadka, *The Protected Malay States, 1874–1895* (Kuala Lumpur, 1968); and an unpublished dissertation by P. L. Burns entitled "The Constitutional History of Malaya with Special Reference to the Malay States of Perak, Selangor, Negri Sembilan and Pahang, 1874–1914" (University of London, 1965). James de V. Allen, "Malayan Civil Service, 1874–1941: Colonial Bureaucracy/Malayan Elite," forthcoming in the journal *Comparative Studies in Society and History*, is an examination of the ambiguous role of the European bureaucracy in Malaya. A nuts-and-bolts description of the administrative system is given in S. W. Jones, *Public Administration in Malaya* (London, 1944), and a critical account of the juridical relationship is provided by R. St. J. Braddell, *The Legal Status of the Malay States* (Singapore, 1932).

The best studies of bureaucratic development in the Philippines are Onofre D. Corpuz, *The Bureaucracy in the Philippines* (Quezon City, 1957), Joseph Ralston Hayden, *The Philippines: A Study in National Development* (New York, 1942). Hayden deals with the development of Philippine government specifically under American rule. Also helpful for the early period of American control are James H. Blount's *American Occupation of the Philippines, 1898–1912* (Manila, 1968 [1st ed., 1912]), Dean C. Worcester, *The Philippines Past and Present* (2 vols., New York, 1914 [rev. ed., edited by J. R. Hayden, New York, 1930]), and Eliodoro G. Robles, *The Philippines in the Nineteenth Century* (Quezon City, 1969).

Economic: In addition to J. S. Furnivall's classic *Colonial Policy and Practice* (New York, 1956), and James R. Andrus's *Burmese Economic Life* (Stanford, Calif., 1947), two more recent works deal with the Burmese economic framework in greater detail: U Tun Wai's *Economic Development of Burma from 1800 to 1940* (Rangoon, 1961), and Maung Shein, *Burma's Transport and Foreign Trade in Relation to the Economic Development of the Country* (Rangoon, 1964). For Thailand, James Ingram's *Economic Change in Thailand Since 1850* (Stanford, Calif., 1955) needs no supplementation.

Perhaps the most serviceable general account of the economic pattern that developed in Indochina is Charles Robequain, *The Economic Development of French Indochina* (New York, 1944). An account of Indochina during the world Depression, which is far less sympathetic than Robequain's to the colonialist point of view, is Paul Bernard, *Le Problème économique indochinois* (Paris, 1934). Yves Henry, *Économie agricole de l'Indochine* (Hanoi, 1932), is an unwieldy but crucial work on the socio-economic world and landholding patterns of the Vietnamese peasant. Pierre Gourou, *Les paysans du delta tonkinois* (Paris, 1936 [reprinted in Paris, 1965]), is another indispensable survey, confined to the peasants of northern Vietnam. The best study of the Cambodian economy is Remy Prud'homme's *Économie du Cambodge* (Paris, 1969), which supersedes Pierre Dreyfus's *Le Cambodge Économique* (Paris, 1910). Jean Delvert's *Le paysan cambodgien* (Paris, 1961) is useful on the rural economy, as are portions of Pierre Gourou's classic *L'Utilisation du sol en Indochine française* (Paris, 1940).

For the Netherlands East Indies and British Malaya, G. C. Allen and Audrey G. Donnithorne, *Western Enterprise in Indonesia and Malaya: A Study in Economic Development* (London, 1957), examines the instruments and methods of European economic penetration. Works specifically on the economic framework of the Netherlands East Indies include: J. H. Boeke, *Indonesian Economics: The Concept of Dualism in Theory and Policy* (The Hague, 1961); *The Structure of the Netherlands Indies Economy* (New York, 1942), by the same author; J. O. M. Broek, *The Economic Development of the Netherlands Indies* (New York, 1942); and G. Gonggrijp, *Schets Ener Economische Geschiedenis van Indonesie* (*Sketch of an Economic History of Indonesia*) (Haarlem, 1957). K. M. Stahl, *The Metropolitan Organisation of British Colonial Trade* (London, 1951), contains substantial material on Malaysia, and T. H. Silcock, *The Commonwealth Economy in Southeast Asia* (Durham, N.C., 1959), discusses the basic economic patterns of the colonial era and also has an excellent bibliography. Wong Lin Ken, "The Trade of Singapore, 1819–69," *Journal of the Malayan Branch Royal Asiatic Society*, XXXIII, 4 (1960), is also helpful. Lim Chong-yah, *Economic Development of Modern Malaya* (Kuala Lumpur, 1967), is an account by a leading Malaysian economist of economic development in the peninsula in the twentieth century. For studies of more specific aspects of the Malayan economy, see the following: C. K. Meek, *Land Law and Custom in the Colonies* (London, 1946), which has two chapters on Malaya: and J. J. Puthucheary, *Ownership and Control in the Malayan Economy* (Singapore, 1960), which is a stimulating and sometimes controversial study with a marked historical perspective. A collection of important articles on many of the more important features of the Malayan economy may be found in T. H. Silcock, ed., *Readings in Malayan Economics* (Singapore, 1961).

A. V. H. Hartendorp's *Short History of Industry and Trade of the Philippines* (Manila, 1953) is a general introduction to Philippine economic development but is very weak on pre-twentieth-century development. Eliodoro G. Robles has written one of the most detailed accounts of *The Philippines in the Nineteenth Century* (Quezon City, 1969), based primarily on the extensive holdings of the Newberry Collection at the University of Chicago and containing a wealth of detail on the administrative development of the late Spanish period. For studies of more specific aspects of the Philippine economic structure, see Benito F. Legarda y Fernandez's "Foreign Trade, Economic Change, and Entrepreneurship in Nineteenth-

Century Philippines" (unpublished Ph.D. dissertation, Harvard University, 1955), which is the most important scholarly work on the nineteenth-century Philippine economy; Frederick Wernstedt, *The Role and Importance of Philippine Interisland Shipping and Trade* (Ithaca, N.Y., 1957); and Mary E. Seymour, "Agricultural Credit and Banking in the Philippines, 1913–1917: an Administrative Study" (unpublished Ph.D. dissertation, University of Chicago, 1962). There are a number of useful firsthand accounts, including W. G. Palgraves's *The Far Off Eden Isles: Country Life in the Philippines Fifty Years Ago, by a British Consul* (Manila, 1929), and the company-prepared *Centenary of Wise and Company in the Philippines (1826–1926)* (Manila, 1926). Documentary data on the Philippine economy during the American period is extensive and readily available, especially in the Annual Reports of the Governors-General. *The Records of the Bureau of Insular Affairs Relating to the Philippine Islands, 1898–1935* (Washington, 1942) compiled by Kenneth Munden, and the companion *Preliminary Inventories of the Records of the Office of the High Commissioner to the Philippines* (Washington, 1963), compiled by Richard S. Maxwell, are introductions to the archival material at the Library of Congress.

Chapter 22. Economic Transformation, 1870–1940

Export Industries: Jonathan Levin, *The Export Economies: their Pattern of Development in Historical Perspective* (Cambridge, Mass., 1960), is a good general study of this subject, and it includes a case study of the Burma export rice industry. For more on that particular industry, see Cheng Siok-hwa's well-researched *The Rice Industry of Burma, 1852–1940* (Kuala Lumpur, 1968), and Michael Adas's forthcoming Ph.D. dissertation (University of Wisconsin). On the rubber export industry, P. T. Bauer has written *The Rubber Industry: A Study in Competition and Monopoly* (London, 1948), and another volume entitled *Report of a Visit to the Rubber Smallholdings of Malaya* (London, 1948), which is one of the few extended discussions of that important section of the economy. A full-scale study of plantation rubber in Malaya has been made by J. H. Drabble, who, in addition to his unpublished Ph.D. dissertation at the University of London, has written an article entitled "The Plantation Rubber Industry in Malaya up to 1922," *Journal of the Malayan Branch Royal Asiatic Society*, XL:1 (July, 1967), 52–77. Also see James C. Jackson's *Planters and Speculators: Chinese and European Agricultural Enterprise in Malaya, 1786–1921* (Kuala Lumpur, 1968), which is a general discussion of a changing agricultural economy. B. J. O. Schrieke's "West Coast Report," in his *Indonesian Sociological Studies*, I (The Hague, 1955), deals with the coffee and rubber industries of Sumatra in the 1910's and 1920's. The definitive account of the early tin industry in Malaya is Wong Lin Ken, *The Malayan Tin Industry to 1914* (Tucson, Ariz., 1965). Clifford Geertz's *The Social Context of Economic Change: An Indonesian Case Study* (Cambridge, Mass., 1956), together with other Geertz works, covers the sugar industry in Java. Benito F. Legarda y Fernandez, "Foreign Trade, Economic Change, and Entrepreneurship in Nineteenth-Century Philippines" (unpublished Ph.D. dissertation, Harvard University, 1955), is perhaps the best study of the development in the early Philippines.

Socio-economic Transformation: Works on the economic development of the individual countries of Southeast Asia have been listed in the bibliography for Chapter 21. Among the socio-economic changes experienced by Southeast Asians was the tremendous rise of population. Charles Fisher, "Some Comments on Population Growth in South-East Asia with Special Reference to the Period Since 1830," in C. D. Cowan, ed., *The Economic Development of Southeast Asia* (New York, 1964), provides a general discussion of this problem. Bram Peper, *Grootte en Groei van Java's Inheemse Bevolking in de Negentiende Eeuw* (*Size and Growth of Java's Native Population in the Nineteenth Century*) (Amsterdam, 1967), is a good example of a number of recent Dutch studies that are among the first serious and deep studies in the historical demography of Southeast Asia. Another aspect of the socio-economic transformation was the influx of aliens into Southeast Asia. For information on the Chinese immigrants, G. William Skinner's study of *Chinese Society in Thailand* (Ithaca, N.Y., 1957) is excellent; see also W. L. Blythe, "Historical Sketch of Chinese Labour in Malaya," *Journal of the Malayan Branch Royal Asiatic Society*, XX:1 (1947) 67–114. (NOTE: For more on overseas Chinese, see Chapter 6, Chapter 23, and Chapter 34 in this Bibliography.) Other works on the influx of immigrants include the following: R. N. Jackson, *Immigrant Labour and the Development of Malaya, 1786–1920* (Kuala Lumpur, 1961); J. Norman Parmer, *Colonial Labour Policy and Administration: A History of Labour in the Rubber Plantation Industry in Malaya c. 1910–1941* (New York, 1960); Kernial Singh Sandhu, *Indians in Malaya: Immigration and Settlement, 1786–1957* (Cambridge, England, 1969); and Tengku Shamsul Bahrin's two articles, "Indonesian Labour in Malaya," *Kajian Ekonomi Malaysia*, II:1 (June, 1965), 53–70, and "The Growth and Distribution of the Indonesian Population in Malaya," *Bijdragen tot de Taal-, Land- en Volkenkunde*, CXXIII:2 (1967), 267–86.

The ways in which Southeast Asians adapted to these changes are studied by Clifford Geertz, *Agricultural Involution* (Berkeley, Calif., 1963), dealing with the intensification of agriculture in Java; by Clark Cunningham, *The Postwar Migration of the Toba-Bataks to East Sumatra* (New Haven, Conn., 1958); by S. Husin Ali, *Social Stratification in Kampong Bagan: A Study of Class, Status, Conflict and Mobility in a Rural Malay Community* (Singapore, 1964); and by Thomas R. McHale, "An Econoecological Approach to Economic Development: The Philippines" (unpublished Ph.D. dissertation, Harvard University, 1960), among others. In his book entitled *Le Problème économique indochinois* (Paris, 1934), Paul Bernard examines the Vietnamese situation during the world Depression. Articles in the *Bulletin économique de l'Indochine* explore some basic areas of colonial Vietnamese socio-economic history.

PART FOUR. SOCIAL CHANGE AND THE EMERGENCE OF NATIONALISM

Chapter 23. Preludes

Nationalism: As a product of the interest aroused within the last two decades, there are now many general studies of nationalism and its processes in the non-Western world, though few with adequate historical perspectives. Among those relevant to the early stages of nationalism in Southeast Asia are the following: Rupert Emerson, *From Empire to Nation: The Rise to Self-Assertion of Asian and African Peoples* (Boston, 1960); Karl W. Deutsch, *Nationalism and Social Communication* (Cambridge, Mass., 1966); Clifford Geertz, ed., *Old Societies and New States: The Quest for Modernity in Asia and Africa* (New York, 1963); Daniel Lerner, *The Passing of Traditional Society* (Glencoe, Ill., 1958); and K. R. Minogue, *Nationalism* (London, 1967). Harry J. Benda's article, "Political Elites in Colonial Southeast Asia: An Historical Analysis," *Comparative Studies in Society and History*, VII (1965), 233–51, is a provocative comparative analysis.

Peasant Risings and Pre-nationalism: For some stimulating studies of peasant unrest and similar phenomena in general, see E. J. Hobsbawm, *Primitive Rebels: Studies in Archaic Forms of Social Movement in the Nineteenth and Twentieth Centuries* (1st ed., 1959 [reprinted in New York, 1965]); Eric Wolf, *Peasant Wars of the Twentieth Century* (New York, 1969); and Peter Worsley, *The Trumpet Shall Sound: A Study of "Cargo" Cults in Melanesia* (London, 1957). For works dealing generally with peasant revolts in Southeast Asia, see Harry J. Benda, "Peasant Movements in Colonial Southeast Asia," *Asian Studies* (Manila), III:3 (1965), 420–34; and Erich H. Jacoby, *Agrarian Unrest in Southeast Asia* (2d ed., New York, 1961).

Studies of peasant movements in Indonesia include: Justus M. van der Kroef, "Javanese Messianic Expectations: Their Origin and Cultural Context," *Comparative Studies in Society and History*, I (1959), 299–323; and Sartono Kartodirdjo, "The Peasants' Revolt of Banten in 1888, Its Conditions, Course and Sequel: A Case Study of Social Movements in Indonesia," No. 50 of *Verhandelingen van het Koninklijk Instituut voor Taal-, Land- en Volkenkunde* (The Hague, 1966). For the Samin movement, see Harry J. Benda and Lance Castles, "The Samin Movement," *Bijdragen tot de Taal-, Land- en Volkenkunde*, CXXV:2 (1969), 207–40; and The Siauw Giap, "The Samin and Samat Movements in Java: Two Examples of Peasant Resistance," *Révue du Sud-Est Asiatique* (1967, no. 2; 1968, no. 1). See also Harry J. Benda and Ruth McVey, eds., *The Communist Uprisings of 1926–1927 in Indonesia: Key Documents* (Ithaca, N.Y., 1960).

The "To' Janggut" movement in Malaya is the subject of James de V. Allen's article entitled "The Kelantan Rising of 1915: Some Thoughts on the Concept of Resistance in British Malayan History," IX:2 (1968), 241–257. For other peasant movements in Malaya and Borneo, see: Dato' Seri Lela Di-Raja, "The Ulu Trengganu Disturbance, May, 1928: Extracts from the Diary of Dato' Seri Lela Di-Raja," *Malaysia in History*, XII:1 (1968), 21–26; and Robert R. Pringle, "Asun's 'Rebellion': The Political Growing Pains of a Tribal Society in Brooke Sarawak." Paper delivered to the International Conference on Asian History, Kuala Lumpur, 1968 (in mimeograph).

The Saya San rebellion in Burma is analyzed in Ma Ma Lay, "The Real Origin and Causes of the Burma Rebellion," *Thu lou lu* (Rangoon) (1953), pp. 371–91. The official report of the movement (Report of the Rebellion in Burma up to 3d May, 1931, and Communique of 19th May, 1931, Parliamentary Paper, House of Commons, Cmd. 3900, 1931) is myopic. The rebellion is covered in greater or lesser detail in the following secondary works: E. Sarkisyanz, *Buddhist Backgrounds of the Burmese Revolution* (The Hague, 1965); and Donald Eugene Smith, *Religion and Politics in*

Burma (Princeton, N.J., 1965). Also see Michael Mendelson's article, "A Messianic Buddhist Association in Upper Burma," *Bulletin of the School of Oriental and African Studies*, XXIV (1961), 560–80.

The best studies of peasant unrest in the Philippines are David R. Sturtevant's numerous works, including his doctoral dissertation, "Philippine Social Structure and its Relation to Agrarian Unrest," (Stanford University, 1958); "Guardia de Honor: Revitalization Within the Revolution," *Asian Studies* (Manila), IV:2 (August, 1966), 342–52; and "Sakdalism and Philippine Radicalism," *JAS*, XXI:2 (February, 1962), 199–213. R. M. Stubbs, "Philippine Radicalism: The Central Luzon Uprisings 1925–1935" (unpublished Ph.D. dissertation, University of California, 1951), and M. C. Guerrero, "The Colorum Uprisings, 1924–1931," *Asian Studies* (Manila), V (1967), 65–78, are also good. The study of local or regional history, as distinct from peasant movements, has been far more scanty. John H. Larkin's "The Place of Local History in Philippine Historiography," *JSEAH*, VIII:2 (September, 1967), 306–17, is an outstanding exception.

The basic Western-language discussion of the Vietnamese Cao Dai movement is that of Gabriel Gobron, *History and Philosophy of Caodaism* (Saigon, 1950 [1st ed. in French, Paris, 1949]). For Vietnamese peasant secret societies, there is a pioneering survey by Georges Coulet, *Les Sociétés secrètes en terre d'Annam* (Saigon, 1926). Up to this point, few if any Western scholars and journalists have commanded a knowledge of Sino-Vietnamese culture adequate to understand its popular revitalization in the Cao Dai and Hoa Hao movements. For example, note the many mistranslations in Bernard Fall's essay, "The Political Religous Sects of Vietnam," *Pacific Affairs*, XXVIII:3 (September, 1955), 235–53.

In Thailand, there were rebellions similar to those mentioned in the text, the chief of them occurring in 1902 in Patani, North Thailand, and the Northeast. See Tej Bunnag, "Khabot phu mi bun phak isan" ("The Holy Men's Rebellion in the Northeast"), *Sangkhomsat parithat*, V:1 (June, 1967), 78–86; and "Khabot ngiao muang phrae" ("The Shan Rebellion at Phrae"), *Sangkhomsat parithat*, VI:2 (September, 1968), 67–80.

The Chinese in Southeast Asia: (NOTE: For other works on the overseas Chinese, see Chapter 6, Chapter 27, and Chapter 34 in the Bibliography.)

The principal compendium of information on the overseas Chinese communities is Victor Purcell, *The Chinese in Southeast Asia* (1st ed., 1951 [revised ed., London, 1965]), which also has a substantial bibliography. A recent brief survey of the Chinese in Southeast Asia may be found in C. P. Fitzgerald, *The Third China* (Melbourne, 1965). On the particular question of Chinese economic capacities, see Maurice Freedman, "The Handling of Money: A Note on the Background to the Economic Sophistication of the Overseas Chinese," *Man*, LIX (1959), pp. 64–65; and on the general problems of association and assimilation, see Alice Tay Ehr Soon, "The Chinese in South-East Asia," *Race*, IV:1 (November, 1962), 34–48.

Descriptions and studies of the Chinese in Singapore and Malaysia are numerous. Some of the most useful may be listed (alphabetically) as follows: W. L. Blythe, *The Impact of Chinese Secret Societies in Malaya* (London, 1969), and "Historical Sketch of Chinese Labour in Malaya," *Journal of the Malayan Branch Royal Asiatic Society*, XX:1 (1947), 67–114, by the same author; Maurice Freedman, *Chinese Family and Marriage in Singapore* (London, 1957), "Immigrants and Associations: Chinese in Nineteenth Century Singapore," *Comparative Studies in Society and History*, 3 (1960–61), 25–48, (reprinted in L. A. Fallers, ed., *Immigrants and Associations* [The Hague and Paris, 1967], pp. 17–48), and "Chinese Kinship and Marriage in Singapore," *JSEAH*, III:2 (1962), 65–73, by the same author; L. A. P. Gosling, "Migration and Assimilation of Rural Chinese in Trengganu," in J. S. Bastin and R. Roolvink, eds., *Malayan and Indonesian Studies* (London, 1964), pp. 201–21; R. N. Jackson, *Pickering: Protector of Chinese* (Kuala Lumpur, 1965); Barrington Kaye, *Upper Nankin Street Singapore: A Sociological Study of Chinese Households Living in a Densely Populated Area* (Singapore, 1960); S. M. Middlebrook, "Yap Ah Loy, 1837–85," *Journal of the Malayan Branch Royal Asiatic Society*, XXIV:2 (1951); William H. Newell, *Treacherous River: A Study of Rural Chinese in North Malaya* (Kuala Lumpur, 1962); Png Poh Seng, "The Kuomintang in Malaya," *JSEAH*, II:1 (1961), 1–32; Victor Purcell, *The Chinese in Malaya* (1st ed., 1948 [reprinted in Kuala Lumpur, 1967]); Song Ong Siang, *One Hundred Years History of the Chinese in Singapore* (1st ed., 1923 [reprinted in Kuala Lumpur, 1967]); Eunice Thio, "The Singapore Chinese Protectorate: Events and Conditions Leading to Its Establishment, 1823–1877," *Journal of the South Seas Society*, XVI:1–2 (1960), 40–80; T'ien Ju-Kang, *The Chinese of Sarawak: A Study of Social Structure* (London, 1953); J. D. Vaughan, *Manners and Customs of the Chinese of the Straits Settlements* (Singapore, 1879); C. S. Wong, *A Cycle of Chinese Festivals* (Singapore, 1967), and *A Gallery of Chinese Kapitans* (Singapore, 1963).

Studies of the Chinese in Indonesia include: Mary Somers, *Peranakan Chinese Politics in Indonesia* (Ithaca, N.Y., 1964); Donald E. Willmott, *The Chinese of Semarang: A Changing Minority Community in Indonesia* (Ithaca, N.Y., 1960); *The National Status of the Chinese in Indonesia, 1900–1958* (Ithaca, N.Y., 1960), by the same author; Tan Giok-Lan, *The Chinese of Sukabumi: a Study of Social and Cultural Accommodation* (Ithaca, N.Y., 1963); Lea Williams, *Overseas Chinese Nationalism: The Genesis of the Pan-Chinese Movement in Indonesia, 1900–1916* (Glencoe, Ill., 1960); W. J. Cator, *The Economic Position of the Chinese in the Netherlands Indies* (Oxford, 1936); and G. W. Skinner, "Change and Persistence in Chinese Culture Overseas: A Comparison of Thailand and Java," *Journal of the South Seas Society*, XVI:1–2 (1960), 86–100, which is commented on by The Siauw Giap, "Religion and Overseas Chinese Assimilation in Southeast Asian Countries," *Révue du Sud-Est Asiatique* (1965, no. 2), 67–84.

For Thailand, the classic work, superior to all others, is G. William Skinner, *Chinese Society in Thailand: An Analytical History* (Ithaca, N.Y., 1957), which for Thailand should be used to the exclusion of Purcell. Also of importance are R. J. Coughlin, *Double Identity: The Chinese in Modern Thailand* (Hong Kong, 1960), and K. P. Landon, *The Chinese in Thailand* (London, 1941). Also note G. W. Skinner's comparative essay "Change and Persistence in Chinese Culture Overseas: A Comparison of Thailand and Java," *Journal of the South Seas Society*, XVI:1–2 (1960), 86–100.

Edgar Wickberg's study of *The Chinese in Philippine Life, 1850–1898* (New Haven, Conn., 1965), and his article entitled "The Chinese Mestizo in Philippine History," *JSEAH*, V:1 (March, 1964), 62–100, are essential reading. Also see Alfonso Felix, Jr., ed., *The Chinese in the Philippines, 1770–1898* (Manila, 1969). Three dissertations are also pertinent: George H. Weightman, "The Philippine Chinese: A Cultural History of a Marginal Trading Community" (Cornell University, 1960); Jacques Amyot, "The Chinese of Manila: A Study of Adaptation of Chinese Familialism to the Philippine Environment" (University of Chicago, 1960); and K. K. M. Jensen, "The Chinese in the Philippines During the American Regime, 1898–1946" (University of Wisconsin, 1956).

The best work on the Chinese in Indochina is W. E. Willmott's *The Chinese in Cambodia* (Vancouver, B. C., 1967). Wang Wen-Yuan, *Les Relations entre l'Indochine française et le Chine* (Paris, 1937), is also helpful.

The Influx of Alien Ideologies: Frank N. Trager, ed., *Marxism in Southeast Asia: A Study of Four Countries* (Stanford, Calif., 1959), discusses Marxist influences and movements in Burma, Thailand, Vietnam, and Indonesia. The early history of the Communist movement in Southeast Asia is dealt with in J. H. Brimmell, *Communism in Southeast Asia: A Political Analysis* (London, 1959); and Malcolm Kennedy, *A Short History of Communism in Asia* (London, 1957). For individual countries, Ruth McVey, *The Rise of Indonesian Communism* (Ithaca, N.Y., 1965), has dealt in great detail with the early years of the Indonesian Communist Party, and Harry J. Benda and Ruth McVey, eds., *The Communist Uprisings of 1926–1927 in Indonesia; Key Documents* (Ithaca, N.Y., 1960), provides some of the source materials for this period, as does B. Schrieke, "The Causes and Effects of Communism on the West Coast of Sumatra," in B. Schrieke, *Indonesian Sociological Studies*, I (The Hague, 1955).

For Chinese nationalism in Southeast Asia, a number of the studies on the overseas Chinese are valuable, particularly G. William Skinner's *Chinese Society in Thailand* (Ithaca, N.Y., 1957); Png Poh Seng, "The Kuomintang in Malaya," *JSEAH*, II:1 (1961), 1–32; and Lea Williams, *Overseas Chinese Nationalism: The Genesis of the Pan-Chinese Movement in Indonesia, 1900–1916* (Glencoe, Ill., 1960). The only work which sets out to examine Indian nationalism in Southeast Asia is Usha Mahajani, *The Role of Indian Minorities in Burma and Malaya* (Bombay, 1960). For the influence of Chettyars in Burma, see Chester L. Cooper, "Moneylenders and the Economic Development of Lower Burma: An Exploratory Historical Study of the Role of the Indian Chettyars" (unpublished Ph.D. dissertation, American University, 1959); and Philip Siegelman, "Colonial Development and the Chettyar; a Study in the Ecology of Modern Burma, 1850–1941" (unpublished Ph.D. dissertation, University of Minnesota, 1963). Kernial Singh Sandhu, *Indians in Malaya: Immigration and Settlement, 1786–1957* (Cambridge, England, 1969), may also be read with advantage. The influence of the overseas Japanese was perhaps most strongly felt in the Philippines, and this subject has been extensively studied by Grant K. Goodman in his *Davao: A Case Study in Japanese-Philippine Relations* (Lawrence, Kans., 1967), and *Four Aspects of Philippine-Japanese Relations, 1930–1940* (New Haven, Conn., 1967). See also Serafin D. Quiason's "Some Notes on the Japanese Community in Manila: 1898–1941," *Solidarity*, III:9 (September, 1968), 39–59.

Masonry enjoyed considerable influence in the Philippines at the turn of the century, and is studied by John N. Schumacher, "Philippine Masonry to 1890," *Asian Studies* (Manila), IV:2 (August, 1966), 328–41; and by Teodoro M. Kalaw, *Philippine Masonry* (Manila, 1956 [reprint]). The impact of Christianity in its various sectarian manifestations is analyzed somewhat less successfully by Richard L. Deats in *Nationalism and Christianity in the Philippines* (Dallas, Tex., 1967).

On the influence of Islamic reform in Indonesia, the best work is Deliar Noer's "The Rise and Development of the Modernist Movement in Indonesia During the Dutch Colonial Period" (unpublished Ph.D. dissertation, Cornell, 1963). The chapter "The Renaissance of Indonesian Islam" in Harry J. Benda, *The Crescent and the Rising Sun* (The Hague, 1958), is a most helpful brief account. For Malaya, see William R. Roff, "Kaum Muda —Kaum Tua: Innovation and Reaction Among the Malays, 1900–1941," in K. G. Tregonning, ed., *Papers on Malayan History* (Singapore, 1962). For some account of ideological life in the Middle East, see William R. Roff, "Indonesian and Malay Students in Cairo in the 1920's," *Indonesia* (Ithaca, N.Y.), IX (March, 1970), 73–87.

Chapter 24. Channels of Change

Urbanization: (NOTE: For more on this topic, see the bibliography for Chapter 34.)

Increasing interest has focused in recent times on the city as an important agent of social change, an interest reflected in studies of the sociology of cities and the processes of urbanization. For some examples of traditional cities, see G. Coedès, *Angkor: An Introduction* (London, 1963); V. C. Scott O'Connor, *Mandalay and Other Cities of Burma* (London, 1907); Paul Wheatley, *The Golden Khersonese* (Kuala Lumpur, 1961); and Hugh Tinker, *The City in the Asian Polity* (London, 1964). The only full-scale study of modern urbanization in the region is T. G. McGee, *The Southeast Asian City* (London, 1967), but a number of shorter articles dealing with general phenomena rather than particular cities are worth attention, and the following may be instanced: D. W. Fryer, "The Million City in Southeast Asia," *Geographical Review* (October, 1953), pp. 474–94; N. S. Ginsburg, "The Great City in Southeast Asia," *American Journal of Sociology*, LX (1955), 455–62; and Nathan Keyfitz, "Political-Economic Aspects of Urbanization in South and Southeast Asia," in Philip M. Hauser and Leo Schnore, eds., *The Study of Urbanization* (New York, 1965).

Of the studies of individual cities in Southeast Asia, those on Singapore are perhaps the most numerous. C. B. Buckley's *Anecdotal History of Old Times in Singapore* (1st ed., 1902 [reprinted in Kuala Lumpur, 1965]), is a rather diffuse but detailed historical background. Other historical studies are: William R. Roff, "The Malayo-Muslim World of Singapore at the Close of the Nineteenth Century," *JAS*, XXIV:1 (1964), 75–90; and Png Poh Seng, "The Straits Chinese in Singapore: A Case of Local Identity and Sociocultural Accommodation," *JSEAH*, X:1 (1969), 95–114. The first issue of the 1969 *Journal of Southeast Asian History* is a commemorative one celebrating the founding of modern Singapore, and it contains many articles of interest. On the integration of immigrant communities to the urban life of Singapore in the nineteenth and twentieth centuries, see Maurice Freedman, "Immigrants and Associations: Chinese in Nineteenth Century Singapore," *Comparative Studies in Society and History*, III

(1960–61), 25–48; and his *Chinese Family and Marriage in Singapore* (London, 1957). Also of interest is Judith Djamour, *Malay Kinship and Marriage in Singapore* (London, 1959). On Bawean patterns of settlement in Singapore, see J. Vredenbregt, "Bawean Migrations: Some Preliminary Notes," *Bijdragen tot de Taal-, Land- en Volkenkunde*, CXX:1 (1964), 109–37; and Mansor b. Haji Fadzal, "My Baweanese People," *Intisari*, II:4 (n.d.), 11–71. For studies of cities in Malaysia, see J. M. Gullick, "Kuala Lumpur, 1880–1895," *Journal of the Malayan Branch Royal Asiatic Society*, XXVIII:4 (1955), 1–172; Kernial Singh Sandhu, "Chinese Colonization of Malacca: A Study in Population Change 1500–1957 A.D.," *Journal of Tropical Geography*, XV (1961), 1–26; and *Penang Past and Present, 1786–1963*, published by the City Council of Georgetown (Penang, 1966).

For urbanization in Indonesia, Lance Castles has written "The Ethnic Profile of Djakarta," *Indonesia*, III (April, 1967), 153–204; and Edward Bruner has studied the social and cultural results of Toba Batak migration to Medan in his article, "Urbanization and Ethnic Identity in North Sumatra," *American Anthropologist*, LXIII:3 (June, 1961), 508–21. Clifford Geertz's *The Social History of an Indonesian Town* (Cambridge, Mass., 1965), is a study of "Modjokuto," a small town in Java. The volume of essays entitled *The Indonesian Town: Studies in Urban Sociology* (The Hague, 1958) presents the work of a number of Dutch scholars.

Philippine urbanization is examined in Robert T. Reed's *Hispanic Urbanism in the Philippines: A Study of the Impact of Church and State* (Manila, 1967); in Donn V. Hart's *The Philippine Plaza Complex: A Focal Point in Culture Change* (New Haven, Conn., 1955); and in Paul F. Cressey's "Urbanization in the Philippines," *Sociology and Social Research*, XLIV (July, 1960), 402–9.

In Burma and Thailand, urbanization is covered only in the secondary accounts listed elsewhere, most notably through the details in Virginia Thompson, *Thailand: The New Siam* (New York, 1941 [reprinted in New York, 1967]); Kenneth P. Landon, *Siam in Transition: A Brief Survey of Cultural Trends in the Five Years since the Revolution of 1932* (Chicago, 1939); and John Christian, *Burma and the Japanese Invader* (Calcutta, 1945).

On urbanization in Cambodia, see Paul Bergue, "L'Habitation Européene au Cambodge," *Revue Indochinoise*, I (1905), 490–99; and R. Garry, "L'Urbanisation au Cambodge," *Civilisations*, XVII (1967), 83–106.

Education and Language: (NOTE: For more on the development of education and national languages in Southeast Asia, see the bibliography for Chapter 35.)

For Southeast Asia in general, the only descriptive work for the period dealt with by this part is J. S. Furnivall, *Educational Progress in Southeast Asia* (New York, 1944). Within Malaysia, "Education in Malaya, 1900–1941," is described by H. R. Cheeseman, *Malayan Historical Journal*, II:1 (1955), 30–47; D. D. Chelliah, *A Short History of the Educational Policy of the Straits Settlements, 1800–1925* (Kuala Lumpur, 1947), gives some account of the early period as well. Both of these accounts embody a colonial point of view, and J. Stewart Nagle's *Educational Needs of the Straits Settlements and Federated Malay States* (Baltimore, 1928) differs little in emphasis. A more recent summary is provided by T. R. Doraisamy, ed., *150 Years of Education in Singapore* (Singapore, 1969). Eugene

Wijeyasingha, *A History of Raffles Institution, 1823–1963* (Singapore, 1963), and N. J. Ryan and Desmond Tate, *Malay College, 1905–1965: Past and Present* (Kuala Kangsar, n.d.), give the history of two of the most influential schools in Singapore and Malaya.

The Taman Siswa movement, which developed a widespread private school system in Indonesia in the 1920's and after and which was founded on ideals of a national culture, is studied by Ruth McVey, "Taman Siswa and the Indonesian National Awakening," *Indonesia*, IV (October, 1967), 128–49.

The only general account of education in Thailand in the years before 1940 is M. L. Manich Jumsai, *Compulsory Education in Thailand* (Paris, 1951). David K. Wyatt's *The Politics of Reform in Thailand* (New Haven, Conn., 1969) is also relevant for developments in education, but only up to 1910. There is no good general work on education in Burma, though much useful information is available through official reports.

For education in Indochina, Henri Froidevaux, *L'Oeuvre scolaire de la France dans nos colonies* (Paris, 1900), is a useful description of a generally torpid endeavor. See also Auguste Rivoalen, "L'Oeuvre française d'enseignement au Viet-Nam," *France-Asie*, XIII (1956), 401–18. For Cambodia, see Humbert Hess, "L'Enseignement au Cambodge," in *Comptes Rendus des Sciences Coloniales*, IV (1924), 335–43; and Jean Delvert, "L'Oeuvre française d'enseignement au Cambodge," *France-Asie*, XIII (1956), 309–22.

In the Philippines, education during the Spanish period is the subject of an article by Henry F. Fox, "Primary Education in the Philippines, 1565–1863," *Philippine Studies*, XIII:2 (April, 1965), 207–31. For a general history, see Encarnacion Alzona's *A History of Education in the Philippines* (Manila, 1932). Joseph Ralston Hayden's monumental book, *The Philippines: A Study in National Development* (New York, 1942), has excellent chapters tracing the development of education and language during the American regime. The annual reports of the American governors-general contain detailed analyses of the school system as it developed after 1900. For a history of the development of *Pilipino*, see Ernest J. Frei's *The Historical Development of the Philippine National Language* (Manila, 1959).

Chapter 25. The Philippines

Philippine nationalism from 1872 to 1941 can be broken into five major periods. The first—1872–96—can be studied in John N. Schumacher, "The Filipino Nationalists' Propaganda Campaign in Europe, 1880–1895" (unpublished doctoral dissertation, Georgetown University, 1965); Josefa Saniel, *Japan and the Philippines, 1868–1898* (Quezon City, 1963); Edmund Plauchet, "The Cavite Uprising of 1872," *Philippine Historical Bulletin*, IV:4 (December, 1960), 1–16; Romeo Cruz, "Philippine Nationalism in the Nineteenth Century," *Philippine Historical Bulletin*, VI:1 (March, 1962), 16–29; Maximo N. Kalaw's classic study *The Development of Philippine Politics, 1872–1920* (Manila, 1926); Teodoro A. Agoncillo's important if somewhat unsatisfactory *The Revolt of the Masses* (Quezon City, 1956); and Eliodoro G. Robles, *The Philippines in the Nineteenth Century* (Quezon City, 1969). The republication of *La Solidaridad* by the University of the Philippines Press in 1967 is of great value as a source. The writings of José P. Rizal, most successfully translated by León Ma. Guerrero as *The Lost Eden* (Bloomington, Ind., 1961), and *The Subversive* (Bloomington, Ind., 1962), are essential reading. The two best biographies of Rizal are Rafael Palma's *The Pride of the Malay Race* (New York, 1949), and León Ma. Guerrero's *The First Filipino* (Manila, 1963). The publications of the National Heroes Commission in Manila, including *The Minutes of the Katipunan* (1964), and the *Memoirs of General Artemio Ricarte* (1963), are important source books. The Philippine Historical Association's special issue of the *Historical Bulletin*, VIII:3 (September, 1963), dealing with Andrés Bonifacio, contains a number of valuable articles.

A detailed overview of the second historical period—1896–1901—can be found in Gregorio F. Zaide's *The Philippine Revolution* (Manila, 1954). Cesar A. Majul's brilliant study entitled *The Political and Constitutional Ideas of the Philippine Revolution* (Quezon City, 1967), examines the intellectual assumptions of the Filipino leadership during this period. The Ateneo de Manila publications of the *Trial of Rizal* (Manila, 1961), edited by Horacio de la Costa, and the *Trial of Andres Bonifacio* (Manila, 1963), edited by Virginia Palma-Bonifacio, are significant volumes dealing with the executions of these two famous Filipinos. Cesar A. Majul's biography of *Apolinario Mabini, Revolutionary* (Manila, 1964), and Mabini's writings, most recently edited by Alfredo S. Veloso in three volumes for the Mabini Centennial (Quezon City, 1964), are also very important. Leandro H. Fernandez's *The Philippine Republic* (New York, 1926), and Teodoro A. Agoncillo's *Malolos: The Crisis of the Republic* (Quezon City, 1960), both trace the struggle in Malolos and against the Americans. General Aguinaldo's *Memoirs of the Revolution* (Manila, 1967) are of little use as a historical source.

The third period—1901–1913—has been studied extensively. The motives behind American intervention are analyzed in Ernest R. May, *Imperial Democracy* (New York, 1961); Julius W. Pratt, *Expansionists of 1898* (Baltimore, 1936); and H. Wayne Morgan, *America's Road to Empire* (New York, 1966); and from a different point of view in Walter LaFeber, *The New Empire: An Interpretation of American Expansion, 1860–1898* (Ithaca, N.Y., 1963), and Thomas J. McCormick, *China Market: America's Quest for Informal Empire 1893–1901* (Chicago, 1967). Many of the American participants wrote of their experiences: James H. Blount in his *American Occupation of the Philippines 1898–1912* (Manila, 1968 [1st ed., 1912]) was critical, while Dean C. Worcester, in his *The Philippines Past and Present* (2 vols., New York, 1914 [rev. ed., edited by J. R. Hayden, New York, 1930]), celebrated intervention; and James A. LeRoy, in his *The Americans in the Philippines* (2 vols., Boston and New York, 1914), reserved judgment. Robert L. Beisner's *Twelve Against Empire* (New York, 1968) helps to shatter long-standing illusions about the anti-imperialists. Among the best political histories of the American era are Dapen Liang's *The Development of Philippine Political Parties* (Hong Kong, 1939), and Garel A. Grunder and William E. Livezey's *The Philippines and the United States* (Norman, Okla., 1951). Bonifacio S. Salamanca's *The Filipino Reaction to American Rule 1901–1913* (n.p., 1968) is a perceptive attempt at revisionist history. Among the many studies of the Aglipayan church, one of the best is Pedro S. de Achútegui and Miguel A. Bernad, *Religious Revolution in the Philippines* (Manila, 1960). The controversy over the friar lands can be followed in W. C. Forbes, D. C. Worcester, and F. W. Carpenter, *The Friar Land Inquiry, Philippine Government* (Manila, 1910); in the

Report of the Committee on Insular Affairs, No. 2289, 61st Congress, 3d session, March 3, 1911; and in "Disposition of the Friar Lands," a speech by Manuel L. Quezon to the United States Congress, May 1, 1912. William Cameron Forbes, an outspoken defender of the Republican Party in the Philippines, wrote *The Philippine Islands* (Cambridge, England, 1945); his effect in the Philippines has been analyzed by Robert M. Spector, "W. Cameron Forbes in the Philippines: A Study in Proconsular Power," *JSEAH*, VII:2 (September, 1966), 74–92. See also Oscar M. Alfonso, *Theodore Roosevelt and the Philippines, 1897–1909* (Quezon City, 1970).

The fourth period—1913–33—has been most thoroughly studied by Michael P. Onorato, who has published in *Asian Studies, Philippine Studies* and elsewhere. See in particular his *A Brief Review of American Interest in Philippine Development and Other Essays* (Berkeley, Calif., 1968). For an analysis of the Democratic Party years, see Roy W. Curry, "Woodrow Wilson and Philippine Policy," *Mississippi Valley Historical Review*, XLI (1954), 435–452; and Francis Burton Harrison's *The Cornerstone of Philippine Independence* (New York, 1922). The protracted struggle between Governor Leonard Wood and the Filipino leadership produced a large and polemical literature. See, for example, Jorge Bocobo's *General Leonard Wood and the Law* (Manila, 1923) and Manuel L. Quezon and Camilo Osias, *Governor-General Wood and the Filipino Cause* (Manila, 1924). Bruno Lasker's *Filipino Immigration* (Chicago, 1931 [reprint, 1969]), and the Occasional Papers of the Institute of Asian Studies, *The Filipino Exclusion Movement 1927–1935* (Quezon City, 1967), examine the problems of the Filipino migration to Hawaii and the United States.

The most literate and perceptive analysis of the transition from American rule to Commonwealth status—the fifth and final historical period—can be found in Theodore Friend's *Between Two Empires* (New Haven, Conn., 1965). See also Friend's four articles dealing with sugar and the independence question: "American Interests and Philippine Independence, 1929–1933," *Philippine Studies*, XI (1963), 505–23; "Philippine Interests and the Mission for Independence, 1929–1932," XII:1 (1964), 63–82; "Philippine Independence and the Last Lame-Duck Congress," XII:2 (April, 1964), 260–76; and "Veto and Repassage of the Hare-Hawes-Cutting Act: A Catalogue of Motives," XII:4 (October, 1964), 666–80. Manuel L. Quezon's autobiography, *The Good Fight* (New York, 1946), is far more revealing than most of the scholarly literature dealing with the Commonwealth President. The detailed analysis by Rōyama Masamichi and Takéuchi Tatsuji in their study *The Philippine Polity: A Japanese View* (New Haven, Conn., 1967), gives the reader a succinct view of the Commonwealth era.

Chapter 26. Burma

For Burma in this period, one must rely for the most part on secondary accounts, notably the excellent general history by John F. Cady, *A History of Modern Burma* (Ithaca, N.Y., 1958), supplemented by the works of John L. Christian, *Modern Burma: A Survey of Political and Economic Development* (Berkeley, Calif., 1942); Donald Eugene Smith, *Religion and Politics in Burma* (Princeton, N.J., 1965); and E. Sarkisyanz, *Buddhist Backgrounds of the Burmese Revolution* (The Hague, 1965). Also useful is John L. Christian's *Burma and the Japanese Invader* (Calcutta, 1945). The best primary sources are U Ba U's *My Burma* (New York, 1959); Dr. Ba Maw, *Breakthrough in Burma: Memoirs of a Revolution, 1939–1946* (New Haven, Conn., 1968); and Maung Maung, ed., *Aung San of Burma* (The Hague, 1962). See also Maurice Collis, *Trials in Burma* (London, 1938), and George Orwell's penetrating novel, *Burmese Days* (New York, 1934).

Chapter 27. Indonesia

The general history of early-twentieth-century Indonesia is most usefully surveyed in George McT. Kahin, *Nationalism and Revolution in Indonesia* (Ithaca, N.Y., 1952). It is complemented by the introductory section of Harry Benda's *The Crescent and the Rising Sun: Indonesian Islam under the Japanese Occupation 1942–1945* (The Hague, 1958), with its Islamic emphasis. There are now a number of excellent modern studies in English on more restricted periods and topics. The social history of the "Ethical Policy" period is explored in Robert Van Niel, *The Emergence of the Modern Indonesian Elite* (The Hague, 1960), and in W. F. Wertheim and The Siauw Giap, "Social Change in Java, 1900–1930," *Pacific Affairs,* XXXV:3 (1962), 223–47. See also Lea Williams, *Overseas Chinese Nationalism: the Genesis of the Pan-Chinese Movement in Indonesia, 1900–1916* (Glencoe, Ill., 1960). Developments among the Chinese of Java and emerging tensions between them and the Javans are treated more analytically by The Siauw Giap in "Group Conflict in a Plural Society," *Revue du Sud-Est Asiatique* (1966, nos. 1 and 2), 1–32, 185–218. The special local pattern in the Kudus area, the scene of Chinese-Javanese riots in 1918, described in The's article, is the subject of Lance Castles, *Religion, Politics and Economic Behavior in Java: The Kudus Cigarette Industry* (New Haven, Conn., 1967). Ruth McVey's *The Rise of Indonesian Communism* (Ithaca, N.Y., 1965) is the definitive work on its subject and related political developments in the turbulence of the late 1910's and early 1920's.

The article entitled "Taman Siswa and the Indonesian National Awakening," *Indonesia,* IV (October, 1967), 128–49, also by Ruth McVey, is a brilliant essay on the intellectual history of the early twentieth century. The literary movements that exemplified the cultural and intellectual changes of these decades are surveyed in A. Teeuw, *Modern Indonesian Literature* (The Hague, 1967), and Anthony Johns, "Genesis of a Modern Literature," in Ruth McVey, ed., *Indonesia* (New Haven, Conn., 1963), both of which carry the narrative forward into the 1940's and after. See also Heather Sutherland, "Pudjangga Baru: Aspects of Indonesian Intellectual Life in the 1930's," *Indonesia,* VI (October, 1968), 106–27.

Perhaps not by chance, most of the best biographical works for Indonesian history center on this period. Raden Adjeng Kartini, *Letters of a Javanese Princess* (New York, 1964), is a classic reissued with a fine introductory essay by Hildred Geertz. Soetan Sjahrir, *Out of Exile* (New York, 1949), is a collection of letters written in the 1930's by the nationalist, later prime minister, and represents the more Western pole in Indonesian intellectual life of the time. The more "Javanese" pole is represented by two volumes about the extraordinary figure of Sukarno: Bernard Dahm, *Sukarno and the Struggle for Indonesian Independence* (Ithaca, N.Y., 1969), deals mainly with his earlier years and emphasizes the links between his nationalist politics and Javanese political culture, while *Sukarno, an Autobiography as told to Cindy Adams* (Indianapolis, Ind., 1965), gives his own version as he saw it in the early 1960's. Of interest also is Muhamad Radjab's engaging book, *Semasa Ketjil Dikampung, 1913–1928: Autobiografi seorang anak Minangkabau* (*Village Childhood, 1913–1928: The Autobiography of a Minangkabau Boy*) (Jakarta, 1950).

Chapter 28. Vietnam

Jean Lacouture, *Ho Chi Minh: A Political Biography* (New York, 1968), is an informal, readable study of Vietnam's most famous anticolonial leader. Bernard B. Fall, ed., *Ho Chi Minh on Revolution, Selected Writings 1920–1966* (New York, 1967), follows Ho's career through his own words and writings: Of particular importance is his "French Colonization on Trial," pp. 68–123. David Marr, *Vietnam's Anti-colonial Movements: The Early Years, 1885–1925* (Berkeley, Calif., forthcoming), offers a serious survey of Vietnamese nationalism in its formative period. John T. McAlister, *Vietnam: The Origins of Revolution* (New York, 1969), is a well-written general study of Vietnamese revolutionary potentialities and actualities. It may be compared with Dennis J. Duncanson, *Government and Revolution in Vietnam* (London, 1968). Louis Roubaud, *Viet Nam: la tragédie indochinoise* (Paris, 1931), was published just after the bloody suppression of the Vietnamese Nationalist Party and offers important insights into the struggle between colonialism and nationalism. Of course, a basic French source for the history of Vietnamese revolutionary politics is the multivolume series of the Gouvernement General de l'Indochine, *Contribution à l'histoire des mouvements politiques de l'Indochine française* (Hanoi, 1933–34). John McAlister and Paul Mus, *The Vietnamese and Their Revolution* (New York, 1970), offers the reflections of a pioneering, philosophically minded French "old Indochina hand" on Vietnamese politics. It is in part a translation of Mus's *Vietnam: sociologie d'une guerre* (Paris, 1952).

One important way of understanding social change in twentieth-century Vietnam is to read the profusion of brilliant Vietnamese novels produced in the 1920's and 1930's by such apostles of reform as Nhat Linh, Khai Hung, Hoang Dao, Thach Lam, To Hoai, and others. Novels were used as reform platforms because colonial authorities were less likely to censor them. Although few Vietnamese novels have yet been translated into English or French, see Hoang Ngoc Thanh, "The Social and Political Development of Vietnam as Seen Through the Modern Novel" (unpublished Ph.D. dissertation, University of Hawaii, 1968).

Chapter 29. Thailand

The only general accounts of this critical period in Thai history are included in the following works: Prince Chula Chakrabongse, *Lords of Life: The Paternal Monarchy of Bangkok, 1782–1932* (New York, 1960); Virginia Thompson, *Thailand: The New Siam* (New York, 1941 [reprinted in New York, 1967]); and Kenneth P. Landon, *Siam in Transition: A Brief Survey of Cultural Trends in the Five Years since the Revolution of 1932* (Chicago, 1939). Of these general works, Landon's is by far the most important. King Vajiravudh's reign is critically important but has not received detailed treatment in Western languages (although work is currently underway on the subject by at least two scholars). Praphat Trinarong's *Chiwit lae ngan khong atsawaphahu* (*The Life and Work of Pegasus* [Rama VI]) (Bangkok, 1963) indicates the great wealth of information available. The memoirs of Rian Sichan and Net Phunwiwat in *Prawat patiwat khrang raek khong thai r.s. 130* (*The History of the First Thai Revolution, 1912*) (Bangkok, 1960) are the most important source for that event, while the reign as a whole is best conveyed in sense and flavor in the memoirs of Phraya Satchaphirom, *Lao hai luk fang* ("*Told to My Children*") (Bangkok, 1955). The revolution of 1932 is the subject of a doctoral dissertation at Indiana University (1963), "The June Revolution of 1932 in Thailand: A Study in Political Behavior," by Thawatt Mokarapong. A recent flood of books in Thai on the 1930's was set off by a venerable old Thai journalist, "Thai Noi," when he wrote *Prasopkan 34 pi haeng rabop prachathipatai* (*The Fruits of 34 Years of Democracy*) (Bangkok, 1966). A great deal of useful coverage of this period is to be found in Pierre Fistie, *L'Évolution de la Thaïlande contemporaine* (Paris, 1967).

Chapter 30. Malaya

The principal study of nationalism in Malaya before World War II is William R. Roff, *The Origins of Malay Nationalism* (New Haven, Conn., and London, 1967), but reference should also be made to T. H. Silcock and Ungku Abdul Aziz, "Malayan Nationalism," in W. L. Holland, ed., *Asian Nationalism and the West* (New York, 1953), and Raden Soenarno, "Malay Nationalism, 1900–1945," *JSEAH*, I:1 (1960), 1–28. Usha Mahajani's *The Role of Indian Minorities in Burma and Malaya* (Bombay, 1960), and Tan Cheng Lock's *Malayan Problems from a Chinese Point of View* (Singapore, 1947), deal to some extent with prewar politics in Malaya.

Chapter 31. Laos and Cambodia

For Laos in this period, the most relevant works are Peter Kemp, *Alms for Oblivion* (London, 1961); Pierre Gentil, *Remous sur le Mekong* (Nancy, 1950); and Katay Don Sasorith, *Le Laos: son évolution politique* (Paris, 1953).

Cambodian nationalism has not yet received a full-scale study. Martin Herz's *Short History of Cambodia* (New York, 1958), although otherwise full of errors, is accurate and perceptive on the 1940's.

PART FIVE. THE PREOCCUPATIONS OF INDEPENDENCE

Chapter 33. The Evolution of New Political Societies

Perhaps the best general introduction to this period in Southeast Asia is George McT. Kahin, ed., *Governments and Politics of Southeast Asia* (2d ed., Ithaca, N.Y., 1964), with individual essays on each country of the region. Annual articles in the January or February issue of *Asian Survey* also merit attention.

The Union of Burma: Wartime and postwar Burmese politics are covered generally in several good secondary accounts, notably Frank N. Trager, *Burma: From Kingdom to Republic* (New York, 1966); John F. Cady, *A History of Modern Burma* (Ithaca, N.Y., 1958); and Hugh Tinker, *The Union of Burma* (4th ed., London, 1968). Lucian W. Pye, *Politics, Personality, and Nation Building: Burma's Search for Identity* (New Haven,

Conn., 1962), has a stimulating discussion of the subjective problems of the period; while Frank N. Trager, *Toward a Welfare State in Burma* (New York, 1958), deals with the construction of Burmese socialism and economic reconstruction. For just the war period, John L. Christian's *Burma and the Japanese Invader* (Calcutta, 1945) is useful. Also see Dorothy H. Guyot's unpublished Ph.D. dissertation entitled "The Political Impact of the Japanese Occupation of Burma" (Yale University, 1966). Dr. Ba Maw, *Breakthrough in Burma: Memoirs of a Revolution, 1939–1946* (New Haven, Conn., 1968); and Maung Maung, ed., *Aung San of Burma* (The Hague, 1962), are good sources for those major figures in Burmese political development. U Nu is the subject of a biography by Richard A. Butwell, *U Nu of Burma* (Stanford, Calif., 1963).

The Kingdom of Thailand: David A. Wilson's *Politics in Thailand* (Ithaca, N.Y., 1962) long has been the standard source for the politics of the postwar period, although it is stronger analytically than descriptively. The detail is provided in better fashion, though tendentiously, in Pierre Fistie, *L'Évolution de la Thaïlande contemporaine* (Paris, 1967), which has a good deal of interesting information on the rule of Phibun. Frank Darling's *Thailand and the United States* (Washington, 1965) is also relevant. Charles F. Keyes, *Isan: Regionalism in Northeastern Thailand* (Ithaca, N.Y., 1967), is an important introduction to Thailand's most important regional problem. Rayne Kruger, *The Devil's Discus* (London, 1964), is the only full discussion on the death of King Ananda but is not the last word on the subject. The issues and problems of the 1960's are discussed in Louis Lomax, *Thailand: The War that Is, the War that Will Be* (New York, 1967); Daniel Wit, *Thailand: Another Vietnam?* (New York, 1968); and David A. Wilson, "China, Thailand and the Spirit of Bandung," *China Quarterly*, XXX (April–June, 1967), 149–69, and XXXI (July–September, 1967), 96–127, as well as his *The United States and the Future of Thailand* (New York, 1970).

The Kingdom of Laos: Material on Laos before independence can be found in Peter Kemp, *Alms for Oblivion* (London, 1961); Pierre Gentil, *Remous sur le Mekong* (Nancy, 1950); and Katay Don Sasorith, *Le Laos: son évolution politique* (Paris, 1953). Events in Laos since independence are best covered in Hugh Toye's concise and excellent study, *Laos: Buffer State or Battleground* (London, 1968). Arthur J. Dommen's *Conflict in Laos* (New York, 1964; rev. ed., 1971), although more journalistic, is also good, as is Bernard Fall's *Anatomy of a Crisis* (Garden City, N.Y., 1969).

For the effect of Lao events on United States foreign policy, see, among others, Roger Hilsman, *To Move a Nation* (New York, 1967), and Arthur Schlesinger, *The Thousand Days* (New York, 1966). A good brief study of Lao politics is E. H. S. Simmonds, "Independence and Political Rivalry in Laos," in Saul Rose, ed., *Politics of Southern Asia* (London, 1963).

Cambodia: The official French weekly *Indochine*, published in Hanoi between 1940 and 1945, is a valuable source for developments in World War II, as is Claude Fillieux's *Merveilleux Cambodge* (Paris, 1962), and Maurice Ducaroy's *Ma Trahison en Indochine* (Paris, 1949). Pierre Christian, "Son Ngoc Thanh," *Indochine Sud-Est Asiatique* (October, 1952), pp. 48–49, is also useful. There are several good studies of postwar Cambodian politics. By far the most valuable is Philippe Preschez, *Essai sur la democratie au Cambodge* (Paris, 1961), supplemented by Roger

Smith's "Cambodia," in George McT. Kahin, *Governments and Politics of Southeast Asia* (2d ed., Ithaca, N.Y., 1964). Michael Leifer's *Cambodia: The Search for Security* (New York, 1967) is also useful, and Philippe Devillers, "Dynamics of Power in Cambodia," in Saul Rose, ed., *Politics of Southern Asia* (London, 1963), is valuable. Achille Dauphin-Meunier's *Le Cambodge de Sihanouk* (Paris, 1965) contains some good insights.

The Democratic Republic of Vietnam; the Republic of Vietnam: Jean Decoux, *À la barre de l'Indochine: histoire du mon gouvernement général 1940–1945* (Paris, 1949), discusses the Japanese occupation of Vietnam from the perspective of the French governor-general who experienced it. Vietnamese history in the 1940's and early 1950's is surveyed more generally in Philippe Devillers, *Histoire du Viet Nam de 1940 à 1952* (Paris, 1952); Ellen J. Hammer, *The Struggle for Indochina 1940–1955* (Stanford, Calif., 1955); and Donald Lancaster, *The Emancipation of French Indochina* (London, 1961). Truong Chinh, *The August Revolution* (Hanoi, 1958), is an interpretation of the Viet Minh's accession to power in 1945 by a senior Party theoretician. But the reader should bear in mind that the nature of the August Revolution is still a matter of some controversy among Vietnamese Marxist writers. Jean Sainteny, *Histoire d'une paix manquée, Indochine 1945–1947* (Paris, 1953), is an important "inside" record of post–August Revolution diplomatic history by one of its French participants. Bernard Fall, *Street Without Joy, Indochina at War 1946–1954* (Harrisburg, Pa., 1961), is a famous military journalist's picture of the Franco-Vietnamese war itself. English-language writings on Vietnamese history increase in quantity for the post–1954 period but do not necessarily improve in quality. Hostile accounts of northern Vietnam since 1954 include P. J. Honey, *North Vietnam Today* (New York, 1962), and Hoang Van Chi, *From Colonialism to Communism, A Case History of North Vietnam* (London, 1964). A much more sympathetic eyewitness account of the north is that of Gerard Chaliand, *The Peasants of North Vietnam* (Baltimore, 1969 [1st ed., Paris, 1968]).

Robert Shaplen, *The Lost Revolution* (New York, 1966), is a superb journalistic narrative and discussion of the politics of the Diem and immediate post-Diem periods in southern Vietnam. Robert Scigliano, *South Vietnam: Nation Under Stress* (Boston, 1963), is relatively balanced in its analysis of the Diem government. Milton Osborne, *Strategic Hamlets in South Vietnam* (Ithaca, N.Y., 1965), describes one of the Diem regime's most disastrous failures and tellingly compares "counterinsurgency" schemes in Vietnam and Malaysia. Douglas Pike, *The Viet Cong* (Cambridge, Mass., 1965), gives a hostile but detailed description of the organizational features, but not the ideological activities, of the National Liberation Front. George McT. Kahin and John Lewis, *The United States in Vietnam* (New York, 1967 [enlarged ed., 1969]), is a critical scholarly review of American intervention in the 1960's war. Thich Nhat Hanh's *Vietnam: Lotus in a Sea of Fire* (New York, 1967) is an important statement of Buddhist opinion on the same subject. Even for the stormy 1960's, there are no English-language discussions of such developments in Vietnamese culture as the novels of Nhat Tien, Duyen Anh, and Duong Nghiem Mau or the work of the "Creation Group" (*nhom Sang Tao*) in postwar Vietnamese poetry. The obsession of most English-language writers on Vietnam with "counter-insurgency," political or military, to the exclusion of almost all other topics, is only too conspicuous to compilers and readers of Southeast Asia bibliographies alike.

Malaysia and Singapore: The Japanese conquest of Malaya and Singapore between December, 1941 and February, 1942 has been the subject of much description and reminiscence, but we refer here only to three firsthand and authoritative accounts: A. E. Perceval, *The War in Malaya* (London, 1949); H. Gordon Bennett, *Why Singapore Fell* (Sydney, 1944); and Masanobu Tsuju, *Singapore: The Japanese Version* (Sydney, 1960). There are also numerous accounts of the Japanese occupation of Malaya by those who experienced it: F. Spencer Chapman's *The Jungle Is Neutral* (London, 1949) is particularly interesting for its account of the formation and activities of Chinese Communist-organized resistance to the Japanese, and Chin Kee Onn's *Malaya Upside Down* (Singapore, 1946) conveys something of life at that time for the civilian. Relatively little scholarly work has been done on the occupation period, but two articles by Japanese writers may be cited: Y. Itagaki, "The Japanese Policy for Malaya Under the Occupation," in K. G. Tregonning, ed., *Papers on Malayan History* (Singapore, 1962); and Yoji Akashi, "Japanese Military Administration in Malaya" (paper presented to the International Conference on Asian History, Kuala Lumpur, August, 1968, mimeograph).

General and summary accounts of postwar Malayan political development, necessarily brief when dealing with particulars, may be found in L. A. Mills, *Malaya: A Political and Economic Appraisal* (Minneapolis, Minn., 1958); and J. Norman Parmer, "Malaya and Singapore," in George McT. Kahin, ed., *Governments and Politics of Southeast Asia* (2d ed., Ithaca, N.Y., 1964). R. S. Milne, *Government and Politics in Malaya* (Boston, 1967), is an extremely useful analytical account of the growth of Malaysia over two decades, with the emphasis on political institutions.

The introduction and abandonment of the Malayan Union scheme and the events leading up to the outbreak of armed rebellion in 1948 have been dealt with in two recent monographs: James de V. Allen, *The Malayan Union* (New Haven, Conn., 1967); and Michael R. Stenson, *Repression and Revolt: The Origins of the 1948 Communist Insurrection in Malaya and Singapore* (Athens, Ohio, 1969). The Communist "emergency," as it was termed, has stimulated a great deal of reflection and writing. Gene Z. Hanrahan, *The Communist Struggle in Malaya* (New York, 1954), is a well-documented account by an American of certain aspects of the guerrilla war. Lucian Pye, *Guerrilla Communism in Malaya* (Princeton, N.J., 1956), is an interesting and important attempt to understand the nature of Chinese participation in the struggle. A number of studies have been made of the processes and problems of rural Chinese "resettlement" during the emergency, notably J. B. Perry Robinson, *Transformation in Malaya* (London, 1955); Kernial Singh Sandhu, "The Saga of the 'Squatter' in Malaya," *JSEAH*, V:1 (March, 1964), 143–77; and Han Suyin's novel, . . . *And the Rain My Drink* (London, 1956). Two general accounts of the politics and administration of the period are Victor Purcell, *Malaya: Communist or Free?* (London, 1954); and Harry Miller, *Menace in Malaya* (London, 1954). An official history of the emergency has been written by Anthony Short but is awaiting publication. In the meantime, two military accounts of these twelve years are Edgar O'Ballance, *The Communist Insurgent War, 1948–1960* (London, 1966), and Richard Clutterbuck, *The Long War:*

The Emergency in Malaya 1948–1960 (London, 1967). An interesting comparison between the Malayan emergency and the American war in Vietnam, by one of the principal participants in the former, is Sir Robert Thompson's *Defeating Communist Insurgency: The Lessons of Malaya and Vietnam* (New York, 1966).

Studies of individual parties and of the party system in Malaysia and Singapore include: for peninsular Malaya, G. S. Maryanov, "Political Parties in Mainland Malaya," *JSEAH*, VIII:1 (1967), 99–110; Margaret Roff, "The Malayan Chinese Association, 1948–65," *JSEAH*, IV:2 (1965), 40–53; Chan Cheng Hee, "The Malayan Chinese Association" (unpublished M.A. thesis, University of Singapore, 1965); and Margaret Roff, "UMNO: The First Twenty Years," *Australian Outlook*, XX:2 (1966), 168–76; for Singapore, Thomas J. Bellows, "The Singapore Party System," *JSEAH*, VIII:1 (1967), 122–38 (Bellow's unpublished Ph.D. dissertation, Yale University, 1968, has the same title); Michael Leifer, "Politics in Singapore: The First Term of the Peoples' Action Party 1959–1963," *Journal of Commonwealth Political Studies*, II (1964), 102–19; Yeo Kim Wah, "A Study of Three Early Political Parties in Singapore," *JSEAH*, X:1 (1969), 115–41; and Pang Cheng Lian, "The People's Action Party, 1954–1963," *JSEAH*, X:1 (1969), 142–54. For the Borneo territories in Malaysia, R. S. Milne, "Party Politics in Sarawak and Sabah," *JSEAH*, VI:2 (1963), 104–17; Craig Lockard, "Parties, Personalities and Crisis Politics in Sarawak," *JSEAH*, VIII:1 (1967), 110–21; and Edwin Lee, "The Emergence of Tokay Leaders in Party Politics in Sabah," *JSEAH*, IX:2 (1968), 306–24. R. S. Milne and K. J. Ratnam, "Politics and Finance in Malaya," *Journal of Commonwealth Political Studies*, III:3 (1965), 182–98, deals with this important question in relation to politics in the peninsula.

There are relatively few political biographies or autobiographies of Malaysian politicians, but the following are of interest: Tan Cheng Lock, *Malayan Problems from a Chinese Point of View* (Singapore, 1947); Soh Eng Lim, "Tan Cheng Lock: His Leadership of the Malayan Chinese," *JSEAH*, I:1 (1960), 29–55; Ishak b. Tadin, "Dato' Onn, 1946–1951," *JSEAH*, I:1 (1960), 56–88; Harry Miller, *Prince and Premier: A Biography of Tunku Abdul Rahman* (London, 1959); and Alex Josey, *Lee Kuan Yew* (Singapore, 1968).

The Philippines: The war years in the Philippines are shrouded in controversy. See, for example, David J. Steinberg's *Philippine Collaboration in World War II* (Ann Arbor, Mich., 1967), and Teodoro A. Agoncillo's *The Fateful Years* (2 vols., Quezon City, 1965). Mauro Garcia has published a valuable collection of *Documents on the Japanese Occupation of the Philippines* (Manila, 1965), and many of the participants including Jorge Vargas, José P. Laurel, and Claro M. Recto have published memoirs. The postwar struggle of the Hukbalahap is equally controversial. Among the more detailed studies are Renze L. Hoeksema's "Communism in the Philippines: a Historical and Analytical Study" (unpublished Ph.D. dissertation, Harvard University, 1956); Alvin H. Scaff's *The Philippine Answer to Communism* (Stanford, Calif., 1955); and Uldarico S. Baclagon's *Lessons From the Huk Campaign in the Philippines* (Manila, 1960). Luis Taruc, the leader of the Huk movement, has written a number of books, the most important being *Born of the People* (New York, 1953). William J. Pomeroy's *The Forest: a Personal Record of the Huk Guerrilla Struggle in the Philippines* (New

York, 1963) is an interesting account of guerrilla life in 1950–52. Alfredo B. Saulo, in his book *Communism in the Philippines* (Manila, 1969), has written a brief introduction to the growth of the Party in the Philippines.

There is no truly satisfactory history of the postwar era. David Bernstein's book, *The Philippine Story* (New York, 1947), gives a good description of the transition to independence but should be supplemented by Violet E. Wurfel, "American Implementation of Philippine Independence" (unpublished Ph.D. dissertation, University of Virginia, 1951). Robert A. Smith's *Philippine Freedom 1946–1958* (New York, 1958) is disappointing. Marcial P. Lichauco's *Roxas: The Story of a Great Filipino and of the Political Era in Which He Lived* (Manila, 1952) is the best eulogy on Roxas. The best work on Magsaysay is Frances L. Starner, *Magsaysay and the Philippine Peasantry: the Agrarian Impact on Philippine Politics, 1953–1956* (Berkeley, Calif., 1961). It has become the fad in recent years for Filipino politicians to commission campaign biographies; like the paper on which they are printed, they are not worth much historically. The *Official Gazette*, the publication of the Republic of the Philippines, is the most detailed and accurate primary source, listing appointments; recording speeches, court cases, and legislative acts; and chronicling the official history of the nation. The daily newspapers and the weekly *Philippines Free Press* serve as a tonic to the *Official Gazette*, which is always accurate but very rarely fair to all positions. Ascertaining the truth in the miasma of "anomalies" is extremely difficult.

Indonesia: A stimulating series of essays provides the best introduction to the manifold and controversial issues involved in interpreting postcolonial Indonesian history. Harry Benda's "Decolonization in Indonesia: The Problem of Continuity and Change," *American Historical Review*, LXX:4 (July, 1965), 1058–73, raises serious questions about the assumptions of much postwar scholarship on Indonesia. Benda and Herbert Feith debate the same issues in *JAS*, XXIII:3 (May, 1964), 449–56, and XXIV:2 (February, 1965), 305–12. Jan Pluvier, *Confrontations: a Study in Indonesian Politics* (Kuala Lumpur, 1965); and David Levine, "History and Social Structure in the Study of Contemporary Indonesia," *Indonesia*, VII (April, 1969), 5–19, approach the question from their own, more radical, points of view. Herbert Feith and Lance Castles, eds., *Indonesian Political Thinking, 1945–1965* (Ithaca, N.Y., 1970), is a superb collection of translated readings.

The exhilaration and trauma of the 1940's, the years of Japanese conquest and revolution against the Dutch, powerfully influenced the course of Indonesian history thereafter. Benedict Anderson probes the implications of the Japanese period in "Japan: 'The Light of Asia,'" in Josef Silverstein, ed., *Southeast Asia in World War II* (New Haven, Conn., 1966). Harry Benda, *The Crescent and the Rising Sun: Indonesian Islam under the Japanese Occupation, 1942–1945* (The Hague, 1958), is the most comprehensive study of the period, but George Kanahele, "The Japanese Occupation of Indonesia: Prelude to Independence" (unpublished Ph.D. dissertation, Cornell University, 1966), also merits attention. The peak of the crisis in late 1945 and early 1946, as the Japanese empire died and the Republic was born in anarchy, is treated in several works. See Benedict Anderson's study, "The Pemuda Revolution: Indonesian Politics 1945–1946" (unpublished Ph.D. dissertation, Cornell University, 1967); John R. W. Smail, *Bandung in the Early Revolution, 1945–46: A Study in the Social History of the*

Indonesian Revolution (Ithaca, N.Y., 1964); Sutan Sjahrir, *Our Struggle* (Ithaca, N.Y., 1968), a translation of the most decisive political manifesto of late 1945; and Idrus's mordant short novel, *Surabaja,* translated in *Indonesia,* V (April, 1968), 1–28, about the revolutionary battle in November, 1945. George McT. Kahin's *Nationalism and Revolution in Indonesia* (Ithaca, N.Y., 1952) is the classic history of the revolution as a whole.

Herbert Feith's *The Decline of Constitutional Democracy in Indonesia* (Ithaca, N.Y., 1962) covers the calmer early years of political independence. Daniel Lev describes *The Transition to Guided Democracy: Indonesian Politics, 1957–59* (Ithaca, N.Y., 1966). Taken together, three works convey some of the complexities of the early 1960's before Armageddon in late 1965: Herbert Feith, "Dynamics of Guided Democracy," in Ruth McVey, ed., *Indonesia* (New Haven, Conn., 1963); J. A. C. Mackie, *Problems of the Indonesian Inflation* (Ithaca, N.Y., 1967), which explores the relation between the economics and politics of the period; and T. K. Tan, ed., *Sukarno's Guided Indonesia* (Brisbane, 1967). Two works of special interest on political topics are Donald Hindley, *The Communist Party of Indonesia, 1951–1963* (Berkeley, Calif., 1966), and William Liddle, "Suku Simalungun: An Ethnic Group in Search of Representation," *Indonesia,* III (April, 1967), 1–28, a study of the development of lower-level political structures in an area of north Sumatra.

The cultural revolution in postcolonial Indonesian life is most broadly and brilliantly treated in Benedict Anderson, "The Languages of Indonesian Politics," *Indonesia,* I (April, 1966), 89–116. Anthony Johns has explored the same cultural revolution in a fine series of literary studies including, "Chairil Anwar: An Interpretation," *Bijdragen tot de Taal-, Land-, en Volkenkunde,* CXX:4 (1964), 393–405; and "A Poet between Two Worlds: The Work of Sitor Situmorang," *Westerly* (November, 1965). One of the major novels of the period has been translated: Mochtar Lubis, *A Road with no End* (London, 1968). John Echols, ed., *Indonesian Writing in Translation* (Ithaca, N.Y., 1956), provides a valuable collection of poems and short stories, mostly from after 1940.

Chapter 34. The Postwar Arena: Domestic and International Themes

Demography: Population growth has been extremely important among the socio-economic factors that have conditioned the political development of Southeast Asian countries since World War II. The standard published work on the demography of peninsular Malaya is T. E. Smith, *Population Growth in Malaya: An Analysis of Recent Trends* (London, 1952), but attention should also be drawn to the important unpublished doctoral dissertation of J. C. Caldwell, "The Population of Malaya" (Australian National University, Canberra). Caldwell also has a very useful article, "The Demographic Background," in T. H. Silcock and E. K. Fisk, eds., *The Political Economy of Independent Malaya* (Canberra, 1963). Two other articles of interest are Kernial Singh Sandhu, "The Population of Malaya: Some Changes in the Pattern of Distribution Between 1947 and 1957," *Journal of Tropical Geography,* XVI (October, 1962), and T. G. McGee, "Population: A Preliminary Analysis," in Wang Gungwu, ed., *Malaysia: A Survey* (New York, 1964). For a stimulating article on demography in Indonesia, see Nathan Keyfitz, "Indonesian Population and the European Industrial Revolution," *Asian Survey,* V:10 (October, 1965), 503–14. The most comprehensive study is Widjojo Nitisastro, *Dynamics of Population in Indonesia* (Ithaca, N.Y., 1970). The best study on this subject in the Philippines is the *First Conference on Population, 1965* (Manila, 1965), published by the Population Institute of the University of the Philippines.

The growing population in postwar Southeast Asia has made changes in land allocation imperative. The two best studies on land allocation in the Philippines are Akira Takahashi's *Land and Peasants in Central Luzon: The Socio-economic Structure of a Bulacan Village* (Tokyo, 1969), and Frances L. Starner's *Magsaysay and the Philippine Peasantry: The Agrarian Impact on Philippine Politics, 1953–1956* (Berkeley, Calif., 1961). Also, see Frederick L. Wernstedt and Paul D. Simkins, "Migrations and the Settlement of Mindanao," *JAS*, XXV (November, 1965), 83–103. For an analysis of the impact of modernization on the rural Philippines, see George M. Guthrie *et al.*, *The Psychology of Modernization in the Rural Philippines* (Quezon City, 1970). Also, the RAND Corporation, commissioned by the Agency for International Development, undertook a detailed social science survey of economic and political conditions in the Philippines. The data, published in H. A. Averch, F. H. Denton, and J. E. Koehler, *A Crisis in Ambiguity: Political and Economic Development in the Philippines* (Santa Monica, Calif., 1970), are very valuable, the conclusions to be drawn from them very controversial. For Vietnam, the two most relevant works are Gerard Chaliand, *The Peasants of North Vietnam* (Baltimore, 1969 [1st ed., Paris, 1968]); and Robert Shaplen, *The Lost Revolution* (New York, 1966). Rémy Prud'homme's *L'Économie du Cambodge* (Paris, 1969) is outstanding, and it contains valuable tables. Some of the problems facing the Malay peasant and his land are discussed in T. B. Wilson, *The Economics of Padi Production in North Malaya, Part I: Land Tenure, Rents, Land Use and Fragmentation* (Kuala Lumpur, 1958); E. K. Fisk, *Studies in the Rural Economy of South East Asia* (London, 1964); E. K. Fisk, "Features of the Rural Economy," in T. H. Silcock and E. K. Fisk, eds., *The Political Economy of Independent Malaya* (Canberra, 1963); M. G. Swift, "Economic Concentration and Malay Peasant Society," in Maurice Freedman, ed., *Social Organization* (London, 1967). Two useful articles dealing with government land development schemes are R. Ho, "Land Settlement Projects in Malaya: An Assessment of the Role of the Federal Land Development Authority," *Journal of Tropical Geography*, XII (1965), 1–15, and R. Wikkramatileke, "State Aided Rural Land Colonisation in Malaya: An Appraisal of the F.L.D.A.," *Annals of the Association of American Geographers*, LV (1965), 377–403.

The Political-Administrative Setting: (NOTE: For studies of earlier bureaucratic development in Southeast Asia, see bibliography for Chapter 21.)

For the problems and transformations of the postwar bureaucracy in Burma, see James Guyot, "Bureaucratic Transformation in Burma," in Ralph Braibanti, ed., *Asian Bureaucratic Systems Emergent from the British Imperial Tradition* (Durham, N.C., 1966). William J. Siffin, *The Thai Bureaucracy* (Honolulu, 1966), is a superb analysis for Thailand. Among many outstanding works published by the Institute of Public Administration in the Philippines, José C. Abueva's *Focus on the Barrio; the Story Behind the Birth of the Philippine Community Development Program Under President Ramon Magsaysay* (Manila, 1959) is perhaps the best for this subject. S. W. Jones, *Public Administration in Malaya* (London, 1953), is historical in treatment and useful for later comparison in Malaysia. Robert O. Tilman, *Bureaucratic Transition in Malaya* (Durham, N.C., 1964), is a study of the process of "Malayanization" of the public services. Gayl Ness, *Bureaucracy and Rural Development in Malaysia* (Berkeley, Calif., 1967), relates planning and administration to economic development. Peter J. Wilson, *A Malay Village and Malaysia: Social Values and Rural Development* (New Haven, Conn., 1967), is an attempt to discuss development administration in the light of established social values. E. K. Fisk, "Special Development Problems of a Plural Society: The Malayan Example," *The Economic Record*, XXXVIII (1962), 209–24, discusses development administration and planning from the point of view of an economist. James C. Scott, *Political Ideology in Malaysia: Reality and the Beliefs of an Elite* (New Haven, Conn., 1968), is an enterprising attempt to determine some of the basic value orientations of the bureaucrats themselves.

Four fine articles on changing legal systems–a subject hardly ever discussed for other Southeast Asian countries, yet one of broad implications—are the following: Daniel Lev, "The Lady and the Banyan Tree: Civil Law Change in Indonesia," *American Journal of Comparative Law*, XIV (spring, 1965), 282–307; M. A. Jaspan, "In Quest of New Law: The Perplexity of Legal Syncretism in Indonesia," *Comparative Studies in Society and History*, VII:3 (April, 1965), 252–66. Daniel Lev, "The Supreme Court and Adat Inheritance Law in Indonesia," *American Journal of Comparative Law*, XI:2 (spring, 1962), 205–44; and Daniel Lev, "The Politics of Judicial Development in Indonesia," *Comparative Studies in Society and History*, VII:2 (January, 1965), 173–202. Also pertinent to the problems and transformations of bureaucracy in Indonesia are Selosoemardjan, *Social Changes in Jogjakarta* (Ithaca, N.Y., 1962); Leslie Palmier, *Social Status and Power in Java* (London, 1960); and Everett Hawkins, "Job Inflation in Indonesia," *Asian Survey*, VI:5 (May, 1966).

For Cambodia, Claude-Gilles Gour, *Institutions Constitutionelles et Politiques du Cambodge* (Paris, 1965), traces developments since independence.

Urban Trends: (NOTE: For other works on this topic, see bibliography for Chapter 24.)

The best general study on this subject is T. G. McGee, *The Southeast Asian City* (New York, 1967). Aprodicio A. Laquian has studied the problems of the city of Manila in his book, *The City in Nation Building: Politics and Administration in Metropolitan Manila* (Manila, 1966). His more recent *Slums Are for People* (Manila, 1969), a detailed analysis of Manila's urban problem and a developmental project in its Tondo section, is part of the growing literature on the urban scene in the Philippines. Richard L. Stone and Joy Marsella offer significant insight into Southeast Asian urbanization in their article "Mahirap: A Squatter Community in a Manila Suburb" in *Modernization: Its Impact in the Philippines* III (Institute of Philippine Culture, Paper No. 6, Quezon City, 1968), 64–91. See also Mary R. Hollnsteiner, "The Urbanization of Metropolitan Manila" in *Modernization: Its Impact in the Philippines* IV (Institute of Philippine Culture, Paper No. 7, Quezon City, 1969), 147–74. Charles Goulin, "Phnom Penh: Notes de Géographie Urbaine," in *Cahiers d'Outre Mer*, LXXVII (January–March, 1967), 5–36, studies Phnom Penh. For urban trends in Malaysia and Singapore, see: R. J. W. Neville, "Singapore: Recent

Trends in the Sex and Age Composition of a Cosmopolitan Community," *Population Studies*, XVII (1963), 99–112; J. C. Caldwell, "Urban Growth in Malaya: Trends and Implications," *Population Review* (January, 1963), pp. 39–50; T. G. McGee, "The Cultural Role of Cities: A Case Study of Kuala Lumpur," *Journal of Tropical Geography*, XVII (1963), 178–96; Hamzah Sendut, "Urbanization," in Wang Gungwu, ed., *Malaysia: A Survey* (New York, 1964), pp. 82–96; and G. J. Missen, "The Big City in Malaya," in J. Rutherford, M. I. Logan, and G. J. Missen, *New Viewpoints in Economic Geography: Case Studies from Australia, New Zealand, Malaysia, North America* (Sydney, 1966), pp. 394–414.

Alien Influences upon Southeast Asian Economies, and Southeast Asian Responses: (NOTE: for works specifically on the overseas Chinese in Southeast Asia, see bibliography for Chapters 22 and 23.)

A good recent analysis of this subject is in Frank Golay, *et al.*, eds., *Underdevelopment and Economic Nationalism in Southeast Asia* (Ithaca, N.Y., 1969). For a good analysis of the continuing Dutch influence in the Indonesian economy, see Hans Schmitt, "Post-colonial Politics: A Suggested Interpretation of the Indonesian Experience, 1950–8," *Australian Journal of Politics and History*, IX:2 (November, 1963). For Malaysia, J. J. Puthucheary's *Ownership and Control of the Malaysian Economy* (Singapore, 1960) examines the structure of ownership. The literature on alien influence in the economic sphere in the Philippines is extensive and often highly emotional. Among the most scholarly works are Remigio E. Agpalo's *The Political Process and the Nationalization of the Retail Trade in the Philippines* (Quezon City, 1962); Shirley Jenkins's *American Economic Policy Toward the Philippines* (Stanford, Calif., 1954); Frank H. Golay's *The Philippines: Public Policy and National Economic Development* (Ithaca, N.Y., 1961); and Sheldon Appleton's "Overseas Chinese and Economic Nationalization in the Philippines," *JAS*, XIX (February, 1960), 151–61. For a different perspective on the issue, see John J. Carroll's *The Filipino Manufacturing Entrepreneur* (Ithaca, N.Y., 1965). Senators Lorenzo Tañada and José W. Diokno are among the most articulate spokesmen of the Filipino nationalist point of view; see, for example, José W. Diokno, "What the Philippines Expects of Foreign Investors," *Solidarity*, IV:6 (June, 1969), 39–45. The volume edited by G. P. Sicat, *The Philippine Economy in the 1960's* (Quezon City, 1964), contains many essays well worth reading. For a current analysis of the Chinese and Chinese *mestizo* communities in the Philippines, see Gerald A. McBeath, "Chinese Integration in Contemporary Philippine Society," *The Annals of the Philippine Chinese Historical Association* (Inaugural Issue, March, 1970), pp. 71–89.

Southeast Asia and International Politics: General works on the centripetal as well as the centrifugal forces at work in Southeast Asia since the war are Russell H. Fifield, *The Diplomacy of Southeast Asia: 1945–1958* (New York, 1958); Bernard K. Gordon, *The Dimensions of Conflict in Southeast Asia* (Englewood Cliffs, N.J., 1966); *Toward Disengagement in Asia* (Englewood Cliffs, N.J., 1969) by the same author; and Werner Levi, *The Challenge of World Politics in South and Southeast Asia* (Englewood Cliffs, N.J., 1968). There is also much useful information in Robert Shaplen's *Time Out of Hand: Revolution and Reaction in Southeast Asia* (New York, 1969). An analysis of the Geneva Conference of 1954, with emphasis on the legal viewpoint, is Robert F. Randle, *Geneva 1954: The Settlement of the Indochinese War* (Princeton, N.J., 1969). Two symposia on the legal aspects of the Vietnam war are found in Richard A. Falk, ed., *The Vietnam War and International Law* (2 vols., Princeton, N.J. 1968 and 1969). Works on specific disputes include Douglas Hyde, *Confrontation in the East* (Singapore, 1965); Nancy McHenry Fletcher, *The Separation of Singapore from Malaysia* (Ithaca, N.Y., 1969); and Michael Leifer, *The Philippine Claim to Sabah* (Switzerland, 1968).

The best single survey of postwar Philippine foreign policy can be found in Milton W. Meyer's *A Diplomatic History of the Philippine Republic* (Honolulu, 1965). The two best volumes dealing with the Philippine-American relationship specifically are George E. Taylor's *The Philippines and the United States: Problems of Partnership* (New York, 1964), and the volume edited by Frank Golay for the Philippine-American Assembly held in Davao in 1966, entitled *The United States and the Philippines* (Englewood Cliffs, N.J., 1966). Published in the Philippines with a number of additional articles, the book is essential reading.

For Malaysia, there are a number of studies of the process by which that state was constructed. Lee Kuan Yew's *The Battle for Merger* (Singapore, 1961) tells the story of Singapore's efforts to join Malaysia, while Milton Osborne's *Singapore and Malaysia* (Ithaca, N.Y., 1964) deals in some detail with Singapore politics during this period. Those interested should see also the very perceptive article by Emily Sadka, "Singapore and the Federation: Problems of Merger," *Asian Survey*, I (January, 1962), 17–25. J. P. Ongkili's *The Borneo Response to Malaysia, 1961–1963* (Singapore, 1967) is a brief but useful study of opinion, principally in Sarawak and Sabah. T. E. Smith, *The Background to Malaysia* (London, 1963), is a brief study undertaken for the Royal Institute of International Affairs. Willard A. Hanna, *The Formation of Malaysia; New Factor in World Politics* (New York, 1964), brings together a number of reports written by Hanna for the American Universities Field Staff between 1962 and 1964. Malaysia's international relations in general have been discussed in two articles in Wang Gungwu, ed., *Malaysia: A Survey* (New York, 1964): Robin W. Winks, "Malaysia and the Commonwealth: An Inquiry into the Nature of Commonwealth Ties," and Zainal Abidin b. Abdul Wahid, "Malaysia, Southeast Asia and World Politics."

Most of the literature on Indonesian foreign policy has a current events rather than historical focus. For the foundations of the Republic's foreign policy, see the *Political Manifesto* of November, 1945, which is still largely valid today. The development of more specific policies is best followed in general works, such as George McT. Kahin, *Nationalism and Revolution in Indonesia* (Ithaca, N.Y., 1952), and Herbert Feith, *The Decline of Constitutional Democracy in Indonesia* (Ithaca, N.Y., 1962). See also Leslie Palmier, *Indonesia and the Dutch* (London, 1962) and Jan M. Pluvier, *Confrontations: A Study in Indonesian Politics* (Kuala Lumpur, 1965).

For Thai foreign relations, see Frank Darling, *Thailand and the United States* (Washington, 1965), Donald Neuchterlein, *Thailand and the Struggle for Southeast Asia* (Ithaca, N.Y., 1965), and David A. Wilson, *The United States and the Future of Thailand* (New York, 1970).

The best analysis of Cambodia's foreign policy since independence is Roger Smith's *Cambodia's Foreign Policy* (Ithaca, N.Y., 1965), and parts of Robert Shaplen's *The Lost Revolution* (New York, 1966) are also good. See also Peter A. Poole, *Cambodia's Quest for Survival* (New York, 1969), and David Chandler, "Cambodia's Strategy of Survival," *Current History* (December, 1969), pp. 344–48. For a Czech viewpoint, see Ivan Dolezal, "The Policy of Neutrality and the International Position of Cambodia," *Asian and African Studies,* IV (1968), 57–79.

Chapter 35. Cultural Reconstruction and Postwar Nationalism

The Expansion of Education: (NOTE: For other studies on this topic, see the bibliography for Chapter 33.)

For Malaysia, two background studies on education are Ho Seng Ong, *Education for Unity in Malaya* (Penang, 1952), an interesting but idiosyncratic study by a prominent Malaysian teacher, and Frederic Mason, *The Schools of Malaya* (Singapore, 1959), which is a brief, factual description. Robert O. Tilman, "Education and Political Development in Malaya," in Robert O. Tilman, ed., *Man, State, and Society in Contemporary Southeast Asia* (New York, 1969), outlines the problems as they existed at independence. Two recent official publications are useful in providing statistical and other information: *Education in Malaysia,* and *Educational Statistics of Malaysia, 1938–1967* (both published in Kuala Lumpur, 1968). There has been a dearth of scholarly articles on education in independent Malaysia, but see R. H. K. Wong, "Education and Problems of Nationhood," in Wang Gungwu, ed., *Malaysia: A Survey* (New York, 1964), and Margaret Roff, "The Politics of Language in Malaya," *Asian Survey,* VII:5 (May, 1967), 316–28.

For Cambodia, see F. Martini, "De la Création actuelle des mots en cambodgien," *Bulletin de la Société Linguistique de Paris,* CLVII (1962), 160–71.

The most useful survey attempting to chart the nature of change not only in education but in all other aspects of Philippine life is John J. Carroll's *Changing Patterns of Social Structure in the Philippines 1896–1963* (Quezon City, 1968). This compendium collates for both target years and has appended an excellent bibliography. See also the articles contained in the two volumes published by the Institute of Philippine Culture entitled, *Modernization: Its Impact in the Philippines* (Quezon City, 1967 and 1968).

For Indonesia, see Murray Thomas, "Effects of Indonesian Population Growth on Educational Development, 1940–1968," *Asian Survey,* IX:7 (July, 1969).

Religion, Politics, and Sociocultural Change: The role of Christianity in contemporary Southeast Asia is examined in Gerald H. Anderson, ed., *Christ and Crisis in Southeast Asia* (New York, 1968).

Those interested in religious change in Malaysia might consult the following: K. J. Ratnam, "Religion and Politics in Malaya," in Robert O. Tilman, ed., *Man, State, and Society in Contemporary Southeast Asia* (New York, 1969); Fred von der Mehden, "Religion and Politics in Malaya," *Asian Survey,* III:12 (December, 1963), 609–15; Charles F. Gallagher, "Contemporary Islam: A Frontier of Communalism. Aspects of Islam in Malaysia," American Universities Field Staff Reports, Southeast Asia Series, XIV:10 (1966); and Manning Nash, "Tradition and Tension in Kelantan," *Journal of Asian and African Studies,* I:4 (October, 1966), 310–14.

For changes in religion in Cambodia, see Thierry de Beaucé, "Le Cambodge: Bouddhisme et Développement," *Esprit*, XXXV:363 (September, 1967), 265–79.

Among the more interesting analyses of modern religion in the Philippines are Jaime Bulatao and Vitaliano Gorospe, *Split-Level Christianity* (Quezon City, 1966), and Marcelino Foronda's "The Canonization of Rizal," *The Journal of History* (Philippines), VIII (1960), 1–48.

Benedict Anderson, "The Languages of Indonesian Politics," *Indonesia*, I (April, 1966), 89–116, merits careful study. James Peacock, *Rites of Modernization: Symbols and Social Aspects of Indonesian Proletarian Drama* (Chicago, 1968), is helpful for understanding changes in Indonesia. Lance Castles, "Notes on the Islamic School at Gontor," *Indonesia*, I (April, 1966), 30–45, provides a fine contemporary picture of a *pondok*, with indications of its economic and political implications.

Nationalism and Its Participants in the Postwar Period: The political process in Malaysia, extremely lively and well-developed since independence, has attracted the interest of many political scientists and other analysts. To most observers, the most important basic theme of Malaysian politics has been the relationship between the communities. The fullest treatment of communalism in Malaya is found in K. J. Ratnam, *Communalism and the Political Process in Malaya* (Kuala Lumpur, 1963), but associated ideas are also developed in two useful articles: M. G. Swift, "Malayan Politics: Race and Class," *Civilisations*, XII:2 (1960), 237–47, and T. H. Silcock, "Communal and Political Structures," in T. H. Silcock and E. K. Fisk, eds., *The Political Economy of Independent Malaya* (Canberra, 1963). Margaret Clark's unpublished M.A. thesis, "The Malayan Alliance and its Accommodation of Communal Pressures" (University of Malaya, 1964), examines some of the specific issues on which political rivalries have turned; and some of the implications of mainland politics for Borneo are developed by Robert O. Tilman in his article, "The Alliance Pattern in Malayan Politics: Bornean Variations on a Theme," *South Atlantic Quarterly*, LXIII:1 (1964), 60–74. Michael Leigh, *The Chinese Community in Sarawak: A Study in Communal Relations* (Singapore, 1964), is a useful short study of the issues in Sarawak, while Margaret Roff, "The Rise and Demise of Kadazan Nationalism," *JSEAH*, X:2 (1969), 243–326, discusses tribal politics in Sabah. John A. McDougall, "Shared Burdens: A Study of Communal Discrimination by the Political Parties of Malaysia and Singapore" (unpublished Ph.D. dissertation, Harvard University), makes a systematic study of party attitudes toward communal discrimination.

John Armstrong's *Sihanouk Speaks* (New York, 1964), should be read alongside Roger Smith's "Prince Norodom Sihanouk of Cambodia," *Asian Survey*, VII:6 (June, 1968), 353–62, for information about the former head of Cambodia. The Cambodian English-language monthly, *Kambuja*, also contains valuable material on Cambodia's leaders.

Two of the most thoughtful Filipinos to write on the meaning of nationalism for their country are Horacio de la Costa in his books, *The Background of Nationalism* (Manila, 1965), and *Asia and the Philippines* (Manila, 1965); and the late Senator Claro M. Recto in the *Recto Reader* (Manila, 1965).

G. William Skinner, ed., *Local, Ethnic, and National Loyalties in Village Indonesia* (New Haven, Conn., 1959), is a particularly fine collection of six papers dealing with the place of national ideologies in Indonesia.

INDEX

For terms referring to major countries and peoples of Southeast Asia—e.g., Malaysia, Indonesia, Filipino, British Burma—it seems of little value to list every place where they are mentioned in the text. Under these terms in the index are listed only references pertaining to the formation or dissolution of the political unit *per se* or to the term itself. General information on these peoples and places will be found under the appropriate subject headings—e.g., administration, international relations, language, nationalism, trade.

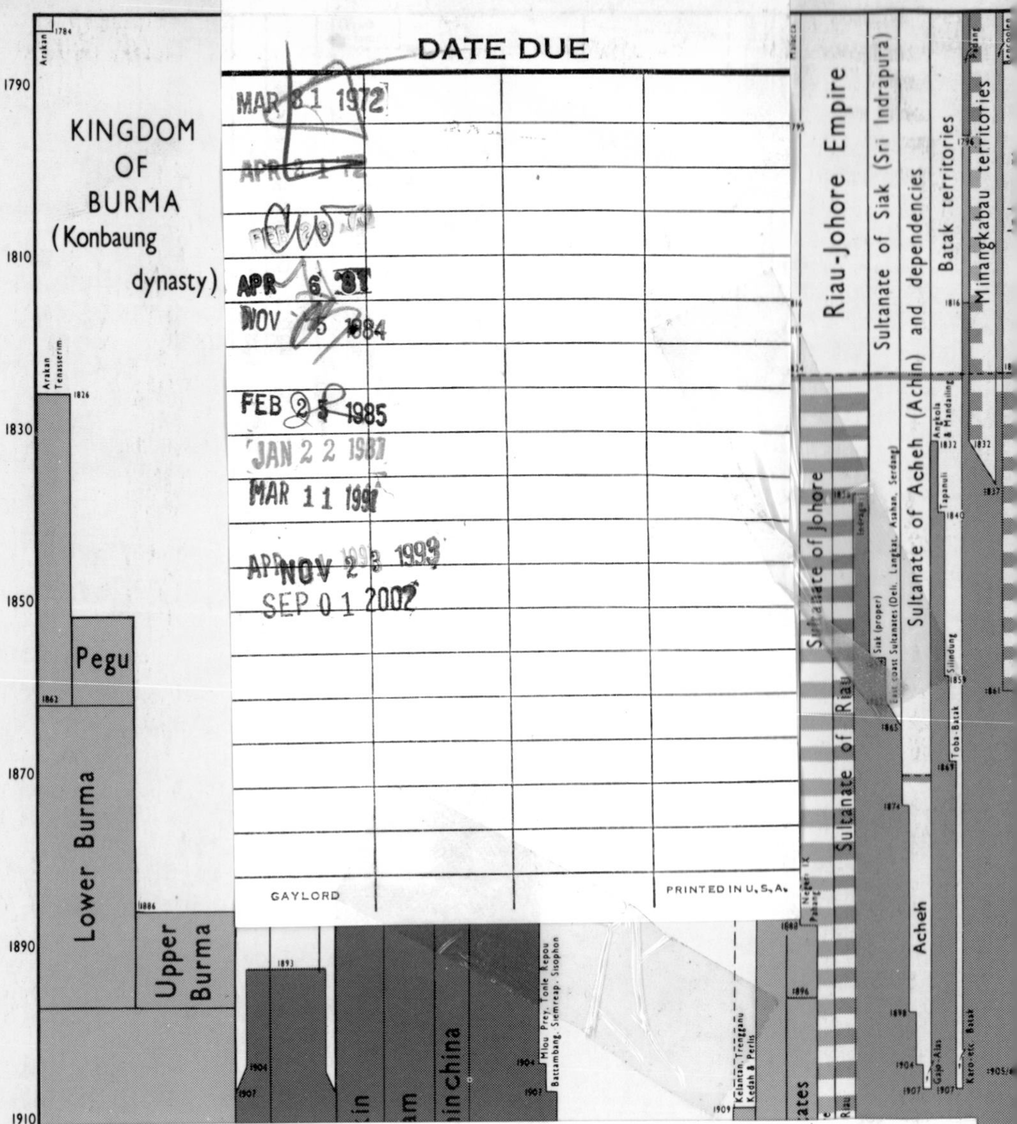

1790

KINGDOM OF BURMA (Konbaung dynasty)

Arakan 1784

1810

Arakan Tenasserim 1826

1830

1850

Pegu

1862

1870

Lower Burma

1886

Upper Burma

1890

1893

1904

1907

1910

1930

1950

Riau-Johore Empire

Sultanate of Siak (Sri Indrapura)

Sultanate of Acheh (Achin) and dependencies

Batak territories

Minangkabau territories

Sultanate of Johore

Sultanate of Riau

Siak (proper)

East coast Sultanates (Deli, Langkat, Asahan, Serdang)

Sultanate of Acheh

Acheh

Angkola & Mandailing

Tapanuli

Silindung

Toba-Batak

Gajo-Alas

Karo-etc. Batak

Mlou Prey, Tonle Repou

Battambang, Siemreap, Sisophon

Kelantan, Trengganu

Kedah & Perlis